Advances in Computational Intelligence in Geotechnical and Geological Engineering

Advances in Computational Intelligence in Geotechnical and Geological Engineering

Editors

Danial Jahed Armaghani
Hadi Khabbaz
Manoj Khandelwal
Niaz Muhammad Shahani
Ramesh Murlidhar Bhatawdekar

 Basel • Beijing • Wuhan • Barcelona • Belgrade • Novi Sad • Cluj • Manchester

Editors

Danial Jahed Armaghani
School of Civil and
Environmental Engineering
University of Technology
Sydney
Ultimo
Australia

Hadi Khabbaz
School of Civil and
Environmental Engineering
University of Technology
Sydney
Ultimo
Australia

Manoj Khandelwal
Institute of Innovation,
Science and Sustainability
Federation University
Australia
Ballarat
Australia

Niaz Muhammad Shahani
School of Mines
China University of Mining
and Technology
Xuzhou
China

Ramesh Murlidhar
Bhatawdekar
Centre of Tropical
Geoengineering
(GEOTROPIK)
School of Civil Engineering
Faculty of Engineering
Universiti Teknologi Malaysia
Johor Bahru
Malaysia

Editorial Office
MDPI AG
Grosspeteranlage 5
4052 Basel, Switzerland

This is a reprint of articles from the Special Issue published online in the open access journal *Mathematics* (ISSN 2227-7390) (available at: https://www.mdpi.com/journal/mathematics/special_issues/CI_Geotech_Geol).

For citation purposes, cite each article independently as indicated on the article page online and as indicated below:

Lastname, A.A.; Lastname, B.B. Article Title. *Journal Name* **Year**, *Volume Number*, Page Range.

ISBN 978-3-7258-2355-0 (Hbk)
ISBN 978-3-7258-2356-7 (PDF)
doi.org/10.3390/books978-3-7258-2356-7

© 2024 by the authors. Articles in this book are Open Access and distributed under the Creative Commons Attribution (CC BY) license. The book as a whole is distributed by MDPI under the terms and conditions of the Creative Commons Attribution-NonCommercial-NoDerivs (CC BY-NC-ND) license.

Contents

About the Editors vii

Preface ix

Yongyi Wang, Bin Gong, Yongjun Zhang, Xiaoyu Yang and Chun'an Tang
Progressive Fracture Behavior and Acoustic Emission Release of CJBs Affected by Joint Distance Ratio
Reprinted from: *Mathematics* **2022**, *10*, 4149, doi:10.3390/math10214149 1

Haoding Xu, Xuzhen He and Daichao Sheng
Rainfall-Induced Landslides from Initialization to Post-Failure Flows: Stochastic Analysis with Machine Learning
Reprinted from: *Mathematics* **2022**, *10*, 4426, doi:10.3390/math10234426 31

Mohamed Elgharib Gomah, Guichen Li, Naseer Muhammad Khan, Changlun Sun, Jiahui Xu, Ahmed A. Omar, et al.
Prediction of Strength Parameters of Thermally Treated Egyptian Granodiorite Using Multivariate Statistics and Machine Learning Techniques
Reprinted from: *Mathematics* **2022**, *10*, 4523, doi:10.3390/math10234523 57

Syed Mujtaba Hussaine and Linlong Mu
Intelligent Prediction of Maximum Ground Settlement Induced by EPB Shield Tunneling Using Automated Machine Learning Techniques
Reprinted from: *Mathematics* **2022**, *10*, 4637, doi:10.3390/math10244637 78

Danial Jahed Armaghani, Biao He, Edy Tonnizam Mohamad, Y X Zhang, Sai Hin Lai and Fei Ye
Applications of Two Neuro-Based Metaheuristic Techniques in Evaluating Ground Vibration Resulting from Tunnel Blasting
Reprinted from: *Mathematics* **2023**, *11*, 106, doi:10.3390/math11010106 103

Haoxuan Yu and Izni Zahidi
Tailings Pond Classification Based on Satellite Images and Machine Learning: An Exploration of Microsoft ML.Net
Reprinted from: *Mathematics* **2023**, *11*, 517, doi:10.3390/math11030517 120

Yigai Xiao, Hongwei Deng, Guanglin Tian and Songtao Yu
Analysis of Microscopic Pore Characteristics and Macroscopic Energy Evolution of Rock Materials under Freeze-Thaw Cycle Conditions
Reprinted from: *Mathematics* **2023**, *11*, 710, doi:10.3390/math11030710 134

Feng Gao, Xin Li, Xin Xiong, Haichuan Lu and Zengwu Luo
Refined Design and Optimization of Underground Medium and Long Hole Blasting Parameters—A Case Study of the Gaofeng Mine
Reprinted from: *Mathematics* **2023**, *11*, 1612, doi:10.3390/math11071612 151

Xin Wei, Niaz Muhammad Shahani and Xigui Zheng
Predictive Modeling of the Uniaxial Compressive Strength of Rocks Using an Artificial Neural Network Approach
Reprinted from: *Mathematics* **2023**, *11*, 1650, doi:10.3390/math11071650 169

Xianan Wang, Shahab Hosseini, Danial Jahed Armaghani and Edy Tonnizam Mohamad
Data-Driven Optimized Artificial Neural Network Technique for Prediction of Flyrock Induced by Boulder Blasting
Reprinted from: *Mathematics* **2023**, *11*, 2358, doi:10.3390/math11102358 186

Abidhan Bardhan, Raushan Kumar Singh, Sufyan Ghani, Gerasimos Konstantakatos and Panagiotis G. Asteris
Modelling Soil Compaction Parameters Using an Enhanced Hybrid Intelligence Paradigm of ANFIS and Improved Grey Wolf Optimiser
Reprinted from: *Mathematics* **2023**, *11*, 3064, doi:10.3390/math11143064 208

Leilei Liu, Guoyan Zhao and Weizhang Liang
Slope Stability Prediction Using *k*-NN-Based Optimum-Path Forest Approach
Reprinted from: *Mathematics* **2023**, *11*, 3071, doi:10.3390/math11143071 231

About the Editors

Danial Jahed Armaghani

Danial Jahed Armaghani is a prominent researcher in the field of civil and geotechnical engineering. His work has made significant contributions to the understanding and mitigation of geotechnical and geological hazards, earning him a reputation as an excellent researcher in his field. Dr. Danial's research focuses on a wide range of topics, including slope stability analysis, rock mechanics, tunnel construction, surface and deep excavations, and applying machine learning models and optimization algorithms to solve various geotechnical problems. Dr. Danial is currently working as a Research Fellow at the School of Civil and Environmental Engineering, University of Technology Sydney, Australia. He has published more than 300 articles in well-established ISI and Scopus journals and at national and international conferences. His published works have received more than 23,000 citations, which indicate the significant impact and influence of his research in the academic and scientific community. He was among the top 2% of scientists for four consecutive years from 2019 to 2024, according to Stanford University. He was also among the top 0.05% of all scholars worldwide according to ScholarGPS Highly Ranked Scholar in Engineering and Computer Sciences.

Hadi Khabbaz

Hadi Khabbaz is a Professor in geotechnical and civil engineering. He received his PhD degree from the University of New South Wales, Australia, in 1997. He has been an academic staff member at the University of Technology Sydney (UTS) since January 2008. Currently, he is the Head of Discipline of Geotechnical and Transport Engineering and the Deputy Director of the Transport Research Centre at UTS. Additionally, he serves as the Vice Chair of the Technical Committee TC211 on Ground Improvement for the International Society for Soil Mechanics and Geotechnical Engineering (ISSMGE). He has made noteworthy contributions in the fields of ground improvement techniques and unsaturated soil mechanics. He is the author or co-author of more than 300 technical papers. Over the last 10 years, he has been a chief investigator in more than 20 research and industry-funded projects in the field of transportation geotechnics. He also served as the Chair of the Australian Geomechanics Society (Sydney Chapter), the Deputy Chair, and the Treasurer of this society. He has been the Chief Editor of the AGS Symposium proceedings for the last 10 years.

Manoj Khandelwal

Manoj Khandelwal is an Associate Professor and Program Coordinator of mining engineering at Federation University Australia and an Australian Endeavour Fellow. With over twenty years of experience in research and teaching across Australia and India, he is a renowned expert in mining geomechanics and rock blasting. He has published over 200 research papers and has more than 7700 citations, with an h-index of 49. Dr. Khandelwal has authored a technical book and completed numerous research and consultancy projects. His accolades include the Young Scientist Award from the President of India, various awards from the Mining Engineers' Association of India, and Endeavour Fellowships, Australia. He also serves on the Editorial Boards of various reputed international journals.

Niaz Muhammad Shahani

Niaz Muhammad Shahani has a PhD in Mining Engineering, and a postdoc in the School of Mines, China University of Mining and Technology. He obtained a Bachelor's degree in Mining Engineering from Mehran University of Engineering and Technology, Jamshoro, Pakistan, in 2015; received a Master's degree in Mining Engineering from China University of Mining and Technology in 2019 and continued his PhD studies at the School of Mines; and attained a PhD in Mining Engineering in December 2022. From 2023 to the present, he has been working as a postdoc in the Department of Mining Engineering, School of Mines, China University of Mining and Technology. Currently, he is mainly engaged in the fields of intelligent mining and surrounding rock control, mine safety and management, and artificial intelligence and optimization algorithms, and he has published more than 50 articles in well-established ISI and Scopus journals and at national and international conferences. His published works have received around 600 citations, which indicates the significant impact and influence of his research in the academic and scientific community.

Ramesh Murlidhar Bhatawdekar

Ramesh Murlidhar Bhatawdekar is a well-known researcher in the field of Civil, Mining, and Geotechnical Engineering. His major contribution is through AI/ML application research in geotechnical issues in civil and mining projects in tropical climates. He collaborates with a good network of researchers to produce high-quality research. Dr. Ramesh graduated with a degree in Mining Engineering from the Indian Institute of Technology, Kharagpur, India. He has vast experience in large opencast mines of limestone and iron ore in India/SEA. Dr. Ramesh has also completed an M. Phil, PhD, and Post Doctorate from the Universiti Technologi Malaysia. He is affiliated with both Universities. Dr. Ramesh has more than 1300 citations. He has published more than 100 research papers in WOS/Scopus. He has also presented research papers at more than 40 international conferences. He has published six book chapters and has been the Guest Editor of certain Special Issues. His research interest includes solving industry-based problems through research by applying AI/ML algorithms.

Preface

This reprint represents a significant step forward in the application of cutting-edge computational intelligence (CI) techniques to solve complex problems in geotechnical and geological engineering. The twelve chapters in this reprint showcase the versatility and power of CI methods across a wide range of geotechnical applications. From predicting slope stability to optimizing blasting parameters, and from modeling soil compaction to analyzing rock microstructures, the innovative approaches presented here demonstrate the immense potential of CI to advance our understanding and capabilities in geotechnical engineering.

We begin with an exploration of slope stability prediction using a novel k-NN-based Optimum-Path Forest approach, offering improved accuracy and efficiency in assessing landslide risks. The reprint then delves into soil compaction modeling using an enhanced hybrid intelligence paradigm that combines ANFIS with an improved Grey Wolf Optimizer, showcasing the power of integrating multiple CI techniques.

Several chapters focus on the application of artificial neural networks and other machine learning techniques in various contexts, including the prediction of flyrock induced by boulder blasting, modeling of uniaxial compressive strength in rocks, and the optimization of underground blasting parameters. These chapters highlight the adaptability of CI methods in addressing diverse geotechnical challenges.

The reprint also explores more specialized topics, such as the analysis of microscopic pore characteristics and macroscopic energy evolution in rock materials under freeze–thaw conditions, and the classification of tailings ponds using satellite imagery and machine learning. These studies demonstrate the broad applicability of CI techniques in geotechnical and geological engineering.

We further examine the use of neuro-based metaheuristic techniques for evaluating ground vibration from tunnel blasting and the application of automated machine learning in predicting maximum ground settlement induced by tunnel construction. The reprint also includes studies on predicting the strength parameters of thermally treated granodiorite and analyzing rainfall-induced landslides using stochastic analysis with machine learning. The final chapter investigates the progressive fracture behavior and acoustic emission release of cemented joint blocks, providing insights into the complex behavior of jointed rock masses.

This collection of chapters represents the forefront of research in applying CI to geotechnical and geological engineering. It is our hope that this reprint will serve as a valuable resource for researchers, practitioners, and students in the field, inspiring further innovations and advancements in the application of CI to solve real-world geotechnical challenges.

Danial Jahed Armaghani, Hadi Khabbaz, Manoj Khandelwal, Niaz Muhammad Shahani, and Ramesh Murlidhar Bhatawdekar
Editors

mathematics

Article

Progressive Fracture Behavior and Acoustic Emission Release of CJBs Affected by Joint Distance Ratio

Yingyi Wang [1], Bin Gong [2,*], Yongjun Zhang [3], Xiaoyu Yang [4] and Chun'an Tang [1]

[1] State Key Laboratory of Coastal and Offshore Engineering, Dalian University of Technology, Dalian 116024, China
[2] College of Engineering, Design and Physical Sciences, Brunel University London, London UB8 3PH, UK
[3] School of Civil Engineering, Qingdao University of Technology, Qingdao 266520, China
[4] School of Civil Engineering, Chongqing Jiaotong University, Chongqing 400074, China
* Correspondence: bin.gong@brunel.ac.uk

Abstract: The progressive collapse behavior and energy release of columnar jointed basalts (CJBs) can be greatly influenced by different joint distance ratios. By adopting the digital image correlation, a series of heterogeneous CJB models are established. The continuous fracture process and acoustic emissions (AEs) are captured numerically under varying lateral pressures. The load curves under different joint distance ratios and model boundaries are analyzed. Meanwhile, the strength, deformation modulus and AE rule are discussed. The data indicate that under plane strain, the troughs of compression strength appear at the column dip angle $\beta = 30°, 150°, 210°$ or $330°$; the equivalent deformation modulus changes in an elliptical way with β increasing; the compression strength and equivalent deformation modulus are higher than the case between plane stress and plane strain under different joint distance ratios. When $\beta = 30°$, the accumulation of AE energy corresponding to the stress peak under plane strain are higher than the case between plane stress and plane strain but becomes lower when β increases to $60°$, which implies the critical transformation of the AE energy-related failure precursor affected by column dip angle. These achievements will contribute to the design, construction and support of slopes and tunnels encountering CJBs.

Keywords: columnar jointed basalt; failure mechanism; acoustic emission; joint distance ratio; numerical simulation

MSC: 74-10

1. Introduction

The columnar jointed basalts (CJBs) generally form because of the condensation and contraction of magma and contain obvious columnar joints. The CJBs are popularly distributed in many sites on this planet, such as Scotland, Siberia, China, Mexico, Australia, the United States, Brazil, India, etc. [1–4]. Columnar joints have even been found on Mars [5]. In the past decades, the columnar jointed rock masses (CJRMs) were encountered in several hydropower stations located in southwest China, such as the Baihetan, Jinanqiao, Wudongde, Xiluodu, and Tongjiezi hydropower stations. Two photographs [5,6] of CJRMs are shown in Figure 1.

Some researchers have investigated the anisotropy, size effect and confining pressure effect of CJBs (or CJRMs). In terms of numerical simulation, insightful achievements have been obtained. However, few studies have been conducted regarding the mechanical responses of CJBs with different joint distance ratios and model boundaries. The homogenization-based model was developed by Meng et al. [7] for studying the effect of discontinuous structures and the elastic parameters. Zheng et al. [1] calculated the influences of size effect and anisotropy using the discrete element method (DEM). Yan et al. [8] modelled the deformation and failure of CJRMs using the finite difference method (FDM).

Li et al. [3] discussed the transient-thermoelastic fractures affected by the highly ti dependent thermal loads by applying the numerical manifold method (NMM). Niu et al. calculated the permeability property of CJRMs with various dip angles numerically, an case study was also carried out. However, the gradual failure process and energy evolut of CJBs have not been understood in depth.

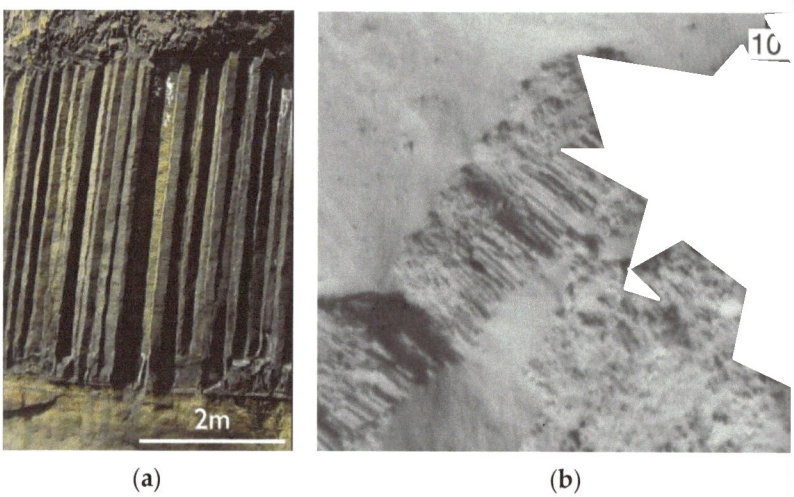

Figure 1. The columnar jointed rock masses observed in field: (**a**) Fingal's Cave on Staffa in ! land [6]; (**b**) the columnar joints discovered on Mars [5].

In terms of physical tests, some useful results have been achieved. With the air understanding the hydraulic fracturing of CJRMs, the compression tests were perform under triaxial stress state by Xiang et al. [10]. Through a series of compression experim under uniaxial stress state, Ke et al. [11] analyzed the anisotropy induced by transv joints. Shi et al. [12] presented an approach to obtain the strengths using the Mohr–Coul and Hoek–Brown criteria under triaxial stresses. A group of laboratory tests were car out by Jin et al. [4] for understanding the anisotropic parameters of CJRMs. To analyze actual geological structures on site, the uniaxial testing was carried out by Ji et al. [13]. quadrangular, pentagonal and hexagonal prisms were also investigated by Que et al. in a laboratory. The anisotropic parameters were discussed by combining the structu features of three kinds of models. In the field tests of CJBs (or CJRMs), many valua results have been obtained. However, the rock masses in nature are generally com cated. The preparation of rock specimens would suffer unexpectable disturbance [2,15- Meanwhile, the AE energy evolution during the fracture process for the CJBs are gre affected by joint distance ratio and model boundary and remains unclear. Moreover, w there are many experimental scheme configurations and specimens, time-consuming uneconomical problems will be encountered.

On the one hand, the influence of column dip angles, joint distance ratios and mo boundaries on the mechanical properties of CJBs should be revealed systematically. the other hand, it will contribute to understand the collapse mechanism to reproduce progressive fracture process and AE energy evolution appropriately. In the enginee projects, the CJBs could not only show significant discontinuity and anisotropy, but a suffer lateral pressure. Hence, it has significant value to reveal the complex deforming bearing features, failure mechanisms and instability precursor of CJBs under lateral press

In this study, to analyze the failure mechanism and AE release rule of CJBs contair various joint distance ratios under different boundary conditions, the digital CJB figu were used for creating the non-homogeneous models. Based on meso-mechanics statistical damage mechanics, a series of numerical tests were conducted. The simulated results were analyzed by comparing with the corresponding tests to verify the rationality and reliability. Furthermore, the continuous failure process and damage failure pattern of the CJB were reproduced. The influence of column dip angles, joint distance ratios and model boundaries on the accumulation of AE energy were comprehensively analyzed to provide the theoretical basis for the treatment measures.

2. Materials and Methods

2.1. The Combination of RFPA and DIC

In terms of the main advances of the rock failure process analysis (RFPA) approach, the assumptions on where and how cracks will occur and propagate are not needed [20,21]. In addition, its effectiveness in modelling the non-linear deforming and bearing of rocks has been verified by many researchers [22,23]. Moreover, RFPA has been adopted in simulating slope instability [24], size effect [25] and zonal disintegration characteristics [26] of rocks. Thus, RFPA has been chosen in this study.

The digital image correlation (DIC) was adopted for building up the RFPA models. Firstly, the vectorized coordinates of elements were obtained through importing and processing the digital figures using the gray-threshold segmentation. Considering the digital figures consist of many square pixels, each pixel corresponds to one finite element, and the spatial coordinates of every pixel corresponds to the node coordinates of the related element. Secondly, the joint or matrix of rocks can be determined by dividing the gray value of pixels, and the related material properties will be assigned. According to the above principle, the creation process of non-homogeneous numerical models is presented in Figure 2a.

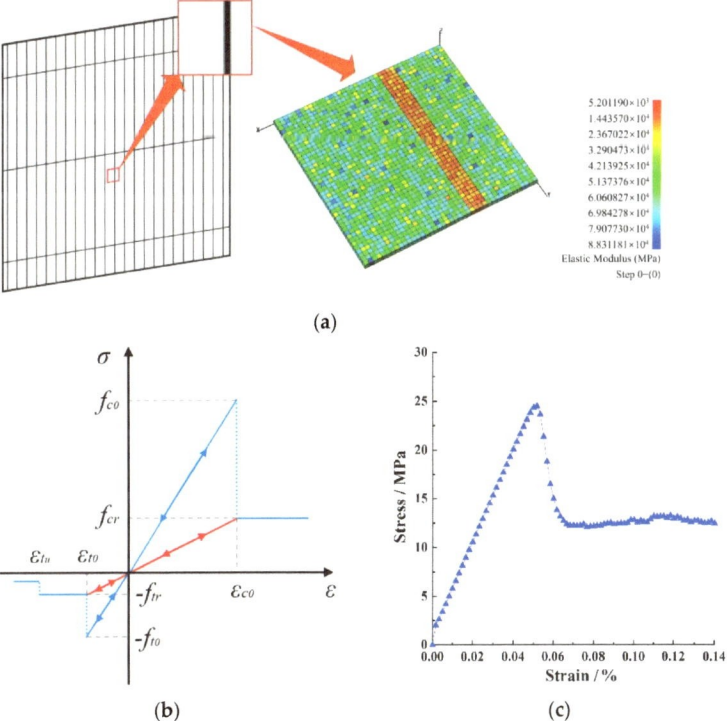

Figure 2. (a) The creation process of non-homogeneous numerical models; (b) the element constitution subject to uniaxial stress; (c) the stress-strain curve.

The element constitution subject to uniaxial stress is depicted in Figure 2b. Through the approach of extending uniaxial constitutive relation to triaxial stress states (Mazars and Pijaudier-Cabot [27]), the constitutive relation shown in Figure 2a can be extended to the triaxial stress states.

2.2. Damage and Failure of One Meso-Element

The rock nonuniformity can be taken into account if the parameter values of meso-elements are assumed to obey the Weibull distribution:

$$f(u) = \frac{m}{u_0}\left(\frac{u}{u_0}\right)^{m-1} exp\left(-\frac{u}{u_0}\right)^m \tag{1}$$

where u is a certain parameter of meso-elements, e.g., compressive strength; u_0 represents the related mean value of u. The notation m represents the heterogeneity index and reflects the nonuniform degree. A higher m implies a higher non-uniformity.

If one element suffers tension along an axis, the elastic-brittle damage constitution described by Equation (2) will be applied.

$$\sigma_3 \leq f_t \tag{2}$$

where f_t represents the unique strength under uniaxial tensile. Note that the stress and strain under compression are positive in this study.

Moreover, the Mohr-Coulomb strength criterion is used for judging the shear damage of one meso-element as shown by Equation (3).

$$\sigma_1 - \frac{1+sin\varphi}{1-sin\varphi}\sigma_3 - f_c \geq 0 \tag{3}$$

where σ_1, σ_3, φ and f_c represents the major principal stress, minor principal stress, internal friction angle and uniaxial compressive strength, respectively. The damage-induced degeneration of element parameter can be computed according to Wang et al. (2022) [28].

2.3. Modeling Effectiveness

The indoor experiment by Ke et al. [11] is adopted to verify the simulation-based approach. Ke et al. [11] made the columns using cement, fine sand, water and water reducer with the mass ratio of 1.0:0.5:0.35:0.002. A regular hexagonal prism containing the section diameter = 10 mm and the length = 50 mm was selected for simulating the actual column. The white cement slurry was used for bonding columns, which simulates joint surface. The ratio of longitudinal to transverse of column was 5. The shift distance of transverse joint was 25 mm. Seven kinds of column-dip angles (β) from 0° to 90° were considered. The rock mass specimens were regular 50 mm × 50 mm × 100 mm quadrangular prisms. The compressive testing was carried out by applying the CSS-3940YJ rock mechanics servo testing machine. The loading method with constant displacement rate of 0.05 mm/min was used. A flat steel cushion block was placed at the rock ends. Then, vertical pressure was applied until the failure of the specimen.

Note that the 50 mm × 100 mm models were used for verification under different load directions subject to plane strain. The inner hexagonal prisms have a diameter of 10 mm. The digital figures were used for creating the numerical samples as displayed in Table 1. The parameter values of the finite element models were determined according to the literatures [8–13,16–19] and presented in Table 2. The displacement load with a ratio of 0.005 mm/step was used until the model failure.

Table 1. The model geometry and load conditions used for verification.

Column Dip Angle (β)	15°	45°	60°
Model			

Table 2. The physical-mechanical parameter values for numerical simulation.

Material Type	Heterogeneity Index	Elastic Modulus (GPa)	Uniaxial Compressive Strength (MPa)	Poisson's Ratio	Friction Angle (°)
Basalt	5	60	120	0.2	56.15
Joint	5	15	30	0.25	36

Table 3 shows the related comparison of the specimen failure modes obtained by simulations and experiments. We can see that the results when $\beta = 15°$ and $\beta = 45°$ in numerical and laboratory physical tests show relatively good similarity. However, for the condition of $\beta = 60°$, there are certain differences between them. This is because of the end effect of the specimen in laboratory test. Namely, there is a certain friction constraint at the ends of both sides of the specimen in laboratory test.

Table 3. The failure modes obtained by simulation and experiment [11].

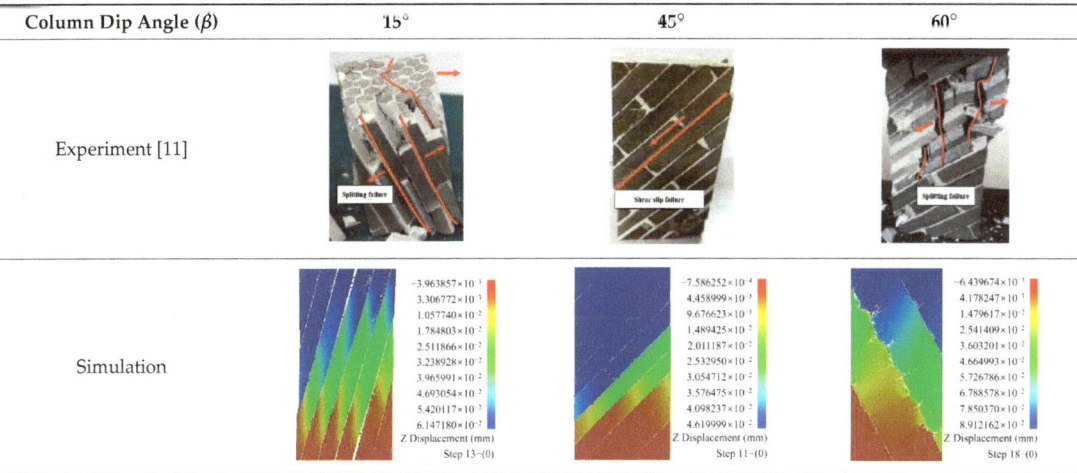

2.4. Numerical Investigation

In this section, the column length and diameter are 0.5~3 m and 13~25 cm, respectively. The specimens for numerical testing are square models and are 4 m in size, and the diameter of columns inside specimens is 20 cm. The rock heterogeneity index is considered as 5. The elastic modulus of joints is 15 GPa. The residual index of strengths after rock failure is taken as 0.5. The dip angles of the column are 0°, 15°, 30°, 45°, 60°, 75° and 90°, respectively. The spacing of the secondary joints is 1.5 m. Simultaneously, the distance ratio of the secondary joints changes from 0% to 50%. The lateral pressure is considered as 4 MPa. In terms of the boundary conditions, two cases are taken into account including the plane strain and the case between plane stress and plane strain.

Moreover, the meso-element size of the models remains the same. For instance, the element number of the 4 m specimen is 1,081,600. The applied configuration for established CJB specimens along the direction parallel to the column axis are presented as Figure 3a–g. For Figure 3e, the normal displacement constraints are applied on the two faces. For Figure 3f, the normal displacement constraint is applied only on one face, and the other normal direction of the plane is free. For Figure 3a–g, the pre-set loading is applied onto the top surface along the vertical direction until the model failure.

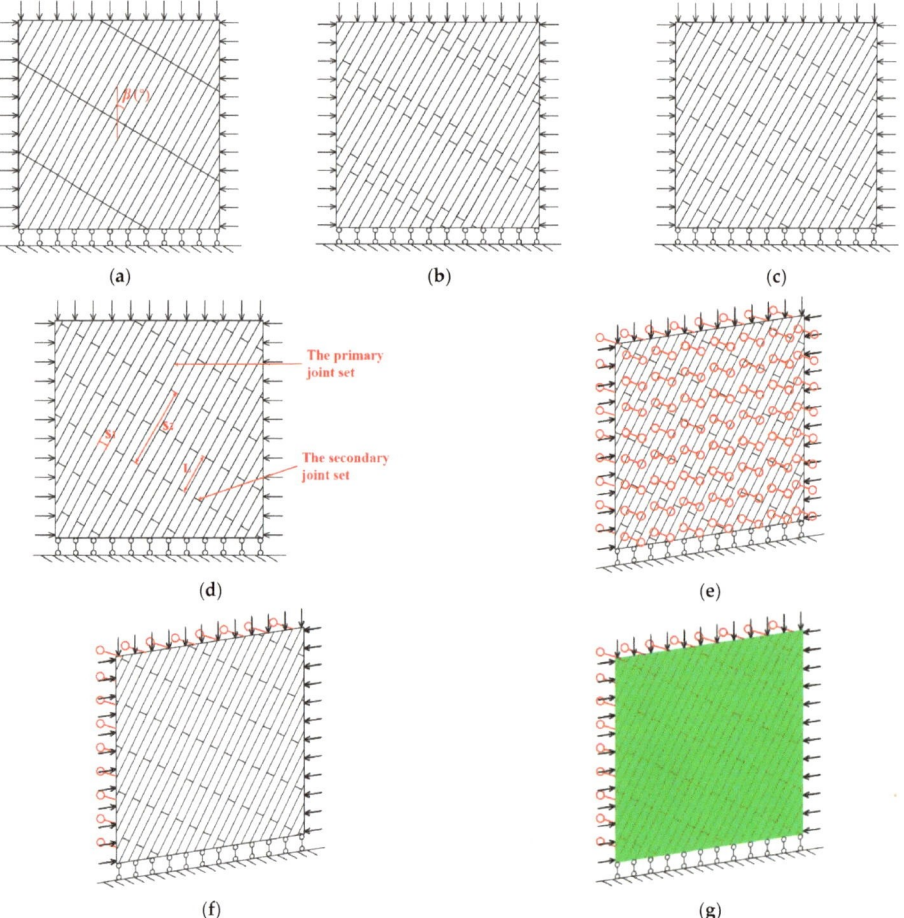

Figure 3. (**a**–**d**) The CJBs containing the joint distance ratios 0%, 20%, 40% and 50%, respectively; (**e**) the model setup under plane strain; (**f**,**g**) the model setup for the case between plane stress and plane strain.

Generally, the parameter values of joints will be lower than rock matrix [29]. The selection of parameters can affect the elastic moduli and compression strengths [30]. According to the corresponding literatures [8–13,16–19], the mechanical parameter values of rock and joint of CJBs are determined (see Table 2).

3. Results

3.1. The Deforming and Bearing under Different Joint Distance Ratios

3.1.1. Under Plane Strain

According to Figure 4a, under the lateral pressure of 4 MPa, in terms of compressive strength (CS), when the joint distance ratio is 0%, the compressive strength of specimen shows a roughly U-shaped trend as β increases; when the joint distance ratio is 20%, 40% and 50%, that changes roughly in a V-shaped trend as β increases. At β of 60° and 75°, compared with the specimen with a joint distance ratio of 0%, for the models with the joint distance ratios of 20%, 40% and 50%, the CS is risen greatly, which is caused by the obvious growth of the effective bearing area. Furthermore, combined with Figure 4c, it is clear that for the CJBs with various joint distance ratios, the troughs of CS appear at β = 30°, 150°, 210° and 330°; the peaks of CS appear at β = 0°, 90°, 180° and 270°. Additionally, for the CJBs with the joint distance ratios of 20%~50%, the CSs of specimens decrease sharply near β = 0° and 180°, which results from the rapid penetration failure of joints. However, they change relatively gently near β = 90° and 270°.

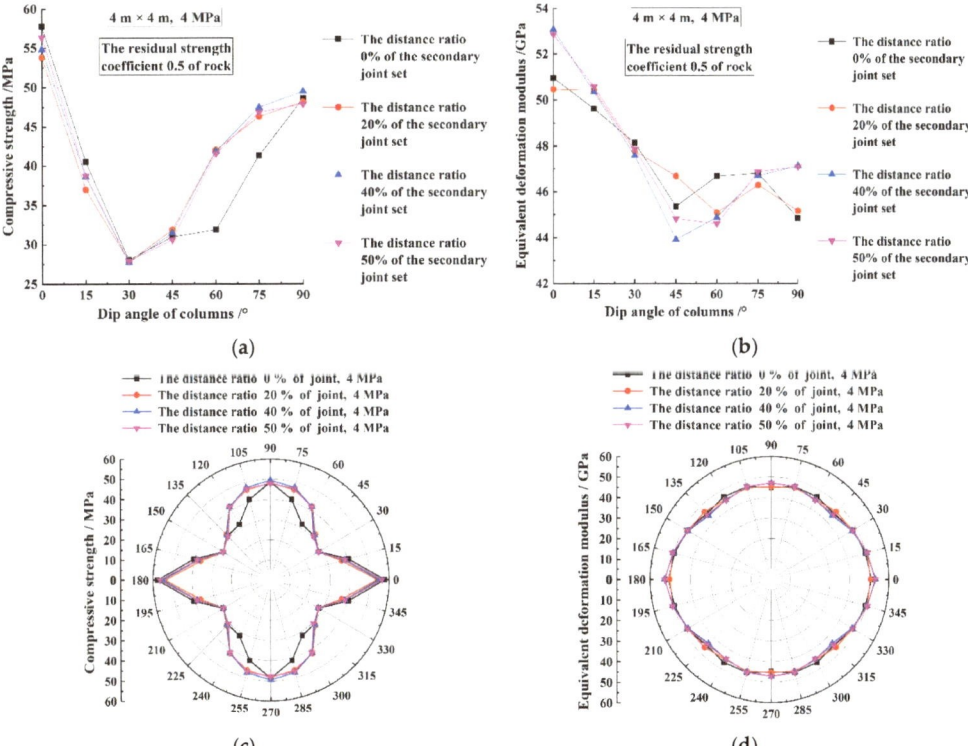

Figure 4. The CJBs with different joint distance ratios: (**a**,**c**) the compressive strength; (**b**,**d**) the equivalent deformation modulus.

Figure 4b shows that under plane strain, in the aspect of equivalent deformation modulus (EDM), when the joint distance ratio is 0%~50%, the EDM of specimen reduces in the beginning, but changes/fluctuates with β increases later. The highest value of EDM appears when β = 0°; the lower values of EDM exist at the range of β = 45°~90°. Moreover, combined with Figure 4d, it is clear that for the CJBs with various joint distance ratios, the EDMs change in elliptical way with β increases. The EDM of the models is less sensitive to the variation in joint distance ratio, which is mainly because the compaction and elastic deformation are not sensitive to joint distance ratio.

Figure 5a,b displays the loading curves of the CJBs owning various joint distance ratios when the lateral pressure = 4 MPa under plane strain. As presented in Figure 5a, when the joint distance ratio = 0%, the loading curve of the CJBs with $\beta = 60°$ show ductile failure characteristic, while the loading curves of other CJBs show basically brittle failure characteristics. In addition, no residual strength stage exists on the loading curves for $\beta = 15°$, 30° and 75°, indicating that the failure and overall instability of specimen occur. As shown in Figure 5b,d, the loading curves for various column dip angles are almost with some characteristics of brittle failure. When the joint distance ratio is 20%, 40% and 50%, there is no residual strength stage in the loading curve when $\beta = 15°$, while regarding the other column dip angles, the residual strength stages exist in the loading curves. If $\beta = 30°$ and 75°, compared with the CJBs with joint distance ratio 0%, for the CJBs with joint distance ratios 20%~50%, the residual strength stability is improved.

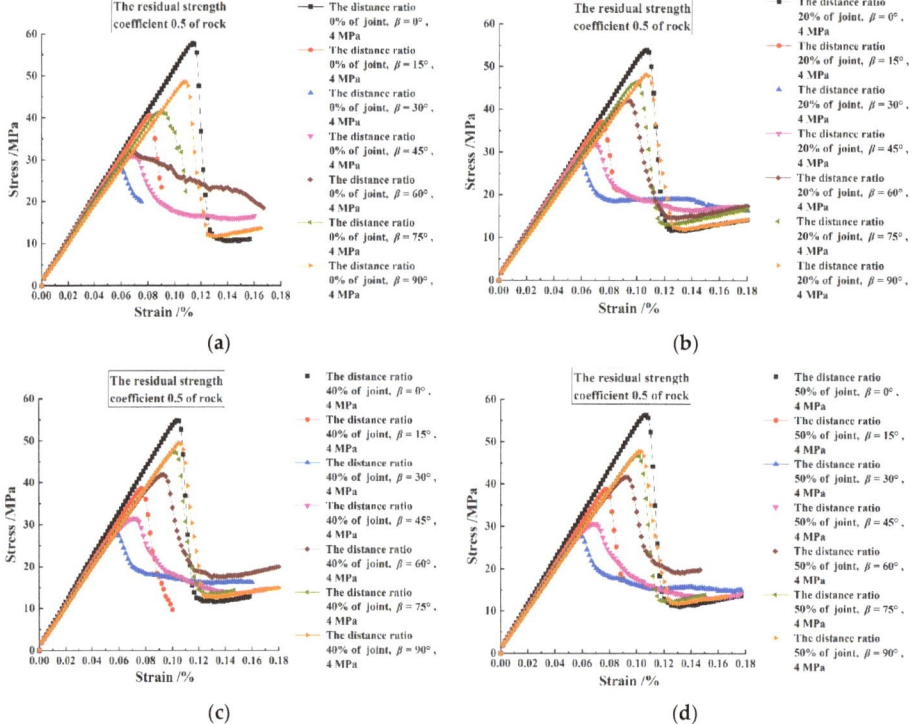

Figure 5. The loading curves of CJBs: (**a**) the joint distance ratio of 0%; (**b**) the joint distance ratio of 20%; (**c**) the joint distance ratio of 40%; (**d**) for the joint distance ratio of 50%.

3.1.2. The Cases of Two Kinds of Model Boundaries

Figure 6 shows the CSs and EDMs of CJBs with different joint distance ratios in the cases of two kinds of model boundaries. As depicted in Figure 6a, in terms of CS, for the CJBs with $\beta = 30°$ under the lateral pressure = 4 MPa, from the perspective of joint distance ratio, if the boundary condition is the case between plane stress and plane strain, the CS of specimen displays a decreasing and increasing fluctuation trend with the growth of joint distance ratio, in which the ratio of the highest CS to the lowest CS is 1.023, indicating the very small fluctuation range. If the boundary condition is plane strain, the model CS reduces in the beginning, but rises as the joint distance ratio increases later. The ratio of the highest value to the lowest value of CS is 1.012, which shows that the variation range is also very small. From the perspective of model boundary condition, the CS under Case II is higher than Case I. If the model boundaries are changed in Case II, the increasing rates of CSs of specimens with joint distance ratios of 0%, 20%, 40% and 50% are 13.41%, 14.56%, 13.22% and 15.23%, respectively.

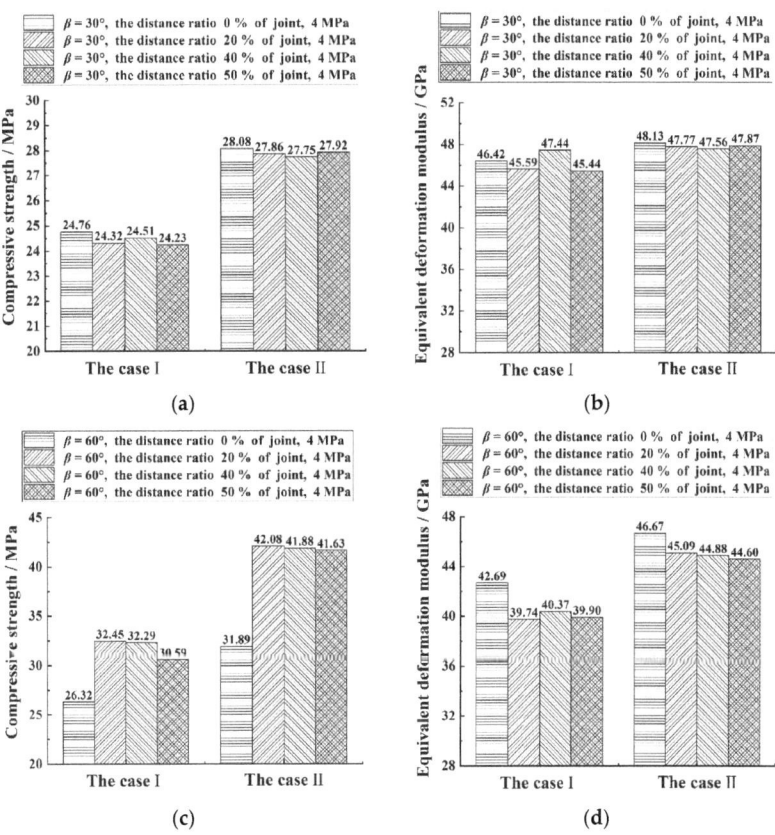

Figure 6. For the cases of two kinds of model boundaries and the CJBs with different joint distance ratios: (a,c) the compressive strength for $\beta = 30°$ and $60°$; (b,d) the equivalent deformation modulus for $\beta = 30°$ and $60°$ (Case I corresponding to the case between plane stress and plane strain and Case II corresponding to the plane strain).

As presented in Figure 6b, for the CJBs with $\beta = 30°$ when the lateral pressure = 4 MPa, from the perspective of joint distance ratio, if the model boundaries are Case II, the EDM of specimen displays a reducing and rising fluctuation trend with the increase in joint distance ratio. If the model boundaries are Case I, the model EDM decreases in the beginning, but increases with the growth of joint distance ratio. From the perspective of model boundary condition, if the model boundaries vary from Case I to Case II, the increasing rates of EDMs of specimens with joint distance ratios of 0%, 20%, 40% and 50% are 3.68%, 4.78%, 0.25% and 5.35%, respectively, indicating that there is no obvious difference for the EDMs of specimens under the two model boundaries.

Figure 6c shows that in terms of CS, for the CJBs with $\beta = 60°$ when the lateral pressure = 4 MPa, from the perspective of joint distance ratio, if the model boundaries are Case between plane stress and plane strain, the model CS rises in the beginning, but reduces as the joint distance ratio increases, in which the ratio of the highest value to the lowest value of CS is 1.233. If the model boundaries are in plane strain, as the joint distance ratio rises, the model CS also increases firstly but decreases later. For this case, the ratio of the highest value to the lowest value of CS is 1.320. From the perspective of model boundary condition, the CS in Case II is higher than that in Case I. If the model boundaries vary from Case I to Case II, the increasing rates of CSs of specimens with joint distance ratios of 0%, 20%, 40% and 50% are 21.16%, 29.68%, 29.70% and 36.09%, respectively.

Figure 6d shows that for the CJBs with $\beta = 60°$ when the lateral pressure = 4 MPa, if the model boundaries are Case II, the EDM of specimen displays a decreasing and increasing fluctuation trend with the growth of joint distance ratio. If the model boundaries are Case I, the model EDM reduces with the increase in joint distance ratio. From the perspective of model boundary condition, if the model boundaries vary from Case I to Case II, the increasing rates of EDMs of specimens with joint distance ratios of 0%, 20%, 40% and 50% are 9.32%, 13.46%, 11.17% and 11.78%, respectively.

Figure 7a,b displays the loading curves influenced by various joint distance ratios in the cases of two kinds of model boundaries. Figure 7a shows that for the CJBs with $\beta = 30°$ when the lateral pressure of 4 MPa, if the model boundaries are Case I, the loading curves of specimens with various joint distance ratios will be closer. For Case II, the loading curves of specimens with different joint distance ratio show relatively obvious difference in the residual strength stage. Significantly, no residual strength stage exists on the loading curve for the joint distance ratio 0%, indicating that the macro instability of the model occurs. Regarding the perspective of model boundary condition, compared with Case I, the stress peak and residual strength of the model boundary condition in the case II are higher. As shown in Figure 7b, for the CJBs with $\beta = 60°$ if the model boundaries are Case I, the loading curves influenced by various joint distance ratios show certain ductile failure characteristics, which is caused by the relatively strong confining pressure. For Case II, the loading curve for joint distance ratio 0% is with ductile failure characteristic, while the stress-strain curves for joint distance ratios 20%, 40% and 50% show brittle failure characteristics, which results from the obvious influence of confining pressure on CJB anisotropy. From the perspective of model boundary condition, compared with Case I, the stress peaks for Case II are higher.

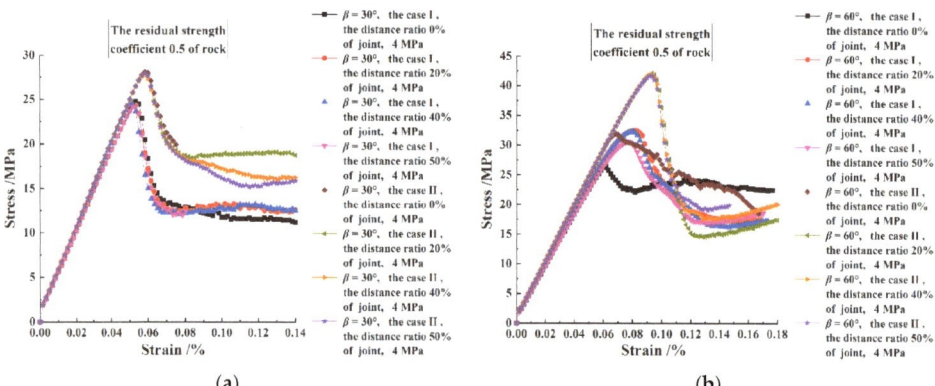

Figure 7. For the two kinds of model boundaries and the loading curves affected by various joint distance ratios: (**a**) for $\beta = 30°$; (**b**) for $\beta = 60°$ (Case I corresponding to the case between plane stress and plane strain and Case II corresponding to the plane strain).

3.2. Fracture Processes and Energy Evolutions under Different Joint Distance Ratios

3.2.1. Failure Modes under Different Column Dip Angles

Figure 8 displays the z-direction displacement contours of the CJBs with the joint distance ratios 0%, 50% and various βs under plane strain when the lateral pressure = 4 MPa. Figure 8a,h shows that for the CJBs with $\beta = 0°$ and the joint distance ratio 0%, the columnar joints in the upper zone of the mode are damaged, and there is a fluctuating strip fracture zone near the top of the model. Meanwhile, the sedimentation inside the model is distributed along the strip fracture zone. When the joint distance ratio is 50%, the fracturing of the columnar joints in the middle of the upper area of the model develops deeper and deeper. As presented in Figure 8b,i, for the CJBs with β = 15° and the joint distance ratio 0%, the columnar joints at the upper area of the model slide and become cracked due to the compression shear. Simultaneously, the sedimentation inside the model mainly develops along the dip angle of the cracked columns. For the condition of the joint distance ratio 50%, the joints within the upper area of the model slide and become damaged. As depicted in Figure 8c,j, for the CJBs with β = 30° and the joint distance ratio 0%, the columnar joints within the model slide under compression and shear, and the sedimentation at the right side of the upper part of the specimen is transmitted to deeper part. When the joint distance ratio is 50%, the joint slip characteristics and sedimentation inside the model are also basically same as the case of the joint distance ratio 0%. As shown in Figure 8d,k, for the CJBs with β = 45° and the joint distance ratio 0%, a relatively straight oblique shear zone appears within the model, which connects the upper left area as well as the lower right area of the specimen. For the condition of the joint distance ratio 50%, the oblique fracture zone inside the specimen is relatively curved, while the sedimentation still mainly developed following the oblique fractured area.

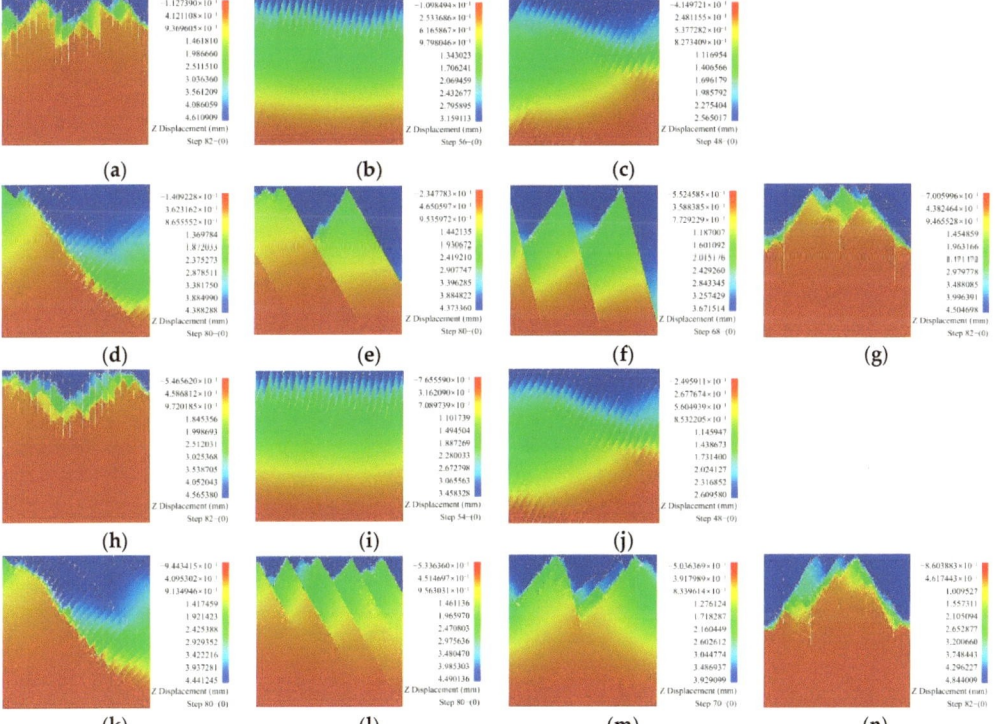

Figure 8. (**a**–**g**) The z-direction displacement diagrams of the CJBs with the joint distance ratio 0% and different column dip angles; (**h**–**n**) the z-direction displacement diagrams of the CJBs with the joint distance ratio 50% and different column dip angles.

As presented in Figure 8e,l, for the CJBs with β = 60° and the joint distance ratio 0%, the shear sliding occurs at the secondary joint set within the model. Additionally, the shear fracture zone exists between the secondary joints in the upper area of the model. The sedimentation is basically distributed within the middle area and the right area of the upper part of the model, along the secondary joint set and shear fracture zone. When the joint distance ratio is 50%, the secondary joint sets at the upper middle part of the model are cut through, and the oblique shear fracture zones appear close to the upper end of the specimen. As depicted in Figure 8f,m, for the CJBs with $\beta = 75°$ and the joint distance ratio 0%, the shear sliding at the secondary joint sets inside the specimen is relatively obvious. Additionally, there are two oblique shear fracture zones between the secondary joints at the upper zone of the model. The sedimentation is mainly distributed along the fracture zones and secondary joint sets, and in the right zone of the model, the sedimentation develops deeper and deeper. For the joint distance ratio = 50%, the shear sliding at the secondary joint sets is less obvious, and there are the oblique shear fracture zones at the upper part of the specimen. As shown in Figure 8g,n, for the CJBs with $\beta = 90°$ and the joint distance ratio 0%, the secondary joint sets at the upper-middle area of the model are damaged, where an M-shaped shear fracture zone appears. The sedimentation mainly develops along the M-shaped shear fractured area. Namely, at the upper part of the model, the sedimentation is transmitted to a deeper depth. When the joint distance ratio is 50%, the secondary joint sets at the upper middle part of the model are also damaged. The M-shaped shear fracture zone and sedimentation distribution characteristics at the upper middle part of the model are also similar as the case of the joint distance ratio 0%.

3.2.2. Fracture Processes and Energy Evolutions under Different Column Dip Angles

(1) For the CJBs with $\beta = 30°$ and the joint distance ratio 0%

Figure 9a displays the schematic diagram of the CJBs model with $\beta = 30°$ and the joint distance ratio 0%, under the lateral pressure = 4 MPa. The stress-strain curve and AE energy are presented in Figure 9b,c. Meanwhile, the minor principal stress contours at the Points A~F are depicted in Figure 9d–i, describing the phenomenon of compression shear, sliding, and cracking of joints, crack initiation, propagation and rupture. The red zones on the minor principal stress diagram reflects the high-stress concentrations.

Combined with Figure 9b,d–i, it can be indicated that at the Point, the corresponding columnar joints and secondary joint sets inside the specimen show stress concentration. At the Point B, the columnar joints at the upper area of the model slide and become cracked. At the upper middle area of the model, high-stress concentration occurs along the edges of some columns, initially forming strip-shaped stress concentrations. When the loading is reduced to the Point C, the fractures generate and develop along the edges of some columns, the stresses is concentrated at the crack tips, and a strip-shaped stress concentration is formed inside the specimen. If the loading reaches the Point D, the fractures propagate further, the concentration extent of the original strip stress decreases, and there are stress concentrations along the edges of some columns at the right middle side of the specimen. When the loading reaches the Point E, the cracks initiate at the secondary joint sets. If the loading reaches the Point F, fractures intensify inside those strip fracture zones above the secondary joint sets. Moreover, there are strip damage zones at the upper surface and middle parts of the model. These columnar joints slide and become cracked in the middle upper part of the specimen. The secondary joint sets in the upper zone and the lower part of the model get damaged, and the secondary joint set at the middle of the model fails.

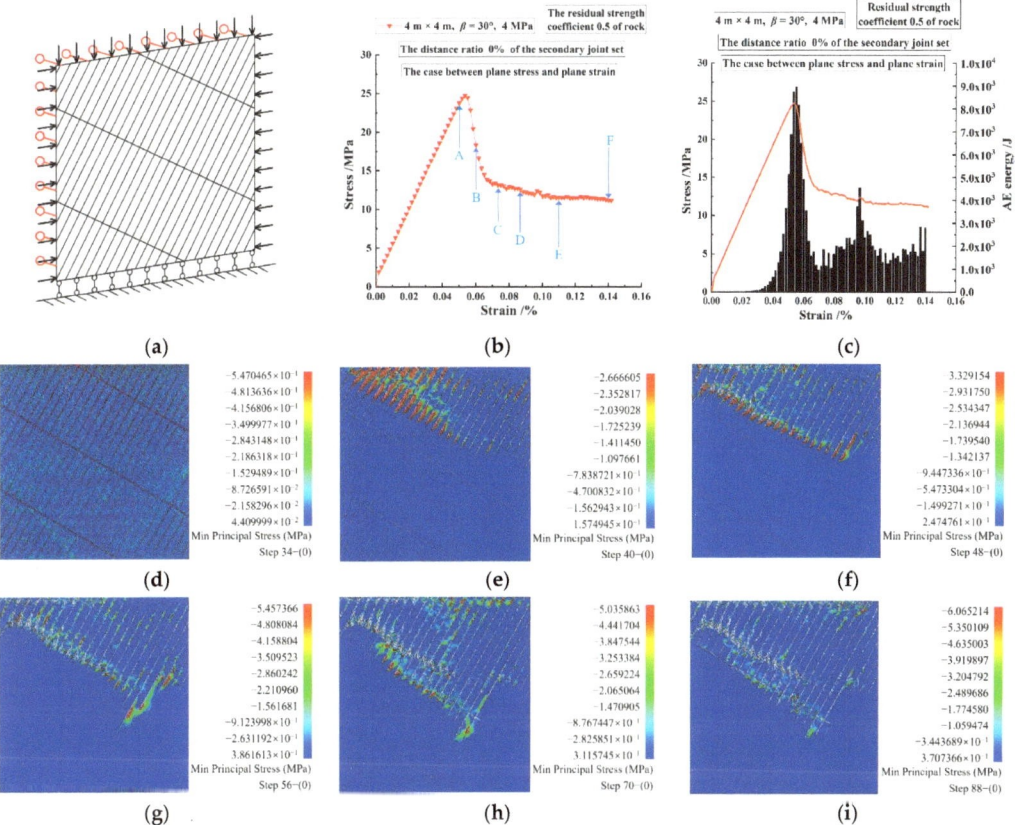

Figure 9. (a) For the case between plane stress and plane strain, the schematic diagram of the CJB model with $\beta = 30°$ and the joint distance ratio 0%; (b,c) the loading curve and AE energy; (d–i) the minor principal stress contours at the Points A~F.

Figure 9c indicates that the AE energy release of the model shows roughly with the double-peak distribution. The 1st peak may be mainly caused by the damage-slip cracking at the upper middle area of the model. Meanwhile, the 2nd AE energy peak is mainly caused by the damage sliding at columnar joints at the middle area of the model and the crack creation and develop along the secondary joints.

(2) For the CJBs with $\beta = 30°$ and the joint distance ratio 50%

Figure 10a shows the schematic diagram of the CJBs model with $\beta = 30°$ and the joint distance ratio 50% when the lateral pressure = 4 MPa. Figure 10b,c displays the loading curve and AE energy. Figure 10d–i shows the minor principal stress contours at the Points A~F. Combined with Figure 10b,d–i, at the Point A, these joint sets and secondary joint sets inside the model show high-stress concentration. If the loading reaches Point B, the trend of compressive shear sliding along the columnar joint sets near the top of the specimen. If the loading reaches the Point C, the joint sets in the upper zone of the sample slide and become cracked, and several columns at the top of the model show stress concentrations. If the loading continues to decrease to the Point D, along the secondary joint set in the upper part of that specimen, cracks initiate and the stresses concentrate, forming a strip stress concentration zone. Near the upper end of the model, the columns also show stress concentration, forming another strip stress concentration zone. If the loading is reduced to the Point E, the stress concentrations are transferred to the vicinity below the position of the secondary joint set. When the stress reaches Point F, in the upper zone of the sample and near the lower position of these secondary joint set, cracks are created and propagate, and the stresses are concentrated at the crack tips. Simultaneously, within the right middle part of the specimen, those joints slide under compression and shear, and the high-stress concentrations appear at the edge of the nearby column. Moreover, there are strip damage and fracture zones in the upper middle area of the model. In this area, the columnar joints are damaged, slide and become cracked. At the position of secondary joint set in the upper area of the model, the damage occurs. As shown in Figure 10c, the AE release of the model shows a single-peak distribution. The peak is as a result of the damaging, sliding and cracking of the columnar joints in the upper area of the sample.

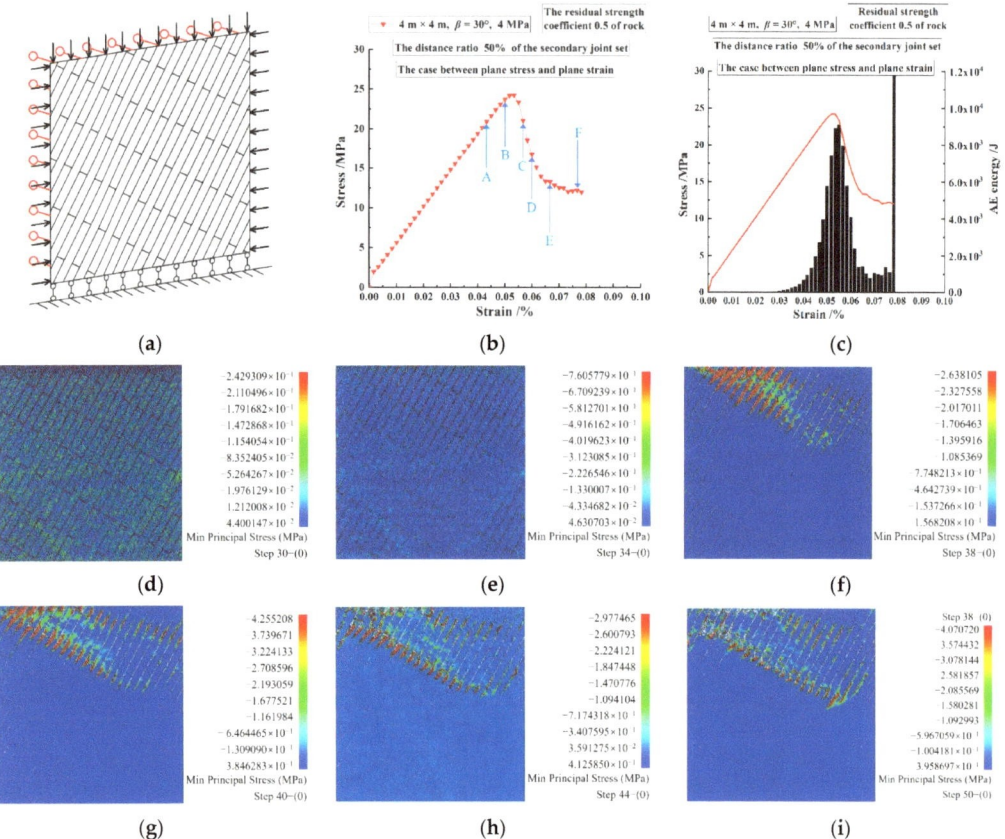

Figure 10. (a) For the case between plane stress and plane strain, the schematic diagram of the CJBs model with $\beta = 30°$ and the joint distance ratio 50%; (b,c) the loading curve and AE energy; (d–i) the minor principal stress contours at the Points A~F.

(3) For the CJBs with $\beta = 75°$ and the joint distance ratio 50%

Figure 11a displays the schematic diagram of the CJBs model with $\beta = 75°$ and the joint distance ratio 50% under the lateral pressure = 4 MPa. The stress-strain curve and AE release are presented (see Figure 11b,c). The minor principal stress contours at the Points A~F are depicted in Figure 11d–i. Combined with Figure 11b,d–i, at the Point, the joints within the model and the secondary joint set at the middle of the model shows high-stress concentration. If the loading reaches the Point B, the secondary joints at the upper middle area of the model are damaged. In the meantime, the columns near it display obvious stress concentration. If the loading drops to the Point C, crack initiation, propagation and penetration occur near the secondary joint set at the upper middle part of the model. In addition, there is an oblique shear fracture zone between the secondary joint sets. If the loading continues to decrease to the Point D, near the middle of the model, crack initiation, propagation and penetration at the secondary joints develop towards the lower area of the model. Simultaneously, crack creation and stress concentration happen near the secondary joints at the right side of the model. If the loading is reduced to the Point E, fractures along the secondary joint set of the specimen are intensified. Moreover, in the right middle part of the specimen, the shear fracture zones develop and the stresses at the tips of cracks are concentrated. If the loading reaches the Point F, the crushing inside the specimen will intensify.

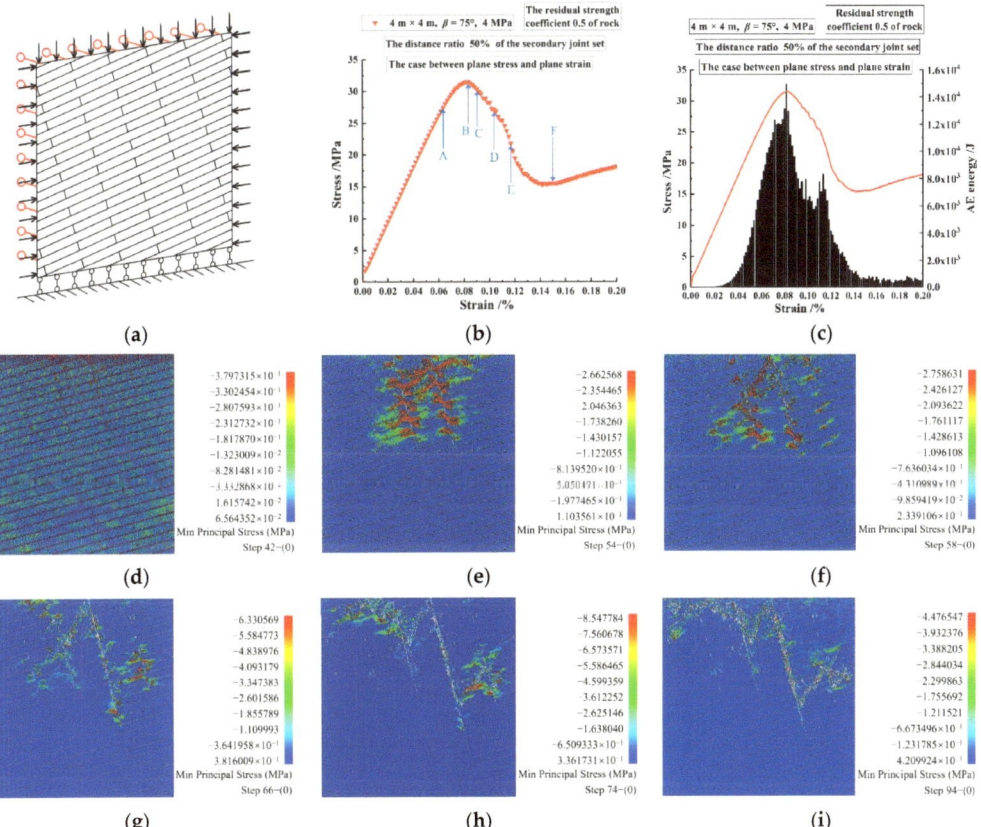

Figure 11. (a) For the case between plane stress and plane strain, the schematic diagram of the CJBs model with $\beta = 75°$ and the joint distance ratio 50%; (b,c) the loading curve and AE energy; (d–i) the minor principal stress contours at the Points A~F.

Meanwhile, the joints within the model are damaged. The secondary joints at the upper area of the model are damaged and cracked, especially at the middle of the upper area of the model, where the damage and fracture penetrate. Close to the upper end of the model and at the right middle part of the model, the damaged zones are developed.

As displayed in Figure 11c, it is clear that the AE energy of the model displays the double-peak distribution. The first energy peak might be induced by the primary joint damage and the cracking of secondary joint set in the upper middle area of the model. The second peak might be as a result of the fracture of the primary joints near the upper left area of the model and the development of the shear fracture zone in the right middle part of the model.

3.2.3. Fracture Processes and Energy Evolutions under Various Joint Distance Ratios and Column Dip Angle of 60°

(1) When the joint distance ratio = 0%

Figure 12a shows the schematic diagram of the CJBs model with $\beta = 60°$ and the joint distance ratio 0% under the lateral pressure = 4 MPa. Figure 12b,c displays the loading curve and AE energy. Figure 12d–I shows the minor principal stress contours at the Points A~F. Combined with Figure 12b,d–i, at the Point A, the secondary joint set within the specimen shows high-stress concentrations, with the trend of compression shear sliding. If the loading goes to the Point B, the secondary joint sets inside the specimen gradually slide, and the high stress concentrations appear near the upper end of the specimen. If the loading reaches the Point C, the cracks are created near the upper end of the specimen. If the loading continues to decrease to the Point D, near the upper end of the model, the cracks propagate, and the stresses at the crack tips are concentrated. If the loading is reduced to the Point E, the cracks further develop in the upper area of the specimen, but the stress concentration reduces. If the loading reaches the Point F, fractures intensify from the secondary joints and fracture zones. At the middle of the right side of the specimen, the cracks initiate, and the stresses are concentrated. Meanwhile, the secondary joint sets slide, are damaged, compressed, and sheared. The damage fracture zones are developed near the top and at the upper area of the specimen.

Figure 12c shows that the AE energy of the specimen is roughly with four-peak distribution (or multi-peak distribution). The first energy peak might be as a result of the compression shear sliding at the secondary joint sets inside the specimen. The second peak might be mainly caused by the damage development of fractured zone near the top of the specimen. The third peak might be mainly as a result of the development of the fracture zone near the upper end of the model, the fracture zone in the upper zone of the model and the damage near the secondary joint sets. The fourth peak might be induced by the fracturing aggravation at the secondary joint sets and the initiation and propagation of cracks in the right middle area of the specimen.

(2) When the joint distance ratio = 20%

Figure 13a displays the schematic diagram of the CJBs model with $\beta = 60°$ and the joint distance ratio 20% under the lateral pressure = 4 MPa. The loading curve and AE energy are shown in Figure 13b,c. The minor principal stress contours at the Points A~F are displayed in Figure 13d–i. Combined with Figure 13b,d–i, at the Point A, the secondary joint sets within the specimen show high-stress concentration. If the loading reaches the Point B, near the upper end of the specimen, the high-stress concentrations appear around the secondary joint sets. If the loading decreases to the Point C, the secondary joint sets get fractured at the upper area of the model. The stress concentration is obvious near the upper end of the model. When the loading continues to drop to the Point D, the creation and propagation of cracks occur within the original stress concentration areas. If the loading is reduced to the Point E, cracks further develop in the upper left and upper right parts of the model. When the loading reaches the Point F, the crushing in the upper zone of the model will intensify. Meanwhile, damage along columnar joint sets inside the specimen develops. The compressive shear fractures appear along the secondary joint sets. The damage fracture zones at the upper part of the model are formed. Figure 13c shows that the elastic energy of the specimen shows the single-peak distribution. The peak is induced by the compression-shear failure of the secondary joint sets, the damage of the primary joints and the columns in the upper part of the model.

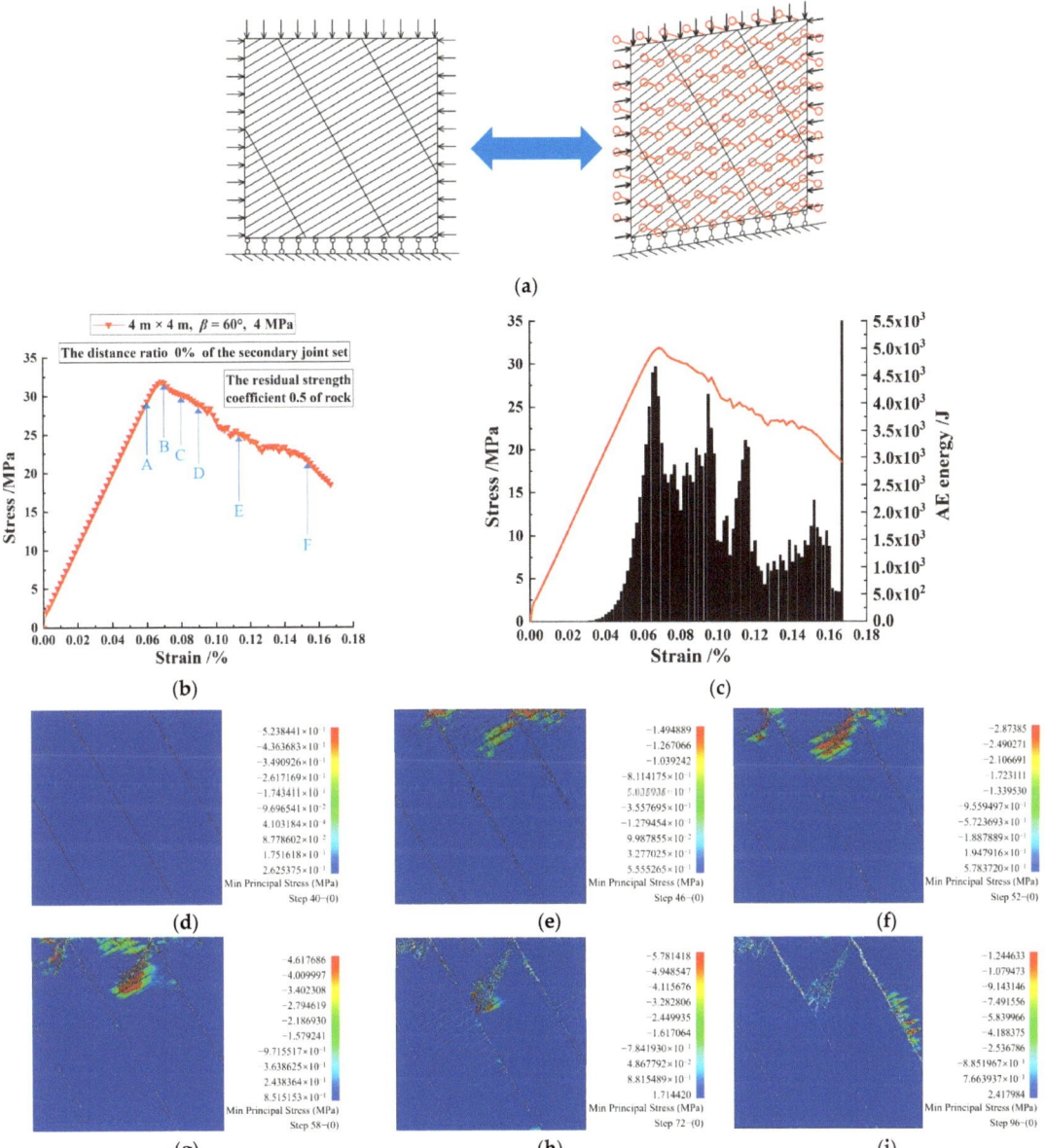

Figure 12. (a) Under plane strain, the schematic diagram of the CJBs model with $\beta = 60°$ and the joint distance ratio 0%; (b,c) the loading curve and AE energy; (d–i) the minor principal stress contours at the Points A~F.

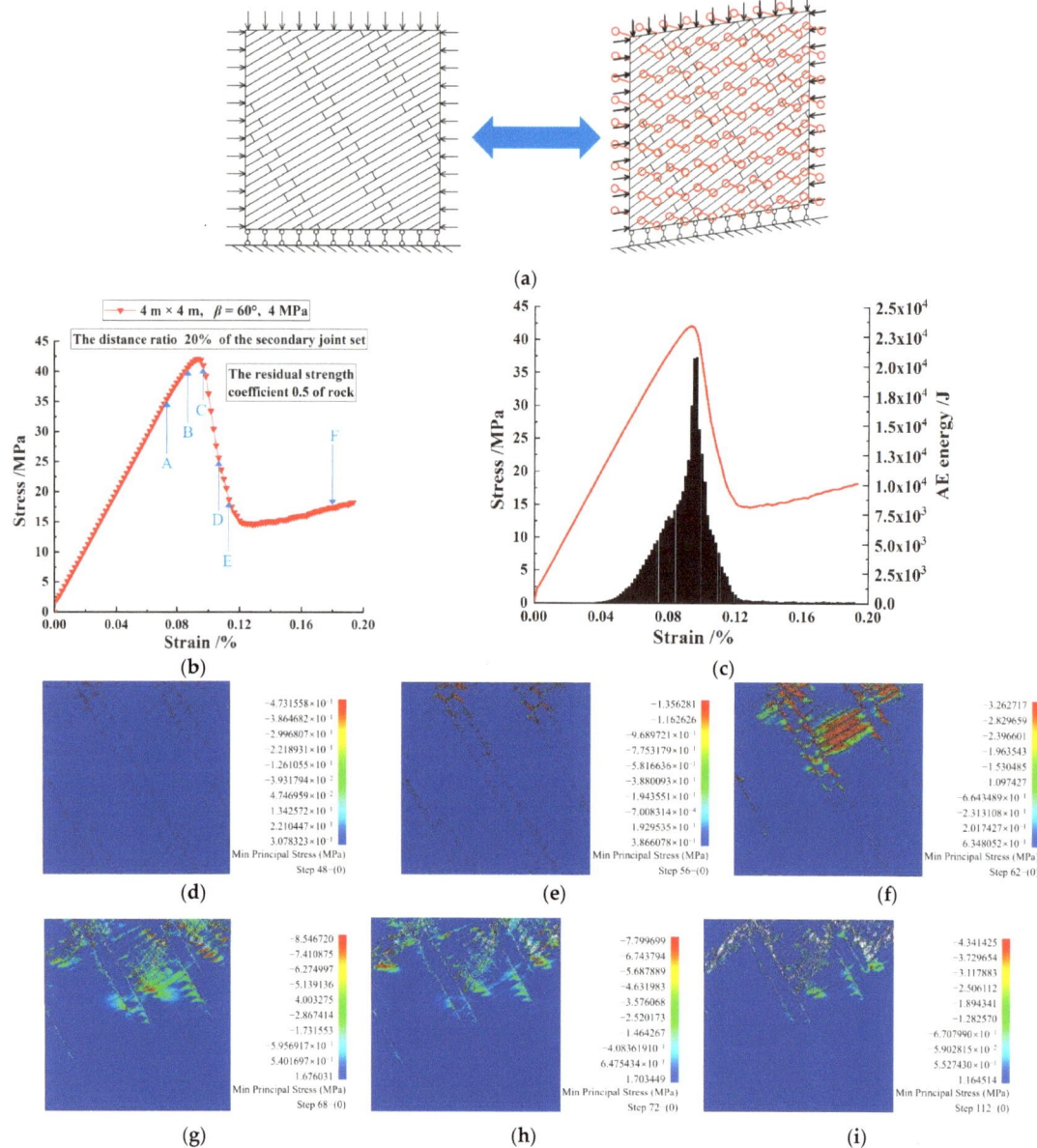

Figure 13. (**a**) Under plane strain, the schematic diagram of the CJBs model with $\beta = 60°$ and the joint distance ratio 20%; (**b**,**c**) the loading curve and AE energy; (**d**–**i**) the minor principal stress contours at the Points A~F.

(3) When the joint distance ratio = 50%

Figure 14a shows the schematic diagram of the CJBs model with $\beta = 60°$ and the joint distance ratio 50% under the lateral pressure = 4 MPa. Figure 14b,c displays the loading curve and AE energy. Figure 14d–i show the minor principal stress contours at the Points A~F. Combined with Figure 14b,d–i, at the Point A, the secondary joint sets within the specimen are with a certain degree of stress concentration. If the loading reaches the Point B, the high stress concentrations are gradually significant near the secondary joint sets. If the loading is reduced to the Point C, the secondary joints slide, are compressed and sheared, and the creation and propagation of cracks and the high-stress concentration appears. If the loading decreases to the Point D, the compression shear and sliding at the secondary joint sets further develop. If the loading further decreases to the Point E, the compression shear and sliding fracture at the secondary joint sets develops towards the lower area of the model, but the extent of high-stress concentration reduces. If the loading is reduced to the Point F, the crushing intensifies near the top of the model and at the secondary joints. Meanwhile, there are the damage fracture zones developing towards the upper end of the model. The compression shear, damage and fracture appear at secondary joint sets. The damage at columnar joints is developed.

As presented in Figure 14c, the elastic energy of the model has a single-peak distribution. The peak is mainly as a result of the compression-shear damage and fracture of the secondary joint sets, as well as the failure of the columns near the upper end of the model.

(4) When the joint distance ratio = 50%

Figure 15a displays the schematic diagram of the CJBs model with $\beta = 60°$ and the joint distance ratio 50%, in the case between plane stress and plane strain, under the lateral pressure = 4 MPa. The stress-strain curve and elastic energy are shown in Figure 15b,c. The minor principal stress contours at the Points A~F are depicted in Figure 15d–i. Combined with Figure 15b,d–i, at the Point A, the high-stress concentrations appear at the primary and secondary joints inside the model. If the loading is reduced to the Point B, the secondary joint sets get cracked in the upper zone of the model, and there will be obvious concentrated stresses around the secondary joint sets at the upper middle area of the model. When the loading decreases to the Point C, the cracks near the secondary joint sets initiate, propagate and penetrate in the upper area of the model, and the concentrated stresses move to the columns near the secondary joint sets. If the loading continues to decrease to the Point D, at the right side of the upper part of the specimen, the creation and propagation of cracks form along the columns around the secondary joints. If the loading reaches the Point F, the damage of the columns will intensify in the top zone of the specimen. Meanwhile, the damage of columnar joints inside the model develops. The secondary joints near the top part of the model are damaged and broken. The damage fracture zones are formed at the columns between the secondary joint sets. As displayed in Figure 15c, the AE energy of the specimen shows roughly the double-peak distribution. The first peak might be caused by the compression damage of primary joints, and the cracking of the secondary joint sets and surrounding columns. The second peak is basically as a result of the crack initiation of the columns at the upper left area of the model, and the crack propagation of the columns at the right side of the model.

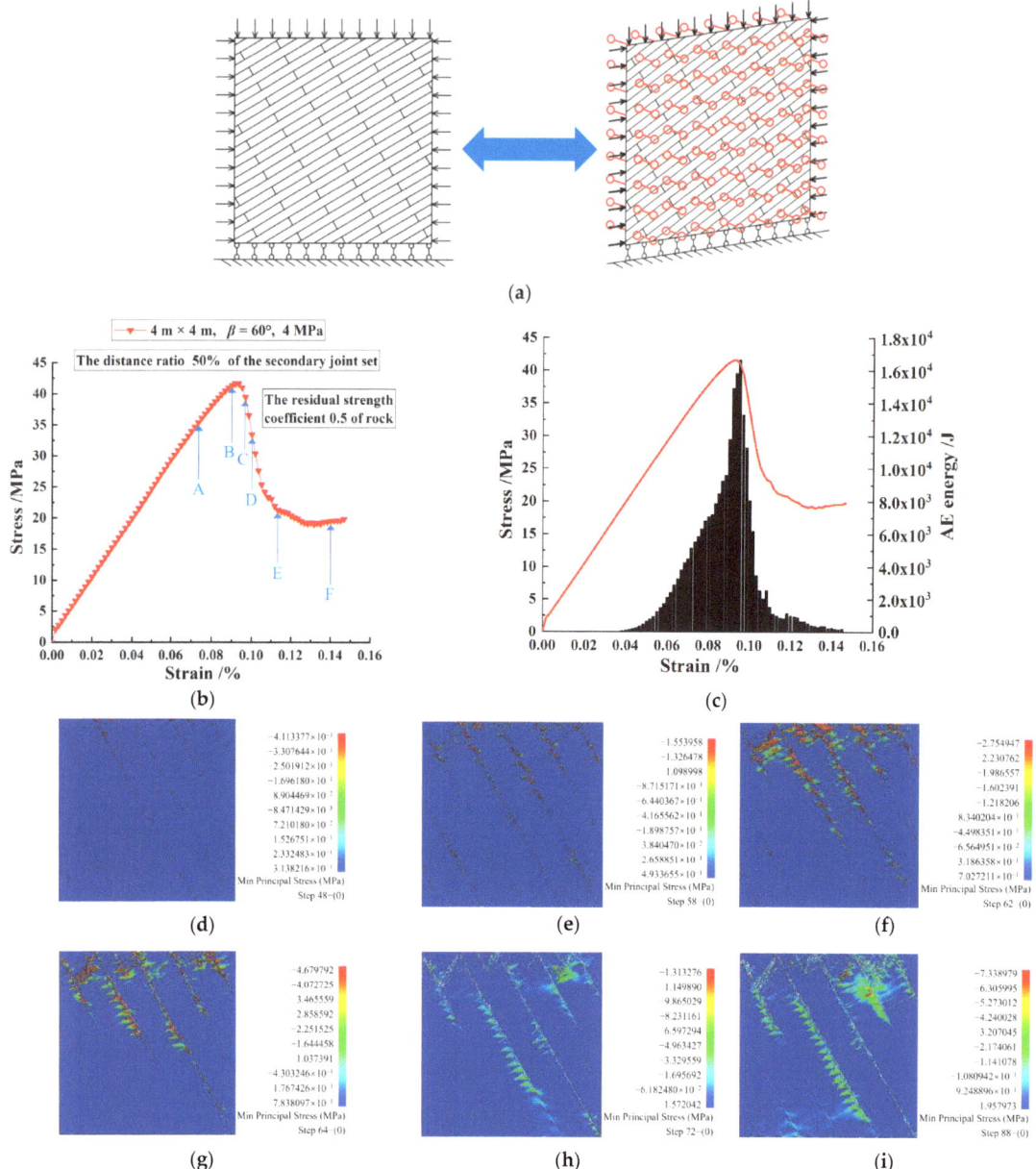

Figure 14. (a) Under plane strain, the schematic diagram of the CJBs model with $\beta = 60°$ and the joint distance ratio 50%; (b,c) the loading curve and AE energy; (d–i) the minor principal stress contours at the Points A~F.

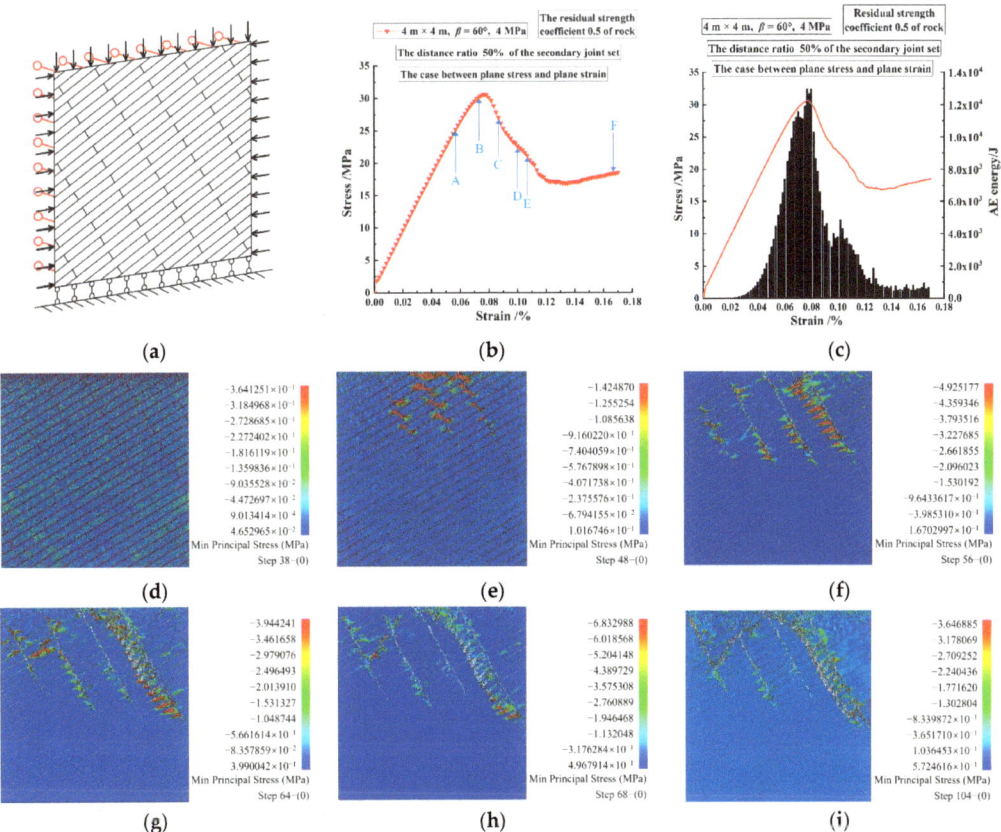

Figure 15. (**a**) For the case between plane stress and plane strain, the schematic diagram of the CJBs model with $\beta = 60°$ and the joint distance ratio 50%; (**b**,**c**) the loading curve and AE energy; (**d**–**i**) the minor principal stress contours at the Points A~F.

3.3. The AE Counts and Energy Accumulations under Different Joint Distance Ratios
3.3.1. For the Case of Plane Strain

From Figure 16a–c, it is clear that for the CJBs with $\beta = 30°$ and the joint distance ratio 0%, the AE count and energy accumulation change slightly in the beginning but increase sharply later. When the joint distance ratio is 20% and 50%, the variation trend of the AE count and energy accumulation is slow change, then shows a steep rise, and then slow growth. In terms of the accumulation magnitude of AE energy, the order from small to large is the joint distance ratios 0%, 20% and 50%, respectively. When the joint distance ratio is 0%, no residual strength stage exists on the loading curve, indicating that the overall instability of the model occurs. Before the instability failure, the AE count and energy accumulation are lower than those for the joint distance ratios 20% and 50%.

Mathematics **2022**, *10*, 4149

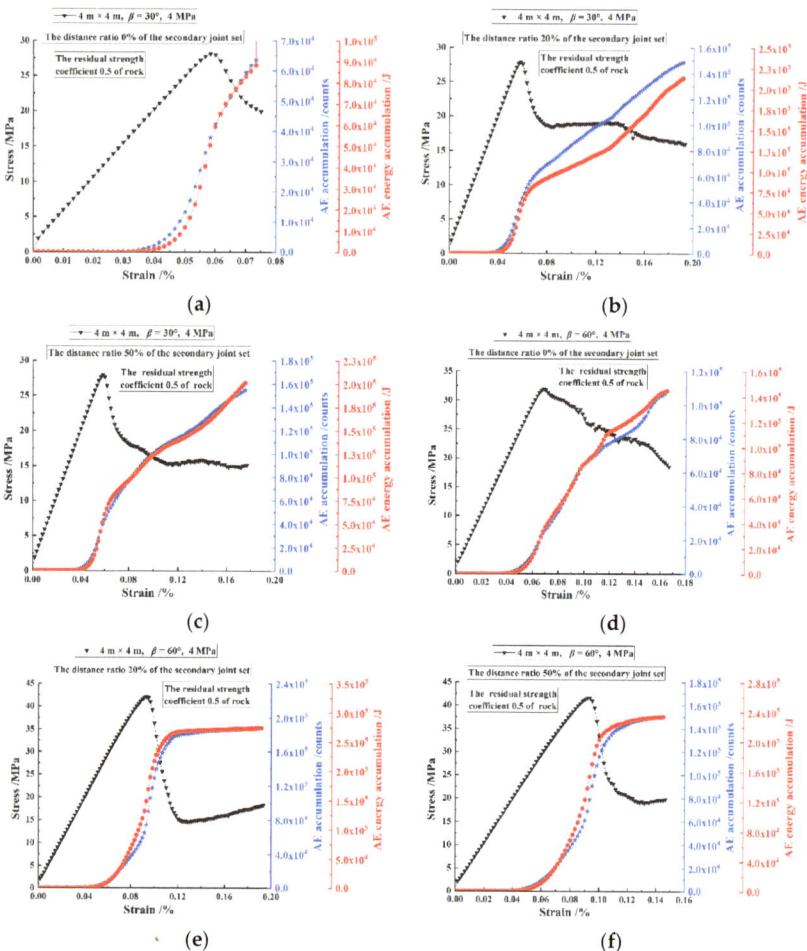

Figure 16. The AE counts and energy accumulations of the CJBs with different joint distance ratios: (**a**–**c**) for $\beta = 30°$ and the joint distance ratios 0%, 20% and 50%, respectively; (**d**–**f**) for $\beta = 60°$ and the joint distance ratios 0%, 20% and 50%, respectively.

As presented in Figure 16d–f, regarding the variation in the AE counts and energy accumulations, for the CJBs with $\beta = 60°$ and the joint distance ratio 0%, the AE count and energy accumulation change gently at first and then grow. When the joint distance ratio is 20% and 50%, the variation trend of the AE count and energy accumulation is a slow change, then it increases, and then shows gentle variation. In terms of the accumulation magnitude of AE energy, the order from small to large is the joint distance ratios 0%, 50% and 20%, respectively. When the joint distance ratio is 20%, there is a higher degree of damage and fragmentation for the specimen under loading. Thus, the AE energy accumulations are higher than those for the joint distance ratios 0% and 50%.

3.3.2. For the Case between Plane Stress and Plane Strain

Figure 17 displays the AE counts and energy accumulations of the CJBs with various joint distance ratios. As depicted in Figure 17a–c, regarding the variation in the AE counts and energy accumulations, for the CJBs with $\beta = 30°$ and the joint distance ratios 0%, 20% and 50%, the AE counts and energy accumulations firstly change slowly, then increase sharply, and then grow gently. When the joint distance ratio is 50%, the residual strength stage of the loading curve is in short duration, the overall instability of the specimen occurs, so the gentle growth stages of the AE counts and energy accumulations are also short. In terms of the accumulation magnitude of AE energy, the order from small to large is the joint distance ratios 50%, 20% and 0%, respectively. For the joint distance ratio 0%, the model is seriously cracked and broken, so the AE counts and energy accumulations are higher than those for the joint distance ratios 50% and 20%.

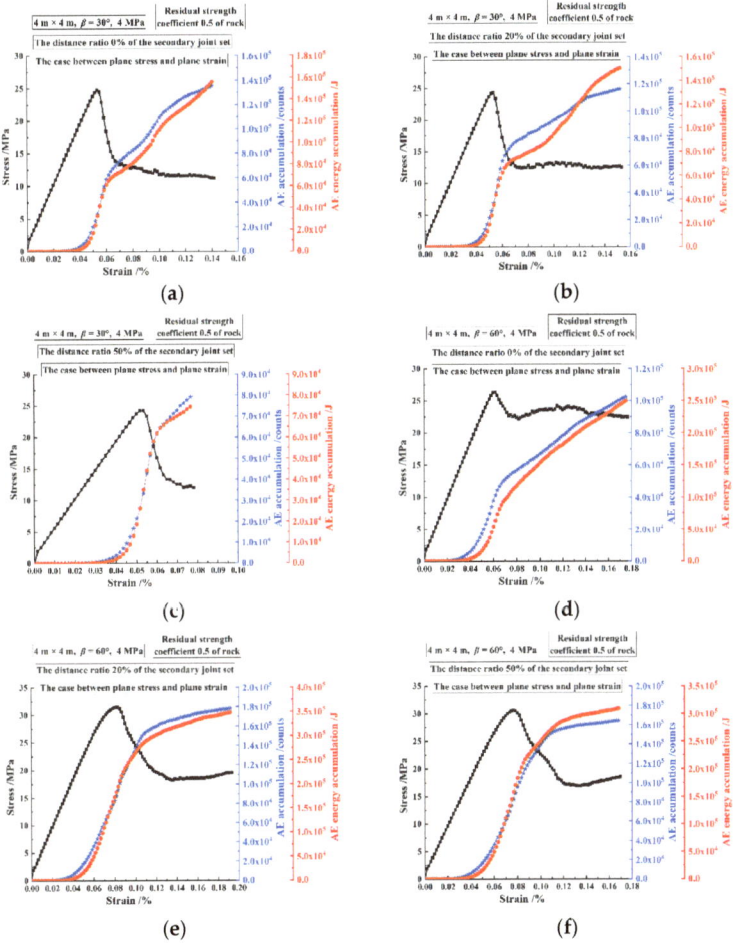

Figure 17. For the case between plane stress and plane strain, the AE counts and energy accumulations of the CJBs with different joint distance ratios: (**a**–**c**) for $\beta = 30°$ and the joint distance ratios 0%, 20% and 50%, respectively; (**d**–**f**) for $\beta = 60°$ and the joint distance ratios 0%, 20% and 50%, respectively.

As shown in Figure 17d–f, regarding the variation in the AE counts and energy accumulations, for the CJBs with $\beta = 60°$ and the joint distance ratio 0%, they change slowly in the beginning, but then rise steeply, and grow gently later. When the joint distance ratio is 20% and 50%, the variation trend of the AE counts and energy accumulations is firstly slow change, then steep increase and then gentle change. In terms of the accumulation magnitude of AE energy, the order from small to large is the joint distance ratios 0%, 50% and 20%, respectively. It can be inferred that for the CJBs with $\beta = 60°$ and the joint distance ratio 20%, there is a higher degree of fragmentation of the model, so the AE counts and energy accumulations are higher than those for the joint distance ratios 0% and 50%.

3.3.3. The AE Energy Accumulations under Compression

(1) For the case of plane strain

Figure 18 shows the accumulation of AE energy of the CJBs with various joint distance ratios, in the case of plane strain. As presented in Figure 18a, the accumulated AE energy corresponding to the stress peaks, occur in order of $\beta = 30°$, $45°$ ($60°$), $15°$, $75°$, $90°$ and $0°$, respectively. From the perspective of their magnitude from small to large, they are in order of $\beta = 75°$, $60°$, $15°$ ($30°$), $0°$, $90°$ and $45°$, respectively. As depicted in Figure 18b, the accumulated AE energy corresponding to the stress peaks occur in order of $\beta = 30°$, $45°$, $15°$, $60°$, $75°$ and $0°$ ($90°$), respectively. From the perspective of their magnitude from small to large, they are in order of $\beta = 15°$, $30°$, $45°$, $90°$, $75°$, $0°$ and $60°$, respectively. According to Figure 18c, the accumulated AE energy corresponding to the stress peaks occur in order of $\beta = 30°$, $45°$, $15°$, $60°$, $75°$, $0°$ and $90°$, respectively. From the perspective of their magnitude from small to large, they are in order of $\beta = 15°$, $30°$, $90°$ ($0°$), $75°$, $45°$ and $60°$, respectively. As displayed in Figure 18d, the accumulated AE energy corresponding to the stress peaks occur in order of $\beta = 30°$, $45°$, $15°$, $60°$, $75°$, $90°$ and $0°$, respectively. From the perspective of their magnitude from small to large, they are in order of $\beta = 15°$, $90°$, $30°$, $75°$, $0°$, $45°$ and $60°$, respectively.

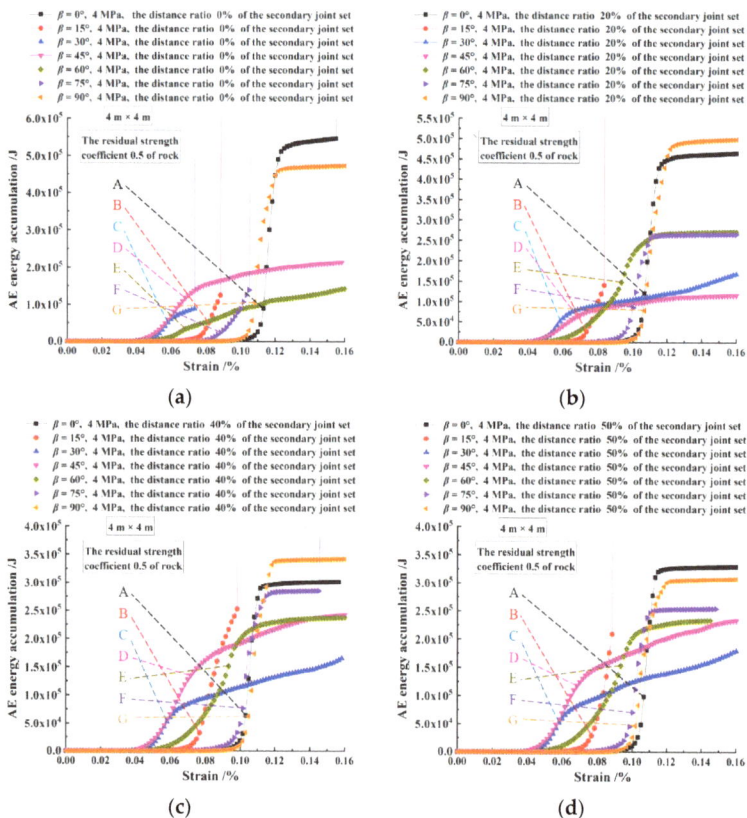

Figure 18. The AE energy accumulations for the peak stresses of the CJBs with different joint distance ratios: (a–d) for the joint distance ratios 0%, 20%, 40% and 50%.

(2) For the case of two kinds of model boundaries

Figure 19 displays the accumulated AE energy corresponding to the stress peaks of the CJBs with various joint distance ratios, in the case of two kinds of model boundaries. Case I is the case between plane stress and plane strain; Case II is the case of plane strain. As depicted in Figure 19a, regarding the CJBs with $\beta = 30°$ when the lateral pressure = 4 MPa under Case I, the accumulated AE energy corresponding to the stress peaks fluctuates with the increase in joint distance ratio, in which the ratio of the highest value to the lowest is 1.284. However, for Case II, the accumulated AE energy corresponding to the stress peaks firstly grows gently, and then changes slowly as the joint distance ratio increases, in which the ratio of the highest value to the lowest is 1.034. Furthermore, the accumulated AE energy corresponding to the stress peaks in Case II is higher than Case I. If the model boundaries vary from Case I to Case II, for the joint distance ratios 0%, 20%, 40% and 50%, the accumulated AE energy corresponding to the stress peaks grow by 53.18%, 46.53%, 89.92% and 48.35%, respectively.

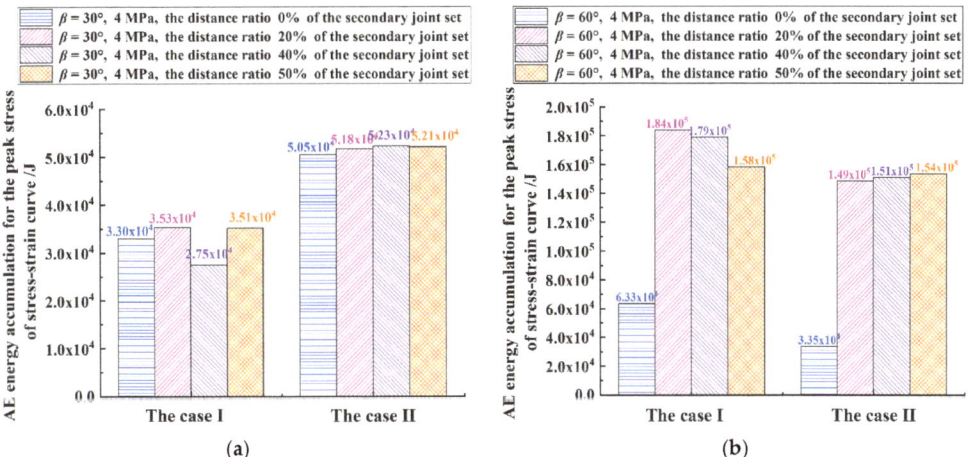

Figure 19. For the case of two kinds of model boundaries, for the CJBs with different joint distance ratios: (a) the accumulated AE energy corresponding to the stress peaks, for $\beta = 30°$; (b) the AE energy accumulations corresponding to the peak stresses, for $\beta = 60°$.

Figure 19b shows that when $\beta = 60°$ and the lateral pressure = 4 MPa under Case I, the AE energy accumulation corresponding to the stress peaks increases sharply but reduces with the growth of joint distance ratio later, in which the ratio of the highest value to the lowest is 2.905, indicating the large variation range. For Case II, the accumulated AE energy corresponding to the stress peaks rises steeply and then grows slowly as the joint distance ratio rises, in which the ratio of the highest value to the lowest is 4.587, implying the great variation range. In addition, the accumulated AE energy corresponding to the stress peaks in Case II is lower than those in Case I. If the model boundaries vary from Case I to Case II, for the joint distance ratios 0%, 20%, 40% and 50%, the AE energy accumulations corresponding to the peak stresses increase by −47.15%, −19.23%, −15.53% and −2.98%, respectively.

4. Discussion

4.1. Influence of Joint Characteristics on CS and EDM

In the case of plane strain, under various joint distance ratios, the troughs of CS appear at $\beta = 30°$, $150°$, $210°$ and $330°$; the peaks of CS appear at $\beta = 0°$, $90°$, $180°$ and $270°$. Additionally, for the CJBs with the joint distance ratios of 20%~50%, the CSs of specimens decrease sharply near $\beta = 0°$ and $180°$, but they change relatively gently near $\beta = 90°$ and

270°. Under various joint distance ratios, the EDMs change in elliptical way as the column dip angle increases. The EDM of model is less sensitive to the variation in joint distance ratio. Moreover, the CS and EDM in Case II are higher than those in Case I.

Zheng et al. [31] performed shear tests on jointed granite samples. Their results showed that the shear strength peak grew with the normal stress or sawtooth angle increasing, but the shear stress-strain curves were not displayed to analyze further. Wang et al. [32] adopted the particle flow code (PFC) for studying the deforming and bearing properties of rock masses with varying joint density and argued that the specimen with a high joint density shows low strength. However, the jointed rock masses were with discrete fracture networks, and it was inconvenient for understanding anisotropy of joined rock masses. Fan et al. [33] adopted the three-dimensional PFC to reproduce the physico-mechanical properties of multiple non-persistent joints subject to uniaxial loading, and analyzed the changing of CSs as the dip-angle and length of joints increase. Moreover, with the increase in joint length, the rock CS will be more and more sensitive to the change of the dip angle. Nevertheless, the influence of lateral pressures on the CS and EDM of rock mass specimens was not taken into account. Wu et al. [34] applied the numerical simulation method to calculate the anisotropy of strength and deformation of jointed rock masses. However, the distribution of joint dip angles, joint trace lengths and joint spacings are different from the specimens in this paper.

4.2. Influence of Joint Characteristics on Fracture Mechanism

Taking the following case in this paper for example: the CJBs models with $\beta = 60°$ and the joint distance ratios 0% and 50% under plane strain. When the joint distance ratio is 0%, with the increase in loading, the secondary joint sets inside the specimen gradually slide under compression and shear, and the high-stress concentrations occur close to the upper end of the specimen. After that, the cracks initiate. As the loading grows, the cracks further develop in the upper zone of the model, but the stress concentration reduces. As the loading further increases, the fracture intensifies along the secondary joints and fractured zones. At the middle of the right side of the specimen, the cracks initiate and the stresses are concentrated.

When the joint distance ratio is 50%, with the growing of loading, the high-stress concentrations are gradually significant near the secondary joint sets. As the loading continues to rise, at the upper area of the model, the secondary joint sets slide, are compressed and sheared, the fractures are created and develop, and the concentrated stresses appear. With the increase in loading, the compression shear and sliding at the secondary joint sets further develop, and the fractures also generate and propagate near the upper end of the model. As the loading further increases, the compression shear and sliding fracture at the secondary joint sets develops towards the lower end of the model, but the extent of high-stress concentration reduces. With the loading further growing, the crushing intensifies towards the upper surface of the model and at the secondary joint sets.

Zhou et al. [35] used the two-dimensional PFC method to compute the physicomechanical parameter values of specimens with single and double joints. However, the influence of lateral pressures on the failure mechanisms of specimens were not taken into account. Wu et al. [34] analyzed the cracking modes of jointed rocky masses subject to lateral pressure by using the numerical simulation method. Nevertheless, the dip angles, trace lengths and spacings of joints obey to the normal, lognormal and negative exponential distributions, respectively. As a result, the fracture features were different from the specimens in this study. Chen et al. [36] suggested that affected by varying lateral pressure, the loading curve of granite specimens containing pre-existing micro-cracks has the feature of stepped brittle drops. Fan et al. [33] discussed the fracture mechanisms and failure patterns of multiple non-persistent joints under uniaxial loading by using the PFC3D method, and analyzed the influence of the dip angles and lengths of joints on the fracture mechanisms. However, the lateral pressures were not taken into account.

4.3. Influence of Joint Characteristics on Acoustic Emission

Taking the following case in this paper for example: the CJBs models with $\beta = 60°$ and the joint distance ratios 0% and 50% under plane strain. When the joint distance ratio is 0%, the AE energy released of the model shows roughly the distribution of four peaks. The first energy peak might result from the fracture and compression shear sliding at the secondary joint sets inside the specimen. The second energy peak might be caused by the damage development of the fracture zone at the upper part of the specimen. The third energy peak might result from the development of the fracture zone close to the upper end of the model, the development of the fracture zone in the top zone of the model and the damage near the secondary joint sets. The fourth energy peak might be caused by the crack aggravation at the secondary joint sets and the creation and propagation of cracks in the middle right zone of the model.

When the joint distance ratio is 50%, the released AE energy of the model shows the single peak distribution. The AE energy peak might mainly result from the compressive shear, damage and fracture of the secondary joint sets, as well as the damage of columns near the upper end of the model.

The tests conducted by Meng et al. [37] show that with the increase in normal stress, the initial slope of shear-stress vs. shear-strain curve of cement mortars increases, while the AE activity gradually lags on the strain axis. However, the stress or damage diagrams corresponding to the AE activities were not displayed to further investigate mechanical behaviors of the specimens. The tests obtained by Guo et al. [38] show that the smaller the joint continuity rate, the more lagging the AE activity for the rock bridge failure point on the time axis. This conclusion is similar with the order of AE energy accumulations in certain cases of this paper. For example, for the CJBs with $\beta=60°$ or $75°$, when the joint distance ratio grows from 0% to 50%, the AE energy accumulation at the peak stresses lags along the strain axis. By the combination of the laboratory physical test and numerical test, Zhang et al. [39] summarized the influences of normal stiffnesses and joint dip angles on the fracture mechanisms and AE energy accumulations of specimens with en-echelon joints. Nevertheless, there are certain differences for the AE energy accumulations due to geometric difference between the en echelon joints and columnar joints. The tests by Wang et al. [40] show that the AE energy accumulation increases with the growth of joint roughness, which provides insights for future related work of CJBs in this study.

5. Conclusions

Based on the meso-damage mechanics and the statistical damage theory, a group of numerical nonuniform CJB samples with various dip angles of columns and distance ratios of secondary joints were established. The continuous fracture and AE release processes of CJBs were captured, and the AE-induced energy release rules were discussed. The conclusions can be drawn as follows:

Under plane strain, the troughs of CS appear at the column dip angles $\beta = 30°, 150°, 210°$ and $330°$; the peaks of CS appear at $\beta = 0°, 90°, 180°$ and $270°$ under different joint distance ratios. Meanwhile, for the CJBs with the joint distance ratios of 20%~50%, the CSs of specimens decrease sharply near $\beta = 0°$ and $180°$, but they change relatively gently near $\beta = 90°$ and $270°$. In terms of EDM, it changes in elliptical way with increasing column dip angle under different joint distance ratios. The EDM of specimen is less sensitive to the variation in joint distance ratio. Under plane strain, the CSs and EDMs are higher than the corresponding values in the case between plane stress and plane strain. These rules can provide the theoretical basis for determining in situ parameters, tunnel axis in transportation engineering, excavation direction in mining engineering and so on.

In the case between plane stress and plane strain, when $\beta = 30°$ and the joint distance ratio = 0%, the columnar joints slide and are compressed; cracks occur near the upper end of the model as the loading grows. Especially, the high stresses will concentrate along the edges of the columns and result in the creation and propagation of cracks at the upper top part of the specimen. As the loading increases, the shear failure happens at the middle part of the model because of high shear stresses. Simultaneously, many fractures develop at the secondary joint sets and the crushing intensifies within the strip fracture zone above the secondary sets. Under plane strain, when $\beta = 60°$ and the joint distance ratio = 50%, the stress concentrations are gradually obvious near the secondary joint sets with the loading increasing. Then, these joints slide, are compressed and sheared. The high stress releases due to the newly formed cracks and rebuilds up at the tips of cracks, which leads the fracture of the secondary joints to developing towards the lower end of the model. However, the extent of stress concentration gradually reduces. With the gradual processes of stress concentration, stress release and stress transfer, the crushing intensifies near the top of the specimen and at the secondary joints. These results will contribute to the maintenance, support design and reinforcement of slopes and tunnels located at CJBs.

Under plane strain, when the joint distance ratio = 50%, the AE energy accumulations corresponding to the stress peaks occur along the strain axis in order of $\beta = 30°, 45°, 15°, 60°, 75°, 90°$ and $0°$. In terms of the magnitude, they occur in the order from small to large when $\beta = 15°, 90°, 30°, 75°, 0°, 45°$ and $60°$, successively. Moreover, when $\beta = 30°$ under the lateral pressure, the accumulated AE energy corresponding to the stress peaks under plane strain is higher than those in the case between plane stress and plane strain. However, when β increases to $60°$, the former ones become lower than the later ones, which implies the critical transformation of the influence of column dip angles on the AE energy-related fracture precursor. These achievements can help to promote the disaster prevention and mitigation for slope sliding, slope toppling and tunnel collapse which may cause severe damage by revealing the failure precursors of rock masses.

Author Contributions: Conceptualization, B.G.; data curation, Y.W.; formal analysis, Y.W.; funding acquisition, B.G. and C.T.; investigation, Y.W. and X.Y.; software, C.T.; supervision, B.G. and C.T.; writing—original draft, Y.W.; writing—review and editing, B.G., Y.Z. and X.Y. All authors have read and agreed to the published version of the manuscript.

Funding: This research was funded by the National Natural Science Foundation of China (Grant Nos. 41941018 and 42102314), the National Basic Research Program of China (Grant No. 2018YFC1505301), and the China Postdoctoral Science Foundation (Grant No. 2020M680950), for which the authors are grateful.

Data Availability Statement: The datasets generated and/or analyzed during the current study are available from the corresponding author upon reasonable request.

Conflicts of Interest: The authors declare no conflict of interest.

Symbol and Abbreviation

Symbol

σ	Stress
f_{c0}	Uniaxial compressive strength
f_{t0}	Uniaxial tensile strength
f_{cr}	Residual compressive strength
f_{tr}	Residual tensile strength
ε	Strain
ε_{c0}	Strain at f_{c0}
ε_{t0}	Strain at f_{t0}
ε_{tu}	Ultimate tensile strain

Abbreviation

CJRM	Columnar jointed rock mass
CJB	Columnar jointed basalt
CS	Compressive strength
EDM	Equivalent deformation modulus

References

1. Zheng, W.T.; Xu, W.Y.; Ning, Y.; Meng, G.T. Scale effect and anisotropy of deformation modulus of closely jointed basaltic mass. *J. Eng. Geol.* **2010**, *18*, 559–565.
2. Jiang, Q.; Feng, X.T.; Hatzor, Y.H.; Hao, X.J.; Li, S.J. Mechanical anisotropy of columnar jointed basalts: An example from the Baihetan hydropower station, China. *Eng. Geol.* **2014**, *175*, 35–45. [CrossRef]
3. Li, G.; Wang, K.; Gong, B.; Tao, Z.G.; Du, K. A multi-temporal series high-accuracy numerical manifold method for transient thermoelastic fracture problems. *Int. J. Solids Struct.* **2021**, *230*, 111151. [CrossRef]
4. Jin, C.Y.; Li, S.G.; Liu, J.P. Anisotropic mechanical behaviors of columnar jointed basalt under compression. *Bull. Eng. Geol. Environ.* **2018**, *77*, 317–330. [CrossRef]
5. Milazzo, M.P.; Keszthelyi, L.P.; Jaeger, W.L.; Rosiek, M.; Mattson, S.; Verba, C.; Beyer, R.A.; Geissler, P.E.; McEwen, A.S.; Hi, R.T. Discovery of columnar jointing on Mars. *Geology* **2009**, *37*, 171–174. [CrossRef]
6. Goehring, L.; Mahadevan, L.; Morris, S.W. Nonequilibrium scale selection mechanism for columnar jointing. *Proc. Natl. Acad. Sci. USA* **2009**, *106*, 387–392. [CrossRef] [PubMed]
7. Meng, Q.X.; Wang, H.L.; Xu, W.Y.; Chen, Y.L. Numerical homogenization study on the effects of columnar jointed structure on the mechanical properties of rock mass. *Int. J. Rock Mech. Min. Sci.* **2019**, *124*, 104127. [CrossRef]
8. Yan, L.; Xu, W.Y.; Wang, R.B.; Meng, Q.X. Numerical simulation of the anisotropic properties of a columnar jointed rock mass under triaxial compression. *Eng. Comput.* **2018**, *35*, 1788–1804. [CrossRef]
9. Niu, Z.H.; Zhu, Z.D.; Que, X.C. Constitutive model of stress-dependent seepage in columnar jointed rock mass. *Symmetry* **2020**, *12*, 160. [CrossRef]
10. Xiang, Z.P.; Wang, H.L.; Xu, W.Y.; Xie, W.C. Experimental study on hydro-mechanical behaviour of anisotropic columnar jointed rock-like specimens. *Rock Mech. Rock Eng.* **2020**, *53*, 5781–5794. [CrossRef]
11. Ke, Z.Q.; Wang, H.L.; Xu, W.Y.; Lin, Z.N.; Ji, H. Experimental study of mechanical behaviour of artificial columnar jointed rock mass containing transverse joints. *Rock Soil Mech.* **2019**, *40*, 660–667.
12. Shi, A.C.; Wei, Y.F.; Zhang, Y.H.; Tang, M.F. Study on the strength characteristics of columnar jointed basalt with a true triaxial apparatus at the Baihetan hydropower station. *Rock Mech. Rock Eng.* **2020**, *53*, 4947–4965. [CrossRef]
13. Ji, H.; Zhang, J.C.; Xu, W.Y.; Wang, R.B.; Wang, H.L.; Yan, L.; Lin, Z.N. Experimental investigation of the anisotropic mechanical properties of a columnar jointed rock mass: Observations from laboratory-based physical modelling. *Rock Mech. Rock Eng.* **2017**, *50*, 1919–1931. [CrossRef]
14. Que, X.C.; Zhu, Z.D.; Niu, Z.H.; Lu, W.N. Estimating the strength and deformation of columnar jointed rock mass based on physical model test. *Bull. Eng. Geol. Environ.* **2020**, *80*, 1557–1570. [CrossRef]
15. Feng, X.T.; Hao, X.J.; Jiang, Q.; Li, S.J.; Hudson, J.A. Rock cracking indices for improved tunnel support design: A case study for columnar jointed rock masses. *Rock Mech. Rock Eng.* **2016**, *49*, 2115–2130. [CrossRef]
16. Hao, X.J.; Feng, X.T.; Yang, C.X.; Jiang, Q.; Li, S.J. Analysis of EDZ development of columnar jointed rock mass in the Baihetan diversion tunnel. *Rock Mech. Rock Eng.* **2016**, *49*, 1289–1312. [CrossRef]
17. Chen, B.R.; Li, Q.P.; Feng, X.T.; Xiao, Y.X.; Feng, G.L.; Hu, L.X. Microseismic monitoring of columnar jointed basalt fracture activity: A trial at the Baihetan Hydropower Station, China. *J. Seismol.* **2014**, *18*, 773–793. [CrossRef]
18. Xiao, Y.X.; Feng, X.T.; Chen, B.R.; Feng, G.L.; Yao, Z.B.; Hu, L.X. Excavation-induced microseismicity in the columnar jointed basalt of an underground hydropower station. *Int. J. Rock Mech. Min. Sci.* **2017**, *97*, 99–109. [CrossRef]
19. Jiang, Q.; Wang, B.; Feng, X.T.; Fan, Q.X.; Wang, Z.L.; Pei, S.F.; Jiang, S. In situ failure investigation and time-dependent damage test for columnar jointed basalt at the Baihetan left dam foundation. *Bull. Eng. Geol. Environ.* **2019**, *78*, 3875–3890. [CrossRef]
20. Liang, Z.Z.; Gong, B.; Li, W. Instability analysis of a deep tunnel under triaxial loads using a three-dimensional numerical method with strength reduction method. *Tunn. Undergr. Space Technol.* **2019**, *86*, 51–62. [CrossRef]
21. Gong, B.; Wang, Y.Y.; Zhao, T.; Tang, C.A.; Yang, X.Y.; Chen, T.T. AE energy evolution during CJB fracture affected by rock heterogeneity and column irregularity under lateral pressure. *Geomat. Nat. Hazards Risk* **2022**, *13*, 877–907. [CrossRef]
22. Feng, X.H.; Gong, B.; Tang, C.A.; Zhao, T. Study on the non-linear deformation and failure characteristics of EPS concrete based on CT-scanned structure modelling and cloud computing. *Eng. Fract. Mech.* **2022**, *261*, 108214. [CrossRef]
23. Liang, Z.Z.; Gong, B.; Wu, X.K.; Zhang, Y.B.; Tang, C.A. Influence of principal stresses on failure behavior of underground openings. *Chin. J. Rock Mech. Eng.* **2015**, *34*, 3176–3187.
24. Gong, B.; Wang, S.Y.; Sloan, S.W.; Shen, D.C.; Tang, C.A. Modelling rock failure with a novel continuous to discontinuous method. *Rock Mech. Rock Eng.* **2019**, *52*, 3183–3195. [CrossRef]
25. Wang, Y.Y.; Gong, B.; Tang, C.A.; Zhao, T. Numerical study on size effect and anisotropy of columnar jointed basalts under uniaxial compression. *Bull. Eng. Geol. Environ.* **2022**, *81*, 41. [CrossRef]
26. Chen, B.P.; Gong, B.; Wang, S.Y.; Tang, C.A. Research on zonal disintegration characteristics and failure mechanisms of deep tunnel in jointed rock mass with strength reduction method. *Mathematics* **2022**, *10*, 922. [CrossRef]
27. Mazars, J.; Pijaudier-Cabot, G. Continuum damage theory-application to concrete. *J. Eng. Mech.* **1989**, *115*, 345–365. [CrossRef]
28. Wang, Y.Y.; Gong, B.; Tang, C.A. Numerical investigation on anisotropy and shape effect of mechanical properties of columnar jointed basalts containing transverse joints. *Rock Mech. Rock Eng.* **2022**, *55*, 7191–7222. [CrossRef]

29. Bahaaddini, M.; Sharrock, G.; Hebblewhite, B.K. Numerical investigation of the effect of joint geometrical parameters on the mechanical properties of a non-persistent jointed rock mass under uniaxial compression. *Comput. Geotech.* **2013**, *49*, 206–225. [CrossRef]
30. Nassir, M.; Settari, A.; Wan, R. Joint stiffness and deformation behaviour of discontinuous rock. *J. Can. Pet. Technol.* **2010**, *49*, 78–86. [CrossRef]
31. Zheng, B.W.; Qi, S.W.; Huang, X.L.; Guo, S.F.; Wang, C.L.; Zhan, Z.F.; Luo, G.M. An advanced shear strength criterion for rock discontinuities considering size and low shear rate. *Appl. Sci.* **2020**, *10*, 4095. [CrossRef]
32. Wang, X.; Yuan, W.; Yan, Y.T.; Zhang, X. Scale effect of mechanical properties of jointed rock mass: A numerical study based on particle flow code. *Geomech. Eng.* **2020**, *21*, 259–268.
33. Fan, X.; Kulatilake, P.; Chen, X. Mechanical behavior of rock-like jointed blocks with multi-non-persistent joints under uniaxial loading: A particle mechanics approach. *Eng. Geol.* **2015**, *190*, 17–32. [CrossRef]
34. Wu, N.; Liang, Z.Z.; Li, Y.C.; Qian, X.K.; Gong, B. Effect of confining stress on representative elementary volume of jointed rock masses. *Geomech. Eng.* **2019**, *18*, 627–638.
35. Zhou, J.X.; Zhou, Y.; Gao, Y.T. Effect mechanism of fractures on the mechanics characteristics of jointed rock mass under compression. *Arab. J. Sci. Eng.* **2018**, *43*, 3659–3671. [CrossRef]
36. Chen, G.Q.; Sun, X.; Wang, J.C.; Wang, D.; Zhu, Z.F. Detection of cracking behaviors in granite with open precut cracks by acoustic emission frequency spectrum analysis. *Arab. J. Geosci.* **2020**, *13*, 258. [CrossRef]
37. Meng, F.Z.; Wong, L.N.Y.; Zhou, H.; Wang, Z.Q.; Zhang, L.M. Asperity degradation characteristics of soft rock-like fractures under shearing based on acoustic emission monitoring. *Eng. Geol.* **2020**, *266*, 105392. [CrossRef]
38. Guo, Q.F.; Pan, J.L.; Cai, M.F.; Zhang, Y. Investigating the effect of rock bridge on the stability of locked section slopes by the direct shear test and acoustic emission technique. *Sensors* **2020**, *20*, 638. [CrossRef] [PubMed]
39. Zhang, Y.C.; Jiang, Y.J.; Asahina, D.; Wang, Z. Shear behavior and acoustic emission characteristics of en-echelon joints under constant normal stiffness conditions. *Theor. Appl. Fract. Mech.* **2020**, *109*, 102772. [CrossRef]
40. Wang, G.; Zhang, Y.Z.; Jiang, Y.J.; Liu, P.X.; Guo, Y.S.; Liu, J.K.; Ma, M.; Wang, K.; Wang, S.G. Shear behaviour and acoustic emission characteristics of bolted rock joints with different roughnesses. *Rock Mech. Rock Eng.* **2018**, *51*, 1885–1906. [CrossRef]

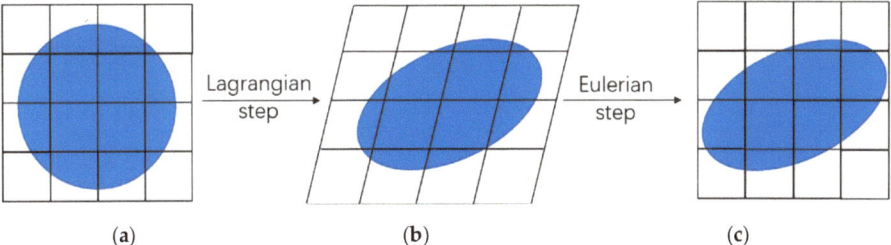

Figure 2. Illustration showing the updating of Eulerian materials in the coupled Eulerian–Lagrangian method: (**a**) first step; (**b**) second step; (**c**) reshaping to the initial mesh.

In the CEL model, the contact between Eulerian domains and Lagrangian domains is modeled using the general contact method, which is based on the penalty method. In this study, the boundaries are modeled as Lagrangian rigid bodies. Seeds are created on the Lagrangian element faces and edges, while anchor points are created on the Eulerian material surface. The penalty method approximates spring deformation. The contact force, Fp, which is enforced between seeds and anchor points, is related to the penetration distance, dp, as:

$$F_p = k_p\, d_p \tag{8}$$

where the factor k_p is the penalty stiffness, which depends on the Lagrangian and Eulerian material properties.

2.4. Transition between Finite Element Analysis and Coupled Eulerian–Lagrangian Analysis

The two steps should have the same physical conditions; the last increment of the first step will be the initial conditions of the second step. Therefore, the results exported from the coupled hydro-mechanical FE analysis will be imported into the CEL simulations. The exported data should include the coordinates, saturation, void ratio, stresses, and strain of each node or element, which is implemented by Python scripts. The nodal displacement and velocity will be ignored because they are too small, compared with the geometry of the slope.

In infiltration analysis, data are saved on the element nodes or integration points, and the deformed mesh has irregular shapes so that the meshes between the two steps are inconsistent. Therefore, the data from the first step cannot be used in the second step directly. The biharmonic spline interpolation method [47] is adopted to remap the data and is implemented using MATLAB scripts:

$$W(x_i) = \sum_{j=1}^{N} \alpha_j\, \phi_m\,(x_i - x_j) \tag{9}$$

where x_i and x_j are the target interpolation points and initial data points, respectively; $W(x_i)$ is the data on each target interpolation point; α_j is found by solving the linear system with all the known element nodal data; ϕ_m is the biharmonic green function for each dimension and can be checked against previous studies [47].

Next, we substitute the effective stress of unsaturated soil (Equation (4)) into the yield strength (Equation (1)):

$$\tau_f = d + \sigma'\tan\beta = d - \chi\, u_w \tan\beta + \sigma_t \tan\beta. \tag{10}$$

As reported in previous studies [48–50], landslides often occur rapidly, meaning that excess pore water pressure does not have time to dissipate. This situation is similar to undrained conditions in soil mechanics [51]. Therefore, after the infiltration analysis, the pore water pressure is assumed to keep constant in post-failure flows, and an equivalent strength method is used [14]. For the soil in each FE element, the equivalent friction angle β_e and equivalent cohesion d_e used in CEL are:

$$d_e = d - \chi\, u_w\, \tan \beta \tag{11}$$

$$\beta_e = \beta \tag{12}$$

Here, the pore water pressure, u_w, and χ (i.e., saturation) are from the last iteration of the FE analysis. Due to the increase in water pressure and saturation, the equivalent cohesion is reduced, compared with that before rainfall occurred.

The equivalent friction and cohesion are based on the total stress; this stress is related to the equivalent density, ρ_e, which is increased due to the rainfall:

$$\rho_e = \rho_s + n\, s\, \rho_w. \tag{13}$$

3. Rainfall-Induced Landslide and Post-Failure Flow

Figure 3a,b shows the geometry of two types of slopes, which have the same sizes but are different in terms of layers. First, the uniform slope is studied. The rise and run of the slope are 10 m and 14 m, respectively. The uniform rainfall boundary condition is enforced on the top surface, while a completely fixed boundary condition is applied to the bottom. The left and right boundaries are fixed in the normal direction. Table 1 shows the parameters used in the simulation of the base model. The soil–water characteristic curve (SWCC) is fitted using the van Genuchten model [52]. The relative permeability is modeled using the Gardner model [22,53]. Further simulations may only vary one parameter at a time and may fix the others. Figure 4 shows the SWCC and hydraulic conductivity that are used in simulations.

The FE mesh contains 440 elements, and the element size is approximately 1 m × 1 m. Each element contains four Gaussian integration points. First, a steady-state step is conducted to obtain an initial stress distribution without rainfall. Then, transient analysis is conducted to simulate the rainfall-induced hydro-mechanical response of the slope.

Table 1. Parameters used in the simulation of rainfall-induced landslides.

Parameters	Values
Young's modulus E	100 MPa
Poisson's ratio v	0.3
Cohesion d in Drucker–Prager	10 kPa
Friction angle β in Drucker–Prager	35°
Dilation angle ψ	0°
Soil particle density ρ_s	2650 kg/m^3
Water density ρ_w	1000 kg/m^3
Initial porosity n	0.3
Rainfall intensity q_r	0.018 m/h
Duration	20 h
Initial matric suction	20 kPa
Hydraulic conductivity k	0.036 m/h
SWCC parameter α'	0.31 m^{-1}
SWCC parameter n'	1.19
Hydraulic conductivity parameter η	1.962 m^{-1}

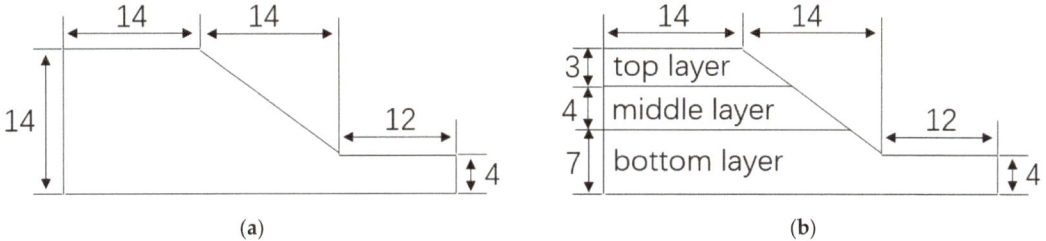

Figure 3. Illustrations of slope geometries: (**a**) uniform slope; (**b**) layered slope.

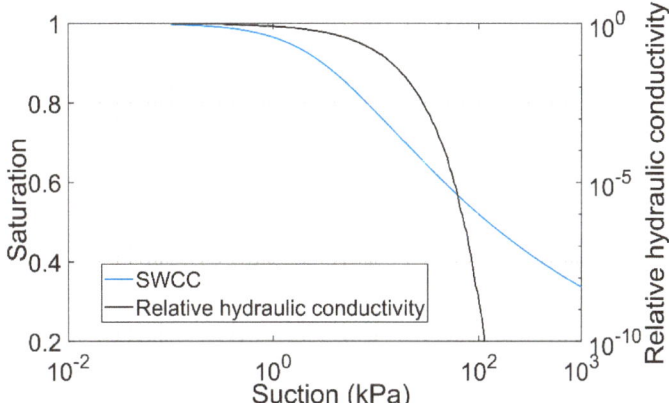

Figure 4. The SWCC and hydraulic conductivity.

The variations in saturation with time are presented in Figure 5. In total, 40 h are simulated (20 h of rainfall and 20 h after rainfall) to check the distribution of saturation. The initial saturation of the slope is uniformly 0.684. After the start of rainfall, the saturation increases rapidly near the surface of the slope, forming a high saturation band (Figure 5a). With time, the high saturation band widens (Figure 5a,b) due to the rainfall. After the rainfall stops, this band will move downward and spread out with a decrease in saturation (Figure 5c).

The predicted displacement from the first step is presented in Figure 6. Figure 6a shows the rainfall of 10.6 h, the slopes have almost no deformation. Figure 6b shows the initial deformation of the slope in 18 h and in Figure 6c the sliding surface can be clearly observed. A scale factor is taken as 100 to amplify the displacement of the slope. Because damping is used, the model can cope with a certain degree of deformation without a failure of convergence. Figure 7a shows the displacement of the slope top and Figure 7b shows that of the slope toe. Figures 6 and 7 illustrate that this failure happens at around 17 h. If the rainfall duration is less than 17 h, the slope is expected to remain stable. In addition, the displacement in the first step is quite small compared with the geometry of the slope; therefore, ignoring this displacement in the second step is reasonable.

A finer mesh size of 0.5 m × 0.5 m is also employed in the first step and the results are shown in Figure 8. Figure 8a,b shows the saturation distribution and displacement in the FE infiltration analysis. The displacement is also amplified by 100 to clearly show the deformation of the slope. According to Figure 8, there is no significant difference between the fine and coarse mesh sizes. Taking into account the computational efficiency of the simulations, a mesh size of 1 m × 1 m is sufficient to address this problem.

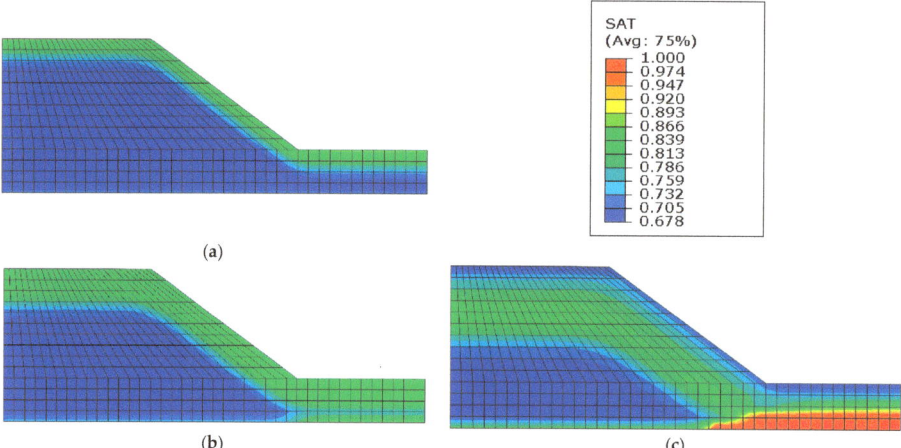

Figure 5. Variations of saturation in the FE infiltration analysis: (**a**) t = 10.6 h; (**b**) t = 20.2 h; (**c**) t = 40 h.

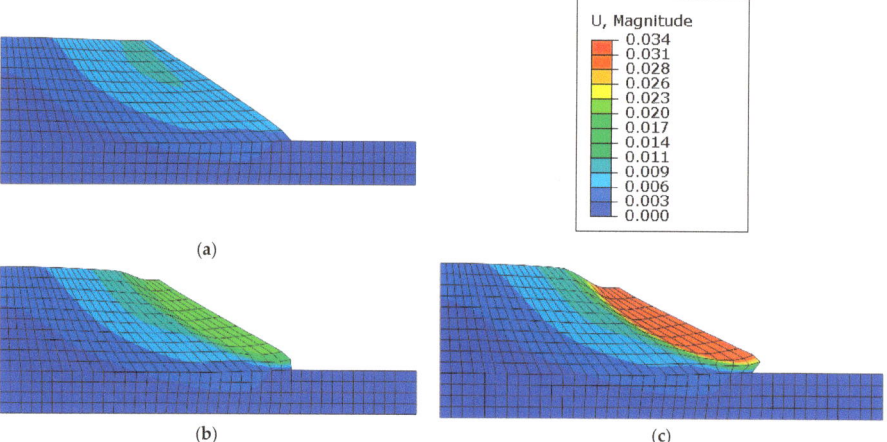

Figure 6. Variations of displacement in the FE infiltration analysis (displacement amplified by 100): (**a**) t = 10.6 h; (**b**) t = 18 h; (**c**) t = 20 h.

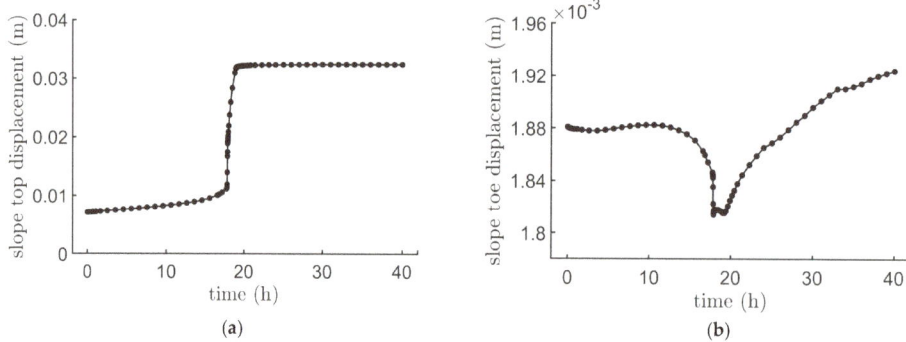

Figure 7. Variations of displacement in tow positions: (**a**) slope top; (**b**) slope toe.

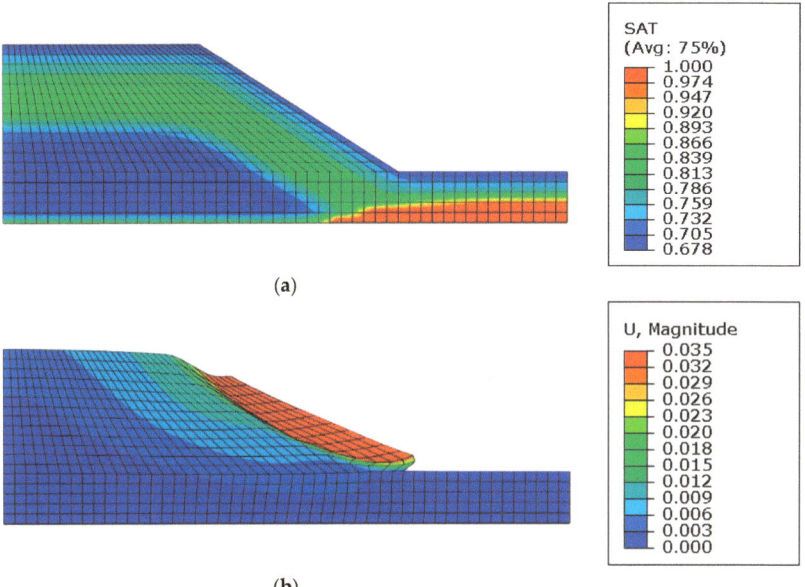

Figure 8. The FE infiltration analysis with a finer mesh size: (**a**) saturation distribution; (**b**) displacement (amplified by 100).

Each element in the CEL method contains only one Gaussian integration point. The CEL simulation domain contains 2400 elements, and the mesh size is 0.5 m × 0.5 m, which is consistent with the integration points in the first step. Initially, 1502 elements contain materials. Additionally, because the pore water pressure and saturation are different at different locations after infiltration, the equivalent cohesion d_e in the CEL method are spatial variables, even if the initial slope has uniform strength parameters; 1502 different materials are filled in the CEL, and each is tracked by its own EVF.

Figure 9 shows the deformation of the slope. The slope does not register the tiny amount of velocity in the first step (Figure 9a). An initial sliding surface is clearly indicated in Figure 9b. The soil slides downward along this sliding surface (Figure 9c). The sliding mass gradually reduces (Figure 9d) and finally stops (Figure 9e).

The determination of runout and influence distance is illustrated in Figure 10. The dots show the sum of all 1502 EVFs for all CEL materials. Elements that are fully occupied by materials have values of EVF = 1, and empty elements have EVF = 0. Therefore, the final slope profile exits at elements that have 0 < EVFs < 1. The Eulerian analysis cannot track the material interface exactly. Instead, it can only be approximately recovered by conducting curve fitting (Figure 10). In order to obtain an accurate influence and runout distance, the top profile and bottom profile are fitted separately (Figure 10). Additionally, because the landslide front is represented by only one or two layers of elements, it is even harder to accurately obtain the runout distance; the different influence distance D_*^i and runout distance D_*^r are defined at different heights (Figure 10) to depict the final slope profile. Here, the superscript i denotes the influence distance, and r denotes the runout distance. Subscript numbers (0, 0.5, 1, 1.5) indicate the vertical distance between the defined height and the initial top and toe of the slope (Figure 10). Figure 11 shows the variations in influence distances (Figure 11a) and runout distances (Figure 11b) over time, which clearly shows that the post-failure flow stops at around 5 s. After 5 s of deformation, the slope head and slope toe stop moving and are finally stable. Additionally, the influence distance is generally larger than the runout distance, which is to be expected because only part of the upper soil eventually accumulates at the toe of the slope.

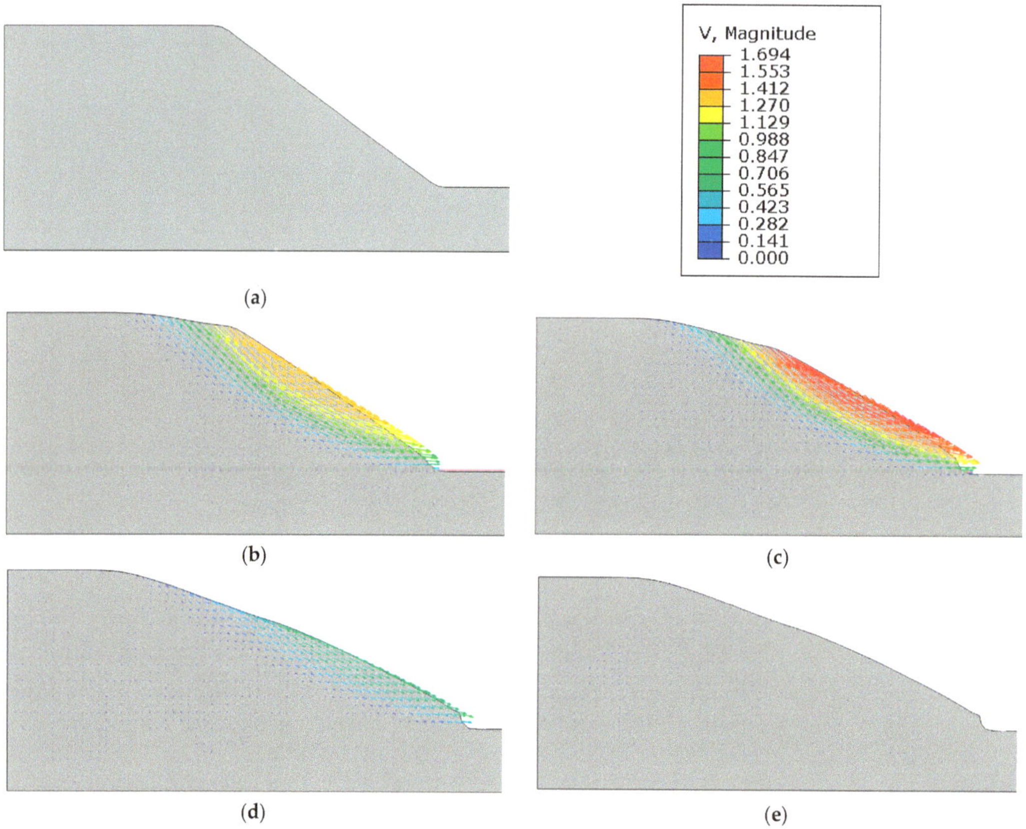

Figure 9. Slope deformation in the CEL simulation: (**a**) t = 0 s; (**b**) t = 1.5 s; (**c**) t = 2.5 s; (**d**) t = 4.5 s; (**e**) t = 5.5 s.

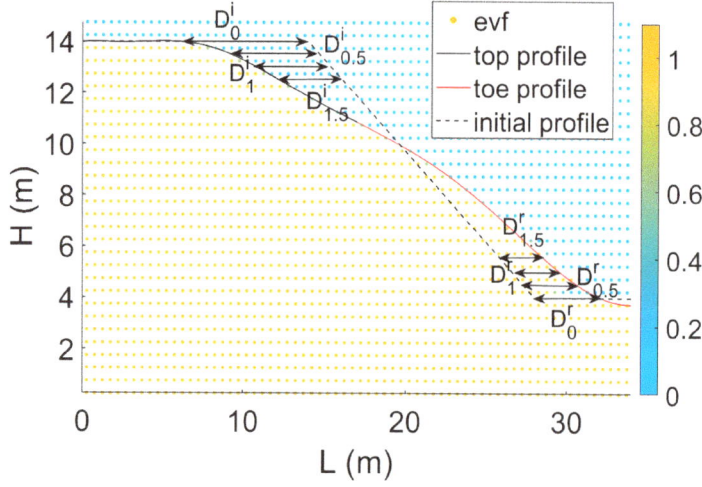

Figure 10. Determination of the slope surface, runout, and influence distance.

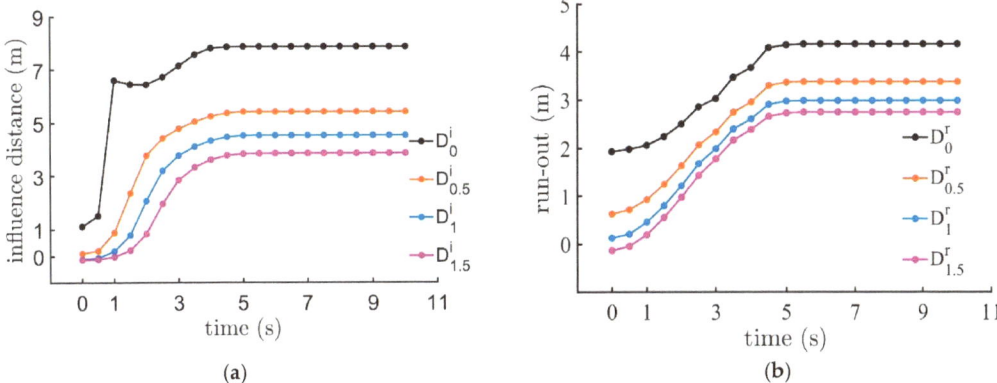

Figure 11. Variation of runout and influence distance with time from CEL simulations: (**a**) distance of the slope top with time (influence distance); (**b**) distance of the slope toe with time (runout distance).

3.1. Effect of Soil and Rainfall Parameters

Rainfall-induced landslides are affected by many factors, including soil parameters, initial saturation, rainfall intensity, rainfall duration, and slope geometry. Therefore, it is necessary to conduct a sensitivity analysis, which is achieved by simply varying one parameter but fixing the other parameters in this study. In this section, seven parameters are studied, including the Drucker–Prager cohesion, d, the Drucker–Prager friction angle, β, soil particle density, ρ_s, hydraulic conductivity, k, initial saturation, S_i, rainfall intensity, q_r and rainfall duration, T_r.

The variation in final influence and runout distance with each different Drucker–Prager cohesion d (from 5 to 100 kPa) in the uniform slopes is presented in Figure 12a,b. When the cohesion is less than 5 kPa, the slope is initially not stable and will fail at the geostatic step. When the cohesion increases (higher strength), the influence distance and runout decrease (i.e., the slope is more stable). When the cohesion is greater than 50 kPa, this rainfall intensity and duration will not cause instability and landslides.

Soil properties usually vary greatly in the vertical direction due to sedimentation history. In this section, layered slopes are also considered (three layers, as in Figure 3b; the parameters for the different layers are listed in Table 2). For example, to study slopes with different cohesion values, d, for different layers, four simulations are conducted. Due to the sedimentation history, the bottom soils usually have greater strength and density, which pattern is followed in the simulations, as in Table 2. Tests D2 and D3 have the same average cohesion as the base model, while D3 has greater variation. Test D1 has smaller average cohesion than the base model, and test D4 has greater average cohesion. Figure 12c,d gives the influence and runout distance for these layered slopes; the horizontal axis is the maximum cohesion for the tests and so, from left to right, tests D1 to D4 are shown. The horizontal dash lines represent the results for the uniform slope (the base model). In Figure 12c,d, the variation of cohesion between layers has limited influence (i.e., D2 and D3 are the same), but the layered slopes (D2 and D3) demonstrate smaller runout distance than the uniform slope (the base model) because of the greater cohesion at the slope toe in D2 and D3. Additionally, in agreement with the trend of increasing cohesion in uniform slopes, the increase in average cohesion in the layered slopes (from D1 to D4) also leads to increased stability and reduced runout.

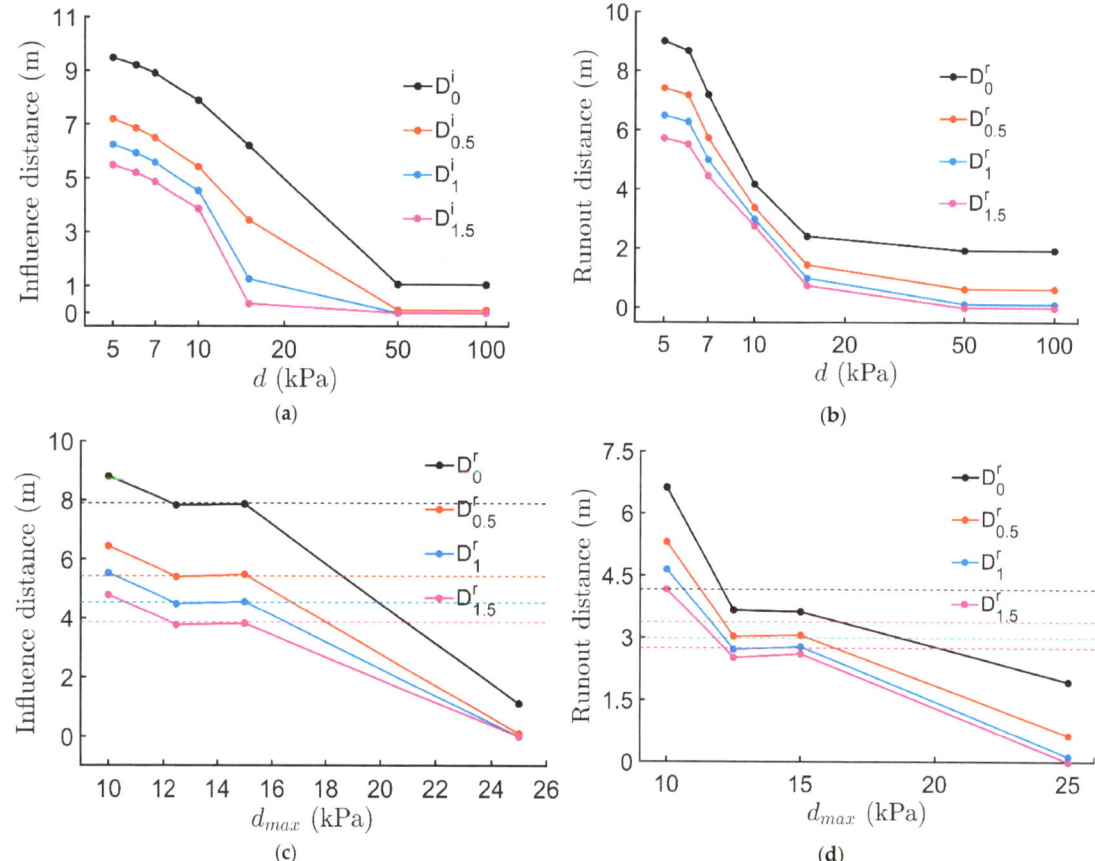

Figure 12. Variation of influence distance and runout with different cohesion in uniform and layered slopes: (**a**) different influence distances in uniform slopes; (**b**) different runout distances in uniform slopes; (**c**) different influence distances in layered slopes; (**d**) different runout distances in layered slopes.

Table 2. Parameters used for the layered slopes.

	Test Label	Top	Middle	Bottom	Mean	Max
Cohesion d (kPa)	D1	5	7.5	10	7.5	10
	D2	7.5	10	12.5	10	12.5
	D3	5	10	15	10	15
	D4	15	20	25	20	25
Friction angle β (°)	F1	31	33	35	33	35
	F2	34	35	36	35	36
	F3	33	35	37	35	37
	F4	35	37	39	37	39
Soil particle density ρ_s (kg/m^3)	R1	2250	2450	2650	2450	2650
	R2	2550	2650	2750	2650	2750
	R3	2450	2650	2850	2650	2850
	R4	2650	2850	3050	2850	3050

The results concerning the different Drucker–Prager friction angles, β (from 32 to 45°), in the uniform slopes are illustrated in Figure 13a,b. The slope will initially be unstable and will fail in the geostatic step if the friction angle is less than 32°. When the friction angle increases (higher strength), the influence and runout distance decrease (i.e., more stable), and a friction angle greater than 45° will not have landslides. Similarly, four-layered slopes are studied with different friction angles, β, for the different layers (parameters are chosen based on the same logic as the study of cohesion), and Figure 13c,d gives the results. Tests F2 and F3 have smaller runout values than the base model (these three tests have the same average friction angle) and F3 is smaller than F2, which is because the larger friction angle at the slope toes is effective in reducing the runout. Additionally, a greater average friction angle (from F1 to F4) will also reduce the runout.

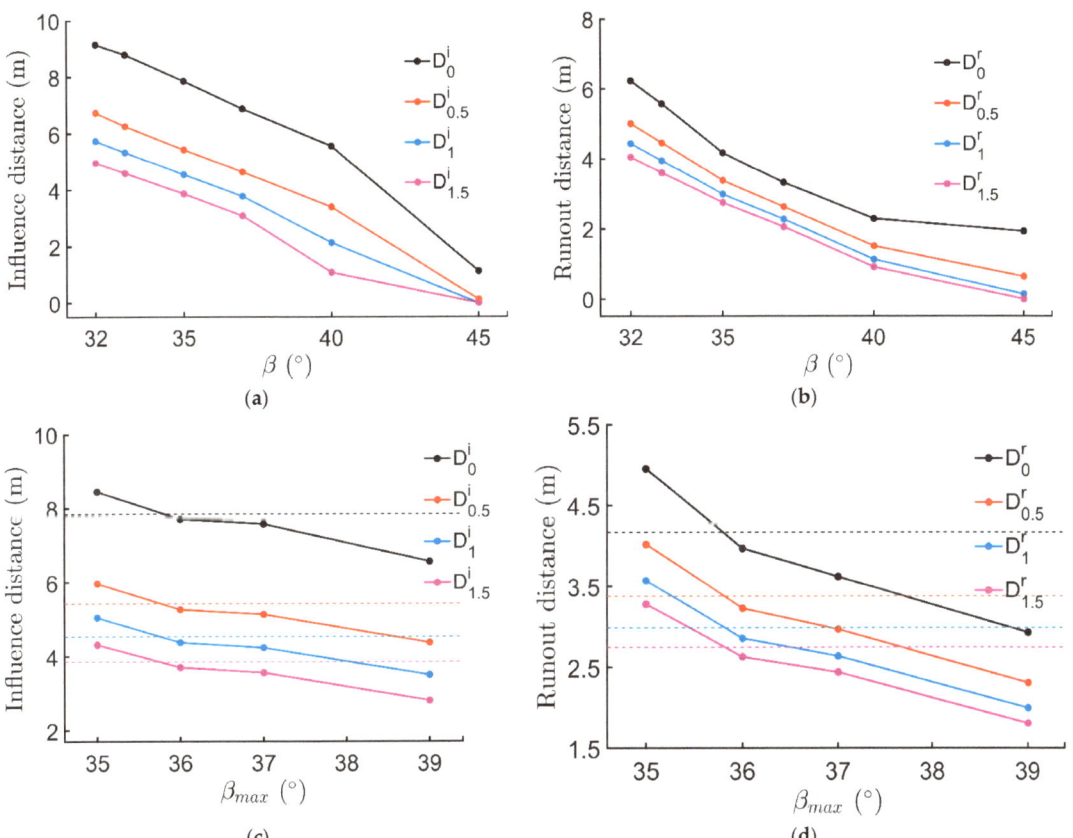

Figure 13. Variations in influence distance and runout with different friction angles: (**a**) different influence distances in uniform slopes; (**b**) different runout distances in uniform slopes; (**c**) different influence distances in layered slopes; (**d**) different runout distances in layered slopes.

The results concerning particle density, ρ_s, in the uniform slopes are illustrated in Figure 14a,b (with values from 1450 to 2950 kg/m³). When the density increases, the influence and runout distance increase (i.e., they become unstable due to the higher gravity load). Their impact on influence distance is very small (Figure 14a) but the density has a great impact on the runout (Figure 14b). Table 2 lists four tests of layered slopes with different particle densities; the values are not far from the typical values for sands and clays (2650 kg/m³), the obtained runout and influence distance only vary slightly

(Figure 14c,d), and this variation is possibly smaller than the error associated with the determination of runout.

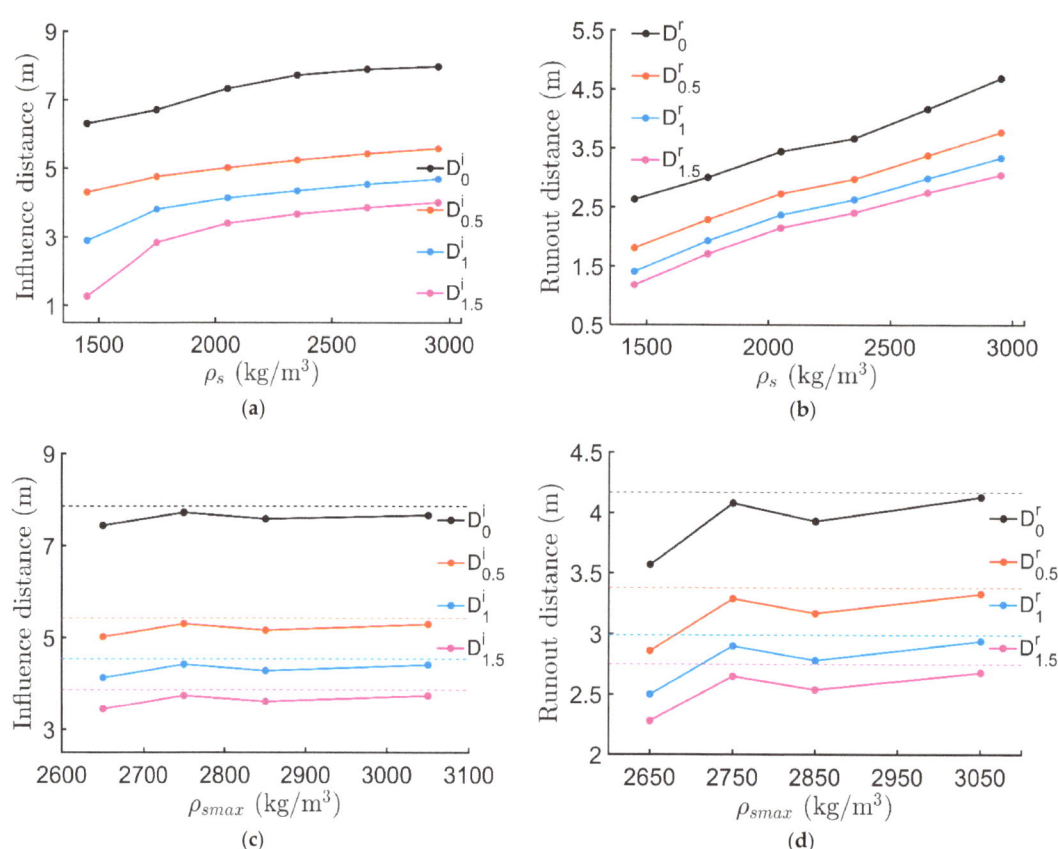

Figure 14. Variations in influence distance and runout with different densities: (**a**) different influence distances in uniform slopes; (**b**) different runout distances in uniform slopes; (**c**) different influence distances in layered slopes; (**d**) different runout distances in layered slopes.

The impact of hydraulic conductivity, k (from 0.018 to 0.7 m/h), is presented in Figure 15. To ensure that no runoff happens on the slope surface, k cannot be less than 0.018 m/h (i.e., the rainfall intensity, q_r). When the hydraulic conductivity increases near the rainfall intensity (0.018 m/h), the runout distance will exhibit a violent drop (Figure 15b). When the hydraulic conductivity continues to increase, the influence and runout distance decrease (i.e., they become more stable), as shown in Figure 15a,b. This is because higher conductivity will let water infiltrate quickly through the slope and reach the bottom, and the growth of saturation in the slope will be reduced.

Initial saturation, S_i, is also a factor that influences the runout. The results are presented in Figure 16a,b (S_i is from 0.512 to 0.83). When the S_i is greater than 0.83, the slope is initially not stable and fails in the geostatic step. When the S_i increases, the influence and runout distance increase slightly.

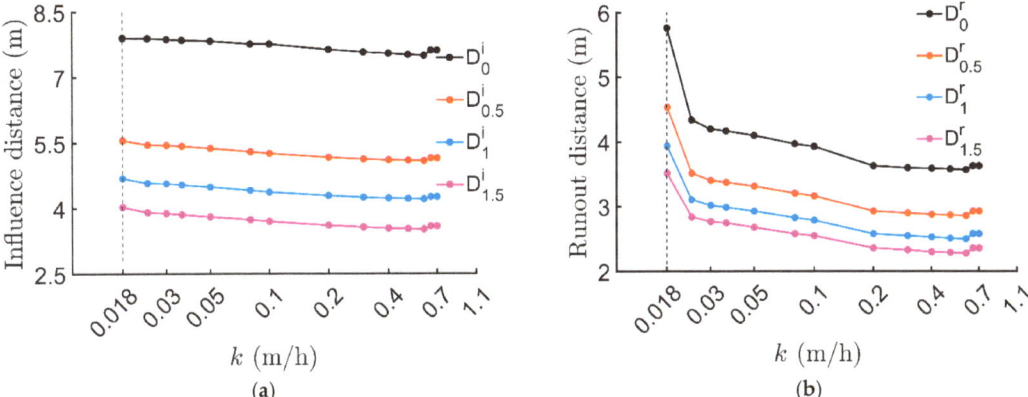

Figure 15. Variations in influence distances and runout with different hydraulic conductivity values: (**a**) different influence distances in uniform slopes; (**b**) different runout distances in uniform slopes.

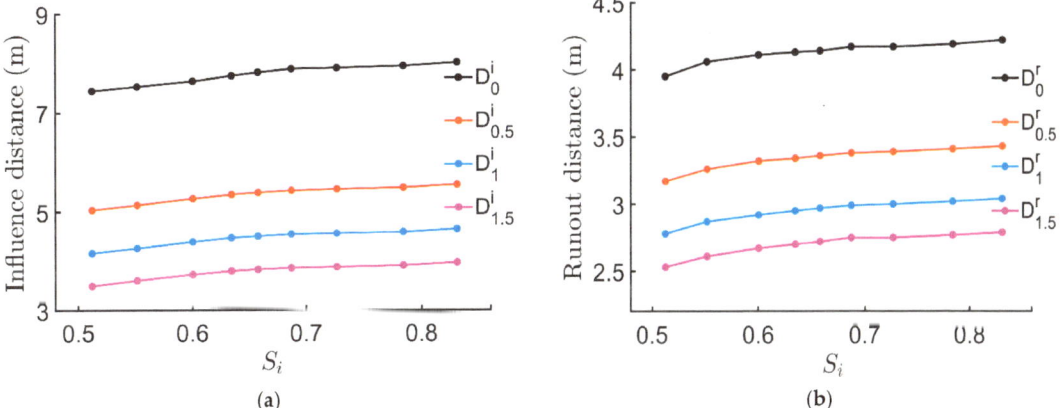

Figure 16. Variations in influence distances and runout with different initial saturation values: (**a**) different influence distances in uniform slopes; (**b**) different runout distances in uniform slopes.

The rainfall intensity (varying from 0.012 to 0.036 m/h) and duration (from 1 to 40 h) were investigated, and the results are presented in Figures 17a,b and 18a,b. The intensity value must be smaller than the hydraulic conductivity value (0.036 m/h), otherwise, surface runoff will occur. Figure 17 shows that when the rainfall intensity increases, the influence and runout distance also increase. In particular, when the rainfall intensity is very close to the maximum possible intensity and is greater than 0.03 m/h, the runout distance will rise dramatically (Figure 17b), which is similar to the drop seen in Figure 14b; in both cases, the rainfall intensity is very close to the hydraulic conductivity. In terms of the impact of rainfall duration, T_r, Figure 18a shows the different influence distances with changing T_r and Figure 18b gives the results of the different runout distances. According to Figure 18, the increase in T_r leads to an increase in influence and runout distance. However, the influence distance is not very sensitive to this variable, while the runout distance increases gradually with persistent rainfall.

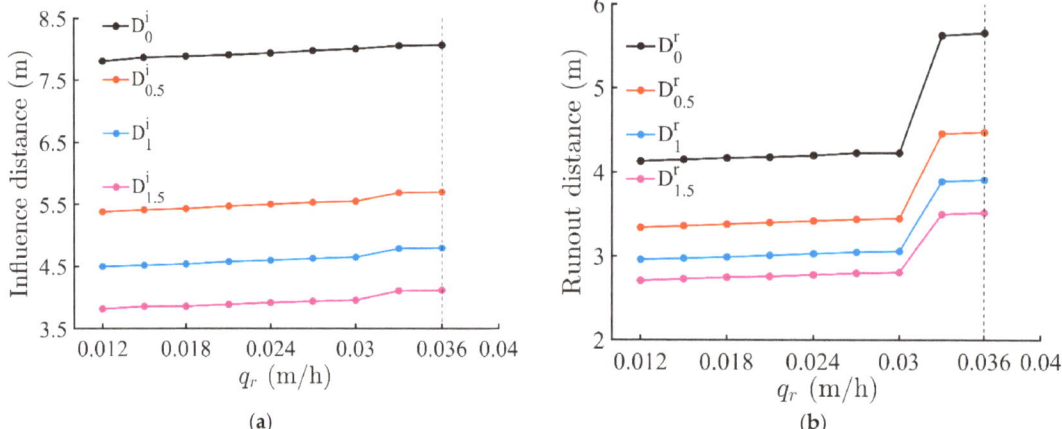

Figure 17. Variations in influence distances and runout with different rainfall intensities: (**a**) different influence distances in uniform slopes; (**b**) different runout distances in uniform slopes.

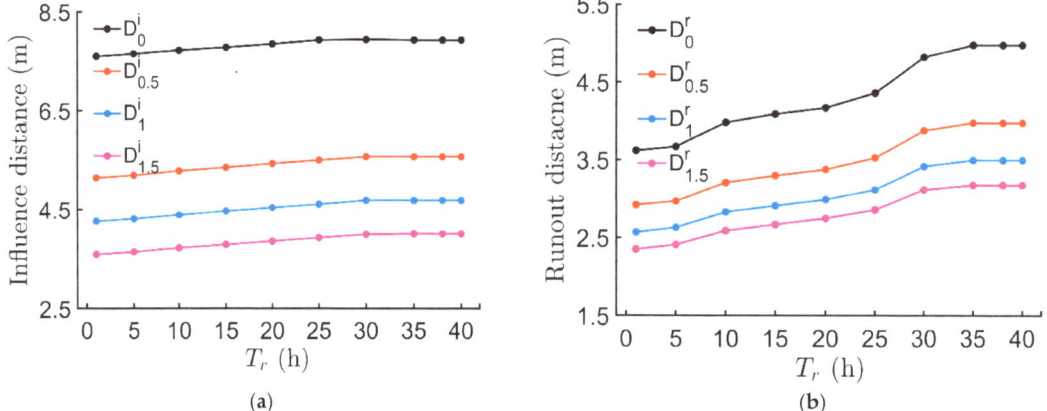

Figure 18. Variations in influence distance and runout with different rainfall duration: (**a**) different influence distances in uniform slopes; (**b**) different runout distances in uniform slopes.

3.2. Effect of Slope Shapes

The previous studies mostly employ two-dimensional (2D) analysis by assuming that the longitudinal length, perpendicular to the slope cross-section, is long, and the problem is simplified into a plane-strain problem. In this section, three-dimensional (3D) slopes are studied, including two types of geometry: a concave slope and a convex slope (Figure 19a,c). The side views of the two slopes are the same as those of the base model. In both tests, the Eulerian domain is discretized into 24,000 elements. Of these, 19,039 elements are initially occupied by materials for the concave slope, and 11,441 elements are occupied by materials for the convex slope. Because tracking tens of thousands of materials and their EVFs requires a large amount of RAM and CPU resources, each initially occupied element will be not modeled as a separate material, as in the 2D simulations; however, every 12 elements (concave) or 8 elements (convex) initially share the same material and are tracked by an EVF. Therefore, 1749 (concave) and 1490 (convex) materials are defined in the CEL. The material parameters are calculated via the same biharmonic spline interpolation method used in the infiltration simulations. The top view of the final profiles is shown in Figure 19b,d. The dash lines represent the contours at the same height as in the initial profile, with magenta

Article

Rainfall-Induced Landslides from Initialization to Post-Failure Flows: Stochastic Analysis with Machine Learning

Haoding Xu, Xuzhen He * and Daichao Sheng

School of Civil and Environmental Engineering, University of Technology Sydney, Ultimo, NSW 2007, Australia
* Correspondence: xuzhen.he@uts.edu.au

Abstract: Rainfall-induced landslides represent a severe hazard around the world due to their sudden occurrence, as well as their widespread influence and runout distance. Considering the spatial variability of soil, stochastic analysis is often conducted to give a probability description of the runout. However, rainfall-induced landslides are complex and time-consuming for brute-force Monte Carlo analyses. Therefore, new methods are required to improve the efficiency of stochastic analysis. This paper presents a framework to investigate the influence and runout distance of rainfall-induced landslides with a two-step simulation approach. The complete process, from the initialization of instability to the post-failure flow, is simulated. The rainfall infiltration process and initialization of instability are first solved with a coupled hydro-mechanical finite element model. The post-failure flow is simulated using the coupled Eulerian–Lagrangian method, wherein the soil can flow freely in fixed Eulerian meshes. An equivalent-strength method is used to connect two steps by considering the effective stress of unsaturated soil. A rigorous method has been developed to accurately quantify the influence and runout distance via Eulerian analyses. Several simulations have been produced, using three-dimensional analyses to study the shapes of slopes and using stochastic analysis to consider uncertainty and the spatial variability of soils. It was found that a two-dimensional analysis assuming plain strain is generally conservative and safe in design, but care must be taken to interpret 2D results when the slope is convex in the longitudinal direction. The uncertainty and spatial variability of soils can lead to the statistic of influence and runout distance. The framework of using machine-learning models as surrogate models is effective in stochastic analysis of this problem and can greatly reduce computational effort.

Keywords: landslides; runout; influence distance; rainfall; stochastic analysis

MSC: 60G60; 65-04

1. Introduction

Rainfall-induced landslides occur frequently around the world; they are a threat to life and cause huge economic losses [1–6]. According to a previous study [7], of the 4862 investigated landslides from 2004 to 2016, 79% were triggered by rainfall and led to the deaths of 55,997 people. Rainfall-induced landslides usually happen so rapidly that no mitigation measures can be introduced after instability is initiated [8,9]. Therefore, active measures (e.g., vegetations, retaining structures, piles, mesh, geocells, etc.) must be erected beforehand and the influence and runout distance must be determined, taking into account the probable soil-loss problems [10]. In addition, effective disaster management and slope stability analysis must be performed [4,11,12].

Rainfall-induced shallow landslides happen in two stages, as pointed out by Cascini [13]: first, the development of a complete shear band in the soil, which is termed the failure stage, and second, rapid post-failure flow, i.e., the post-failure stage. The second stage is the result of the failure stage. Therefore, the entire process of rainfall-induced landslides can be simulated according to two interrelated steps, which are rainfall infiltration analysis and

post-failure large deformation analysis. The same two-step calculation has been validated with two case studies in China and Japan, respectively [14]. The fracture behavior that normally occurs in rocks is not considered in this study [15–17]. The finite element (FE) method, using coupled hydro-mechanical models, is usually adopted for slope stability analysis under rainfall infiltration [18–20] and is also employed in this study. Several numerical models have been developed to simulate the large deformation of post-failure flows, including but not limited to the particle finite element method [21], material point method [22], and smoothed-particle hydrodynamics [23]. The coupled Eulerian–Lagrangian (CEL) method is a technique used to model the flow of Eulerian materials through a fixed mesh by tracking the Eulerian volume fraction (EVF); it is also suitable for simulating the post-failure large deformation of landslides. An equivalent strength method is used to connect the two steps (infiltration analysis and post-failure flow analysis), which considers the variations in soil material properties caused by rainfall infiltration.

Most previous rainfall-induced landslide simulations employ deterministic analysis [24–26]. However, due to the limited number of tests conducted for most projects, soil properties cannot be precisely determined in practice, so stochastic analysis is often conducted using Monte Carlo simulations. Additionally, soil properties often vary spatially, due to the sediment history, and soil parameters are regarded as random fields [27–30]. Therefore, this study presents a framework for conducting stochastic analysis of runout distance and the influence distance of landslides, considering the spatial variability of soils. Additionally, three-dimensional simulations are conducted to study how the slope shape can influence the stability and runout of landslides.

One challenge of Monte-Carlo-based stochastic analysis with spatial variability is the high sampling demand, i.e., a large number of samples; therefore, simulations are needed for a single analysis, which demand considerable computing resources and time. Some efforts have been made to reduce the number of simulations [31,32]. Meanwhile, surrogate models and regression models are also used to replace the time-consuming numerical simulations [33,34]. The stochastic analysis framework was proposed as a result of training machine-learning models as surrogate models, using the framework to study slope stability [35].

The two-step calculations of rainfall-induced landslides are time-consuming in every simulation. However, an accurate probability density function (PDF) requires large sample sizes, which may require years to complete brute-force Monte Carlo analyses (directly simulated from the two-step calculations). The aim of this paper is to build a framework for a rainfall-induced landslide problem to significantly improve the efficiency of stochastic analysis: for this purpose, a small number of simulations are conducted to obtain the influence and runout distance. Then, the random fields of soil parameters and the calculated influence and runout distance are treated as the input and output to train a machine-learning (ML) model. This model will be used to predict the influence and runout distance for many samples and, thus, to estimate the PDF.

The structure of this paper is as follows. Soil models, the hydro-mechanical model, the CEL method, and, particularly, the method used to connect the infiltration analysis and post-failure flows are explained in Section 2. A deterministic analysis and parametric analysis are presented in Section 3, while three-dimensional analyses are conducted to examine how three-dimensional shape effects the accuracy of predictions. A stochastic analysis is presented in Section 4, including the generation of random fields, brute-force stochastic analysis, a brief introduction to neural networks, and stochastic analysis with machine learning.

2. Method

In this study, the rainfall infiltration process and the initialization of instability are simulated with a coupled hydro-mechanical FE model. The coupled Eulerian–Lagrangian method is used for post-failure flows.

inside and outside is connected, the air pressure can be ignored, and the effective stress principle is:

$$\sigma' = \sigma_t - \chi\, u_w\, I \tag{4}$$

where χ is Bishop's parameter, which is approximately the value of the saturation in previous studies [38,39]. According to Arifin and Schanz [38], χ (ranging from 0 to 1) can be measured in the laboratory and $\chi = 1$ means full saturation; I is the second-order identity tensor.

Darcy's law is expressed as:

$$sn\mathbf{v}_w = -k_d \frac{\partial h}{\partial \mathbf{x}} \tag{5}$$

$$h = z + \frac{u_w}{|\mathbf{g}|\, \rho_w} \tag{6}$$

$$k_d = k_s\, \overline{k_d} \tag{7}$$

where s is the saturation; n is the porosity; $\mathbf{v}_w$ is the seepage velocity of water; k_d is the permeability of the soil; h is the hydraulic head in the soil; $\mathbf{x}$ is the coordinate; z is the elevation above the reference elevation; $\mathbf{g}$ is the acceleration of gravity; ρ_w is the density of the water; k_s is the relative permeability and its cubic power of saturation for the uniform pore-size distribution [40]; $\overline{k_d}$ is the permeability of fully saturated soil.

Porosity has a significant effect on slope stability. Soils with greater porosity have a larger water-retention capacity; therefore, for a certain rainfall intensity, slopes take longer to become saturated and, thus, unstable [41]. This phenomenon can be reproduced with the present model. However, some effects are hard to implement in this kind of two-step analysis, and are, therefore, ignored. For example, the soil–water characteristic curve is greatly influenced by porosity [42], which is not considered in the FE model. Some researchers [43,44] have considered the spatial variability of the porosity and proved that this variability may lead to some unexpected effective stress distribution and may make the failure process more complicated. Our stochastic analysis considers the spatial variability of soil strength parameters and permeability, but not their porosity. In the post-failure stage, the porosity of soils will also undergo dramatic change because of the rearrangement of soil particles and segregation [45,46]. The variation of porosity is difficult to establish, especially considering the effect of segregation [14]. In this study, porosity is assumed to be constant in post-failure flows.

The Abaqus FE software [37] with a coupled hydro-mechanical model is used to simulate rainfall infiltration. With the rainfall continuing, the deformation of the slope may increase rapidly, leading to instability at some stage, and finally, to landslides. This post-failure flow is large deformation, in which a traditional FE simulation may suffer mesh distortion and, thus, non-convergence. The results of the coupled analysis after slope failure would be mapped into the CEL model as the initial conditions.

2.3. Coupled Eulerian–Lagrangian (CEL) Method

In the CEL method, a mesh is fixed for the Eulerian domain, and materials such as soils can move freely in the mesh, which can help to avoid the mesh distortion problem near slip surfaces (where the shear behavior concentrates). Each iteration of the CEL model is illustrated in Figure 2. The configuration of a specific material in the Eulerian domain is tracked by its Eulerian volume fraction (EVF). A value of EVF = 1 for an element means that this element is totally occupied by the materials. The sum of EVFs in each element cannot exceed 1, and EVF = 0 means that this element is empty. The first step in the CEL method is similar to an updated Lagrangian FE simulation (Figure 2a); in the second step of the CEL method, as shown in Figure 2b (sometimes termed the Eulerian step), the mesh is reset, and a transfer algorithm is used to update all the variables and EVFs (Figure 2c).

2.1. Soil Constitutive Model

The Mohr–Coulomb model has been widely used in geotechnical engineering because (i) it has a small number of parameters that can be determined easily, and (ii) the concept is simple and can reflect the characteristics of both frictional and cohesive materials, such as soils. However, its yield surface does not employ continuous derivatives, which leads to the difficulty of convergence in some simulations. The Drucker–Prager model can, then, be used as an alternative way to avoid this problem, especially in large deformation simulations [36,37]. In this study, an extended Drucker-Prager model with a non-associated flow rule is used in both the first step (rainfall infiltration) and the second step (post-failure flows), and the yield function is:

$$f = t + p \tan \beta - d \tag{1}$$

$$t = \frac{q}{2}\left[1 + \frac{1}{k_t} - \left(1 - \frac{1}{k_t}\right)\left(\frac{J_3}{q}\right)^3\right] \tag{2}$$

where t is the effective shear stress; J_2 and J_3 are the second and third invariants of deviatoric stress; q is generalized shear stress; p is the mean stress; k_t is the ratio of the yield stress in triaxial tension to that in triaxial compression and it controls the shape of the yield stress in the π plane. When $k_t = 1$ (as used in this study), this reduces to the convectional Drucker–Prager model where $t = q = \sqrt{3J_2}$. The Drucker–Prager friction angle, β, is the slope of the linear yield surface in the p-t plane and is related to the true friction angle of the material; the Drucker–Prager intercept, d, is related to the true cohesion and friction angle of the material. Figure 1a shows the linear Drucker–Prager model in the meridional plane, while Figure 1b shows a comparison of the linear Drucker–Prager model ($k_t = 1$) with the Mohr–Coulomb model ($\varphi = 20°$).

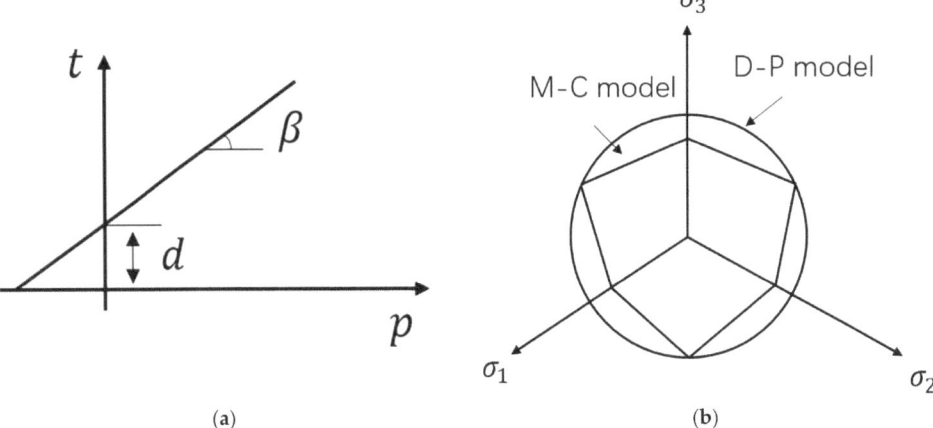

(a)   (b)

Figure 1. The illustration of linear Drucker–Prager model: (**a**) linear Drucker-Prager model on the meridional plane; (**b**) comparison of linear Drucker–Prager model ($k = 1$) and the Mohr–Coulomb model ($\varphi = 20°$).

The flow potential, G, is:

$$G = t - p \tan \psi \tag{3}$$

where ψ is the dilation angle.

2.2. Coupled Hydro-Mechanical Analysis

The soil is a three-phase mixture with the soil skeleton, water, and air. The total stress σ_t is related to the water pressure u_w, air pressure, u_a, and the effective stress, σ'. If the air for the top contour, red for the mid-segment, and blue for the bottom. The solid lines use the same contours for the final profile, while the dotted lines are drawn from the 2D predictions (i.e., the base model). The black arrows indicate the sliding directions. In both cases (concave and convex), the runout distances are smaller than in the 2D prediction; in particular, the runout distances at the corner are almost negligible. Therefore, the runout distance predicted by the 2D analysis is conservative and leads to safe design in practice. In terms of the influence distance, for those sections away from the corner, the predictions from 3D and 2D analyses are almost identical, with a 1.5% difference. For the concave slope, the top corner does not move, so the conservative prediction from the 2D analysis is safe in practice. However, in the case of the convex slope, the influence distance at the top corner is larger than in the 2D analysis. Therefore, great care must be taken to interpret the 2D analysis when the slope is convex in the longitudinal direction.

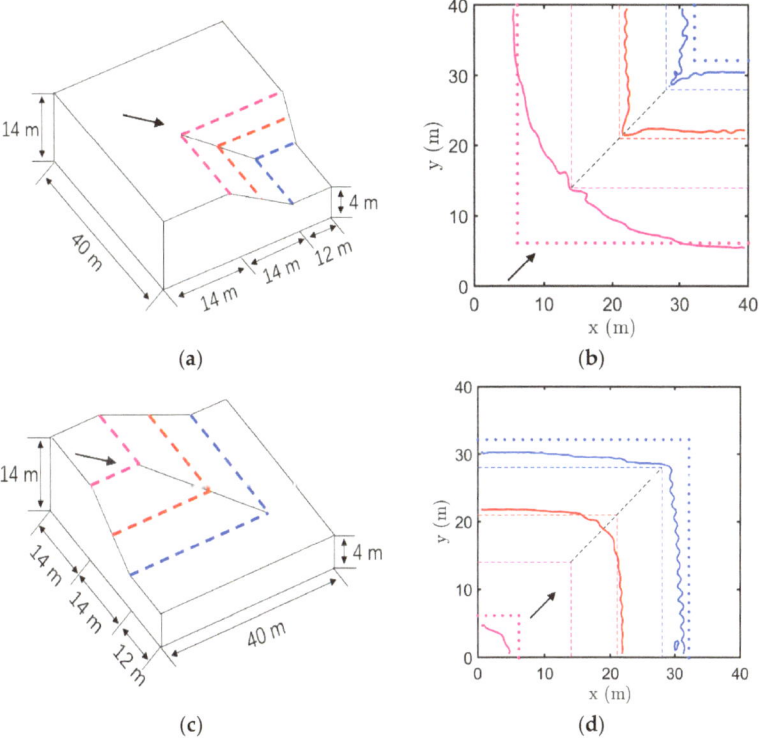

Figure 19. Runout and influence distances of the 3D slopes (dashed lines: initial contours; solid lines: final contours; dotted lines: 2D predictions): (**a**) concave slope shape; (**b**) top view of the final profile of the concave slope; (**c**) convex slope shape; (**d**) top view of the final profile of the convex slope.

4. Stochastic Analysis with Machine Learning

Soil parameters are often associated with uncertainty and spatial variability. The proposed two-step framework is used to conduct stochastic analysis, wherein the initial parameters, including cohesion, d, friction angle, β, soil particle density, ρ_s, and hydraulic conductivity, k, are modeled with random fields. The material parameters are assumed to follow log-normal distributions. The exponential autocorrelation function $(\rho(x, x') = \exp\left(-\frac{|x-x'|}{l_H} - \frac{|x-x'|}{l_v}\right))$ is used, where l_H and l_v are the horizontal and vertical correlation lengths. These correlation lengths reflect the rate at which the correlation is delayed between two points in space. In other words, soil particles will be more similar with a shorter distance from each other. In the infiltration analysis, there are 440 elements;

therefore, 440 materials are defined, which are spatial variables. The open-source software GSTools [54] was used to generate random field samples. Figure 20 shows the random fields of cohesion in the simulations. The parameters used in this stochastic analysis are listed in Table 3. At this point, 1000 random fields are generated, and the corresponding simulations are performed. Each two-step simulation in this study is conducted on a laptop computer, with an Intel Core 7 CPU @ 2.80GHz and 16 GB of random-access memory (RAM). Each simulation takes 20–30 min to complete, meaning that 1000 simulations cost 16 days of computation.

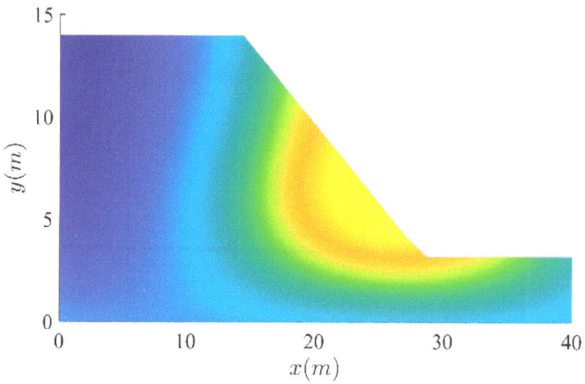

Figure 20. The generation of random fields of cohesion.

Table 3. The parameters for the stochastic analysis.

Parameter	Mean μ	COV	l_H	l_v
Cohesion d	10 kPa	0.1	16 m	8 m
Friction angle β	35°	0.05	16 m	8 m
Soil particle density ρ_s	2650 kg/m^3	0.05	16 m	8 m
Hydraulic conductivity k	0.036 m/h	0.3	16 m	8 m

The numerically estimated PDF of the influence and runout distance are illustrated in Figures 21 and 22, respectively. The mean values of influence distance are larger than the runout distance, which is consistent with the results of the deterministic analysis. In addition, the standard deviation of influence distance is smaller than that of runout distance, which means that the uncertainty and spatial variable of soil parameters have a stronger impact on the uncertainty of runout distance than the influence distance. These simulations took over two weeks and the estimated PDFs are not very accurate, compared with the solid lines shown in Figures 21 and 22, which were obtained from machine-learning-aided stochastic analysis using 10^5 Monte Carlo samples.

Machine learning (ML) algorithms can build mathematical models, based on existing sample input-output pairs [35]. For the rainfall-induced landslides presented in this study, the inputs are the material parameters, which are spatially variable, and the outputs are the influence and runout distance. In the framework of machine-learning-aided stochastic analysis, the input data (spatially variable material parameters) and calculated influence and runout distance from a small number of two-step simulations are fed into the ML algorithms as training data. A general mathematical relationship will then be found and can be used as a surrogate model to predict the influence and runout distance, which is more effective than the two-step simulations.

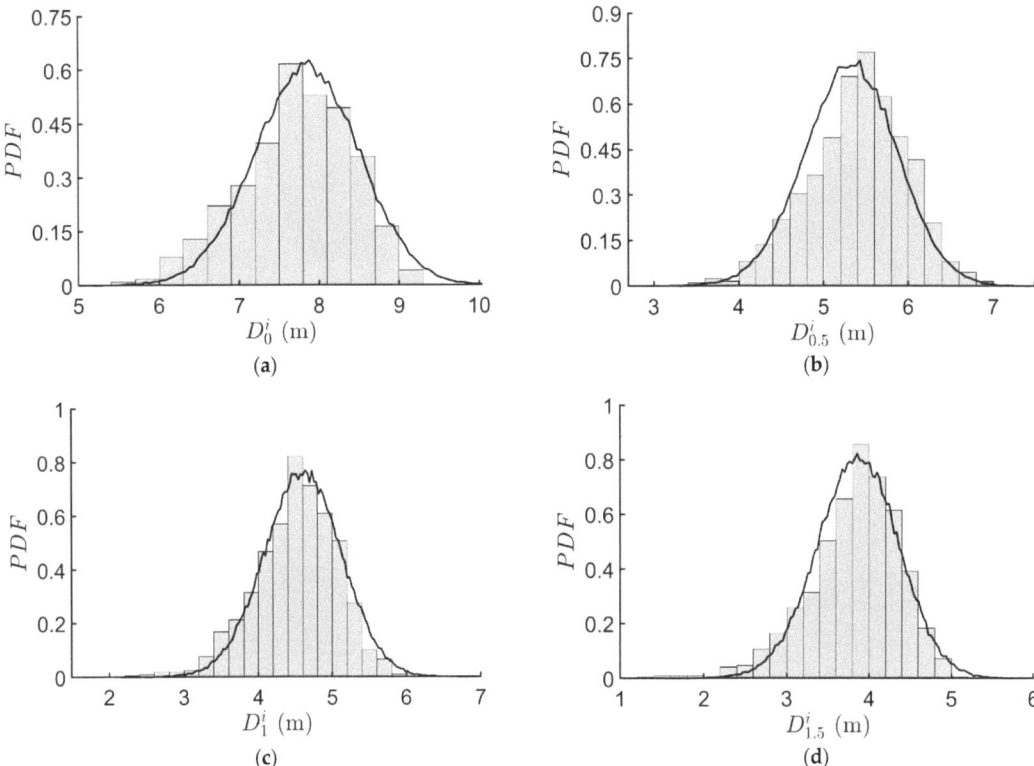

Figure 21. The estimated probability density function of influence distance (histogram: 1000 samples with brute-force simulations; solid line: 10^5 samples, evaluated with the machine-learning model): (**a**) PDF of D_0^i; (**b**) PDF of $D_{0.5}^i$; (**c**) PDF of D_1^i; (**d**) PDF of $D_{1.5}^i$.

An artificial neural network (ANN) is used in this study, which is inspired by the biological neural networks that constitute animal brains [35]. It is similar to the human brain's neural network, from the perspective of information processing. A neural network is an operation model, which is composed of a large number of nodes (or neurons) connected with each other. These artificial neurons receive the signal, process it, and pass the signal on to adjacent neurons. ANNs can have multiple input and output connections and the connections between neurons are called "edges". Signals are transferred from the input layer to the output layer. The connection between every two nodes represents a weighted value for the signal passing through the connection, which is called weight and is similar to the memory of the artificial neural network. Each node has a specific output function called the activation function. Before the output is produced, the weighted sum is combined with this neuron's internal state (or activation) by using this activation function. Non-linear activation functions can help ANNs to learn more complex data and give exact predictions. The loss function is used to define the accuracy and ANNs are trained to minimize the loss function. The learning rate defines the size of the corrective steps that the model must take to adjust for errors in each observation. A high learning rate shortens the training time but may cause an unstable training process and may lead to a local minimum other than a global minimum, while a lower learning rate results in a long training process. The open-source library, TensorFlow, which implements the ANNs is used in the present study.

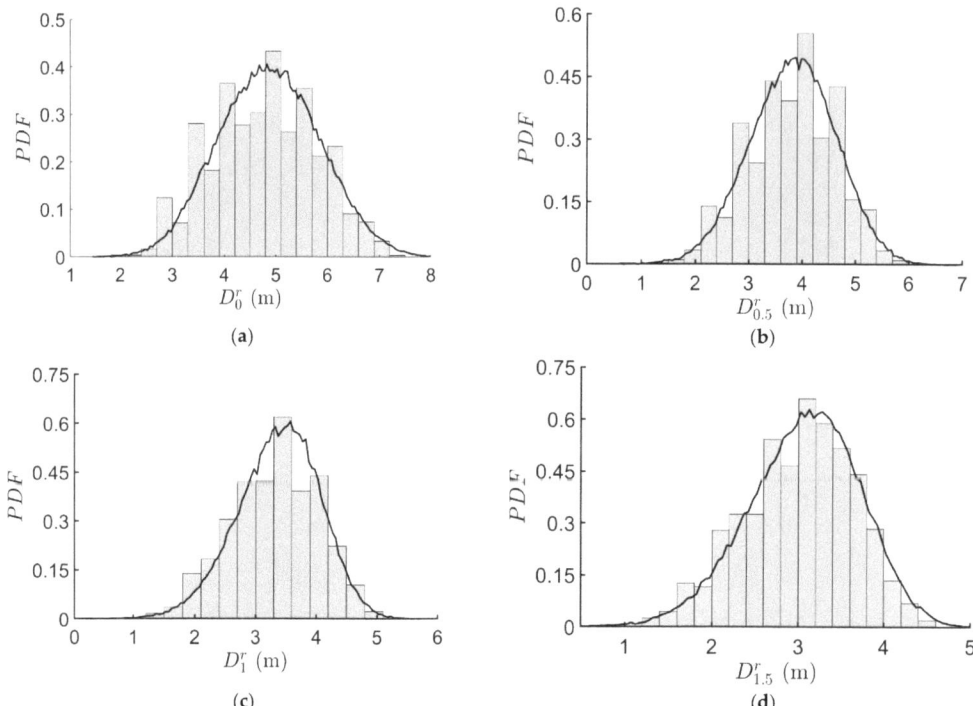

Figure 22. The estimated probability density function of runout (histogram: 1000 samples with brute-force simulations; solid line: 10^5 samples, evaluated with the machine-learning model): (**a**) PDF of D_0^r; (**b**) PDF of $D_{0.5}^r$; (**c**) PDF of D_1^r; (**d**) PDF of $D_{1.5}^r$.

The FE model in infiltration analysis contains 440 elements and 4 random fields. Therefore, the input size of ML algorithms is 1760 and the output size is 8, which are the influence and runout distance defined at different heights. For this analysis, 1000 input–output pairs were obtained from two-step simulations, of which 500 samples were first used as training samples and 500 were validation samples. It was shown that deep learning neural networks can perform very complex tasks [55], but in the case of the simple problem in the present study, ANNs with only one hidden layer were enough. The activation function is the rectified linear unit (ReLU), while the mean absolute percentage error (MAPE) was chosen as the loss function. The Adam learning-rate optimization algorithm [56] was used and a learning rate of 0.001 was adopted in this study. An early-stop technique (with a maximum of 5000 epochs of training) was also used to stop the training after the loss function did not change.

The number of neurons is a tuneable hyperparameter in ANNs. Figure 23 shows the variety of MAPEs possible when the neurons change from 20 to 100. The increase in neurons will lead to more complex models and is expected to improve the accuracy. However, when the neurons are more than 60, no significant improvement can be observed. Therefore, an ANN with 60 hidden neurons is optimal. This size of ANN can handle very complex problems because it has more than 10^5 trainable parameters. Figures 24 and 25 compare the influence and runout distance calculated with two-step simulations with those predicted from machine-learning surrogate models. It is clear that the mean absolute percentage error (MAPEs) of runout distance (about 9%–10%) is greater than that of influence distance (4%–8%). This is because in Eulerian simulations, the interface and the profile cannot be exactly tracked but are instead recovered from the positions of elements where the 0 < EVFs < 1, using curve fitting. Therefore, there are errors when determining the runout or influence distance and this noise in the input data prevents the ML algorithms from producing very accurate models. The errors here (of around 10% for the runout distance and 6% for the influence distance) from machine-learning surrogate models are, thus, considered acceptable.

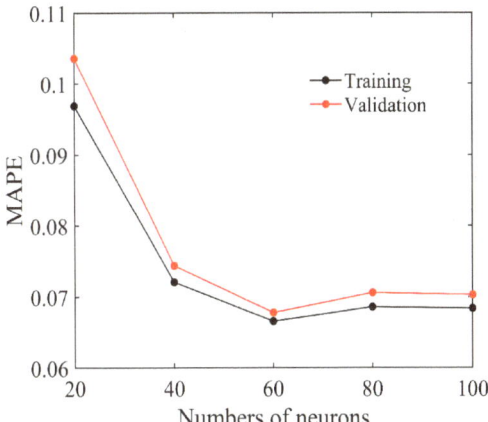

Figure 23. Errors in artificial neural networks with various hyperparameters.

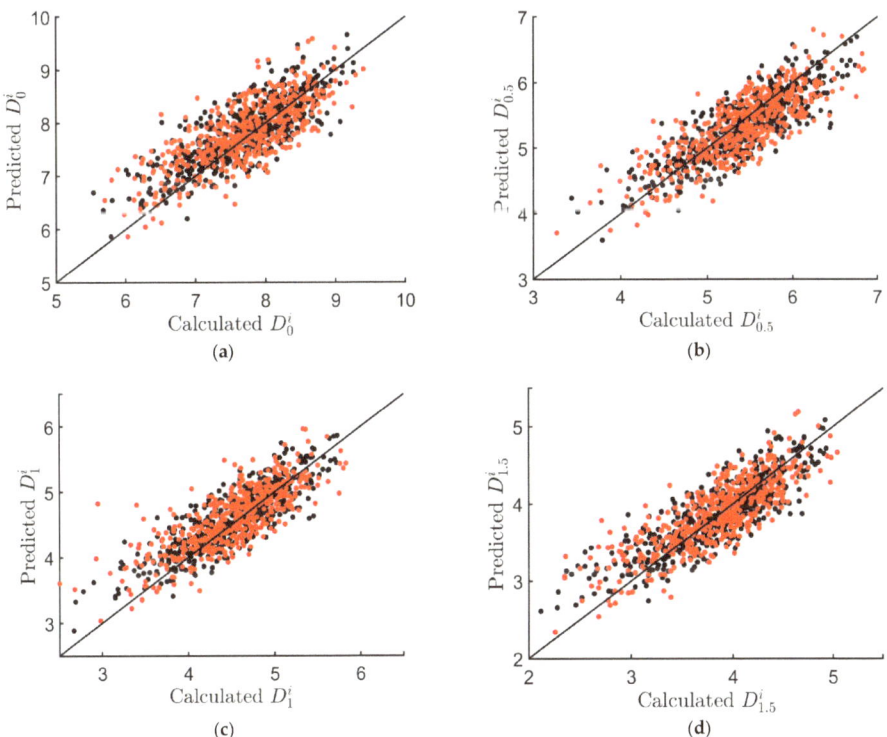

Figure 24. The predictions of influence distance from the numerical simulations and the machine-learning model (black dots = training; red dots = validation): (a) MAPE = 4.85% with D_0^i; (b) MAPE = 5.28% with $D_{0.5}^i$; (c) MAPE = 6.45% with D_1^i; (d) MAPE = 7.81% with $D_{1.5}^i$.

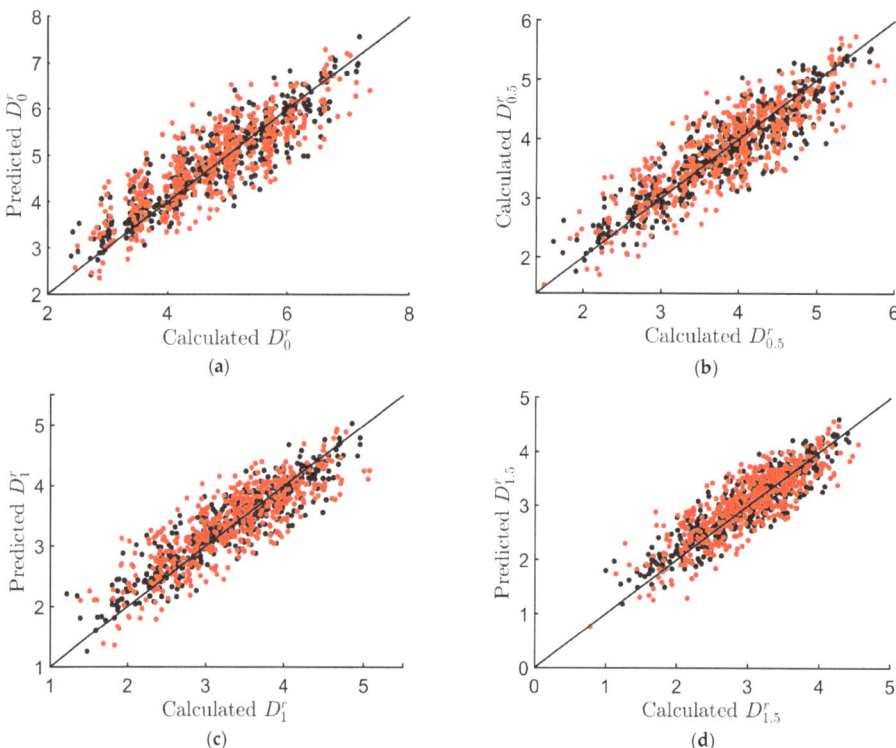

Figure 25. Predictions of runout from the numerical simulations and the machine-learning model (black dots = training; red dots = validation): (**a**) MAPE = 9.45% with D_0^r; (**b**) MAPE = 9.24% with $D_{0.5}^r$; (**c**) MAPE = 10.03% with D_1^r; (**d**) MAPE = 10.04% with $D_{1.5}^r$.

With this ANN as a surrogate model, the influence and runout distance for the millions of Monte Carlo samples can be easily evaluated. In Figures 21 and 22, the black solid lines are the PDFs of influence and runout distances for the 10^5 Monte Carlo samples, which are evaluated with the machine-learning surrogate model. The computation time for 500 simulations is about 7–10 days, while the time needed for the training and prediction of 10^5 samples using ML is only about 10 min.

Table 4 shows the mean and standard deviations for the influence and runout distance. The errors between the brute-force stochastic analysis and machine-learning-aided stochastic analysis are smaller than 2%. However, machine-learning-aided analysis is able to obtain an accurate PDF, due to the larger number of samples used. Therefore, this framework greatly reduces the amount of computation necessary and ensures higher accuracy with a large number of Monte Carlo samples.

After the PDFs of influence and runout distance are obtained, the probability that an infrastructure (i.e., a house, railway, etc.) lies within the influence of landslides can be estimated using the following function:

$$p_f = \int_a^\infty f_{PDF}(x)\,dx \tag{14}$$

where a is the distance between the infrastructure and the slope top and toe, and $f_{PDF}(x)$ is the probability density function of the influence and runout distance.

Table 4. The statistics of influence distance and runout.

Random Variable of Interest	Brute-Force Analysis		Machine-Learning-Aided	
	Mean	Standard Deviation	Mean	Standard Deviation
D_0^i	7.72 m	0.72 m	7.85 m	0.66 m
$D_{0.5}^i$	5.40 m	0.60 m	5.32 m	0.55 m
$D_{1.5}^i$	3.81 m	0.58 m	3.86 m	0.49 m
D_0^r	4.79 m	1.02 m	4.88 m	0.97 m
$D_{0.5}^r$	3.80 m	0.82 m	3.82 m	0.80 m
D_1^r	3.32 m	0.73 m	3.37 m	0.68 m
$D_{1.5}^r$	3.00 m	0.65 m	3.07 m	0.65 m

5. Conclusions

This paper presents a study of the influence and runout distance of rainfall-induced landslides. In particular, the effect of the 3D slope shape was studied and stochastic analysis was conducted.

A two-step approach was adopted for rainfall-induced landslides. This approach can simulate the entire process, from initialization to post-failure flows. A coupled hydro-mechanical FE model was used to simulate the infiltration of rainfall, which can evaluate the pore pressure, displacement, and plastic strain of the slope. The coupled Eulerian–Lagrangian (CEL) method was used as the second step to simulate the post-failure flows. An equivalent strength method was used to build a connection between the infiltration analysis and the post-failure flow. A method was also developed to more accurately quantify the influence and runout distance using Eulerian analysis.

The sensitivity analysis showed that the influence and runout distance are affected by many factors, including the soil strength parameters (cohesion and friction angle), soil permeability and density, initial slope saturation, and rainfall intensity and duration. Two 3D slopes were studied with different shapes in the direction perpendicular to the cross-section (a concave slope and a convex one); it was found that the runout predicted from the 3D analysis is smaller than in the predictions of the 2D analysis, assuming plain strain; therefore, 2D analysis is conservative and is safe for design. In terms of the influence distance, the 2D analysis agreed with the 3D analysis regarding sections away from the intersecting corner, but the 2D analysis was conservative for the concave slope and was optimistic for the convex slope. Therefore, great care must be taken when interpreting the 2D analysis results when the slope is convex in the longitudinal direction.

Stochastic reliability analysis was conducted to consider both the uncertainty and spatial variability of soils. An example is given herein, where the four material parameters (cohesion, friction angle, particle density, and permeability) are modeled as random fields. Monte-Carlo simulations were conducted to investigate the statistics of the influence and runout distance, associated with the uncertainty of the material properties. Brute-force analysis and machine-learning-aided analysis were compared. For the brute-force analysis, simulations of 1000 samples needed 16 days of computation. However, the estimated probability density function (PDF) of influence and runout distance were still not satisfactory, due to the small sampling size. Therefore, a larger number of samples are required to obtain an accurate PDF. However, traditional stochastic reliability analysis requires a great deal of computing resources and time to achieve a higher accuracy—10^5 samples require 4–6 years to finish, whereas machine-learning-aided analysis is very efficient.

A neural network was used to establish the relationship between the material properties (which are spatially variable) and the influence and runout distance. With only 500 samples for use as training datasets, the ML algorithms could train a model that predicted the influence and runout distance with good accuracy. With this machine-learning model as a surrogate model to predict the influence and runout distance of millions of samples, a PDF with high accuracy was obtained. Once such a PDF is obtained, a complete stochastic examination can then be conducted, including the mean values of influence and runout distance, identifying the probability that infrastructure lies within the influence of landslides.

Author Contributions: Conceptualization, X.H.; methodology, H.X.; software, H.X.; validation, H.X.; data curation, H.X.; writing—original draft preparation, H.X.; writing—review and editing, X.H. and D.S.; supervision, X.H. and D.S.; funding acquisition, D.S. All authors have read and agreed to the published version of the manuscript.

Funding: This research received no external funding.

Data Availability Statement: The datasets generated during or analysed during the current study are available from the corresponding author on reasonable request.

Conflicts of Interest: The authors declare that they have no known competing financial interest or personal relationships that could have appeared to influence the work reported in this paper.

References

1. Ekanayake, J.C.; Phillips, C.J. Slope Stability Thresholds for Vegetated Hillslopes: A Composite Model. *Can. Geotech. J.* **2002**, *39*, 849–862. [CrossRef]
2. Take, W.A.; Bolton, M.D.; Wong, P.C.P.; Yeung, F.J. Evaluation of Landslide Triggering Mechanisms in Model Fill Slopes. *Landslides* **2004**, *1*, 173–184. [CrossRef]
3. Wang, F.W.; Sassa, K.; Wang, G. Mechanism of a Long-Runout Landslide Triggered by the August 1998 Heavy Rainfall in Fukushima Prefecture, Japan. *Eng. Geol.* **2002**, *63*, 169–185. [CrossRef]
4. Nwazelibe, V.E.; Unigwe, C.O.; Egbueri, J.C. Integration and Comparison of Algorithmic Weight of Evidence and Logistic Regression in Landslide Susceptibility Mapping of the Orumba North Erosion-Prone Region, Nigeria. *Model. Earth Syst. Environ.* **2022**, 1–20. [CrossRef]
5. Egbueri, J.C.; Igwe, O.; Unigwe, C.O. Gully Slope Distribution Characteristics and Stability Analysis for Soil Erosion Risk Ranking in Parts of Southeastern Nigeria: A Case Study. *Environ. Earth Sci.* **2021**, *80*, 292. [CrossRef]
6. Lacerda, W. The Behavior of Colluvial Slopes in a Tropical Environment. In *Landslides: Evaluation and Stabilization/Glissement de Terrain: Evaluation et Stabilisation, Set of 2 Volumes*; CRC Press: Boca Raton, FL, USA, 2004; pp. 1315–1342. [CrossRef]
7. Froude, M.J.; Petley, D.N. Global Fatal Landslide Occurrence from 2004 to 2016. *Nat. Hazards Earth Syst. Sci.* **2018**, *18*, 2161–2181. [CrossRef]
8. Schuster, R.L.; Highland, L.M. The Third Hans Cloos Lecture. Urban Landslides: Socioeconomic Impacts and Overview of Mitigative Strategies. *Bull. Eng. Geol. Environ.* **2007**, *66*, 1–27. [CrossRef]
9. Huang, B.; Yin, Y.; Du, C. Risk Management Study on Impulse Waves Generated by Hongyanzi Landslide in Three Gorges Reservoir of China on June 24, 2015. *Landslides* **2016**, *13*, 603–616. [CrossRef]
10. Egbueri, J.C.; Igwe, O.; Ifediegwu, S.I. Erosion Risk Mapping of Anambra State in Southeastern Nigeria: Soil Loss Estimation by RUSLE Model and Geoinformatics. *Bull. Eng. Geol. Environ.* **2022**, *81*, 91. [CrossRef]
11. Nebeokike, U.C.; Igwe, O.; Egbueri, J.C.; Ifediegwu, S.I. Erodibility Characteristics and Slope Stability Analysis of Geological Units Prone to Erosion in Udi Area, Southeast Nigeria. *Model. Earth Syst. Environ.* **2020**, *6*, 1061–1074. [CrossRef]
12. Unigwe, C.O.; Igwe, O.; Onwuka, O.S.; Egbueri, J.C.; Omeka, M.E. Roles of Hydro-Geotechnical and Slope Stability Characteristics in the Erosion of Ajali and Nanka Geologic Formations in Southeastern Nigeria. *Arab. J. Geosci.* **2022**, *15*, 1492. [CrossRef]
13. Cascini, L.; Cuomo, S.; Pastor, M.; Sorbino, G. Modeling of Rainfall-Induced Shallow Landslides of the Flow-Type. *J. Geotech. Geoenviron. Eng.* **2010**, *136*, 85–98. [CrossRef]
14. Chen, X.; Zhang, L.; Zhang, L.; Zhou, Y.; Ye, G.; Guo, N. Modelling Rainfall-Induced Landslides from Initiation of Instability to Post-Failure. *Comput. Geotech.* **2021**, *129*, 103877. [CrossRef]
15. Li, H.; Tang, H.; Qin, Q.; Zhou, J.; Qin, Z.; Fan, C.; Su, P.; Wang, Q.; Zhong, C. Characteristics, Formation Periods and Genetic Mechanisms of Tectonic Fractures in the Tight Gas Sandstones Reservoir: A Case Study of Xujiahe Formation in YB Area, Sichuan Basin, China. *J. Pet. Sci. Eng.* **2019**, *178*, 723–735. [CrossRef]
16. Li, H. Research Progress on Evaluation Methods and Factors Influencing Shale Brittleness: A Review. *Energy Rep.* **2022**, *8*, 4344–4358. [CrossRef]
17. Li, J.; Li, H.; Yang, C.; Wu, Y.; Gao, Z.; Jiang, S. Geological Characteristics and Controlling Factors of Deep Shale Gas Enrichment of the Wufeng-Longmaxi Formation in the Southern Sichuan Basin, China. *Lithosphere* **2022**, *2022*, 4737801. [CrossRef]
18. Schrefler, B.A.; Scotta, R. A Fully Coupled Dynamic Model for Two-Phase Fluid Flow in Deformable Porous Media. *Comput. Methods Appl. Mech. Eng.* **2001**, *190*, 3223–3246. [CrossRef]
19. Yang, K.-H.; Uzuoka, R.; Thuo, J.N.; Lin, G.-L.; Nakai, Y. Coupled Hydro-Mechanical Analysis of Two Unstable Unsaturated Slopes Subject to Rainfall Infiltration. *Eng. Geol.* **2017**, *216*, 13–30. [CrossRef]
20. Zhang, L.L.; Zhang, J.; Zhang, L.M.; Tang, W.H. Stability Analysis of Rainfall-Induced Slope Failure: A Review. *Proc. Inst. Civ. Eng.-Geotech. Eng.* **2011**, *164*, 299–316. [CrossRef]

21. Zhang, X.; Krabbenhoft, K.; Sheng, D.; Li, W. Numerical Simulation of a Flow-like Landslide Using the Particle Finite Element Method. *Comput. Mech.* **2015**, *55*, 167–177. [CrossRef]
22. Liu, X.; Wang, Y. Probabilistic Simulation of Entire Process of Rainfall-Induced Landslides Using Random Finite Element and Material Point Methods with Hydro-Mechanical Coupling. *Comput. Geotech.* **2021**, *132*, 103989. [CrossRef]
23. He, X.; Liang, D.; Bolton, M.D. Run-out of Cut-Slope Landslides: Mesh-Free Simulations. *Geotechnique* **2018**, *68*, 50–63. [CrossRef]
24. Bandara, S.; Soga, K. Coupling of Soil Deformation and Pore Fluid Flow Using Material Point Method. *Comput. Geotech.* **2015**, *63*, 199–214. [CrossRef]
25. Bandara, S.; Ferrari, A.; Laloui, L. Modelling Landslides in Unsaturated Slopes Subjected to Rainfall Infiltration Using Material Point Method. *Int. J. Numer. Anal. Methods Geomech.* **2016**, *40*, 1358–1380. [CrossRef]
26. Wang, B.; Vardon, P.J.; Hicks, M.A. Rainfall-Induced Slope Collapse with Coupled Material Point Method. *Eng. Geol.* **2018**, *239*, 1–12. [CrossRef]
27. Srivastava, A.; Babu, G.L.S.; Haldar, S. Influence of Spatial Variability of Permeability Property on Steady State Seepage Flow and Slope Stability Analysis. *Eng. Geol.* **2010**, *110*, 93–101. [CrossRef]
28. Li, H.; Zhou, J.; Mou, X.; Guo, H.; Wang, X.; An, H.; Mo, Q.; Long, H.; Dang, C.; Wu, J. Pore Structure and Fractal Characteristics of the Marine Shale of the Longmaxi Formation in the Changning Area, Southern Sichuan Basin, China. *Front. Earth Sci.* **2022**, *10*, 1018274. [CrossRef]
29. Egbueri, J.C.; Igwe, O. The Impact of Hydrogeomorphological Characteristics on Gullying Processes in Erosion-Prone Geological Units in Parts of Southeast Nigeria. *Geol. Ecol. Landsc.* **2021**, *5*, 227–240. [CrossRef]
30. Cho, S.E. Probabilistic Analysis of Seepage That Considers the Spatial Variability of Permeability for an Embankment on Soil Foundation. *Eng. Geol.* **2012**, *133–134*, 30–39. [CrossRef]
31. Huang, J.; Fenton, G.; Griffiths, D.V.; Li, D.; Zhou, C. On the Efficient Estimation of Small Failure Probability in Slopes. *Landslides* **2017**, *14*, 491–498. [CrossRef]
32. Wang, Y.; Zhao, T.; Hu, Y.; Phoon, K.-K. Simulation of Random Fields with Trend from Sparse Measurements without Detrending. *J. Eng. Mech.* **2019**, *145*, 04018130. [CrossRef]
33. Kang, F.; Xu, Q.; Li, J. Slope Reliability Analysis Using Surrogate Models via New Support Vector Machines with Swarm Intelligence. *Appl. Math. Model.* **2016**, *40*, 6105–6120. [CrossRef]
34. Liu, L.; Zhang, S.; Cheng, Y.-M.; Liang, L. Advanced Reliability Analysis of Slopes in Spatially Variable Soils Using Multivariate Adaptive Regression Splines. *Geosci. Front.* **2019**, *10*, 671–682. [CrossRef]
35. He, X.; Xu, H.; Sabetamal, H.; Sheng, D. Machine Learning Aided Stochastic Reliability Analysis of Spatially Variable Slopes. *Comput. Geotech.* **2020**, *126*, 103711. [CrossRef]
36. Zhang, X.; Chen, Z.; Liu, Y.; Liao, J. *The Material Point Method: A Continuum-Based Particle Method for Extreme Loading Cases*; Elsevier Science & Technology: San Diego, CA, USA, 2016; pp. 196–205. ISBN 9780124077164.
37. Systèmes, D. *Abaqus/CAE User's Manual*; Dassault Systèmes Simulia Corp: Providence, RI, USA, 2014.
38. Arifin, Y.F.; Schanz, T. Osmotic Suction of Highly Plastic Clays. *Acta Geotech.* **2009**, *4*, 177–191. [CrossRef]
39. Borja, R.I.; White, J.A. Continuum Deformation and Stability Analyses of a Steep Hillside Slope under Rainfall Infiltration. *Acta Geotech.* **2010**, *5*, 1–14. [CrossRef]
40. Fredlund, D.G. Unsaturated Soil Mechanics in Engineering Practice. *J. Geotech. Geoenviron. Eng.* **2006**, *132*, 286–321. [CrossRef]
41. Mukhlisin, M.; Taha, M.R.; Kosugi, K. Numerical Analysis of Effective Soil Porosity and Soil Thickness Effects on Slope Stability at a Hillslope of Weathered Granitic Soil Formation. *Geosci. J.* **2008**, *12*, 401–410. [CrossRef]
42. Sheng, D.; Zhou, A.-N. Coupling Hydraulic with Mechanical Models for Unsaturated Soils. *Can. Geotech. J.* **2011**, *48*, 826–840. [CrossRef]
43. Zhu, H.; Zhang, L.M.; Xiao, T. Evaluating Stability of Anisotropically Deposited Soil Slopes. *Can. Geotech. J.* **2019**, *56*, 753–760. [CrossRef]
44. Le, T.M.H.; Gallipoli, D.; Sanchez, M.; Wheeler, S. Rainfall-Induced Differential Settlements of Foundations on Heterogeneous Unsaturated Soils. *Géotechnique* **2013**, *63*, 1346–1355. [CrossRef]
45. Marks, B.; Eriksen, J.; Dumazer, G.; Sandnes, B.; Måløy, K.J. Size Segregation of Intruders in Perpetual Granular Avalanches. *J. Fluid Mech.* **2017**, *825*, 502–514. [CrossRef]
46. Yang, Q.; Su, Z.; Cheng, Q.; Ren, Y.; Cai, F. High Mobility of Rock-Ice Avalanches: Insights from Small Flume Tests of Gravel-Ice Mixtures. *Eng. Geol.* **2019**, *260*, 105260. [CrossRef]
47. Sandwell, D.T. Biharmonic Spline Interpolation of GEOS-3 and Seasat Altimeter Data. *Deep. Sea Res. Part B Oceanogr. Lit. Rev.* **1987**, *34*, 763. [CrossRef]
48. Cascini, L.; Cuomo, S.; di Mauro, A.; di Natale, M.; di Nocera, S.; Matano, F. Multidisciplinary Analysis of Combined Flow-like Mass Movements in a Catchment of Southern Italy. *Georisk Assess. Manag. Risk Eng. Syst. Geohazards* **2021**, *15*, 41–58. [CrossRef]
49. Zhao, N.; Yan, E.; Cai, J. A Quasi Two-Dimensional Friction-Thermo-Hydro-Mechanical Model for High-Speed Landslides. *Eng. Geol.* **2018**, *246*, 198–211. [CrossRef]
50. van Asch, T.W.J.; Malet, J.-P.; van Beek, L.P.H. Influence of Landslide Geometry and Kinematic Deformation to Describe the Liquefaction of Landslides: Some Theoretical Considerations. *Eng. Geol.* **2006**, *88*, 59–69. [CrossRef]
51. Llano-Serna, M.A.; Farias, M.M.; Pedroso, D.M. An Assessment of the Material Point Method for Modelling Large Scale Run-out Processes in Landslides. *Landslides* **2016**, *13*, 1057–1066. [CrossRef]

52. van Genuchten, M.T. A Closed-Form Equation for Predicting the Hydraulic Conductivity of Unsaturated Soils. *Soil Sci. Soc. Am. J.* **1980**, *44*, 892–898. [CrossRef]
53. Gardner, W.R. Some Steady-State Solutions of the Unsaturated Moisture Flow Equation with Application to Evaporation from a Water Table. *Soil Sci.* **1958**, *85*, 228–232. [CrossRef]
54. Müller, S.; Schüler, L.; Zech, A.; Heße, F. GSTools v1.3: A Toolbox for Geostatistical Modelling in Python. *Geosci. Model Dev. Discuss.* **2021**, *2021*, 1–33. [CrossRef]
55. He, X.; Wang, F.; Li, W.; Sheng, D. Deep Learning for Efficient Stochastic Analysis with Spatial Variability. *Acta Geotech.* **2021**, *17*, 1031–1051. [CrossRef]
56. Kingma, D.P.; Ba, J. Adam: A Method for Stochastic Optimization. In Proceedings of the 3rd International Conference on Learning Representations (ICLR 2015), San Diego, CA, USA, 7–9 May 2015.

Article

Prediction of Strength Parameters of Thermally Treated Egyptian Granodiorite Using Multivariate Statistics and Machine Learning Techniques

Mohamed Elgharib Gomah [1,2,†], Guichen Li [1,*], Naseer Muhammad Khan [3,†], Changlun Sun [1], Jiahui Xu [1], Ahmed A. Omar [4], B. G. Mousa [2], Marzouk Mohamed Aly Abdelhamid [2] and M. M. Zaki [2,5]

[1] Key Laboratory of Deep Coal Resource Mining, School of Mines, China University of Mining and Technology, Ministry of Education of China, Xuzhou 221116, China
[2] Department of Mining and Petroleum Engineering, Faculty of Engineering, Al-Azhar University, Cairo 11884, Egypt
[3] Department of Sustainable Advanced Geomechanical Engineering, Military College of Engineering, National University of Sciences and Technology, Risalpur 23200, Pakistan
[4] Housing and Building National Research Center, Cairo 12622, Egypt
[5] College of Energy and Mining Engineering, Shandong University of Science and Technology, Qingdao 266590, China
* Correspondence: liguichen@cumt.edu.cn; Tel.: +86-158-0521-5566
† These authors contributed equally to this work.

Citation: Gomah, M.E.; Li, G.; Khan, N.M.; Sun, C.; Xu, J.; Omar, A.A.; Mousa, B.G.; Abdelhamid, M.M.A.; Zaki, M.M. Prediction of Strength Parameters of Thermally Treated Egyptian Granodiorite Using Multivariate Statistics and Machine Learning Techniques. *Mathematics* **2022**, *10*, 4523. https://doi.org/10.3390/math10234523

Academic Editors: Danial Jahed Armaghani, Hadi Khabbaz, Manoj Khandelwal, Niaz Muhammad Shahani and Ramesh Murlidhar Bhatawdekar

Received: 28 October 2022
Accepted: 28 November 2022
Published: 30 November 2022

Publisher's Note: MDPI stays neutral with regard to jurisdictional claims in published maps and institutional affiliations.

Copyright: © 2022 by the authors. Licensee MDPI, Basel, Switzerland. This article is an open access article distributed under the terms and conditions of the Creative Commons Attribution (CC BY) license (https://creativecommons.org/licenses/by/4.0/).

Abstract: The mechanical properties of rocks, such as uniaxial compressive strength and elastic modulus of intact rock, must be determined before any engineering project by employing lab or in situ tests. However, there are some circumstances where it is impossible to prepare the necessary specimens after exposure to high temperatures. Therefore, the propensity to estimate the destructive parameters of thermally heated rocks based on non-destructive factors is a helpful research field. Egyptian granodiorite samples were heated to temperatures of up to 800 °C before being treated to two different cooling methods: via the oven (slow-cooling) and using water (rapid cooling). The cooling condition, temperature, mass, porosity, absorption, dry density (D), and P-waves were used as input parameters in the predictive models for the UCS and E of thermally treated Egyptian granodiorite. Multi-linear regression (MLR), random forest (RF), k-nearest neighbor (KNN), and artificial neural networks (ANNs) were used to create predictive models. The performance of each prediction model was also evaluated using the (R^2), (RMSE), (MAPE), and (VAF). The findings revealed that cooling methods and mass as input parameters to predict UCS and E have a minor impact on prediction models. In contrast, the other parameters had a good relationship with UCS and E. Due to severe damage to granodiorite samples, many input and output parameters were impossible to measure after 600 °C. The prediction models were thus developed up to this threshold temperature. Furthermore, the comparative analysis of predictive models demonstrated that the ANN pattern for predicting the UCS and E is the most accurate model, with R^2 of 0.99, MAPE of 0.25%, VAF of 97.22%, and RMSE of 2.04.

Keywords: Egyptian granodiorite; thermal treatments; predictive models; multivariate statistics; machine learning techniques

MSC: 62H10

1. Introduction

With the advancement of thermal engineering applications, such as geothermal energy extraction, deep nuclear waste storage, and coal mining, a more in-depth understanding of rocks' strength and index properties are essential. High-temperature conditions distinguish these applications and may extend to 1000 °C, as in the coal gasification process [1]. Temperature can cause damage to the rock's surface and internal structure, which could induce instability and rock failure [2,3]. Moreover, during the evaluation process of the strength properties of rock, it is not always possible to extract drilled cores significantly to apply the destructive tests if the rock is deteriorated due to high-temperature exposure. Hence, it is crucial to develop alternative strategies to conduct a trial for recognizing the behavior of rocks after exposure to high-temperature circumstances. On the other hand, the rock's uniaxial compressive strength (UCS) and elastic modulus (E) are the two most critical rock properties in mining engineering applications. Hence, the strength parameters of rock material are essential for geotechnical engineering designs such as mechanical excavation, the design and construction of foundations, slope stability examinations, etc. [4–8]. Furthermore, UCS is one of the fundamental parameters used in the designing and planning stages [9] through rock mass classification systems, e.g., rock mass rating (RMR) [10,11], geological strength index (GSI) [12], and rock mass index (RMI) [13]. The direct estimation of UCS during the preliminary design step is too expensive, time-consuming, and complicated, mainly when conducting this test following standard procedures such as ISRM and ASTM [14–18]. The indirect evaluation of UCS supports mining engineers in overcoming the challenge of using traditional laboratory tests to calculate UCS and E. Therefore, the quick and inexpensive prediction of UCS and E from simple indirect tests that need limited preparation of the specimen through alternative and indirect methods, such as simple and multiple regression models and soft computing techniques, is an attractive trend for scholars [19–23], etc.

Many efforts have been made to forecast the UCS and E of different types of rock through various indices to individually reveal the correlation between the index and the predicted parameter by traditional regression [14,24–30]. However, there are many complexities in the application and generalization of the former statistical models, and it can be recommended only for specific rock types [5,31–33]. Furthermore, for several rock types, there is no agreement regarding the equations obtained from regression analysis. In addition, one disadvantage related to the update of statistical model equations concerning new data is that, when different from the original data, "site-specific data may be inappropriate for users to evaluate UCS and E in another site" [34–37]. Many recent studies have highlighted using soft computation techniques due to their feasible, fast, and promising means for resolving complex geotechnical engineering problems to surmount the challenges of these traditional techniques [38–40]. For instance, artificial neural networks (ANNs), Adaptive Network-based Fuzzy Inference System (ANFIS), Genetic Programming (GP), and Regression Tree methods in predicting UCS and E of rock in an objective and practical approach [15,21,22,35,41–60]. These methods are receiving more attention in resolving challenging rock engineering issues. As a result, numerous researchers use statistical approaches to extrapolate rocks' strength and informational qualities from their physical properties. In comparison to multilinear regression and the adoptive neural-fuzzy inference system, it has been suggested that an artificial neural network-based prediction model is the most effective model for measuring granite thermal damage factors based on porosity [61]. A prediction model for uniaxial compressive strength and the static Young's modulus utilizing multilinear regression, artificial neural networks, random forest, and k-nearest neighbor is proposed by [62] after evaluating the heat effect on the physical, chemical, and mechanical properties of marble rock. According to the results, MLR and ANNs provided R^2 values of 0.81 and 0.90 for MLR and 0.85 and 0.95 for ANNs for both ES and UCS, while E and UCS prediction have an R^2 of 0.94 and 0.97 for KNN and RF, respectively. As input variables for these characteristics, density, porosity, and ultrasonic wave velocities were used [63–65]. Such studies opine that the predictive abilities of artificial intelligence techniques outperform statistical methods. According to the results of these studies, soft computing techniques are more effective at predicting mechanical properties than statistical methodologies.

Rocks can be exposed to high temperatures and either slow or rapid cooling, such as after fires. Accordingly, the physical and mechanical properties of these rocks will be affected. In addition, Young's modulus and uniaxial compressive strength are crucial variables for the efficient design of engineering applications in rock mass environments. These two factors require labor-intensive and expensive laboratory analysis, and if the testing procedure is not carried out correctly, the results could be inaccurate. Furthermore, drilled cores may not always be significantly recoverable if the rock has been damaged by exposure to high temperatures. The tendency to estimate the destructive parameters of thermally heated rocks based on non-destructive parameters is a hot research topic and is very limited. Moreover, after performing an intensive literature review regarding the prediction of uniaxial compressive strength and Young's modulus of rocks under different thermal conditions based on non-destructive parameters (as illustrated in Table 1), it was seen that there are rare studies related to this research area. Thus, this paper uses different prediction models to predict the UCS and E based on the physical parameters of Egyptian granodiorite after thermal and cooling treatments. Predictive models were created using multi-linear regression (MLR), random forest (RF), k-nearest neighbor (KNN), and artificial neural networks (ANNs). The coefficient of determination (R^2), root mean square error (RMSE), mean absolute percentage error (MAPE), and variance accounted for (VAF) were used to assess the effectiveness of each prediction model. The findings of this research will make it simpler to efficiently deal with the rocks in engineering construction projects under high-temperature rock mechanics conditions and help to predict UCS and E without the need to estimate them in the laboratory.

Table 1. Summary of some recent related studies in various locations.

Rock Type (Region)	Reference	Conditions	Input Parameters	Output Parameters
Travertine (Haji a bad, Iran).	Dehghan et al., 2010 [49]	25 °C	V_p, n, I_s, SH	UCS, E
Carbonate rocks (southwestern Turkey).	Yagiz et al., 2012 [20]	25 °C	n, SH, I_d, V_p	UCS, E
Granite (Peninsular Malaysia).	Jahed et al., 2015 [22]	25 °C	ρ_{dry}, Qtz, Plg, V_p	UCS, E
"Gabbro, limestone, granite, sandstone, quartzite, tuff, diabase, etc. (Turkey)	Teymen, et al., 2020 [51]	25 °C	BTS, SH, SSH, I_s, V_p, UW	UCS
Basalt stones (Jordan)	Barham, et al., 2020 [60]	25 °C	ρ_{dry}, SH, BTS, I_d, I_s	UCS
limestone, sandstone, marl, and dolomite (Khewra Gorge)	Umer et al., 2020 [66]	200 °C	BTS, UCS	E_d
Granite (Pakistan)	Naseer et al., 2022 [61]	25–900 °C	ρ_{dry}, n, V_p	DT
Marble (Pakistan)	Naseer et al., 2022 [62]	25–500 °C	T, V_p, ρ_{dry}, n, E_d	UCS, E

P-wave velocity (V_p), porosity (n), point load index (I_s), Schmidt hammer (SH), slake durability index (I_d), dry density (ρ_{dry}), quartz content (Qtz), plagioclase content (Plg), Shore hardness (SSH), Brazilian tensile strength (BTS), unit weight (UW), and dynamic elastic modulus (E_d).

2. Rock Description and Experimental Data

2.1. Geological Setting

Granodiorite is an igneous rock that has recently been used in various projects such as ladders, hydro-engineering constructions, road paving materials, construction, and monuments. A silica-rich intrusion of magma that cools in batholiths beneath the surface produces granodiorite, a plutonic igneous rock. Tonalite and granodiorite are two granitoid rocks that make up Egypt's Arabian-Nubian Shield. They make up more than 40% of the subsurface system in the Sinai and Eastern Desert [67]. In terms of structure, granodiorite is an intrusive igneous rock similar to granite. However, it contains more plagioclase-feldspar than orthoclase-feldspar in appearance and varies in type from granitic to alkali granite and old granite, which is dark gray [68]. In Egypt's Eastern Desert, granodiorite samples were collected from old granite (near Gabel Abu Marwa). The study region is located between 23°00′ and 23°10′ north latitudes and 33°17′ and 33°28′ east longitudes (130 Km southeast of Aswan, Egypt), as illustrated in Figure 1a.

Figure 1. (**a**) Geological map of the studied area, (**b**) granodiorite appearance, and (**c**) a thin section micrograph of granodiorite.

2.2. Rock Description

The studied granodiorite samples were grey, as shown in Figure 1b, and had an average porosity of 0.54%, absorption wt. of 0.34, a dry density of 2610 kg/m^3, P-wave velocities of 5120 m/s, uniaxial compressive strength of 64 MPa, and Young's modulus of 48.8 GPa at room temperature. Employing a Bruker D8 Advance X-ray Diffractometer, X-ray diffraction (XRD) analysis revealed the rock's content to be quartz (Q), plagioclase feldspar (Pl), potassium feldspar (Kf), biotite (Bi), etc. (Figure 1c). Before testing, the samples were dried for at least 24 h at 105 °C.

2.3. Experimental Data

Based on the results obtained by Gomah et al. [2,69], the input and output data were used to build up the prediction models in this study. In these investigations, a high-temperature furnace (Nabertherm electric furnace-B410) with a thermal precision of ±3 °C and a maximum temperature of 1300 °C was used for the heating process. Further, granodiorite samples were separated into five groups to ensure measurement accuracy, each with two subgroups of three samples for each target temperature. These groups were all then subjected to the same heating process. Granodiorite specimens were heated to the target temperatures of 200, 400, 600, and 800 °C, at a rate of 5 °C/min to prevent any potential thermal shock caused by the furnace's sharp thermal gradient. The temperature was held constant for 2 h, and the heated samples were then cooled to room temperature using slow cooling by natural air in the oven (hereinafter called slow-cooling samples or S-C samples) and rapid cooling by water (hereinafter called rapid-cooling samples or R-C samples), as illustrated in Table 2.

Table 2. Input and output data of prediction models.

Method	Temperature (°C)	Input Data					Output Data	
		Mass (g)	Density (g/cm³)	P-Wave Velocity (m/s)	Porosity %	Absorption wt. %	UCS (MPa)	E (GPa)
-	25 °C	779	2.69	5619.82	1.33	0.50	66.9	50.7
		803	2.70	5645.16	0.00	0.00	65.9	47.8
		800	2.69	5633.80	1.35	0.53	59.2	48.0
S-C	200 °C	789	2.67	4455.88	1.20	0.46	66.3	41.1
		779.15	2.67	4450.37	1.29	0.50	67.1	44.1
		784.25	2.67	4454.55	1.25	0.48	67.6	43.0
R-C	200 °C	796	2.67	4039.74	0.00	0.00	70.2	41.8
		799	2.67	4070.00	1.27	0.51	71.6	50.2
		799.3	2.68	4050.00	1.29	0.50	67.4	45.1
S-C	400 °C	791	2.65	3482.81	1.32	0.51	75.9	31.5
		790	2.64	3495.68	1.43	0.56	67.9	28.9
		790.9	2.64	3384.83	1.32	0.51	73.9	31.2
R-C	400 °C	788	2.63	2911.69	0.00	0.00	55.0	24.7
		787	2.63	2606.52	2.48	0.98	56.1	25.1
		786.7	2.60	2613.88	2.57	1.00	69.3	26.5
S-C	600 °C	793	2.54	855.17	5.49	2.09	31.6	9.1
		793	2.54	1098.21	3.77	1.45	26.1	9.5
		783.9	2.54	815.49	5.17	2.03	26.8	8.6
R-C	600 °C	784	2.56	909.63	3.82	1.48	20.8	4.3
		783	2.42	754.55	3.80	1.45	19.4	3.9
		801.8	2.57	725.43	5.13	1.97	20.0	3.2
S-C	800 °C	787	2.24	0.00	10.85	4.17	2.7	-
		787	2.29	0.00	14.38	5.56	2.8	-
R-C	800 °C	786	2.22	0.00	16.88	5.64	1.5	-
		775	2.19	0.00	16.47	6.50	1.1	-

According to the International Society for Rock Mechanics (ISRM)'s suggested methods, the physical parameters of the granodiorite samples were calculated, both before and after the thermal treatments. Pundit PL-2 with two transducers (a transmitter and a receiver) was used as the ultrasonic pulse generator and acquisition system to quantify P-wave velocity along the specimen's axis [70]. R-C and S-C granodiorite samples underwent uniaxial compressive strength tests following the ASTM D7012-14 specifications. The mechanical properties were tested using a compression testing machine with a 200 T loading capacity. Two strain gauges were used, with a data-collection system linked to the device, to identify the axial and lateral displacements of the specimen. Finally, the mass, size, longitudinal wave velocity, absorption, porosity, UCS, and E of the granodiorite specimens were recorded and compared to their initial values after being subjected to different heating and cooling methods.

2.4. Prediction Models

2.4.1. Multiple-Linear Regression (MLR)

MLR is frequently employed to forecast relevant parameters. Simple linear regression, utilized in the case of numerous predictive variables, is expanded by MLR. Hence, it can be used to find the most pertinent and suitable equation when more than one independent variable is available as input parameters. In this study, a set of MLR was run using many independent variables to predict UCS and E. Equation (1) illustrates how it can describe the input without variables while considering how they relate.

$$Y = c + B_1 X_1 + B_2 X_2 + \ldots + B_n X_n \tag{1}$$

where the partial regression coefficients are B_1 to B_n, Y is the dependent variable, c is constant, and X_1 to X_n are the independent variables.

2.4.2. Random Forest Regression (RFR)

One of the most accurate prediction techniques for classification and regression among the numerous machine-learning algorithms is the emerging random forest (RF) algorithm, which was first implemented by Leo Breiman and Cutler Adele in 2001 [71]. This is because it can simulate complex interactions between input variables and thus is comparatively robust to outliers. The RFR algorithm has many benefits, including the ability to handle massive databases efficiently, the lack of sensitivity to noise or over-fitting [72], the ability to deal with thousands of input variables without deleting any, and the fact that it has lower complexity than other machine-learning algorithms (e.g., ANN). The RFR method is frequently used in geotechnical engineering [73]. For example, RFR was applied to the stability of rock pillars, and also in assessing landslide susceptibility and evaluating the potential for soil liquefaction [73–76].

The decision tree (DT) method and the bagging technique are the two fundamental parts of RF. The DT algorithm can be used for classification and regression issues depending on the dataset. The feature space is divided into smaller sections before applying the DT algorithm. Until the stop threshold is satisfied, the partitioning is carried out iteratively. Three parts—internal, external, and branches—are built when a DT is constructed. The internal nodes are constantly connected with decision-making functions to choose which node to contact next. The output nodes, also known as terminals or leaf nodes, are DT nodes that can no longer be split. The DT method is helpful in many civil engineering situations. However, the RF algorithm is more potent and reliable in many data mining tasks than a single tree [75]. RF is a technique for ensemble learning that builds on bagging to anticipate outputs [77]. Using various data from the bagging approach, several connected DTs are built in RF. The modeling accuracy is improving through the outcome averaging of all DTs, and overfitting is controlled. The overall structure of RF is shown in Figure 2, where n indicates the total number of trees built in RF and k1, k2, and kn are the outcomes of each DT.

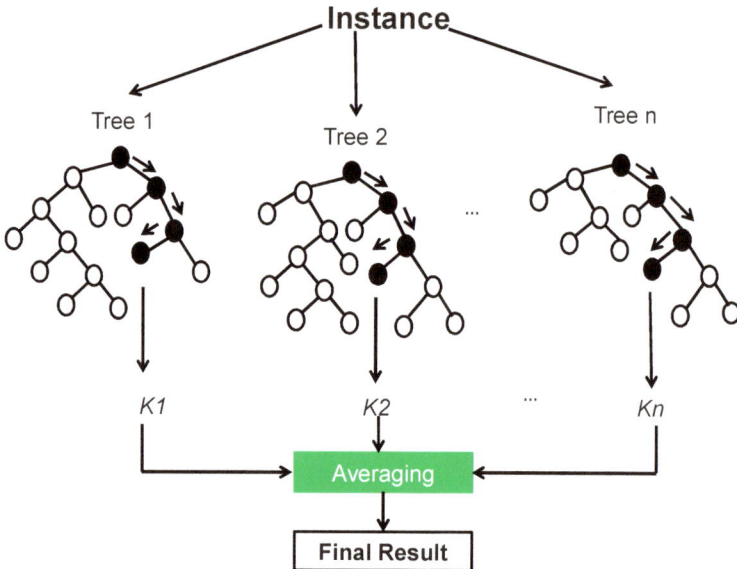

Figure 2. Fundamental design of the RF algorithm.

2.4.3. The K-Nearest Neighbor (KNN)

The labels of the K-nearest patterns in the data space are the foundation of nearest neighbor algorithms. In the context of large datasets and low dimensions, most relative neighbor techniques are known to be effective local procedures. An extensive range of machine learning issues can be applied thanks to variations for multi-label classification, regression, and semi-supervised learning cases. The k-nearest neighbor (KNN) approach is easy to use, practical, and implementable [78]. This technique is utilized for classification and regression, much like ANN and RF. The fundamental idea behind KNN is to identify a set of "k" samples near unknown samples in the calibration dataset (for instance, by using distance functions). Finding collections of models that are identical to one another can help with this.

Furthermore, KNN establishes the category of unknown samples by averaging the relevant variables and contrasting the outcomes with the "k" samples. Because of this, the efficiency of the KNN depends significantly on the k value [79]. Employing the KNN approach has certain advantages, such as it being simple to understand and put into practice. Additionally, it can comprehend non-linear decision boundaries when used for classification and regression, and by varying the value of K, it can provide a very flexible choice limit. Additionally, there is not a phase in the KNN architecture solely for training; hence, adjusting the other hyperparameters is relatively easy. The three-distance function, which calculates the distance between nearby locations and is shown in the following Formulas (2)–(4), is used for the regression problem.

$$F(e) = \sqrt{\sum_{i=0}^{f} (x_i - y_i)^2} \qquad (2)$$

$$F(ma) = \sum_{i=0}^{f} |x_i - y_i| \qquad (3)$$

$$F(ma) = \left(\sum_{i=0}^{f} (|x_i - y_i|)^q \right)^{\frac{1}{q}} \qquad (4)$$

where x_i and y_i represent the ith dimension, q indicates the order between the points x and y, and $F(e)$ stands for the Euclidean function. $F(ma)$ and $F(mi)$ are for the Manhattan and Minkowski functions, respectively.

2.4.4. Artificial Neural Network (ANN)

The artificial neural network is a soft computing technique that has recently been widely accepted as a predicting method in rock engineering applications such as tunnels, slope stability, and underground openings. ANN proffers better aptitudes in dealing with the nonlinear relationship between parameters than the traditional regression approaches. ANN models possess capabilities in processing the information pertinent to high parallelism and their ability to learn. Furthermore, solving the complex or imprecise data and grouping and filtration of noisy data to build the underlying correlation between the datasets [80] provide the extraordinary prediction efficiency of ANN models. Any artificial neural network is formed from several quite simple and highly interconnected processors, also neurons, due to their similarity to the biological neurons in the human brain [81,82]. A traditional ANN is usually represented by three principal components: network architecture, transfer function, and learning code [83].

Multi-layered perception (MLP) is employed in this section. It is made up of the following three layers: (1) an input layer for providing data; (2) a hidden layer using an algorithm and a set of features, neurons, and the hidden layer chosen through trial-and-error techniques [84]; and (3) an output layer for providing the input data's output. The number of neurons in each layer varies according to the application. Each link between a layer neuron and the one below it is connected and has weight [85]. The ANN model also employs several other algorithms. However, due to its straightforward training function, backpropagation (BP) is the most effective and is frequently utilized in engineering challenges. Previous research has shown that the BP approach considers and presupposes a random value. The NN process uses that random value to calculate the result after that. Hence, the weight value will be changed to reduce the error margin. This process will be performed as often as necessary until the minimal result is achieved [86]. Supervised learning techniques must be employed throughout the training stage to guarantee the precision and efficacy of each classification and operation in ANN. The BP algorithm's networking is trained using a set of instances to connect and link the nodes and identify the parametric function, also known as weight inadequacies methods. The mean square error (MSE) is repeatedly reduced to reduce the difference between the actual and the predicted output. Training also helps in determining each iteration's weight.

This study produced a self-generated ANN code with n numbers of networks while maintaining the same training and activating function for a single loop, as illustrated in Figure 3. This code has a loop function that can run for many networks. Even though the data type may change, this code's essential activation function was constant, and the code was once run over 100 networks. The number of neurons for each network in a loop rose for each successor; as a result, network (1) had one neuron, network (2) had two, and so on. Several ANN algorithms are available; however, the recommendation [74] of using BP with the Levenberg–Marquardt algorithm is the most practical. Compared to other algorithms, Levenberg–Marquardt (LM) is more effective, requires a shorter time, and produces superior results. As a result, LM was applied to both the hidden and the output layers of the current model.

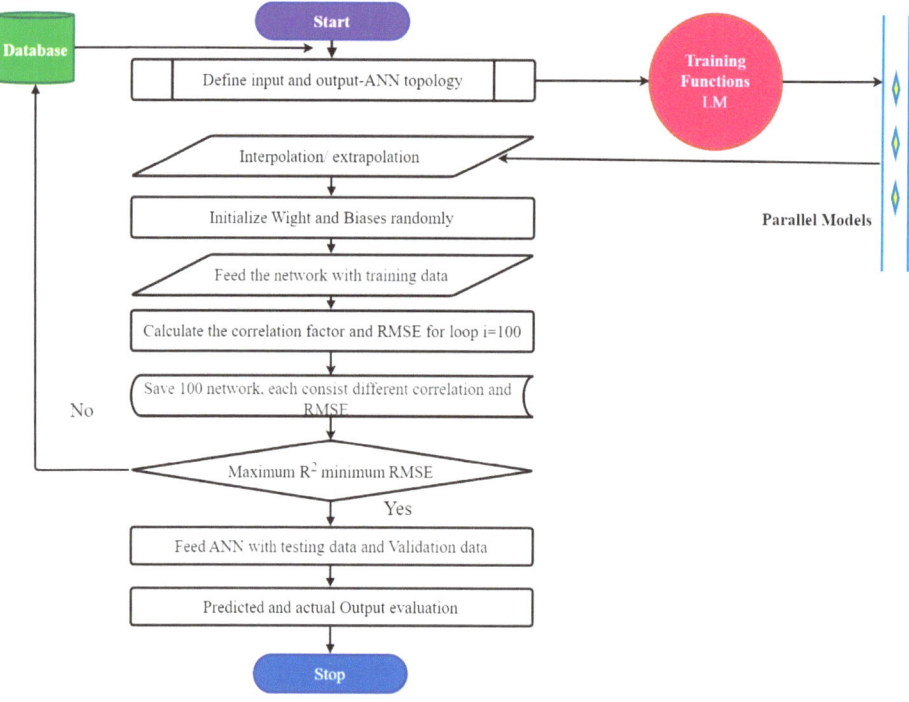

Figure 3. ANN flowchart for the UCS and E prediction model.

Figure 4 depicts an example of an ANN model's flowchart. A set of input layers, a predetermined number of hidden layers, and a bunch of output layers make up the usual ANN structure. The primary neuron is processed to estimate the output by linking the multiple layers of inputs with the proper weights (W) and biases (b). As shown, the basic structure of this analysis consists of two outputs (uniaxial compressive strength (UCS) and elastic modulus (E)) and five inputs (temperature, absorption, porosity, dry density, and P-wave velocity). There was a total of 42 data points in the dataset. The following three categories of data were created: validation (15%), testing (15%), and training (70%).

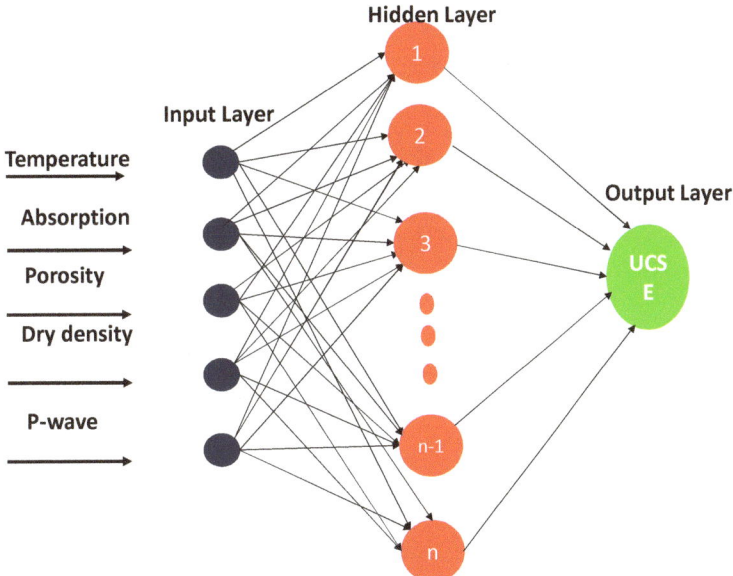

Figure 4. The structure of ANN for UCS and E predictions.

3. Results

3.1. Data Analysis

Thermal treatment significantly impacts the rock porosity and, consequently, water absorption of granodiorite. The porosity of the granodiorite specimens generally increased steadily for the both rapid- and slow-cooling methods, with temperatures rising but at different rates. Changes in linked mass and volume are the most significant influence on rock density. After being heated, the granodiorite's density gradually reduced compared to room temperature. Furthermore, thermal treatments significantly affected the granodiorite's ultrasonic wave velocities, and that behavior was noticed for both cooling methods studied. Summary of findings: The P-wave velocity of rocks decreases concurrently with temperature increases. Due to the severity of the thermal fissures, it was impossible to quantify the longitudinal wave velocity at 800 °C (assumed 0 m/s). Consequently, the degradation of the longitudinal wave velocity of granodiorite is caused by the physical and chemical alterations that occur after 600 °C, as displayed in Figure 5.

On the other hand, the mechanical properties of Egyptian granodiorite deteriorate primarily under the influence of temperature as the thermal expansion of its minerals change through their microstructure. Because of the mismatched growth during heating, thermal stresses are produced inside the granodiorite. When thermal stresses within or between minerals exceed the maximum strength of the minerals, microcracks and microfractures initiate and expand because thermal treatments induce mineral growth and chemical reactions [87]. As opposed to slow-cooled samples, rapid-cooled samples generally had lower uniaxial strength and elastic modulus, proving that the created microstructural alteration resulted from the thermal treatments and cooling methods, as shown in Figure 5. At 800 °C, the effects of high temperatures grew increasingly noticeable for both cooling techniques, and inter- and trans-granular cracks quickly developed, creating a network of microcracks. Furthermore, the granodiorite specimens' internal structures were destroyed, making them impossible to measure E (Table 1).

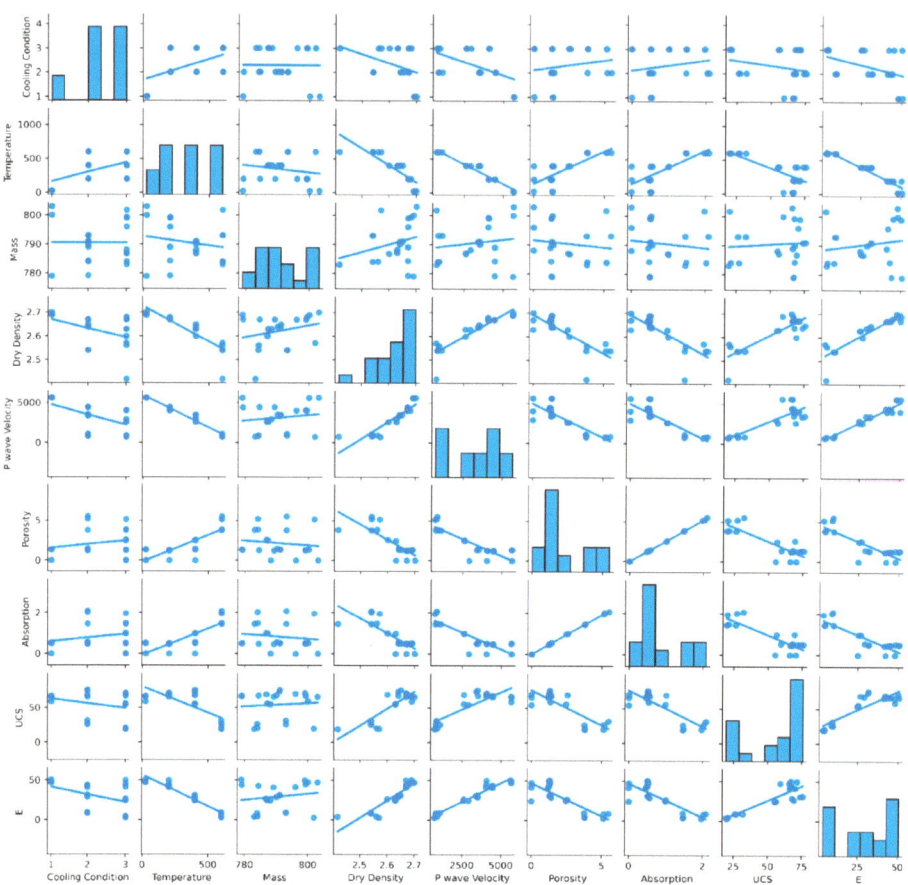

Figure 5. Input and output distributions as a pairwise correlation matrix.

For machine learning and statistical techniques, the parameters used in this work include the cooling method, temperature, mass, P-wave velocity, density, porosity, absorption, UCS, and E. The prediction of UCS and E is meant to employ the other parameters as inputs. Using a correlation matrix, a descriptive statistical technique, users may learn more about the variance and covariance of the regressions, which are part of the prediction model. Alongside other statistical matrices, it is frequently utilized. The correlation matrix typically explains each variable's fluctuation. Figures 5 and 6 can demonstrate this using correlation and paired correlation. The relationships between the input variables and the output include negative, positive, or no connections. For instance, variables that exhibit a negative correlation include temperature, absorption, and porosity. In contrast, the P-wave velocity and density had positive relations, while the mass and cooling method revealed poor relations with UCS and E. As they have a poor impact on both USC and E, as shown in Figure 6, the cooling method and mass of specimens were excluded from the following machine learning prediction as input parameters. Furthermore, after 600 °C, the model efficiency was minimized due to many input and output parameters being corrupted, such as Pv and E. Figures 5 and 6 make it simple for a researcher to grasp the impact of inputs on the expected model's output findings. The larger the negative or positive link, the more critical the model efficiency.

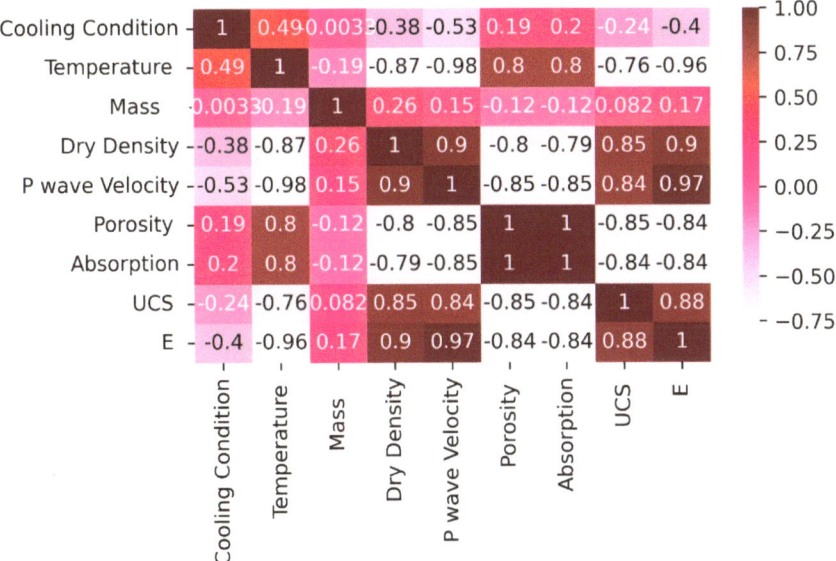

Figure 6. Inputs and outputs correlation matrix.

3.2. Model Performance

This study used statistical (MLR) and intelligent models (RFR, KNN, and ANNs) to create predictive models for the UCS and E of Egyptian granodiorite. The performance of predicted models is then investigated by comparing the correlation efficiencies of various generated models. The efficiency indices (R^2), (MAPE), (VAF), and (RMSE) were used to perform the evaluations for this comparison. The accuracy of model fitting is evaluated by the coefficient of determination (R^2). The linear fit equation represents this, and is defined as the ratio of actual data variation to estimated value variance. Less than 30% is regarded as suspicious, above 75% is regarded as remarkable, and a model with an R^2 of at least 55% is accepted. In addition, the efficiency of a prediction system is measured by the mean absolute percentage error (MAPE), also known as the mean absolute percentage deviation (MAPD). It can be expressed as the average absolute percent inaccuracy for every period, minus the actual values divided by the true values, and it describes this accuracy as a percentage. The standard deviation of the residuals is represented by the root mean square error (RMSE) (prediction errors). In a perfect scenario, the RMSE would be zero, a common indicator of the discrepancies between predicted or expected values and actual values. The variance accounted for (VAF) is typically used to verify that the predictive model is accurate. This is accomplished by comparing the outputs as anticipated and measured [88]. A VAF rating of 100 indicates that the predictive model accurately predicts the outcome. Consequently, the more accurately the forecast is made, the closer the predictive model's VAF is to 100 (i.e., lower variance). Hence, $R^2 = 1$, MAPE = RMSE = 0, and VAF = 100% are performance indicators that can be used to describe an outstanding model. Equations (5)–(8) were used to compute the performance indices, as shown below:

$$R^2 = \frac{\sum_{i=1}^{n}(y_i)^2 - \sum_{i=1}^{n}(y_i - k'_i)^2}{\sum_{i=1}^{n}(y_i)^2} \tag{5}$$

$$\text{MAPE} = \frac{1}{2}\sum_{i=1}^{n}\left|\frac{y_i - k'_i}{y_i}\right| \times 100 \tag{6}$$

$$RMSE = \sqrt{\frac{\sum_{i=1}^{n}(y_i - k'_i)}{n}} \quad (7)$$

$$VAF = \left[1 - \frac{var(y - k')}{var(y)}\right] \times 100 \quad (8)$$

where (y) is the actual value and (k') is the predicted value.

3.3. Prediction Models of UCS and E

3.3.1. Multilinear Regression Prediction Models

Two distinct multilinear regression equations were created for the prediction of UCS and E. Equations (9) and (10) can be used to express these mathematically, as follows:

$$UCS = -259.79 + 12.93 Temp + 0.20 density + 35.21 velocity + 0.04 porosity + 7.69 Absorption \quad (9)$$

$$E = -62.51 + 5.02 Temp - 0.003 density + 16.12 velocity + 0.01 porosity + 4.50 Absorption \quad (10)$$

A coefficient of determination (R^2) of 0.86 for the relationship between actual and predicted UCS (Figure 7a) and 0.96 for the relationship between actual and predicted E (Figure 7b) indicate the relation between actual and predicted UCS and E.

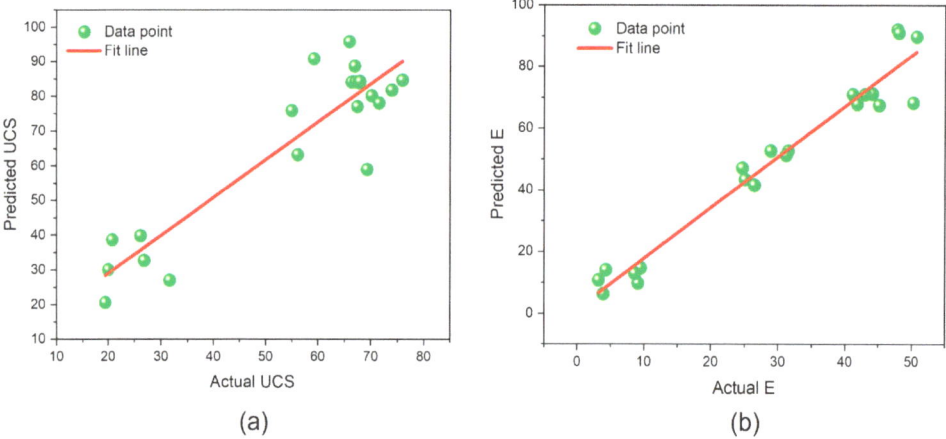

Figure 7. MLR model for actual and predicted UCS (**a**) and E (**b**).

3.3.2. Random Forest Technique

The random forest (RF) and k-nearest neighbor's regressions (KNN) models were built using Python's Scikit-Learn module. The python package includes many machine-learning techniques readily usable in various applications. The data were normalized to convert the values collected on diverse scales to a standard scale at the beginning of this analysis. Following that, 70% of the data were used to train the models, and the remaining 30% were divided into the testing set (15%) and the validation group (15%). With the aid of the testing set, the hyper-parameters were adjusted. The RF model's (n estimators) and (max depth) hyperparameters were varied throughout a range of possible values. The number of estimators, which is directly linked to the number of decision trees built by the random forest regression model, is determined before computing the maximum averages of forecasts. As the number of trees rises, the model becomes more computationally expensive while offering better performance. The max depth hyperparameters indicate the depth of every decision tree in a random forest. Because the max depth hyperparameter was allocated a very high value, the model is overfitted. Table 3 lists the ideal values for n estimators, max depth, and random state. Additionally, as seen in Figure 8, the predicted values for USC and E have a strong correlation coefficient ($R^2 = 0.98$) for the actual parameter value.

Table 3. Optimized RFR hyperparameters.

Parameters	Values	Details
n-estimators	100	Number of trees in RFR
Max-depth	12	Maximum depth of tree
Random state	10	Random state

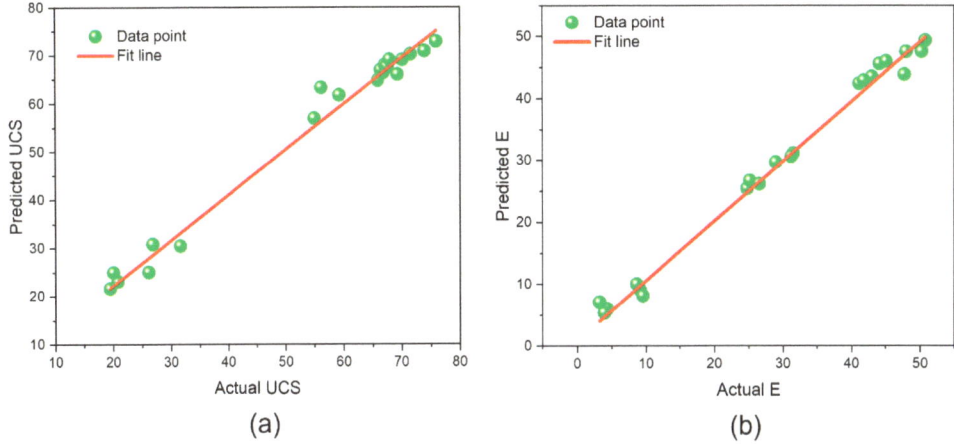

Figure 8. Relationship between the predicted and actual UCS (**a**) and E (**b**) of Egyptian granodiorite using random forest technique.

3.3.3. K-Nearest Neighbor Technique

The variable "n neighbors" in the KNN model represented the number of neighbors, which might vary. The "number of neighbors" hyperparameter determines the number of neighbors that should be considered while averaging data for a forecast. The approach becomes more accurate and computationally costly when the value of the n neighbors hyperparameter is raised to a large amount. A grid search strategy was applied to find the ideal values for the hyperparameters. The grid search strategy tests a wide range of potential values for each hyperparameter being adjusted before choosing one to represent the perfect combination. The value was experimented with on various levels, while other hyperparameters stayed the same to establish a workable limit for each hyperparameter. The optimum pairing of n neighbors and metric values is described in Table 4. Additionally, as can be observed in Figure 9 that the predicted value at this parameter-optimal value has a good correlation coefficient ($R^2 = 0.95$) for both USC and E.

Table 4. Optimized KNN hyperparameters.

Parameters	Values	Descriptions
n-neighbors	11	Number neighbors
Metric	Minkowski	The distance metric to use

3.3.4. Neural Network Model

Figure 10 displays the regression values for the UCS and E models of granodiorite during each phase of the ANN, including training, validation, testing, and regression results.

Excellent regression was obtained during training, validation, and testing combinations between the predicted and measured measurements of UCS and E.

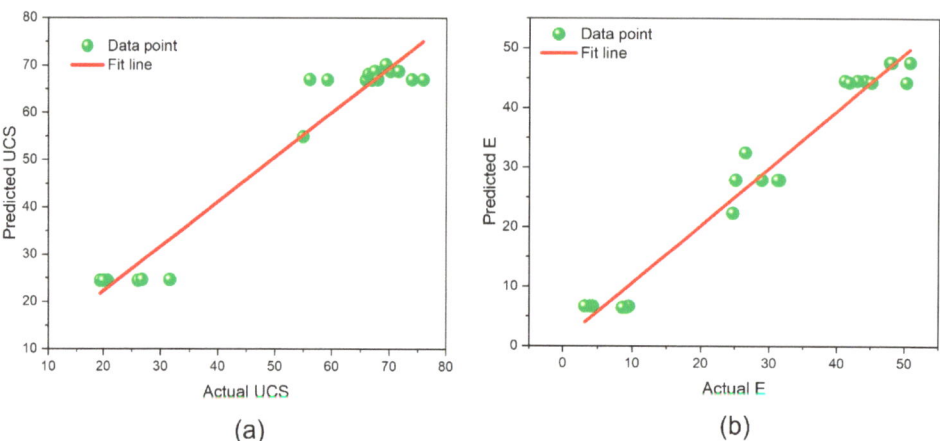

Figure 9. Relationship between expected and real UCS (**a**) and E (**b**) based on the KNN approach.

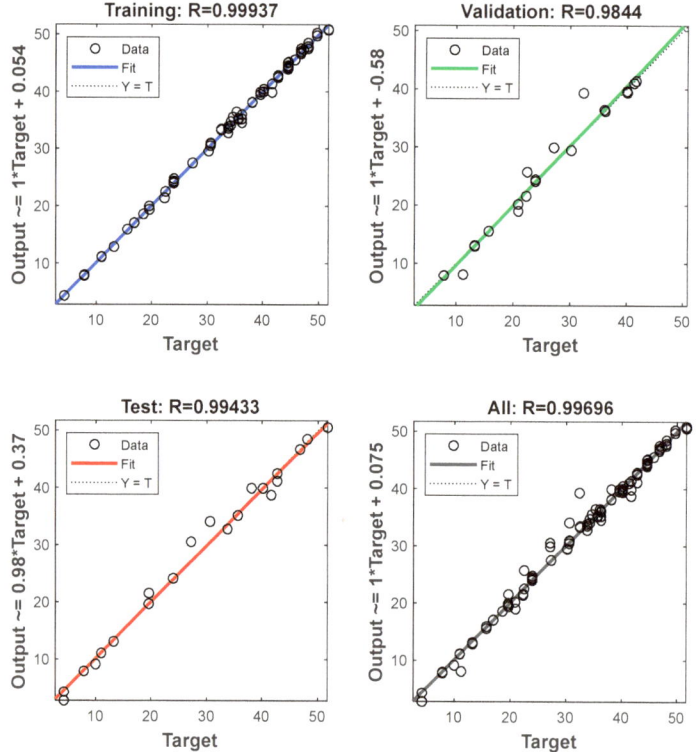

Figure 10. ANN training, validation, and testing stages with the related regression coefficient for UCS and E.

Consequently, as shown in Figure 11, an exceptional R^2 value (0.99) between the expected and actual (UCS and E) data is observed (Table 5).

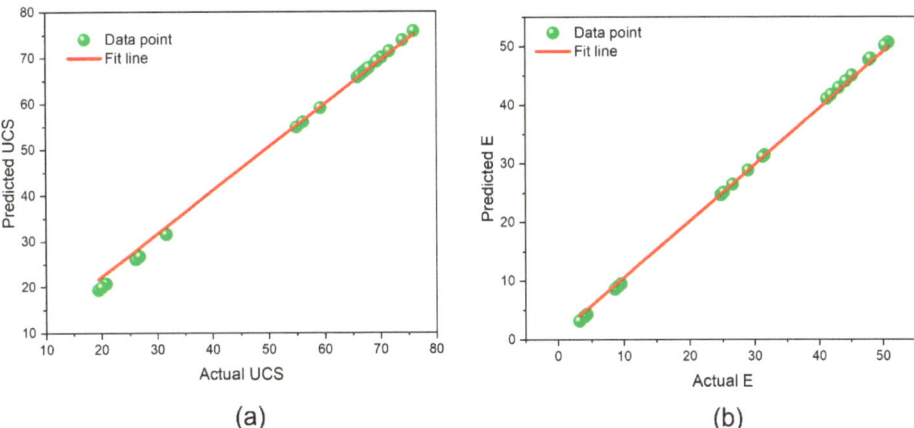

Figure 11. Relationship between the predicted and actual UCS (**a**) and E (**b**) using ANN approach.

Table 5. Relation between the actual and the predicted values of UCS and E for used intelligent methods.

Temperature (°C)	Actual UCS (MPa)	Actual E (GPa)	Predicted UCS (KNN)	Predicted E (KNN)	Predicted UCS (RFR)	Predicted E (RFR)	Predicted UCS (ANN)	Predicted E (ANN)
25 °C	66.85	50.73	66.95	47.68	66.43	49.38	66.79	50.68
	65.89	47.75	66.95	47.68	64.85	43.90	65.82	47.70
	59.2	48	66.95	47.68	61.84	47.59	59.14	47.95
200 °C	66.34	41.1	68.16	44.60	67.02	42.44	66.27	41.06
	67.08	44.1	68.16	44.60	68.04	45.64	67.01	44.06
	67.64	43	68.16	44.60	67.61	43.53	67.57	42.96
	70.15	41.8	68.78	44.30	69.13	42.91	70.08	41.76
	71.56	50.2	68.78	44.30	70.28	47.62	71.49	50.15
	67.41	45.1	68.78	44.30	67.75	46.05	67.34	45.05
400 °C	75.92	31.5	67.02	27.90	72.93	31.17	75.84	31.47
	67.91	28.9	67.02	27.90	69.17	29.72	67.84	28.87
	73.93	31.2	67.02	27.90	70.95	30.65	73.86	31.17
	54.95	24.7	54.89	22.35	57.02	25.47	54.89	24.67
	56.11	25.1	67.03	27.90	63.40	26.75	56.05	25.07
	69.32	26.5	70.20	32.48	66.10	26.21	69.25	26.47
600 °C	31.61	9.1	24.66	6.48	30.51	9.11	31.58	9.09
	26.11	9.5	24.49	6.70	25.10	8.16	26.08	9.49
	26.8	8.6	24.66	6.48	30.89	10.04	26.77	8.59
	20.79	4.3	24.49	6.70	23.17	6.02	20.77	4.30
	19.44	3.9	24.49	6.70	21.70	5.41	19.42	3.90
	20.01	3.2	24.49	6.70	25.01	7.11	19.99	3.20

The MSE (mean squared error) metric was used to assess network accuracy and efficiency. Increasing the neuron count in the hidden layer reduced the MSE value as the number of iterations rose. The MSE for each UCS and E model was assessed. A lower MSE number at 11 epochs for UCS and E resulted in the best regression model, as illustrated in Figure 12.

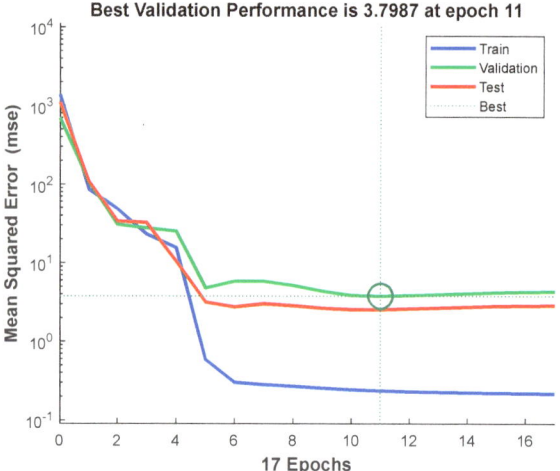

Figure 12. ANN Performance based on the mean squared error metric.

According to the neuron convergence investigation, as seen in Figure 13, the UCS and E best regression and least MSE were achieved on 17 neurons. This demonstrates that the number of iterations and the number of neurons critically influence the model's accuracy.

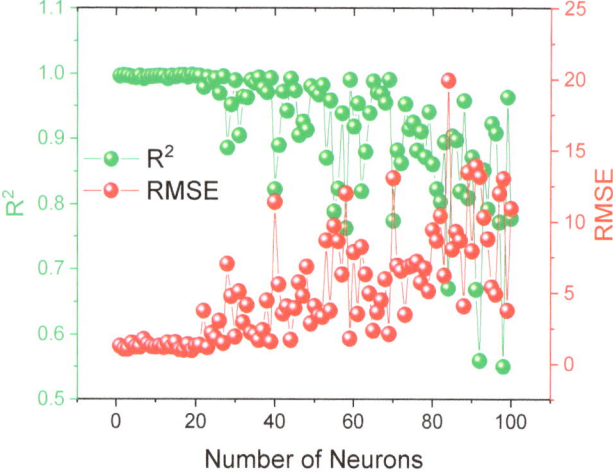

Figure 13. Impact of neuron convergence in the hidden layer.

4. Discussion

Thermal treatment causes mineral expansions and chemical reactions, which results in the formation and propagation of microcracks and microfractures. Mineral grains grow, and the thermal expansion characteristics of distinct minerals vary. Anisotropic thermal expansion along separate crystallographic axes of the same mineral under heating further contributes to uneven growth. Furthermore, the evaporation of free and constitutional water raises the micro-pores in granodiorite, which could affect the texture, such as in damage to the mineral silicate frame. As a result, microcracks occur between or inside the mineral grains. Hence, this can cause mineralogical, physical, and mechanical changes in rocks significantly different from those at room temperature.

Testing the UCS and E to gain more knowledge about the mechanical behavior of rock is more difficult in high-temperature deep geotechnical applications. Therefore, a more critical research aspect is the propensity to evaluate the destructive parameters of thermally treated rocks based on non-destructive factors. The UCS and E are thus predicted in this paper using various prediction models derived from the physical characteristics of Egyptian granodiorite following thermal and cooling treatments. The cooling technique, temperature, mass, P-wave velocity, density, porosity, and absorption to forecast the UCS and E were the input parameters used in this study. Prediction model effectiveness was reduced after 600 °C because many input and output variables, such as Pv and E, were hard to measure due to severe degradation to granodiorite specimens. As a result, the prediction models were built up to this critical temperature, which can be considered a threshold temperature point. The relationships between the input and the output variables indicated negative, positive, or no relations. In the prediction models, temperature, absorption, and porosity are factors that have a negative connotation. On the other hand, the density and P-wave velocity were positive. However, the mass and cooling technique demonstrated weak relationships with UCS and E; hence, they were eliminated from the soft computing prediction models. Moreover, as illustrated in Figure 6, temperature and P-wave velocity actively contributed to the elastic modulus prediction model. On the contrary, porosity, absorption, and density showed a less significant predictive impact. In contrast, porosity and density were the most efficient characteristics for predicting uniaxial compressive strength.

The greater the magnitude of the negative or positive relationship, the more crucial the model performance. As demonstrated in the results in Table 6, the MLR prediction models' performance coefficients for UCS and E are 0.86% and 0.96%, respectively. In contrast, intelligent models for UCS and E, such as RFR, KNN, and ANN, have higher performance coefficients of 0.98%, 0.95%, and 0.99%, demonstrating that their models for UCS and E prediction are more rational than the statistical model. Hence, the obtained results from this study are better than those concluded by [62]. Furthermore, after comparing the results obtained from the statistical (MLR) and soft computed models, it is concluded that the intelligent models perform better at predicting UCS and E than the MLR, whereas ANN provides a high coefficient of determination for UCS and ES, and the MLR provides a lower coefficient for both predicted parameters. Hence, based on these performance indexes, the ANN performed excellently.

Table 6. Performance indices of the developed models.

Predicted Parameter	Models	R^2	RMSE	MAPE (%)	VAF (%)
UCS	MLR	0.86	27.15	34.53	81.02
E		0.96	0.90	23.15	31.53
UCS, E	RFR	0.98	0.14	1.18	94.23
	KNN	0.95	3.02	0.94	94.01
	ANN	0.99	2.04	0.25	97.22

5. Conclusions

This article suggests a new predictive model quantifying the preheated Egyptian granodiorite's uniaxial compressive strength and its elastic modulus. Four prediction models were created: multi-linear regression (MLR), random forest (RF), k-nearest neighbor (KNN), and artificial neural networks (ANNs). These models were developed using five input parameters as a base (temperature, porosity, absorption, density, and p-wave). Each prediction model's efficiency was evaluated using the coefficient of determination (R^2), root mean square error (RMSE), mean absolute percentage error (MAPE), and variance accounted for (VAF). The principal conclusions are listed as follows:

(1) Due to the close results of the slow cooling by the oven and rapid cooling by the water of thermally treated granodiorite, the cooling method and mass as input parameters to predict UCS and E have a minor effect on the prediction models of UCS and E. In

contrast, the temperature, porosity, absorption, dry density, and P-wave velocity had good relations with UCS and E.

(2) After 600 °C, the performance of the prediction models was diminished because many input and output parameters, such as Pv and E, were impossible to measure due to the severe damage to granodiorite samples. The prediction models were therefore developed up to this threshold temperature, which can be regarded as a threshold temperature point.

(3) The inconsistent performance for the MLR model demonstrates that the temperature and P-wave velocity actively contributed to the prediction models of elastic modulus. In contrast, the porosity, absorption, and density had a less significant predictive impact. In comparison, porosity and density were the best effective parameters to predict the uniaxial compressive strength.

(4) The performance coefficients for the MLR prediction models for UCS and E are 0.86% and 0.96%, respectively. In contrast, the intelligent models for UCS and E, including RFR, KNN, and ANN, provide a better performance coefficient (9–13%), indicating that their models for UCS and E prediction are more reasonable than the statistical model (MRL).

(5) The comparative analysis of predictive models revealed that the ANN model used for predicting the UCS and E is the most accurate model, with R^2 of 0.99, MAPE of 0.25%, VAF of 97.22%, and RMSE of 2.04.

Recommendation: This study mainly discusses three artificial intelligence techniques (RFR, KNN, and ANNs) and a conventional linear regression model (MLR). Other methods, such as the adoptive neural-fuzzy inference system (ANFIS model), may be employed to predict the mechanical parameters based on the non-destructive parameters. Moreover, as well known, rocks' chemical, physical, and mechanical behavior vary by region. This study examined Egyptian granodiorite. Hence, the study could be more general by considering different rocks in other locations. Moreover, future research may incorporate the sparse principal component analysis (PCA), one of the most commonly operated unsupervised machine learning algorithms for dimensionality reduction and visualize multidimensional data.

Author Contributions: Conceptualization, M.E.G.; methodology, M.E.G.; validation, M.E.G., N.M.K., B.G.M., M.M.A.A., M.M.Z. and G.L.; analysis, M.E.G., G.L., N.M.K., C.S., J.X., A.A.O., B.G.M., M.M.A.A. and M.M.Z.; writing—original draft, M.E.G.; writing—review and editing, M.E.G., G.L., N.M.K., C.S., J.X., A.A.O., B.G.M., M.M.A.A. and M.M.Z.; supervision, M.E.G. and G.L.; funding acquisition, G.L. All authors have read and agreed to the published version of the manuscript.

Funding: This research was funded by National Natural Science Foundation of China grant number [U22A20165, 52174089] and Fundamental Research Funds for the Central Universities [2020ZDPY0221].

Data Availability Statement: All the data and models employed and/or generated during the study appear in the submitted article.

Acknowledgments: The authors gratefully acknowledge the financial support from the National Natural Science Foundation of China (No. U22A20165, No. 52174089), and the Fundamental Research Funds for the Central Universities (No. 2020ZDPY0221).

Conflicts of Interest: The authors declare no conflict of interest.

References

1. Verma, A.K.; Gautam, P.; Singh, T.N.; Bajpai, R.K. Discrete element modelling of conceptual deep geological repository for high-level nuclear waste disposal. *Arab. J. Geosci.* **2015**, *8*, 8027–8038. [CrossRef]
2. Gomah, M.E.; Li, G.; Bader, S.; Elkarmoty, M.; Ismael, M. Damage Evolution of Granodiorite after Heating and Cooling Treatments. *Minerals* **2021**, *11*, 779. [CrossRef]
3. Gomah, M.E.; Li, G.; Sun, C.; Xu, J.; Yang, S.; Li, J. On the Physical and Mechanical Responses of Egyptian Granodiorite after High-Temperature Treatments. *Sustainability* **2022**, *14*, 4632. [CrossRef]
4. Ceryan, N. Application of support vector machines and relevance vector machines in predicting uniaxial compressive strength of volcanic rocks. *J. Afr. Earth Sci.* **2014**, *100*, 634–644. [CrossRef]

5. Wang, Y.; Aladejare, A.E. Selection of site-specific regression model for characterization of uniaxial compressive strength of rock. *Int. J. Rock Mech. Min. Sci.* **2015**, *75*, 73–81. [CrossRef]
6. Vasanelli, E.; Calia, A.; Colangiuli, D.; Micelli, F.; Aiello, M.A. Assessing the reliability of non-destructive and moderately invasive techniques for the evaluation of uniaxial compressive strength of stone masonry units. *Constr. Build. Mater.* **2016**, *124*, 575–581. [CrossRef]
7. Liu, B.; Zhao, Y.; Zhang, C.; Zhou, J.; Li, Y.; Sun, Z. Characteristic strength and acoustic emission properties of weakly cemented sandstone at different depths under uniaxial compression. *Int. J. Coal Sci. Technol.* **2021**, *8*, 1288–1301. [CrossRef]
8. Jangara, H.; Ozturk, C.A. Longwall top coal caving design for thick coal seam in very poor strength surrounding strata. *Int. J. Coal Sci. Technol.* **2021**, *8*, 641–658. [CrossRef]
9. Zhang, Q.; Huang, X.; Zhu, H.; Li, J. Quantitative assessments of the correlations between rock mass rating (RMR) and geological strength index (GSI). *Tunn. Undergr. Sp. Technol.* **2019**, *83*, 73–81. [CrossRef]
10. Bieniawski, Z.T. Engineering classification of jointed rock masses. *Civ. Eng. S. Afr.* **1973**, *15*, 335–343.
11. Bieniawski, Z.T. *Engineering Rock Mass Classifications: A Complete Manual for Engineers and Geologists in Mining, Civil, and Petroleum Engineering*; John Wiley & Sons: Hoboken, NJ, USA, 1989; ISBN 0471601721.
12. Hoek, E. Strength of Rock and Rock Masse. 1994. Available online: https://www.sid.ir/paper/546357/en (accessed on 1 October 2022).
13. Palmstrøm, A. Characterizing rock masses by the RMi for use in practical rock engineering: Part 1: The development of the Rock Mass index (RMi). *Tunn. Undergr. Sp. Technol.* **1996**, *11*, 175–188. [CrossRef]
14. Yılmaz, I.; Sendır, H. Correlation of Schmidt hardness with unconfined compressive strength and Young's modulus in gypsum from Sivas (Turkey). *Eng. Geol.* **2002**, *66*, 211–219. [CrossRef]
15. Baykasoğlu, A.; Güllü, H.; Çanakçı, H.; Özbakır, L. Prediction of compressive and tensile strength of limestone via genetic programming. *Expert Syst. Appl.* **2008**, *35*, 111–123. [CrossRef]
16. Karaman, K.; Kesimal, A. A comparative study of Schmidt hammer test methods for estimating the uniaxial compressive strength of rocks. *Bull. Eng. Geol. Environ.* **2015**, *74*, 507–520. [CrossRef]
17. Wang, Y.; Aladejare, A.E. Bayesian characterization of correlation between uniaxial compressive strength and Young's modulus of rock. *Int. J. Rock Mech. Min. Sci.* **2016**, *85*, 10–19. [CrossRef]
18. Yang, D.; Ning, Z.; Li, Y.; Lv, Z.; Qiao, Y. In situ stress measurement and analysis of the stress accumulation levels in coal mines in the northern Ordos Basin, China. *Int. J. Coal Sci. Technol.* **2021**, *8*, 1316–1335. [CrossRef]
19. Diamantis, K.; Gartzos, E.; Migiros, G. Study on uniaxial compressive strength, point load strength index, dynamic and physical properties of serpentinites from Central Greece: Test results and empirical relations. *Eng. Geol.* **2009**, *108*, 199–207. [CrossRef]
20. Yagiz, S.; Sezer, E.A.; Gokceoglu, C. Artificial neural networks and nonlinear regression techniques to assess the influence of slake durability cycles on the prediction of uniaxial compressive strength and modulus of elasticity for carbonate rocks. *Int. J. Numer. Anal. Methods Geomech.* **2012**, *36*, 1636–1650. [CrossRef]
21. Mishra, D.A.; Basu, A. Estimation of uniaxial compressive strength of rock materials by index tests using regression analysis and fuzzy inference system. *Eng. Geol.* **2013**, *160*, 54–68. [CrossRef]
22. Jahed Armaghani, D.; Tonnizam Mohamad, E.; Momeni, E.; Narayanasamy, M.S.; Mohd Amin, M.F. An adaptive neuro-fuzzy inference system for predicting unconfined compressive strength and Young's modulus: A study on Main Range granite. *Bull. Eng. Geol. Environ.* **2015**, *74*, 1301–1319. [CrossRef]
23. Armaghani, D.J.; Tonnizam Mohamad, E.; Momeni, E.; Monjezi, M.; Sundaram Narayanasamy, M. Prediction of the strength and elasticity modulus of granite through an expert artificial neural network. *Arab. J. Geosci.* **2016**, *9*, 48. [CrossRef]
24. Deere, D.U.; Miller, R.P. *Engineering Classification and Index Properties for Intact Rock*; Illinois Univ At Urbana Dept Of Civil Engineering: Urbana, IL, USA, 1966.
25. Sheorey, P.R. Schmidt hammer rebound data for estimation of large scale in situ coal strength. *Int. J. Rock Mech. Min. Sci. Geomech. Abstr.* **1984**, *21*, 10–28. [CrossRef]
26. Sachpazis, C.I. Correlating Schmidt hardness with compressive strength and Young's modulus of carbonate rocks. *Bull. Int. Assoc. Eng. Geol. l'Association Int. Géologie l'Ingénieur* **1990**, *42*, 75–83. [CrossRef]
27. Katz, O.; Reches, Z.; Roegiers, J.-C. Evaluation of mechanical rock properties using a Schmidt Hammer. *Int. J. Rock Mech. Min. Sci.* **2000**, *37*, 723–728. [CrossRef]
28. Yagiz, S. Predicting uniaxial compressive strength, modulus of elasticity and index properties of rocks using the Schmidt hammer. *Bull. Eng. Geol. Environ.* **2009**, *68*, 55–63. [CrossRef]
29. Fattahi, H. Applying soft computing methods to predict the uniaxial compressive strength of rocks from schmidt hammer rebound values. *Comput. Geosci.* **2017**, *21*, 665–681. [CrossRef]
30. Demirdag, S.; Sengun, N.; Ugur, I.; Altindag, R. Estimating the uniaxial compressive strength of rocks with Schmidt rebound hardness by considering the sample size. *Arab. J. Geosci.* **2018**, *11*, 502. [CrossRef]
31. Fener, M.; Kahraman, S.; Bilgil, A.; Gunaydin, O. A comparative evaluation of indirect methods to estimate the compressive strength of rocks. *Rock Mech. Rock Eng.* **2005**, *38*, 329–343. [CrossRef]
32. Maji, V.B.; Sitharam, T.G. Prediction of elastic modulus of jointed rock mass using artificial neural networks. *Geotech. Geol. Eng.* **2008**, *26*, 443–452. [CrossRef]

33. Beiki, M.; Majdi, A.; Givshad, A.D. Application of genetic programming to predict the uniaxial compressive strength and elastic modulus of carbonate rocks. *Int. J. Rock Mech. Min. Sci.* **2013**, *63*, 159–169. [CrossRef]
34. O'Rourke, J.E. Rock index properties for geoengineering in underground development. *Min. Eng.* **1989**, *41*, 106–109.
35. Rezaei, M.; Majdi, A.; Monjezi, M. An intelligent approach to predict unconfined compressive strength of rock surrounding access tunnels in longwall coal mining. *Neural Comput. Appl.* **2014**, *24*, 233–241. [CrossRef]
36. Feng, X. Application of Bayesian Approach in Geotechnical Engineering (Doctoral Dissertation, Caminos). 2015. Available online: https://oa.upm.es/37270/ (accessed on 1 October 2022).
37. Aladejare, A.E.; Wang, Y. Estimation of rock mass deformation modulus using indirect information from multiple sources. *Tunn. Undergr. Sp. Technol.* **2019**, *85*, 76–83. [CrossRef]
38. Gorai, A.K.; Raval, S.; Patel, A.K.; Chatterjee, S.; Gautam, T. Design and development of a machine vision system using artificial neural network-based algorithm for automated coal characterization. *Int. J. Coal Sci. Technol.* **2021**, *8*, 737–755. [CrossRef]
39. Zhou, J.; Lin, H.; Jin, H.; Li, S.; Yan, Z.; Huang, S. Cooperative prediction method of gas emission from mining face based on feature selection and machine learning. *Int. J. Coal Sci. Technol.* **2022**, *9*, 51. [CrossRef]
40. Xie, J.; Ge, F.; Cui, T.; Wang, X. A virtual test and evaluation method for fully mechanized mining production system with different smart levels. *Int. J. Coal Sci. Technol.* **2022**, *9*, 41. [CrossRef]
41. Grima, M.A.; Babuška, R. Fuzzy model for the prediction of unconfined compressive strength of rock samples. *Int. J. Rock Mech. Min. Sci.* **1999**, *36*, 339–349. [CrossRef]
42. Singh, V.K.; Singh, D.; Singh, T.N. Prediction of strength properties of some schistose rocks from petrographic properties using artificial neural networks. *Int. J. Rock Mech. Min. Sci.* **2001**, *38*, 269–284. [CrossRef]
43. Gokceoglu, C. A fuzzy triangular chart to predict the uniaxial compressive strength of the Ankara agglomerates from their petrographic composition. *Eng. Geol.* **2002**, *66*, 39–51. [CrossRef]
44. Lee, S.-C. Prediction of concrete strength using artificial neural networks. *Eng. Struct.* **2003**, *25*, 849–857. [CrossRef]
45. Gokceoglu, C.; Zorlu, K. A fuzzy model to predict the uniaxial compressive strength and the modulus of elasticity of a problematic rock. *Eng. Appl. Artif. Intell.* **2004**, *17*, 61–72. [CrossRef]
46. Karakus, M.; Tutmez, B. Fuzzy and multiple regression modelling for evaluation of intact rock strength based on point load, Schmidt hammer and sonic velocity. *Rock Mech. Rock Eng.* **2006**, *39*, 45–57. [CrossRef]
47. Yılmaz, I.; Yuksek, A.G. An example of artificial neural network (ANN) application for indirect estimation of rock parameters. *Rock Mech. Rock Eng.* **2008**, *41*, 781–795. [CrossRef]
48. Gokceoglu, C.; Sonmez, H.; Zorlu, K. Estimating the uniaxial compressive strength of some clay-bearing rocks selected from Turkey by nonlinear multivariable regression and rule-based fuzzy models. *Expert Syst.* **2009**, *26*, 176–190. [CrossRef]
49. Dehghan, S.; Sattari, G.H.; Chehreh Chelgani, S.; Aliabadi, M.A.; Chelgani, S.C.; Aliabadi, M.A. Prediction of uniaxial compressive strength and modulus of elasticity for Travertine samples using regression and artificial neural networks. *Min. Sci. Technol.* **2010**, *20*, 41–46. [CrossRef]
50. Cevik, A.; Sezer, E.A.; Cabalar, A.F.; Gokceoglu, C. Modeling of the uniaxial compressive strength of some clay-bearing rocks using neural network. *Appl. Soft Comput. J.* **2011**, *11*, 2587–2594. [CrossRef]
51. Teymen, A.; Mengüç, E.C. Comparative evaluation of different statistical tools for the prediction of uniaxial compressive strength of rocks. *Int. J. Min. Sci. Technol.* **2020**, *30*, 785–797. [CrossRef]
52. Armaghani, D.J.; Amin, M.F.M.; Yagiz, S.; Faradonbeh, R.S.; Abdullah, R.A. Prediction of the uniaxial compressive strength of sandstone using various modeling techniques. *Int. J. Rock Mech. Min. Sci.* **2016**, *85*, 174–186. [CrossRef]
53. Li, W.; Tan, Z. Research on rock strength prediction based on least squares support vector machine. *Geotech. Geol. Eng.* **2017**, *35*, 385–393. [CrossRef]
54. Mohamad, E.T.; Armaghani, D.J.; Momeni, E.; Yazdavar, A.H.; Ebrahimi, M. Rock strength estimation: A PSO-based BP approach. *Neural Comput. Appl.* **2018**, *30*, 1635–1646. [CrossRef]
55. Umrao, R.K.; Sharma, L.K.; Singh, R.; Singh, T.N. Determination of strength and modulus of elasticity of heterogenous sedimentary rocks: An ANFIS predictive technique. *Meas. J. Int. Meas. Confed.* **2018**, *126*, 194–201. [CrossRef]
56. Çelik, S.B. Prediction of uniaxial compressive strength of carbonate rocks from nondestructive tests using multivariate regression and LS-SVM methods. *Arab. J. Geosci.* **2019**, *12*, 193. [CrossRef]
57. Mokhtari, M.; Behnia, M. Comparison of LLNF, ANN, and COA-ANN techniques in modeling the uniaxial compressive strength and static Young's modulus of limestone of the Dalan formation. *Nat. Resour. Res.* **2019**, *28*, 223–239. [CrossRef]
58. Ceryan, N.; Samui, P. Application of soft computing methods in predicting uniaxial compressive strength of the volcanic rocks with different weathering degree. *Arab. J. Geosci.* **2020**, *13*, 288. [CrossRef]
59. Ebdali, M.; Khorasani, E.; Salehin, S. A comparative study of various hybrid neural networks and regression analysis to predict unconfined compressive strength of travertine. *Innov. Infrastruct. Solut.* **2020**, *5*, 93. [CrossRef]
60. Barham, W.S.; Rabab'ah, S.R.; Aldeeky, H.H.; Al Hattamleh, O.H. Mechanical and Physical Based Artificial Neural Network Models for the Prediction of the Unconfined Compressive Strength of Rock. *Geotech. Geol. Eng.* **2020**, *38*, 4779–4792. [CrossRef]
61. Khan, N.M.; Cao, K.; Emad, M.Z.; Hussain, S.; Rehman, H.; Shah, K.S.; Rehman, F.U.; Muhammad, A. Development of Predictive Models for Determination of the Extent of Damage in Granite Caused by Thermal Treatment and Cooling Conditions Using Artificial Intelligence. *Mathematics* **2022**, *10*, 2883. [CrossRef]

62. Khan, N.M.; Cao, K.; Yuan, Q.; Bin Mohd Hashim, M.H.; Rehman, H.; Hussain, S.; Emad, M.Z.; Ullah, B.; Shah, K.S.; Khan, S. Application of Machine Learning and Multivariate Statistics to Predict Uniaxial Compressive Strength and Static Young's Modulus Using Physical Properties under Different Thermal Conditions. *Sustainability* **2022**, *14*, 9901. [CrossRef]
63. Singh, R.; Kainthola, A.; Singh, T.N. Estimation of elastic constant of rocks using an ANFIS approach. *Appl. Soft Comput.* **2012**, *12*, 40–45. [CrossRef]
64. Jahed Armaghani, D.; Tonnizam Mohamad, E.; Hajihassani, M.; Yagiz, S.; Motaghedi, H. Application of several non-linear prediction tools for estimating uniaxial compressive strength of granitic rocks and comparison of their performances. *Eng. Comput.* **2016**, *32*, 189–206. [CrossRef]
65. Barzegar, R.; Sattarpour, M.; Nikudel, M.R.; Moghaddam, A.A. Comparative evaluation of artificial intelligence models for prediction of uniaxial compressive strength of travertine rocks, case study: Azarshahr area, NW Iran. *Model. Earth Syst. Environ.* **2016**, *2*, 76. [CrossRef]
66. Waqas, U.; Ahmed, M.F. Prediction Modeling for the Estimation of Dynamic Elastic Young's Modulus of Thermally Treated Sedimentary Rocks Using Linear–Nonlinear Regression Analysis, Regularization, and ANFIS. *Rock Mech. Rock Eng.* **2020**, *53*, 5411–5428. [CrossRef]
67. Helmy, H.M.; Ahmed, A.F.; El Mahallawi, M.M.; Ali, S.M. Pressure, temperature and oxygen fugacity conditions of calc-alkaline granitoids, Eastern Desert of Egypt, and tectonic implications. *J. Afr. Earth Sci.* **2004**, *38*, 255–268. [CrossRef]
68. El-Taher, A.; Uosif, M.A.M.; Orabi, A.A. Natural radioactivity levels and radiation hazard indices in granite from Aswan to Wadi El-Allaqi southeastern desert, Egypt. *Radiat. Prot. Dosim.* **2007**, *124*, 148–154. [CrossRef] [PubMed]
69. Gomah, M.E.; Li, G.; Sun, C.; Jiahui, X.; Sen, Y.; Jinghua, L.; Ismael, M.; Elkarmoty, M. Macroscopic and microscopic research on Egyptian granodiorite behavior exposed to the various heating and cooling strategies. *Geomech. Geophys. Geo-Energy Geo-Resour.* **2022**, *8*, 158. [CrossRef]
70. ASTM Committee D-18 on Soil and Rock. *Standard Test Method for Laboratory Determination of Pulse Velocities and Ultrasonic Elastic Constants of Rock*; ASTM International: West Conshohocken, PA, USA, 2008.
71. Breiman, L. Random forests. *Mach. Learn.* **2001**, *45*, 5–32. [CrossRef]
72. Jin, X.; Diao, W.; Xiao, C.; Wang, F.; Chen, B.; Wang, K.; Li, S. Estimation of wheat agronomic parameters using new spectral indices. *PLoS ONE* **2013**, *8*, e72736. [CrossRef]
73. Qi, C.; Fourie, A.; Du, X.; Tang, X. Prediction of open stope hangingwall stability using random forests. *Nat. Hazards* **2018**, *92*, 1179–1197. [CrossRef]
74. Ullah, H.; Khan, I.; AlSalman, H.; Islam, S.; Asif Zahoor Raja, M.; Shoaib, M.; Gumaei, A.; Fiza, M.; Ullah, K.; Rahman, M. Levenberg–Marquardt backpropagation for numerical treatment of micropolar flow in a porous channel with mass injection. *Complexity* **2021**, *2021*, 5337589. [CrossRef]
75. Qi, C.; Tang, X. Slope stability prediction using integrated metaheuristic and machine learning approaches: A comparative study. *Comput. Ind. Eng.* **2018**, *118*, 112–122. [CrossRef]
76. Zhang, K.; Wu, X.; Niu, R.; Yang, K.; Zhao, L. The assessment of landslide susceptibility mapping using random forest and decision tree methods in the Three Gorges Reservoir area, China. *Environ. Earth Sci.* **2017**, *76*, 405. [CrossRef]
77. Brokamp, C.; Jandarov, R.; Rao, M.B.; LeMasters, G.; Ryan, P. Exposure assessment models for elemental components of particulate matter in an urban environment: A comparison of regression and random forest approaches. *Atmos. Environ.* **2017**, *151*, 1–11. [CrossRef] [PubMed]
78. Wu, X.; Kumar, V.; Ross Quinlan, J.; Ghosh, J.; Yang, Q.; Motoda, H.; McLachlan, G.J.; Ng, A.; Liu, B.; Yu, P.S. Top 10 algorithms in data mining. *Knowl. Inf. Syst.* **2008**, *14*, 1–37. [CrossRef]
79. Akbulut, Y.; Sengur, A.; Guo, Y.; Smarandache, F. NS-k-NN: Neutrosophic set-based k-nearest neighbors classifier. *Symmetry* **2017**, *9*, 179. [CrossRef]
80. Basheer, I.A.; Hajmeer, M. Artificial neural networks: Fundamentals, computing, design, and application. *J. Microbiol. Methods* **2000**, *43*, 3–31. [CrossRef]
81. Wasserman, P.D. *Neural Computing: Theory and Practice*; Van Nostrand Reinhold Co.: Washington, DC, USA, 1989; ISBN 0442207433. Available online: https://dl.acm.org/doi/abs/10.5555/63484 (accessed on 1 October 2022).
82. Negnevitsky, M. *Artificial Intelligence A Guide to Intelligent Systems*; Addison-Wesley: Harlow, UK, 2002.
83. Simpson, P.K. *Artificial Neural Systems: Foundations, Paradigms, Applications, and Implementations*; Elsevier Science Inc.: San Diego, CA, USA, 1989; ISBN 0080378951.
84. Aboutaleb, S.; Behnia, M.; Bagherpour, R.; Bluekian, B. Using non-destructive tests for estimating uniaxial compressive strength and static Young's modulus of carbonate rocks via some modeling techniques. *Bull. Eng. Geol. Environ.* **2018**, *77*, 1717–1728. [CrossRef]
85. Atkinson, P.M.; Tatnall, A.R.L. Introduction neural networks in remote sensing. *Int. J. Remote Sens.* **1997**, *18*, 699–709. [CrossRef]
86. Facchini, L.; Betti, M.; Biagini, P. Neural network based modal identification of structural systems through output-only measurement. *Comput. Struct.* **2014**, *138*, 183–194. [CrossRef]
87. Tian, H.; Kempka, T.; Yu, S.; Ziegler, M. Mechanical properties of sandstones exposed to high temperature. *Rock Mech. rock Eng.* **2016**, *49*, 321–327. [CrossRef]
88. Armaghani, D.J.; Mohamad, E.T.; Narayanasamy, M.S.; Narita, N.; Yagiz, S. Development of hybrid intelligent models for predicting TBM penetration rate in hard rock condition. *Tunn. Undergr. Sp. Technol.* **2017**, *63*, 29–43. [CrossRef]

Article

Intelligent Prediction of Maximum Ground Settlement Induced by EPB Shield Tunneling Using Automated Machine Learning Techniques

Syed Mujtaba Hussaine [1] and Linlong Mu [2,*]

[1] College of Civil Engineering, Tongji University, Shanghai 200092, China
[2] Department of Geotechnical Engineering, Tongji University, Shanghai 200092, China
* Correspondence: mulinlong@tongji.edu.cn; Tel.: +86-21-65982005

Citation: Hussaine, S.M.; Mu, L. Intelligent Prediction of Maximum Ground Settlement Induced by EPB Shield Tunneling Using Automated Machine Learning Techniques. *Mathematics* 2022, *10*, 4637. https://doi.org/10.3390/math10244637

Academic Editors: Danial Jahed Armaghani, Hadi Khabbaz, Manoj Khandelwal, Niaz Muhammad Shahani and Ramesh Murlidhar Bhatawdekar

Received: 11 October 2022
Accepted: 1 December 2022
Published: 7 December 2022
Corrected: 12 April 2023

Publisher's Note: MDPI stays neutral with regard to jurisdictional claims in published maps and institutional affiliations.

Copyright: © 2022 by the authors. Licensee MDPI, Basel, Switzerland. This article is an open access article distributed under the terms and conditions of the Creative Commons Attribution (CC BY) license (https:// creativecommons.org/licenses/by/ 4.0/).

Abstract: Predicting the maximum ground subsidence (Smax) in the construction of soil pressure balanced shield tunnel, particularly on soft foundation soils, is essential for safe operation and to minimize the possible risk of damage in urban areas. Although some research has been done, this issue has not been solved because of its complexity and many other influencing factors. Due to the increasing accuracy of machine learning (ML) in predicting surface deformation of shield tunneling and the development of automated machine learning (AutoML) technology. In the study, different ML prediction models were constructed using an open source AutoML framework. The prediction model was trained by the dataset, which contains 14 input parameters and an output (i.e., Smax). Different AutoML frameworks were employed to compare their validities and efficiencies. The performance of the model is estimated by contrasting the prediction accuracy parameters, including root mean square error (RMSE), mean absolute error (MAE) and determinant coefficient (R^2). With a coefficient of determination (R^2) of 0.808, MAE of 3.7, and RMSE of 5.2 on the testing dataset, the best prediction model i.e., extra tree regressor showed better performance, proving that our model has advantages in predicting Smax. Furthermore, the SHAP analysis reveal that the soil type (ST), torque (To), cover depth (H), groundwater level (GW), and tunneling deviation have a significant effect on Smax compared to other model inputs.

Keywords: maximum surface settlement; tunneling; auto machine learning; feature selection; shapley additive explanations (SHAP) analysis

MSC: 65Z05

1. Introduction

With the acceleration of urban construction, the construction of subway networks has become one of the most practical methods to alleviate traffic jam and shortages of land resources [1–5]. These excavation systems are generally built as twin tunnels and the excavation is carried out through soft soils or weak rocks at shallow depths. For urban subway tunnels, the shield tunneling method (especially the earth pressure balance (EPB) shield tunneling) is one of the most widely used construction methods due to its little impact on the surrounding environment. The advantages of less influence and a high degree of mechanization are widely applied to the actual engineering projects. However, in weak strata, the shield tunneling method can still cause a lot of land subsidence [6,7]. The surface subsidence mechanism [8,9] and development process caused by shield tunneling is complex, which can be seen in Figure 1, including (1) preemptive settlement; (2) settlement in front of excavation; (3) settling during propulsion; (4) shield tail gap settlement; and (5) subsequent settlement. Each stage's surface subsidence involves geological conditions, shield parameters, on-site construction, and other factors. Predicting surface deformation during the shield construction process reasonably and accurately has always been a problematic issue in research.

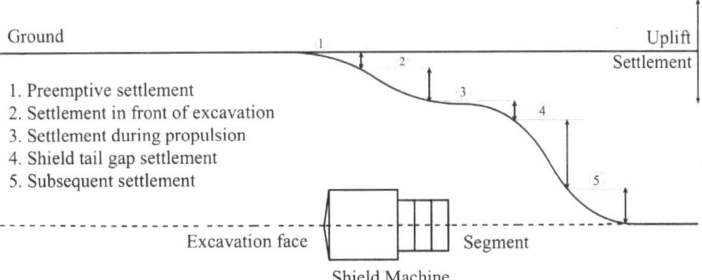

Figure 1. Schematic diagram of longitudinal settlement caused by shield tunneling.

The ground settlement caused by shield tunneling, apart from empirical, traditional theoretical calculations, numerical simulations, and other research methods, has been analyzed [10,11]. The empirical formula [12,13] describes the general ground subsidence caused by shield tunneling because the geological conditions in different regions are quite different, and the numerical value of the parameters varies widely. However, the empirical models adopted in engineering often ignore the influence of parameters used to adjust the settlement during shield tunneling. Therefore, the accuracy of surface subsidence prediction based on the empirical formula method is unacceptable. Due to the limitations of empirical methods, many studies have proposed analytical methods to estimate the settlement induced by shield excavation [14,15].

In the analytical method, it is difficult for simplified computational models to accurately account for the complex interactions between shield and soil, which affects the application of the analytical method in practical engineering problems [16]. Compared with empirical and analytical methods, numerical simulation methods can simulate the dynamic construction process of shield tunnels and comprehensively consider the interaction between tunnel construction and soil layers [17]. However, calculating the numerical model is time-consuming, and the constitutive model is difficult to accurately simulate the response of the soil layer on the macroscopic scale [2,18,19].

In shield tunneling, which is a dynamic process, the tunneling parameters and geological parameters change in real-time, and the surface subsidence due to shield excavation can be predicted in real-time. The parameter adjustment plan can be given to guide the shield tunneling in an absolute sense. In the construction process, traditional methods are difficult to achieve in this regard. Machine learning algorithms have developed rapidly in recent years and are gradually being applied in geotechnical engineering due to their nonlinear solid fitting capabilities and the simultaneous consideration of the influence of multiple parameters [20]. Because machine algorithms can obtain accurate results quickly, machine learning algorithms provide new ideas for intelligently controlling the shield tunneling process. Regarding the prediction of surface subsidence caused by shield tunneling, the widely used machine learning algorithms include artificial neural networks (ANN) and support vector machines (SVM). Recent research shows that ML methods have great application prospects in analyzing complex geotechnical problems, such as deformation caused by landslide [21,22] and underground soil structure interaction caused by tunnel excavation [23]. In early investigations, Shi et al. [24] used the artificial neural network method (ANNs) to calculate the maximum ground settlement due to shield tunneling accurately. In addition, the same method is also used to calculate the width of the settlement tank induced by shield excavation. Suwansawat et al. [25] systematically expounded the application of artificial neural network method in earth pressure balance shield tunnel based on a substantial amount of measured engineering data. Santos et al. [26] obtained the correlation between the excavation parameters and the ground subsidence based on the artificial neural network model, which fits the actual theoretical results. Many studies have combined a variety of optimization methods, for instance, genetic algorithms, particle swarm algorithms, with ANNs to optimize the accuracy of the prediction model [27,28].

However, a significant challenge in using ANN is to determine the optimal network framework [29]. In addition, due to its complex nature, the output from an ANN model is usually inexplicable; therefore, complicated ML models such as ANN are often referred to as a "black box" model. Zhang et al. [30] accurately predicted the development law of the ground subsidence due to shield excavation by integrating the wavelet function and the support vector machine algorithm. The study of machine learning methods to predict ground subsidence caused by shield tunneling is shown in Table 1.

Table 1. Development and Application of Machine Learning Algorithms in Shield Tunnels.

Related Literature	Method	Output Parameters	Data Points
Shi (1998) [24]	BP	S_c, S_i, S_f	356
Suwansawat (2006) [31]	BP	G	49
Santos (2008) [26]	BP	G	81
Darabi (2012) [32]	BP	G	53
Pourtaghi (2012) [33]	Wavelet, BP	G	49
Ahangari (2015) [28]	ANFIS, GEP	G	53
Zhou (2016) [34]	RF	G	66
Bouayad (2017) [27]	ANFIS	G	95
Zhang (2017) [30]	LSSVM	G	55

Note: G = surface subsidence; S_c = Surface subsidence when passing through the monitoring section; S_i = Surface subsidence after the completion of the monitoring section segment assembly; S_f = Surface subsidence after stabilization.

Random Forest (RF) is another integrated ML algorithm that can process a large amount of data in a short time. The final prediction result integrates multiple embedded calculation results with high accuracy and is used to calculate the settlement caused by shield tunnel construction [34]. Shao et al. [35] optimized the ANN model through the particle swarm optimization (PSO) method and founded the optimum transfer speed of the screw conveyor to ensure the safety of the tunnel face. In order to guarantee the tunneling efficiency of the shield tunneling machine, Armaghani et al. [36] proposed the use of PSO-ANN and the Imperial Competitive Algorithm (ICA)-ANN method to estimate the tunnel speed of the shield tunneling facility. At the same time, the method of PSO-SVM is also applied to calculate and improve the tunnel parameters of the shield machine during the tunnel construction. At the same time, the method of PSO-SVM is also applied to calculate and improve the tunnel parameters of the shield machine during the tunnel construction [37]. However, there are many new machine learning algorithms at this stage, and the prediction performance of different algorithms is different.

Although abundant highly effective studies have been introduced above, there is still a lack of research on performance differences of different machine learning algorithms in predicting the maximum ground subsidence due to shield tunneling; secondly, the current research mainly focuses on the final output results, and there is a lack of research on the correlation between input and output parameters. Therefore, constructing an interpretable ML model can reveal the connection between input and output parameters, thereby helping engineering designers to make the best decisions to ensure that soil settlement is limited within the expected range throughout the construction process. At present, a feature selection method, that is, the Pearson correlation method, has been used to detect and control the influencing parameters of the surface settlement caused by the tunnel excavation process. But the defect of this method is that it can only consider the linear relationship between two parameters, while ignoring the influence of feature interaction between parameters [6]. So academia began to use explainable artificial intelligence (XAI) to study this problem. It allows humans to understand the output of complex ML models [38]. The Shapley Additive Interpretation (SHAP) proposed by [39], is one such XAI-based algorithm. The SHAP method can measure how each input feature affects the dependent variable (output).

Owing to the importance of predicting settlements due to shield tunneling in geotechnical engineering, more and more people are trying to use machine learning algorithms to build predictive models that can accurately estimate influencing variables. Currently, selecting a suitable model requires the process of sample characterization, parameter fine-tuning, and configuration comparison. These steps are complicated and difficult for non-experts in machine learning to follow. For this reason, the research of automatic machine learning (AutoML) has attracted more and more attention. The advantage of AutoML is that it can automatically match the most suitable model and hyperparameters on the basis of complex datasets, thus simplifying the process of selecting the best model and optimize the performance of the model. On the whole, the structure of our study is organized as follows. Firstly, the database and data pre-processing methods we utilize are explained. Secondly, this study compares the differences of two feature selection methods (Pearson correlation and SHAP algorithm) in analyzing the same project datasets collected from two EPB tunnel projects completed in Hangzhou, China. The SHAP algorithm is applied to analyze the impact of the input feature parameters on the overall prediction results. In the end, considering the advantages of AutoML, based on the AutoML method, this research uses the PyCaret [40], a low-code machine learning library to construct a shield tunnel prediction model based on monitored data. Subsequently, a comparative analysis of various types of developed ML methods was accomplished to evaluate their performance and select the best-performing model in this problem, and remarkable conclusions are ultimately summarized.

2. Establishment of Surface Deformation Database for Shield Tunneling

2.1. Project Overview

The dataset used in this research was collected from two metro line tunneling projects in Hangzhou, China [41]. As shown in Figure 2, metro line two (project-1) was excavated from Gucui station to Xueyuan station, while metro line six (project-2) was excavated from Shangpu station to Heshan Road station. Figure 3 outlines the construction plan implemented during the excavation of Projects 1 and 2. The twin tunnels excavated for Project 1 (de-noted as downlink and uplink in Figure 3a) were initiated in January 2016 and completed in June 2016. The twin tunnels considered in Project 2 (namely, the left and right tunnels in Figure 3b) commenced on 15 April 2017, and were completed on 15 October 2017. The downlink of Project 1 and both tunnels in Project 2 were excavated using two "Shichuandao" type EPB shield machines. In contrast, the "Kawasaki" EPB shield was used to excavate the uplink of Project 1. The inner diameter of each twin tunnel in both projects was 5.5 m, while the outer diameter was 6.2 m. The total excavation length of the twin tunnels for Project 1 was 1950 m, and that for Project 2 was 2486 m. Note to avoid any effect of secondary disturbance due to the second excavation; this analysis only considered the data from the first excavation of each project (i.e., downlink in Project 1 and left tunnel in Project 2).

2.2. Engineering Geology

To determine the geological conditions at the proposed site, the construction unit conducted comprehensive field and laboratory testing. The cross-sectional geological profile of the tunnel section observed in Projects 1 and 2 is shown in Figure 4, which shows the main soil layers of the site, including soil fill (mixed soil and pure soil), sandy silt, silty sandy silt, sandy silt, silt, boulders1, silty silt, silty clay, and boulders 2 observed at a depth of around 30 m. From Figure 4a, it can be seen that Project 1 started excavation from the downlink route, covering a depth of 10.6 m to 18.7 m. The soil layer of this route is mainly muddy silty clay and muddy clay. Project 2 is excavated from the left line and covers a depth of 9 m to 16.6 m, passing through sandy silt and silt layers, as shown in Figure 4b.

Figure 2. Hangzhou metro system map [41].

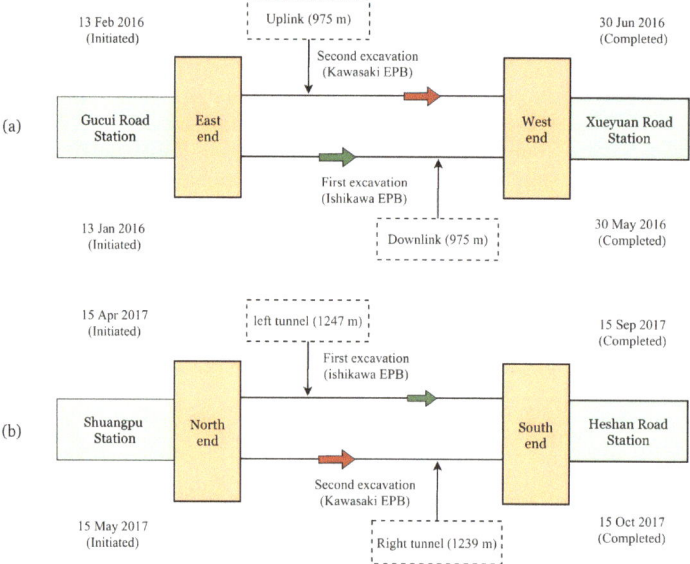

Figure 3. Construction plan of twin tunnels for (**a**) Project 1 and (**b**) Project 2 [41].

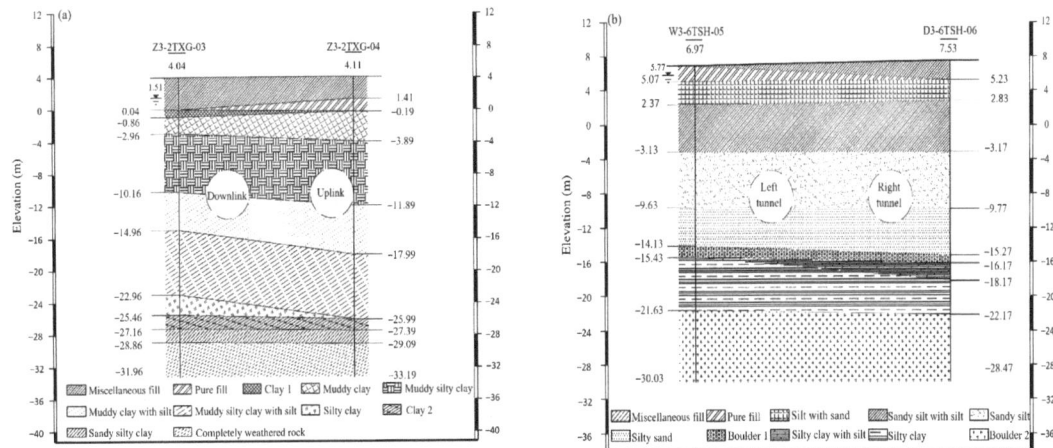

Figure 4. Cross-sectional geological profiles for (**a**) Project 1 and (**b**) Project 2 (unit: m) (Kannangara et al., 2022) [41].

Based on the Chinese National Standard (CNS) GB/T50123-1999 (standard for soil test methods) [42], the laboratory tests was carried out to measure the physical and mechanical properties of the soil layers of the project 1 and project 2, as shown in Table 2. The shear strength parameters (i.e., c and φ) of the soil can be measured through a series of direct shear tests. The direct shear tests require the soil samples to be pre-consolidated for 24 hours and sheared rapidly (0.8–1.2 mm/min) under undrained conditions. The average groundwater levels of Project 1 and Project 2 were −2.14 m and −1.8 m, respectively. It is worth noting that the groundwater levels remained stable during excavation.

Table 2. Soil physical properties of projects (1 and 2) [41].

Project	Soil Type	γ (kN/m^3)	φ°	c (kPa)	G_s	e
1	Miscellaneous fill	(18)				
	Pure fill	(18.5)				
	Clay 1	18.2	10	12	2.74	1.095
	Muddy clay	17.6	13	10	2.73	1.247
	Muddy silty clay	17.6	14	10	2.72	1.218
	Muddy clay with silt	17.5	14	11	2.72	1.22
	Muddy silty clay with silt	18.1	18	12	2.71	1.067
	Silty clay	17.6	14	12	2.73	1.204
	Clay 2	17.4	12	15	2.74	1.243
	Sandy silty clay	20.2	22	14	2.69	0.608
	Completely weathered rock					
2	Miscellaneous fill	(18)				
	Pure fill	(17.5)				
	Silt with sand	19.4	26	8	2.69	0.768
	Sandy silt with silt	19.5	28	5.5	2.69	0.742
	Sandy silt	19.7	29	4.5	2.68	0.706
	Silty sand	19.7	31.5	4	2.68	0.687
	Boulder 1		36	5		
	Silty clay with silt	17.1	13	14	2.71	1.283
	Silty clay	20.1	21	28	2.71	0.66
	Boulder 2		40	6		

Note: γ is the unit weight of soil, φ is the soil internal frictional angle, c is the cohesion of the soil, G_s is the specific gravity, and e is the void ratio. Data within round brackets are the empirical values.

2.3. Preliminary Selection of Input Parameters

Previous studies discovered that in the shield tunneling process, the main factors affecting the surface deformation could be roughly divided into three categories [31,43]: (1) tunnel geometric parameters (such as tunnel burial depth, shield diameter, section form, etc. [44,45]; (2) stratum parameters (such as cover soil type, face soil type, soil compressive modulus, elastic modulus, cohesion, internal friction angle, groundwater level, etc.); (3) shield construction parameters (shield thrust, advanced rate, shield attitude, cutter head torque, thrust, jack pressure, horizontal deviation (front), vertical deviation (front), horizontal deviation (back), vertical deviation (back) [46], grouting pressure, grouting volume, etc.). The 14 input features by their respective categories and the target variable (i.e., Smax) as shown in Table 3 are considered for the analysis.

Table 3. List of input features and target variable considered for analysis [41].

Category	Parameters	Symbol	Unit
Tunnel geometry	Cover depth	H	m
Geological conditions	Soil type [a]	ST	-
	Groundwater level	GW	m
Shield operational parameters	Face pressure (top)	FPt	kPa
	Face pressure (center) [b]	FPc	kPa
	Advance rate	AR	mm/min
	Pitching angle	PA	°
	Thrust	Th	kN
	Torque	To	kN m
	Jack pressure	JP	kPa
	Horizontal deviation (front)	HDf	mm
	Vertical deviation (front)	VDf	mm
	Horizontal deviation (back)	HDb	mm
	Vertical deviation (back)	VDb	mm
Target variable	Maximum surface settlement	S_{max}	mm

[a] Categorical feature. [b] Computed by taking the average of face pressures recorded at left and right positions.

In order to observe the ground subsidence, an optical level (Suguang DS05, China, accuracy 0.5 mm/km) and an electronic level (Trimble DINI 03, USA, 0.3 mm/km) were used to measure the site subsidence. Surface settlements were measured twice daily, once at 8:00 a.m. and again at 4:00 p.m. The allowable values for the surface settlement and uplift were set at 35 mm and 10 mm, respectively.

Since the specifications of the entire tunnel are the same, the burial depth and diameter of the tunnel (D) are constantly changing. Considering that the buried depth and diameter of the tunnel will affect the development model of the stratum subsidence and the size of the final settlement during the shield tunnel process [31,47], these two parameters are selected as the only geometric parameters. Since the tunnels in this study were constructed by shield tunneling, their outer diameters are the same, both are 6.2 m, the influence of parameter D can be ignored.

Geological parameters include the depth of groundwater (GW) level, and physical and mechanical properties of rock and soil. In machine learning algorithms, the geological parameters need to be quantified. The physical and mechanical properties of the rock and soil layer, along with the thickness and location of the soil layer, will influence the subsidence induced by shield tunnel. Commonly used is the direct input of the soil layer c, φ value [28,30], or directly using numbers to indicate the type of soil layer (ST) [35]. The soil types mainly traversed during the EPB shield excavation for the two projects in this study were "silty clay" and "silt sand". For the convenience of description, they are coded as 0 and 1 respectively.

In this study, a total of 11 shield operating parameters were considered as the input features of the model. The four operational parameters, i.e., thrust, torque, tunneling rate, and jack pressure, affect the degree of disturbance to the stratum during the shield tunneling process [48]. The soil pressure will affect the stability of the tunnel face [49,50]. Project 2 uses the "Ishikawa" EPB shield. In order to measure the surface pressure during its working process, three earth pressure gauges were installed on the top, left and right sides of the shield machine [51]. The "face pressure (top)" and "face pressure (center)" are used as input parameters to analyze the effect of face pressure on the settlement caused by excavation. The shield machine must advance strictly along the design route (DTA) during the working process. The attitude and position of the shield machine are described by vertical deviation (front), horizontal deviation (front), vertical deviation (back), horizontal deviation (back), rolling angle, and pitch angle [52]. The pitch and rolling angles describe the attitude of the shield machine relative to the horizontal and vertical axes, respectively. For each parameter taken into account in the dataset, the corresponding symbol and its unit are displayed in Table 3. It is to be noted that the data preparation process were carried out as recommended by kannangara. et. al. [41] and the data is further refined as explained in Section 2.4 below.

2.4. Data Pre-Processing

A major problem of machine learning prediction models is that the learning curve is difficult to converge. In order to improve the probability of curve convergence, the data set must be preprocessed to reduce data inconsistency [53]. In the cause of probe critical information from the shield-soil interplay for surface subsidence prediction, a total of 264 data samples were collected, which were further divided into two subsets to evaluate a model's generalization ability. Randomly select 80% of the samples in the constructed data sample library as the training and testing set of the model (211 observations per feature). It should be noted that the test set must be referred to evaluate the model's behavior. The remaining 20% (53 data samples) have been retained from the basic dataset to be adopted for predictions, the data should not be confused with a training/test segmentation. According to the 264 surface subsidence measurement data chosen in this study, the input and output data of first 25 points are shown in Table 4. The limits of mentioned parameters to construct the predictive models for all 264 data samples, including average, standard deviation (Std.), maximum (Max.), minimum (Min.) and three percentiles (75%, 50%, and 25%) are summarized in Table 5.

Table 4. Dataset samples used for creating intelligent model.

No.	Ring	H (m)	ST	GW (m)	FPt (kPa)	FPc (kPa)	AR (mm/min)	PA (°)	Th (kN)	To (kN/m)	JP (kPa)	HD (mm)	VDF (mm)	HD (mm)	VDB (mm)	Smax (mm)
1	5	9.03	1	1.46	40	95	0	−0.1	9345	1937	8700	−34	53	27	−53	4.65
2	9	9.05	1	1.57	0	70	7	−0.22	27,124	1305	24,600	−63	−67	5	−55	5.52
3	14	9.07	1	1.68	80	140	31	0	19,986	2310	17,700	−80	−43	−23	−62	40.11
4	18	9.09	1	1.79	110	180	59	−0.1	16,804	1965	4700	−78	−43	−46	−48	8.8
5	22	9.1	1	1.9	110	180	45	−0.2	20,275	1937	18,500	−49	−31	−62	−44	8.76
6	26	9.13	1	2.01	120	190	32	−0.2	17,478	2529	16,075	−37	−17	−54	42	18.67
7	30	9.25	1	2.12	110	180	34	−0.6	18,907	2289	null	−31	−45	−37	−15	16.16
8	34	9.36	1	2.22	110	195	30	−0.77	17,459	2567	16,200	−32	−46	−29	−21	6.45
9	39	null	1	2.33	120	190	42	−0.7	19,564	2036	18,050	−15	−20	−51	2.41
10	43	9.6	1	2.44	110	170	29	−0.7	null	2874	18,250	−8	−53	−13	−57	3.18
11	51	9.83	1	2.66	130	205	36	−1	19,344	2853	17,800	−1	−55	5	−46	1.58
12	55	9.94	1	2.49	130	205	48	−1	19,726	2153	18,000	1	−58	17	−55	7.61
13	59	10.04	1	2.33	130	205	41	−1	17,758	2250	16,300	14	−47	16	−49	10.12
14	64	10.14	1	2.16	130	200	38	−1	18,297	2778	16,900	−18	−45	−8	−44	11.77
15	68	10.24	1	2	130	205	38	−1.1	18,597	2657	16,975	4	−35	7	−31	12.97
16	72	10.34	1	1.84	120	190	35	−1.2	18,693	2278	17,225	−18	−39	16	−13	15.45
17	76	10.43	1	1.67	130	205	46	−1.2	17,618	2095	15,750	−42	−44	−5	−14	21.3
18	80	10.53	1	1.51	130	200	45	null	17,885	1953	15,775	−31	−47	−29	−19	16.11
19	84	null	1	1.34	130	200	43	−1.1	18,490	2567	16,900	−15	−47	−30	−33	11.6
20	89	10.73	1	1.21	140	205	44	−1.1	18,923	2049	17,400	−18	−39	−16	−32	14.35
21	50	10.91	0	112.0	60	160	51	−1.33	10,655	481	9500	13	−55	10	−4	12.1
22	55	11.05	0	240.0	50	170	50	−1.42	11,270	506	10,100	29	−48	42	2	16.7
23	85	11.89	0	12.2	50	190	62	−1.49	10,307	518	9100	4	−87	17	−31	26.9
24	90	12.03	0	11.9	60	215	63	−1.17	10,703	522	9525	21	−69	35	−60	28.5
25	100	12.31	0	32.4	40	170	57	−1.31	12,307	569	10,875	−22	−66	47	−40	40.2

Table 5. Descriptive statistical description of the dataset used.

Parameter Count	Count	Mean Count	Std. Count	Min. Count	25% Count	50% Count	75% Count	Max. Count
H	264	14.5	2.7	9.03	11.98	15.07	16.71	18.70
ST	264	0.52	0.5	0	0	1	1	1
GW	264	1.96	0.6	0.36	1.63	1.93	2.40	3.18
FPt	264	122.6	62.12	0	70	110	182.5	230
FPc	264	232.3	37	70	205	240	260	310
AR	264	58.40	11.76	0	53	60	66	80
PA	264	−0.09	0.78	−1.49	−0.77	−0.20	0.38	1.37
Th	264	19,592.6	4404.27	0	17,194.0	19,331.0	23,280.0	27433.0
To	264	1537.85	956.04	0	569.75	19,210.0	2481.5	3180
JP	264	17,862.2	3992.54	25	15,750.0	17,850.0	21,131.25	24950.0
HDf	264	−8.74	23.70	−80	−22.25	−12	2.25	69
VDf	264	−47.14	39.57	−125	−76	−48	−14	36
HDb	264	22.97	25.57	−62	8	23	39.25	107
VDb	264	−25.07	35.80	−126	−51	−26	−4	54
Smax	264	20.87	12.48	1.58	11.225	16.95	28082	55.30

For data cleansing, the shield parameters obtained from the shield site often contain many invalid data and cannot be used directly, so the data must be cleaned. PyCaret by default utilizes the drop_duplicates () function for the cleaning process, which includes the removal of nulls and outlier rejection. Table 6 lists the data samples obtained after cleansing. We performed all analyses using the default settings; for example, the test/hold-out set was 80/20, with 10-fold cross-validation for model comparison. The preprocessing methods that were employed are discussed next.

Table 6. Cleaned dataset samples used for creating intelligent model.

No.	Ring	H (m)	ST	GW (m)	FPt (kPa)	FPc (kPa)	AR (mm/min)	PA (°)	Th (kN)	To (kN/m)	JP (kPa)	HD (mm)	VDF (mm)	HD (mm)	VDB (mm)	Smax (mm)
1	5	9.03	1	1.46	40	95	0	−0.1	9345	1937	8700	−34	53	27	−53	4.65
2	9	9.05	1	1.57	0	70	7	−0.2	27,124	1305	24,600	−63	−67	5	−55	5.52
3	14	9.07	1	1.68	80	140	31	0	19,986	2310	17,700	−80	−43	−23	−62	40.11
4	18	9.09	1	1.79	110	180	59	−0.1	16,804	1965	4700	−78	−43	−46	−48	8.8
5	22	9.1	1	1.9	110	180	45	−0.2	20,275	1937	18,500	−49	−31	−62	−44	8.76
6	26	9.13	1	2.01	120	190	32	−0.2	17,478	2529	16,075	−37	−17	−54	−42	18.67
7	30	9.25	1	2.12	110	180	34	−0.6	18,907	2289	17,950	−31	−45	−37	−15	16.16
8	34	9.36	1	2.22	110	195	30	−0.77	17,459	2567	16,200	−32	−46	−29	−21	6.45
9	39	9.48	1	2.33	120	190	42	−0.7	19,564	2036	18,050	−15	−65	−20	−51	2.41
10	43	9.6	1	2.44	110	170	29	−0.7	19,778	2874	18,250	−8	−53	−13	−57	3.18
11	51	9.83	1	2.66	130	205	36	−1	19,344	2853	17,800	−1	−55	5	−46	1.58
12	55	9.94	1	2.49	130	205	48	−1	19,726	2153	18,000	1	−58	17	−55	7.61
13	59	10.04	1	2.33	130	205	41	−1	17,758	2250	16,300	14	−47	16	−49	10.12
14	64	10.14	1	2.16	130	200	38	−1	18,297	2778	16,900	−18	−45	−8	−44	11.77
15	68	10.24	1	2	130	205	38	−1.1	18,597	2657	16,975	4	−35	7	−31	12.97
16	72	10.34	1	1.84	120	190	35	−1.2	18,693	2278	17,225	−18	−39	16	−13	15.45
17	76	10.43	1	1.67	130	205	46	−1.2	17,618	2095	15,750	−42	−44	−5	−14	21.3
18	80	10.53	1	1.51	130	200	45	−1.2	17,885	1953	15,775	−31	−47	−29	−19	16.11
19	84	10.63	1	1.34	130	200	43	−1.1	18,490	2567	16,900	−15	−47	−30	−33	11.6
20	89	10.73	1	1.21	140	205	44	−1.1	18,923	2049	17,400	−18	−39	−16	−32	14.35
21	50	10.91	0	112.0	60	160	51	−1.33	10,655	481	9500	13	−55	10	−4	12.1
22	55	11.05	0	240.0	50	170	50	−1.42	11,270	506	10,100	29	−48	42	2	16.7
23	85	11.89	0	12.2	50	190	62	−1.49	10,307	518	9100	4	−87	17	−31	26.9
24	90	12.03	0	11.9	60	215	63	−1.17	10,703	522	9525	21	−69	35	−60	28.5
25	100	12.31	0	32.4	40	170	57	−1.31	12,307	569	10,875	−22	−66	47	−40	40.2

2.4.1. Data Normalization

Cleaned data is often different and affects the result of machine learning. In order to eliminate this influence and improve the convergence speed to a certain extent, it is necessary to normalize the data. In statistics, the more commonly used normalization methods include dispersion standardization and Z-score standardization. Dispersion standardization is widely used in deformation prediction, and its data normalization interval may be different but mainly normalized to $[-1, 1]$ or $[0, 1]$. For any parameter x, the normalized value is given as:

$$X_{norm} = \frac{X - X_{min}}{X_{max} - X_{min}} (\overline{X}_{max} - \overline{X}_{min}) + \overline{X}_{min} \tag{1}$$

In the formula, X_{max}, X_{min} is the maximum and minimum values of variable x, where $\overline{X}_{max}$, $\overline{X}_{min}$ is the maximum and minimum values of normalized variables X. For the normalization process of measured data, we employed PyCaret, which uses the "Zscore" function by default to normalize the data in the range of $[0, 1]$.

2.4.2. Cross-Validation Method

Building a machine learning model is mainly composed of 3 phases: training, testing, and validation. The validation process mainly solves the problems of overfitting and under fitting in machine learning. Machine learning validation methods primarily include simple cross-validation (hold-out cross-validation), k-fold cross-validation, and leave-one-out cross-validation [54]. In order to improve the generalization performance of the ML model and overcome the deficiencies of data, k-fold cross-validation is the most popular cross-validation method used in the model training phase [55,56]. In order to test the performance of the entire prediction model more accurately, the original training data set constructed is stochastically divided into k parts. For each calculation, k-1 subsets are provided for training, and the remaining subset is used for verification. This procedure is used to test the ability of the sub-models. Repeat the calculation k times so that each sub-dataset can be used as a validation. Summarize and calculate the average ability of k sub-models to measure the performance of the entire prediction model. The formula is shown as follows:

$$T = \frac{1}{k} \sum_{i=1}^{k} MSE_i \tag{2}$$

where, T = fitness function, MSE_i = prediction error for the ith validation set. The performance of the k-fold cross-validation method depends on the number of subsets. However, fewer subsets cannot eliminate the problem of overfitting or underfitting, which will affect the model's accuracy. Too many subsets will significantly increase the model's performance computation time. Considering the limited amount of data in this study, in order to obtain reliable results, we finally adopted the 10-fold cross-validation method.

3. Feature Selection

Feature selection plays a significant role in machine learning because it manually or automatically chooses the input features that contribute significantly to the target variable. It is a desirable step to consider when building an ML model [34]. After the primary selection of input parameters in the surface deformation prediction of shield tunneling, the model may still face the problem of having too many input parameters. In order to avoid the dimensionality and the occurrence of overfitting and improve the model's accuracy, it is necessary to rely on feature selection for input parameter further filtering. Tan et al. [57] used grey relational analysis and sorted them by the degree of relevance to determine the main factor influencing the amount of deformation. Moreover, the commonly used feature selection methods include Filter, Wrapper, the principal component analysis method, Sobol sensitivity analysis [58], recursive feature elimination, the tree model-based feature selection method, etc.

3.1. Analysis 1: Pearson Correlation Method

Feature selection methods are numerous and complex in predicting the surface deformation of shield tunnels. The linear correlation between the x and y variables can be measured by the Pearson correlation coefficient, whose formula is given in Equation (3) [59].

$$r = \frac{\sum (X_i - \overline{X})(Y_i - \overline{Y})}{\sqrt{(X_i - \overline{X})^2 (Y_i - \overline{Y})^2}} \qquad (3)$$

In the formula, r represents the Pearson correlation coefficient; X_i and Y_i represent the values of the X and Y variables in the sample respectively; $\overline{X}$ and $\overline{Y}$ are the average values of the variable values.

The closer the absolute value of the correlation coefficient r is to 1, the stronger the linear correlation between the variables. When $r = 0$, it means that there is no linear correlation between the two variables. The correlation coefficient was calculated using the corr(.) function provided in the Pandas library, and the results are listed in Figure 5. In this study, the guidelines recommended by Zhang et al. [6], were used to select the characteristic variables. From the calculation results of the correlation coefficient, it can be seen that among the listed features, only ST is strongly linearly correlated with Smax ($|r| = 0.63$), while FPt, Th, To, JP, and VDf are moderately correlated with Smax ($|r| = 0.42 \sim 0.56$). In addition, the parameters H, AR, HDb, and VDb are weakly correlated with Smax ($|r| = 0.23 \sim 0.36$), and the remaining characteristic variables GW, FPc, PA, and HDf show very weak correlations with Smax ($|r| < 0.19$). In this analysis, the feature variables with a medium correlation with the output variable Smax ($|r| \geq 0.4$) are selected as effective features for predicting Smax, and the rest of the input features are not used as effective variables for prediction analysis due to small correlation coefficient and weak correlation. There is some difficulty in using the Pearson correlation coefficient feature selection method when a large number of analyzed features are poorly correlated with the predictor variables, as shown in this study.

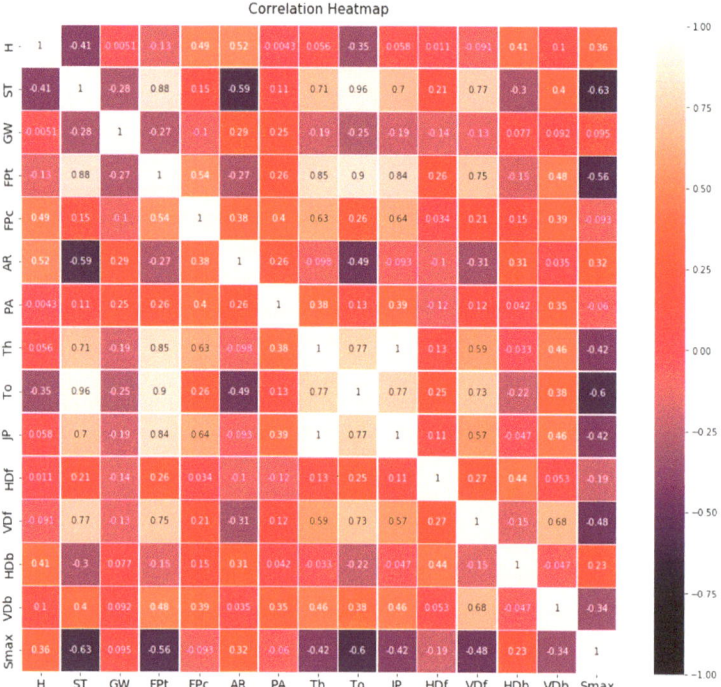

Figure 5. Inter-correlations of Pearson correlation coefficients among input data.

3.2. Analysis 2: Shapley Additive Explanations (SHAP)

Although the machine learning model based on the ensemble algorithm has relatively good performance, with the increase in model complexity, the interpretability of the model is reduced, which makes the regression model a black-box model. To solve the challenge of poor interpretability of the model, the SHAP framework is introduced to explain the model results and to provide support for the reliability of the model results. SHAP (Shapley additive explanations) is an interpretive framework proposed by Lundberg and Lee [39] for interpreting black-box models. The SHAP method is widely used in coalition game theory, which evaluates the degree of influence of input features on output parameters through Shapley values [60]. The basic method is to calculate the contribution value of each input feature and add the influence value of each feature to obtain the final prediction of the model [61].

For an ensemble tree model, when doing a regression task, the model outputs a probability value. SHAP can calculate the Shapley value to measure the influence value of each input variables to the final prediction. Assume that g represents the explanatory model, M represents the number of features, and z indicates whether the feature exists (value 0 or 1); φ is the original value when all the inputs are absent, for each feature Shapley value, the formula can be given as follows:

$$g(z) = \varphi_0 + \sum_i^M \varphi_i z_i \quad (4)$$

For each feature, the SHAP value describes the expected change in model predictions when conditioned on this feature. For each function, the SHAP value describes the feature's contribution to the overall prediction outcome to account for the distinction between the average model calculation and the actual calculation. When $i > 0$; it shows that this feature has an improving effect on the predicted value, and conversely when $i < 0$, it shows that this feature reduces the contribution. The model importance given by the regressor model only shows which input variable is essential but does not show how the variable influences the calculation results. The most significant superiority of the SHAP model is that it can show the influence of input variables in each data, as well as the positive or negative effect of this influence on the final prediction result.

Figure 6 is a summary graph of SHAP features, which analyzes factors affecting surface deformation according to feature importance.

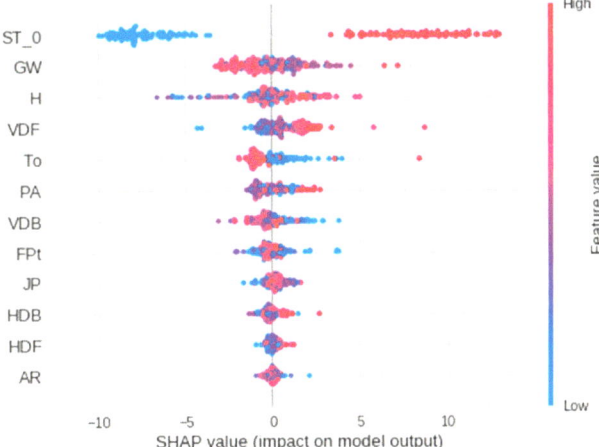

Figure 6. Summary plot obtained from SHAP analysis.

As shown in Figure 6 the soil type (ST), Torque (To) cover depth (H), ground water level (GW), and other characteristics have a significant effect on the model. The most important feature of SHAP that affects settlement prediction is the soil type (ST). Therefore, silty clay with a higher positive SHAP value has a greater influence on the mod-el output result than silty sand. Torque (To) and Cover depth (H) in the current model (ET) also have a significant impact on predicting Smax. Positive SHAP values are observed when Torque values are low, while negative SHAP values are observed when Torque values are high, which means that a smaller torque will induce greater surface settlement. In the same way, it can be seen that when H is larger, the corresponding SHAP value is positive, which means that the output value of the prediction model will increase.

The SHAP values for PA, VDB, AR, JP, HDB, and HDF mainly converge near zero. The zero SHAP value stands that there is no effect on the model's calculation. To better understand the dependency of each feature in the model's output a simplified version of the above plot is shown in Figure 7. It can be found that in the current model, ST, To, H, GW, and VDF are the most important features in predicting Smax, while the importance of other features is less in comparison to ST.

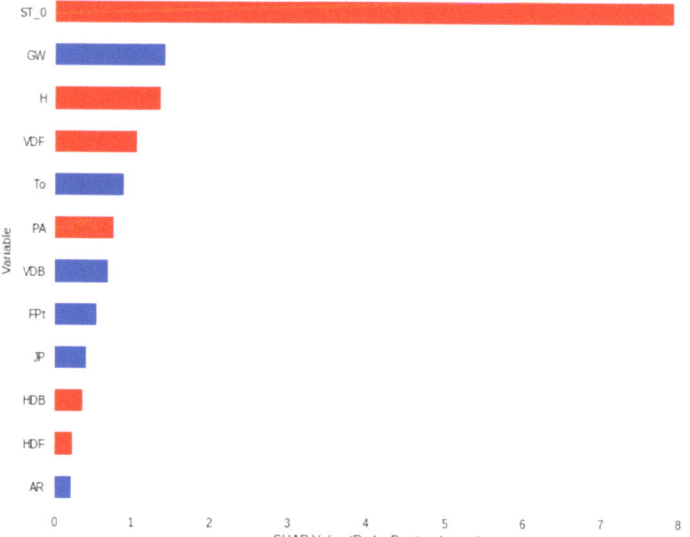

Figure 7. Feature Importance by SHAP Values of designed ET model.

Figure 8 shows the SHAP dependency graph between features ST, H, and GW, which have a high impact on the model and are selected to draw the SHAP feature dependency graph, where the third axis of the dependency graph is the categorical variable. Figure 8a, shows the correlation data of silty clay (labeled 0, represented by blue dots) and silty sand (labeled 1, represented by red dots). It can be found that the EPB operates at low VDf values while traversing the silty clay formation in Project 1, and calculates a large negative SHAP value. Conversely, when the TBM was operating at high VDf values while traversing the silty sand formation in Project 2, a large positive SHAP value was calculated.

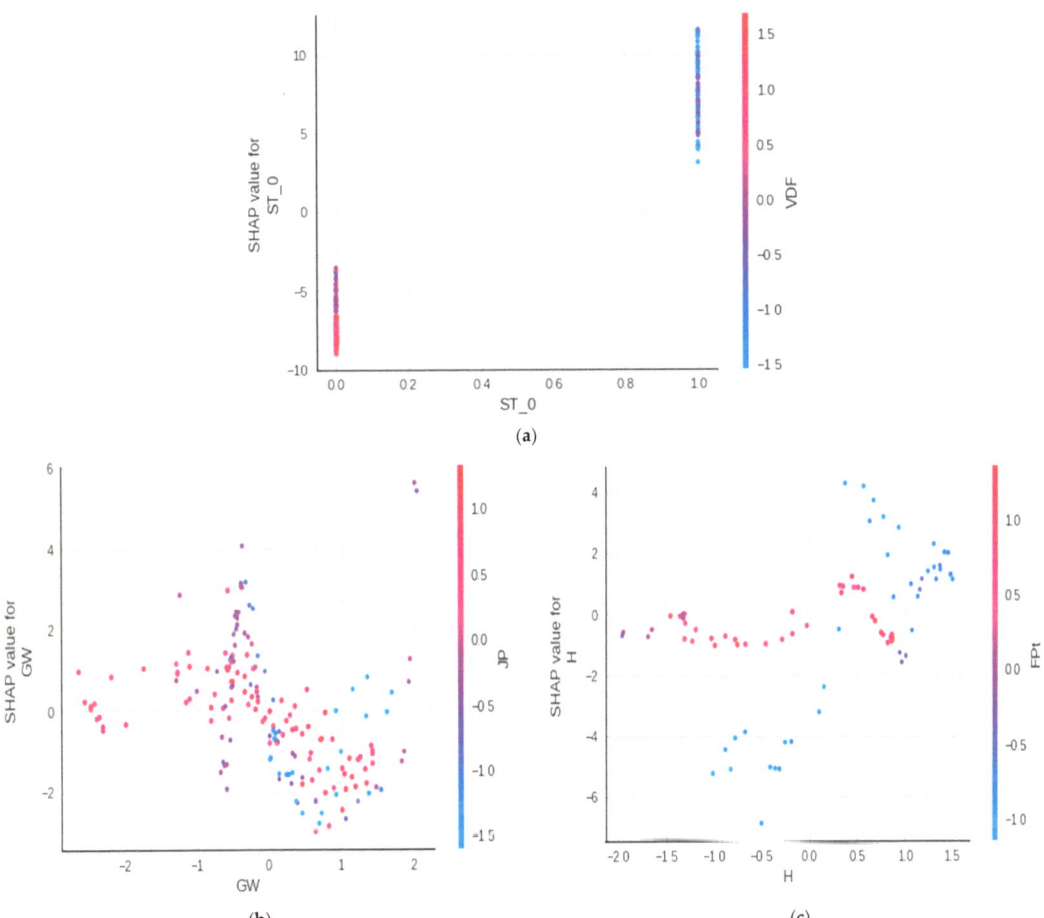

Figure 8. Dependency plots for (**a**) ST_0, (**b**) GW, and (**c**) H.

Figure 8b shows how the SHAP value increases and then decreases as the GW value increases. Similarly, Figure 8c shows that SHAP values for H are primarily close to 0, corresponding to FPt, which means that the cover depth (H) has zero impact on the model's output Smax when sufficient face pressure is present. Also, as the FPt values decrease at greater depths (>12 m), the Smax increases, indicating a larger positive SHAP value for H.

Therefore, as with analysis 1 and analysis 2, five variables (i.e. ST, To, H, GW, and VDF) were considered important for predicting tunnelling-induced settlements and are selected as final input parameters for building a ML models.

4. Research Methodology

Despite the numerous research conducted in the past, it is essential to carry on with the ongoing efforts of developing newer and faster machine learning techniques that are more effective and can also be developed and deployed with ease. In this analysis, three commonly used statistical evaluation parameters, i.e., coefficient of determination (R^2), mean absolute error (MAE), and root mean square error (RMSE), were used to evaluate the accuracy of the calculation results generated by the intelligent method, as given by equations.

$$R^2 = 1 - \frac{\sum_{i=1}^{N}\left(y_i^{act} - y_i^{pred}\right)^2}{\sum_{i=1}^{N}\left(y_i^{act} - \overline{y_i^{act}}\right)} \tag{5}$$

$$MAE = \left(\frac{1}{n}\right)\sum_{i=1}^{N}\left|y_i^{act} - y_i^{pred}\right| \tag{6}$$

$$RMSE = \sqrt{\left(\frac{1}{N}\right)\sum_{i=1}^{N}\left(y_i^{act} - y_i^{pred}\right)^2} \tag{7}$$

where y_i^{act} signifies the measured value of the i_{th} output feature, y_i^{pred} is the predicted value of the i_{th} output feature, and N is the number of data in the dataset. MAE, RMSE, and R^2 represent the average value, standard deviation, and correlation degree of the difference between the measured value and the predicted value, respectively.

4.1. Machine Learning Techniques

A new Python library (PyCaret) [40], offers a majority of machine learning techniques to construct a new prediction model. 21 ML algorithms were optimized through a comprehensive search of multiple ML methods, bypassing the whole dataset to the regression module of PyCaret (2.3.10), which divides the dataset into train and testing sets of 80% (211) and 20% (53) records, respectively, by calling the 'setup' function. 20% of the samples (53 data) are reserved from the original data set to demonstrate the predictive effect of the predict_model() function. This process is independent of the train/test phase, since this particular split is done to simulate a real engineering environment. Another reason for this approach is that these 53 samples are not available when doing machine learning model building. In order to analyze and calculate the relationship between multiple input variables and output variable when using machine learning methods to build prediction models, regression analysis algorithms are often adopted [62,63]. Regression analysis statistics method determines the distribution relationship of data through known datasets, measures the contribution of input features to output features, and has been widely verified in ML methods [64,65]. Regression method can be used for making predictions on continuous data (time-series) in ML, especially when the regression relationship line of variables does not pass through the origin, regression analysis is more accurate. In addition, with the development of mathematical statistics theory, ML algorithm is often used in nonlinear regression estimation. Table 7 lists the regression estimators and other algorithms that were used in this study [40].

After performing the feature selection methods using analysis 1 and 2 as discussed in Section 3, all the models from the available machine learning libraries and frameworks were trained on datasets containing the selected features from Pearson correlation method and SHAP algorithm. Based on their R^2 values, the top five models were selected for further optimization. The hyperparameter adjustment method is used to improve the R^2 value of the selected model. Furthermore, tuned models were trained using 10-fold cross-validation to use all of the samples as training and testing, as the number of samples in the database is not enough. All of the tuned models were ensembled. Ensemble modeling is a technique in which various models are built to predict an output variable. This is accomplished through the use of various modeling methods or samples of training databases. The aggregated model then summarizes the predictions for each submodel, resulting in a single eventual prediction for the unknown data. The method of ensemble model can effectively reduce the generalization error of calculation, provided that the sub models built in the process of ensemble model are independent and diversified. The two most common methods in ensemble learning are bagging and boosting [66,67]. Stacking [68] is also a type of ensemble learning where predictions from multiple models are used as input features for a meta-model that predicts the final outcome. After the ensemble technique, the best of all the models were calculated and selected using the AutoML function, improving the R^2 value before determining the model for saving.

Table 7. Introduction to various ML algorithms (regression estimators).

No.	Estimator	Description
1	Extra tree Regressor	A regressor with multiple decision trees, which is highly randomized, is only used in the ensemble methods.
2	Random Forest Regressor	The algorithm establishes multiple decision trees by randomly sampling, and obtains the overall regression prediction results by averaging the results of all trees.
3	Gradient Boosting Regressor	An algorithm for combining multiple simple models into a composite model.
4	Light Gradient Boosting Machine	The algorithm adopts a distributed gradient lifting framework based on decision tree algorithm, which can solve the problems encountered by GBDT in massive data.
5	AdaBoost Regressor	This algorithm trains different weak regressors for the same training set and combines them to form a stronger final regressor.
6	Extreme gradient boosting	The algorithm is optimized on the framework of GBDT, which is efficient, flexible and portable.
7	K neighbors Regressor	A simple algorithm for predicting the target value on all available cases based on a similarity measure.
8	Decision Tree Regressor	A method of approximating the value of a discrete function. The induction algorithm is used to generate readable rules and decision trees, and the decision is used to analyze new data.
9	Support vector machine	A generalized linear classifier for binary classification of data according to supervised learning.
10	Bayesian Ridge	A probability model for estimating regression problems.
11	Ridge Regression	A biased estimation regression method dedicated to the analysis of collinearity data is essentially an improved least squares estimation method.
12	CatBoost Regressor	An algorithm based on symmetric decision tree, which can efficiently and reasonably handle categorical features.
13	Linear Regression	A linear approach that shows the relationship between a dependent variable and one or more independent variables.
14	Least Angle Regression	A statistical analysis method that uses regression analysis to determine the quantitative relationship between multiple variables.
15	Huber Regressor	A linear regression that replaces the loss function of MSE with huber loss.
16	Orthogonal Matching Pursuit	A nonlinear adaptive algorithm using a super complete dictionary for signal decomposition.
17	Elastic Net	A linear regression model applied to multiple correlated features.
18	Lasso Regression	A compressed estimate. It constructs a penalty function to obtain a more refined model, which is a biased estimate for processing data with complex collinearity.
19	Passive aggressive Regressor	Online learning algorithms for both classification and regression.
20	Random sample consensus	An iterative method that estimates the parameters of a mathematical model from a set of observed data containing outliers that do not affect the estimates.
21	Theil-Sen regressor	A robust model for fitting straight lines in nonparametric statistics.

5. Results and Discussion

The experimental work was performed by employing a Python library (PyCaret). The regression module of PyCaret is a supervised ML module that forecasts continuous values. It has over 21 ML algorithms and various plots to analyze the model's performance.

5.1. Experimental Design

Figure 9 depicts an experimental design flow diagram with seven major components: data collection, data pre-processing (data cleaning, normalization, and cross-validation), feature selection, hyper-parameter tuning, data partitioning, model development, model selection, and future prediction.

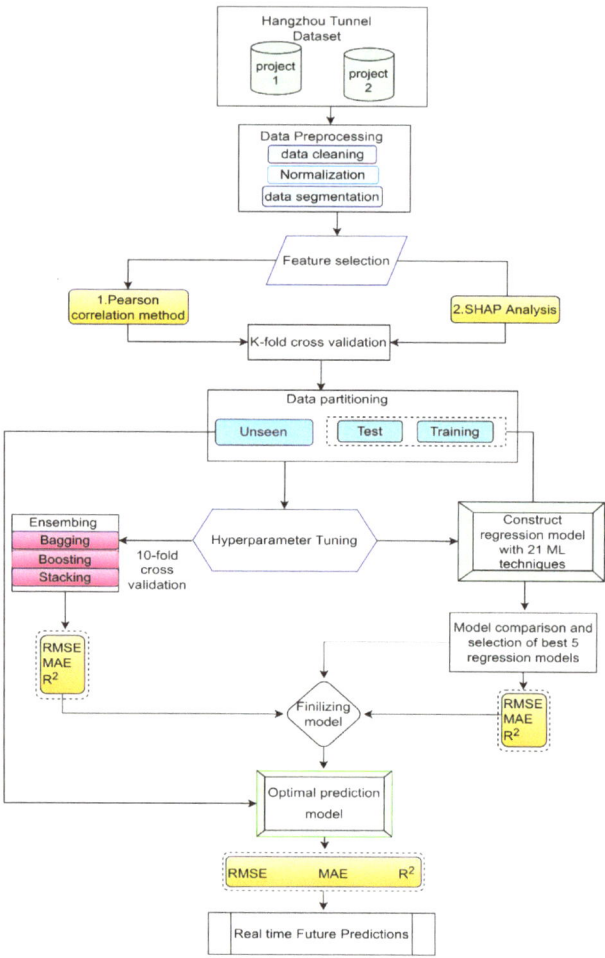

Figure 9. Flow chart of developed prediction model.

As described in Section 2.1, data from metro line tunneling projects in Hangzhou for predicting tunnel-induced settlements were collected. Data were cleaned first, which included the removal of nulls and outlier rejection. All the data are of integer datatype and were normalized to $[-1, 1]$ as discussed in Section 2.4.2 and then divided into training and testing samples. As discussed in Section 3, feature selection methods using Pearson correlation and SHAP were applied to find relevant features. Five features (i.e. ST, To, H, GW, and VDF) were considered important for predicting Smax, and were selected as final input parameters for building ML models. ML models were then developed with 21 ML estimators, as explained in Section 4.1, and performance was recorded based on the MAE, RMSE, and R^2 values the results that were obtained are presented in Table 8. Among the 21 developed ML models, the best five models were selected: the extra tree regressor, Random Forest Regressor, AdaBoost Regressor, Light Gradient Boosting Machine, and Gradient Boosting Regressor. All the best five selected models were then subjected to hyper-parameter tuning to maximize the model's performance without overfitting by using the tune_model function, which will automatically tune the hyper-parameters of a model using a random grid search on a pre-defined search space. Furthermore, the 10-fold cross-validation technique is utilized for a dynamic partitioning of data and for improving the tuned model's performance. The tuned models were then ensemble which is well known in improving the stability and accuracy of regression models (primarily tree-based) using various ensemble techniques; these include Bagging, Boosting, and Stacking. Table 8 presents the results obtained after adopting the corresponding techniques. Finally, forecasting was performed through the best-selected model (i.e., the extra trees regressor model). The model was also validated with unseen data for predictions to check the robustness of the model and it was found to be satisfactory.

Table 8. Statistical values of the 21 developed ML prediction models on Training and Test set.

No.	Model	MAE Training	R^2 Training	RMSE Training	MAE Test	R^2 Test	RMSE Test
1	Extra tree Regressor	3.7	0.891	4.5	3.8	0.791	5.5
2	Random Forest Regressor	4.2	0.857	5.0	4.3	0.753	6.1
3	Gradient Boosting Regressor	4.3	0.846	5.1	3.8	0.788	5.6
4	Light Gradient Boosting Machine	4.5	0.826	5.5	3.97	0.762	6.0
5	AdaBoost Regressor	4.4	0.834	5.2	5	0.736	6.4
6	Extreme gradient boosting	4.3	0.845	5.2	5.1	0.742	6.41
7	K neighbors Regressor	4.28	0.831	5.5	4.76	0.732	6.48
8	Decision Tree Regressor	4.7	0.691	5.5	5.67	0.599	8.0
9	Support vector machine	4.7	0.655	5.6	5.82	0.582	8.0
10	Bayesian Ridge	7.54	0.603	8.46	7.1	0.47	9.02
11	Ridge Regression	7.59	0.602	8.48	6.80	0.51	8.74
12	CatBoost Regressor	7.62	0.592	8.52	6.72	0.55	8.77
13	Linear Regression	7.70	0.57	8.76	6.76	0.50	8.82
14	Least Angle Regression	7.70	0.57	8.76	6.76	0.51	8.82
15	Huber Regressor	7.57	0.57	8.73	6.61	0.51	8.73
16	Orthogonal Matching Pursuit	7.9	0.55	9.23	7.6	0.36	10.1
17	Elastic Net	8.1	0.52	9.31	7.62	0.40	9.6
18	Lasso Regression	7.70	0.57	8.76	7.77	0.40	9.63
19	Passive aggressive Regressor	8.1	0.42	10.44	8.56	0.19	11.20
20	Random sample consensus	7.43	-0.33	8.43	10.10	-0.10	12.49
21	Theil-Sen regressor	7.43	-0.33	8.43	10.10	-0.10	12.49

5.2. Performance Analysis

The model's performance was analyzed across different aspects, as discussed below.

5.2.1. Performance of Regression Models

The regression models for the given dataset were developed using PyCaret; for a diverse dataset, the coefficient of determination (R^2), mean absolute error (MAE), and root mean square error (RMSE) are considered reliable statistics for evaluating the prediction model. Among the 21 different generated continuous models on the training set and the test set, the statistical significance of the best five selected models after being subjected to hyperparameter tuning, 10-fold cross-validation, and various ensemble techniques, giving their coefficient of determination (R^2), the mean absolute error (MAE), and the root mean square error (RMSE), is given in Table 9 below. Based on the statistical values, it appears that the extra tree regressor (ET) outperformed in all cases at the training and testing stages, with an R^2 of 0.808, MAE of 3.7, and an RMSE of 5.2 on the test set. The extra tree regressor, which outperformed in all the cases, was finalized as the best model.

5.2.2. Performance of the Extra Tree Regressor

The extra tree regressor model was also analyzed graphically using residual graphs, prediction error plots, and validation curve plots. Plotting uses the trained model object and generates a plot based on the testing dataset. Figure 10 depicts the plots between the experimental and predicted Smax as predicted by the generated models. The x-axis and y-axis represent the experimental and predicted values, respectively, and the blue and green colors represent the training and testing sets, respectively. The black diagonal line represents the identity line.

Table 9. Statistical values of the best five selected prediction Models on Training and Test set.

No.	Model	MAE Training	R^2 Training	RMSE Training	MAE Test	R^2 Test	RMSE Test
1	Extra tree Regressor	3.4	0.913	4.04	3.7	0.808	5.2
2	Random Forest Regressor	4.2	0.861	5.0	4.3	0.786	5.4
3	Gradient Boosting Regressor	4.3	0.854	5.1	3.8	0.792	5.5
4	AdaBoost Regressor	4.4	0.849	5.1	5.0	0.763	5.9
5	Light Gradient Boosting Machine	4.5	0.842	5.5	3.9	0.778	6.0

A prediction error plot compares actual targets to the values predicted by our model. This demonstrates the model's variance. We can identify regression models using this plot by comparing them to the 45-degree slanting line and determining whether the prediction exactly matches the model.

A residual plot is a graphical representation of the relationship between an independent variable and its corresponding response variable. A residual value is a measure of how well a regression line fits the dataset, with a few data points fitting and others missing. The x-axis in the residual plot represents the residual values, and the y-axis represents the independent variable.

The validation curve is the learning curve calculated from a holdout validation dataset that gives an idea of how well the model is generalizing dataset. The validation curve plots the score over a varying hypermeter. It is more convenient to plot the influence of a single hypermeter on the training score and the validation score to determine whether the estimator is overfitting or underfitting for some hypermeter values. From Figure 10c, both the validation curves are becoming narrower with the increased value of max_depth.

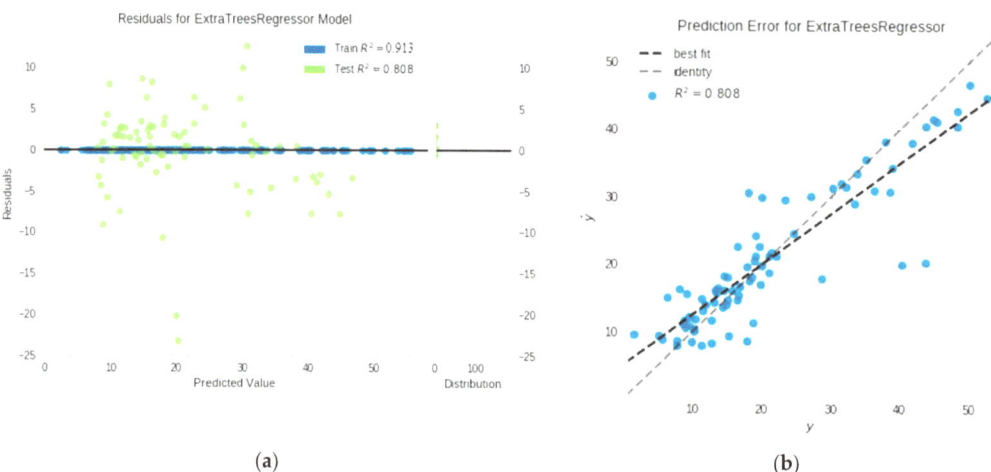

(a) (b)

Figure 10. Cont.

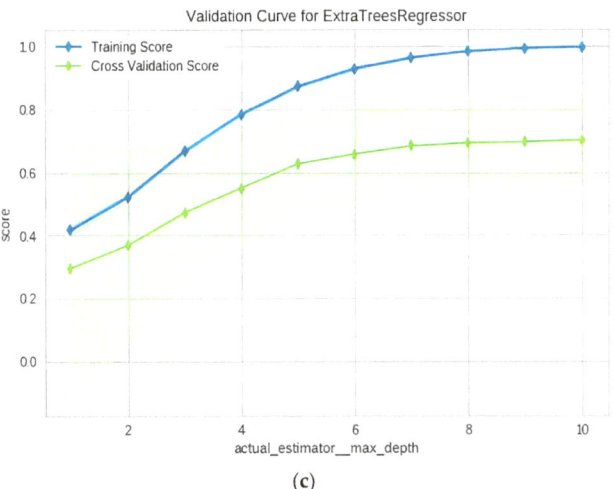

(c)

Figure 10. (**a**) Residuals for extra tree regressor; (**b**); Prediction error for extra tree regressor (**c**) Validation curve for extra tree regressor.

5.2.3. Prediction of Unseen Data

To finalize the model and predict based on unseen data (the 20% of data) that we detached at the start and never revealed to PyCaret. The finalize_model () function fits the model to the full dataset containing the test/holdout samples. The predict_model () function is employed to make predictions on the unseen data, this time we will pass the data_unseen parameter. Data_unseen is the variable created at the beginning and contains 20% (53 samples) of the original dataset that was never exposed to PyCaret. Although the model is same, we can see that R^2 increased from 0.913 to 0.96 in the final ET model. This is because the final ET variable is trained on the entire dataset including the test/hold-out set. The plot of prediction error is shown in Figure 11. After testing the models on the unseen data subset, the results we obtained are summarized in Table 10 below. At the unseen_data stage, the model performed well with MAPE of 2.10, R^2 of 0.961, and RMSE of 3.94.

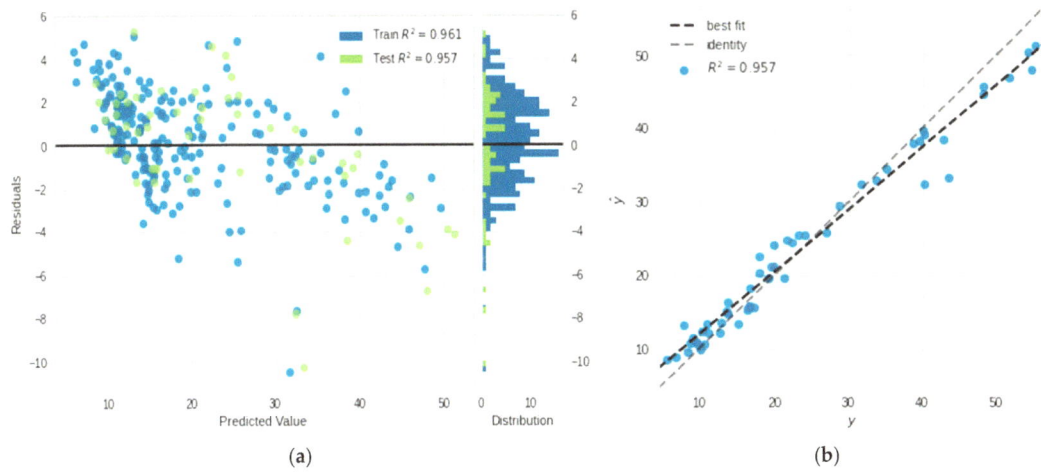

Figure 11. (**a**) Residuals for extra tree regressor; (**b**) Prediction error for extra tree regressor.

Table 10. Statistical values of the Generated prediction Models on unseen data.

	MAE	MSE	RMSE	R^2	RMSLE	MAPE
Extra tree regressor	2.1023	15.5794	3.9471	0.961	0.1664	0.1053

According to Table 10 and Figure 11, the mean absolute error (MAE) between predicted and measured maximum surface subsidence is less than 3%, indicating that the predictive performance of the model is acceptable and satisfactory for the given project. Given the statistical results and graphical plots, the models generated by PyCaret can be used to predict ground subsidence's caused by shield tunneling.

5.3. Analysis of Model on Entire Dataset

As it is known that PyCaret wraps a number of machine learning frameworks and libraries, the model built by PyCaret is evaluated to learn about the details of the best algorithm selected by the AutoML function. The extra tree regressor is identified to be the best-selected model based on the statistical R^2 value of 0.961. Furthermore, our best model was finalized for deployment and saved for making new predictions over the whole dataset, including (training, test, and unseen_data sets). An actual vs. predicted value plot is plotted for visualization as a histogram, as shown in Figure 12a, where the brown bars represent the actual values, the blue bars represent the predicted values, and the purple bars represent the error. A regression plot is plotted over the entire dataset to show the linear relationship between the Actual Value and the Predicted Value of Smax, and the dots are not far in the hyperplane of the linear line, which indicates that the regression model is good as shown in Figure 12b. Further, we can compare the predicted values and residuals in an error plot over the entire dataset, shown in Figure 12c. The statistical R^2 value of 1 and the actual vs. predicted value plot on our entire dataset indicate that the selected model i.e. extra tree regressor (ET) is highly significant in predicting the surface settlements induced by tunneling when compared to our other models.

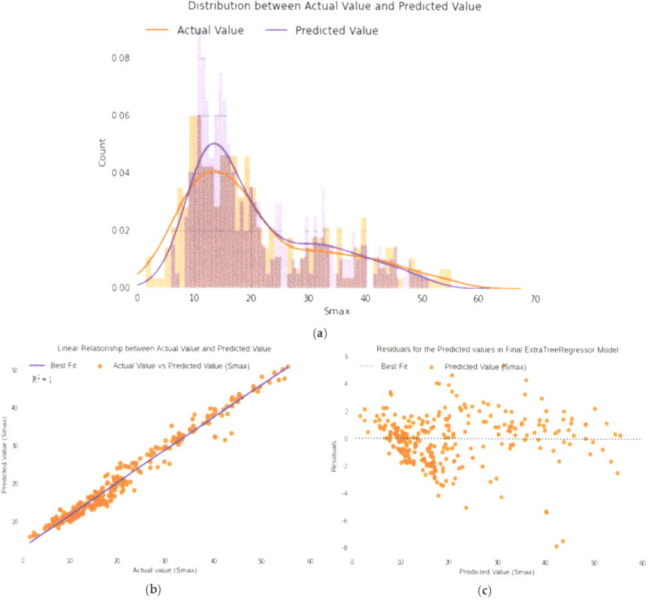

Figure 12. (a) Distribution between Actual value and Predicted value; (b) Regression plot; (c) Residual plot.

6. Conclusions

This study systematically illustrates the process of application of Auto machine learning (AutoML)-based method to precisely predict tunneling-induced settlement using EPB shield machines. The 10-fold cross-validation method is utilized to overcome the scarcity of data and promote the robustness of the model. The coefficient of determination (R^2), mean absolute error (MAE), and root mean square error (RMSE), are selected as three quantificational evaluation indices. Feature selection methods (i.e., Pearson correlation, and the SHAP framework) were employed to select features from a dataset with 14 input features (i.e., H, ST, GW, FPt, FPc, AR, PA, Th, To, JP, HDf, VDf, HDb, and VDb). Subsequently, AutoML-based models were built and trained on the selected features from the corresponding feature selection method. Then, the five best models were selected among 21 developed ML prediction models, and performances were compared by computing the R^2, RMSE, and MAE. According to the analysis, the extra tree regressor outperformed the other four models. Finally, the extra tree regressor model was used to make predictions on unseen data to simulate a real-life scenario and highlight the strengths of the model's predicted performance.

The following conclusions are provided based on the results of the model comparison and analysis:

- Feature selection is essential to address when predicting Smax due to shield tunneling. It is recommended to compare at least two feature selection methods, especially when there needs to be more information about the relationship between input and output parameters. Herein, H, ST, GW, FPt, PA, To, JP, VDF, and VDb significantly impact the maximum surface settlement caused by tunneling based on the features selected from the Pearson correlation method. However, deciding which feature to select may be challenging when there is a weak correlation with the desired output.
- SHAP-based feature selection algorithms comprehend the output of a complex ML model and facilitate model validation by allowing the user to investigate how various features contribute to the model's prediction. The SHAP analysis performed in this study revealed that the most critical parameters affecting tunneling-induced ground settlements were soil type (ST), torque (To), cover depth (H), groundwater level (GW), and tunneling deviation. These prudent factors identified by the model enable engineers and shield operators to reasonably manage shield operations.
- It is feasible and most reliable to calculate the maximum ground settlement (Smax) during the construction of earth pressure balanced (EPB) shield tunneling by the proposed AutoML models. According to the statistical and graphical results, the extra-tree regressor's predictive ability is the best among all 21 AutoML models. Furthermore, the prediction results on unseen data indicate that the model's predicted performance is acceptable and within the project's tolerances. As a result, the prediction results generated from the AutoML-based extra tree regressor model are the most reliable, indicating that the model can be employed in real projects when completely-new deep excavation data are imported.

Limitations

Because of the lack of a professional public database and the irregular quality of engineering data, this study excludes the meta-learning submodule in AutoML. More work should be done to collect similar data and create a database that can provide prior experience.

This study does not investigate the impact of tunneling operations with parameters related to grouting quality (e.g., large grout filling percentage and grouting pressure), which can significantly reduce settlements developed after the shield passing, as they were unavailable for Project 1. In order to enhance the effectiveness of the ML models, it is recommended to consider the effects of these parameters in future research.

Author Contributions: Conceptualization, S.M.H.; methodology, S.M.H.; software, S.M.H., L.M.; validation, S.M.H.; formal analysis, L.M.; investigation, S.M.H.; resources, L.M.; data curation, S.M.H.; writing—original draft preparation, S.M.H.; writing—review and editing, S.M.H.; visualization, L.M.; supervision, L.M.; project administration, L.M.; funding acquisition, L.M. All authors have read and agreed to the published version of the manuscript.

Funding: This research was funded by the National Natural Science Foundation of China under Grant No. 51738010, the Shanghai Natural Science Foundation (no. 22ZR1464600).

Data Availability Statement: The dataset used in this study is available on GitHub at https://github.com/umgeotech/Database/tree/master/Surface%20Settlement (accessed on: 6 September 2022). For any inquiries, please contact the corresponding author of the current manuscript.

Acknowledgments: The authors appreciate the five anonymous reviewers for the valuable suggestions that greatly improved this article. The dataset used in this research consists of 264 data samples adopted from the following study by Professor Wanhuan Zhou (State Key Laboratory of Internet of Things for Smart City and Department of Civil and Environmental Engineering, University of Macau, Macau, China) and her team, to whom we are grateful: Kannangara, K.P.M.; Zhou, W.H.; Ding, Z.; Hong, Z.H. Investigation of feature contribution to shield tunnelinginduced settlement using Shapley additive explanations method. *J. Rock Mech. Geotech. Eng.* **2022**, *14*, 1052–1063.

Conflicts of Interest: The authors declare no conflict of interest.

References

1. Zhang, P. A novel feature selection method based on global sensitivity analysis with application in machine learning-based prediction model. *Appl. Soft Comput.* **2019**, *85*, 105859. [CrossRef]
2. Chen, R.P.; Lin, X.T.; Kang, X.; Zhong, Z.Q.; Liu, Y.; Zhang, P.; Wu, H.N. Deformation and stress characteristics of existing twin tunnels induced by close-distance EPBS under-crossing. *Tunn. Undergr. Space Technol.* **2018**, *82*, 468–488. [CrossRef]
3. Chen, D.F.; Feng, X.T.; Xu, D.P.; Jiang, Q.; Yang, C.X.; Yao, P.P. Use of an improved ANN model to predict collapse depth of thin and extremely thin layered rock strata during tunnelling. *Tunn. Undergr. Space Technol.* **2016**, *51*, 372–386. [CrossRef]
4. Zhang, Z.; Huang, M. Geotechnical influence on existing subway tunnels induced by multiline tunneling in Shanghai soft soil. *Comput. Geotech.* **2014**, *56*, 121–132. [CrossRef]
5. Jiang, M.; Yin, Z.Y. Influence of soil conditioning on ground deformation during longitudinal tunneling. *C. R. Mec.* **2014**, *342*, 189–197. [CrossRef]
6. Zhang, W.G.; Li, H.R.; Wu, C.Z.; Li, Y.Q.; Liu, Z.Q.; Liu, H.L. Soft computing approach for prediction of surface settlement induced by earth pressure balance shield tunneling. *Undergr. Space* **2021**, *6*, 353–363. [CrossRef]
7. Liang, R.Z.; Xia, T.D.; Lin, C.G.; Yu, F. Analysis of surface deformation and horizontal displacement of deep soil caused by shield driving. *J. Rock Mech. Eng.* **2015**, *34*, 583–593.
8. Mair, R.J. Subsurface settlement profiles above tunnels in clays. *Geotechnique* **1993**, *43*, 315–320. [CrossRef]
9. Standing, J.R. Greenfield ground response to EPBM tunnelling in London Clay. *Geotechnique* **2013**, *63*, 989–1007.
10. Zhu, C.H.; Li, N. Estimation and regularity analysis of maximal surface settlement induced by subway construction. *Chin. J. Rock Mech. Eng.* **2017**, *1*, 3543–3560.
11. Karakus, M.; Fowell, R.J. 2-D and 3-D finite element analyses for the settlement due to soft ground tunnelling. *Tunn. Undergr. Space Technol.* **2006**, *21*, 392. [CrossRef]
12. Peck, R.B. Deep excavations and tunneling in soft ground. In Proceedings of the 7th ICSMFE, Mexico City, Mexico, 25–29 August 1969; pp. 225–290.
13. Attewell, P.B.; Yeates, J.; Selby, A.R. Soil Movements Induced by Tunnelling and Their Effects on Pipelines and Structures. United States; 1986. Available online: https://www.osti.gov/biblio/7052176 (accessed on 1 August 2022).
14. Mindlin, R.D. Force at a point in the interior of a semi-infinite solid. *Physics* **1936**, *7*, 195–202. [CrossRef]
15. Hagiwara, T.; Grant, R.J.; Calvello, M.; Taylor, R.N. The effect of overlying strata on the distribution of ground movements induced by tunnelling in clay. *Soils Found.* **1999**, *39*, 63–73. [CrossRef] [PubMed]
16. Cheng, C.Y.; Dasari, G.R.; Chow, Y.K.; Leung, C.F. Finite element analysis of tunnel–soil–pile interaction using displacement controlled model. *Tunn. Undergr. Space Technol.* **2007**, *22*, 450–466. [CrossRef]
17. Kasper, T.; Meschke, G. A 3D finite element simulation model for TBM tunnelling in soft ground. *Int. J. Numer. Anal. Methods Geomech.* **2004**, *28*, 1441–1460. [CrossRef]
18. Ng, C.W.; Fong, K.Y.; Liu, H.L. The effects of existing horseshoe-shaped tunnel sizes on circular crossing tunnel interactions: Three-dimensional numerical analyses. *Tunn. Undergr. Space Technol.* **2018**, *77*, 68–79. [CrossRef]
19. Jin, Y.F.; Zhu, B.Q.; Yin, Z.Y.; Zhang, D.M. Three-dimensional numerical analysis of the interaction of two crossing tunnels in soft clay. *Undergr. Space* **2019**, *4*, 310–327. [CrossRef]
20. Qi, C.; Tang, X. Slope stability prediction using integrated metaheuristic and machine learning approaches: A comparative study. *Comput. Ind. Eng.* **2018**, *118*, 112–122. [CrossRef]

21. Zhang, L.; Shi, B.; Zhu, H.; Yu, X.B.; Han, H.; Fan, X. (PSO-SVM-based deep displacement prediction of Majiagou landslide considering the deformation hysteresis effect. *Landslides* **2021**, *18*, 179–193. [CrossRef]
22. Zhang, L.; Shi, B.; Zhu, H.; Yu, X.; Wei, G. A machine learning method for inclinometer lateral deflection calculation based on distributed strain sensing technology. *Bull. Eng. Geol. Environ.* **2020**, *79*, 3383–3401. [CrossRef]
23. Zhang, W.; Li, Y.; Wu, C.; Li, H.; Goh AT, C.; Liu, H. Prediction of lining response for twin tunnels constructed in anisotropic clay using machine learning techniques. *Undergr. Space* **2020**, *7*, 122–133. [CrossRef]
24. Shi, J.; Ortigao JA, R.; Bai, J. Modular neural networks for predicting settlements during tunneling. *J. Geotech. Geoenviron. Eng.* **1998**, *124*, 389–395. [CrossRef]
25. Suwansawat, S.; Einstein, H.H. Describing settlement troughs over twin tunnels using a superposition technique. *J. Geotech. Geoenviron. Eng.* **2007**, *133*, 445–468. [CrossRef]
26. Santos, O.J., Jr.; Celestino, T.B. Artificial neural networks analysis of Sao Paulo subway tunnel settlement data. *Tunn. Undergr. Space Technol.* **2008**, *23*, 481–491. [CrossRef]
27. Bouayad, D.; Emeriault, F. Modeling the relationship between ground surface settlements induced by shield tunneling and the operational and geological parameters based on the hybrid PCA/ANFIS method. *Tunn. Undergr. Space Technol.* **2017**, *68*, 142–152. [CrossRef]
28. Ahangari, K.; Moeinossadat, S.R.; Behnia, D. Estimation of tunnelling-induced settlement by modern intelligent methods. *Soils Found.* **2015**, *55*, 737–748. [CrossRef]
29. Goh, A.T.; Zhang, W.; Zhang, Y.; Xiao, Y.; Xiang, Y. Determination of earth pressure balance tunnel-related maximum surface settlement: A multivariate adaptive regression splines approach. *Bull. Eng. Geol. Environ.* **2018**, *77*, 489–500. [CrossRef]
30. Zhang, L.; Wu, X.; Ji, W.; AbouRizk, S.M. Intelligent approach to estimation of tunnel-induced ground settlement using wavelet packet and support vector machines. *J. Comput. Civ. Eng.* **2017**, *31*, 04016053. [CrossRef]
31. Suwansawat, S.; Einstein, H.H. Artificial neural networks for predicting the maximum surface settlement caused by EPB shield tunneling. *Tunn. Undergr. Space Technol.* **2006**, *21*, 133–150. [CrossRef]
32. Darabi, A.; Ahangari, K.; Noorzad, A.; Arab, A. Subsidence estimation utilizing various approaches—A case study: Tehran No. 3 subway line. *Tunn. Undergr. Space Technol.* **2012**, *31*, 117–127. [CrossRef]
33. Pourtaghi, A.; Lotfollahi-Yaghin, M.A. Wavenet ability assessment in comparison to ANN for predicting the maximum surface settlement caused by tunneling. *Tunn. Undergr. Space Technol.* **2012**, *28*, 257–271. [CrossRef]
34. Zhou, J.; Shi, X.; Du, K.; Qiu, X.; Li, X.; Mitri, H.S. Feasibility of Random-Forest approach for prediction of ground settlements induced by the construction of a shield-driven tunnel. *Int. J. Geomech.* **2016**, *17*, 04016129. [CrossRef]
35. Shao, C.; Lan, D. Optimal control of an earth pressure balance shield with tunnel face stability. *Autom. Constr.* **2014**, *46*, 22–29. [CrossRef]
36. Armaghani, D.J.; Mohamad, E.T.; Narayanasamy, M.S.; Narita, N.; Yagiz, S. Development of hybrid intelligent models for predicting TBM penetration rate in hard rock condition. *Tunn. Undergr. Space Technol.* **2017**, *63*, 29–32. [CrossRef]
37. Zhang, P.; Chen, R.P.; Wu, H.N. Real-time analysis and regulation of EPB shield steering using Random Forest. *Autom. Constr.* **2019**, *106*, 102860. [CrossRef]
38. Linardatos, P.; Papastefanopoulos, V.; Kotsiantis, S. Explainable AI: A review of machine learning interpretability methods. *Entropy* **2021**, *23*, 18. [CrossRef]
39. Lundberg, S.M.; Lee, S.I. A Unified Approach to Interpreting Model Predictions. *Advances in Neural Information Processing Systems*. 2017, Volume 30. Available online: https://papers.nips.cc/paper/2017 (accessed on 1 August 2022).
40. Ali, M. (April 2022). PyCaret: An Open Source, Low-Code Machine Learning Library in Python. (PyCaret Version 2.3.5). Available online: https://www.pycaret.Org (accessed on 1 August 2022).
41. Kannangara, K.P.M.; Zhou, W.H.; Ding, Z.; Hong, Z.H. Investigation of feature contribution to shield tunneling-induced settlement using Shapley additive explanations method. *J. Rock Mech. Geotech. Eng.* **2022**, *14*, 1052–1063.
42. GB/T50123-1999; Standard for Soil Test Method. China Planning Press: Beijing, China, 1999. (In Chinese)
43. Kim, C.Y.; Bae, G.J.; Hong, S.W.; Park, C.H.; Moon, H.K.; Shin, H.S. Neural network based prediction of ground surface settlements due to tunnelling. *Comput. Geotech.* **2001**, *28*, 517–547. [CrossRef]
44. Ding, L.; Wang, F.; Luo, H.; Yu, M.; Wu, X. Feedforward analysis for shield-ground system. *J. Comput. Civ. Eng.* **2013**, *27*, 231–242. [CrossRef]
45. Chen, R.; Meng, F.; Li, Z.; Ye, Y.; Ye, J. Investigation of response of metro tunnels due to adjacent large excavation and protective measures in soft soils. *Tunn. Undergr. Space Technol.* **2016**, *58*, 224–235. [CrossRef]
46. Feng, X.T.; Zhang, C.; Qiu, S.; Zhou, H.; Jiang, Q.; Li, S. Dynamic design method for deep hard rock tunnels and its application. *J. Rock Mech. Geotech. Eng.* **2016**, *8*, 443–461. [CrossRef]
47. Morovatdar, A.; Palassi, M.; Ashtiani, R.S. Effect of pipe characteristics in umbrella arch method on controlling tunneling-induced settlements in soft grounds. *J. Rock Mech. Geotech. Eng.* **2020**, *12*, 984–1000. [CrossRef]
48. Meng, F.Y.; Chen, R.P.; Kang, X. Effects of tunneling-induced soil disturbance on the post-construction settlement in structured soft soils. *Tunn. Undergr. Space Technol.* **2018**, *80*, 53–63. [CrossRef]
49. Dammyr, Ø.; Nilsen, B.; Gollegger, J. Feasibility of tunnel boring through weakness zones in deep Norwegian subsea tunnels. *Tunn. Undergr. Space Technol.* **2017**, *69*, 133–146. [CrossRef]

50. Qin, S.; Xu, T.; Zhou, W.H. Predicting pore-water pressure in front of a TBM using a deep learning approach. *Int. J. Geomech.* **2021**, *21*, 04021140. [CrossRef]
51. Kannangara, K.K.P.M.; Ding, Z.; Zhou, W.H. Surface settlements induced by twin tunneling in silty sand. *Undergr. Space* **2022**, *7*, 58–75. [CrossRef]
52. Zhou, C.; Xu, H.; Ding, L.; Wei, L.; Zhou, Y. Dynamic prediction for attitude and position in shield tunneling: A deep learning method. *Autom. ConStruct.* **2019**, *105*, 102840. [CrossRef]
53. Nawi, N.M.; Atomi, W.H.; Rehman, M.Z. The effect of data pre-processing on optimized training of artificial neural networks. *Procedia Technol.* **2013**, *11*, 32–39. [CrossRef]
54. Braga-Neto, U.; Hashimoto, R.; Dougherty, E.R.; Nguyen, D.V.; Carroll, R.J. Is cross-validation better than resubstitution for ranking genes. *Bioinformatics* **2004**, *20*, 253–258. [CrossRef]
55. Zhang, P.W. Hybrid meta-heuristic and machine learning algorithms for tunneling-induced settlement prediction: A comparative study. *Tunn. Undergr. Space Technol.* **2020**, *99*, 103383. [CrossRef]
56. Zhang, P.Y. Intelligent modelling of clay compressibility using hybrid meta-heuristic and machine learning algorithms. *Geosci. Front.* **2021**, *12*, 441–452. [CrossRef]
57. Tan, C.P. Surface subsidence prediction based on grey relational support vector machine. *J. Cent. South Univ. (Nat. Sci. Ed.)* **2012**, *43*, 632–637.
58. Cheng, Z.L.; Zhou, W.H.; Ding, Z.; Guo, Y.X. Estimation of spatiotemporal response of rooted soil using a machine learning approach. *J. Zhejiang Univ. Sci. A* **2020**, *21*, 462–477. [CrossRef]
59. Pearson, K. Notes on Regression and Inheritance in the Case of Two Parents. *Proc. R. Soc. Lond.* **1895**, *58*, 240–242. [CrossRef]
60. Štrumbelj, E.; Kononenko, I. Explaining prediction models and individual predictions with feature contributions. *Knowl. Inf. Syst.* **2014**, *41*, 647–665. [CrossRef]
61. Parsa, A.B.; Movahedi, A.; Taghipour, H.; Derrible, S.; Mohammadian, A.K. Toward safer highways, application of XGBoost and SHAP for real-time accident detection and feature analysis. *Accid. Anal. Prev.* **2020**, *136*, 105405. [CrossRef]
62. Siew, H.L.; Nordin, M.J. Regression techniques for the prediction of stock price trend. In Proceedings of the International Conference on Statistics in Science, Langkawi, Malaysia, 10–12 September 2012.
63. Jiang, P.; Chen, J. Displacement prediction of landslide based on generalized regression neural networks with K-fold cross-validation. *Neurocomputing* **2016**, *198*, 40–47. [CrossRef]
64. Handa, R. Prediction of Foreign Exchange Rate Using Regression Techniques. 2017. Available online: https://www.semanticscholar.org/paper/PREDICTION-OF-FOREIGN-EXCHANGE-RATE-USING-Sharma/f3feac47eafb58a1c200082c895cd591b09e020a (accessed on 1 August 2022).
65. Han, J.; Pei, J.; Kamber, M. *Data Mining: Concepts and Techniques*; Elsevier: Amsterdam, The Netherlands, 2011.
66. Breiman, L. Bagging predictors. *Mach. Learn.* **1996**, *24*, 123–140. [CrossRef]
67. Yoav Freund, R.E. A Decision-Theoretic Generalization of On-Line Learning and an Application to Boosting. *J. Comput. Syst. Sci.* **1997**, *55*, 119–139. [CrossRef]
68. Wang, G.; Hao, J.; Ma, J.; Jiang, H. A comparative assessment of ensemble learning for credit scoring. *Expert Syst. Appl.* **2011**, *38*, 223–230. [CrossRef]

Article

Applications of Two Neuro-Based Metaheuristic Techniques in Evaluating Ground Vibration Resulting from Tunnel Blasting

Danial Jahed Armaghani [1,2,*], Biao He [3], Edy Tonnizam Mohamad [1], Y.X Zhang [4], Sai Hin Lai [3] and Fei Ye [5]

[1] Centre of Tropical Geoengineering (GEOTROPIK), Institute of Smart Infrastructure and Innovative Engineering (ISIIC), Faculty of Civil Engineering, Universiti Teknologi Malaysia, Johor Bahru 81310, Malaysia
[2] Department of Urban Planning, Engineering Networks and Systems, Institute of Architecture and Construction, South Ural State University, 76, Lenin Prospect, Chelyabinsk 454080, Russia
[3] Department of Civil Engineering, Faculty of Engineering, Universiti Malaya, Kuala Lumpur 50603, Malaysia
[4] School of Engineering, Design and Built Environment, Western Sydney University, Kingswood, NSW 2751, Australia
[5] School of Highway, Chang'an University, Xi'an 710064, China
* Correspondence: jadanial@utm.my or danialarmaghani@susu.ru

Abstract: Peak particle velocity (PPV) caused by blasting is an unfavorable environmental issue that can damage neighboring structures or equipment. Hence, a reliable prediction and minimization of PPV are essential for a blasting site. To estimate PPV caused by tunnel blasting, this paper proposes two neuro-based metaheuristic models: neuro-imperialism and neuro-swarm. The prediction was made based on extensive observation and data collecting from a tunnelling project that was concerned about the presence of a temple near the blasting operations and tunnel site. A detailed modeling procedure was conducted to estimate PPV values using both empirical methods and intelligence techniques. As a fair comparison, a base model considered a benchmark in intelligent modeling, artificial neural network (ANN), was also built to predict the same output. The developed models were evaluated using several calculated statistical indices, such as variance account for (VAF) and a-20 index. The empirical equation findings revealed that there is still room for improvement by implementing other techniques. This paper demonstrated this improvement by proposing the neuro-swarm, neuro-imperialism, and ANN models. The neuro-swarm model outperforms the others in terms of accuracy. VAF values of 90.318% and 90.606% and a-20 index values of 0.374 and 0.355 for training and testing sets, respectively, were obtained for the neuro-swarm model to predict PPV induced by blasting. The proposed neuro-based metaheuristic models in this investigation can be utilized to predict PPV values with an acceptable level of accuracy within the site conditions and input ranges used in this study.

Keywords: tunnel blasting; Peak particle velocity; metaheuristic algorithms; neuro-swarm; neuro-imperialism

MSC: 68Uxx

1. Introduction

Blasting operations are frequently used in mines, quarries, and tunnels to excavate rock mass, due to their economy and efficiency. An important control object during blasting is the magnitude of ground vibration, as this is related to the safety of the surrounding buildings and equipment [1]. During blasting operations, the blast-induced ground vibration can propagate in three directions: transverse, longitudinal, and vertical direction [2]. When the vibration starts to propagate, each particle has its velocity. The peak particle velocity (PPV) is defined as the highest velocity of the particles, which is the base factor to assess the magnitude of ground vibration produced by blasting events [3–6]. Dozens of investigations were carried out to determine the PPV magnitude [7], and they included three types:

empirical/experimental methods, statistical-based methods, and artificial intelligence (AI) techniques.

In the case of empirical/experimental methods, many researchers [8,9] suggested a uniform style, which works based on only two parameters, namely, the distance of the measuring transducer from the blasting face and the explosive weight (charge amount). This uniform style was introduced by Duvall and Petkof [10], and it is known as the USBM equation form. The scaled distance (SD) is the main term of the USBM equation, which can relate the two mentioned parameters to predict PPV values. However, average performance accuracy was reported by the researchers for different proposed empirical equations, whereas a high prediction capacity is required for such techniques to minimize the risk associated with ground vibration produced by blasting. In addition, typically, these empirical/experimental equations were proposed for the conditions of the specific site, which has a unique geological structure and setting [11]. It seems that these empirical/experimental formulas cannot predict PPV with a satisfactory level of accuracy in the other blasting locations, and there is a need to try other available techniques to get more reliable results with higher accuracy.

Statistical regression methods have also been used to predict blast-induced PPV. For example, Hasanipanah et al. [12] developed a multiple linear regression (MLR) model/equation to forecast blast-induced PPV in the Miduk copper mine, in Iran. In their research, 69 data samples were allocated to the training (development) data sets for constructing the MLR model, while 17 data sets were apportioned to the testing (assessment) data sets to evaluate the MLR model. The results showed that the constructed MLR model had favorable accuracy (coefficient of determination, R^2 = 0.883) by comparing the measured PPV values with the predicted PPV values. Similarly, Ram Chandar et al. [13] proposed another MLR model to forecast PPV values in three mines. Their applied input variables included the maximum charge per delay, distance, burden, spacing, amplitude, and frequency. The results indicated that MLR was a reliable tool that can produce good accuracy and can be applied at any mine site. However, PPV is a sensitive indicator that can significantly characterize the influence of the ground vibration resulting from blasting on the safety of a building or equipment.

Some researchers [14] mentioned that the accuracy level of statistical models and MLR techniques in predicting PPV was inadequate compared to AI techniques, which can yield more reliable results. For example, Khandelwal and Singh [15] compared the PPV prediction results of both artificial neural networks (ANN) and MLR and found that the corresponding coefficients of correlation for predicting PPV are 0.994 by ANN and 0.4971 by MLR. It showed that the ANN model had a greater accuracy, whereas the proposed MLR equation had a higher error. Similar results were seen by Xue and Yang [16], Parida and Mishra [17], and Lawal and Idris [18].

In recent years, many models and studies have been developed using AI techniques for solving civil and mining problems [19–37] and specifically for predicting PPV produced by blasting. These models mainly include ANN, gene expression programming (GEP), neuro-fuzzy, decision tree, support vector machine (SVM), fuzzy logic, genetic algorithm (GA), and genetic programming [38–40]. The studies highlighted the feasibility and applicability of AI models in solving PPV produced by mine or quarry blasting. However, the AI studies for predicting PPV induced by tunnel blasting are limited to a few investigations only, as presented in Table 1. For instance, Monjezi et al. [41] attempted to use ANN to predict PPV values produced by tunnel blasting in a project carried out in Iran. They reported that the ANN technique was a powerful and easy-to-use method for solving such problems. Lawal et al. [42] conducted research to predict tunnel blast-induced PPV in the Daejeon tunnel, in South Korea. They proposed different techniques, i.e., ANN, moth-flame optimization (MFO)-ANN, and GEP, and used the controllable (e.g., hole depth) and uncontrollable (e.g., rock mass rating) factors. The results showed that the MFO-ANN model performed better in predicting PPV compared with ANN and GEP. In another work, Jelušič et al. [43] used a neuro-fuzzy model to predict PPV values in two tunnels located in Slovenia. In their study, the charge and the distance from the blast face to the monitoring positions were allocated as model predictors. It was found that the neuro-fuzzy model can well predict PPV. Rana et al. [39] compared two AI techniques (ANN and decision tree) for forecasting the PPV values in six tunnels in India. They used a database comprising 137 data samples. The results showed that the decision tree model outperformed the ANN model. Hasanipanah et al. [44] developed two forms of the GA model (linear and power) to estimate PPV in a tunneling project at the Bakhtiari dam region in Iran. The results indicated that the performance of the GA power form outperformed the GA linear form. More information regarding the available studies for estimating blast-induced PPV in tunnels can be found in Table 1.

Table 1. Some relevant investigations for predicting tunnel blast-induced PPV.

Reference	Technique	Input Parameter	Database No.	Site Location/Country
Monjezi et al. [41]	ANN	MC, DI, ST, HD	182	Located in Iran
Li et al. [45]	SVM	MC, DI	32	Located in Guiyang, China
Mohamadnejad et al. [46]	GRNN, SVM	MC, DI	37	Located in Iran
Hasanipanah et al. [47]	SVM	DI, MC	80	Located in Iran
Yin et al. [48]	BP-NN	DI, HD, MC, TC	40	Located in Beijing, China
Hasanipanah et al. [44]	GA	MC, DI	85	Located in Iran
Abbaszadeh Shahri and Asheghi [49]	ANN	TC, CPD, DI	37	Located in Iran
Rajabi and Vafaee [50]	ANN	MC, DI	64	Located in Lorestan Province, Iran
Jelušič et al. [43]	Neuro-fuzzy	TC, DI	48	Located in Slovenia
Lawal et al. [42]	MFO-ANN, GEP	HL, CPD, ND, TC, DI, RMR	56	Located in KAERI, Daejeon, South Korea

CPD: charge per delay, CPH: charge per hole, TC: total charge, DI: distance from blast face, MC: maximum charge per delay, RMR: rock mass rating, H: hole diameter, HD: hole depth, HL: hole length, NH: number of holes, TCS: tunnel cross-section, ST: stemming, BP: back-propagation, NN: neural network, GRNN: generalized regression neural network.

It is obvious that ANN is the main model developed by many researchers to estimate PPVs. However, this technique includes some drawbacks that influence its results considerably [51–53]. Combining some optimization techniques can yield more sustainable results from ANNs and higher-performing predictions. In the present study, we aimed to develop more accurate PPV prediction models based on several advanced neural network models, including the neuro-swarm and neural-imperialism models. To achieve this goal, we prepared a comprehensive PPV dataset of tunnel blasting to establish these two neural-based models. These two models are based on particle swarm optimization (PSO) and the imperialism competitive algorithm (ICA) as two powerful metaheuristic techniques. Additionally, we developed an empirical equation based on the collected database and compared its performance with the neural-based models, to verify which model is best for predicting blast-induced PPV in tunnel blasting operations.

2. Methods and Materials

2.1. ANN

An artificial neural network, or ANN, is a type of artificial intelligence (AI) system that can imitate a specific organizational notion of how the nervous system works. Unlike the traditional AI model that came before it, the ANN is able to learn the pattern from the training that it is given and estimate the underlying relationship that exists between the input variables and the output variables. This characteristic gives these approaches a big advantage over the other intelligence models that exist in this field. The ANN models use the artificial neurons as basic units to process the available data (i.e., input and output variables) in a way similar to a human being's brain. For the first time, McCulloch and Walter [54] modeled the behaviors of artificial neurons by gathering and applying a binary decision unit for input/output variables. The network they developed is capable of obtaining outputs with the minimum error (i.e., the difference between the target of the data and system output). This can be done through the employment of an artificial node or neuron.

The signal can be received at each artificial node in the network, and then the signal can be processed by an activation function, such that an estimate of the output can be generated [55]. Every output of a neuron will be taken as the input for the subsequent neuron. Ch and Mathur [56] successfully showed that the most significant factor in ANN performance and capability is the neuron/node connection patterns and their process of design. The ANN model can be iteratively trained multiple times to reduce the imperfection of the outputs. This process will continue until the preferred error of the network or the number of iterations (i.e., repetition) is obtained. Amarghani et al. [57] recommended applying the sigmoid transfer function to predict non-linear relationships. An artificial neuron j with inputs (X_i), weights (W_{ij}), bias (b_j), and system output (O_j) is presented in Figure 1.

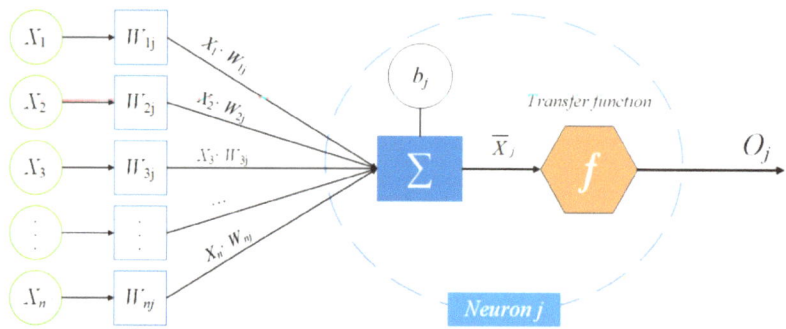

Figure 1. An artificial node used in the ANN system.

2.2. PSO

Kennedy and Eberhart [58] pioneered particle swarm optimization (PSO) as an effective, applicable, and powerful metaheuristic algorithm (i.e., optimization technique). Swarms or particles in PSO search for optimal values/targets in a repetitive manner. Throughout the search operation, the particles change their positions depending on the experiences they have obtained up to that moment. Each particle learns to obtain its best position, which is divided into two locations. The first one is named $\overrightarrow{p_{best}}$ (or the best personal position) and the second one is named $\overrightarrow{g_{best}}$ (or the best global position). During the learning stage, the particles are trained to enhance the speed of their movement to get better positions of $\overrightarrow{g_{best}}$ and $\overrightarrow{p_{best}}$. In this way, in each iteration, their locations (distance between each swarm) and velocities can be computed. Therefore, their new locations can be obtained using their previous locations and their velocities. The updated velocity and location of the particles in PSO can be easily calculated using Equations (1) and (2). $\overrightarrow{v_{new}}$ in Equation (1) is the updated velocity in each swarm, which can be calculated using velocity confidence (C_1 and C_2), present velocity and location of the swarm ($\vec{v}$ and $\vec{p}$, respectively), and the discussed $\overrightarrow{g_{best}}$ and $\overrightarrow{p_{best}}$. Then, $\overrightarrow{p_{new}}$ needs to be calculated as the updated position or location of each swarm. The literature consists of numerous studies that have explained PSO and its structure in more detailed ways [59].

$$\overrightarrow{v_{new}} = \vec{v} + C_1 \times \left(\overrightarrow{p_{best}} - \vec{p}\right) + C_2 \times \left(\overrightarrow{g_{best}} - \vec{p}\right) \qquad (1)$$

$$\overrightarrow{p_{new}} = \vec{p} + \overrightarrow{v_{new}} \qquad (2)$$

2.3. ICA

Atashpaz-Gargari and Lucas [60] designed the first imperialist competitive algorithm (ICA) as another metaheuristic algorithm to behave/solve various minimization or maximization issues. Like other metaheuristic algorithms, ICA works based on population (i.e., the number of countries), where each country is considered as a possible solution. The algorithm implementation starts using a random number of countries as initial solutions. The individuals of the population in ICA are countries, among which the best ones (i.e., those of the highest power) are selected and assigned as imperialists. The rest of the countries play the role of colonies of the imperialists. The most powerful countries in ICA are those with minimum cost; these countries can take ownership/control of more colonies. In general, ICA comprises three main machinists/operators: assimilation, revolution, and competition. The assimilation operator directs the colonies through the path of growing into imperialists to achieve more control and power, a better cultural level, and an enhanced economy. During the first two operators, the colonies will have a high chance of reaching a better position (i.e., solution) compared to that of their imperialists; in this condition, a colony will take the control of the empire. Finally, during the competition process, the imperialists will also have a high chance of adopting more colonies. During the competition process, the weakest empire collapses, and, at the same time, the strongest ones can take possession of more colonies, which leads to the increase of their control/power. The mentioned procedure is repeated until the strongest empire or the only one can control all countries. In this condition, the rest of the empires, which are weak, will collapse and their role will change as a colony. The literature contains more details and explanations regarding different applications of ICA in solving optimization problems [61].

2.4. Neuro-Based Models

The ANN models could be more powerful when being integrated with some other optimization algorithms, such as PSO and ICA [62]. The ANN models might attain a wrong or unacceptably inaccurate prediction because of the weakness of back-propagation models in the exploration of the global minimum [63]. It is highly probable for the ANN models to give strong local minima during training; however, the metaheuristic techniques have the capacity of managing this situation by determining the ANN's biases and weights. Therefore, the search space in this case encounters global minima owing to the implementation of PSO/ICA (i.e., optimization algorithms). In the current paper, two neuro-based approaches, PSO-ANN and ICA-ANN, are used to predict the PPV values induced by tunnel blasting. Then, the results attained by both hybrid models are compared in a way that selects the one with higher accuracy. In the rest of this paper, the terms neuro-swarm and neuro-imperialism will be utilized instead of PSO-ANN and ICA-ANN models, respectively. More information regarding the mixing of PSO and ICA with the ANN model for prediction-based problems can be found elsewhere [64,65].

2.5. Statistical Indices

In general, the performance quality of hybrid neuro-based or other predictive techniques is assessed using some statistical indices. Two of the most famous indices are the root mean square error ($RMSE$) and the coefficient of determination (R^2). Lower $RMSE$ values show higher accuracy of the predictions made; on the other hand, higher values of R^2 show a good covenant between the actual and estimated values. These two statistical parameters are calculated using Equations (3) and (4). In these equations, S is the total no. of samples, estimated PPV and measured PPV are presented by z' and z, respectively, and $\bar{z}$ presents the mean values of measured PPV.

$$RMSE = \sqrt{\frac{1}{n}\sum_{i=1}^{S}(z' - z)^2} \qquad (3)$$

$$R^2 = 1 - \frac{\sum_i (z - z')^2}{\sum_i (z - \bar{z})^2} \quad (4)$$

The other widely used statistical index is the variance account for (VAF), which is based on percentage. The formula of VAF is expressed as follows:

$$VAF = \left[1 - \frac{var(z - z')}{var(z)}\right] \times 100\% \quad (5)$$

The perfect value for VAF is 100% for a model with $R^2 = 1$ and $RMSE = 0$. Apart from these indices, the authors decided to use an a-20 index as a new and powerful index. This is defined in the following equation, where m^{20} signifies the rate of experimental value/predicted value that lies between the range of 0.80 to 1.20 and S is the total no. of samples.

$$a20 - index = \frac{m^{20}}{S} \quad (6)$$

2.6. Case Study and Database

In this study, the data was collected from Shi Ban Gou Tunnel, which is located in Qinghai Province, China. The Shi Ban Gou Tunnel is a highway tunnel constructed on G6 National Highway to connect region 1 (Zamalong) to region 2 (Daotang river). The route of the tunnel crosses the ridge from east to west. The basic information of the tunnel is as follows: the total length is 525 m; the design elevation of the starting point is 2478.64 m; the design elevation of the ending point is 2490.8 m; and the maximum overburden distance of the tunnel is 204 m. The route map of the tunnel is shown in Figure 2.

Figure 2. Route map of the tunnel (via Google Earth Pro).

According to the information from a geological survey, the tunnel exit is located on the Huangshui River valley slope. The natural slope angle of the mountain is about 34–70 degrees, with scattered piles of broken boulders on the right-hand slope and exposed bedrock on the left-hand slope, which indicates the poor stability of the natural slope at the tunnel entrance. In the exit section of the tunnel, the surrounding rock is composed of a mixed-medium weathered and slightly weathered gneiss with complex lithology, broken rock mass, developed joints and fissures, and a blocky or laminated structure. The rock and soil mass wave velocity of this section is 1–2.9 km·s^{-1}.

The tunnel entrance is located around 20 m up from the cliff face, next to the Temple of the Holy Ancestors of Buddha (the temple is 8 m in height and covers a total area of 52 m^2). Because the mountain is steep and the rock above the tunnel entrance is broken, the tunnel excavation by blasting increases the disturbance to the mountain. This may cause landslides, rock falls, and other hazards, seriously threatening the safety of the thousand-year-old temple. The relative positions of the tunnel and the temple are shown in Figure 3. Owing to the blasting operation, vibrations propagate not only along the tunnel axis but also far upward to the ground around the temple. The PPV values produced by blasting in the tunnel may have an undesired influence on the safety of the temple, thereby raising administrators' complaints. Since the safety of the described temple is a primary concern in this project, the values of PPV should be controlled and minimized when the tunnel is being excavated. For the safety of the temple, the field measurement of PPV was carried out using a seismograph, as shown in Figure 4. This type of seismograph is a measuring instrument for ultra-low or low-frequency vibrations. It is mainly used for the measurement of pulsations generated from the ground and structures, and it has three measurement levels of velocity: small, medium, and large velocity.

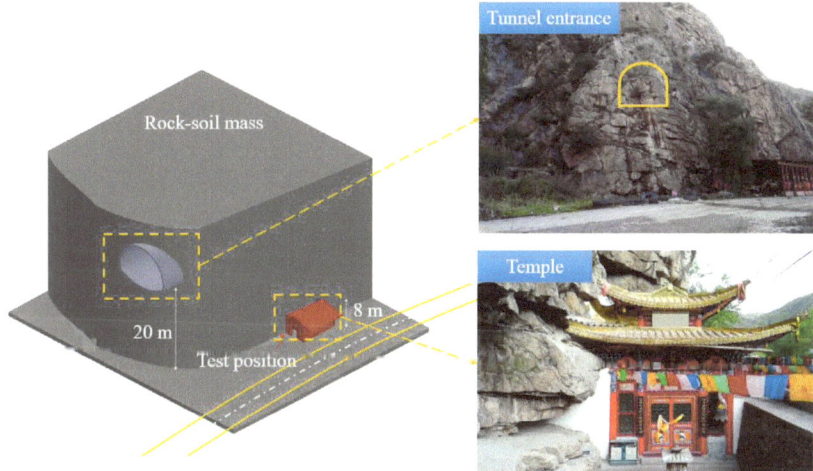

Figure 3. Positions of the tunnel and temple.

Figure 4. A measurement and monitoring point of PPV values induced by blasting.

To establish a database to forecast PPV values, the results of the Shi Ban Gou Tunnel during blasting operations were considered and used. Three hundred and one blasting operations in the mentioned tunnel with the relevant blasting parameters were observed. The blasting design factors include charge (C), rock mass rating, number of holes, and the distance from the measuring station (DI) to the blasting point, together with their relevant PPV values. It is important to mention that the distance from the measuring station is the horizontal distance between the blasting face and the monitoring point inside the temple. In the available data, a maximum distance of 745 m was recorded for DI, and, since there is an inverse relationship between PPV and DI, the authors decided to use a DI range of 49–397 m. In this way, the total number of blasting events was reduced to 154. It is worth noting that the safety of the temple presented in Figure 3, because of the close distance to the tunnel, was the main concern for the tunnel construction team. Therefore, blasting pattern parameters, as well as geological conditions of the tunnel face, were carefully designed and monitored.

Although there are several parameters measured in the tunnel site, many researchers in their empirical and computational PPV models suggested using only two predictors: DI and C [66,67]. Therefore, these two variables were used in this study, as well, to forecast PPV results produced by blasting. The statistical information of the adopted data used in this study and its modeling part are shown in Table 2. In the following section, different models will be applied to estimate PPV values and select the most accurate model for PPV prediction.

Table 2. Input and output variables and their relevant statistical information.

Parameters	Unit	Group	Max	Min	Mean	SD
Total charge (C)	kg	Input	150	45	121	39.05
Distance from the measuring station (DI)	m	Input	397	49	227	91.97
Peak particle velocity (PPV)	mm/s	Output	23.06	10	13	2.88

Max: maximum; Min: minimum; SD: standard deviation.

3. Analysis and Prediction of PPV Values

This section presents the procedures of PPV estimation using two different approaches, empirical and intelligent. The empirical approach, which is still a commonly utilized technique, will be described first. Then, intelligence systems comprising two neuro-based models—neuro-swarm and neuro-imperialism—will be constructed with their influential parameters to predict PPV values.

3.1. Empirical Approach

It is a common practice of mining engineers or designers to use an empirical equation for PPV prediction in mines, quarries, tunnels, etc. This is an essential task to be implemented before blasting operations and after the design of blasting pattern parameters. The process of estimation of PPV based on an empirical approach is not difficult, and, according to many well-known references [4,6,68], it can be computed using only two predictors (i.e., variables): distance (DI) from the blast-face and charge (C) weight. Therefore, in this study, as the empirical approach, an established equation formed by USBM [10], $PPV = zSD^x$, was used. In the mentioned equation form, z and x are site constants that can be obtained from the power structure of the equation, and SD is defined as the scaled distance, which should be calculated using DI (m) and C (kg) in a form of thfe following equation:

$$SD = \left(\frac{DI}{\sqrt{C}}\right) \quad (7)$$

Therefore, if the results of DI and C are available, it is possible to propose an empirical equation for forecasting PPV values. The proposed equations for predicting PPV values with $z = 30.584$ and $x = -0.293$ is expressed as $PPV = 30.584 SD^{-0.293}$. The SD values, together with their PPV values, are displayed in Figure 5. In this figure, the evaluation is only based on R^2, which is sufficient for a single equation. As a result, $R^2 = 0.615$ can be considered a suitable prediction level for estimating PPV induced by tunnel blasting. This level of accuracy may be applicable for predicting PPV values by designers before blasting events; however, a forecasting model with a higher accuracy/performance level would be of interest and importance for a better determination of the safety region of blasting. This can be done through the applications of neuro-based approaches, i.e., neuro-swarm and neuro-imperialism, using the same input variables (including DI and C). The modeling process of these techniques in forecasting PPV results will be described in detail, later.

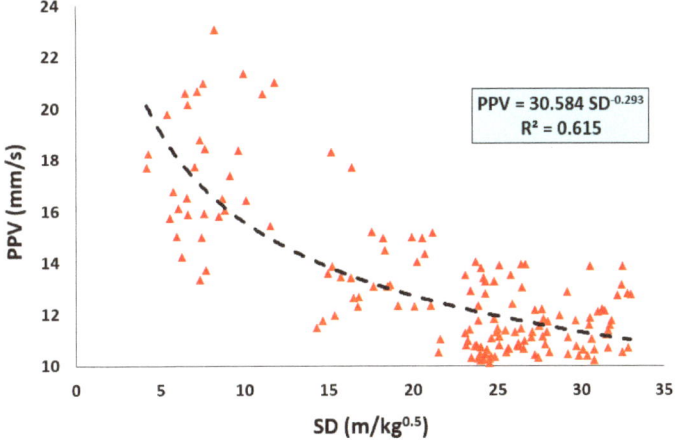

Figure 5. PPV values as a function of scaled distance based on 154 data samples.

3.2. Neuro-Based Approach

From our findings and discussion in the previous section, it was observed that a prediction technique that can provide a higher accuracy degree is needed to estimate blast-induced PPV. Hence, two neuro-based models, neuro-swarm and neuro-imperialism, were selected to do this task. The same models were highlighted in previous studies as powerful and applicable techniques in solving other geotechnical and mining engineering problems [69]. The process of modeling begins with determining the most effective parameters of the ANN approach, which is the base model in neuro-based structures. Nevertheless, before that procedure, the data need to be subjected to a normalization process to help make the modeling faster and easier. The proposed equation to normalize the datasets can make the following processes simplified [70,71]:

$$O_{norm} = \frac{O - O_{min}}{O_{max} - O_{min}} \tag{8}$$

where O_{min} and O_{max} stand for the minimum and maximum values of O, respectively; O denotes the measured value, and O_{norm} represents the normalized one. Many studies in the literature have suggested the use of only a single hidden layer in ANN [72], and some others have suggested multiple hidden layers to solve their problems [73]. As a result, the PPV data in the current study were exposed to one, two, and three hidden layers for prediction purposes. The obtained results confirmed that the use of only one hidden layer can result in predicting more accurately in comparison with two or three layers. Therefore, only a single hidden layer was considered in solving the PPV issue using neuro-based models.

In ANN design, another significant factor is the number of neurons that needs to be well determined with the help of a parametric study (a common way of designing the number of neurons). Considering the previously conducted studies and using only two input variables (*DI* and *C*), values ranging from 1 to 5 were applied to the modeling of this part, and the *RMSE* and R^2 values in each case were calculated. The results confirmed that the use of 4 hidden neurons provided closer PPV values to the measured ones; for that reason, regarding this parameter, the best number of neurons in the ANN model was set to 4. After designing the ANN structure (2-4-1 as input variables-number of hidden neurons-output variable, respectively), the rest of the modeling processes in the present study were carried out by referring to this structure as the base model. Note that the total number of data samples for modeling was 154; 80% of the total data samples were considered as the training data samples, and the rest (another 20%) were considered as the testing set.

The first step in neuro-swarm and neuro-imperialism modeling is selecting their most effective factors. In the case of neuro-swarm, iteration number, size of particle or swarm (SS), velocity coefficients, and inertia weight can influence the model performance (capability), as highlighted by various scholars [64,74]. However, several investigations suggested default values or fixed values for velocity coefficients and inertia weight to solve the problems [75]. Therefore, in this research, the velocity coefficient of 2 and the inertia weight of 0.25 were applied for all neuro-swarm models. Two other effective factors in the neuro-swarm model were designed later. In the case of neuro-imperialism, three factors—the number of countries (NOC), the number of decades (NOD), and the number of imperialists (NOI)—can have a great affect on the modeling results. Similar to the neuro-swarm model, NOI = 10 was utilized for all neuro-imperialism models, based on previous investigations [74], and NOD and NOC parameters were determined later.

As mentioned in the previous paragraph, the SS and the number of iterations should be designed for the neuro-swarm model, while these parameters are NOD and NOC for the neuro-imperialism model. In conducting two parametric studies, SS and NOC values in the range of 50 and 500, with the incremental step of 50, were used for modeling. In these parametric studies, a maximum value of 500 was assigned to the number of iterations/decades. Therefore, ten neuro-swarm and ten neuro-imperialism predictive models were created to estimate PPV values, and their *RMSE*s were recorded as shown in Figure 6a,b, respectively for neuro-swarm and neuro-imperialism methods. From Figure 6, two parameters, the number of population and the number of model repetitions, can be determined for each neuro-based model. It is obvious that for all models, the *RMSE* values were significantly reduced in the beginning iterations/decades until reaching a constant *RMSE*, and, after that, there is no change in the results of the *RMSE*. However, the constant point is different for each neuro-based model. For example, for SS = 50 (Figure 6a), the results of the *RMSE* were not changed after iteration number = 100. This is the way of selecting the best iteration/decade number. On the other hand, the best SS and NOC values are related to those with the lowest *RMSE* values. In this way, the neuro-swarm model and the neuro-imperialism model received the lowest *RMSE* values when SS = 450 and NOC = 400, respectively. Therefore, they were selected as the best populations in these two models. Regarding iteration and decade number: conservatively, iteration number = 400 and NOD = 300 were selected for neuro-swarm and neuro-imperialism methods, respectively, in estimating PPV. By determining these parameters, there is no more effective parameter that needs to be designed. The results obtained by these two neuro-based models in forecasting PPV induced by tunnel blasting will be discussed in the following section.

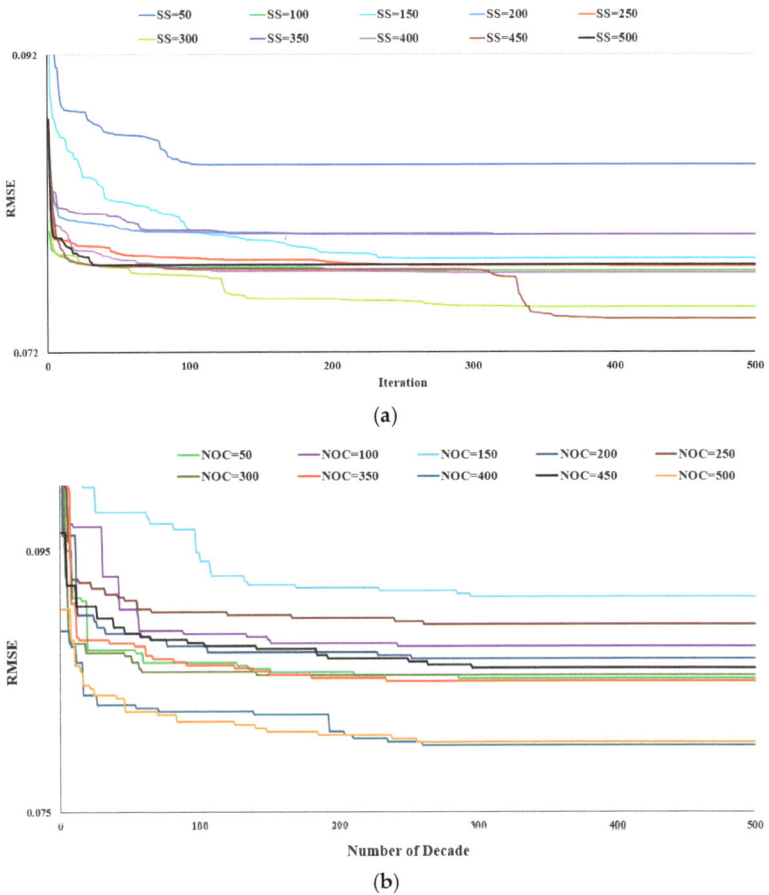

Figure 6. Results of hybrid neuro-based models to predict PPV values. (**a**) 10 models of neuro-swarm; (**b**) 10 models of neuro-imperialism.

4. Results and Discussion

This section discusses the results obtained from both the empirical and computational models in terms of estimating the PPV values produced by tunnel blasting. To show that the databases used in the modeling are suitable and to understand more about the effective parameters of PPV, an empirical equation was also proposed to predict PPV values. However, it was highlighted in past studies that these empirical equations are not strong enough for solving ground vibration problems in blasting sites. With this in mind, the evaluation process of the proposed empirical equation was performed, and, based on the obtained R^2 (0.615), it was found that the empirical equation includes a wide range of errors. This may be because the nature of rock mass, which is site-specific or based on geological conditions of the blast face, is not considered in the empirical equation.

Therefore, to increase the performance prediction and to have a fair comparison, the same model inputs (DI and C) were utilized in two neuro-based techniques. The idea behind that is to propose a computational model which can increase the accuracy level and at the same time be applicable and easy to implement. Needless to mention, an exact or near-to-exact determination of blast safety zone is always a challenge for civil and mining engineers. It means that the designers are looking for a reliable and applicable methodology with the lowest error level. Both neuro-based techniques were designed with the mentioned aim to predict PPV induced by tunnel blasting. As discussed earlier, four statistical indices were used for assessing intelligent models, and their results are tabulated in Table 3. Note that an ANN as the base model was also designed in this investigation to better realize the roles of PSO and ICA in optimizing ANN weights and biases. In fact, by selecting the optimum weight and bias for ANN, an increase in the accuracy level of the proposed models can be seen.

Table 3. Results of the developed models in forecasting PPV values.

Set	Statistical Index	ANN	Neuro-Swarm	Neuro-Imperialism
Train	R^2	0.615	0.904	0.896
	RMSE	0.138	0.072	0.079
	VAF (%)	61.368	90.318	89.515
	a-20 index	0.195	0.374	0.374
Test	R^2	0.687	0.913	0.822
	RMSE	0.126	0.075	0.077
	VAF (%)	68.073	90.606	80.77
	a-20 index	0.161	0.355	0.258

Table 3 presents statistical indices results for the model training and model testing parts. In addition, Figures 7–9 display the results of the measured and predicted PPV values with the use of the neuro-swarm, neuro-imperialism, and ANN techniques, respectively. In addition, the statistical indices (i.e., R^2, VAF, RMSE, and a-20 index) results for the introduced models are depicted in these figures. In terms of the prediction capacity, the neuro-swarm model was found to have a higher capability to present a better relationship (higher performance) between the predicted and measured PPV values. Regarding the model training part, the R^2 values of 0.615, 0.896, and 0.904 for ANN, neuro-imperialism, and neuro-swarm models, respectively, were obtained, which showed that the neuro-swarm was superior to the other ones in this part. Similarly, the same trend in R^2 results can be found for the model testing part (Table 3), which confirmed the high-reliability level of the model during development. In addition, the same neuro-swarm model received the lowest RMSE and highest VAF results for both the training and testing stages. As a new and powerful indicator for assessing model accuracy, the a-20 index was calculated for all proposed models. The ideal value for an a-20 index is 1.0, and it is related to a model with equal measured and predicted values. Therefore, values closer to 1.0 are set as more accurate models. Based on this discussion, the neuro-swarm model with a-20 index values of 0.374 and 0.355 is the best among all applied models.

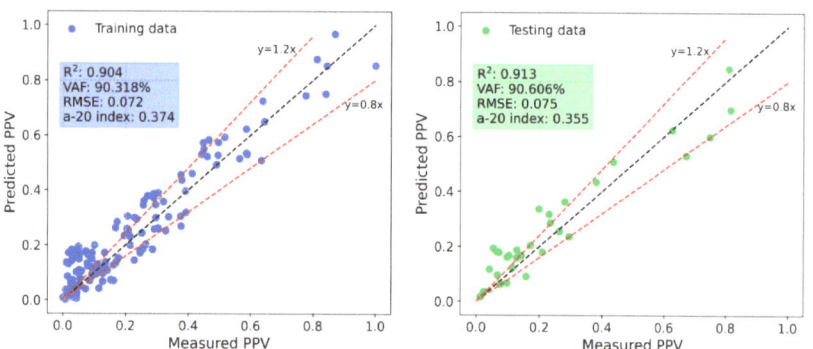

Figure 7. Predicted PPV values by the neuro-swam model VS measured ones.

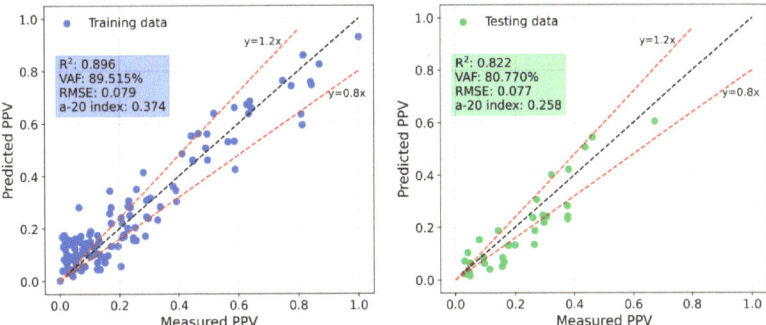

Figure 8. Predicted PPV values by the neuro-imperialism model VS measured ones.

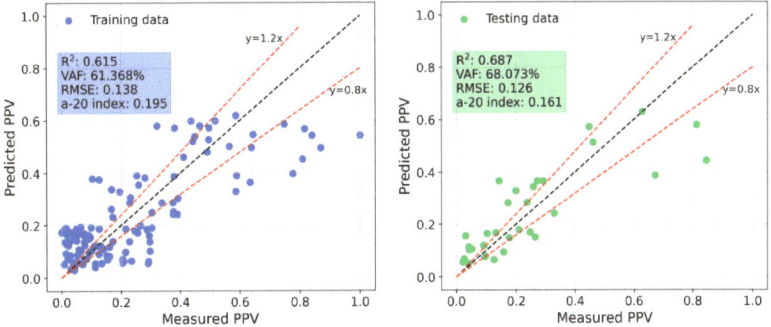

Figure 9. Predicted PPV values by the ANN model VS measured ones.

From the results, it is clear that both neuro-based models are strong enough to increase performance prediction of the base model (i.e., ANN) in predicting PPV values obtained by tunnel blasting. The estimated PPV values and their close agreement with the measured ones reveal that PSO and ICA are highly capable of optimizing the biases and weights of ANN. However, in cases where new data was accessible, the neuro-swarm with PSO as an optimization algorithm outperformed the other one. The techniques in this study, with their detailed design process, can be utilized in tunnel blasting for determining PPV values with a low level of error. In this way, the safety zone of blasting related to only ground vibration can be determined to check the locations of important structures, equipment, and products.

In terms of model accuracy and the ability for prediction purposes, note that the findings achieved in this paper are better than some other techniques published in the literature. For instance, Jelušič et al. [43] received an $R^2 = 0.87$ for their neuro-fuzzy model in estimating PPV. Li et al. [45] proposed a SVM model with $R^2 = 0.910$ for the same problem. Moreover, our study used only two variables as inputs to solve the PPV problem, which means that our study is simpler compared with other studies, such as Yin et al. [48], with four inputs, and Lawal et al. [42], with six inputs. It is concluded that our study is superior to the available studies and techniques in the literature, and it can be utilized by engineers and researchers.

5. Limitations and Future Studies

The proposed model in this work is based on an analysis of a database of 154 data samples gathered from a single tunnel in China. As a result, the proposed model is applicable to the same or similar geological and blasting pattern conditions. If other researchers want to adopt the proposed model, the range of input parameters is sensitive to the PPV results. The similar approach described in this study can be expanded upon using a larger number of data samples compiled from other tunnel sites (obviously with various geological conditions) to develop a more generalized model. In addition, some other optimized hybrid models, such as neuro-fuzzy-based, fuzzy-based, SVM-based, and random forest-based, can also be applied to examine their capabilities and power in increasing the performance of PPV prediction compared with the models proposed in this study.

6. Summary and Conclusions

The idea of proposing an intelligence model that can enjoy the advantages of at least two models was performed in this study to predict PPV values induced by blasting events in a tunnel. To do this, a total of 154 data samples were used in the modeling. According to previous studies, an equation was proposed empirically for the prediction of PPV using two model predictors (*DI* and *C*). Then, two neuro-based models were modeled in detail for the same aim (using *DI* and *C* values). The following concluding remarks can be derived from this study:

(1) The prediction level of the proposed empirical model in predicting PPV values is not strong enough ($R^2 = 0.615$). However, the same can be used by mining and civil engineers to temporarily predict PPV values or to have an approximate determination of the blast safety zone.

(2) Using the same input variables, neuro-based metaheuristic models received a higher performance degree to predict PPV induced by tunnel blasting. The neuro-swarm model was able to increase the performance capacity of the empirical equation from $R^2 = 0.615$ to $R^2 = 0.904$ and $R^2 = 0.913$ for training and testing, respectively. Similarly, $R^2 = 0.896$ and 0.822 were obtained for training and testing parts of the developed neuro-imperialism model, respectively.

(3) It was observed that both PSO and ICA algorithms are strong enough to optimize the weights and biases of the ANN model (the base model). However, the highest capacity for predicting PPV values can be obtained using the PSO algorithm in a form of the neuro-swarm model.

Author Contributions: Conceptualization, D.J.A., B.H., E.T.M.; methodology, D.J.A., B.H.; software, D.J.A., B.H.; validation, D.J.A., B.H.; formal analysis, D.J.A., B.H.; data curation, F.Y.; writing—original draft preparation, D.J.A., B.H., E.T.M., Y.X.Z., S.H.L., F.Y.; writing—review and editing, D.J.A., B.H., E.T.M., Y.X.Z., S.H.L., F.Y.; supervision, D.J.A., E.T.M., Y.X.Z., S.H.L. All authors have read and agreed to the published version of the manuscript.

Funding: This research received no external funding.

Data Availability Statement: The data is available upon request.

Acknowledgments: The authors of this study wish to express their appreciation to the University of Malaya for supporting this study and making it possible.

Conflicts of Interest: The authors declare no conflict of interest.

References

1. Siskind, D.E.; Stagg, M.S.; Kopp, J.W.; Dowding, C.H. *Structure Response and Damage Produced by Ground Vibration from Surface Mine Blasting*; Technical Report; U.S. Department of the Interior: Washington, DC, USA; United States Bureau of Mines: Washington, DC, USA, 1980.
2. Bhandari, S. *Engineering Rock Blasting Operations*; AA Balkema: Rotterdam, The Netherlands, 1997.
3. Davies, B.; Farmer, I.; Attewell, P. Ground vibration from shallow sub-surface blasts. *Engineer* **1964**, *217*, 553–559.
4. Roy, P. Putting ground vibration predictions into practice. *Colliery Guard.* **1993**, *241*, 63–67.
5. Singh, T.N.; Singh, V. An intelligent approach to prediction and control ground vibration in mines. *Geotech. Geol. Eng.* **2005**, *23*, 249–262. [CrossRef]
6. *IS-6922*; Criteria for Safety and Design of Structures Subjected to under Ground Blast. Bureau of Indian Standards: New Delhi, India, 1973.

7. Chen, W.; Hasanipanah, M.; Nikafshan Rad, H.; Jahed Armaghani, D.; Tahir, M. A new design of evolutionary hybrid optimization of SVR model in predicting the blast-induced ground vibration. *Eng. Comput.* **2021**, *37*, 1455–1471. [CrossRef]
8. Armaghani, D.; Momeni, E.; Abad, S. Feasibility of ANFIS model for prediction of ground vibrations resulting from quarry blasting. *Environ. Earth Sci.* **2015**, *74*, 2845–2860. [CrossRef]
9. Zhou, J.; Asteris, P.G.; Armaghani, D.J.; Pham, B.T. Prediction of ground vibration induced by blasting operations through the use of the Bayesian Network and random forest models. *Soil Dyn. Earthq. Eng.* **2020**, *139*, 106390. [CrossRef]
10. Duvall, W.; Petkof, B. *Spherical Propagation of Explosion-Generated Strain Pulses in Rock*; Bureau of Mines: Washington, DC, USA, 1958.
11. Kostić, S.; Vasović, N.; Franović, I.; Samčović, A.; Todorović, K. Assessment of blast induced ground vibrations by artificial neural network. In Proceedings of the 12th Symposium on Neural Network Applications in Electrical Engineering (NEUREL), Belgrade, Serbia, 25–27 November 2014; pp. 55–60. [CrossRef]
12. Hasanipanah, M.; Faradonbeh, R.S.; Amnieh, H.B.; Armaghani, D.J.; Monjezi, M. Forecasting blast-induced ground vibration developing a CART model. *Eng. Comput.* **2017**, *33*, 307–316. [CrossRef]
13. Ram Chandar, K.; Sastry, V.R.; Hegde, C.; Shreedharan, S. Prediction of peak particle velocity using multi regression analysis: Case studies. *Geomech. Geoengin.* **2017**, *12*, 207–214. [CrossRef]
14. Khandelwal, M.; Singh, T.N. Prediction of blast-induced ground vibration using artificial neural network. *Int. J. Rock Mech. Min. Sci.* **2013**, *46*, 1214–1222. [CrossRef]
15. Khandelwal, M.; Singh, T.N. Prediction of blast induced ground vibrations and frequency in opencast mine: A neural network approach. *J. Sound Vib.* **2006**, *289*, 711–725. [CrossRef]
16. Xue, X.; Yang, X. Predicting blast-induced ground vibration using general regression neural network. *J. Vib. Control.* **2014**, *20*, 1512–1519. [CrossRef]
17. Parida, A.; Mishra, M.K. Blast Vibration Analysis by Different Predictor Approaches-A Comparison. *Procedia Earth Planet. Sci.* **2015**, *11*, 337–345. [CrossRef]
18. Lawal, A.I.; Idris, M.A. An artificial neural network-based mathematical model for the prediction of blast-induced ground vibrations. *Int. J. Environ. Stud.* **2020**, *77*, 318–334. [CrossRef]
19. Asteris, P.G.; Rizal, F.I.M.; Koopialipoor, M.; Roussis, P.C.; Ferentinou, M.; Armaghani, D.J.; Gordan, B. Slope Stability Classification under Seismic Conditions Using Several Tree-Based Intelligent Techniques. *Appl. Sci.* **2022**, *12*, 1753. [CrossRef]
20. Mahmood, W.; Mohammed, A.S.; Asteris, P.G.; Kurda, R.; Armaghani, D.J. Modeling Flexural and Compressive Strengths Behaviour of Cement-Grouted Sands Modified with Water Reducer Polymer. *Appl. Sci.* **2022**, *12*, 1016. [CrossRef]
21. Chen, L.; Asteris, P.G.; Tsoukalas, M.Z.; Armaghani, D.J.; Ulrikh, D.V.; Yari, M. Forecast of Airblast Vibrations Induced by Blasting Using Support Vector Regression Optimized by the Grasshopper Optimization (SVR-GO) Technique. *Appl. Sci.* **2022**, *12*, 9805. [CrossRef]
22. Skentou, A.D.; Bardhan, A.; Mamou, A.; Lemonis, M.E.; Kumar, G.; Samui, P.; Armaghani, D.J.; Asteris, P.G. Closed-Form Equation for Estimating Unconfined Compressive Strength of Granite from Three Non-destructive Tests Using Soft Computing Models. *Rock Mech. Rock Eng.* **2022**. [CrossRef]
23. Koopialipoor, M.; Asteris, P.G.; Mohammed, A.S.; Alexakis, D.E.; Mamou, A.; Armaghani, D.J. Introducing stacking machine learning approaches for the prediction of rock deformation. *Transp. Geotech.* **2022**, *34*, 100756. [CrossRef]
24. Yang, H.; Song, K.; Zhou, J. Automated Recognition Model of Geomechanical Information Based on Operational Data of Tunneling Boring Machines. *Rock Mech. Rock Eng.* **2022**, *55*, 1499–1516. [CrossRef]
25. Yang, H.; Wang, Z.; Song, K. A new hybrid grey wolf optimizer-feature weighted-multiple kernel-support vector regression technique to predict TBM performance. *Eng. Comput.* **2020**, *38*, 2469–2485. [CrossRef]
26. Yang, H.; Liu, J.; Liu, B. Investigation on the cracking character of jointed rock mass beneath TBM disc cutter. *Rock Mech. Rock Eng.* **2018**, *51*, 1263–1277. [CrossRef]
27. Shan, F.; He, X.; Armaghani, D.J.; Zhang, P.; Sheng, D. Success and challenges in predicting TBM penetration rate using recurrent neural networks. *Tunn. Undergr. Space Technol.* **2022**, *130*, 104728. [CrossRef]
28. Cavaleri, L.; Barkhordari, M.S.; Repapis, C.C.; Armaghani, D.J.; Ulrikh, D.V.; Asteris, P.G. Convolution-based ensemble learning algorithms to estimate the bond strength of the corroded reinforced concrete. *Constr. Build. Mater.* **2022**, *359*, 129504. [CrossRef]
29. Indraratna, B.; Armaghani, D.J.; Correia, A.G.; Hunt, H.; Ngo, T. Prediction of resilient modulus of ballast under cyclic loading using machine learning techniques. *Transp. Geotech.* **2022**, *38*, 100895. [CrossRef]
30. Khanmohammadi, M.; Armaghani, D.J.; Sabri Sabri, M.M. Prediction and Optimization of Pile Bearing Capacity Considering Effects of Time. *Mathematics* **2022**, *10*, 3563. [CrossRef]
31. Jolfaei, S.; Lakirouhani, A. Sensitivity Analysis of Effective Parameters in Borehole Failure, Using Neural Network. *Adv. Civ. Eng.* **2022**, *2022*, 4958004. [CrossRef]
32. Ikram, R.M.A.; Dai, H.-L.; Ewees, A.A.; Shiri, J.; Kisi, O.; Zounemat-Kermani, M. Application of improved version of multi verse optimizer algorithm for modeling solar radiation. *Energy Rep.* **2022**, *8*, 12063–12080. [CrossRef]
33. Adnan, R.M.; Ewees, A.A.; Parmar, K.S.; Yaseen, Z.M.; Shahid, S.; Kisi, O. The viability of extended marine predators algorithm-based artificial neural networks for streamflow prediction. *Appl. Soft Comput.* **2022**, *131*, 109739. [CrossRef]
34. Fakharian, P.; Rezazadeh Eidgahee, D.; Akbari, M.; Jahangir, H.; Ali Taeb, A. Compressive strength prediction of hollow concrete masonry blocks using artificial intelligence algorithms. *Structures* **2023**, *47*, 1790–1802. [CrossRef]

35. Rezazadeh Eidgahee, D.; Jahangir, H.; Solatifar, N.; Fakharian, P.; Rezaeemanesh, M. Data-driven estimation models of asphalt mixtures dynamic modulus using ANN, GP and combinatorial GMDH approaches. *Neural Comput. Appl.* **2022**, *34*, 17289–17314. [CrossRef]
36. Jahangir, H.; Nikkhah, Z.; Rezazadeh Eidgahee, D.; Esfahani, M.R. Performance Based Review and Fine-Tuning of TRM-Concrete Bond Strength Existing Models. *J. Soft Comput. Civ. Eng.* **2022**, *7*, 43–55.
37. Alzubi, Y.; Al Adwan, J.; Khatatbeh, A.; Al-kharabsheh, B. Parametric Assessment of Concrete Constituent Materials Using Machine Learning Techniques. *J. Soft Comput. Civ. Eng.* **2022**, *6*, 39–62.
38. Dindarloo, S.R. Prediction of blast-induced ground vibrations via genetic programming. *Int. J. Min. Sci. Technol.* **2015**, *25*, 1011–1015. [CrossRef]
39. Rana, A.; Bhagat, N.K.; Jadaun, G.P.; Rukhaiyar, S.; Pain, A.; Singh, P.K. Predicting Blast-Induced Ground Vibrations in Some Indian Tunnels: A Comparison of Decision Tree, Artificial Neural Network and Multivariate Regression Methods. *Min. Metall. Explor.* **2020**, *37*, 1039–1053. [CrossRef]
40. Faradonbeh, R.S.; Armaghani, D.J.; Monjezi, M.; Mohamad, E.T. Genetic programming and gene expression programming for flyrock assessment due to mine blasting. *Int. J. Rock Mech. Min. Sci.* **2016**, *88*, 254–264. [CrossRef]
41. Monjezi, M.; Ghafurikalajahi, M.; Bahrami, A. Prediction of blast-induced ground vibration using artificial neural networks. *Tunn. Undergr. Space Technol.* **2011**, *26*, 46–50. [CrossRef]
42. Lawal, A.I.; Kwon, S.; Kim, G.Y. Prediction of the blast-induced ground vibration in tunnel blasting using ANN, moth-flame optimized ANN, and gene expression programming. *Acta Geophys.* **2021**, *69*, 161–174. [CrossRef]
43. Jelušič, P.; Ivanič, A.; Lubej, S. Prediction of blast-induced ground vibration using an adaptive network-based fuzzy inference system. *Appl. Sci.* **2021**, *11*, 203. [CrossRef]
44. Hasanipanah, M.; Golzar, S.B.; Larki, I.A.; Maryaki, M.Y.; Ghahremanians, T. Estimation of blast-induced ground vibration through a soft computing framework. *Eng. Comput.* **2017**, *33*, 951–959. [CrossRef]
45. Li, D.; Yan, J.; Zhang, L. Prediction of blast-induced ground vibration using support vector machine by tunnel excavation. *Appl. Mech. Mater.* **2012**, *170–173*, 1414–1418. [CrossRef]
46. Mohamadnejad, M.; Gholami, R.; Ataei, M. Comparison of intelligence science techniques and empirical methods for prediction of blasting vibrations. *Tunn. Undergr. Space Technol.* **2012**, *28*, 238–244. [CrossRef]
47. Hasanipanah, M.; Monjezi, M.; Shahnazar, A.; Armaghani, D.J.; Farazmand, A. Feasibility of indirect determination of blast induced ground vibration based on support vector machine. *Measurement* **2015**, *75*, 289–297. [CrossRef]
48. Yin, Z.; Wang, D.; Gao, Z.; Li, S. Prediction and Analysis of Blast-Induced Vibration for Urban Shallow Buried Tunnel Using Various Types of Artificial Neural Networks. In Proceedings of the 8th International Conference on Intelligent Computation Technology and Automation, Nanchang, China, 14–15 June 2015; Volume 3, pp. 642–646. [CrossRef]
49. Abbaszadeh Shahri, A.; Asheghi, R. Optimized developed artificial neural network-based models to predict the blast-induced ground vibration. *Innov. Infrastruct. Solut.* **2018**, *3*, 34. [CrossRef]
50. Rajabi, A.M.; Vafaee, A. Prediction of blast-induced ground vibration using empirical models and artificial neural network (Bakhtiari Dam access tunnel, as a case study). *J. Vib. Control.* **2020**, *26*, 520–531. [CrossRef]
51. Wang, X.; Tang, Z.; Tamura, H.; Ishii, M.; Sun, W.D. An improved backpropagation algorithm to avoid the local minima problem. *Neurocomputing* **2004**, *56*, 455–460. [CrossRef]
52. Momeni, E.; Nazir, R.; Armaghani, D.J.; Maizir, H. Prediction of pile bearing capacity using a hybrid genetic algorithm-based ANN. *Measurement* **2014**, *57*, 122–131. [CrossRef]
53. Momeni, E.; Yarivand, A.; Dowlatshahi, M.B.; Armaghani, D.J. An Efficient Optimal Neural Network Based on Gravitational Search Algorithm in Predicting the Deformation of Geogrid-Reinforced Soil Structures. *Transp. Geotech.* **2020**, *26*, 100446. [CrossRef]
54. McCulloch, W.S.; Pitts, W. A logical calculus of the ideas immanent in nervous activity. *Bull. Math. Biophys.* **1943**, *5*, 115–133. [CrossRef]
55. Zhang, G.; Patuwo, B.E.; Hu, M.Y. Forecasting with artificial neural networks: The state of the art. *Int. J. Forecast.* **1998**, *14*, 35–62. [CrossRef]
56. Ch, S.; Mathur, S. Particle swarm optimization trained neural network for aquifer parameter estimation. *KSCE J. Civ. Eng.* **2012**, *16*, 298–307. [CrossRef]
57. Armaghani, D.J.; Mohamad, E.T.; Narayanasamy, M.S.; Narita, N.; Yagiz, S. Development of hybrid intelligent models for predicting TBM penetration rate in hard rock condition. *Tunn. Undergr. Space Technol.* **2017**, *63*, 29–43. [CrossRef]
58. Kennedy, J.; Eberhart, R.C. A discrete binary version of the particle swarm algorithm. In Proceedings of the IEEE International Conference on Systems, Man, and Cybernetics. Computational Cybernetics and Simulation, Orlando, FL, USA, 12–15 October 1997; IEEE: Piscataway, NJ, USA, 1997; pp. 4104–4108.
59. Hajihassani, M.; Jahed Armaghani, D.; Kalatehjari, R. Applications of Particle Swarm Optimization in Geotechnical Engineering: A Comprehensive Review. *Geotech. Geol. Eng.* **2018**, *36*, 705–722. [CrossRef]
60. Atashpaz-Gargari, E.; Lucas, C. Imperialist competitive algorithm: An algorithm for optimization inspired by imperialistic competition. In Proceedings of the 2007 IEEE Congress on Evolutionary Computation, Singapore, 25–28 September 2007; IEEE: Piscataway, NJ, USA, 2007; pp. 4661–4667.

61. Taghavifar, H.; Mardani, A.; Taghavifar, L. A hybridized artificial neural network and imperialist competitive algorithm optimization approach for prediction of soil compaction in soil bin facility. *Meas. J. Int. Meas. Confed.* **2013**, *46*, 2288–2299. [CrossRef]
62. Bashir, Z.A.; El-Hawary, M.E. Applying wavelets to short-term load forecasting using PSO-based neural networks. *IEEE Trans. Power Syst.* **2009**, *24*, 20–27. [CrossRef]
63. Liou, S.W.; Wang, C.M.; Huang, Y.F. Integrative discovery of multifaceted sequence patterns by frame-relayed search and hybrid PSO-ANN. *J. Univers. Comput. Sci.* **2009**, *15*, 742–764. [CrossRef]
64. Mohammed, A.; Kurda, R.; Armaghani, D.J.; Hasanipanah, M. Prediction of compressive strength of concrete modified with fly ash: Applications of neuro-swarm and neuro-imperialism models. *Comput. Concr.* **2021**, *27*, 489–512.
65. Al-Bared, M.A.M.; Mustaffa, Z.; Armaghani, D.J.; Marto, A.; Yunus, N.Z.M.; Hasanipanah, M. Application of hybrid intelligent systems in predicting the unconfined compressive strength of clay material mixed with recycled additive. *Transp. Geotech.* **2021**, *30*, 100627. [CrossRef]
66. Khandelwal, M.; Lalit Kumar, D.; Yellishetty, M. Application of soft computing to predict blast-induced ground vibration. *Eng. Comput.* **2011**, *27*, 117–125. [CrossRef]
67. Iphar, M.; Yavuz, M.; Ak, H. Prediction of ground vibrations resulting from the blasting operations in an open-pit mine by adaptive neuro-fuzzy inference system. *Environ. Geol.* **2008**, *56*, 97–107. [CrossRef]
68. Dowding, C.H. Suggested method for blast vibration monitoring. In *International Journal of Rock Mechanics and Mining Sciences & Geomechanics Abstracts*; Elsevier: Amsterdam, The Netherlands, 1992; Volume 29, pp. 145–156.
69. Paji, M.K.; Gordan, B.; Biklaryan, M.; Armaghani, D.J.; Zhou, J.; Jamshidi, M. Neuro-swarm and Neuro-imperialism Techniques to Investigate the Compressive Strength of Concrete Constructed by Freshwater and Magnetic Salty Water. *Measurement* **2021**, *182*, 109720. [CrossRef]
70. Ikram, R.M.A.; Dai, H.-L.; Al-Bahrani, M.; Mamlooki, M. Prediction of the FRP Reinforced Concrete Beam shear capacity by using ELM-CRFOA. *Measurement* **2022**, *205*, 112230. [CrossRef]
71. Lapedes, A.; Farber, R. How Neural Nets Work. In Proceedings of the 1987 International Conference on Neural Information Processing Systems, Denver, CO, USA, 8–12 November 1987.
72. Hecht-Nielsen, R. Kolmogorov's mapping neural network existence theorem. In Proceedings of the International Conference on Neural Networks, San Diego, CA, USA, 21–24 June 1987; IEEE Press: New York, NY, USA, 1987; Volume 3, pp. 11–13.
73. Ebrahimi, E.; Monjezi, M.; Khalesi, M.R.; Armaghani, D.J. Prediction and optimization of back-break and rock fragmentation using an artificial neural network and a bee colony algorithm. *Bull. Eng. Geol. Environ.* **2016**, *75*, 27–36. [CrossRef]
74. Armaghani, D.J.; Hajihassani, M.; Mohamad, E.T.; Marto, A.; Noorani, S.A. Blasting-induced flyrock and ground vibration prediction through an expert artificial neural network based on particle swarm optimization. *Arab. J. Geosci.* **2014**, *7*, 5383–5396. [CrossRef]
75. Eberhart, R.; Kennedy, J. A new optimizer using particle swarm theory. In *MHS'95, Proceedings of the Sixth International Symposium on Micro Machine and Human Science, Nagoya, Japan, 4–6 October 1995*; IEEE: Piscataway, NJ, USA, 1995; pp. 39–43.

Disclaimer/Publisher's Note: The statements, opinions and data contained in all publications are solely those of the individual author(s) and contributor(s) and not of MDPI and/or the editor(s). MDPI and/or the editor(s) disclaim responsibility for any injury to people or property resulting from any ideas, methods, instructions or products referred to in the content.

Article

Tailings Pond Classification Based on Satellite Images and Machine Learning: An Exploration of Microsoft ML.Net

Haoxuan Yu and Izni Zahidi *

Civil Engineering Discipline, School of Engineering, Malaysia Campus, Monash University, Bandar Sunway 47500, Malaysia
* Correspondence: izni.mohdzahidi@monash.edu

Abstract: Mine pollution from mining activities is often widely recognised as a serious threat to public health, with mine solid waste causing problems such as tailings pond accumulation, which is considered the biggest hidden danger. The construction of tailings ponds not only causes land occupation and vegetation damage but also brings about potential environmental pollution, such as water and dust pollution, posing a health risk to nearby residents. If remote sensing images and machine learning techniques could be used to determine whether a tailings pond might have potential pollution and safety hazards, mainly monitoring tailings ponds that may have potential hazards, it would save a lot of effort in tailings ponds monitoring. Therefore, based on this background, this paper proposes to classify tailings ponds into two categories according to whether they are potentially risky or generally safe and to classify tailings ponds with remote sensing satellite images of tailings ponds using the DDN + ResNet-50 machine learning model based on ML.Net developed by Microsoft. In the discussion section, the paper introduces the environmental hazards of mine pollution and proposes the concept of "Healthy Mine" to provide development directions for mining companies and solutions to mine pollution and public health crises. Finally, we claim this paper serves as a guide to begin a conversation and to encourage experts, researchers and scholars to engage in the research field of mine solid waste pollution monitoring, assessment and treatment.

Keywords: mine geology; computational intelligence; remote sensing; environment management

MSC: 68T20

Citation: Yu, H.; Zahidi, I. Tailings Pond Classification Based on Satellite Images and Machine Learning: An Exploration of Microsoft ML.Net. *Mathematics* 2023, *11*, 517. https://doi.org/10.3390/math11030517

Academic Editors: Danial Jahed Armaghani, Hadi Khabbaz, Manoj Khandelwal, Niaz Muhammad Shahani and Ramesh Murlidhar Bhatawdekar

Received: 18 November 2022
Revised: 4 January 2023
Accepted: 17 January 2023
Published: 18 January 2023

Copyright: © 2023 by the authors. Licensee MDPI, Basel, Switzerland. This article is an open access article distributed under the terms and conditions of the Creative Commons Attribution (CC BY) license (https://creativecommons.org/licenses/by/4.0/).

1. Introduction

1.1. Research Background

With the increasing frequency of mining activities worldwide, mine discharge brings plenty of environmental problems. Among these, mine solid waste discharge is considered one of the most serious environmental problems, and as mine solid waste has a low reuse rate compared to other solid waste, tailings ponds generally need to be built to stockpile mine solid waste [1,2].

There is no doubt that the construction of tailings ponds, while allowing for the storage of mine solid waste, is not a good thing for the environment and human beings: the construction of tailings ponds takes up a lot of land and causes damage to vegetation cover, while the leachate from the ponds can have a serious negative impact on the environment and public health. There are many cases (as shown in Table 1) which confirm this.

In 2003, Agrawal, A. et al. [3] introduced the world to the environmental impact and damage caused by solid waste discharge from the non-ferrous metal industry in India, such as leachate pollution; their research showed that metal recycling of solid waste from the non-ferrous metals industry would be effective in mitigating environmental pollution, and Shengo's [4] review endorsed this practice of recovering metal resources from solid waste. In 2016, Liu, Y. et al. [5] suggested that solid waste discharges can lead to damage to the surface landscape, for example, tailings pond stockpiles, which not only occupy surface space but also bring a major safety hazard that would result in serious human casualties at the mine site in the event of a tailings pond failure; in the same year, 2016, Asif, Z. and Chen, Z. [6] argued that the land occupation of tailings pond stockpiles is indeed a nuisance, and therefore they advocated the use of mine solid waste for land reclamation.

Table 1. Research cases on the mine solid waste pollution.

Pollution Issue	Research Cases	Research Area	Research Purpose	Research Findings
Mine Solid Waste Pollution (Tailings Ponds)	Agrawal, A. et al., 2004 [3]	India: Non-ferrous metals Industry	To study solid waste pollution and management in the non-ferrous metals industry in India.	The results showed that solid waste polluted surface water as well as groundwater, primarily through leachate, thus affecting farmland, rivers and public health. Additionally, the authors advocated that mines should commit to metal recycling of non-ferrous solid waste, which would mitigate solid waste pollution.
	Liu, Y. et al., 2016 [5]	China: Mining Industry	To study the pollution of industrial solid waste in general (mining solid waste in particular) and to make recommendations related to solid waste management based on the current state of the resource and environmental development in China.	The authors suggested that the problem of land occupation by solid waste (tailings pond stockpiling) from mines is very serious, especially in China; at the same time, tailings ponds are a major safety hazard that would result in serious human casualties at the mine site in the event of a tailings pond failure.
	Asif, Z. et al., 2016 [6]	North America: Mining Industry	To discuss the challenges of environmental management, particularly solid waste management, in the North American mining industry.	The author highlighted the hazards of land occupation from tailings pond accumulation, and the author recommended the use of non-hazardous mine solid waste for land reclamation.
	Shengo, L. M. 2021 [4]	Democratic Republic of the Congo: Mining Industry	In order to explore the environmental issues related to the management of mineral waste in the mining industry in the Democratic Republic of the Congo.	The recycling and reuse of non-ferrous solid waste were very important, not only to mitigate the problem of solid waste pollution but also to bring potential resource value.

In addition to the potential environmental pollution and health risks associated with tailings ponds, they are also a potential source of danger and can lead to potential safety incidents. If a tailings pond were to fail, it would be a huge disaster for the environment and the people living in the vicinity of the mine. In Brazil, serious tailings pond failures occurred in 2015 and 2019 [7], causing massive damage to homes and vehicles. In China, a tailings pond failure accident occurred in 2008 in Xiangfen Country, Shanxi, resulting in a large number of casualties and environmental damage [8,9].

Since 2010, the safety and environmental pollution hazards of tailings ponds have received increasing attention from researchers [10,11]. Based on the Google Scholar database (https://scholar.google.com; accessed on 14 November 2022), using "tailings ponds and safety" and "tailings ponds and environment" as the keywords, the number of studies related to both keywords for each three-year period from 2010 to 2020 was found, as shown in Figure 1. The number of related literature results in the last 10 years clearly has an upward trend, showing that the safety and environmental pollution hazards of tailings ponds are receiving the public's increasing attention.

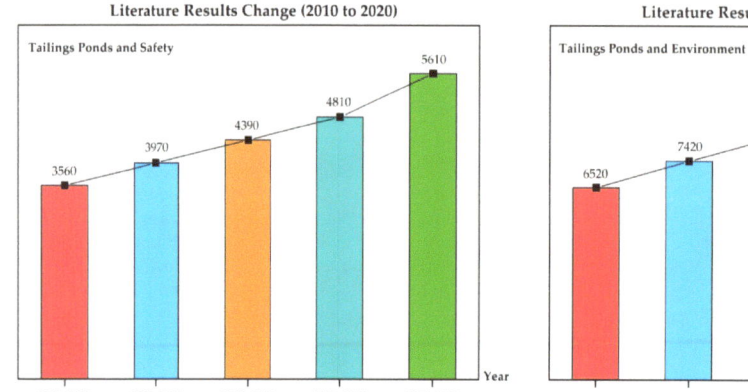

Figure 1. Literature results change of keywords "tailings ponds and safety" and "tailings ponds and environment".

1.2. Research Purpose and Significance

Monitoring and management of tailings ponds are particularly important in order to avoid environmental pollution and safety accidents in tailings ponds [12]. However, monitoring tailings ponds is often very time-consuming and labour-intensive [13]; if remote sensing images and machine learning could be used to determine whether a tailings pond might have potential pollution and safety hazards and then mainly monitoring tailings ponds that may have potential hazards, it would save a lot of effort in tailings ponds monitoring [14,15].

As a result, this paper divides tailings ponds into two categories according to whether they are potentially risky: 1# Tailings Pond, which has potential environmental and safety hazards, and 2# Tailings Pond which has no obvious potential environmental and safety hazards. Combining the remote sensing images (satellite maps) with the results of the field surveys (as shown in Figure 2): it defines that 1# Tailings Pond is an unclosed tailings pond that has significant surface water leaching, thus posing a potential contamination and safety hazard (as shown in Figure 2A); it defines that 2# Tailings Pond is generally a closed (almost closed) tailings pond or a dry stockpile pond with no significant surface water leaching, which may show signs of land reclamation and can generally be considered to have no obvious potential environmental and safety hazards (as shown in Figure 2B).

Based on the features of the two categories of tailings ponds, this paper planned to implement the image identification and classification function of tailings ponds by building a machine learning model via ML.Net developed by Microsoft [16]. At the same time, this paper planned to explore the accuracy of the ML.Net machine learning framework and its machine learning model in classifying and identifying the two types of tailings ponds with different characteristics, providing a starting point for future remote sensing techniques to monitor tailings pond risk and pollution.

Figure 2. Examples: (**A**) 1# Tailings Pond; (**B**) 2# Tailings Pond. Satellite images from tianditu.gov.cn (accessed on 10 November 2022).

2. Materials and Methods

2.1. Machine Learning Model

The training environment used was local training on a computer using a CPU (Intel Core i7-9750H; Memory: 16 GB). Additionally, the study was carried out on Visual Studio 2022 Professional, based on ML.Net developed by Microsoft [17]:

ML.Net is a machine learning framework developed by Microsoft for the new ".Net" platform and provides a low-code development tool called "Model Builder", an intuitive graphical Visual Studio extension for generating, training and deploying custom machine learning models [18]. Therefore, for ".Net" platform developers, using the ML.Net machine learning framework is an excellent choice in terms of ease of use, performance and accuracy [19]. The ML.Net machine learning framework uses a DNN (Deep Neural Network) and Resnet 50 model (DNN + Resnet-50) to implement image classification functions so the study was based on DNN and the ResNet-50 model to categorise two types of tailings ponds with different features:

ResNet-50 is a residual network that uses a shortcut connection to connect the inputs directly to the outputs (as shown in Figure 3A), which effectively solves the problem of performance degradation due to the deepening of the network as the shortcut connection does not increase the amount of computation [20].

In essence, the idea of residual network learning can be understood as a block, which can be defined by Equation (1) [21], where y represents the output, $F(x, \{W_i\})$ represents the residual component and x represents the sample:

$$y = F(x, \{W_i\}) + x. \tag{1}$$

As a result, the ResNet-50 residual network is well suited for feature extraction of the data sets [22]. Additionally, regarding structure, the ResNet-50 network is divided into six parts, of which Stage 1 is the input module, consisting of Conv and Max Pool, Stage 2 to Stage 5 are the residual modules, containing both Conv Block and Identity Block, and Stage 6 is the output module [22,23]. The structure of ResNet-50 is shown in Figure 3B.

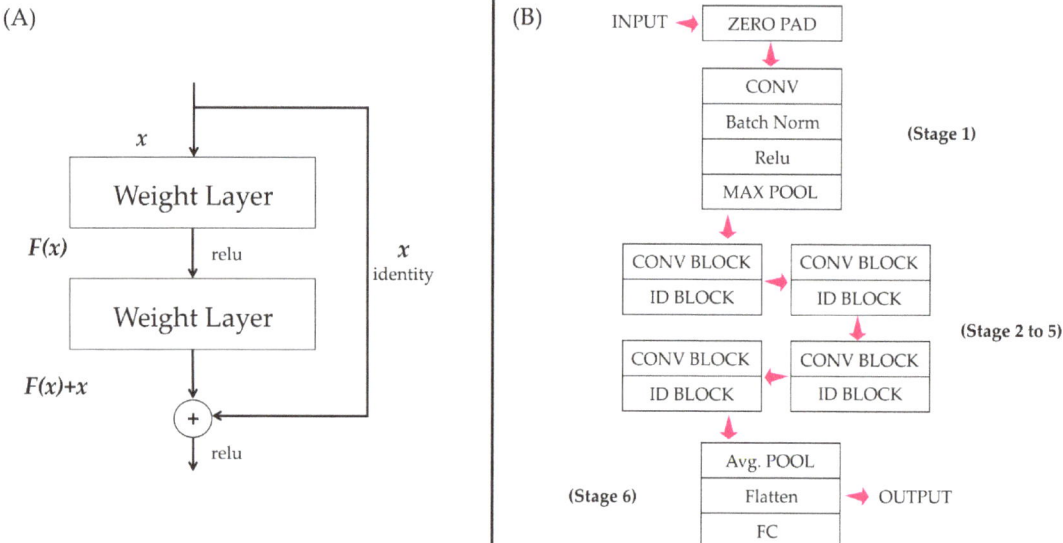

Figure 3. (**A**) The structure of the shortcut connection; (**B**) the structure of the ResNet-50 network.

2.2. Training Set and Test Set

The data chosen for the study were satellite images of tailings ponds within China from Geovis (http://www.geovis.com.cn/ (accessed on 10 November 2022) and Tianditu (https://www.tianditu.gov.cn/ (accessed on 10 November 2022), with a total of 30 sets of both the 1# tailings pond (15 sets) and the 2# tailings pond (15 sets). The two different categories of data in the training set have their own distinctive features: the data in the category 1# Tailings Pond are all unclosed tailings ponds, with significant surface water leaching on the satellite images; the data in the category 2# Tailings Pond are generally closed (or almost closed) tailings ponds or dry storage tailings ponds, with no significant surface water leaching on the satellite images and signs of land reclamation. For data set details, please refer to http://dx.doi.org/10.13140/RG.2.2.26494.87367 (accessed on 10 November 2022).

2.3. Validation Methods

To further validate the accuracy of the image recognition and classification function of the ML.NET machine learning framework [24,25], the cross-validation method was chosen to randomly disrupt the data from training sets and the test sets, re-train the new training sets with DDN + ResNet-50 machine learning framework, test with the new test sets and repeat another 19 times (total 20 times) to find the mean value of the accuracy as an estimate of the accuracy [26]. The entire study process is shown in Figure 4.

After training, the accuracy was tested with the test sets in the intuitive graphical Visual Studio extension module of ML.Net. If the model determines that a satellite image of a tailings pond has a greater than 50% probability of belonging to its original category, then the model is considered to have correctly identified and categorised the tailings pond for this time (as shown in Figure 5).

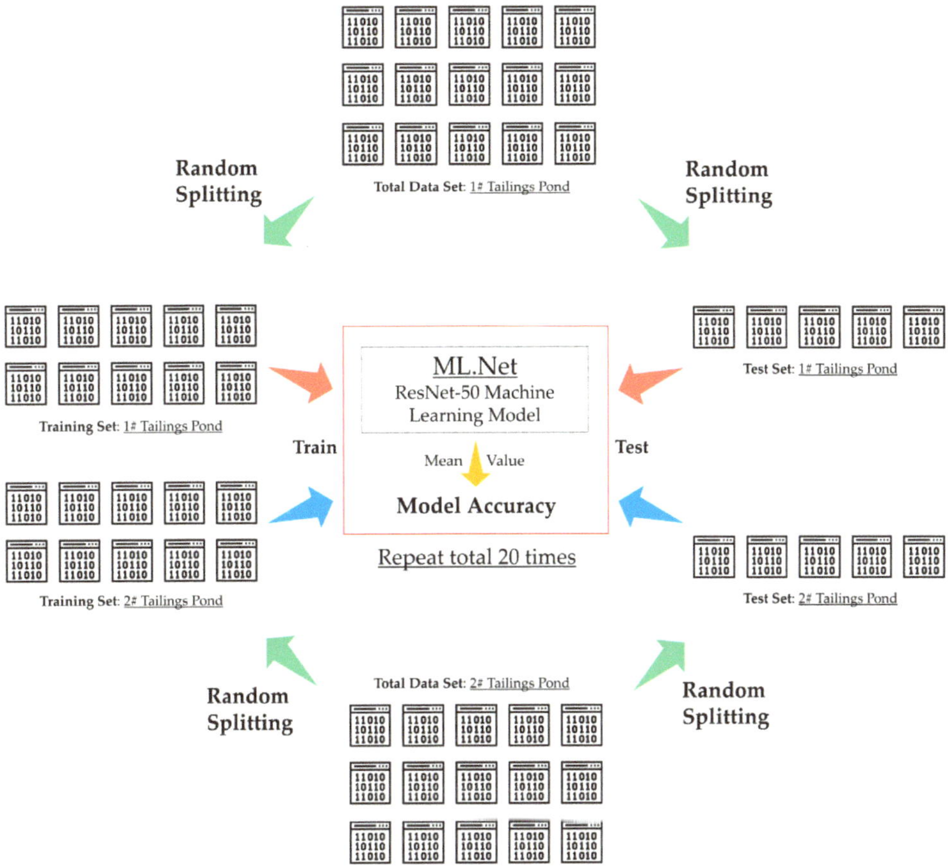

Figure 4. The cross-validation of the machine learning model.

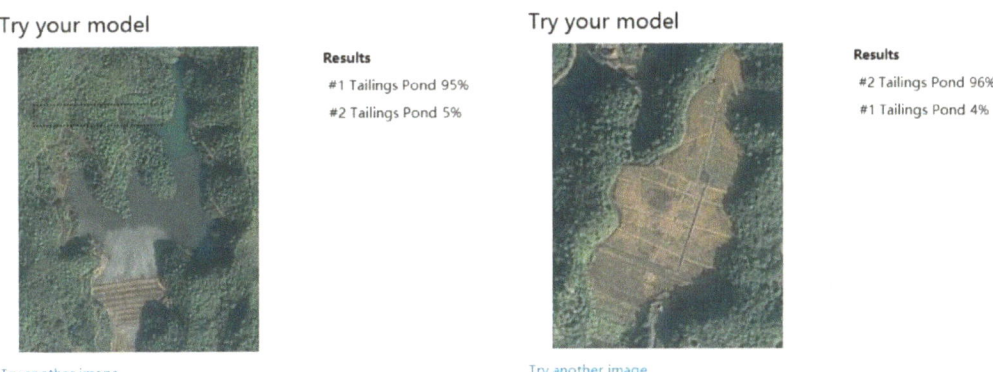

Figure 5. The intuitive graphical Visual Studio extension module of ML.Net. Satellite images from tianditu.gov.cn (accessed on 10 November 2022).

3. Results and Discussion

3.1. Test Accuracy

According to Figure 4, each dataset of the 1# Tailings Pond and 2# Tailings Pond was randomly divided into a training set (10 sets of data) and a test set (5 sets of data), respectively, and each training set was trained by the built DDN + ResNet-50 machine learning model. The model was then tested through the intuitive graphical Visual Studio extension module of ML.Net using the test set according to Figure 5. The whole process was repeated a total of 20 times.

After 20 times cross-validation, the DDN + ResNet-50 network model was found to perform well for the identification and classification of satellite images of tailings ponds, with an average test accuracy of 83.5%: 84% for the 1# Tailings Pond and 83% for the 2# Tailings Pond. The test accuracy data for the 20 times cross-validation are shown in Figure 6.

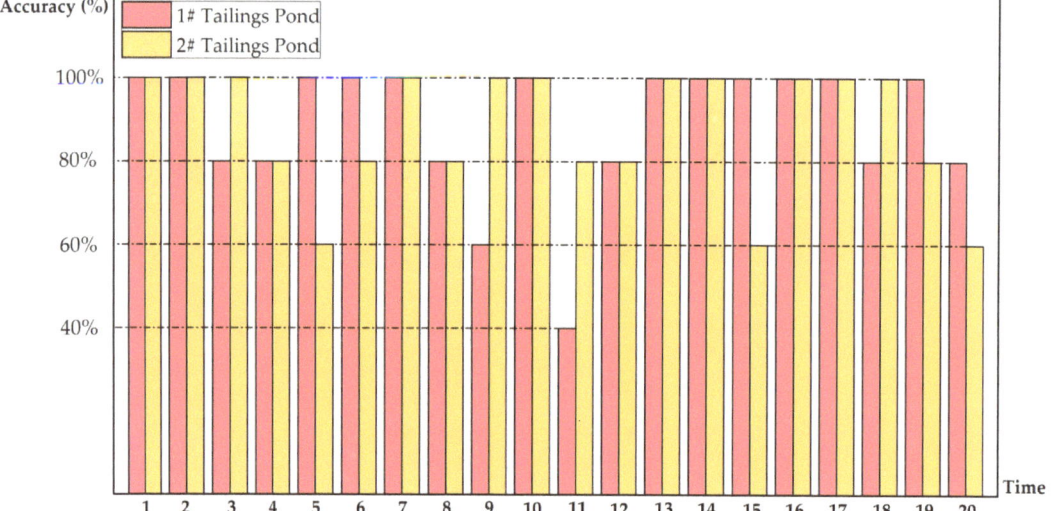

Figure 6. The results of the cross-validation.

3.2. Analysis

The results show that the test accuracy of identification and classification of satellite images of tailings ponds based on the DDN + ResNet-50 machine learning model can reach 83.5%; however, in the cross-validation, the identification accuracy of test sets under different training sets has a relatively large difference. For example, as shown in Figure 6: in the 1st, 2nd, 7th, 10th, 13th, 14th, 16th and 17th time of the cross-validation, the identification accuracy of both categories reached 100%; however, in the 4th, 8th, 11th and 20th time of the cross-validation, the identification accuracy for both categories was lower, with a low identification rate of 40% for the 1# Tailings Pond and a low identification rate of 60% for the 2# Tailings Pond.

This may occur because of the presence of data with insignificant features in the dataset, resulting in insufficient generalisation of the model [27]. For example, in Figure 7, Tailings Pond A below has no significant surface water leaching compared to Tailings Pond B, although it belongs to the category of the 1# Tailings Pond. However, cross-validation solved this problem well; as the number of cross-validation times increased, the test accuracy reached closer to the true value.

Figure 7. Tailings ponds in the datset. (**A**): Source from tianditu.gov.cn; (**B**) source from geovis.com.cn (accessed on 10 November 2022).

Therefore, if further validation and improvement of the accuracy of machine learning models are required, the following measures are worth considering.

- Using the cross-validation method, the total data set is split and combined into different training and testing sets, with the training set being used to train the model and the testing set being used to evaluate how well the model identifies and categorises, which further reflects the accuracy of the model [28]. S-fold cross-validation is a common form of cross-validation in which the total data set is randomly divided into S mutually exclusive subsets of equal size, and each time S-1 copies are randomly selected as the training set and the remaining 1 copy as the test set [29]. When the round is completed, S-1 copies are randomly selected again to train the data [30].
- Expanding the dataset to allow the model to be more aware of the features of the data in the training set can improve the accuracy of the model. Among the ways to expand the dataset may be finding more relevant data, as well as data augmentation [31,32].

3.3. Optimisation

In order to further validate the accuracy of the image recognition and classification functions of the ML.NET machine learning framework and to optimise the original method of cross-validation, in this part, the three-fold cross-validation method was chosen to be used by randomly dividing the total data set into three equally sized sets, randomly selecting two each time as the training set and the remaining one as the test set, and the cycle was repeated three times to determine the accuracy mean value as the accuracy estimate. The three-fold cross-validation method was also repeated three times by randomly disrupting the data inside the A/B/C/D/E/F sets three times, as shown in Figure 8.

After three times three-fold cross-validation, the DDN + ResNet-50 network model was still found to perform well for the identification and classification of satellite images of tailings ponds, with an average test accuracy of 87.8%: 88.9% for the 1# Tailings Pond and 86.7% for the 2# Tailings Pond. The test accuracy data for the three times three-fold cross-validation are shown in Figure 9.

We then explored further and improved the accuracy of the ML.NET machine learning framework and its DNN + Resnet-50 model for the identification and classification of tailings ponds by expanding the dataset (training set and test set). The data for the new dataset were satellite images of tailings ponds within China, Australia and Malaysia from Geovis (http://www.geovis.com.cn/ (accessed on 10 November 2022), Tianditu (https://www.tianditu.gov.cn/ (accessed on 10 November 2022) and Google Earth (https://earth.google.com/ (accessed on 10 November 2022), with a total of 42 sets of both the 1#

tailings pond (21 sets) and 2# tailings pond (21 sets). For data set details, please refer to http://dx.doi.org/10.13140/RG.2.2.27124.01928 (accessed on 10 November 2022).

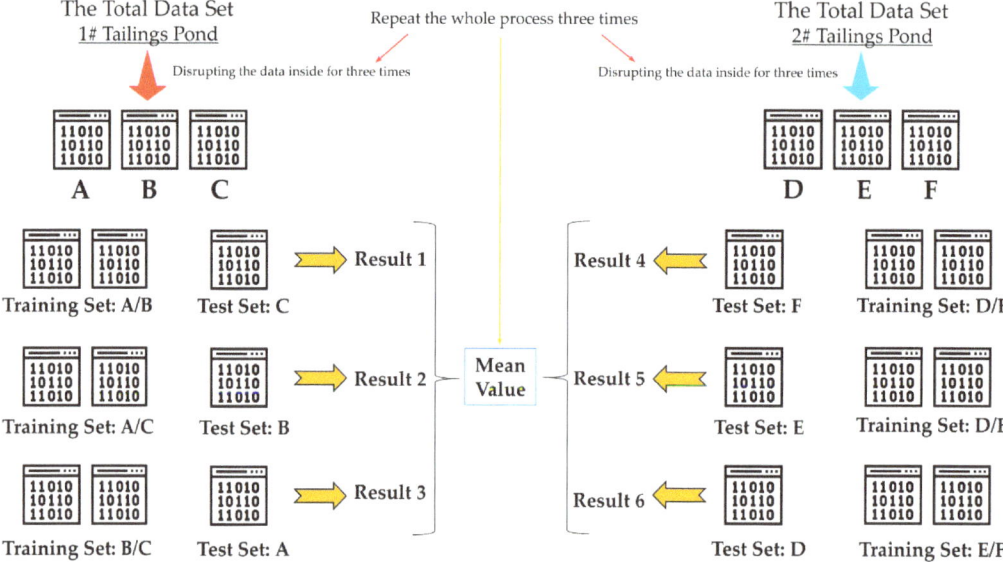

Figure 8. The 3-fold cross-validation schematic diagram.

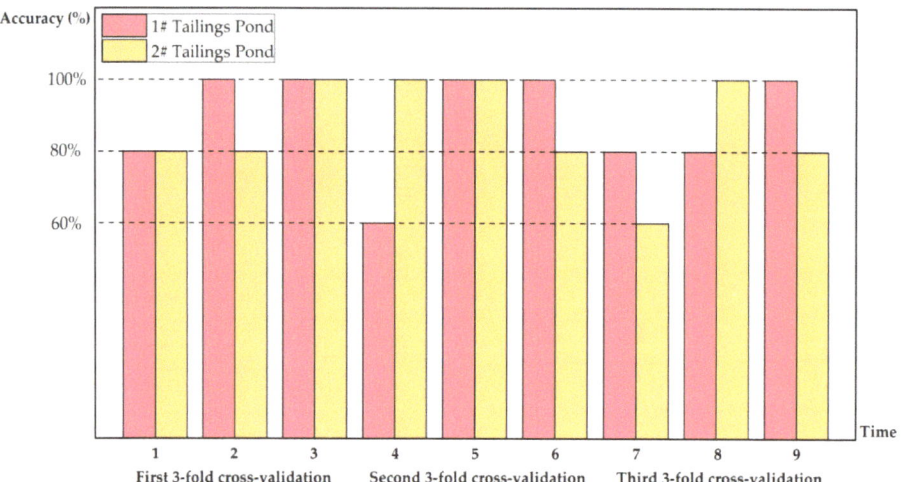

Figure 9. The results of the 3-fold cross-validation.

The new dataset likewise underwent three times three-fold cross-validation (as shown in Figure 8). The DDN + ResNet-50 network model was still found to perform well for the identification and classification of satellite images of tailings ponds, with an average test accuracy of 87.3%: 90.5% for the 1# Tailings Pond and 84.1% for the 2# Tailings Pond. The test accuracy data for the three times three-fold cross-validation are shown in Figure 10.

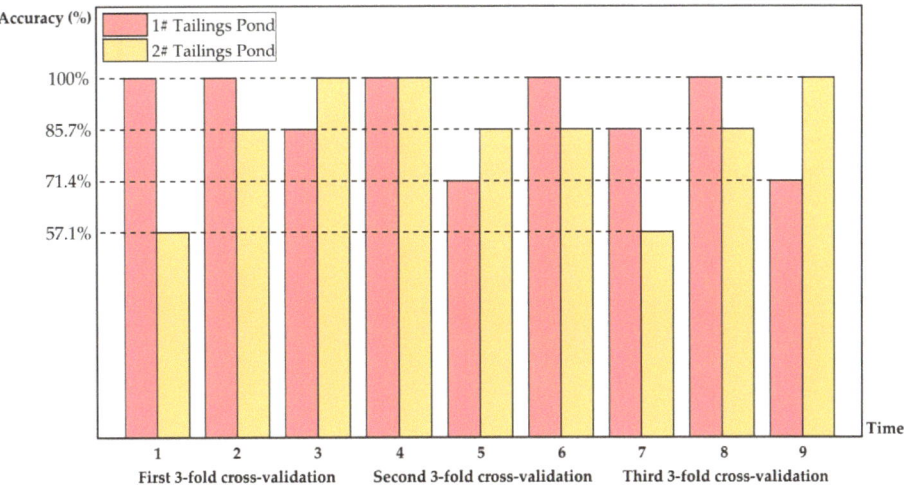

Figure 10. The results of the 3-fold cross-validation for the expanded dataset.

The results showed that the ML.Net machine learning framework and its DDN + ResNet-50 machine learning model performed very well in the recognition and classification of satellite images of tailings ponds, with accuracies above 80% for all three validations (including the validation after expanding the database). However, the identification accuracy for the 2# Tailings Ponds was slightly lower than that for the 1# Tailings Ponds in all three validations. This may be due to the fact that the 2# Tailings Pond is not well characterised, which is exactly the case: some 2# Tailings Ponds, which are about to be closed or have just been closed, are not very different from 1# Tailings Ponds; while some 2# Tailings Ponds, which has been closed for some time, generally already show signs of extensive land reclamation, which are all different. This problem may need to be solved in the future by other methods, but there is no doubt that ML.Net has done an excellent job of identifying and classifying tailings ponds.

4. Discussion: Research Implications and Other Types of Mine Pollution

The monitoring and management of tailings ponds are particularly important in order to avoid environmental pollution and safety accidents in tailings ponds. However, monitoring tailings ponds is often very time-consuming and labour-intensive. This paper explored the accuracy of the ML.Net machine learning framework and its machine learning model in classifying and identifying the two types of tailings ponds with different characteristics, providing a starting point for future remote sensing techniques to monitor tailings pond risk and pollution [33,34].

It is also important to introduce the public to the severity of the current worldwide mine pollution and its hazards to the environment and public health because, in addition to mine solid waste pollution, mine wastewater and mine dust are also serious threats to the environment and the health of residents [35,36]: Mine wastewater pollution causes serious environmental problems (e.g., heavy metal pollution) to rivers, agricultural soils, the surrounding environment and drinking water for people living nearby; mine dust pollution can affect the safety of mining production and can also have a negative impact on the health of miners, for example by causing them to suffer from occupational diseases such as pneumoconiosis [37].

With the introduction of "Sustainable Development" [38] and "One Health" [39], issues related to mine pollution, environmental damage and public health are receiving increasingly widespread attention worldwide that more and more people are becoming aware of the negative health effects of mine pollution and they are trying to take precautions, while researchers are noticing the ecological and public health risks posed by mine pollution, so more and more research related to mine pollution, environmental damage and public health is being carried out. Additionally, many experts in the field of environmental engineering and public health have proposed measures based on their research expertise to address the problems associated with environmental pollution and health crises in mining; they have mostly focused their research on their own single area of study. For example, Li, S. et al. [40,41] have been working on Green Mine Construction and the elimination of mine pollution, but their research has remained focused on improving mining methods and thus mitigating mine pollution, without taking into account emissions pollution and the impact of emissions on public health; furthermore, Sahu, K et al. [42,43] were among the first researchers to propose the reuse of metal mine solid waste for metal resource recovery as well as to mitigate mine solid waste pollution, but their research was limited to chemical recovery processes, and no further research or discussion of mine pollution or public health threats was undertaken [44,45].

Consequently, in the discussion, we propose the concept of a "Healthy Mine" to provide a direction for development and solutions to the mine pollution and public health crises for mining companies to follow and to raise public awareness of mine pollution.

We define a "Healthy Mine" as a mine that actively addresses and mitigates the impact of mine environmental pollution from the mine discharge (water, solid and dust) on the ecological environment, residents' health and the occupational health of miners through company management, pollution treatment technologies and employee education in the process of resource development. We advocate all existing mines in the world today should be moving in this direction so that environmental pollution problems and public health crises can be well alleviated.

By definition, a mine is considered a "Healthy Mine" if it meets the following basic conditions: (A) Wastewater and Leachate Treatment: the wastewater and leachate generating from mine solid waste should be treated, so the mine should actively introduce wastewater treatment technology, and the quality of discharged wastewater and leachate should meet the emission standard; (B) "Healthcare": the mine should ensure that the surrounding population is not affected by pollution from the mine wastewater pollution and the leachate pollution; (C) Solid Waste Management: the mine should have strict management of solid waste discharge sites, and actively implement the land reclamation; (D) Solid Waste Recycle: the mine should be active in the reuse of mine solids, for example in the preparation of construction (or backfill) materials; (E) Dust Control: the mine should actively introduce dust control measure, such as spraying covering agents on the surface of dusty materials; (F) Company Management and Employee Education: the mine should make regulations to strictly manage pollution and discharge control during the mining process, and also strengthen health education for mine employees, for example by strictly requiring them to wear dust filtering masks during mining operations. Thus, the concept diagram of the "Healthy Mine" is as follows in Figure 11:

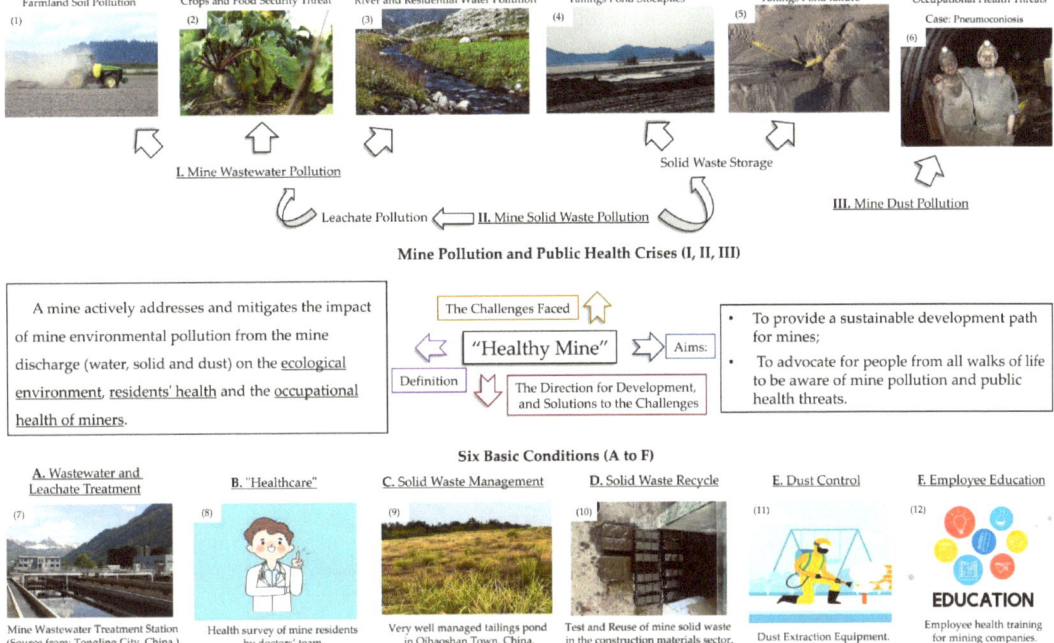

Figure 11. The concept diagram of the "Healthy Mine".

5. Conclusions

As the construction of tailings ponds is a potential environmental and safety hazard, their monitoring is very necessary. Against this background, this paper proposes to classify tailings ponds into two categories according to whether they are potentially risky or generally safe and to classify tailings ponds' remote sensing satellite images using DDN + ResNet-50 machine learning model based on ML.Net developed by Microsoft. Meanwhile, this paper also explored the accuracy of the ML.Net machine learning framework and its machine learning model in classifying tailings pond types according to the different characteristics of the 1# Tailings Pond and 2# Tailings Pond.

The conclusions we have drawn are as follows:

- ResNet-50 is a residual network that uses a shortcut connection to connect the inputs directly to the outputs. Its classification is more accurate, solves the problem of deep network degradation and is well suited to studying the identification and classification of tailings ponds' satellite images.
- DDN + ResNet-50 was found to perform well in the identification and classification of satellite images of tailings ponds. The ML.Net machine learning framework and its model achieved an accuracy of 83.5% for the identification and classification of tailings ponds in the case of 20 times cross-validation, achieved an accuracy of 87.8% for the identification and classification of tailings ponds in the case of three-fold cross-validation and achieved an accuracy of 87.3% for the identification and classification of tailings ponds in the case of three-fold cross-validation after expanding the dataset.
- In this study, the identification accuracy of the 2# Tailings Ponds was slightly lower than that of the 1# Tailings Ponds. This may be due to the fact that the characteristics of 2# Tailings Ponds are not obvious on the satellite maps: some 2# Tailings Ponds that are about to be closed or have just been closed do not differ much from 1# Tailings Ponds on the satellite maps, while some 2# Tailings Ponds that have been closed for

some time generally already show signs of extensive land reclamation on the satellite maps, which are different from each other.

In a nutshell, we claim that this research serves as a guide to starting a conversation, and we hope more and more experts, researchers and scholars will be interested and engage in research in this field of mine pollution assessment using remote sensing technologies and machine learning models.

Author Contributions: Conceptualisation: H.Y.; methodology: H.Y.; writing—original draft preparation: H.Y.; writing—review and editing: H.Y. and I.Z.; supervision: I.Z.; project administration: I.Z. All authors have read and agreed to the published version of the manuscript.

Funding: This research received no external funding.

Data Availability Statement: Data will be made available on request.

Acknowledgments: First, the authors would like to thank the Graduate Research Excellence Scholarship (GRES) from Monash University. Second, the authors express their gratitude to the experts in the research field of mine pollution and public health for their effort.

Conflicts of Interest: The authors declare no conflict of interest.

References

1. Small, C.C.; Cho, S.; Hashisho, Z.; Ulrich, A.C. Emissions from oil sands tailings ponds: Review of tailings pond parameters and emission estimates. *J. Pet. Sci. Eng.* **2015**, *127*, 490–501. [CrossRef]
2. Liu, J.; Liu, R.; Zhang, Z.; Cai, Y.; Zhang, L. A Bayesian Network-based risk dynamic simulation model for accidental water pollution discharge of mine tailings ponds at watershed-scale. *J. Environ. Manag.* **2019**, *246*, 821–831. [CrossRef]
3. Agrawal, A.; Sahu, K.K.; Pandey, B.D. Solid waste management in non-ferrous industries in India. *Resour. Conserv. Recycl.* **2004**, *42*, 99–120. [CrossRef]
4. Shengo, L.M. Review of practices in the managements of mineral wastes: The case of waste rocks and mine tailings. *Water Air Soil Pollut.* **2021**, *232*, 273. [CrossRef]
5. Liu, Y.; Guo, D.; Dong, L.; Xu, Y.; Liu, J. Pollution status and environmental sound management (ESM) trends on typical general industrial solid waste. *Procedia Environ. Sci.* **2016**, *31*, 615–620. [CrossRef]
6. Asif, Z.; Chen, Z. Environmental management in North American mining sector. *Environ. Sci. Pollut. Res.* **2016**, *23*, 167–179. [CrossRef] [PubMed]
7. Porsani, J.L.; Jesus, F.A.N.D.; Stangari, M.C. GPR survey on an iron mining area after the collapse of the tailings dam I at the Córrego do Feijão mine in Brumadinho-MG, Brazil. *Remote Sens.* **2019**, *11*, 860. [CrossRef]
8. Shen, L.; Luo, S.; Zeng, X.; Wang, H. Review on anti-seepage technology development of tailings pond in China. *Procedia Eng.* **2011**, *26*, 1803–1809. [CrossRef]
9. Wei, Z.; Yin, G.; Wang, J.G.; Wan, L.; Li, G. Design, construction and management of tailings storage facilities for surface disposal in China: Case studies of failures. *Waste Manag. Res.* **2013**, *31*, 106–112. [CrossRef]
10. Wang, T.; Zhou, Y.; Lv, Q.; Zhu, Y.; Jiang, C. A safety assessment of the new Xiangyun phosphogypsum tailings pond. *Miner. Eng.* **2011**, *24*, 1084–1090. [CrossRef]
11. Fennell, J.; Arciszewski, T.J. Current knowledge of seepage from oil sands tailings ponds and its environmental influence in northeastern Alberta. *Sci. Total Environ.* **2019**, *686*, 968–985. [CrossRef] [PubMed]
12. Che, D.; Liang, A.; Li, X.; Ma, B. Remote sensing assessment of safety risk of iron tailings pond based on runoff coefficient. *Sensors* **2018**, *18*, 4373. [CrossRef] [PubMed]
13. Zhang, L.; Huang, Y.; Wu, X.; Skibniewski, M.J. Risk-based estimate for operational safety in complex projects under uncertainty. *Appl. Soft Comput.* **2017**, *54*, 108–120. [CrossRef]
14. Lyu, J.; Hu, Y.; Ren, S.; Yao, Y.; Ding, D.; Guan, Q.; Tao, L. Extracting the tailings ponds from high spatial resolution remote sensing images by integrating a deep learning-based model. *Remote Sens.* **2021**, *13*, 743. [CrossRef]
15. Yan, D.; Zhang, H.; Li, G.; Li, X.; Lei, H.; Lu, K.; Zhang, L.; Zhu, F. Improved Method to Detect the Tailings Ponds from Multispectral Remote Sensing Images Based on Faster R-CNN and Transfer Learning. *Remote Sens.* **2021**, *14*, 103. [CrossRef]
16. Ahmed, Z.; Amizadeh, S.; Bilenko, M.; Carr, R.; Chin, W.S.; Dekel, Y.; Dupre, X.; Eksarevskiy, V.; Filipi, S.; Finley, T.; et al. Machine learning at Microsoft with ML. NET. In Proceedings of the 25th ACM SIGKDD International Conference on Knowledge Discovery & Data Mining, Anchorage, AK, USA, 4–8 August 2019; Association for Computing Machinery: New York, NY, USA, 2019; pp. 2448–2458.
17. Capellman, J. *Hands-On Machine Learning with ML. NET: Getting Started with Microsoft ML*; NET to implement popular machine learning algorithms in C; Packt Publishing Ltd.: Birmingham, UK, 2020.
18. Magdin, M.; Benc, J.; Koprda, Š.; Balogh, Z.; Tuček, D. Comparison of Multilayer Neural Network Models in Terms of Success of Classifications Based on EmguCV, ML. NET and Tensorflow. Net. *Appl. Sci.* **2022**, *12*, 3730. [CrossRef]

19. Alexan, A.; Alexan, A.; Stefan, O. Soc based iot sensor network hub for activity recognition using ml. net framework. In *2020 IEEE 26th International Symposium for Design and Technology in Electronic Packaging (SIITME)*; IEEE: Pitesti, Romania, 2020; pp. 184–187.
20. Wen, L.; Li, X.; Gao, L. A transfer convolutional neural network for fault diagnosis based on ResNet-50. *Neural Comput. Appl.* **2020**, *32*, 6111–6124. [CrossRef]
21. Wu, Z.; Nagarajan, T.; Kumar, A.; Rennie, S.; Davis, L.S.; Grauman, K.; Feris, R. Blockdrop: Dynamic inference paths in residual networks. In Proceedings of the IEEE Conference on Computer Vision and Pattern Recognition, Salt Lake City, UT, USA, 18–23 June 2018; pp. 8817–8826.
22. Bin, L.; Lima, D. Facial expression recognition via ResNet-50. *Int. J. Cogn. Comput. Eng.* **2021**, *2*, 57–64.
23. Yu, H.; Zhao, C.; Li, S.; Wang, Z.; Zhang, Y. Pre-Work for the Birth of Driver-Less Scraper (LHD) in the Underground Mine: The Path Tracking Control Based on an LQR Controller and Algorithms Comparison. *Sensors* **2021**, *21*, 7839. [CrossRef]
24. Li, X.X.; Li, D.; Ren, W.X.; Zhang, J.S. Loosening Identification of Multi-Bolt Connections Based on Wavelet Transform and ResNet-50 Convolutional Neural Network. *Sensors* **2020**, *22*, 6825. [CrossRef]
25. Alexan, A.; Alexan, A.; Oniga, Ș. Smartwatch activity recognition feature comparison using ML. net. In Proceedings of the 2022 IEEE International Conference on Automation, Quality and Testing, Robotics (AQTR), Cluj-Napoca, Romania, 19–21 May 2022; pp. 1–6.
26. Rajpal, S.; Lakhyani, N.; Singh, A.K.; Kohli, R.; Kumar, N. Using handpicked features in conjunction with ResNet-50 for improved detection of COVID-19 from chest X.-ray images. *Chaos Solitons Fractals* **2021**, *145*, 110749. [CrossRef] [PubMed]
27. Du, J.; Chen, Q.; Peng, Y.; Xiang, Y.; Tao, C.; Lu, Z. ML-Net: Multi-label classification of biomedical texts with deep neural networks. *J. Am. Med. Inform. Assoc.* **2019**, *26*, 1279–1285. [CrossRef] [PubMed]
28. Ramezan, C.A.; Warner, T.A.; Maxwell, A.E. Evaluation of sampling and cross-validation tuning strategies for regional-scale machine learning classification. *Remote Sens.* **2019**, *11*, 185. [CrossRef]
29. Ping, X.; Yang, F.; Zhang, H.; Zhang, J.; Zhang, W.; Song, G. Introducing machine learning and hybrid algorithm for prediction and optimization of multistage centrifugal pump in an ORC system. *Energy* **2021**, *222*, 120007. [CrossRef]
30. Vu, H.L.; Ng, K.T.W.; Richter, A.; An, C. Analysis of input set characteristics and variances on k-fold cross validation for a Recurrent Neural Network model on waste disposal rate estimation. *J. Environ. Manag.* **2022**, *311*, 114869. [CrossRef]
31. Shorten, C.; Khoshgoftaar, T.M. A survey on image data augmentation for deep learning. *J. Big Data* **2019**, *6*, 1–48. [CrossRef]
32. Zhong, Z.; Zheng, L.; Kang, G.; Li, S.; Yang, Y. Random erasing data augmentation. In Proceedings of the AAAI Conference on Artificial Intelligence, New York, NY, USA, 7–12 February 2020; Volume 34, pp. 13001–13008.
33. Ghanizadeh, A.R.; Delaram, A.; Fakharian, P.; Armaghani, D.J. Developing Predictive Models of Collapse Settlement and Coefficient of Stress Release of Sandy-Gravel Soil via Evolutionary Polynomial Regression. *Appl. Sci.* **2022**, *12*, 9986. [CrossRef]
34. Wang, Y.; Zhao, Y.; Xu, S. Application of VNIR and machine learning technologies to predict heavy metals in soil and pollution indices in mining areas. *J. Soils Sediments* **2022**, *22*, 2777–2791. [CrossRef]
35. Skentou, A.D.; Bardhan, A.; Mamou, A.; Lemonis, M.E.; Kumar, G.; Samui, P.; Armaghani, D.J.; Asteris, P.G. Closed-Form Equation for Estimating Unconfined Compressive Strength of Granite from Three Non-destructive Tests Using Soft Computing Models. *Rock Mech. Rock Eng.* **2022**, 1–28. [CrossRef]
36. Indraratna, B.; Armaghani, D.J.; Correia, A.G.; Hunt, H.; Ngo, T. Prediction of resilient modulus of ballast under cyclic loading using machine learning techniques. *Transp. Geotech.* **2022**, *38*, 100895. [CrossRef]
37. Cavaleri, L.; Barkhordari, M.S.; Repapis, C.C.; Armaghani, D.J.; Ulrikh, D.V.; Asteris, P.G. Convolution-based ensemble learning algorithms to estimate the bond strength of the corroded reinforced concrete. *Constr. Build. Mater.* **2022**, *359*, 129504. [CrossRef]
38. Pindór, T.; Preisner, L. Coal Sector Restructuring due to Sustainable Development. *People* **2000**, *1990*, 2005–2006.
39. Frank, D. One world, one health, one medicine. *Can. Vet. J.* **2008**, *49*, 1063. Available online: https://www.ncbi.nlm.nih.gov/pmc/articles/PMC2572090/ (accessed on 10 November 2022). [PubMed]
40. Li, S.; Yu, L.; Jiang, W.; Yu, H.; Wang, X. The Recent Progress China Has Made in Green Mine Construction, Part I: Mining Groundwater Pollution and Sustainable Mining. *Int. J. Environ. Res. Public Health* **2022**, *19*, 5673. [CrossRef]
41. Yu, H.; Li, S.; Yu, L.; Wang, X. The Recent Progress China Has Made in Green Mine Construction, Part II: Typical Examples of Green Mines. *Int. J. Environ. Res. Public Health* **2022**, *19*, 8166. [CrossRef]
42. Agrawal, A.; Kumari, S.; Sahu, K.K. Iron and copper recovery/removal from industrial wastes: A review. *Ind. Eng. Chem. Res.* **2009**, *48*, 6145–6161. [CrossRef]
43. Agrawal, A.; Sahu, K.K. Problems, prospects and current trends of copper recycling in India: An overview. *Resour. Conserv. Recycl.* **2010**, *54*, 401–416. [CrossRef]
44. Haoxuan, Y.; Zahidi, I. Environmental hazards posed by mine dust, and monitoring method of mine dust pollution using remote sensing technologies: An overview. *Sci. Total Environ.* **2022**, 161135. [CrossRef]
45. Haoxuan, Y.; Zahidi, I. Spatial and temporal variation of vegetation cover in the main mining area of Qibaoshan Town, China: Potential impacts from mining damage, solid waste discharge and land reclamation. *Sci. Total Environ.* **2023**, *859*, 160392.

Disclaimer/Publisher's Note: The statements, opinions and data contained in all publications are solely those of the individual author(s) and contributor(s) and not of MDPI and/or the editor(s). MDPI and/or the editor(s) disclaim responsibility for any injury to people or property resulting from any ideas, methods, instructions or products referred to in the content.

Article

Analysis of Microscopic Pore Characteristics and Macroscopic Energy Evolution of Rock Materials under Freeze-Thaw Cycle Conditions

Yigai Xiao [1,2], Hongwei Deng [1,*], Guanglin Tian [1,*] and Songtao Yu [3]

[1] School of Resources and Safety Engineering, Central South University, Changsha 410083, China
[2] Sinosteel Maanshan General Institute of Mining Research Co., Ltd., Maanshan 243000, China
[3] School of Emergency Management, Jiangxi University of Science and Technology, Ganzhou 341000, China
* Correspondence: denghw208@126.com or 207010@csu.edu.cn (H.D.); tgl15352006270@163.com or 215501027@csu.edu.cn (G.T.)

Abstract: The repeated cyclic freeze-thaw effect in low-temperature environments causes irreversible damage and deterioration to the microscopic pore structure and macroscopic mechanical properties of a rock. To study the effects of the freeze-thaw cycle on the porosity and mechanical properties, the indoor freeze-thaw cycle test and mechanical tests of sandstone-like materials were conducted. Based on nuclear magnetic resonance, the influence of the freeze-thaw cycle on microscopic pores was analyzed, and the intrinsic relationship between porosity and mechanical strength was discussed. Meanwhile, the energy change in the uniaxial compression test was recorded using the discrete element software (PFC2D). The influence of freeze-thaw cycles on different types of energy was analyzed, and the internal relationship between different energies and freeze-thaw cycles was discussed. The results showed that the microscopic pore structure is dominated by micropores, followed by mesopores and the smallest macropores. With an increase in the freeze-thaw cycle, both micropores and mesopores showed an increasing trend. The porosity showed an exponentially increasing trend with the increase in freeze-thaw cycles. The peak strength and elastic modulus decreased exponentially with the increase in freeze-thaw times, while the peak strain showed an exponentially increasing trend. The strain energy and bond strain energy showed a trend of increasing and decreasing in the front and back stages of the peak strength, respectively. However, the frictional energy always showed an increasing trend. The total energy, strain energy, bond strain energy, and friction energy all showed exponential increases with the increase in the number of freeze-thaw cycles.

Keywords: freeze-thaw cycle; microscopic porosity; nuclear magnetic resonance; mechanical properties; energy evolution

MSC: 74S30

Citation: Xiao, Y.; Deng, H.; Tian, G.; Yu, S. Analysis of Microscopic Pore Characteristics and Macroscopic Energy Evolution of Rock Materials under Freeze-Thaw Cycle Conditions. *Mathematics* 2023, 11, 710. https://doi.org/10.3390/math11030710

Academic Editors: Danial Jahed Armaghani, Niaz Muhammad Shahani, Ramesh Murlidhar Bhatawdekar, Hadi Khabbaz and Manoj Khandelwal

Received: 29 November 2022
Revised: 19 January 2023
Accepted: 22 January 2023
Published: 31 January 2023

Copyright: © 2023 by the authors. Licensee MDPI, Basel, Switzerland. This article is an open access article distributed under the terms and conditions of the Creative Commons Attribution (CC BY) license (https://creativecommons.org/licenses/by/4.0/).

1. Introduction

With the continuous development of human society, the scale of infrastructure construction and the degree of resource development and utilization in cold regions will be further improved. However, in low-temperature environments, all geotechnical engineering will inevitably face the unique effects of freeze-thaw cycles. Rocks in their natural environment are a kind of porous material with internal defects, such as microcracks and pores. This repeated rise and decrease in temperature change will lead to water-ice phase changes in porous or crack water inside the engineering bearing unit with porous characteristics. The volume expansion generated by the phase change can cause damage to the initial microscopic pore structure of the rock and soil elements, which can eventually have an important impact on the mechanical characteristics of the bearing unit and the safety and stability of the project [1]. Therefore, it is of great significance to study the effect of cyclic freeze-thaw on the microscopic structure and macroscopic mechanical parameters for the stability of geotechnical engineering in low-temperature regions.

In recent years, the research on the influence of F-T cycle microscopic pore structure in rocks has attracted attention. Li and Zhou [2–5] analyzed the effect of freeze-thaw cycles on the microscopic pore structure of sandstone. The research showed that with the increase in F-T cycles, the porosity increased and the pore sizes of micropores and macropores increased significantly. Gao [6] took red sandstone as the research object and conducted a study on the influence of the F-T cycle on the microscopic pore structure under the action of the chemical environment. The results showed that, under the action of the freeze-thaw cycle, the porosity showed a linear growth trend. Meanwhile, new micropores were constantly emerging inside the specimen. In the study of the influence of F-T cycles on granite, repeated freezing and thawing of pore water generated damage to the microscopic pore structure. Among them, the porosity gradually increased with the increase in the number of cycles, and the micropores gradually developed into macropores [7].

The mechanical strength of the bearing unit in geotechnical engineering plays an important role in the safety and stability of the project. It is of great significance for the safe and efficient operation of rocks to study the influence of the freeze-thaw cycle on mechanical properties. Related research directions have always been the focus of experts and scholars. Gao [8,9] discussed the variation of internal porosity of sandstone under the action of the freeze-thaw cycle and established a strength degradation model of water-saturated sandstone by taking porosity as the dependent variable. At the same time, based on the statistical damage mechanical model of strain equivalence, a constitutive model of sandstone segmentation under freeze-thaw conditions was proposed and verified by the experimental results. Based on the combination of NMR and infrared thermal imaging detection, Yang [10] analyzed the change trend of porosities and mechanical characteristics of marble, granite, and sandstone under the action of F-T cycle and discussed the failure process and failure mode of different rock samples. Through the creep test of sandstone under the F-T cycle, Li [11] established a constitutive model of nonlinear creep damage in sandstone.

Previous studies have shown that the process of rock loading and destruction is accompanied by the release and dissipation of energy, in which the process of energy dissipation can indicate the continuous development of microscopic defects and the weakening of the macroscopic strength until the final destruction [12,13]. From the above research, it can be seen that during F-T cycles, the physical parameters of different rock samples had a certain degree of attenuation. In the same way, the energy release and dissipation laws also have changed accordingly. In recent years, more and more attention has been paid to the effects of cyclic freeze-thaw on energy release and dissipation laws. Taking sandstone as the research object, Deng [14] calculated the strain energy, the elastic strain energy, and the dissipative energy released by using the stress-strain curve, finally analyzing the influence of the freeze-thaw cycle on different types of energy. The results suggested that the strain energy, the elastic strain energy, and the dissipative energy all showed a decreasing trend with an increase in the F-T cycle. Feng [15] discussed the evolution of specimen porosity, mechanical strength, and energy under F-T cycles. Gao [16] conducted uniaxial compression tests on blue sandstone under F-T cycles and explored the influence of cyclic freeze-thaw on the evolution of strain energy, releasable elastic strain energy, and dissipative energy. The damage model of peak stress and peak strain of specimens under freeze-thaw action was established by the ratio of dissipative energy to strain energy, verified with laboratory tests. In summary, the F-T cycle has an important impact on the microscopic pore characteristics, macroscopic mechanical strength, and energy evolution of rock samples. However, in previous studies on the energy evolution of rocks under F-T cycle conditions, most researchers calculated strain energy, releasable strain energy, and dissipative energy through stress-strain curves in mechanical tests. In this study, the uniaxial compression process of sandstone-like material under different freeze-thaw cycles was simulated based on the particle flow code. Different types of energy parameters during the loading process were tracked through the internal energy recording module of the program. Combined with the NMR detection of microscopic pore parameters under different freeze-thaw cycles, the influence of the freeze-thaw cycle on porosity was analyzed from a microscopic perspective. At the same time, the influence of cyclic freeze-thaw on mechanical properties and energy evolution was discussed from a macroscopic perspective. The influence mechanism of the freeze-thaw cycle on the microscopic pores and macroscopic mechanical characteristics of sandstone was revealed from multiple angles. The results of this paper can provide reference and guidance for safety and stability analysis and instability prevention of open-pit mine slopes, highway shoulder slopes, and other geotechnical engineering structures in low-temperature environments [17].

2. Experimental Progress and Methodology

2.1. Raw Materials Selection and Sample Preparation

The sample studied in this paper is a sandstone-like material. The original rock is yellow sandstone from the slope of an open slope in Shandong Province, China. According to the current research on rock-like materials, the cementitious material is ordinary Portland cement (P.O 42.5) [18–24]. The aggregate is a yellow-white spherical quartz sand with a particle size of 0.5~1 mm, and the spherical shape can make it fully wrapped by the cementitious material. The admixtures selected for the test were a yellow-brown, naphthalene-based high-efficiency water reducer and a white, micron-sized silica powder. The specific parameters of raw materials are shown in Tables 1 and 2. In the sample production, the mass matching ratio of different raw materials is 0.32:1.00:1.30:0.10:0.01 (water:cement:quartz sand:silica powder:naphthalene water reducer). First of all, different raw materials are weighed according to different proportions. Then stirring, filling, vibration, demolding, numbering, and curing were carried out in turn. Finally, different physical and mechanical parameters of the sample were tested and compared with the original rock. The test procedures are shown in Figure 1. Table 3 shows the test results for sandstone and sandstone-like materials. Based on the statistical results, it can be seen that the different physical parameters of sandstone-like material are basically close to those of sandstone.

Table 1. Chemical composition of Portland cement.

Material	Traits	Main Ingredients			
		$3CaO \cdot SiO_2$	$2CaO \cdot SiO_2$	$3CaO \cdot Al_2O_3$	$4CaO \cdot Al_2O_3 \cdot Fe_2O_3$
Portland cement	Taupe powder	52.8%	20.7%	11.5%	8.8%

Table 2. Detailed parameters of aggregate and admixture.

Material	Traits	Main Ingredients	Particle Size	Density (g/cm^3)
Quartz sand	Yellow and white particles	Quartz > 99%	0.5–1.0 mm	1.49
Naphthalene water reducer	Brown-yellow powder	β-Naphthalenesulfonate sodium formaldehyde condensate	-	-
Silica fume	White powder	SiO_2 > 99%	1 μm	2.2–2.6

2.2. Laboratory Test

2.2.1. Freeze-Thaw Cycle Test

The freeze-thaw test equipment used in this experiment is the TDS-300 concrete freeze-thaw testing machine produced by Suzhou Donghua Test Instrument Co., Ltd., and the working mode of the equipment is air freezing and water thawing. It takes 12 h for the test equipment to accomplish a full freeze-thaw cycle. Among them, the freezing temperature is −20 °C, and the low-temperature holding time is 4 h. The melting temperature is 20 °C, and the high-temperature holding time is 4 h. A complete freeze-thaw cycle is shown in Figure 2.

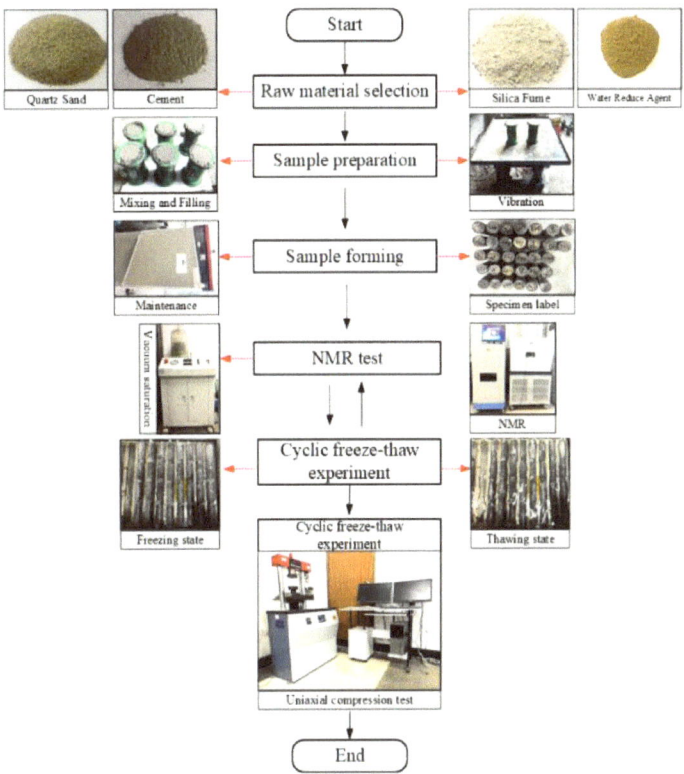

Figure 1. Test procedures.

Table 3. Statistics test results of a sandstone-like material and sandstone.

Material	Density (g/cm^3)	Porosity (%)	Uniaxial Compressive Strength (MPa)
Sandstone	2.33	3.186	32.01
Sandstone-like material	2.31	3.431	33.64

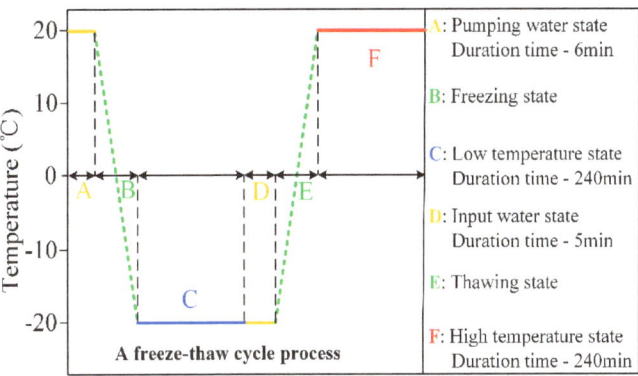

Figure 2. Complete freeze—thaw cycle process.

2.2.2. NMR Test

The NMR analysis device is MesoMR23-060H produced by Suzhou Newmai Analytical Instrument Co., Ltd. The instrument uses the H+ atomic probe of pore water inside rocks to measure the pore water content of different radii, which is inverted into the pore signal (T_2 relaxation time). In the process of sample detection, the magnetic field strength was 0.3 T, and the central principal frequency of NMR was 12.8 MHZ. The diameter of the probe coil was 60 mm and the sampling number was 4 times greater. The sampling interval was 6000 ms and the number of echoes was 7000 times. In addition, to saturate the rock sample, the specimens need to be vacuum saturated before the NMR test. The vacuum pressure inside the instrument cover was 0.1 MPa. The dry pumping time was set to 360 min and the wet pumping time was 240 min.

2.2.3. Uniaxial Compressive Strength Test

The equipment for uniaxial compression test was WHY-300 microcomputer-controlled pressure test equipment produced by Shanghai Hualong Testing Instrument Co., Ltd. The control mode was displacement, and the loading speed was 1 mm/min. The basis for the determination of the end of loading was 40% of the peak strength. According to the test standard specifications [25], the width of test specimen was 50 mm and the length was 100 mm. The uniaxial compressive strength is calculated as follows:

$$f_{cc} = \frac{F}{A} \quad (1)$$

In the formula, f_{cc} is the uniaxial compressive strength. F is the failure load of the rock sample. A is the loading area.

2.3. Pore Radius Decision

According to the basic principle of NMR, the relaxation time (T_2) of pore water inside the rock is mainly affected by the surface relaxation ($T_{2\text{surface}}$) of pore water. During the test, the surface relaxation conforms to the following expression:

$$\frac{1}{T_2} = \frac{1}{T_{2\text{surface}}} = \rho_2 \left(\frac{S}{V}\right) \quad (2)$$

In the formula, ρ_2 is the relaxation strength of the rock particle surface, which is mainly controlled by the lithology of the rock. S is the pore surface area, and V is the pore volume. The NMR testing generally treats the pore shape as spherical, so the formula can be changed to:

$$\frac{1}{T_2} = \rho_2 \frac{F_s}{r_c} \quad (3)$$

F_s is the pore shape factor (spherical pores, $F_s = 3$) and r_c is the pore radius. Since ρ_2 and F_s are constants in the formula, the formula can be reduced to:

$$r_c = C T_2 \quad (4)$$

As can be seen from Equation (4), the relaxation time is linearly related to the pore radius and corresponds one by one. Based on the relaxation time distribution characteristics of the 0-cycle rock sample, the pores are divided into three types of pores: miacropore ($T_2 < 1.5$ ms), mesopore (1.5 ms $\leq T_2 < 16$ ms), and macropores (16 ms $\leq T_2$). The result of pore radius decision is shown in Figure 3.

2.4. Model Description

The software PFC is a particle flow analysis program developed based on the discrete element method, which is widely used in the study of microscopic and macroscopic damage evolution, crack propagation, and failure modes in the processing of rock material [26].

In numerical simulations, the microparticles of different radii are taken as the basic units. The mechanical parameters between the units are used to characterize the macroscopic mechanical properties of rocks. The mechanical parameter relationship between particles is the relationship between force and displacement, and its equation of motion conforms to Newton's second law [27,28]. In addition, the mechanical parameters of different particle units are not directly related to the macroscopic mechanical properties of rock samples. Therefore, in numerical simulations, the trial-and-error method is needed to modify the microscopic parameters of particles until the results are basically consistent with the laboratory test results [29].

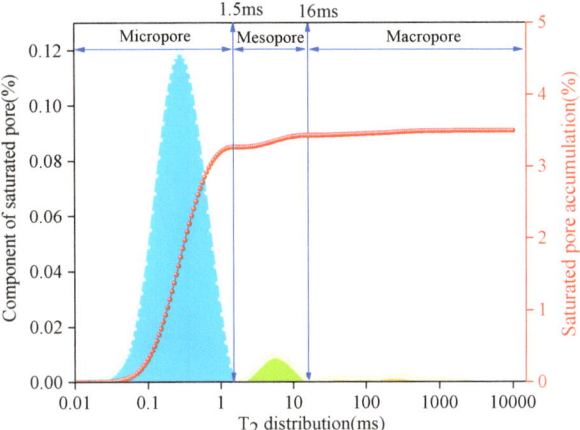

Figure 3. Pore radius division.

The parallel bonding model is one of the important models of the built-in constitutive relationships of PFC systems, which can simulate solid materials (rock, concrete, etc.) with cementing properties. It is a commonly used model for the numerical simulation of current rock and soil materials. The schematic diagram is shown in Figure 4.

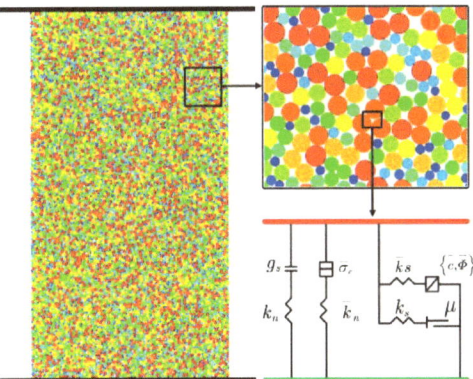

Figure 4. The diagram of the parallel bond model. g_s is the surface gap between particles and k_n is the normal stiffness of a linear spring. k_s is the shear stiffness of a linear spring, and $\bar{k}_n$ is the normal stiffness of the parallel bond. $\bar{k}_s$ and $\bar{\sigma}_c$ are the shear stiffness and the normal strength of the parallel bonds. $\{\bar{c}, \bar{\phi}\}$ is the shear strength of the parallel bond and μ is the coefficient of friction.

3. Results and Discussions

3.1. The Effects of the Freeze-Thaw Cycle on Microscopic Pore Structure

In NMR detection, the relaxation distribution is an important parameter that reflects the internal pore signal in rocks. Figure 5 shows the influence of the microscopic pore structure under different freeze-thaw cycles. As can be seen from Figure 5a, the T_2 distribution basically presents a three-peak feature character. The peak value of the micropore signal was significantly higher than that of mesopores and macropores. The internal microscopic pores are mainly micropores, followed by mesopores, and lastly macropores. As the number of freeze-thaw cycles increased, the T_2 distribution shifted significantly to the right, causing the microscopic pores inside the sample to change from a smaller radius to a larger radius. In addition, except for individual data points, with the increase in F-T cycles, the signal peak of micropores and mesopores also showed a significant increase. However, the change in the peak signal in macropores was not obvious.

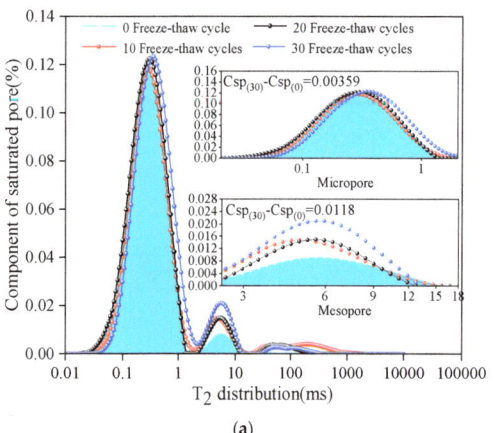
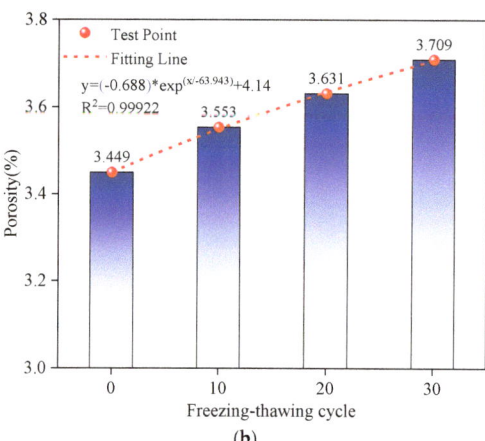

Figure 5. The effect of freezing-thaw cycles on microscopic pore structure. (**a**) Relaxation distribution; (**b**) porosity.

Table 4 shows the statistical results of the pore peak signals of pores of different radii and porosities under the action of the freeze-thaw cycle. According to the analysis of statistical results, when the number of freeze-thaw cycles increased from 0 to 30, the average porosity increased from 3.449% to 3.709%. The increase rate was 7.54%. In the variation law of peak signals of pores of different radii, except for 10 cycles of the peak signal of the micropore slightly less than 0 cycles, the peak value of the micropore signal increased from 0.1197% to 0.12323%, and the increase rate was 2.95%. The peak value of the mesopore signal increased from 0.00922% to 0.02102%, and the increase rate was 1.28%. Although the signal peaks of the 10, 20, and 30 cycles of the macropore were greater than 0 cycles, the change in trend from 10 cycles to 30 cycles was not obvious.

Table 4. The test results of microscopic pores under different freezing-thawing cycles.

F-T Cycle	Porosity (%)	The Peak of Micropore (%)	The Peak of Mesopore (%)	The Peak of Macropore (%)
0	3.449	0.1197	0.00922	0.00188
10	3.553	0.11857	0.01483	0.00411
20	3.631	0.12249	0.01491	0.00366
30	3.709	0.12329	0.02102	0.00284

As the temperature decreased, the pore water and crack water inside the sample began to gradually change from the liquid water state to the solid ice state (Figure 6). At the same time, the change in water ice morphology in pores or cracks leads to an increase in the volume of pore or crack fillers, which causes ice crystals in the pore or crack to generate corresponding pressure on the inner walls of the pore or crack. Studies have shown that a phase change from water to ice increases the volume by 9% [30–33], and the ice crystallization pressure can reach several hundred megapascals. When the pressure of the pore ice crystals in the internal micropores and mesopores on the inner wall was greater than the ultimate tensile strength of the wall, the radius of the micropores and mesopores expanded, and the pore volume continued to increase. Therefore, in the NMR test results, the signal peak of the relaxation time of micropores and mesopores increased, and the porosity increased. Moreover, with the continuous expansion of the pore radius of micropores and mesopores, pore communication occurred between different micropores and mesopores. The micropores and mesopores continued to develop into mesopores and macropores. Finally, in the NMR test, the relaxation time distribution shifted to the right as a whole. In addition, there are microcracks of different sizes in the internal microstructure of the sample. When the pressure of the crack ice of the microcrack on the inner wall was greater than the ultimate tensile strength, the microcrack also expanded in different directions, and the volume of the microcrack increased continuously. The NMR results also showed that the peak signal increased in micropores and mesopores. Similarly, as the volume of microcracks continued to increase, microcracks of different scales expanded and connected, and cracks of smaller sizes gradually developed into larger sizes. The test results also showed that the relaxation distribution began to shift to the right. Moreover, the porosity and the number of the F-T cycle were fitted. The results showed that the number of F-T cycles and porosity had a good exponential relationship ($R^2 = 0.9982$), and the porosity increased exponentially with the increase in the number of F-T cycles.

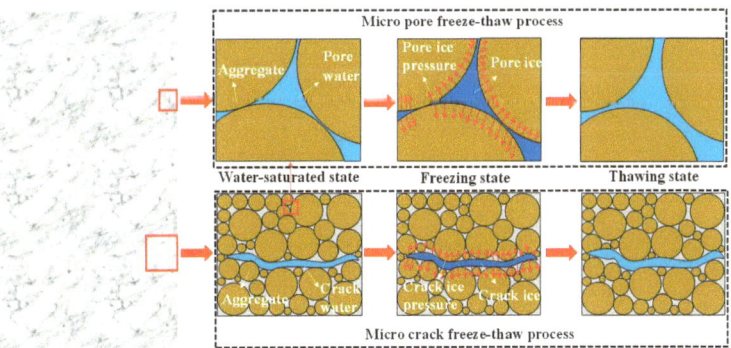

Figure 6. Propagation and development of pores and cracks under freeze-thaw cycles.

It can be seen that in low-temperature environments, there is a good exponential relationship between porosity and F-T cycles; the porosity increases with the increase in the F-T cycle. The results of this experiment can provide reference and support for the subsequent study of the evolution law of microscopic pore structure in low-temperature environments.

3.2. The Effects of the Freeze-Thaw Cycle on Macroscopic Properties
3.2.1. The Effects of the Freeze-Thaw Cycle on Mechanical Properties

Figure 7a shows the stress-strain curve under different freeze-thaw cycles. It can be seen that the stress-strain curves have obvious pores compaction, elastic deformation, stable development of fractures and unstable development stages of fractures under different freeze-thaw cycles. Meanwhile, with the increase in the number of freeze-thaw cycles, the strain in the pore compaction stage increased significantly. The peak strength decreased, and the peak strain increased observably. Table 5 shows the statistical results of the peak strength, elastic modulus, and peak strain under different freeze-thaw cycles. When the number of the F-T cycle increased from 0 to 30, the peak strength decreased from 40.75 MPa to 17.87 MPa with a reduction rate of 56.15%. The elastic modulus was reduced from 41.73 MPa to 12.63 MPa with a reduction rate of 69.73%. The peak strain increased from 1.40612% to 2.25087%, with an increase rate of 60.08%. According to the influence of freeze-thaw on the change rate of different mechanical parameters, the F-T cycle had the largest influence on the elastic modulus, followed by the peak strain, which had the least influence on the peak strength.

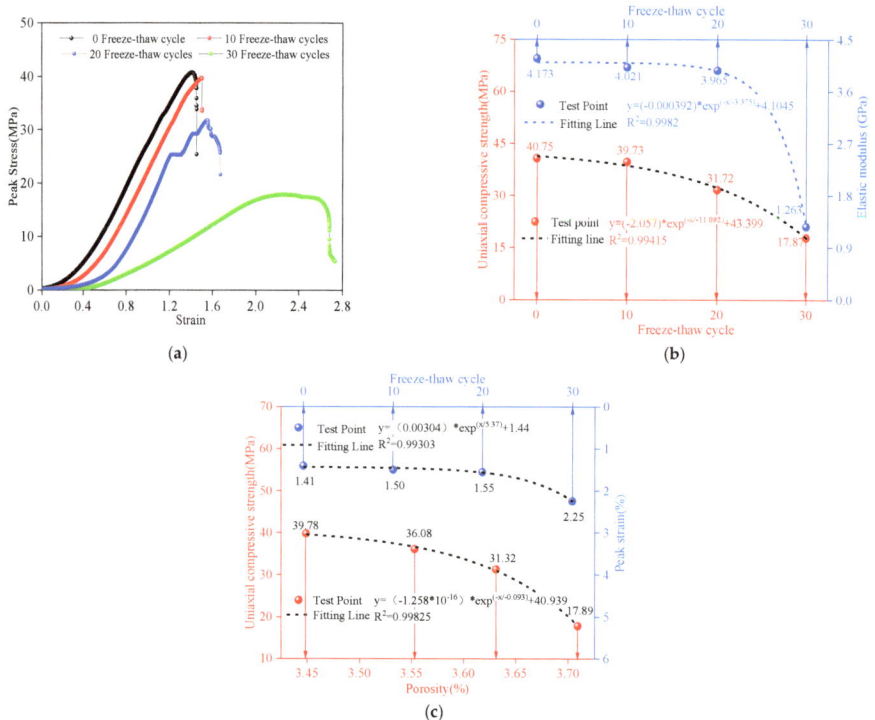

Figure 7. The influence of the number of freeze-thaw cycles on physical and mechanical parameters. (**a**) Stress-strain curve; (**b**) peak strength and elastic modulus; and (**c**) peak strain and porosity.

Table 5. The statistical results of mechanical parameters under different freeze-thaw cycles.

F-T Cycle	Peak Strength (MPa)	Elastic Modulus (GPa)	Peak Strain (%)
0	40.75	4.173	1.40612
10	39.73	4.021	1.49959
20	31.72	3.965	1.55147
30	17.87	1.263	2.25087
Change Ratio	56.15%	69.73%	60.08%

The pore compaction stage is a nonlinear deformation stage in which the original open cracks or pores gradually close during the initial stage of rock loading. With the increase in the F-T cycle, the number of microscopic pores inside the sample gradually increased, which also increased the deformation of the pore compaction stage of the sample. As a result, there was a significant increase in strain during the pore compaction phase, which ultimately led to an increase in peak strain. Moreover, the peak strain had a good exponential relationship with the number of F-T cycles, which increased exponentially with the increase in the cycles. In order to explore the intrinsic relationship between peak strength and elastic modulus and the F-T cycle, different mechanical parameters and freeze-thaw cycles were fitted (Figure 7b,c). The results showed that the peak strength and elastic modulus have a high exponential relationship with freeze-thaw cycles, and the fitting correlation coefficient is above 0.99. While the number of F-T cycles gradually increased, the peak strength and elastic modulus showed an exponential decrease. In previous studies, it was generally believed that the deterioration of the macroscopic mechanical properties under low-temperature environments was the result of the changes in the microscopic pore structure caused by the F-T cycle [34]. Consequently, the relationship between porosity and uniaxial compressive strength was also considered. The results showed that there was a good exponential relationship between porosity and compressive strength, and the fitting coefficient was 0.99825. When the repeated F-T cycle caused the number of microscopic pores to increase, the mechanical strength showed an exponentially decreasing trend, which finally affected the safety and stability of the project.

3.2.2. The Effects of Freeze-Thaw Cycles on Energy Evolution

When the particle flow program simulates rock damage under load, the evolution of different types of energy can be tracked by setting the energy command. Therefore, before tracing the energy evolution, a numerical simulation of the uniaxial compression test should be carried out by the trial-and-error method. When the numerical simulation results are basically consistent with the indoor test results, the energy evolution can be recorded by turning. Table 6 shows the particle flow simulation parameters of the uniaxial compression test under different freeze-thaw cycles. In this numerical simulation, the radius, density, normal and tangential stiffness ratios, porosity, and friction coefficient of the particle element were kept unchanged. The parameters affecting its peak strength and peak strain (Emod, pb_Emod, pb_coh, and pb_ten) were changed to simulate the uniaxial compression test under different cycles.

Table 6. Numerical simulation parameters under different freeze-thaw cycles.

F-T Cycle	Density (kg/m^3)	Radius (m)	Kratio	Porosity	Fric	Emod\Pb-Emod (GPa)	Pb_coh/Pb_ten (MPa)	pb_fa (°)
0						5.66	37.7	20
10	2000	0.002–0.005	1.5	0.03	0.5	5.53	42.6	50
20						5.12	30.7	40
30						1.16	16.3	20

Figure 8 shows the stress-strain curve and numerical simulation stress-strain curve of the mechanical test of the 10 cycles. From the figure, the variation trend of the stress-strain curve simulated by the discrete element program is basically consistent with that of the indoor mechanical test curve. The values of the elastic modulus and peak strength of the discrete element program were basically consistent with those of the indoor mechanical test. The indoor mechanical test results and numerical simulation results of other freeze-thaw cycles are shown in Table 7. It can be seen that the indoor mechanics test results with different cycles were basically similar to the numerical simulation results. The errors in elastic modulus and peak strength were less than 1 MPa and 0.1 Gpa, respectively. Figure 9 shows the final failure mode under different freeze-thaw cycles of internal mechanical testing and numerical simulation. The failure mode of the numerical simulation under different cycles was basically consistent with the results of internal mechanics tests. Furthermore, the cracks caused by internal force failure were mainly tensile cracks, accounting for 85.74~64%. There are fewer shear cracks, accounting for 6~14.26%. Combined with the failure mode and crack type analysis in the indoor test and numerical simulation, it can be seen that the failure mode under different cycles was mainly a tensile splitting failure, accompanied by local shear failure.

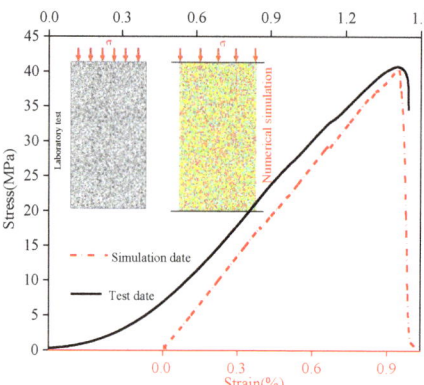

Figure 8. Indoor mechanics test and numerical simulation.

Table 7. Indoor mechanics test results and numerical simulation results under different freeze-thaw cycles.

Mechanical Properties	Peak Stress (MPa)				Elastic Modulus (GPa)			
F-T cycle	0	10	20	30	0	10	20	30
Laboratory test	40.75	39.73	31.72	17.87	4.173	4.021	3.965	1.263
Numerical simulation	40.19	38.95	32.62	17.78	4.259	4.017	3.909	1.312
Differential value	0.56	0.78	0.9	0.09	0.086	0.004	0.056	0.049

In the numerical simulation of the particle flow program, mechanical energy can be divided into body energy and contact energy. Body energy is a change in energy caused by a gravitational load or an applied load. Contact energy is the energy distribution defined in the contact model. In this law of energy evolution, the total energy is a kind of body energy, which is the energy generated by the boundary movement of the wall. Therein, the strain energy and the bond strain energy are the contact energies in the parallel bond model, which are stored in the linear spring and parallel spring, respectively.

Figure 10 shows the evolution of the number of cracks and four types of energies under different freeze-thaw cycles. From the figure, although the F-T cycle is different, the number of cracks in the process of load failure and the evolution of different types of energy are consistent. Based on the crack propagation of the 0 cycle, the crack propagation and energy evolution were divided into four stages. The first stage is the crack-free stage (0–$0.44\sigma_c$). As the force of the specimen gradually increased, the total energy, strain energy, and bond strain energy showed an increasing trend. At this stage, there were no cracks and no frictional energy. The total energy was basically converted into strain energy and cementation energy, which were stored in linear springs and parallel linear springs. The second stage is the slow growth of cracks ($0.44\sigma_c$–$0.75\sigma_c$). At this stage, the energy absorption rates for total energy, strain energy, and cementation energy increased, and the different energies showed an increasing trend. Cracks and frictional energy appeared inside the specimen, and there was a slow, increasing trend. It can be seen that the friction energy was synchronized with the crack propagation. When cracks appeared, the friction energy also appeared. Moreover, the friction energy showed an increasing trend with the increase in the number of cracks. When the strain between particles reached a certain degree, cracks occurred between different particles. The energy consumed by friction between particles when they are cracked is generated by both friction energies. Since the cracks inside the specimen were in the stage of germination and slow growth, the frictional energy was small. Therefore, the cementation energy and strain energy were much greater than the friction energy. The third stage is the crack acceleration growth stage ($0.75\sigma_c$–σ_c). In the stage of accelerated crack growth, the total energy, strain energy, and bond strain energy continued to show an increasing trend. The number of cracks increased, and the growth rate of friction energy increased gradually. More and more of the total energy is dissipated by the frictional energy that overcomes the sliding of the particles. The fourth stage is the rapid growth of cracks (σ_c). In the post-peak phase, the crack spread rapidly, and the friction energy increased rapidly. The bearing capacity of the specimen was weakened, and the rate of total energy growth decreased. The strain energy and boundary energy stored by the linear spring and parallel bond spring were released rapidly due to the failure, and the variation trend changed from increasing to decreasing.

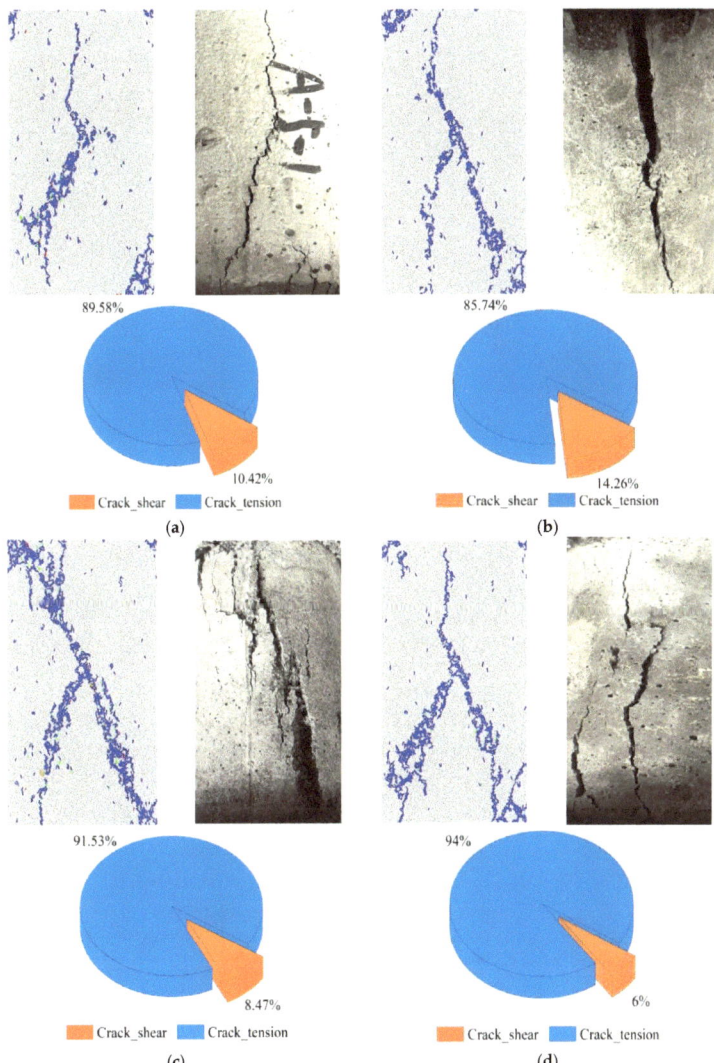

Figure 9. Sample destruction mode under different freeze-thaw cycles: (**a**) 0 F-T cycle; (**b**) 10 F-T cycle; (**c**) 20 F-T cycle; and (**d**) 30 F-T cycle.

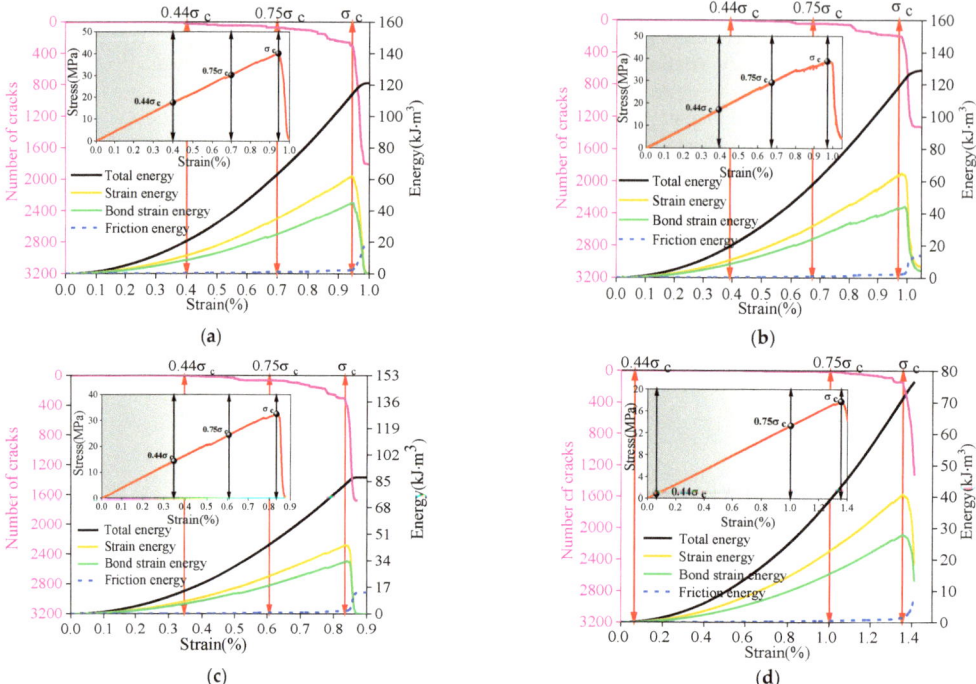

Figure 10. The evolution of different types of energy in different F-T cycles: (**a**) 0 cycle; (**b**) 10 cycle; (**c**) 20 cycle; and (**d**) 30 cycle.

In order to explore the intrinsic relationship between the number of freeze-thaw cycles and different types of energy, the energy values of different stages were fitted to the F-T cycle. The fitting results are shown in Figure 11. The results showed that when the value points are $0.44\sigma_c$ and $0.75\sigma_c$, the total energy, strain energy, bond strain energy, and friction energy have a good exponential relationship with the freeze-thaw cycles, the fitting coefficients of which are above 0.94. With the gradual increase in the number of freeze-thaw cycles, the total energy, strain energy, bond strain energy, and friction energy all showed an exponentially decreasing trend. At the point of peak strength (σ_c), the number of freeze-thaw cycles was exponentially related to the total energy and strain energy, and the fitting coefficient was 0.81964~0.86064. However, the bond strain energy and friction energy conformed severally to a good exponential relationship with freeze-thaw cycles, for which the fitting coefficient was above 0.95. While the number of freeze-thaw cycles gradually increased, the total energy, strain energy, bond strain energy, and friction energy all showed the law of exponential decrease.

In conclusion, peak compressive strength and different types of energy have a good exponential relationship with the F-T cycle. The peak strength and different types of energy showed a decreasing trend with the increase in the number of freeze-thaw cycles. The test results can provide data support for the safety and stability analysis of rock slopes, such as mine slopes and highway shoulder slopes in low-temperature environments, providing guidance for their instability prevention.

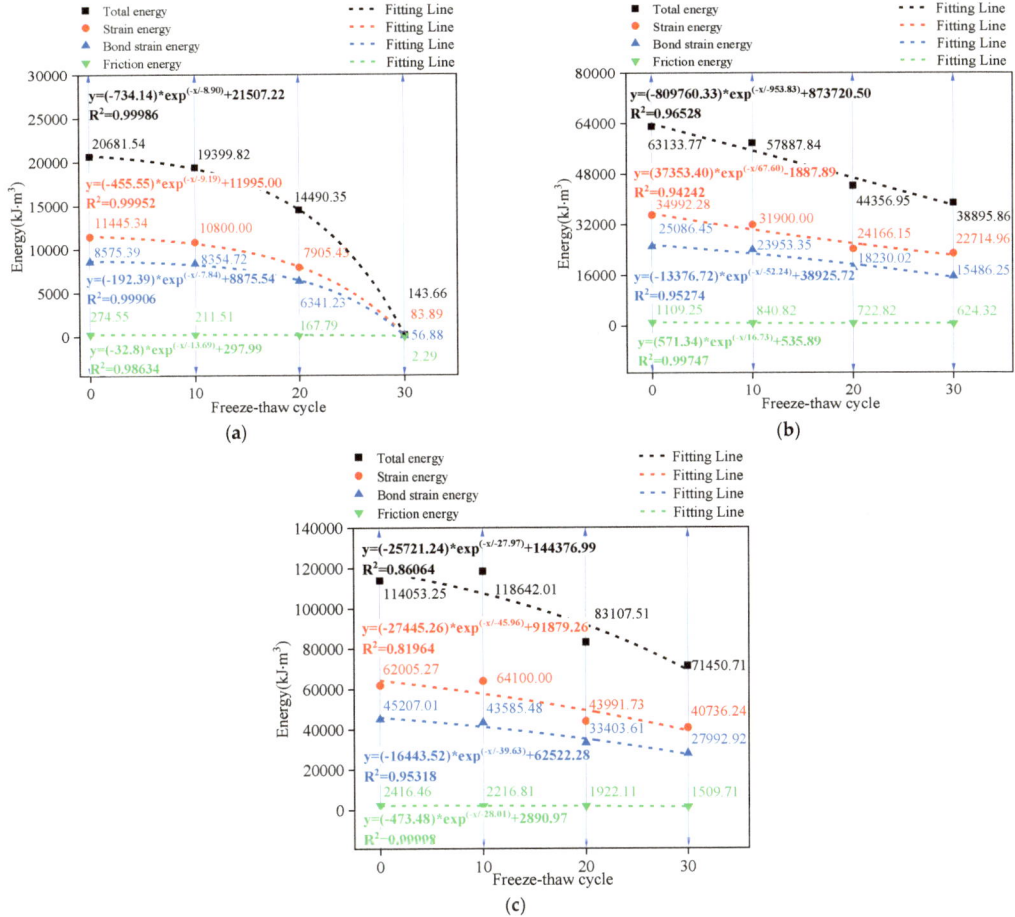

Figure 11. The intrinsic relationship between the number of freeze-thaw cycles and different types of energy: (**a**) $0.44\sigma_c$; (**b**) $0.75\sigma_c$; and (**c**) σ_c.

4. Conclusions

In this paper, the effects of the F-T cycle on the micropore structure and macroscopic mechanical properties of specimens were analyzed by carrying out nuclear magnetic resonance detection and mechanical tests of sandstone-like materials. The intrinsic relationship between porosity and compressive strength was explored. Simultaneously, the discrete element software (PFC2D) was used to simulate the stress-strain curve of the uniaxial compression test under different freeze-thaw times. Based on the built-in energy tracking command of the particle flow software, the evolution of different energies under load was analyzed. The influence of the F-T cycle on different energies was studied. Finally, the intrinsic relationship between the number of freeze-thaw cycles and the existence of different energies was discussed. The main conclusions are as follows:

(1) The microscopic structure is mainly composed of micropores, followed by mesopores, and lastly macropores. The micropores and mesopores showed an increasing trend with the increase in the number of freeze-thaw cycles, while the change in large porosity was not obvious. In addition, the porosity conformed to a good exponential relationship with the number of freeze-thaw cycles and increased exponentially with the increase in the cycles.

(2) The influence of the F-T cycle on elastic modulus is the largest, followed by peak strength, and the influence of peak strain is the least. The peak strength and elastic modulus had a good exponential relationship with the number of freeze-thaw cycles. With the increase in the number of freeze-thaw cycles, the peak strength and elastic modulus showed an exponentially decreasing trend, while the peak strain showed an exponentially increasing trend. In addition, there was a good exponential relationship between the porosity and the uniaxial compressive strength. The uniaxial compressive strength decreases exponentially with the increase in porosity.

(3) The failure mode of mechanical testing under different F-T cycle conditions was similar to that of numerical simulation. The failure is mainly tensile, accompanied by shear failure locally. The failure mode is mainly tensile failure, accompanied by shear failure. In energy evolution, strain energy and bond strain energy showed an increasing trend before the peak intensity and a decreasing trend after the peak intensity. The friction energy and crack synchronously showed an accelerated increasing trend before the peak strength and a rapid increasing trend after the peak. The total, strain, bond strain, and friction energy had an exponential relationship with the number of freeze-thaw cycles. With the increasing number of freeze-thaw cycles, different types of energy showed an exponentially decreasing trend.

Author Contributions: Conceptualization, H.D. and S.Y.; methodology, Y.X. and G.T.; software, G.T.; validation, Y.X. and G.T.; formal analysis, G.T.; investigation, Y.X.; resources, G.T.; data curation, G.T.; writing—original draft preparation, G.T.; writing—review and editing, Y.X.; visualization, G.T.; supervision, H.D.; project administration, H.D.; funding acquisition, H.D. and S.Y. All authors have read and agreed to the published version of the manuscript.

Funding: This research was supported by the National Natural Science Foundation of China (Grant No. 51874352, 52004327), the China National Key R&D Program during the 14th Five-year Plan Period (Grant No. 2021YFC2900400), Science and Technology Project of the Education Department of Jiangxi Province (Grant No. GJJ210867) and Doctoral Scientific Research Foundation of Jiangxi University of Science and Technology (Grant No. 2021003, 205200100581).

Data Availability Statement: The data presented in this study are available on request from the corresponding author.

Conflicts of Interest: The authors declare no conflict of interest.

Abbreviations

NMR	Nuclear magnetic resonance
F-T cycle	Freeze-thaw cycle
Kratio	Normal-to-shear stiffness ratio
Emod	Effective modulus
Pb_Emod	Bond effective modulus
Pb_coh	Cohesion
Pb_ten	Tensile strength
pb_fa	Friction angle

References

1. Al-Omari, A.; Beck, K.; Brunetaud, X.; Török, Á.; Al-Mukhtar, M. Critical degree of saturation: A control factor of freeze-thaw damage of porous limestones at Castle of Chambord, France. *Eng. Geol.* **2015**, *185*, 71–80. [CrossRef]
2. Li, J.; Kaunda, R.; Zhou, K. Experimental investigations on the effects of ambient freeze-thaw cycling on dynamic properties and rock pore structure deterioration of sandstone. *Cold Reg. Sci. Technol.* **2018**, *154*, 133–141. [CrossRef]
3. Li, J.; Zhu, L.; Zhou, K.; Liu, H.W.; Cao, S.P. Damage characteristics of sandstone pore structure under freeze-thaw cycles. *Rock Soil Mech.* **2020**, *9*, 3524–3532.
4. Zhou, K.; Li, B.; Li, J.; Deng, H.; Bin, F. Microscopic damage and dynamic mechanical properties of rock under freeze-thaw environment. *Trans. Nonferrous Met. Soc. China* **2015**, *25*, 1254–1261. [CrossRef]

5. Li, J.; Zhou, K.; Liu, W.; Deng, H. NMR research on deterioration characteristics of microscopic structure of sandstones in freeze-thaw cycles. *Trans. Nonferrous Met. Soc. China* **2016**, *26*, 2997–3003. [CrossRef]
6. Gao, F.; Wang, Q.; Deng, H.; Zhang, J.; Tian, W.; Ke, B. Coupled effects of chemical environments and freeze–thaw cycles on damage characteristics of red sandstone. *Bull. Eng. Geol. Environ.* **2017**, *76*, 1481–1490. [CrossRef]
7. Liu, C.; Deng, H.; Zhao, H.; Zhang, J. Effects of freeze-thaw treatment on the dynamic tensile strength of granite using the Brazilian test. *Cold Reg. Sci. Technol.* **2018**, *155*, 327–332. [CrossRef]
8. Gao, F.; Xiong, X.; Xu, C.; Zhou, K. Mechanical property deterioration characteristics and a new constitutive model for rocks subjected to freeze-thaw weathering process. *Int. J. Rock Mech. Min. Sci.* **2021**, *140*, 104642. [CrossRef]
9. Gao, F.; Xiong, X.; Zhou, K.; Li, J.; Shi, W. Strength deterioration model of saturated sandstone under freeze-thaw cycles. *Rock Soil Mech.* **2019**, *40*, 926–932.
10. Yang, C.; Zhou, K.; Xiong, X.; Deng, H.; Pan, Z. Experimental investigation on rock mechanical properties and infrared radiation characteristics with freeze-thaw cycle treatment. *Cold Reg. Sci. Technol.* **2021**, *183*, 103232. [CrossRef]
11. Li, J.; Zhu, L.; Zhou, K.; Chen, H.; Gao, L.; Lin, Y.; Shen, Y. Non-linear creep damage model of sandstone under freeze-thaw cycle. *J. Cent. South Univ.* **2021**, *28*, 954–967. [CrossRef]
12. Xie, H.; Ju, Y.; Li, L. Criteria for strength and structural failure of rocks based on energy dissipation and energy release principles. *Chin. J. Rock Mech. Eng.* **2005**, *17*, 3003–3010. (In Chinese)
13. Xie, H.; Ju, Y.; Li, L.; Peng, R.D. Energy mechanism of deformation and failure of rock masses. *Chin. J. Rock Mech. Eng.* **2008**, *9*, 1729–1740. (In Chinese)
14. Deng, H.; Yu, S.; Deng, J.; Ke, B.; Bin, F. Experimental Investigation on Energy Mechanism of Freezing-Thawing Treated Sandstone under Uniaxial Static Compression. *KSCE J. Civ. Eng.* **2019**, *23*, 2074–2082. [CrossRef]
15. Feng, Q.; Jin, J.; Zhang, S.; Liu, W.; Yang, X.; Li, W. Study on a Damage Model and Uniaxial Compression Simulation Method of Frozen–Thawed Rock. *Rock Mech. Rock Eng.* **2022**, *55*, 187–211. [CrossRef]
16. Gao, F.; Cao, S.; Zhou, K.; Lin, Y.; Zhu, L. Damage characteristics and energy-dissipation mechanism of frozen-thawed sandstone subjected to loading. *Cold Reg. Sci. Technol.* **2020**, *169*, 102920. [CrossRef]
17. Lazar, M.; Apostu, I.; Faur, F.; Rotunjanu, I. Factors influencing the flooding process of former coal open-pits. *Min. Miner. Depos.* **2021**, *15*, 124–133. [CrossRef]
18. Jiang, C.; Guo, W.; Chen, H.; Zhu, Y.; Jin, C. Effect of filler type and content on mechanical properties and microstructure of sand concrete made with superfine waste sand. *Constr. Build. Mater.* **2018**, *192*, 442–449. [CrossRef]
19. Diambra, A.; Festugato, L.; Ibraim, E.; Peccin da Silva, A.; Consoli, N.C. Modelling tensile/compressive strength ratio of artificially cemented clean sand. *Soils Found.* **2018**, *58*, 199–211. [CrossRef]
20. Ueyendah, S.; Lezgy-Nazargah, M.; Eskandari-Naddaf, H.; Emamian, S.A. Predicting the mechanical properties of cement mortar using the support vector machine approach. *Constr. Build. Mater.* **2021**, *291*, 123396. [CrossRef]
21. Chuta, E.; Colin, J.; Jeong, J. The impact of the water-to-cement ratio on the surface morphology of cementitious materials. *J. Build. Eng.* **2020**, *32*, 101716. [CrossRef]
22. Deng, H.; Tian, G.; Yu, S.; Jiang, Z.; Zhong, Z.; Zhang, Y. Research on Strength Prediction Model of Sand-like Material Based on Nuclear Magnetic Resonance and Fractal Theory. *Appl. Sci.* **2020**, *10*, 6601. [CrossRef]
23. Tian, G.; Deng, H.; Xiao, Y. Correlation Analysis between Microscopic Pore Parameters and Macroscopic Mechanical Properties of Rock-like Materials from the Perspective of Water-Cement Ratio and Sand-Cement Ratio. *Materials* **2022**, *15*, 2632. [CrossRef] [PubMed]
24. Tian, G.; Deng, H.; Xiao, Y.; Yu, S. Experimental Study of Multi-Angle Effects of Micron-Silica Fume on Micro-Pore Structure and Macroscopic Mechanical Properties of Rock-like Material Based on NMR and SEM. *Materials* **2022**, *15*, 3388. [CrossRef]
25. *SL/T 264-2020*; Rock Test Regulations for Water Conservancy and Hydropower Engineering. People's Republic of China Ministry of Water Resources: Beijing, China, 2020. (In Chinese)
26. Cundall, P.; Strack, O. A discrete numerical model for granular assemblies. *Geotechnique* **1979**, *29*, 47–65. [CrossRef]
27. Zhao, Z.; Wang, X.; Wen, Z. Analysis of Rock Damage Characteristics Based on Particle Discrete Element Model. *Geotech. Geol. Eng.* **2018**, *36*, 897–904. [CrossRef]
28. Ning, J.; Liu, X.; Tan, Y.; Wang, J.; Tian, C. Relationship of box counting of fractured rock mass with Hoek–Brown parameters using particle flow simulation. *Geomech. Eng.* **2015**, *9*, 619–629. [CrossRef]
29. Chen, P.Y. Effects of microparameters on macroparameters of flat-jointed bonded-particle materials and suggestions on trial-and-error method. *Geotech. Geol. Eng.* **2017**, *35*, 663–677. [CrossRef]
30. Tan, X.; Chen, W.; Liu, H.; Wang, L.; Ma, W.; Chan, A.H.C. A unified model for frost heave pressure in the rock with a penny-shaped fracture during freezing. *Cold Reg. Sci. Technol.* **2018**, *153*, 1–9. [CrossRef]
31. Huang, S.; Ye, Y.; Cui, X.; Cheng, A.; Liu, G. Theoretical and experimental study of the frost heaving characteristics of the saturated sandstone under low temperature. *Cold Reg. Sci. Technol.* **2020**, *174*, 103036. [CrossRef]
32. Deprez, M.; Kock, T.; De Schutter, G.; Cnudde, V. A review on freeze-thaw action and weathering of rocks. *Earth-Sci. Rev.* **2020**, *203*, 103143. [CrossRef]

33. Huang, S.; Lu, Z.; Ye, Z.; Xin, Z. An elastoplastic model of frost deformation for the porous rock under freeze-thaw. *Eng. Geol.* **2020**, *278*, 105820. [CrossRef]
34. Huang, S.; Yu, S.; Ye, Y.; Ye, Z.; Cheng, A. Pore structure change and physico-mechanical properties deterioration of sandstone suffering freeze-thaw actions. *Constr. Build. Mater.* **2022**, *330*, 127200. [CrossRef]

Disclaimer/Publisher's Note: The statements, opinions and data contained in all publications are solely those of the individual author(s) and contributor(s) and not of MDPI and/or the editor(s). MDPI and/or the editor(s) disclaim responsibility for any injury to people or property resulting from any ideas, methods, instructions or products referred to in the content.

Article

Refined Design and Optimization of Underground Medium and Long Hole Blasting Parameters—A Case Study of the Gaofeng Mine

Feng Gao [1,2], Xin Li [1,2], Xin Xiong [1,2,*], Haichuan Lu [3] and Zengwu Luo [3]

1. School of Resources and Safety Engineering, Central South University, Changsha 410083, China
2. Hunan Provincial Key Laboratory of Resources Exploitation and Hazard Control for Deep Metal Mines, Central South University, Changsha 410083, China
3. Guangxi Gaofeng Mining Co., Ltd., Nandan 547051, China
* Correspondence: xiongxin@csu.edu.cn; Tel.: +86-152-7496-1487

Abstract: Previously conducted studies have established that the rationality of the parameters of medium-deep hole blasting is one of the main factors affecting the blasting effect. To solve the problem of the parameter design and optimization design of medium-deep hole blasting in underground mines, a method of parameter design and the optimization of medium-deep hole blasting based on the blasting crater tests and numerical simulation analyses has been proposed in this study. Based on the background of deep underground mining in Gaofeng Mine, a two-hole blasting model has been established, and the blasting parameters are simulated and analyzed by the damage stress variation of the two-hole model. During the study, the initial values of blasting parameters were first obtained from the field blasting crater test, then the blasting parameters were optimized and analyzed by LS-DYNA software, and finally, the optimization scheme was demonstrated by the corresponding blasting test. The results of the field test showed that the design method of integrated blast crater test and numerical simulation analysis can effectively optimize the design of medium-deep hole blasting parameters and improve the blasting effect to a large extent. This study also provides an effective design system for the design of deep hole blasting parameters in similar mines.

Keywords: medium-deep hole blasting parameters; parameter design and optimization; blast crater test; LS-DYNA numerical simulation optimization; analysis of rock breaking by blasting

MSC: 74-10; 74G15

Citation: Gao, F.; Li, X.; Xiong, X.; Lu, H.; Luo, Z. Refined Design and Optimization of Underground Medium and Long Hole Blasting Parameters—A Case Study of the Gaofeng Mine. *Mathematics* 2023, 11, 1612. https://doi.org/10.3390/math11071612

Academic Editors: Danial Jahed Armaghani, Hadi Khabbaz, Manoj Khandelwal, Niaz Muhammad Shahani, Ramesh Murlidhar Bhatawdekar and Andrey Jivkov

Received: 22 February 2023
Revised: 18 March 2023
Accepted: 22 March 2023
Published: 27 March 2023

Copyright: © 2023 by the authors. Licensee MDPI, Basel, Switzerland. This article is an open access article distributed under the terms and conditions of the Creative Commons Attribution (CC BY) license (https://creativecommons.org/licenses/by/4.0/).

1. Introduction

In mining engineering, medium-deep hole blasting has been widely used in mining. Compared with shallow hole blasting, medium-deep hole blasting has a larger one-time blasting amount, more ore caving, low explosive consumption, and high production efficiency. Moreover, the mining cycle is reduced and the production auxiliary system is simplified [1,2].

It has been proved that reasonable blasting parameters are core to ensuring the quality of medium-deep hole blasting, and the design and optimization of blasting parameters are of great significance to mining [3,4]. In recent years, a lot of work has been carried out to determine the parameters of blasting and the impact of disturbances on the rock mass. Stanković et al. [5] have studied the effect of vibration monitoring instruments positioning on burst vibration, and give recommendations for vibration monitoring instruments positioning during test blasts on any new site, to optimize charge weight per delay for future blasting works without increasing the possibility of damaging surrounding structures. Sołtys [6] has used a matching pursuit algorithm to assess the impact of blasting in open-pit mines on the surrounding area and has proved that by taking into account frequency changes over time, vibration analysis can help make much more profound and reliable predictions in this field.

In traditional blasting parameter optimization and design, mines mainly design blasting parameters based on empirical formulas and adjust blasting parameters according to geological conditions and other conditions. Himanshu et al. [7] have designed the blasting parameters for Ring holes on underground slopes based on empirical formulas and projected the rock fragmentation effect using the Kuz-Ram model, which has also achieved some success. However, the empirical formula method is simple to operate, but the method is subjective to human influence, lacks the corresponding theoretical support, and the effect of optimization also has certain limitations [8]. Nowadays, blasting projects have higher requirements in terms of fragmentation, explosive energy control, blasting efficiency, and safety and environmental protection, and traditional methods can no longer achieve the requirements, so a fine blasting theory has gradually been developed that is more compatible with modern blasting requirements [9].

Up to now, the refined blasting design and optimization system have been applied to more and more blasting fields. Pal et al. [10] have conducted a systematic study on drilling, blasting parameters, gas hazards, strata behavior, and ground vibration to solve the design problem of underground-induced blasting, providing a research idea for a similar blast design. Widodo et al. [11] have analyzed the overbreak and underbreak of each scheme during field blasting, and obtained the optimal scheme under different explosives and blasting parameters, which effectively improved the blasting effect. These methods have achieved good results, but there are some shortcomings that do not reflect the optimization work of blasting parameters. Instead, the common method used in field blasting test research is to design and optimize blasting parameters based on blast crater tests. Jeon et al. [12] have conducted a blasting crater test in underground mines and calculated the minimum explosive quantity of rocks according to the characteristics of rock blasting damage. This method effectively improved the blasting charge. Zhang et al. [13] have conducted blast crater tests under different stress load conditions and proposed a design method for blast parameters considering field stresses based on the test results. The design method based on field blasting tests makes the blasting parameters closer to the actual conditions of the mine, but the method is also subjectively influenced by humans and may produce some errors. Thus, based on the blasting crater test, an intelligent algorithm-based parameter optimization method is proposed. Monjezi et al. [14] have used a genetic algorithm to optimize blasting parameters, which effectively reduced blasting fly rock generation. Dehghani et al. [15] have optimized blasting parameters by a cuckoo optimization algorithm, which effectively reduced blasting fly rock. Saghatforoush et al. [16] have used artificial neural networks for the prediction of blasting fly rock and achieved optimization of blasting parameters by the ant colony optimization algorithm. Bastami et al. [17] have used gene expression programming and particle swarm optimization to predict and optimize blasting costs and obtained optimized blasting parameter designs through blasting cost optimization analysis, which effectively improved blasting fragmentation and reduced the adverse consequences of the blasting process. Sirjani [18] has used the artificial neural network (ANN) model and statistical models to study the anti-rupture in the blasting process. According to the prediction and analysis of the model, the optimal blast pattern design parameters are determined.

These algorithms have greatly improved the rationality of blasting parameters, but the optimization scheme based on intelligent algorithm still has problems such as incomplete analysis and evaluation of the influence factors of blasting parameters, and the intelligent algorithm only focuses on the data itself without linking the relationship between the data, Therefore, the analysis system of blasting parameter optimization based on numerical simulation was gradually formed in the subsequent research [19]. Huang et al. [20] have used PFC2D to optimize blasting parameters and obtained the optimal blasting parameters by analyzing the simulated blasting effects and stress values at monitoring points under different parameters. Jiang et al. [21] have analyzed the damage characteristics of VCR blasting surrounding rocks using FLAC3D and derived the relationship between explosive quantity and damage radius of surrounding rocks, which provides a theoretical basis for optimizing blasting parameters. Mejía et al. [22] have simulated the blasting of different shaped explosive charges using CFD and ANSYS, and obtained Characterization of Blast Wave Parameters of Shaped Charges through the analysis of shock wave stresses to provide support for the design of charging parameters of poly energy charges. The blasting can be simulated by FLAC3D, PFC2D, and other software, but LS-DYNA is the most widely used software in research and practical application. LS-DYNA can clearly show the formation process of fracture area and the development of damage fracture in rock during blasting and can also monitor the stress at key points during the simulation process [23–25]. Huo et al. [26] have analyzed the rock damage of lateral blasting using LS-DYNA and improved the blasting parameters based on the simulation results. Sun et al. [27] have used LS-DYNA software to carry out numerical simulation analysis on the influence of different factors on the blasting presplitting process and have determined the best parameters for blasting drilling. The practice has proven that LS-DYNA software can easily and accurately simulate the process of blasting and rock breaking, and now it has become a common analysis tool in blasting research. However, the optimization of blasting parameters based on numerical simulation greatly improves the rationality of the parameters, but the simulation requires certain initial parameter data, and most of the initial parameter data in the study come from empirical design, lacking the corresponding experimental basis, and to a certain extent, it is also detached from the actual situation of the mine site.

Analyzing the above, it can be noted that the design of medium-deep hole blasting parameters is a very topical issue. Therefore, the purpose of this study is to obtain reasonable parameters for medium-deep hole blasting underground in the Gaofeng Mine, and to achieve this, it is necessary to solve the following tasks: (1) carry out field engineering geological investigation and field blasting crater test; (2) carry out a numerical simulation to optimize blasting parameters; (3) and carry out field blasting tests and analyze blasting results. The specific blasting parameter optimization design process is demonstrated in Figure 1.

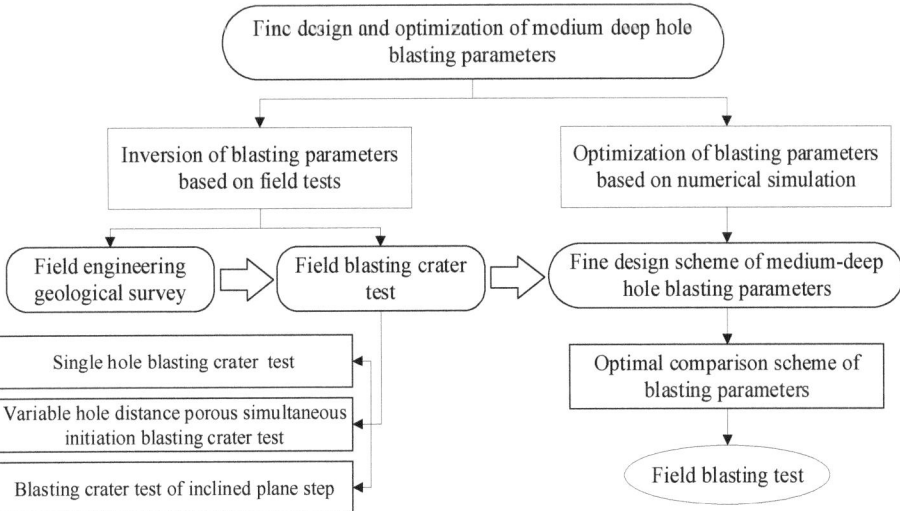

Figure 1. Fine design and optimization flow chart of medium-deep hole blasting parameters (done by the authors).

2. Inversion of Medium-Deep Hole Blasting Parameters Based on Blasting Crater Test

This blasting crater test includes a single-hole blasting crater test, variable hole distance porous simultaneous initiation blasting crater test, and blasting crater test of the inclined plane step. The blasting crater test is based on the Livingston blasting crater theory, also known as the energy balance theory. According to Livingston, when a spherical charge explodes inside the rock, the degree of deformation and destruction of the rock depends largely on the amount of energy that passes through it. Livingston studied the effect of changing the embedment depth of the charge on rock failure with the weight of the charge unchanged and proposed that the relationship between the critical embedment depth of the charge L_e and the charge quantity Q can be expressed by the following formula [28]:

$$L_e = E \times Q^{1/3} \tag{1}$$

where L_e is the critical burial depth, E is the strain energy coefficient, and E is constant for specific rocks and explosives. Q is the weight of the globular package.

Livingston's blasting crater theory is based on the ball charge test. The charge quantity for the blasting of spherical charge is calculated according to the law of cubic root similarity. That is, when the same explosive explodes in the same kind of rock, each parameter of the blasting crater with a certain effect is exploded when the amount of explosive is Q_0, and each parameter of the other blasting crater when the amount of explosive is changed to Q_1 and meets the cubic formula [28]:

$$\frac{(L_{j1})^3}{(L_{j0})^3} = \frac{(Q_{j1})^3}{(Q_{j0})^3} = \frac{(R_{j1})^3}{(R_{j0})^3} = \frac{V_1}{V_0} = \frac{Q_1}{Q_0} \tag{2}$$

where subscriptions 0 and 1 represent the original blasting model and derived model, respectively. L_j is the best burying depth of explosives for blasting crater tests. Q_j is the best charge quantity for the blasting crater test. R_j is the best radius of the blasting crater. V_j is the optimum volume of the blasting crater.

According to the basic principle that the shape of the blasting crater is similar under different charge amounts and the optimum consumption per unit is unchanged, the parameter relation of different blasting craters under different cylindrical charge conditions can be obtained by replacing the buried depth of spherical charge with the depth of blasting hole. Finally, according to the blasting similarity principle, the blasting parameters of medium-deep holes under the same geological conditions can be derived from the blasting parameters of spherical charge [29].

2.1. Engineering Background

The average thickness of the ore body at the test mining site of the medium-deep hole blasting drop at the Guangxi Summit Mine is about 10 m. The ore body elevation is −110 m~−134 m, the length of the ore body is about 21 m, the middle thickness is thin at both ends, and it is an independent small orebody. Minerals and surrounding rocks are more moderately stable than those affected by historical excavation. Depending on the shape distribution of the ore body and mining equipment, mining is divided into upper and lower parts, and a blasting network is used for ore falling. In the design, the depth of the deep hole is 12 m and the diameter of the hole is 65 mm. The details of the ore body are demonstrated in Figure 2.

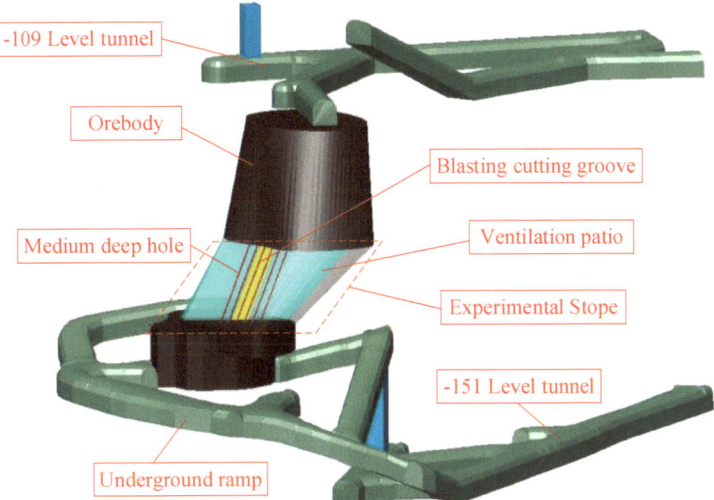

Figure 2. Three-dimensional model of orebody (done by the authors).

The deposit type of the Gao Feng mine is a cassiterite-sulfide type deposit, with a clear boundary between the ore body and the surrounding rocks. The underground ore is mainly cassiterite, with a saturated compressive strength of 80~100 MPa, and the ore is dense and massive with good solidity. The rock quality is above medium, and most of the rock body is above medium integrity. The enclosing rocks are mainly biogenic reef tuffs with a saturated compressive strength of 58 to 90.1 MPa. For hard rocks, the rock quality is above medium, and the enclosing rocks are mostly of good integrity and high compressive strength.

Medium-deep hole blasting has been attempted in the Gaofeng Mine. Due to various factors, it results in a high block rate and an unsatisfactory blasting effect. Because of the above problems, this test carries out a fine design of medium-deep hole blasting parameters through field tests and numerical simulation methods to improve the blasting effect

2.2. Blasting Crater Test Scheme

Firstly, through the single-hole blasting crater tests, the optimum buried depth of the charge center, the volume, and the radius of the blasting crater are determined under the condition of the single hole. Secondly, based on the parameters of single-hole series blasting crater tests, the variable-spacing multi-hole and same-stage blasting crater tests are carried out, and the optimum hole spacing and explosive consumption under this test condition are deduced. Finally, the minimum resistance line parameters of blasting are determined by the crater test of inclined step blasting. According to the blasting similarity theory, the optimum range of medium-deep hole blasting parameters can be calculated. There are 20 holes with 40 mm diameters in this series of hole crater tests. The specific arrangement of the test holes is demonstrated in Figure 3.

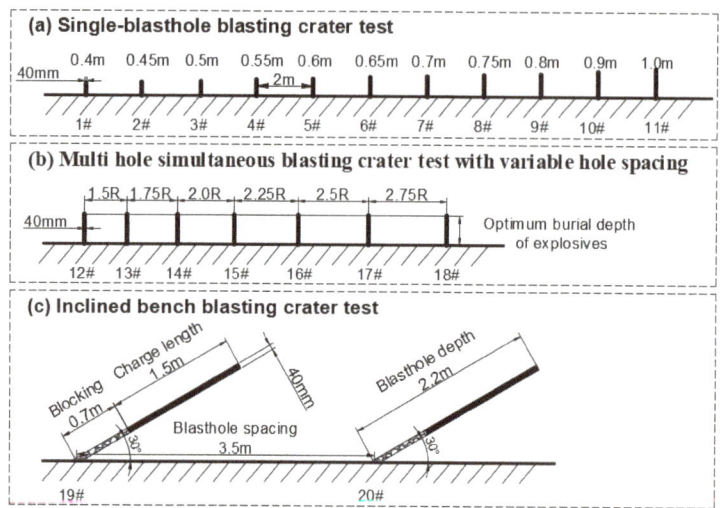

Figure 3. Blasthole arrangement for series blasting crater tests.

2.3. Analysis of Experimental Results

As demonstrated in Figure 4, the field test data collected are processed by CAD, 3D MINE, and MATLAB. The final series of test results are yielded in Table 1.

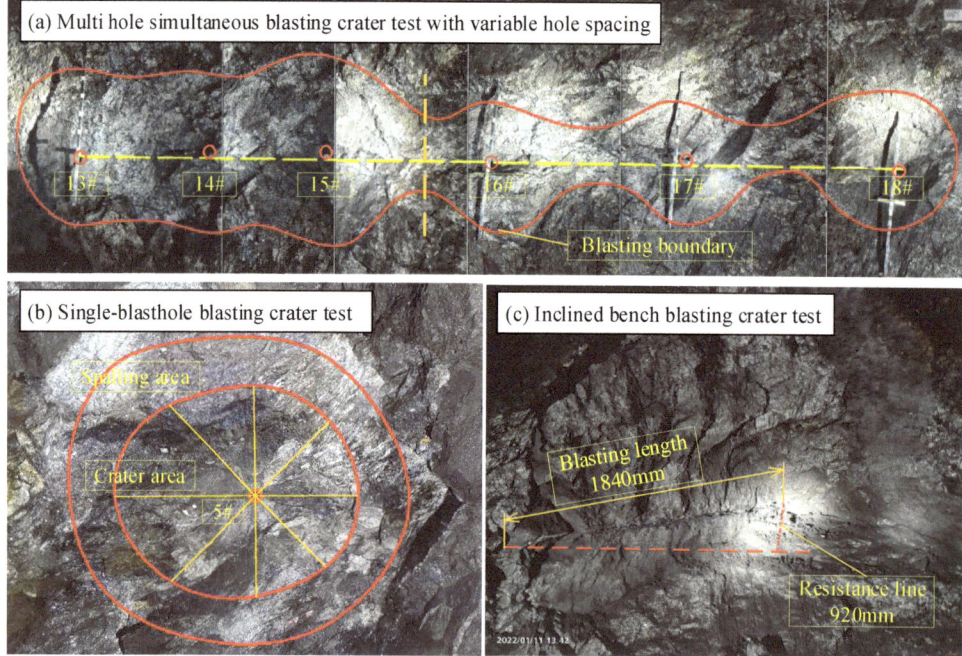

Figure 4. Field effect of series blasting crater tests.

Table 1. Series blasting crater test results.

Parameter	Unit	Value	Parameter	Unit	Value
Optimum depth of explosive	L_j/m	0.5	Optimum crater radius	R_j/m	0.58
Critical burial depth of explosives	L_e/m	0.67	Optimal crater volume	V_j/m	0.32
Optimum depth ratio	Δ_j	0.74	Strain energy coefficient	E	1.01
Optimum hole base spacing	a_j/m	1.0	Optimum resistance line	W_j/m	0.9

According to the blasting similarity theory, the average charge required to break a rock per cubic meter is a fixed value for a given rock. In cylindrical charge, when the charge parameter is changed to the charge quantity per unit length, the proportional relation changes from cubic relation to square relation. That is, the blasting similarity relationship can be expressed by the following formula [30]:

$$\frac{L_x}{L_y} = \left(\frac{q_x}{q_y}\right)^{1/2} \qquad (3)$$

where L_x and L_y are the linear parameters of the bore corresponding to the cylindrical charge blasting model and the blasting test model, such as resistance line, hole bottom distance, etc. q_x and q_y are the charge quantities of the cylindrical charge blasting model and the blasting test model, respectively.

Therefore, based on the above analysis, when the hole diameter is 65 mm, the parameters of medium-deep hole blasting are calculated as follows:

(1) Unit loading q = 1.58 kg/m.
(2) Hole distance a = 1.6 m.
(3) Resistance line b = 1.4 m.

3. Blasting Parameter Optimization Based on Numerical Simulation

3.1. Model Building

LS-DYNA nonlinear finite element software was used to optimize the parameters obtained from the blasting test. At present, the blasting method of row by row is mainly adopted for medium-deep holes under the Gaofeng Mine, and there are only two free planes in each row, and there is a certain stage difference between front and back blasting. Therefore, in order to facilitate more convenient simulation analysis and be more suitable for the actual mine production, the model is simplified to analyze the first-row blasting problem, and a double-hole blasting model is established. At the same time, since the hole depth was much larger than the aperture in the test, the numerical model was simplified into a two-dimensional calculation model without affecting the accuracy of the simulation [31]. In the simulation, the fluid-structure coupling calculation method was used for modeling, the Lagrange algorithm model was set for rock, the Euler algorithm model for explosive, and the 1/2 symmetric grid model was adopted. Since the blasting model was based on the plane stress problem of the infinite body, in addition to the free plane of the cutting groove, no reflection boundary conditions are set in the other three directions, and normal constraints are set in the Z direction [32]. The middle part of the model is the ore area, and the two sides are the surrounding rock area to simulate the blasting and crushing environment of the ore under the surrounding rock clip production. The front area of the model is the free surface area, which is used to simulate the free surface formed by the blasting and cutting groove. The specific model settings are yielded in Figure 5.

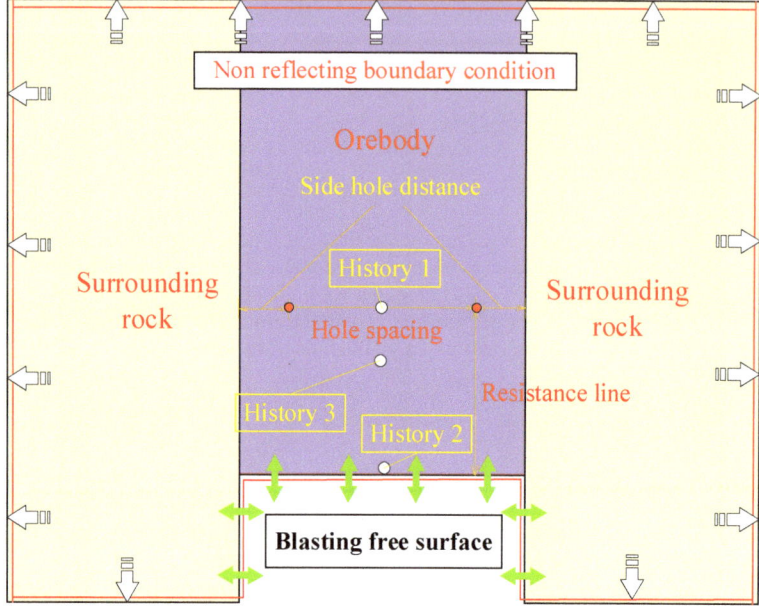

Figure 5. Numerical calculation model.

3.2. Material Parameter

3.2.1. Rock Material Model

RHT (Riedel-Hiermaier-Thoma) constitutive model was selected for rock materials, which was proposed by Riedel, Hiermaier, and Thoma on the basis of the HJC (Holmquist-Johnson-Cook) model. The influence of the third invariant of the deviatoric stress tensor J3 on the shape of the failure surface was introduced to determine the strain type and stress state of the material, and the strength of the material was elucidated by the yield surface, failure surface, and residual strength surface [33,34]. This model is also used to simulate damage constitutive models of rock impact and blasting.

There are many parameters of the RHT model, including default parameters, physical and mechanical property parameters, calculation and derivation parameters, equation-of-state parameters, damage parameters, and strength-related parameters. In the early stage of this test, relevant indoor rock mechanics tests have been completed, and specific mechanical property parameters have been obtained. By referring to relevant literature and similar model parameter design experience [35–37] and determining the values of all parameters of the model, as yielded in Table 2.

3.2.2. Explosive Material Model

During simulation, the HIGH-EXPLOSIVE model in the LS-DYNA material library is used to describe the constitutive relation of explosive, and the Jones-Wilkins-Lee (JWL) equation of state (EOS) is used to describe the relationship between explosive volume expansion and explosive pressure. This equation can fully reflect the stress variation process of explosives in the process of the explosion and is widely used in simulated blasting models [38–40].

Table 2. RHT material parameters input in LS-DYNA.

Parameter	Value	Parameter	Value
Mass density (kg/m^3)	4530	Tensile strain rate dependence exponent BETAT	0.0189
Elastic shear modulus (GPa)	17.39	Pressure influence on plastic flow in tension PTF	0.001
Eroding plastic strain EPSF	2.0	Compressive yield surface parameter GC*	0.53
Parameter for polynomial EOS B_0	1.2	Tensile yield surface parameter GT*	0.7
Parameter for polynomial EOS B_1	1.2	Shear modulus reduction factor XI	0.5
Parameter for polynomial EOS T_1 (GPa)	39.15	Damage parameter D_1	0.04
Failure surface parameter A	2.1	Damage parameter D_2	1
Failure surface parameter N	0.125	Minimum damaged residual strain EPM	0.015
Compressive strength FC (GPa)	85.62	Residual surface parameter AF	1.6
Relative shear strength FS*	0.2311	Residual surface parameter NF	0.61
Relative tensile strength FT*	0.048	Gruneisen gamma GAMMA	0
Lode angle dependence factor Q_0	0.68	Hugoniot polynomial coefficient A_1 (GPa)	39.15
Lode angle dependence factor B	0.05	Hugoniot polynomial coefficient A_2 (GPa)	46.98
Parameter for polynomial EOS T_2	0	Hugoniot polynomial coefficient A_3 (GPa)	9.004
Reference compressive strain rate EOC	3×10^{-5}	Crush pressure PEL (MPa)	57.08
Reference tensile strain rate EOT	3×10^{-6}	Compaction pressure PCO (GPa)	6.0
Break compressive strain rate EC	3×10^{25}	Porosity exponent NP	3.0
Break tensile strain rate ET	3×10^{25}	Initial porosity ALPHA	1.1
Compressive strain rate dependence exponent BETAC	0.0144		

3.3. Modeling Scheme

The corresponding simulation scheme is set up according to the initial blasting parameters obtained from the field blasting crater test. During the simulation, the blasting schemes with different resistance lines are first compared and analyzed, and the parameters of the best resistance lines are determined. Then, the blasting schemes with different hole distances are simulated and analyzed, so as to attain the best blasting hole network parameter scheme. In addition, according to the related research, increasing the hole density coefficient can effectively improve in medium-deep hole blasting effect and decrease the rate of large blocks, but the first row of the blast hole density coefficient should not be too big, the first row of the best hole density coefficient of between 0.9 and 1.1 [41]. Therefore, in order to avoid invalid pore mesh parameter schemes and simplify the workload of numerical simulation, when setting relevant pore mesh parameter schemes, the shot hole density coefficient of the simulation scheme should be kept within the range of the best shot hole density coefficient.

3.4. Analysis of Numerical Simulation Results

3.4.1. Blasting Rock-Breaking Analysis

In numerical simulation blasting, the rock is generally considered to be broken if the damage coefficient of the rock is above 0.6 [26]. Therefore, the rock breakage in the blasting process can be demonstrated in a more comprehensive way according to the cloud map of rock damage fissure changes. According to modern blasting rock-breaking theory, rock destruction is mainly formed by the combined action of explosion shock wave and detonation gas [42]. According to the blasting rock-breaking theory, taking the initial blasting parameter model of 1.6m×1.4m as the research object, the blasting rock-breaking process is divided into 4 stages, as yielded in Figure 6.

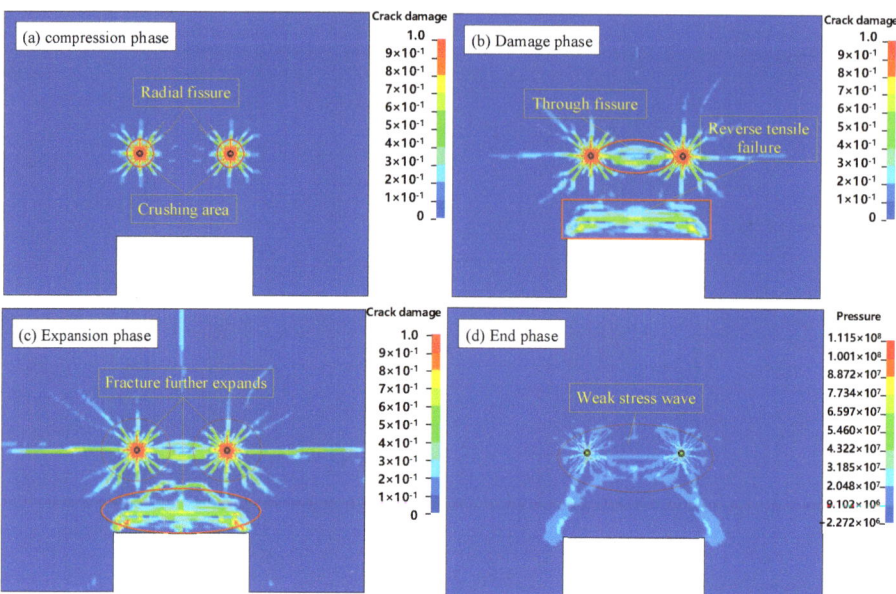

Figure 6. Simulated blasting rock-breaking process.

The first stage is the compression stage, as yielded in Figure 6a. Under the action of a high-pressure shock wave, the surrounding rock near the gun hole is compacted to form a compressible crushing zone. Since the crushing zone absorbs most of the energy of the blasting shock wave, the explosion shock wave rapidly attenuates into stress waves. Although the strength of the stress wave is not enough to compress the rock, the outer rock of the crushing zone is still subjected to strong radial compression, and radial cracks are generated to form the cracked zone.

The second stage is the damage stage, as yielded in Figure 6b. This stage is the main rock-breaking stage. The stress waves between the two holes begin to superposition, and the cracks are connected, resulting in rock failure. Moreover, when the stress waves are transmitted to the free surface, reflections are generated, and the compressive stress waves become tensile stress waves, resulting in large area tensile failure of the free surface rock under the action of reflected tensile force.

The third stage is the expansion stage, as yielded in Figure 6c. At this stage, with the continuous action of stress waves and blasting gas, the cracks continue to expand, resulting in further rock damage.

The fourth stage is the end stage, as yielded in Figure 6d. At this stage, the stress wave and blasting gas have attenuated to the point that the rock cannot be damaged and the crack cannot continue to expand.

Through the simulation of the rock-breaking process of blasting, it can be seen that the position of the free surface during blasting is mainly caused by the tensile failure caused by the reflection of the tensile stress wave. The damage distribution area of this part of the rock is large, and the rock-breaking condition is relatively good. However, the rock between the holes is mainly caused by the mutual penetration of radial cracks caused by the blasting shock wave. This part of the damage mainly depends on the combined action of radial compression stress and detonation gas. The damaged area is small, and the crushing effect is worse than that of the free surface.

3.4.2. Influence of Resistance Line on Blasting Effect

According to the above-simulated rock-breaking analysis process, the effect of the damage fracture program and stress monitoring curve on different resistance lines is simulated and analyzed. The hole spacing was set at 1.6 m, and the resistance lines were set at 1.5 m, 1.4 m, and 1.3 m, respectively. The simulated damage results of each scheme are yielded in Figure 7.

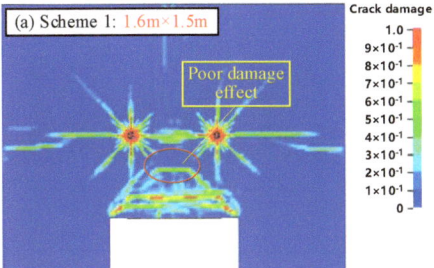
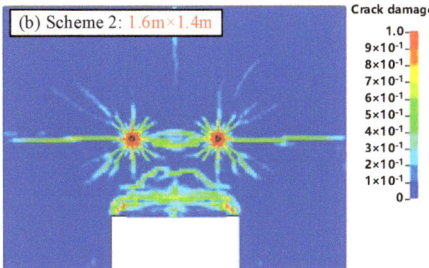
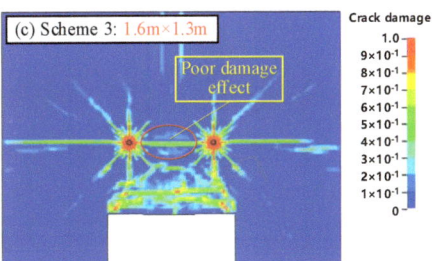

Figure 7. Simulation results of rock damage fracture.

It can be seen from Figure 7 that as the resistance line decreases, the crushing effect of the free surface rock body is also better, but the analysis from Figure 7c demonstrated that when the free surface resistance line is smallest, the rock crushing degree between the gun holes is poorer, which indicates that not the smaller the resistance line, the better the overall crushing effect. This may be due to the resistance line being small or the free-face reverse tensile stress wave having prematurely destroyed the free-face rock, resulting in the premature release of blast gas from the free face, thus affecting the effect of rock fragmentation between the shell holes. Therefore, from the perspective of the development of damage crushing, when the resistance line is 1.3 m, the simulation obtained the best damage-crushing effect of the free face, and when the resistance line is 1.4 m, the overall damage-crushing effect of blasting is the best.

In order to compare and analyze the damage effects of each scheme more accurately, corresponding stress monitoring points (history one and history two) are set in the middle of the hole and in the middle of the free surface during the simulation process. The blasting damage of rock mass between the free surface and the hole can be judged by the stress of the blasting shock wave. The shock wave monitored by each scheme is yielded in Figure 8.

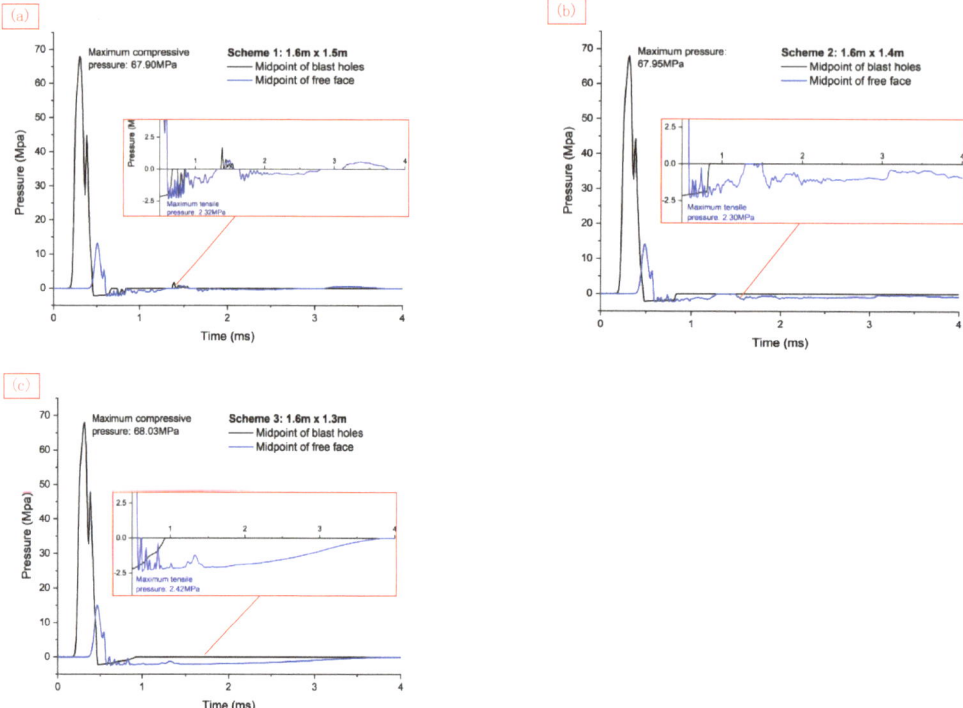

Figure 8. The results of the blast wave monitoring.

Figure 8 demonstrated that around 0.4 ms after blasting, the blasting shock wave is transmitted to the free surface and rapidly increases to the maximum value. Then, the reflection begins to decrease to form a tensile stress wave, which gradually decays to 0. The tensile stress wave also fluctuates up and down due to the interaction between the blast wave in the gun hole. By comparing and analyzing the stress monitored by the free surface, it can be seen that when the hole distance is fixed at 1.6 m, the smaller the resistance line, the longer the action time of the free surface tensile stress wave, and the more uniform the change. According to the blasting mechanism, the damage to the free surface rock is mainly caused by reflecting the tensile stress wave. Therefore, from the perspective of the tensile stress wave, the smaller the resistance line is. The damage and crushing effect of free-face rock are also better.

According to the stress distribution monitoring at the intermediate point of the hole, it can be seen that at about 0.3 ms, the blasting shock wave is transmitted to the intermediate point of the hole and quickly reaches the maximum value, about 70 MPa. Although the stress value of the shock wave at this time is less than the compressive strength of the rock, which is not enough to damage the rock, according to the analysis of blasting rock breakage, blasting rock breakage is not a single impact failure but rather the combined action of shock waves and detonation gas. Therefore, it can be seen from the damage fracture diagram that, although a shock wave is not enough to damage rock, the rock still suffers damage and failure under comprehensive action conditions. It can be seen from the analysis of the graph that the cracks between the two holes are free planes of each other to a certain extent, so a certain reflected tensile stress also appears in the monitoring stress. However, the free plane conditions formed by the holes are limited, and the tensile stress generated between the holes is small.

3.4.3. Analysis of Hole Distance Simulation Results

According to the above simulation results, under the condition that the optimal resistance line is 1.4 m, the hole spacing is set at 1.6 m, 1.5 m, and 1.4 m, respectively, to conduct the simulation test. In order to fully verify the influence of the resistance line, another 3 models with 1.6 m, 1.5 m, and 1.4 m hole spacing were set under the condition of the 1.3 m resistance line. The simulated damage results of each scheme are yielded in Figure 9.

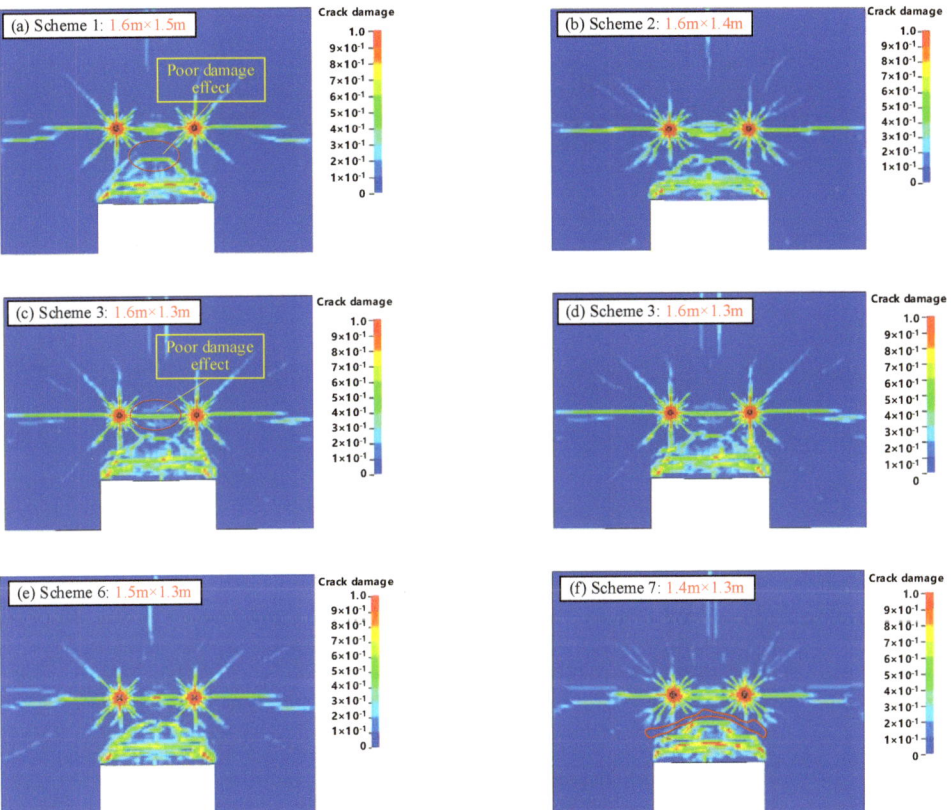

Figure 9. Simulation results of rock damage fracture.

As can be seen from Figure 9, when the resistance line is 1.4 m, the damaging effect of free-face rock in Scheme 2 is slightly worse than that in Scheme 4 and Scheme 5, but the damage condition is also in a good state. According to the damaging effect of the rock between the holes, the damaging effect of Scheme 4 is better than that of Scheme 2 and Scheme 5. It is analyzed that the interaction between the holes may be weakened when the hole distance is too large. However, when the hole distance is small, the shock wave forms the penetrating fissure on the line between holes too early, resulting in the explosion of energy escaping in advance. Therefore, when the resistance line is 1.4 m, the rock blasting damage effect is the best when the hole distance in Scheme 4 is set at 1.5 m.

Compared with the analysis of each scheme in Figure 9, it can be seen that when the resistance line is 1.3 m, the free surface blasting damage effect of each scheme is better than that of the scheme with the resistance line being 1.4 m. Meanwhile, the rock damage and breakage effect between the free surface and the hole is better as the hole distance is smaller. To a certain extent, it promotes the damage and crushing effect of rock between holes and free face. Therefore, when the resistance line is 1.3 m, the rock damage effect is the best when the hole spacing in Scheme 7 is 1.4 m.

Comprehensive comparative analysis of Scheme 4 and Scheme 7, although the 2 schemes are the best schemes at the resistance line of 1.4 m and 1.3 m, respectively, there are still some differences, as can be seen from Figure 9b,f, there is a certain weak damage zone between the gun hole and the free surface damage for both schemes (red circled part in the figure), and obviously, the comparison can be seen that compared with Scheme 4, the weak damage zone area of Scheme 7 is smaller, so the overall blast damage effect of Scheme 7 is better from the blast damage point of view.

In order to determine the blasting effect of the two schemes in the weak damage area more accurately, the corresponding blasting shock wave monitoring point (history 3) is established in the weak fracture area in the simulation, and the blasting damage situation is judged by analyzing the shock wave stress there. The specific distribution of the shock wave is yielded in Figure 10.

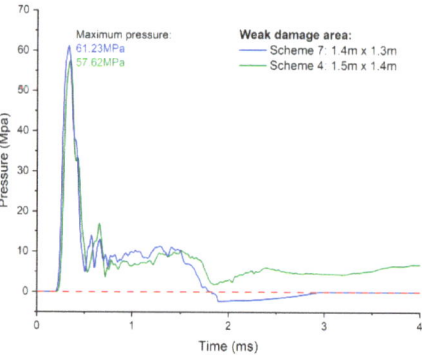

Figure 10. The results of the blast wave monitoring.

It can be seen from Figure 10, the pressure of the blasting shock wave rapidly increases to the maximum value of about 60 MPa at 0.4 ms after detonation, and the maximum pressure value of Scheme 7 is slightly larger than Scheme 4, and then decreases rapidly. Affected by the free surface reflected tensile stress wave, it fluctuates up and down to a certain extent. Some tensile stress even appears in Scheme 7 at 1.8 m. The reason may be that Scheme 7 is more strongly influenced by the free surface reflection tensile stress, which leads to the rapid reduction of compressive stress. From this aspect, it can also be demonstrated that, under the condition that the total blasting energy remains unchanged, the reverse tensile effect generated by Scheme 7 is stronger, and the tensile force transmitted to the weak crushing zone is also larger. Therefore, it can be said that the damage-crushing effect of Scheme 7 in the weak crushing zone is better than that of Scheme 4.

Based on the above analysis, it can be seen from the blasting damage and stress distribution of Scheme 4 and Scheme 7 that the optimal hole mesh parameter scheme should be Scheme 7: 1.4 m × 1.3 m.

4. Field Blasting Test

To further verify the reliability of the theoretical analysis and numerical simulation test results, the optimal Scheme 7 obtained by numerical simulation and the initial Scheme 2 obtained by blasting crater test are selected for the field blasting test. Two rows of holes were arranged in each scheme, and parallel medium-deep holes were arranged in the middle of the rear plate. To better control the footplate boundary, fan-shaped holes were set near the footplate boundary. To avoid excessive concentration of explosives, a cross-charging structure was adopted in the fan-shaped holes. The hole layout is yielded in Figure 11.

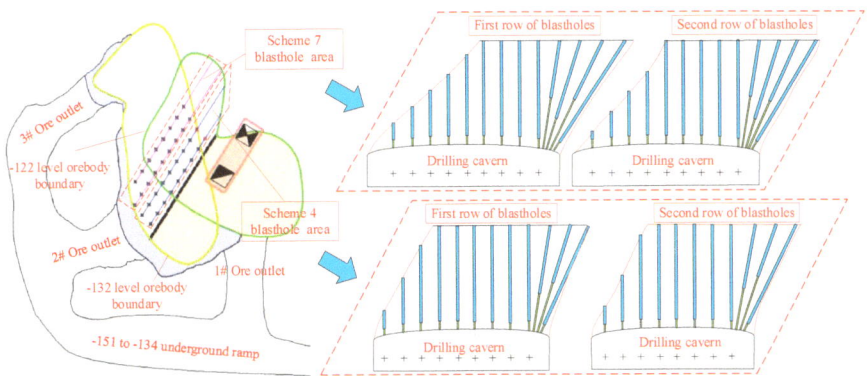

Figure 11. Field blasting hole layout.

The site blasting situation is yielded in Figure 12. According to the analysis of the field blasting effect, most of the blasting fragmentation of Option 2 obtained by the blast crater test are more uniform, but local blasting chunks are still generated, as yielded in Figure 12a. However, in Scheme 7, which is obtained by numerical simulation optimization, there are almost no blasting chunks after blasting. The blasting fragmentation is more uniform on the whole, and the blasting effect is better than Scheme 2, as yielded in Figure 12b.

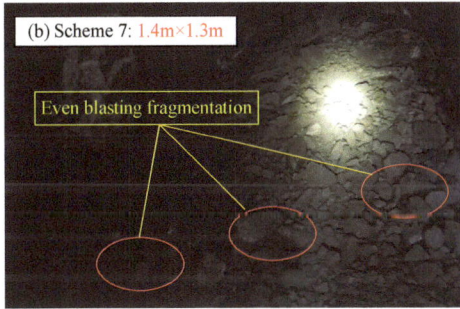

Figure 12. Field blasting test results.

Comparing the blasting results of the two schemes, Scheme 2 obtained by the blast crater test produced some blast chunks, while the optimized hole network parameters achieved a better crushing result. According to the numerical simulation results, the reasons for the large blast chunks are largely due to the weakening of the reverse tensile stress wave caused by the large resistance line, and the large hole network parameters also mean that more rock volume needs to be crushed per unit of explosive, thus leading to insufficient crushing. The numerical simulation results also show that the blast fragmentation in the hole spacing direction is the same for Scheme 2 and Scheme 7, while there is a large difference in the weak fragmentation zone in the resistance line direction, so it can be indicated that the blasting chunks at the site may originate from the weak fragmentation zone.

Through the field blasting test, it is proved that the parameters of medium-deep hole blasting based on the blasting crater test cannot accurately represent the optimal parameter scheme, and it is also proved that the combination of the blasting crater test and numerical simulation method can effectively carry out fine design and optimization of medium-deep hole blasting parameters.

5. Discussion

The design and optimization of blasting parameters are still the key issues limiting the application and development of medium-deep blasting. Some studies use the blast crater test to design the parameters of medium-deep hole blasting, the test results of this method can better reflect the actual situation of the mine site, but it is easily be affected by human subjective factors during data collection, and the integrity of the test site surrounding rock is required by the blast crater test, so this method does not accurately obtain the optimal parameter scheme. Some studies have also used numerical simulations to optimize blasting parameters, and this method has greatly improved the rationality of the blasting parameter design. The analysis of blasting damage by numerical simulation is also more accurate, but numerical simulation requires a certain amount of simulation data, which is generally obtained by empirical design, and these data lack the corresponding experimental basis. Therefore, only using numerical simulation can neither reflect the actual situation of the mine nor accurately calculate the optimal parameter scheme.

In a similar study on the design and optimization of blasting parameters, Wang et al. [43] used numerical simulation and blast crater tests to optimize the blasting parameters of deep holes in the bottomless column segmental collapse method. He used a combination of a series of blast crater tests and LS-DYNA numerical simulation, but unlike this paper, he first analyzed the blasting parameters by numerical simulation analysis and then optimized the parameters based on the blast crater tests to verify them. The research idea of this method is clear in principle, and its biggest advantage is that the numerical simulation results can be verified by blast crater tests. However, the method faces the same problem as described above, which requires a reasonable source of simulation data to ensure the validity of the simulation. Secondly, the optimization of the parameters through blast crater tests requires strict requirements for blast crater tests and certain measures in the quarry to reduce the errors generated by human subjective factors. In this study, reasonable data sources were obtained through blast crater tests, numerical simulations were used to optimize the test data to eliminate errors in blast crater tests, and the optimized data were verified through field blast tests, which overall solved the related problems more reasonably.

6. Conclusions

This article discusses the design and optimization of medium-deep hole blasting parameters in underground mines. The article proposes a method of parameter design and optimization of medium-deep hole blasting based on the blasting crater test and numerical simulation analysis. This study effectively addresses the parameter issues in medium-deep hole blasting in the Gaofeng mines, improving blasting efficiency. The following conclusions have been drawn:

(1) It is obtained that the optimum hole network parameter of the medium-deep hole in the Gaofeng Mine is 1.4 m × 1.3 m, and the reliability of this parameter has been verified through on-site blasting tests. The blasting parameters are applicable to medium-deep hole blasting under similar test conditions in the Gaofeng mines.

(2) It has been demonstrated that the blasting parameter design method based on the blast crater test has some errors and does not accurately represent the optimal blasting solution. It is necessary to optimize the obtained parameters.

(3) The study provides a comprehensive and systematic method for the design and optimization of medium-deep hole blasting parameters and offers valuable insights into the design of deep hole blasting parameters in similar mines. By using the proposed method, the rationality and reliability of the blasting parameters can be improved immensely, which can help to ensure the safety and efficiency of underground mining operations.

Author Contributions: F.G.: Conceptualization, Methodology, Investigation, Supervision, Project administration, Funding acquisition. X.L.: Investigation, Data curation, Writing—original draft, Funding acquisition, Software. X.X.: Validation, Investigation, Data curation, Writing—review & editing. H.L.: Investigation, Resources. Z.L.: Investigation, Resources. All authors have read and agreed to the published version of the manuscript.

Funding: This work was supported by the Hunan Provincial Natural Science Foundation of China (Grant No. 2020JJ4704) and Fundamental Research Funds for the Central Universities of Central South University (Grant No. 2022ZZTS0592).

Data Availability Statement: Not applicable.

Conflicts of Interest: The authors declare that they have no known competing financial interest or personal relationships that could have appeared to influence the work reported in this paper.

References

1. Jiang, Y.H.; Lei, H.Y.; Yang, J.; Song, Y.S.; Ye, G.X. Numerical Simulation of Zhenyuan Gold Mine Blasting Parameters. *Blasting* **2019**, *36*, 77–83.
2. Gen, G.G.; Chi, E.A.; Liu, F.Q. Analysis on Causes of Producing Boulder in Medium-length Hole Blasting and the Technical Measures for Reducing Boulder Yield. *Min. Res. Dev.* **2011**, *4*, 104–106.
3. Zhao, G.Y.; Zhang, L.; Chen, Z.Q.; Wu, J.J.; Dong, L.J. Nonlinear Prediction of Mefium-depth Hole Blasting Effects. *Min. Metall. Eng.* **2010**, *30*, 1–4.
4. Ren, G.F.; Wang, W.; Feng, H.Y.; Yuan, Y.Q. Optimization Study on Mid-length Hole BlastParameters in Rongguan No. 1 Mine. *Blasting* **2011**, *28*, 34–35.
5. Stanković, S.; Dobrilović, M.; Škrlec, V. Optimal positioning of vibration monitoring instruments and their impact on blast-induced seismic influence results. *Arch. Min. Sci.* **2019**, *64*, 591–607.
6. Sołtys, A. Assessment of the impact of blasting works on buildings locatedin the vicinity of open-pit mines using matching pursuit algorithm. *Arch. Min. Sci.* **2020**, *65*, 199–212.
7. Himanshu, V.K.; Roy, M.P.; Shankar, R.; Mishra, A.K.; Singh, P.K. Empirical approach based estimation of charge factor and dimensional parameters in underground blasting. *Min. Metall. Explor.* **2021**, *38*, 1059–1069. [CrossRef]
8. Guo, J.P.; Wang, J.; Li, J.Q. Study on Optimum Design of Blasting Hole Arrangement in Medium-length Hole Blasting. *Blasting* **2017**, *34*, 79–84.
9. Xie, X.Q.; Lu, W.B. 3P (PRECISE, PUNCTILIOUS, AND PERFECT) BLASTING. *Eng. Blasting* **2008**, *14*, 1–7.
10. Pal Roy, P.; Sawmliana, C.; Bhagat, N.K.; Madhu, M. Induced caving by blasting: Innovative experiments in blasting gallery panels of underground coal mines of India. *Min. Technol.* **2003**, *112*, 57–63. [CrossRef]
11. Widodo, S.; Anwar, H.; Syafitri, N.A. *Comparative Analysis of ANFO and Emulsion Application on Overbreak and Underbreak at Blasting Development Activity in Underground Deep Mill Level Zone (DMLZ) PT Freeport Indonesia*; IOP Conference Series: Earth and Environmental Science; IOP Publishing: Bristol, UK, 2019; Volume 279, p. 012001.
12. Jeon, S.; Kim, T.H.; You, K.H. Characteristics of crater formation due to explosives blasting in rock mass. *Geomech. Eng* **2015**, *9*, 329–344. [CrossRef]
13. Zheng, X.S.; Wang, J.; Zhou, N.S. Serial Blasting Crate Tests Confirm Medium-length Hole Blasting Parameter of Non-pillar Sublevel Caving Method. *Blasting* **2009**, *26*, 50–53.
14. Monjezi, M.; Khoshalan, H.A.; Varjani, A.Y. Optimization of open pit blast parameters using genetic algorithm. *Int. J. Rock Mech. Min. Sci.* **2011**, *48*, 864–869. [CrossRef]
15. Dehghani, H.; Pourzafar, M. Prediction and minimization of blast-induced flyrock using gene expression programming and cuckoo optimization algorithm. *Environ. Earth Sci.* **2021**, *80*, 12. [CrossRef]
16. Saghatforoush, A.; Monjezi, M.; Shirani Faradonbeh, R.; Jahed Armaghani, D. Combination of neural network and ant colony optimization algorithms for prediction and optimization of flyrock and back-break induced by blasting. *Eng. Comput.* **2016**, *32*, 255–266. [CrossRef]
17. Bastami, R.; Bazzazi, A.A.; Shoormasti, H.H.; Ahangari, K. Predicting and minimizing the blasting cost in limestone mines using a combination of gene expression programming and particle swarm optimization. *Arch. Min. Sci.* **2020**, *65*, 835–850.
18. Sirjani, A.K.; Sereshki, F.; Ataei, M.; Hosseini, M.A. Prediction of Backbreak in the Blasting Operations using Artificial Neural Network (ANN) Model and Statistical Models (Case study: Gol-e-Gohar Iron Ore Mine No. 1). *Arch. Min. Sci.* **2022**, *67*, 107–121.
19. An, H.M.; Liu, H.Y.; Han, H.; Zheng, X.; Wang, X.G. Hybrid finite-discrete element modelling of dynamic fracture and resultant fragment casting and muck-piling by rock blast. *Comput. Geotech.* **2017**, *81*, 322–345. [CrossRef]
20. Huang, C.; Li, J.T.; Zhao, Y.; Liu, S.F. Optimization of Blasting Parameters for Dongguashan Copper Mine Based on PFC^{2D}. *Min. Metall. Eng.* **2022**, *42*, 1–4.
21. Jiang, N.; Zhou, C.; Luo, X.; Lu, S. Damage characteristics of surrounding rock subjected to VCR mining blasting shock. *Shock. Vib.* **2015**, *2015*, 373021. [CrossRef]

22. Mejía, N.; Mejía, R.; Toulkeridis, T. Characterization of Blast Wave Parameters in the Detonation Locus and Near Field for Shaped Charges. *Mathematics* **2022**, *10*, 3261. [CrossRef]
23. He, L.; Wang, J.; Xiao, J.; Tang, L.; Lin, Y. Pre-splitting blasting vibration reduction effect research on weak rock mass. *Disaster Adv.* **2013**, *6*, 338–343.
24. Ma, G.W.; An, X.M. Numerical simulation of blasting-induced rock fractures. *Int. J. Rock Mech. Min. Sci.* **2008**, *45*, 966–975. [CrossRef]
25. Zhao, D.; Shen, Z.; Li, M.; Liu, B.; Chen, Y.; Xie, L. Study on parameter optimization of deep hole cumulative blasting in low permeability coal seams. *Sci. Rep.* **2022**, *12*, 5126. [CrossRef]
26. Huo, X.; Shi, X.; Qiu, X.; Zhou, J.; Gou, Y.; Yu, Z.; Ke, W. Rock damage control for large-diameter-hole lateral blasting excavation based on charge structure optimization. *Tunn. Undergr. Space Technol.* **2020**, *106*, 103569. [CrossRef]
27. Sun, Q.; Shan, C.; Wu, Z.; Wang, Y. Case Study: Mechanism and Effect Analysis of Presplitting Blasting in Shallow Extra-Thick Coal Seam. *Arch. Min. Sci.* **2022**, *67*, 381–399.
28. Zhang, X.L.; Yi, H.B.; Ma, H.H.; Shen, Z.W. Blast parameter optimization study based on a blast crater experiment. *Shock. Vib.* **2018**, *2018*, 8031735. [CrossRef]
29. Jiang, F.L.; Zhou, K.P.; Deng, H.W.; Pan, D.; Li, K. Blasting Crater Test for Underground Mine's Long-hole Caving. *Min. Metall. Eng.* **2010**, *30*, 10–13.
30. Zhi, W.; Luo, J.; Wang, L.H. Experimental Study on Medium and Deep Hole Blasting Parameters in Panlong Lead Zinc Mine. *Min. Technol.* **2016**, *16*, 83–86.
31. You, Y.Y.; Cui, Z.R.; Zhang, X.L.; You, S.; Kang, Y.Q.; Xiao, C.L.; Lu, F.X. Optimum seam forming angle of double-linear shaped charge in engineering blasting. *Explos. Shock. Waves* **2023**, *43*, 025201-1–025201-15.
32. Gao, F.; Tang, L.; Yang, C.; Yang, P.; Xiong, X.; Wang, W. Blasting-induced rock damage control in a soft broken roadway excavation using an air deck at the blasthole bottom. *Bull. Eng. Geol. Environ.* **2023**, *82*, 97. [CrossRef]
33. Abdel-Kader, M. Modified settings of concrete parameters in RHT model for predicting the response of concrete panels to impact. *Int. J. Impact Eng.* **2019**, *132*, 103312. [CrossRef]
34. Ding, Y.Q.; Tang, W.H.; Zhang, R.Q.; Ran, X.W. Determination and validation of parameters for Riedel-Hiermaier-Thoma concrete model. *Def. Sci. J.* **2013**, *63*, 524–530. [CrossRef]
35. Xie, L.X.; Lu, W.B.; Zhang, Q.B.; Jiang, Q.H.; Chen, M.; Zhao, J. Analysis of damage mechanisms and optimization of cut blasting design under high in-situ stresses. *Tunn. Undergr. Space Technol.* **2017**, *66*, 19–33. [CrossRef]
36. Wang, H.C.; Wang, Z.L.; Wang, J.G.; Wang, S.M.; Wang, H.R.; Yin, Y.G.; Li, F. Effect of confining pressure on damage accumulation of rock under repeated blast loading. *Int. J. Impact Eng.* **2021**, *156*, 103961. [CrossRef]
37. Li, H.C.; Liu, D.S.; Zhao, L. Study on parameters determination of marble RHT model. *Trans. Beijing Inst. Technol* **2017**, *37*, 801–806.
38. Sanchidrian, J.A.; Castedo, R.; Lopez, L.M.; Segarra, P.; Santos, A.P. Determination of the JWL constants for ANFO and emulsion explosives from cylinder test data. *Cent. Eur. J. Energetic Mater.* **2015**, *12*, 177–194.
39. Esmaeili, M.; Tavakoli, B. Finite element method simulation of explosive compaction in saturated loose sandy soils. *Soil Dyn. Earthq. Eng.* **2019**, *116*, 446–459. [CrossRef]
40. Yang, X.; Shao, Z.; Mi, J.; Xiong, X. Effect of adjacent hole on the blast-induced stress concentration in rock blasting. *Adv. Civ. Eng.* **2018**, *2018*, 5172878. [CrossRef]
41. Guo, Z.W. The Application of Deep Hole Blasting Parameter Optimization in BaRun Mining Fracture Rock. Ph.D. Thesis, Inner Mongolia University of Science and Technology, Baotou, China, 2016.
42. Liu, C.Y.; Yang, J.X.; Yu, B. Rock-breaking mechanism and experimental analysis of confined blasting of borehole surrounding rock. *Int. J. Min. Sci. Technol.* **2017**, *27*, 795–801.
43. Wang, P. Parameter–Optimization in Medium-Length Hole of Sublevel Caving without Sill Pillar. Master's Thesis, China University of Geosciences, Wuhan, China, 2009.

Disclaimer/Publisher's Note: The statements, opinions and data contained in all publications are solely those of the individual author(s) and contributor(s) and not of MDPI and/or the editor(s). MDPI and/or the editor(s) disclaim responsibility for any injury to people or property resulting from any ideas, methods, instructions or products referred to in the content.

Article

Predictive Modeling of the Uniaxial Compressive Strength of Rocks Using an Artificial Neural Network Approach

Xin Wei [1], Niaz Muhammad Shahani [1,2,*] and Xigui Zheng [1,2,3,4,*]

1. School of Mines, China University of Mining and Technology, Xuzhou 221116, China
2. The State Key Laboratory for Geo Mechanics and Deep Underground Engineering, China University of Mining & Technology, Xuzhou 221116, China
3. School of Mines and Civil Engineering, Liupanshui Normal University, Liupanshui 553001, China
4. Guizhou Guineng Investment Co., Ltd., Liupanshui 553001, China
* Correspondence: shahani.niaz@cumt.edu.cn (N.M.S.); 3774@cumt.edu.cn (X.Z.)

Abstract: Sedimentary rocks provide information on previous environments on the surface of the Earth. As a result, they are the principal narrators of the former climate, life, and important events on the surface of the Earth. The complexity and cost of direct destructive laboratory tests adversely affect the data scarcity problem, making the development of intelligent indirect methods an integral step in attempts to address the problem faced by rock engineering projects. This study established an artificial neural network (ANN) approach to predict the uniaxial compressive strength (UCS) in MPa of sedimentary rocks using different input parameters; i.e., dry density (ρ_d) in g/cm^3, Brazilian tensile strength (BTS) in MPa, and wet density (ρ_{wet}) in g/cm^3. The developed ANN models, M1, M2, and M3, were divided as follows: the overall dataset, 70% training dataset and 30% testing dataset, and 60% training dataset and 40% testing dataset, respectively. In addition, multiple linear regression (MLR) was performed for comparison to the proposed ANN models to verify the accuracy of the predicted values. The performance indices were also calculated by estimating the established models. The predictive performance of the M2 ANN model in terms of the coefficient of determination (R^2), root mean squared error (RMSE), variance accounts for (VAF), and a20-index was 0.831, 0.27672, 0.92, and 0.80, respectively, in the testing dataset, revealing ideal results, thus it was proposed as the best-fit prediction model for UCS of sedimentary rocks at the Thar coalfield, Pakistan, among the models developed in this study. Moreover, by performing a sensitivity analysis, it was determined that BTS was the most influential parameter in predicting UCS.

Keywords: artificial neural network; multiple linear regression; sedimentary rocks; Thar coalfield; uniaxial compressive strength

MSC: 86-10

1. Introduction

Sedimentary rocks provide information about the previous environment of the Earth's surface. As such, they are the primary narrators of climate, life, and important events that occurred prior to the Earth's surface being formed. Uniaxial compressive strength (UCS) is an essential rock strength parameter widely used in the design of rock structures [1,2]. UCS is an integral parameter in rock characterization, tunnel construction, slope stability analysis, construction, bridges, and other rock-related complications [3–8]. Direct estimation of UCS based on the principles of ISRM (International Society of Rock Mechanics) and ASTM (American Society for Testing and Materials) is a complex, time-consuming, and expensive procedure. It makes testing infeasible for engineering projects where large amounts of data are needed.

To overcome these shortcomings, this study establishes artificial neural network (ANN) predictive models for the estimation of UCS. Many research scholars have established predictive methods to deal with such complex problems using various statistical methods such as ANN and adaptive neuro-fuzzy interference system (ANFIS) [9–17]. Currently, intelligent methods such as ANN, ANFIS, PSO (particle swarm optimization), and GA (genetic algorithm) are frequently applied to solve problems related to rock structure design [2], and these methods are considered to be fast and economical, as well as to have achieved good agreement between the measured and predicted values of rock mechanical properties, i.e., UCS and E (modulus of elasticity in MPa), among others [13]. Torabi-Kaveh employed ANN and multiple regression methods to estimate UCS, and their findings indicated that the ANN method performed better [18]. Yagiz analyzed ANN and multiple regression for predicting UCS of carbonate rocks and found that the ANN method is in good agreement with traditional multiple regression [19]. Ceryan also employed the ANN and regression methods to predict UCS of carbonate rocks and proposed that the ANN results were significantly accurate [20]. Mohamad used a PSO-based ANN method to estimate UCS of soft rocks with input parameters of Brazilian tensile strength (BTS) in MPa, point load index ($Is_{(50)}$) in MPa, and ultrasonic (Vp) in m/s, and demonstrated the high performance of the proposed model [21]. The ANN method has proved to be a key method among all intelligent methods and is thus mostly used to solve challenging problems that are reliant on laboratory experimental data because of their high efficiency and ability to learn from inputs [22]. Based on the reliable predictions of ANN methods, some researchers have estimated various mechanical properties of rocks by analyzing the correlation among various physical parameters [23,24]. Yin employed an ANN back-propagation algorithm, which has been considered as the best prediction method based on previous studies [25]. Skentou used hybrid ANN models for predicting UCS of granite rocks with optimal results. Similarly [26], Kaloop developed six hybrid ANN models to predict UCS of different rock types. Based on the performance indicators, such as R^2 and $RMSE$ [27], the multivariate adaptive regression splines (MARS) revealed ideal results compared with other models developed in the study. Xiang estimated the in situ rock strength from borehole geophysical logs using ANN models [28]. KÖKEN used different soft computing models including ANN for estimating the fracture toughness of rocks [29]. Table 1 shows previous studies using intelligent methods to predict UCS.

Table 1. Previous studies using intelligent methods to predict UCS.

Method	Input	Output	R^2	References
ANN	n, Is, μ, ρ, Vp	UCS	0.97	(Madhubabu et al., 2016) [1]
ANN	ρ, n, Vp, Ab	UCS	0.93	(Abdi et al., 2018) [4]
ANN	n, r, Wabs	UCS	0.92	(Kamani et al., 2020) [14]
ANN	$Vp, Is_{(50)}$, BTS	UCS	0.97	(Mohamad et al., 2015) [21]
ANN	Rn, Vp, DD	UCS	0.82	(Li et al., 2020) [30]
ANN	Is, Vp, Rn, n	UCS	0.93	(Dehghan et al., 2010) [31]
ANFIS	BTS, Vp	UCS	0.60	(Yesiloglu-Gultekin et al., 2013) [32]
PSO-BP	$DD, MC, Vp, Is_{(50)}, Id_2$	UCS	0.999	(Mohamad et al., 2018) [33]
ICA-ANN	$Rn, Vp, Is_{(50)}$	UCS	0.949	(Armaghani et al., 2016a) [34]
ICA-ANN	$n, Rn, Vp, Is_{(50)}$	UCS	0.915	(Armaghani et al., 2016b) [35]
MLR	n, Is, μ, ρ, Vp	UCS	0.91	(Madhubabu et al., 2016) [1]
MLR	ρ, n, Vp, Ab	UCS	0.88	(Abdi et al., 2018) [4]
MLR	$Vp, Is_{(50)}$, SHN, BPI	UCS	0.91	(Heidari et al., 2018) [36]
MLR	$Id_2, Is_{(50)}, N, é$	UCS	0.58	(Yılmaz et al., 2008) [37]

This study applied the ANN approach to estimate UCS with different input parameters such as dry density (ρ_d) in g/cm^3, Brazilian tensile strength (BTS) in MPa, and wet density (ρ_{wet}) in g/cm^3. A total of 78 sedimentary rock samples, i.e., claystone, sandstone, and siltstone, of each type of core rock were selected from Block IX of the Thar coalfield. For the developed ANN models, the dataset is distributed as follows: model 1 (M1) is the overall dataset, model 2 (M2) consists of 70% as the training dataset and 30% as the testing dataset, and model 3 (M3) consists of 60% as the training dataset and 40% as the testing dataset. Similarly, multiple linear regression (MLR) analyses are performed for comparison to the proposed ANN model to check the accuracy of the predicted values. The performance indices are also calculated by estimating the established models. Furthermore, to determine the effect of each variable on the estimated values of UCS, a sensitivity analysis was performed. The complexity and cost of direct destructive laboratory tests adversely affect the data scarcity problem, making the development of intelligent indirect methods an integral step in attempts to address the problem faced by rock engineering projects. In this study, we apply, for the first time, an intelligent prediction method to predict UCS of sedimentary rocks from Block IX of the Thar coalfield. To the best of the authors' knowledge, there is no such application of intelligent prediction techniques.

2. Materials and Methods

2.1. Building Dataset

In this study, sedimentary rock samples, i.e., claystone, sandstone, and siltstone, were collected from Block IX of the Thar coalfield, Pakistan. Figure 1 represents the geological site of the collected rock samples [38]. Initially, a total of 78 core rock samples of each type were prepared and subdivided into standardized samples according to ISRM and ASTM standards to maintain the same rock core dimensions as well as geological and geotechnical features [39,40]. Next, these rock samples were tested in the laboratory at the Department of Mining Engineering, Mehran University of Engineering and Technology, to determine the physical and mechanical parameters, including ρ_d in g/cm^3, BTS in MPa, ρ_{wet} in g/cm^3, and UCS in MPa, using a universal testing machine (UTM), as shown in Figure 2a,b. Figure 2a,b represent the deformed rock core specimen for UCS and BTS tests, respectively. Table 2 presents the five heads and five tails of the dataset of physical and mechanical parameters. Table 3 shows the minimum, maximum, average, and standard deviation of parameters of rock samples determined in the laboratory.

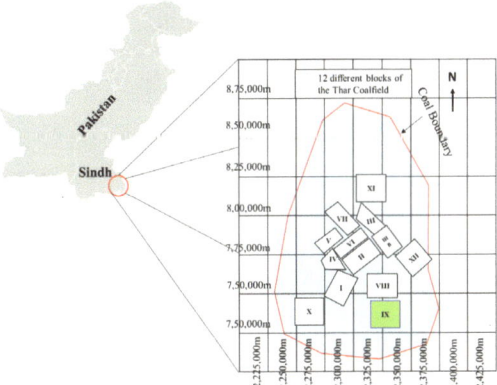

Figure 1. Geological site of the collected rock samples [38].

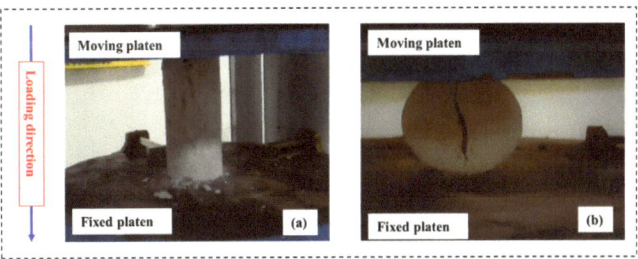

Figure 2. (**a**) Deformed rock core specimen for Brazilian tensile strength test and (**b**) deformed rock core specimen for UCS test.

Table 2. Physical and mechanical parameters of the dataset.

Dataset	ρ_d (g/cm³)	BTS (MPa)	ρ_{wet} (g/cm³)	UCS (MPa)
1	1.91	0.305	2.13	0.404
2	1.75	0.217	2.01	0.491
3	1.77	0.318	2.04	0.531
4	1.78	0.271	2	0.579
5	1.76	0.292	2.04	0.557
...	...	...	...	...
74	1.81	0.178	2.1	0.541
75	1.84	0.189	2.11	0.476
76	1.96	0.2	2.18	0.508
77	1.78	0.108	2.09	0.511
78	1.84	0.138	2.09	1.415

Table 3. The minimum, maximum, average, and standard deviation of the dataset.

Parameters	ρ_d (g/cm³)	BTS (MPa)	ρ_{wet} (g/cm³)	UCS (MPa)
Minimum	1.22	0.023	1.63	0.304
Maximum	2.12	0.627	2.3	3.55
Average	1.76	0.32	2.04	1.38
Standard deviation	0.22	0.13	0.15	0.98

Figure 3 represents histogram plots of the original dataset in this study: (a) dry density (g/cm³), (b) BTS (MPa), (c) wet density (g/cm³), and (d) UCS (MPa). Figure 4 presents the pairwise plot of the original dataset of different parameters and UCS under this study. Notably, none of the parameters are well-correlated to the UCS, thus all of the parameters are analyzed for UCS prediction. In addition, Figure 4 represents a moderate positive correlation of BTS with UCS; however, the dry density and wet density show a negative correlation with UCS.

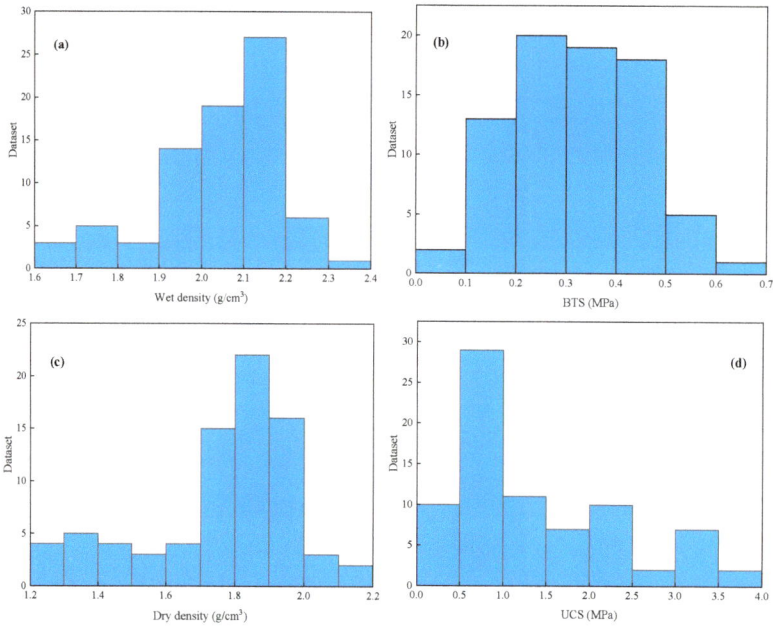

Figure 3. Histogram plots of the original dataset in this study: (**a**) dry density (g/cm³), (**b**) BTS (MPa), (**c**) wet density (g/cm³), and (**d**) UCS (MPa).

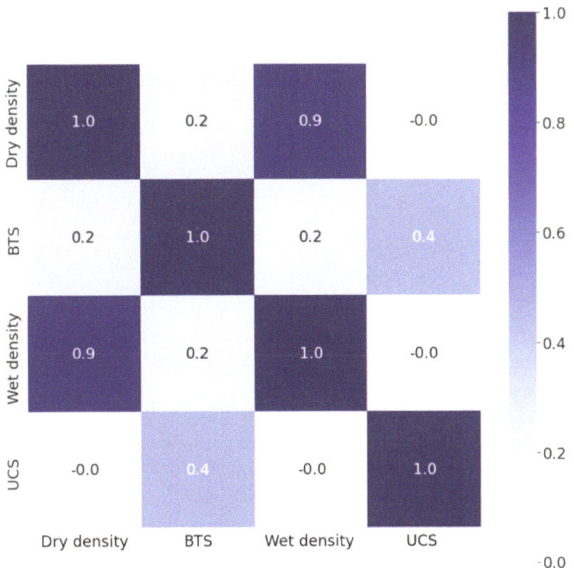

Figure 4. Correlation plot of inputs (dry density (g/cm^3), BTS (MPa), and wet density (g/cm^3)) and output (UCS (MPa)) of the original dataset in this study.

2.2. Methods

The artificial neural network (ANN) approach was employed to predict UCS with three corresponding inputs: ρ_d (g/cm^3), BTS (MPa), and ρ_{wet} (g/cm^3). Figure 5 demonstrates the flow chart of the predictive modeling process for UCS. Owing to the small number of resources available for collecting samples, the current study used a limited dataset, that is, 78 samples divided for the established models, including M1, M2, and M3, as presented in Table 4. M1 means the model was trained on the overall dataset. M2 means the model was trained on 70% (55 datasets) of the dataset and tested on 30% (23 datasets) of the dataset, and M3 means the model was trained on 60% (47 datasets) of the dataset and tested on 40% (31 datasets) of the dataset. In addition, Taylor diagram representation was used, which explains a brief qualitative depiction of the best fit of the model to standard deviations and correlations. Moreover, cosine amplitude method (CAM)-based sensitivity analysis was carried out in order to estimate the influence of each input variable on output UCS.

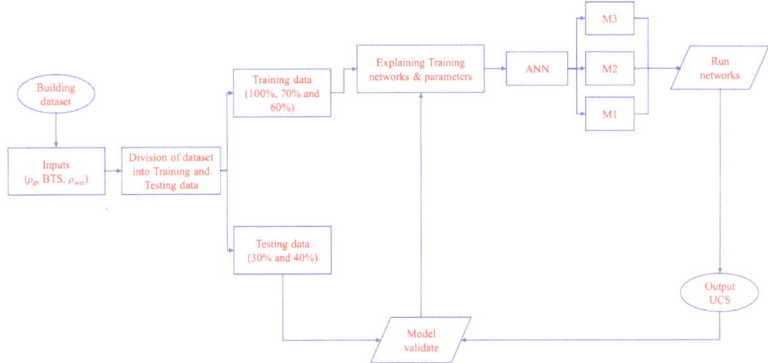

Figure 5. Flow chart of the predictive modeling process for UCS.

Table 4. The dataset distribution for the ANN and MLR models.

Model Code	Dataset	Dataset Distribution (%)	Total Dataset
Model 1 (M1)	Overall	100	78
Model 2 (M2)	Train	70	55
	Test	30	23
Model 3 (M3)	Train	60	47
	Test	40	31

2.2.1. Artificial Neural Network

The concept of ANN was originally introduced by Frank Rosenblatt in 1958 [41]. ANN is considered to be the most common and effective soft computing technique based on the function of the human brain's nervous system [42–47]. This technique is mainly used to solve complex rock structure design problems, i.e., mining, civil, geotechnical, geological engineering, and so on. The ANN structure is an essential factor in designing the ultimate prediction model, as the structure affects the learning capability and performance when estimating the network data. The ANN is structured with three layers (i.e., input layer, hidden layer, and output layer) with a number of interrelated units, called neurons, and the method is used to classify the appropriate correlation between the specified input and output parameters [48]. Figure 6 shows the structure of the ANN to estimate UCS in this research. Because of the complexity of the problem, each neuron has sufficient neuron capacity, and each neuron is related to the weight of the next layer [49–51]. Equation (1) is used to evaluate the approximate number of neurons in the hidden layer, as the improper selection of the number of neurons in the hidden layer often leads to "under-fitting" and "over-fitting" and must be avoided.

$$N_H \leq 2N_1 + 1 \qquad (1)$$

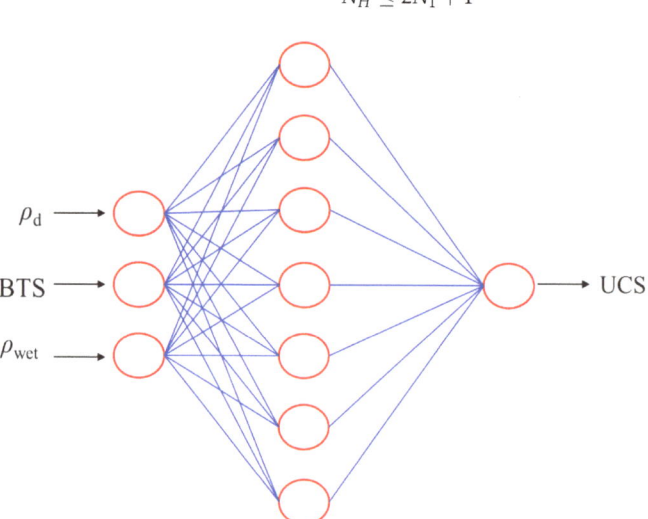

Figure 6. Structure of the artificial neural network.

ANN toolbox in MATLAB package 2018a was used in this study to develop the feed-forward back propagation (FFBP) ANN model with 3-7-1. BP is the most commonly applied powerful learning algorithm in multilayer networks [52,53]. The predictive input parameters, ρ_d, BTS, and ρ_{wet}, were allocated to an input layer composed of three neurons to predict UCS of the output layer. The ANN models, M1, M2, and M3, were trained, tested, and validated. One hundred epochs were used to train the models and the minimum validation error was considered as a stopping point to prevent overfitting. Figure 7 represents the validation curves for the training performance of the ANN models of UCS. Therefore, model M2 demonstrates the best performance curve of UCS, with validation error equal to 0.14562, which is reached at 0 epochs. Figure 8 illustrates the training scatter plots of predicted UCS against measured UCS, as M1 for overall dataset and as M2 and M3 for the training and testing dataset, respectively.

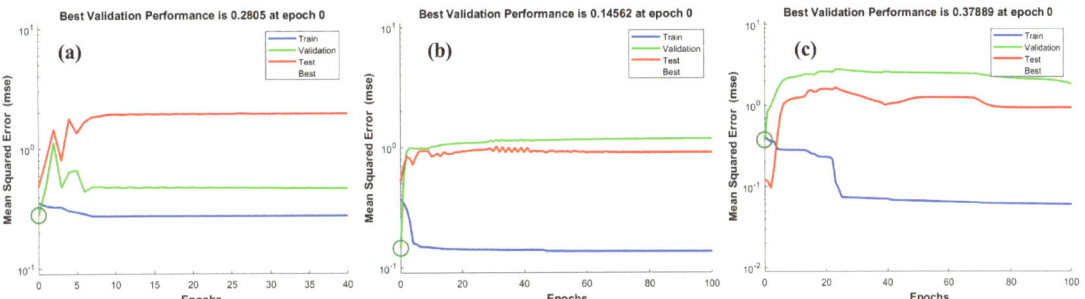

Figure 7. Validation performance curves of UCS at (**a**) M1, (**b**) M2, and (**c**) M3.

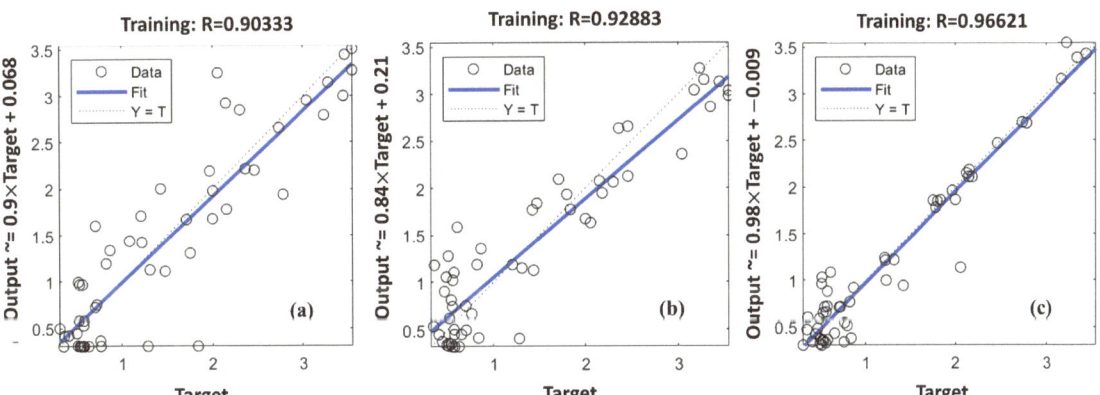

Figure 8. ANN training scatter plots of predicted UCS against measured UCS for (**a**) M1, (**b**) M2, and (**c**) M3.

2.2.2. Multiple Linear Regression

SPSS (version 23) was used to conduct a multiple linear regression (MLR) analysis to determine the existence of a linear relationship between the dependent variable and the independent variables. Regression analysis is used to determine the independent variables' significance in determining the dependent variable's values [54]. More precisely, the purpose of regression analysis in this study was to compare the performance of the ANN analysis to that of conventional linear regression. This approach has also been used in several recent studies on the application of ANNs and linear regression analysis [55]. The basic linear regression equation (Equation (2)), modified to include our dependent and independent variables, is as follows:

$$D = \alpha + B_1 T_1 + B_2 T_2 + B_3 T_3 + \ldots B_n T_n + e \qquad (2)$$

where D represents the dependent variable, α represents the regression constant, B represents the regression coefficient, and T represents the value of the independent variable.

2.2.3. Model Evaluation

This study used ANN and MLR methods. To verify the prediction results of models M1, M2, and M3, the performance indices were calculated. The outcomes of all established models are illustrated as measured and predicted values. Equations (3)–(6) were used to find the coefficient of determination (R^2), root mean squared error ($RMSE$), variance accounts for (VAF), and $a20$-index of each model, respectively. Table 5 represents the performance indices of the ANN and MLR models for predicting UCS on the overall dataset, training dataset, and testing dataset.

$$R^2 = \frac{\sum_{i=1}^{n}\left(UCS_o - \overline{UCS_o}\right)\left(UCS_p - \overline{UCS_p}\right)}{\sqrt{\sum_{i=1}^{n}\left(UCS_o - \overline{UCS_o}\right)^2 \left(UCS_p - \overline{UCS_p}\right)^2}} \quad (3)$$

$$RMSE = \sqrt{\frac{\sum_{i=1}^{n}(UCS_o - UCS_p)^2}{n}} \quad (4)$$

$$VAF = \left[1 - \frac{var(UCS_o - UCS_p)}{var(UCS_o)}\right] \times 100 \quad (5)$$

In addition, to further assess the reliability of the model, a new engineering index, $a20$-index, was applied to the studied models.

$$a20 - index = \frac{m20}{N} \quad (6)$$

where UCS_o is the measured value; $\overline{UCS_p}$ is the predicted value; $\overline{UCS_p}$ and $\overline{UCS_o}$ are the mean of the measured and predicted value, respectively; and n shows the number of the dataset. $m20$ denotes the dataset with a value rate of measured UCS/predicted UCS between 0.80 and 1.20 and N represents the dataset number.

3. Prediction and Discussion of Uniaxial Compressive Strength

The main objective of this study is to investigate the capability of an intelligent model, i.e., ANN, for predicting UCS of sedimentary rocks. The actual and predicted output values were later collated and plotted to ease the performance analysis and correlation studies of these developed models. Various analytical metrics including R^2, $RMSE$, VAF, and $a20$ index were used as performance criteria to examine the final output, to analyze and compare the expected models, and to evaluate the optimal model for data prediction. Model 1 (M1) is the overall dataset, model 2 (M2) consists of 70% as the training dataset and 30% as the testing dataset, and model 3 (M3) consists of 60% as the training dataset and 40% as the testing dataset.

Figure 9 indicates the predicted values of the ANN model M1 for UCS against the measured UCS for the overall dataset. The predicted correlation coefficient of M1 is $R^2 = 0.793$. Based on the M1 predicted outputs, Figure 10a shows the aggregated comparison of predicted versus measured values for UCS. Figure 10b specifies the change in relative error between the measured and predicted values. The MSE value of model M1 achieved is 0.00599. Figure 10c illustrates the error histogram of the established model M1. Here, it can be considered that the distribution of the errors is approximately zero, which is in good agreement with the performance of model M1.

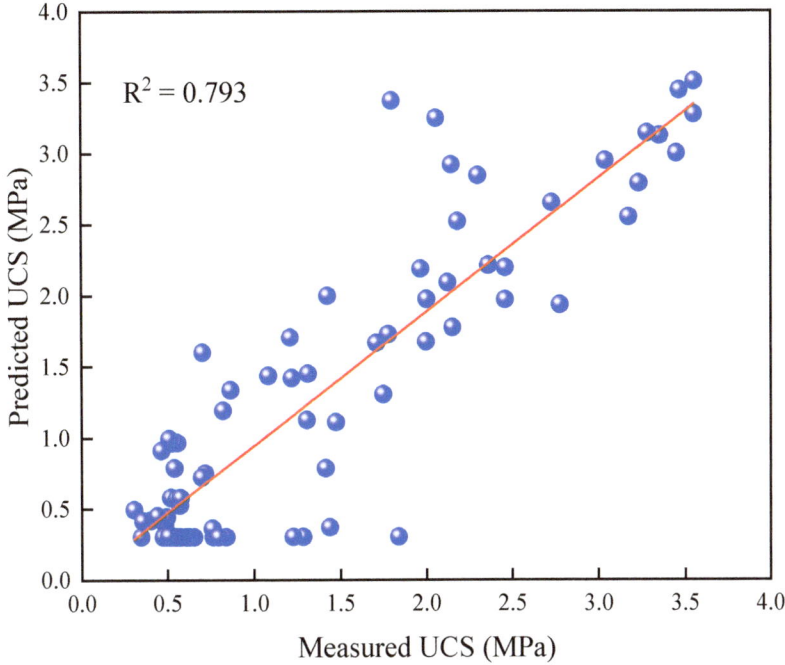

Figure 9. ANN model M1 results for UCS plotted against the measured data.

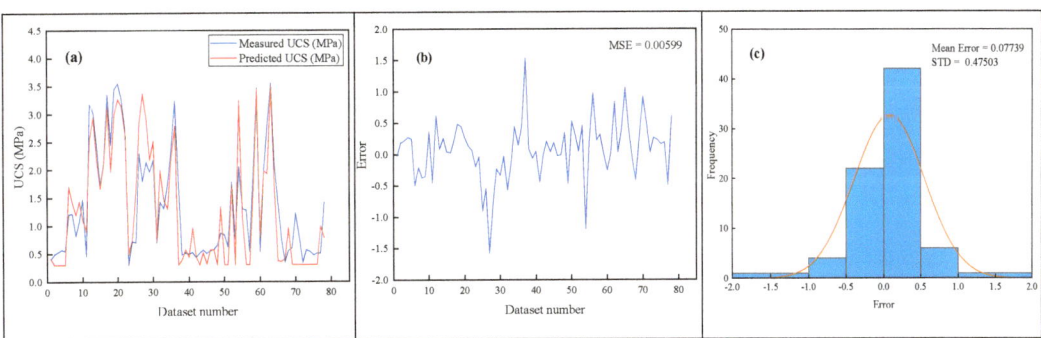

Figure 10. The demonstration of ANN model M1 for UCS. (**a**) Model M1 results aggregated with measured UCS. (**b**) The variation in error between the measured and predicted values. (**c**) Error histogram.

Figure 11 shows the predicted outputs of the ANN model M2 for UCS versus measured data for the training and testing data. For the training and testing data, the predicted R^2 values of model M2 are 0.834 and 0.831, respectively. According to the M2 estimated results for the training data, Figure 12a displays the aggregated comparison of the predicted against measured values for UCS. Figure 12b shows the change in relative error between the measured and predicted values. The MSE value of model M2 is 0.00002. Figure 12c denotes the error histogram of model M2. It can be seen that the distribution of the errors is almost zero, which indicates that the performance of the proposed model M2 is satisfactory and reliable. Similarly, Figure 12d exhibits the aggregated comparison of the predicted against measured values for UCS of estimated outputs of M3 for the testing data. Figure 12e denotes the change in relative error between the measured and predicted values.

The MSE value is achieved as 0.07657. Figure 12f represents the error histogram of model M3. Consequently, it can be seen that the distribution of the errors is nearly zero, which indicates that the performance of the proposed model M2 is acceptable.

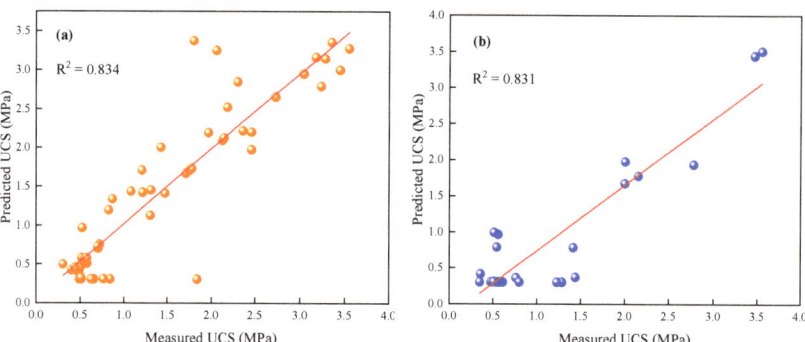

Figure 11. ANN model M2 results for UCS plotted against the measured data for the (**a**) training and (**b**) testing data.

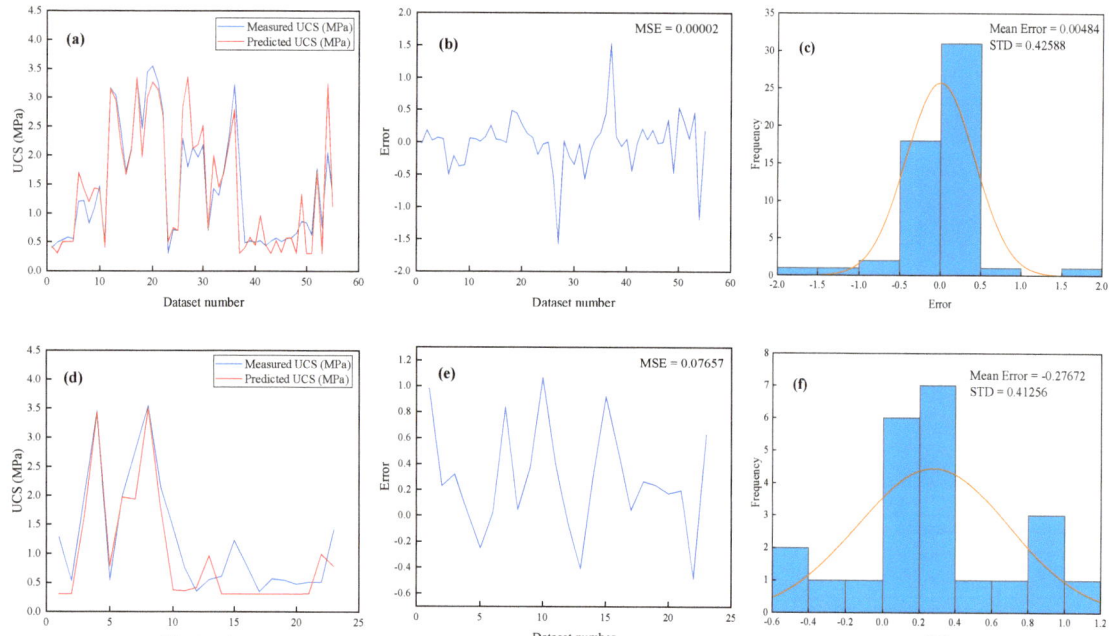

Figure 12. The demonstration of ANN model M2 for UCS. (**a**) The model M2 results aggregated with the measured UCS. (**b**) The variation in error between the measured and predicted values. (**c**) Error histogram for the training data and (**d**) model M2 results aggregated with the measured data. (**e**) The variation in error between the measured and predicted values. (**f**) Error histogram for the testing data.

In Figure 13, the predicted outputs of the ANN model M3 for UCS versus measured data for the training and testing data are presented. Thus, the predicted R^2 values of model M3 are 0.807 and 0.775 for the training and testing data, respectively. Regarding the estimated results of M3 for the training data, Figure 14a shows the aggregated comparison of the predicted against measured values of UCS. Figure 14b shows the change in relative error between the measured and predicted values. The MSE value of M3 is 0.00015. Figure 14c signifies the error histogram of the developed model M3. Hence, it can be noted that the error distribution approaches zero, which shows that the performance of model M3 is adequate. Likewise, for predictive outputs of M3 for the testing data, Figure 14d reveals the aggregated comparison of the predicted against measured values for UCS. Figure 14e indicates the change in relative error between the measured and predicted values. The MSE value of M3 is 0.04541. Figure 14f presents the error histogram of model M3. Thus, the distribution of the errors is nearly zero, which indicates that the performance of the established model M3 is satisfactory.

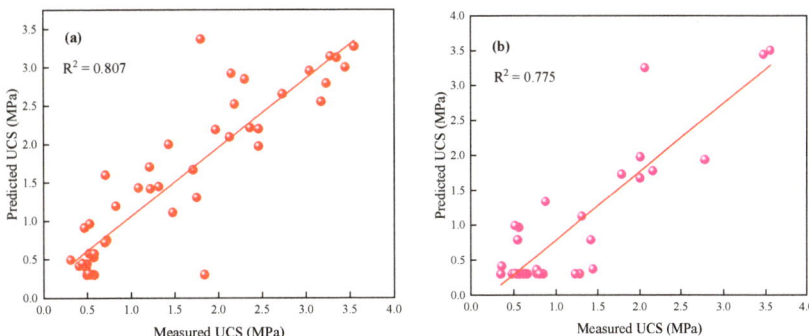

Figure 13. ANN model M3 results for UCS plotted against the measured data for the (**a**) training and (**b**) testing data.

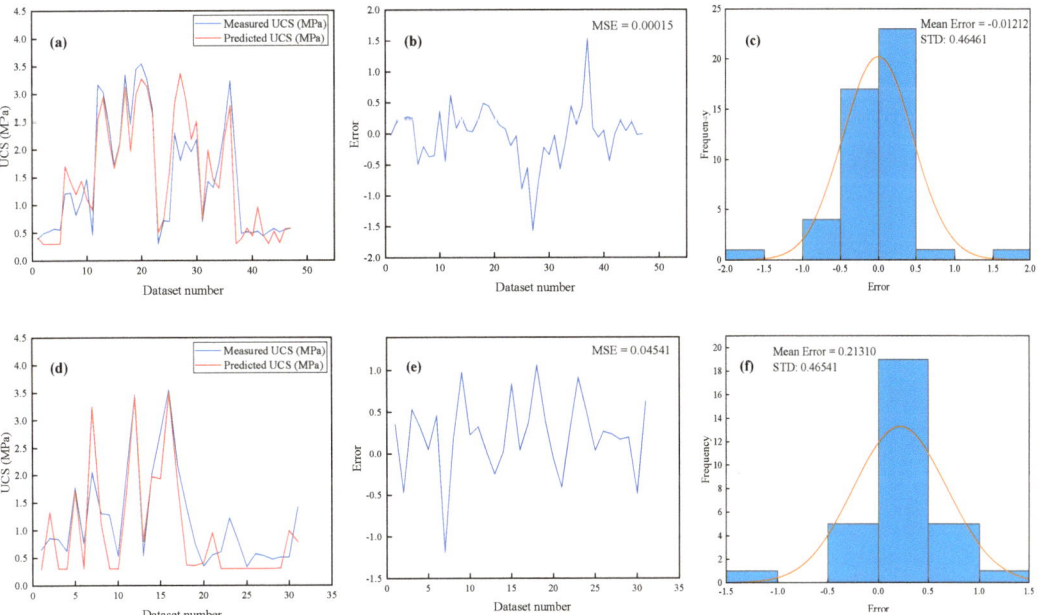

Figure 14. The demonstration of ANN model M3 for UCS. (**a**) Model M3 results aggregated with the measured UCS. (**b**) The variation in error between the measured and predicted values. (**c**) Error histogram for the training data and (**d**) model M3 results aggregated with the measured data. (**e**) The variation in error between the measured and predicted values. (**f**) Error histogram for the testing data.

The first step is to determine whether the data under consideration are appropriate for linear regression analysis. Numerous tests are suggested in the literature for this purpose. Apart from R^2, another very commonly used test is the ANOVA test. In the first case, linear regression was used to determine the relationship between the dependent variable measured UCS and the three independent variables: ρ_d, BTS, and ρ_{wet}. In Table 6, the R^2 values of UCS are estimated using different equations of the MLR models, including M1, M2, and M3, for the overall dataset and training and testing data, i.e., 0.187 for M1, 0.292 and 0.066 for M2, and 0.425 and 0.062 for M3, respectively. Therefore, the R^2 values of UCS are quite satisfactory in models M1, M2, and M2. Furthermore, the ANOVA test also rejected the null hypothesis at a significance value of $p < 0.001$.

Table 5. Performance indices of the ANN and MLR models for predicting UCS for the overall dataset, training dataset, and testing dataset.

	Model		UCS			
			R^2	RMSE	VAF (%)	a20-index
ANN	M1	Overall dataset	0.793	0.07739	0.96	0.95
	M2	Train	0.834	0.00484	0.99	0.99
		Test	0.831	0.27672	0.92	0.80
	M3	Train	0.807	0.01211	0.99	0.99
		Test	0.775	0.21311	0.90	0.80
MLR	M1	Overall dataset	0.187	6.70404	0.98	1.07
	M2	Train	0.292	3.33067	0.77	0.80
		Test	0.066	1.40950	0.81	0.99
	M3	Train	0.425	1.32518	0.82	1.05
		Test	0.062	7.12692	0.99	0.99

Table 6. Multiple linear regression analysis for UCS in MPa; ρ_d (g/cm^3), BTS (MPa), and ρ_{wet} (g/cm^3) are the dry density, Brazilian tensile strength, and wet density, respectively.

Model Code	Dataset	Equation	R^2
M1	Overall	UCS = 1.49 − 0.93ρ_d + 3.12BTS + 0.26ρ_{wet}	0.187
M2	Train	UCS = 1.04 − 1.11ρ_d + 4.35BTS + 0.41ρ_{wet}	0.292
	Test	UCS = 7.83 − 7.24ρ_{wet} + 4.61ρ_d + 0.80BTS	0.066
M3	Train	UCS = 0.72 − 1.80ρ_d + 0.80ρ_{wet} + 6.17BTS	0.425
	Test	UCS = 0.59 − 4.05ρ_{wet} + 4.90ρ_d + 0.24BTS	0.062

Taylor Diagram

The Taylor diagram provides a short numerical explanation of how the fit patterns match their connection and standard deviation. The Taylor diagram can be expressed as follows:

$$R = \frac{\frac{1}{Z}\sum_{z}^{Z}\left(l_n - \bar{l}\right)\left(m_n - \bar{m}\right)}{\sigma_l \sigma_m} \quad (7)$$

where R denotes the correlation; Z denotes the discrete points; l_n and m_n represent two variables; σ_l and σ_m show the standard deviation of l and m, respectively; and $\bar{l}$ and $\bar{m}$ denote the average of σ_l and σ_m, respectively.

Figure 15 indicates the Taylor diagrammatic correlation between the R^2, RMSE, and standard deviation of the original and predicted UCS for the M2 and M3 ANN and MLR models for the testing stage. The prediction of ANN model M3 is highly correlated with the original values and, compared with the other developed models, the standard deviation is similar to the original value. Thus, ANN model M2 with $R^2 = 0.831$ is the most suitable for predicting UCS of sedimentary rocks in the Thar coalfield, Pakistan, among the developed models.

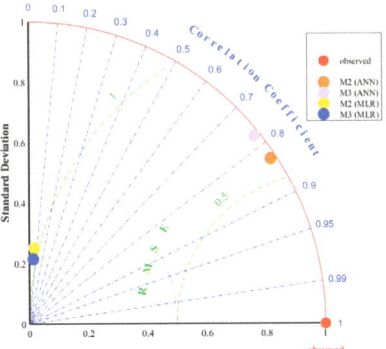

Figure 15. Demonstration of the Taylor diagram for the testing data based on ANN and MLR.

In an ideal scenario, the best-fit prediction model is considered as the one in which the R^2 value is highest, the *RMSE* is lowest, the *VAF* is at a maximum, and the *a*20-index is reliable. Therefore, according to Figure 15, ANN model M2 for the testing dataset revealed the optimal results and is proposed as the best-fit prediction model for UCS in this study.

4. Sensitivity Analysis

It is crucial to accurately analyze the most important parameters that have a great influence on UCS of rock, which can certainly be problematic in the design of structures. Therefore, in this study, the cosine amplitude method was used to investigate the relative influence of the input parameters on the output [56,57]. The general formula of the adopted method can be expressed as follows:

$$r_{ij} = \frac{\sum_{k=1}^{n}\left(\text{UCS}_{ik}\text{UCS}_{jk}\right)}{\sqrt{\sum_{k=1}^{n}\text{UCS}_{ik}^2 \sum_{k=1}^{n}\text{UCS}_{jk}^2}} \qquad (8)$$

where UCS_i and UCS_j are input and output values, respectively, and n denotes the dataset number during the testing stage. Finally, r_{ij} ranges between 0 and 1, specifying additional evidence of the accuracy between each variable and the target. According to Equation (6), if the r_{ij} of any parameter is 0, this indicates that there is no significant relationship between this parameter and the target. On the contrary, when r_{ij} is equal to 1 or approximately 1, a significant relationship can be considered that can greatly influence UCS of the rocks.

Figure 16 shows the relationship between each input parameter (ρ_d, BTS, and ρ_{wet}) of the developed model and the output (UCS). Therefore, it can be seen from the figure that BTS is the most influential parameter in predicting UCS. The corresponding coefficient values are ρ_d = 0.0437, BTS = 0.485, and ρ_{wet} = 0.0435.

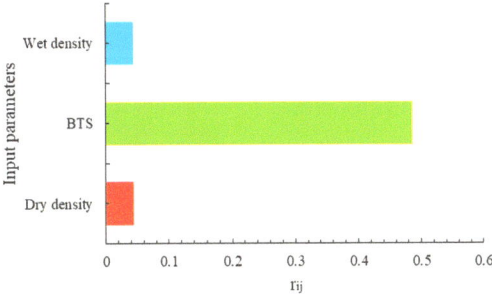

Figure 16. The effect of input variables on the result of the established model.

5. Conclusions

In this study, an intelligent method was used to predict the output, UCS, of sedimentary rocks collected from Block IX of the Thar coalfield, using ρ_d, BTS, and ρ_{wet} as input parameters. The physical and mechanical properties of rock samples were determined in a laboratory in accordance with ISRM and ASTM standards. This study determined the predictive performance of ANN and MLR models by determining the highest R^2, the smallest RMSE, the highest VAF, and a reliable a20-index as follows:

For ANN models, R^2, RMSE, VAF, and a20-index were 0.793, 0.07739, 0.96, and 0.95, respectively, for M1; 0.834 and 0.831, 0.00484 and 0.27672, 0.99 and 0.92, and 0.99 and 0.80, respectively, for the training and testing dataset of M2; and 0.807 and 0.775, 0.01211 and 0.21311, 0.99 and 0.90, and 0.99 and 0.80, respectively, for the training and testing dataset of M3.

In comparison, for the MLR models, R^2, RMSE, VAF, and a20-index were 0.187, 6.70404, 0.98, and 1.07, respectively, for M1; 0.292 and 0.066, 3.33067 and 1.40950, 0.77 and 0.81, and 0.80 and 0.99, respectively, for the training and testing dataset of M2; and 0.425 and 0.062, 1.32518 and 7.12692, 0.82 and 0.99, and 1.05 and 0.99, respectively, for the training and testing dataset of M3.

Thus, the proposed ANN model M2 for the testing dataset yielded the optimal results and is proposed as the best fit prediction model for UCS in this study.

Finally, by performing a sensitivity analysis, it was concluded that BTS was the most influential parameter in predicting UCS.

The current study used only ANN to predict UCS, in comparison with MLR, which could have produced more suitable results. However, future work will focus on predicting UCS using metaheuristic techniques and enhancing the accuracy of the model prediction and model performance in heterogeneous and big datasets. Moreover, the author plans to investigate UCS using optimized machine learning algorithms as well as hybrid and ensemble learning. Furthermore, some other influential attributes will be added to the UCS database to further understand the nature of this study area.

Author Contributions: Conceptualization, N.M.S.; methodology, N.M.S.; software, X.W.; validation, N.M.S.; formal analysis, X.W.; investigation, N.M.S.; resources, X.Z.; data curation, N.M.S. and X.W.; writing—original draft preparation, N.M.S.; writing—review and editing, X.W. and X.Z.; visualization, X.W.; supervision, X.Z.; project administration, X.Z.; funding acquisition, X.Z. All authors have read and agreed to the published version of the manuscript.

Funding: This research was supported by the Science and Technology Innovation Project of Guizhou Province (Qiankehe Platform Talent [2019] 5620 to X.Z.). No additional external funding was received for this study.

Data Availability Statement: Some or all of the data, models, or code that support the findings of this study are available from the corresponding author upon reasonable request.

Conflicts of Interest: The author declares no competing interests.

Nomenclature

Abbreviation/Symbol	Parameter Name	Abbreviation/Symbol	Parameter Name
UCS	Uniaxial compressive stregth	R^2	Coefficient of determination
ISRM	International Society of Rock Mechanics	RMSE	Root mean squared error
ASTM	American Society for Testing and Materials	VAF	Variance accounts for
ANN	Artificial neural network	μ	Poisson's ratio
ANFIS	Adaptive neuro-fuzzy interference system	ρ and r	Density
PSO	Particle swarm optimization	BTS	Brazilian tensile strength
GA	Genetic algorithm	SHN	Schmidt hardness
MARS	multivariate adaptive regression splines	ρ_{wet}	Wet density
ICA	Imperialist competitive algorithm	N	Porosity
Is	Point load strength index	$I_{s(50)}$	Point load index
Rn	Schmidt hammer rebound number	Vp	P-wave velocity
BPI	Block punch index	Ab and Wabs	Water absorption
DD, ρ_d	Dry density		

References

1. Madhubabu, N.; Singh, P.K.; Kainthola, A.; Mahanta, B.; Tripathy, A.; Singh, T.N. Prediction of compressive strength and elastic modulus of carbonate rocks. *Measurement* 2016, 88, 202–213. [CrossRef]
2. Asheghi, R.; Shahri, A.A.; Zak, M.K. Prediction of uniaxial compressive strength of different quarried rocks using metaheuristic algorithm. *Arab. J. Sci. Eng.* 2019, 44, 8645–8659. [CrossRef]
3. Abdi, Y.; Taheri-Garavand, A. Application of the ANFIS Approach for Estimating the Mechanical Properties of Sandstones. *Emir. J. Eng. Res.* 2020, 25, 1.
4. Abdi, Y.; Garavand, A.T.; Sahamieh, R.Z. Prediction of strength parameters of sedimentary rocks using artificial neural networks and regression analysis. *Arab. J. Geosci.* 2018, 11, 587. [CrossRef]
5. Shahri, A.A.; Asheghi, R.; Zak, M.K. A hybridized intelligence model to improve the predictability level of strength index parameters of rocks. *Neural Comput. Appl.* 2020, 33, 3841–3854. [CrossRef]
6. Barzegar, R.; Sattarpour, M.; Deo, R.; Fijani, E.; Adamowski, J. An ensemble tree-based machine learning model for predicting the uniaxial compressive strength of travertine rocks. *Neural Comput. Appl.* 2019, 32, 9065–9080. [CrossRef]
7. Gockceoglu, C.; Zorlu, K. A fuzzy model to predict the uniaxial compressive strength and the modulus of elasticity of a problematic rock. *Eng. Appl. Artif. Intell.* 2004, 17, 61–72. [CrossRef]
8. Baykasoğlu, A.; Güllü, H.; Çanakçi, A.; Özbakir, A. Predicting of compressive and tensile strength of limestone via genetic programming. *Expert Syst. Appl.* 2008, 35, 111–112. [CrossRef]
9. Tiryaki, B. Predicting intact rock strength for mechanical excavation using multivariate statistics, artificial neural networks and regression trees. *Eng. Geol.* 2008, 99, 51–60. [CrossRef]
10. Ozcelik, Y.; Bayram, F.; Yasitli, N.E. Prediction of engineering properties of rocks from microscopic data. *Arab. J. Geosci.* 2013, 6, 3651–3668. [CrossRef]
11. Rajesh-Kumar, B.; Vardhan, H.; Govindaraj, M.; Vijay, G.S. Regression analysis and ANN models to predict rock properties from sound levels produced during drilling. *Int. J. Rock Mech. Min. Sci.* 2013, 58, 61–72. [CrossRef]
12. Kong, F.; Shang, J. A validation study for the estimation of uniaxial compressive strength based on index tests. *Rock Mech. Rock Eng.* 2018, 51, 2289–2297. [CrossRef]
13. Teymen, A.; Mengüç, E.C. Comparative evaluation of different statistical tools for the prediction of uniaxial compressive strength of rocks. *Int. J. Min. Sci. Technol.* 2020, 30, 785–797. [CrossRef]
14. Ajalloeian, R.; Kamani, M. An investigation of the relationship between Los Angeles abrasion loss and rock texture for carbonate aggregates. *Bull. Eng. Geol. Env.* 2019, 78, 1555–1563. [CrossRef]
15. Cabalar, A.F.; Cevik, A.; Gokceoglu, C. Some applications of Adaptive Neuro-Fuzzy Inference System (ANFIS) in geotechnical engineering. *Comput. Geotech.* 2012, 40, 14–33. [CrossRef]
16. Bashari, A.; Beiki, M.; Talebinejad, A. Estimation of deformation modulus of rock masses by sing fuzzy clustering-based modeling. *Int. J. Rock Mech. Min. Sci.* 2011, 48, 1224–1234. [CrossRef]
17. Umrao, R.K.; Sharma, L.K.; Singh, R.; Singh, T.N. Determination of strength and modulus of elasticity of heterogenous sedimentary rocks: An ANFIS predictive technique. *Measurement* 2018, 126, 194–201. [CrossRef]
18. Torabi-Kaveh, M.; Naseri, F.; Saneie, S.; Sarshari, B. Application of artificial neural networks and multivariate statistics to predict UCS and E using physical properties of Asmari limestones. *Arab. J. Geosci.* 2015, 8, 2889–2897. [CrossRef]
19. Yagiz, S.; Sezer, E.A.; Gokceoglu, C. Artificial neural networks and nonlinear regression techniques to assess the influence of slake durability cycles on the prediction of uniaxial compressive strength and modulus of elasticity for carbonate rocks. *Int. J. Numer. Anal. Methods Geomech.* 2012, 36, 1636–1650. [CrossRef]
20. Ceryan, N.; Okkan, U.; Kesimal, A. Prediction of unconfined compressive strength of carbonate rocks using artificial neural networks. *Environ. Earth Sci.* 2013, 68, 807–819. [CrossRef]
21. Mohamad, E.T.; Armaghani, D.J.; Momeni, E.; Abad, S.V.A.N.K. Prediction of the unconfined compressive strength of soft rocks: A PSO-based ANN approach. *Bull. Eng. Geol. Environ.* 2015, 74, 745–757. [CrossRef]
22. Aboutaleb, S.; Behnia, M.; Bagherpour, R.; Bluekian, B. Using non-destructive tests for estimating uniaxial compressive strength and static Young's modulus of carbonate rocks via some modeling techniques. *Bull. Eng. Geol. Environ.* 2018, 77, 1717–1728. [CrossRef]
23. Bejarbaneh, B.Y.; Bejarbaneh, E.Y.; Fahimifar, A.; Armaghani, D.J.; Abd Majid, M.Z. Intelligent modelling of sandstone deformation behaviour using fuzzy logic and neural network systems. *Bull. Eng. Geol. Environ.* 2018, 77, 345–361. [CrossRef]
24. Fakir, M.; Ferentinou, M.; Misra, S. An investigation into the rock properties influencing the strength in some granitoid rocks of KwaZulu-Natal, South Africa. *Geotech. Geol. Eng.* 2017, 35, 1119–1140. [CrossRef]
25. Han, H.; Yin, S. In-situ stress inversion in Liard Basin, Canada, from caliper logs. *Petroleum* 2020, 6, 392–403. [CrossRef]
26. Skentou, A.D.; Bardhan, A.; Mamou, A.; Lemonis, M.E.; Kumar, G.; Samui, P.; Armaghani, D.J.; Asteris, P.G. Closed-Form Equation for Estimating Unconfined Compressive Strength of Granite from Three Non-destructive Tests Using Soft Computing Models. *Rock Mech. Rock Eng.* 2022, 11, 487–514. [CrossRef]

27. Kaloop, M.R.; Bardhan, A.; Samui, P.; Hu, J.W.; Zarzoura, F. Computational intelligence approaches for estimating the unconfined compressive strength of rocks. *Arab. J. Geosci.* **2023**, *16*, 37. [CrossRef]
28. Xiang, Z.; Yu, Z.; Kang, W.H.; Si, G.; Oh, J.; Canbulat, I. Estimation of in-situ rock strength from borehole geophysical logs in Australian coal mine sites. *Int. J. Coal Geol.* **2023**, *269*, 104210. [CrossRef]
29. Köken, E.; Koca, T.K. A comparative study to estimate the mode I fracture toughness of rocks using several soft computing techniques. *Turk. J. Eng.* **2023**, *7*, 296–305. [CrossRef]
30. Li, D.; Armaghani, D.J.; Zhou, J.; Lai, S.H.; Hasanipanah, M. A GMDH predictive model to predict rock material strength using three non-destructive tests. *J. Nondestruct. Eval.* **2020**, *39*, 81. [CrossRef]
31. Dehghan, S.; Sattari, G.H.; Chelgani, S.C.; Aliabadi, M.A. Prediction of uniaxial compressive strength and modulus of elasticity for Travertine samples using regression and artificial neural networks. *Min. Sci. Technol.* **2010**, *20*, 41–46. [CrossRef]
32. Yesiloglu-Gultekin, N.; Gokceoglu, C.; Sezer, E.A. Prediction of uniaxial compressive strength of granitic rocks by various nonlinear tools and comparison of their performances. *Int. J. Rock Mech. Min. Sci.* **2013**, *62*, 113–122. [CrossRef]
33. Mohamad, E.T.; Armaghani, D.J.; Momeni, E.; Yazdavar, A.H.; Ebrahimi, M. Rock strength estimation: A PSO-based BP approach. *Neural Comput. Appl.* **2018**, *30*, 1635–1646. [CrossRef]
34. Armaghani, D.J.; Amin, M.F.M.; Yagiz, S.; Faradonbeh, R.S.; Abdullah, R.A. Prediction of the uniaxial compressive strength of sandstone using various modeling techniques. *Int. J. Rock Mech. Min. Sci.* **2016**, *85*, 174–186. [CrossRef]
35. Armaghani, D.J.; Mohamad, E.T.; Momeni, E.; Monjezi, M.; Narayanasamy, M.S. Prediction of the strength and elasticity modulus of granite through an expert artificial neural network. *Arab. J. Geosci.* **2016**, *9*, 48. [CrossRef]
36. Heidari, M.; Mohseni, H.; Jalali, S.H. Prediction of uniaxial compressive strength of some sedimentary rocks by fuzzy and regression models. *Geotech. Geol. Eng.* **2018**, *36*, 401–412. [CrossRef]
37. Yılmaz, I.; Yuksek, A.G. An example of artificial neural network (ANN) application for indirect estimation of rock parameters. *Rock Mech. Rock Eng.* **2008**, *41*, 781–795. [CrossRef]
38. Shahani, N.M.; Zheng, X.; Guo, X.; Wei, X. MachineLearning-Based Intelligent Predictionof Elastic Modulus of Rocks at Thar Coalfield. *Sustainability* **2022**, *14*, 3689. [CrossRef]
39. Brown, E.T. *Rock Characterization Testing & Monitoring—ISRM Suggested Methods*; ISRM—International Society for Rock Mechanics/Pergamon Press: London, UK, 2007; p. 211.
40. ASTM—American Society for Tenting and Materials. *Standard Practices for Preparing Rock Core as Cylindrical Test Specimens and Verifying Conformance to Dimensionaland Shape Tolerances*; ASTM: West Conshohocken, PA, USA, 2013.
41. Alexx, K. Artificial Neural Networks. Available online: https://www.computerworld.com/article/2591759/artificial-neural-networks.html#:~:text=One%20answer%20is%20to%20use,and%20learned%20to%20recognize%20objects (accessed on 3 July 2021).
42. Alizadeh, M.; Alizadeh, E.; Asadollahpour Kotenaee, S.; Shahabi, H.; Beiranvand Pour, A.; Panahi, M.; Bin Ahmad, B.; Saro, L. Social vulnerability assessment using artificial neural network (ANN) model for earthquake hazard in Tabriz city, Iran. *Sustainability* **2018**, *10*, 3376. [CrossRef]
43. Asteris, P.G.; Mokos, V.G. Concrete compressive strength using artificial neural networks. *Neural Comput. Appl.* **2019**, *32*, 11807–11826. [CrossRef]
44. Pham, B.T.; Singh, S.K.; Ly, H.B. Using Artificial Neural Network (ANN) for prediction of soil coefficient of consolidation. *Vietnam J. Earth Sci.* **2020**, *42*, 311–319. [CrossRef]
45. Pham, T.A.; Ly, H.B.; Tran, V.Q.; Giap, L.V.; Vu, H.L.T.; Duong, H.A.T. Prediction of pile axial bearing capacity using artificial neural network and random forest. *Appl. Sci.* **2020**, *10*, 1871. [CrossRef]
46. Le, V.M.; Pham, B.T.; Le, T.T.; Ly, H.B.; Le, L.M. Daily rainfall prediction using nonlinear autoregressive neural network. *Micro-Electron. Telecommun. Eng.* **2020**, *106*, 213–221.
47. Le, T.T.; Pham, B.T.; Le, V.M.; Ly, H.B.; Le, L.M. A robustness analysis of different nonlinear autoregressive networks using Monte Carlo simulations for predicting high fluctuation rainfall. *Micro-Electron. Telecommun. Eng.* **2020**, *106*, 205–212.
48. Ly, H.B.; Le, T.T.; Vu, H.L.T.; Tran, V.Q.; Le, L.M.; Pham, B.T. Computational hybrid machine learning based prediction of shear capacity for steel fiber reinforced concrete beams. *Sustainability* **2020**, *12*, 2709. [CrossRef]
49. Rashidian, V.; Hassanlourad, M. Application of an artificial neural network for modeling the mechanical behavior of carbonate soils. *Int. J. Geomech.* **2014**, *14*, 142–150. [CrossRef]
50. Fidan, S.; Oktay, H.; Polat, S.; Ozturk, S. An artificial neural network model to predict the thermal properties of concrete using different neurons and activation functions. *Adv. Mater. Sci. Eng.* **2019**, *2019*, 3831813. [CrossRef]
51. Gowida, A.; Moussa, T.; Elkatatny, S.; Ali, A. A hybrid artificial intelligence model to predict the elastic behavior of sandstone rocks. *Sustainability* **2019**, *11*, 5283. [CrossRef]
52. Hajihassani, M.; Armaghani, D.J.; Sohaei, H.; Mohamad, E.T.; Marto, A. Prediction of airblast-overpressure induced by blasting using a hybrid artificial neural network and particle swarm optimization. *Appl. Acoust.* **2014**, *80*, 57–67. [CrossRef]
53. Ekemen Keskin, T.; Özler, E.; Şander, E.; Düğenci, M.; Ahmed, M.Y. Prediction of electrical conductivity using ANN and MLR: A case study from Turkey. *Acta Geophys.* **2020**, *68*, 811–820. [CrossRef]
54. Sajid, M.J. Modelling best fit-curve between China's production and consumption-based temporal carbon emissions and selective socio-economic driving factors. *IOP Conf. Series Earth Environ. Sci.* **2020**, *431*, 012061. [CrossRef]
55. Sajid, M.J. Machine Learned Artificial Neural Networks Vs Linear Regression: A Case of Chinese Carbon Emissions. *IOP Conf. Series Earth Environ. Sci.* **2020**, *495*, 012044. [CrossRef]

56. Momeni, E.; Nazir, R.; Armaghani, D.J.; Maizir, H. Prediction of pile bearing capacity using a hybrid genetic algorithm-based ANN. *Measurement* **2014**, *57*, 122–131. [CrossRef]
57. Ji, X.; Liang, S.Y. Model-based sensitivity analysis of machining-induced residual stress under minimum quantity lubrication. *Proc. Inst. Mech. Eng. Part B J. Eng. Manuf.* **2017**, *231*, 1528–1541. [CrossRef]

Disclaimer/Publisher's Note: The statements, opinions and data contained in all publications are solely those of the individual author(s) and contributor(s) and not of MDPI and/or the editor(s). MDPI and/or the editor(s) disclaim responsibility for any injury to people or property resulting from any ideas, methods, instructions or products referred to in the content.

Article

Data-Driven Optimized Artificial Neural Network Technique for Prediction of Flyrock Induced by Boulder Blasting

Xianan Wang [1], Shahab Hosseini [2,*], Danial Jahed Armaghani [3,*] and Edy Tonnizam Mohamad [3]

[1] School of Civil and Architectural Engineering, Anyang Institute of Technology, Anyang 455000, China; 20160424@ayit.edu.cn
[2] Faculty of Engineering, Tarbiat Modares University, Tehran 14115-175, Iran
[3] Centre of Tropical Geoengineering (GEOTROPIK), Institute of Smart Infrastructure and Innovative Engineering (ISIIC), Faculty of Civil Engineering, Universiti Teknologi Malaysia, Johor Bahru 81310, Malaysia; edy@utm.my
* Correspondence: h.seyyedshahab@modares.ac.ir (S.H.); jadanial@utm.my (D.J.A.)

Citation: Wang, X.; Hosseini, S.; Jahed Armaghani, D.; Tonnizam Mohamad, E. Data-Driven Optimized Artificial Neural Network Technique for Prediction of Flyrock Induced by Boulder Blasting. *Mathematics* **2023**, *11*, 2358. https://doi.org/10.3390/math11102358

Academic Editor: Xiang Li

Received: 17 April 2023
Revised: 13 May 2023
Accepted: 15 May 2023
Published: 18 May 2023

Copyright: © 2023 by the authors. Licensee MDPI, Basel, Switzerland. This article is an open access article distributed under the terms and conditions of the Creative Commons Attribution (CC BY) license (https:// creativecommons.org/licenses/by/ 4.0/).

Abstract: One of the most undesirable consequences induced by blasting in open-pit mines and civil activities is flyrock. Furthermore, the production of oversize boulders creates many problems for the continuation of the work and usually imposes additional costs on the project. In this way, the breakage of oversize boulders is associated with throwing small fragments particles at high speed, which can lead to serious risks to human resources and infrastructures. Hence, the accurate prediction of flyrock induced by boulder blasting is crucial to avoid possible consequences and its' environmental side effects. This study attempts to develop an optimized artificial neural network (ANN) by particle swarm optimization (PSO) and jellyfish search algorithm (JSA) to construct the hybrid models for anticipating flyrock distance resulting in boulder blasting in a quarry mine. The PSO and JSA algorithms were used to determine the optimum values of neurons' weight and biases connected to neurons. In this regard, a database involving 65 monitored boulders blasting for recording flyrock distance was collected that comprises six influential parameters on flyrock distance, i.e., hole depth, burden, hole angle, charge weight, stemming, and powder factor and one target parameter, i.e., flyrock distance. The ten various models of ANN, PSO–ANN, and JSA–ANN were established for estimating flyrock distance, and their results were investigated by applying three evaluation indices of coefficient of determination (R^2), root mean square error (RMSE) and value accounted for (VAF). The results of the calculation of evaluation indicators revealed that R^2, values of (0.957, 0.972 and 0.995) and (0.945, 0.954 and 0.989) were determined to train and test of proposed predictive models, respectively. The yielded results denoted that although ANN model is capable of anticipating flyrock distance, the hybrid PSO–ANN and JSA–ANN models can anticipate flyrock distance with more accuracy. Furthermore, the performance and accuracy level of the JSA–ANN predictive model can estimate better compared to ANN and PSO–ANN models. Therefore, the JSA–ANN model is identified as the superior predictive model in estimating flyrock distance induced from boulder blasting. In the final, a sensitivity analysis was conducted to determine the most influential parameters in flyrock distance, and the results showed that charge weight, powder factor, and hole angle have a high impact on flyrock changes.

Keywords: flyrock; blasting; soft computing; ANN; jellyfish research algorithm; particle swarm

MSC: 68T20; 68T01

1. Introduction

Blasting works typically involve applying the intensity of an explosion to rock masses in order to break them apart and displace them. Some of the explosives' strength is employed in these operations to accomplish the targeted objectives, and a considerable amount of them is wasted [1]. In addition, blasting energies have an effect on a wide variety of places in the surrounding blasting area, the majority of which are undesired and ruinous. The wasted blasting energy is applied to release undesirable environmental and destructive side effects such as flyrock, dust emission, toxic gas pollution, ground vibration, backbreaks, toe problems, boulders, etc. [2–5].

The term "fly rock" describes the egregious fragmentation that produces under random status at the place beyond the intended explosion-safe boundary [6]. This undesirable problem of blasting poses a significant risk, particularly when machinery and buildings are positioned near the locations of the blasting sites [7]. The boulders that are formed as a result of blasting are referred to as "oversize boulders" in the mining industry. Only specific transportation machines and crusher tools can manage the large fragmentation (oversize boulders) in any way, including loading, transporting, or loading operations. When viewed from a more pragmatic perspective, oversize boulders are considered fragmented sizes that must undergo repeated blasting and breakage to be processed further—this process is named secondary blasting. Due to the difference in types of transportation and crushing machinery utilized varies from one activity to the other, it is difficult and impractical to assign a dimension or range of measurements of the oversize boulders [8]. The appropriate rock particles to standard and optimum equipment's loading and hauling cause enhance the productivity and effectiveness of the transporting machines and crushers and reduce the practical costs of processing. Furthermore, the best import rock sizes into a crusher are the size that decrements its maximum efficiency, power consumption, and the amount of wear and tear due to crushing rocks.

Oversize boulders may cause a variety of effects on the efficiency of operational mining processes, including the necessity for supplemental time required for separating chunks, inadequate loading works, secondary blasting, the imposition of additional costs, additional wear on transportation machines and their possible destruction, and incrementing in the amortization of the trucks, shovels and crushes. The formation of oversize boulders in mine and quarry sites will actually occur based on different factors, which can be divided into the following four categories (Figure 1): (1) geologically associated circumstances; (2) blasting design pattern parameters; (3) type and characteristics of explosive; and (4) human-related factors [9].

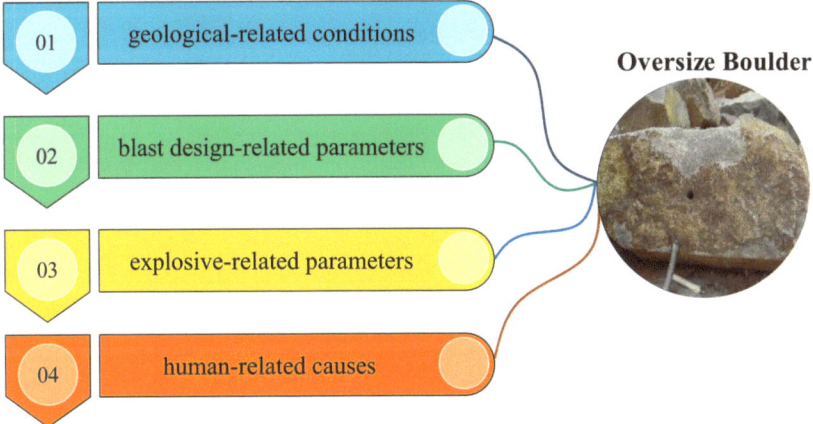

Figure 1. Factors to produce blast-induced oversize boulders.

One of the most significant parameters that affect the production of oversized boulders is the descriptive geology situation. Geological conditions play a crucial role in the generation of blast-induced oversize boulders, not just near the blasting faces but additionally from inside the shot. Nevertheless, controlling geological conditions during designing and performing blasting operations is impossible because it is classified as a group of uncontrollable parameters [10]. Blasting pattern design parameters are an additional category of important parameters that are used for producing oversize boulders. These parameters should be adjusted optimally to generate appropriate fragment size distribution.

Some of the blasting pattern design factors, including stemming, hole depth, hole diameter, burden, and spacing, are illustrated in Figure 2, and categorized in the controllable parameters of blasting rounds and can be determined by the designer and mine engineers to obtain optimum rock fragmentation.

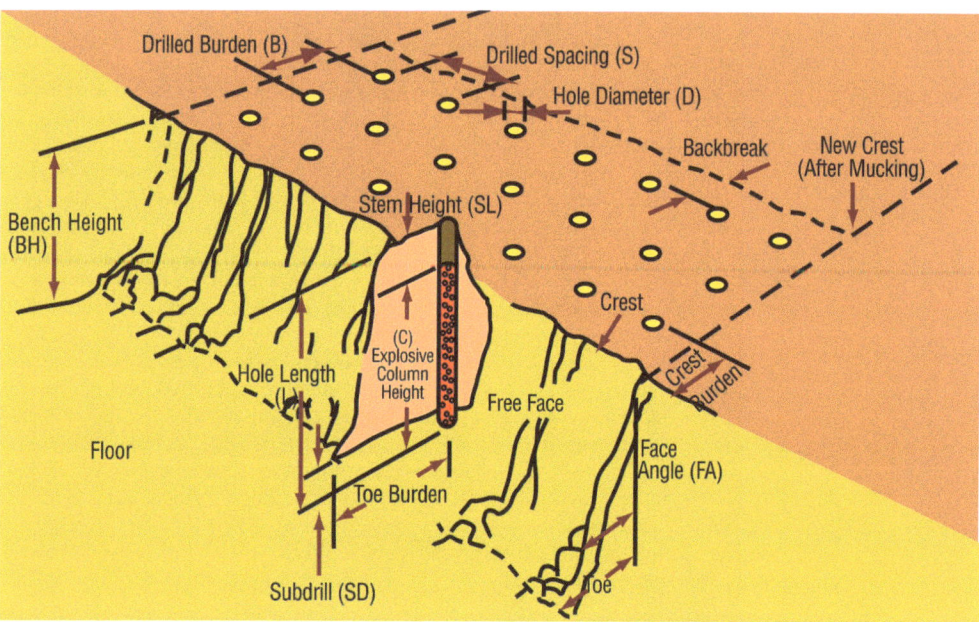

Figure 2. A view of blasting bench and pattern design parameters.

The characteristics of explosives are discussed in the third category. The widest explosives used in mine blasting are dynamite, water gel, and ANFO, which have different densities, resistivities, and specific charges. Therefore, these parameters also have considerable effects on oversize boulders due to bench blasting [9]. Mistakes that were caused by human intervention in the designing and carrying out of blasting activities are other affecting parameters on oversize boulders. The blasting team constantly maintains control over the performance of the blasting designs and ensures that they are finished [11].

Over the past several decades, there have been numerous experimental and empirical systems proposed with the intention of forecasting the particle size distribution and flyrock produced by bench blasting [11–13]. On the other hand, because of the present complicated circumstances of the blast design process, the findings of the proposed experimental systems were not satisfactory [14]. As a result, presenting a unique empirical model for the purpose of predicting flyrock and rock fragmentation is unacceptable and unexpected [15]. In addition to empirical approaches, many studies developed statistical models and formulas to determine the flyrock and fragment rock sizes (see Table 1). Nonetheless, using statistically based methods to solve a highly non-linear issue such as flyrock and rock fragmentation can be a challenging and difficult endeavor. Many attempts are conducted to solve engineering problems by using artificial intelligence and soft computing techniques [16–25]. Therefore, the application of intelligent machine learning, such as artificial intelligence (AI) and soft computing (SC), could have relevance and benefit when attempting to solve issues related to this type. These methods have successfully been applied to effectively apply in a variety of disciplines of engineering, and the conclusions drawn from those applications have been advocated as solutions to real-world issues (see Table 1). In the last decade, numerous attempts have been conducted to model blast-induced flyrock phenomena in mines and predict its' distance utilizing artificial intelligence techniques (Table 1).

Table 1. Some studies conducted in the field of flyrock prediction.

Reference	Year	Inputs	AI Algorithm
[1]	1975	HD	Empirical
[26]	1981	HD, SC	Empirical
[2]	1988	ST/B	Empirical
[27]	2005	B, ST, HD	Empirical
[15]	2009	HD, Fs	Empirical
[28]	2010	HD, ST, BS, SD, PF, Qmax, N, RD	ANN
[7]	2011	B, S, HD, ST, SD, PF, Qmax, RD	FIS, SM
[8]	2011	B, S, HD, ST, PF, Qmax, BI, RMR	ANN
[9]	2011	d, B, HD, ST, BS, SD, PF, Qmax, BI	ANN
[29]	2012	B, S, HD, ST, SD, PF, Qmax, RMR	ANN-GA
[10]	2012	PF, HD, SD, S, d, B, ST	ANN, SVM
[30]	2012	B, S, ST, HD, HD, SC, Q	Empirical
[31]	2013	HD, S, B, d, Qmax	ANN
[32]	2013	HD, S, B, ST, PF, SD	SVM
[13]	2014	B, S, CPM, Q, σ_c, RQD	MVRA
[14]	2014	PF, S, HD, ST, B, Qmax	FIS, ANN
[33]	2015	d, B, S, HD, Q, CPM, σ_c, RQD	ANN, ANFIS
[34]	2016	BDF, EDF, RMR	Empirical
[35]	2016	B, S, CPM, PF, σ_c, RQD	MVRA, BPNN
[36]	2018	B/S, H/B, SD, PF, Qmax RD	LS-SVM, SVR
[37]	2019	B/d, S/B, ST/B, H/B, PF, Xb	MDA
[38]	2020	B, S, ST, PF RD	ELM
[39]	2020	B, S/B, ST/B, H/B, d, B/d, PF, Qmax, VoD RMR, BI	FRES
[6]	2022	B, S, ST, PF, Q	Z-FCM-ANN
[3]	2022	N, HD, B, S, ST, BRH, PF, Q	ANN
[40]	2022	ST, Q, PF	ANN
[41]	2022	d, HD, S, PF, B/S, ST, Qmax	ANFIS, HGSO-ANFIS
[42]	2023	HD, S, B, ST, PF	DT, XGBoost, AdaBoost

According to the abovementioned literature and Table 1, although a precise and smart model for estimating oversize boulders and flyrock is of relevance in mining operations, there is no research that considers the resulting flyrock from boulder blasting. Hence, this study focuses on structuring a smart system for the accurate prediction of flyrock after boulder blasting. The phase of proposing a predictive model is organized using the present optimized multi-layer perception neural network by three optimization algorithms, i.e., PSO and jellyfish search algorithm (JSA). The method employed in this research to anticipate flyrock after oversize boulder blasting is transferable to the solution of various unwelcome problems that can arise from blasting operations in mine and quarry sites. The remainder of the paper is organized as follows: Section 2 provides Methods and Materials. The description of the case study and analysis of the required data are presented in Section 3. The model development and performance of developed models in this study are presented in Section 4. Section 5 addresses the results and discussions. Finally, the obtained results are concluded in Section 6.

2. Methods and Materials

2.1. Jellyfish Search

Chou and Truong [43] presented an Artificial Jellyfish Search (JSA) algorithm in 2021 by modeling it after the predatory procedures carried out by jellyfish, which comprises three involvement of behaviors: (i) jellyfish generally observe a single regulating point, which may be the ocean current or the movement of individuals within the group, as well as a temporal control mechanism, (ii) jellyfish are more interested in locations in which there is a greater quantity of food available, and (iii) the quantity of food is allotted, and the fitness function for it is calculated in accordance with the allocation.

2.1.1. Population Initialization

The initializing of the individuals in JSA is performed using the information on a logical diagram [44], which removes the adverse impacts of randomly generated initial values commonly approved by conventional metaheuristics, such as a minimal convergence speed and a local optimum that can present a fall hazard as a consequence of an absence of the jellyfish variety. The following is an expression of the JSA-based rational diagram [43]:

$$X_{i+1} = \vartheta X_i (1 - X_i), \quad 0 \leq X_0 \leq 1 \tag{1}$$

in which X_i signifies the chaotic position values of the ith jellyfish, X_0 indicates the initially generated jellyfish, and the ϑ is equal to 4.0 [43].

2.1.2. Ocean Current

Ocean currents that include significant quantities of nutrients attract jellyfish to a location and update their position based on the trend that ocean currents are moving in. The following equation can serve as a model for it:

$$X_i(t+1) = X_i(t) + rand(0,1) \times (X^* - \beta \times rand(0,1) \times \mu) \tag{2}$$

where X^* indicates the populations of jellyfish optimal position, μ denotes the average location of the jellyfish swarm, and β stands for the distribution-related factor, which number is fixed to 3.

2.1.3. Jellyfish Swarm

There are two categories of jellyfish motion in swarms: passive and active motions. Throughout repetitions, the position of a particular jellyfish is updated as follows:

$$X_i(t+1) = X_i(t) + \gamma \times rand(0,1) \times (U_b - L_b) \tag{3}$$

where Ub and Lb stand the upper and lower bounds of the search area, and c refers to the motion-related factor, which is fixed at 0.1.

The following equation simulates the jellyfish in the swarm's active motion:

$$X_i(t+1) = X_i(t) + rand(0,1) \times \overrightarrow{direction} \tag{4}$$

A jellyfish swarm perpetually proceeds in the path in which there is a greater supply of food, which displays the direction of the motions of jellyfish within the population. The following objective function (OF) equation is used to determine the motions direction of individual jellyfish:

$$\overrightarrow{direction} = \begin{cases} if \ f(X_j) \geq f(X_i) & X_j(t) - X_i(t) \\ if \ f(X_j) < f(X_i) & X_i(t) - X_j(t) \end{cases} \tag{5}$$

where f is the OF related to location X.

2.1.4. Time Control Mechanism

The timing control scheme in JSA has been modified such that it may be used to direct the motion of jellyfish in response to ocean currents and among swarms of jellyfish. The execution of JSA is heavily reliant on the timing regulating function c(t), which arbitrarily vacillates between the range of 0–1 and may be represented as follows:

$$c(t) = \left|\left(1 - \frac{k}{k_{max}}\right) \times (2 \times rand(0,1) - 1)\right| \qquad (6)$$

where k represents the total number of repetitions, k_{max} signifies the maximum number of iterations, and Figure 3 presents the flowchart of JSA. The pseudocode of the jellyfish search algorithm is shown in Figure 4.

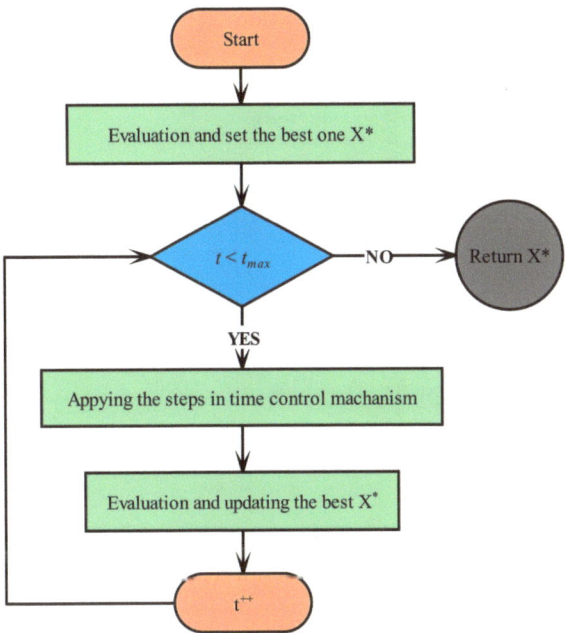

Figure 3. Algorithmic flowchart of the jellyfish search algorithm.

2.2. Particle Swarm Optimization

Particle swarm optimization, abbreviated as PSO, is a metaheuristic algorithm that was first introduced by Kennedy and Eberhart [45]. The accumulated behavior of particles served as motivation for the development of PSO. PSO has a significantly higher learning performance and uses much less memory than the other algorithms, such as the genetic algorithm. These are just two of the many benefits of adopting PSO. This algorithm uses a population of particles to search for the best personal (p_{best}) and best global (g_{best}) coordinates in order to determine the optimal location. In other words, throughout every repetition of the process, the particles advance in the direction of discovering the optimal places. The following are the formulas that can be used to calculate the speed and location of the particles:

$$V_{new} = w \times V + C_1 \cdot r_1(p_{best} - X) + C_2 \cdot r_2(g_{best} - X) \qquad (7)$$

$$X_{new} = X + V_{new} \qquad (8)$$

in which V is the first velocity, X denotes the particles' positions, C_1 and C_2 indicate the constants related to positive acceleration, V_{new} signifies the new velocity, X_{new} represents the location of particles, w is the inertial weight, and r_1 and r_2 stand the random numbers in the range of (0, 1). The diagram and flowchart of PSO are illustrated in Figures 5 and 6, respectively.

Input:	n_{pop}: Population size	Dim: number of dimensions of search space
	Max $_{iter}$: Maximum number of iterations	UB: Upper bound on search space
		LB: Lower bound on search space
		f(**X**): Objective function
	Initialize population of jellyfish $\mathbf{X}_i$ (i=1, 2,…, n_{Pop}) using logistic chaotic map	
	Calculate the quantity of food at each $\mathbf{X}_i$ as f($\mathbf{X}_i$)	
	Find the jellyfish at the location currently with the most food ($\mathbf{X}^*$)	
	For t = 1 to Max $_{iter}$ **do**	
	For i = 1 to n_{pop} **do**	
	Calculate the time control c(t) using	
	$c(t) = \left\| \left(1 - \dfrac{t}{\text{Maxiter}}\right) \times (2 \times \text{rand}(0,1) - 1) \right\|$	
	If c(t)≥ C_0:	
	Jellyfish follows ocean current	
	Determine ocean current	
	$\overrightarrow{\text{trend}} = \mathbf{X}^* - \beta \times \text{rand}(0,1) \times \mu$	
	New location of jellyfish is given by	
	$\mathbf{X}_i(t+1) = \mathbf{X}_i(t) + \text{rand}(0,1) \times \overrightarrow{\text{trend}}$	
	Else	
	Jellyfish moves inside a swarm	
	If rand(0,1)>(1-c(t))	
	Jellyfish exhibits type A motion (passive motion)	
	$\mathbf{X}_i(t+1) = \mathbf{X}_i(t) + \gamma \times \text{rand}(0,1) \times (\mathbf{Ub} - \mathbf{Lb})$	
	Else	
	Jellyfish exhibits type B motion (active motion)	
	Determine direction of jellyfish using	
	$\overrightarrow{\text{Direction}} = \begin{cases} \mathbf{X}_j(t) - \mathbf{X}_i(t) & \text{if } f(\mathbf{X}_i) \geq f(\mathbf{X}_j) \\ \mathbf{X}_i(t) - \mathbf{X}_j(t) & \text{if } f(\mathbf{X}_i) < f(\mathbf{X}_j) \end{cases}$	
	$\overrightarrow{\text{step}} = \text{rand}(0,1) \times \overrightarrow{\text{Direction}}$	
	$\mathbf{X}_i(t+1) = \mathbf{X}_i(t) + \overrightarrow{\text{step}}$	
	End if	
	End for	
	Check whether boundary conditions are satisfied and calculate quantity of food at new location	
	Calculate quantity of food at new location f($\mathbf{X}_i$)	
	End for	
Output:	The best solution so far	

Figure 4. Pseudocode of the jellyfish search algorithm.

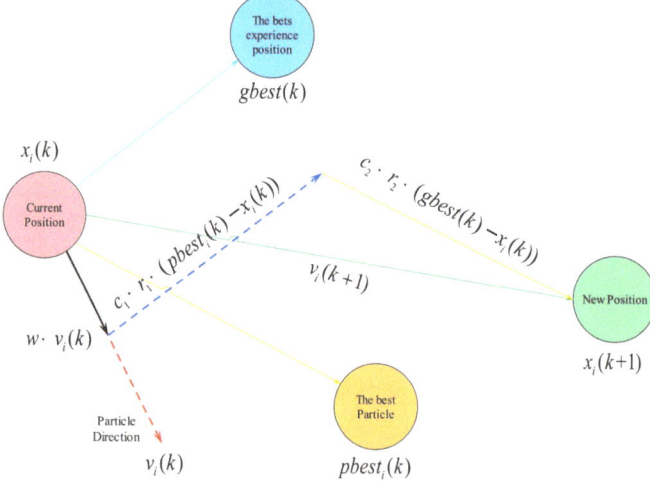

Figure 5. The diagram of the PSO algorithm.

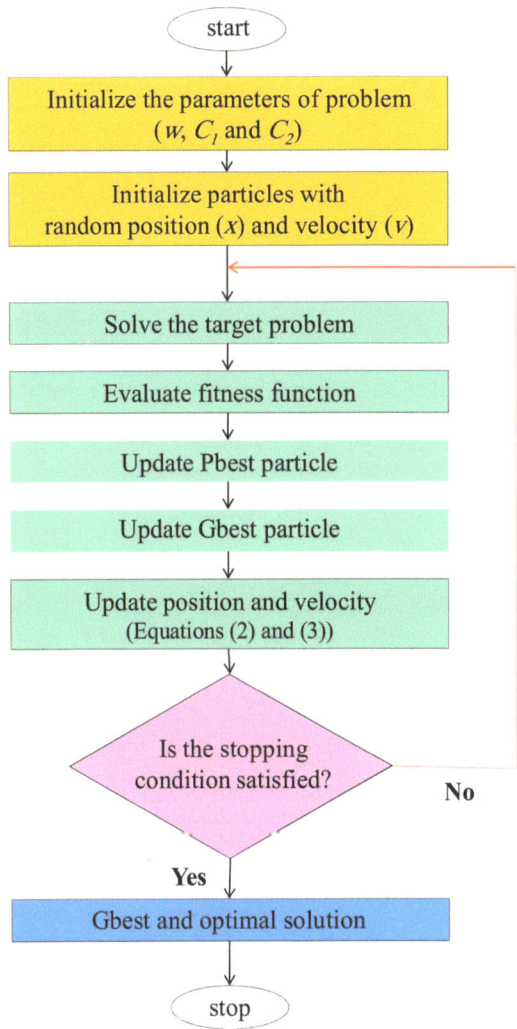

Figure 6. The flowchart of the PSO algorithm.

2.3. Artificial Neural Network

Artificial neural networks (ANN) originate from the structure of human brains in information processing. In the human brain, first, the information is imported and then proceed by neurons. Finally, the output information is output to execute commands. In the processing step, a training process is performed by neurons to obtain accurate and correct information. This process is also conducted for neural networks. ANNs comprise the main three layers involving inputs, output(s), and hidden layers. The main role of each layer is to keep the neurons (binding components) together in each layer and connect them through the weights. The neurons pass the information received from the input source to the next level (layers) [46]. The available data are transmitted from the input neurons to the hidden neurons and, subsequently, to the output neurons (last layer). This data transfer from one layer to another is associated with oscillation (strengthening or weakening), which is controlled by the weights in each layer. However, the main core of neural network processing is the neural computations performed in each layer; meanwhile, in the first step, the imported data into the system is weighted. Then, the linear or sigmoid transfer function is utilized to pass data to the first hidden layer. Finally, the new data generated in the hidden layer are transferred to the output layer based on a similarly expressed process. It is noteworthy that the important components in the ANNs are the neurons' number in layers because the neurons affect the network performances [47]. Based on this, the number of input and output neurons is equal to the number of imported input and outputs to the system, respectively. However, the hidden neurons are determined according to a trial–error procedure. In the mentioned explanation, the data processing is conducted based on the available training algorithms, in which the feedforward-backpropagation (BP) algorithm is widely applied in network training because of its accuracy and speed.

It should be noted that the weighting of neurons during transmitting data is performed randomly; the random weights and biases are generated and modified in the training step. The design of the network structure and the calculation of the appropriate weight are the two primary components that constitute the ANN modeling process. The BP training method applies adjustments to the network weights in order to minimize error levels by using those values. The values that are acquired at each step are compared with the values that are wanted for the output at the end of the process. In the event that the errors are undesirable, the procedure should be repeated to obtain the required values and bring the system error to an acceptable level.

2.4. Hybrid System

Several studies have been conducted in the field of engineering applications to improve the capabilities of ANNs models by using optimization techniques (Table 1). It is possible that the ANN model can also provide unacceptable predictions due to the fact that BP is not really that efficient at locating the precise global minimum. However, the ANN technique has a greater propensity to get stuck in local minima, whereas optimization algorithms, by adjusting the weight and bias of ANNs, can overcome this problem. In the current research, a JSA as a novel metaheuristic algorithm is combined with the ANN, named the JSA–ANN hybrid system, to predict flyrock distance from boulder blasting. Then, the prediction result of JSA–ANN was compared to the PSO algorithm. The hybrid systems search a global minimum, and then ANN selects the method that has the potential to provide the highest accuracy.

3. Case Study and Data Analysis

For access to the required datasets, the Ulu Tiram quarry mine was considered, which is explored in the Johor site in Malaysia. The geographical location of the Ulu Tiram quarry mine is at a latitude of $1°36'41''$ N and a longitude of $103°49'0''$ E. The main ore extraction in this mine is granite, with rock strength ranging from 50–90 MPa. The production rate of Ulu Tiram quarry mine for each month is 15,000–35,000 tons, which is supplied through the implementation of blasting operations. The boulder production-induced mine blasting was regarded as one of the most significant ecological challenges in the aforementioned locations. Normally, after several blasting (i.e., primary blasting), there is a need to blast the boulders produced by these primary blasts. The site's regular hauling and crushing equipment are unable to manage the enormous boulder in any way, including loading, transporting, or handling it. From a more pragmatic standpoint, an oversize boulder can be thought of as a fragment size that must first be subjected to secondary blasting and fracture before any further processing can take place. It is not possible to assign a size or set of dimensions to the oversize boulder since the method of loading, transferring, and crushing the rock varies from one operation to the next. In the mentioned quarry, a total number of 20 boulders with a volume ranging between 2.1–3.8 m^3 were investigated, and the relevant information, together with their flyrock values, were measured.

In total, sixty-five blast datasets were gathered, with each containing information on the hole diameter, hole depth, burden, hole angle, charge weight, stemming, powder factor, and boulder distance as an output. Ammonium nitrate and fuel oil (ANFO) were charged as explosives in blasting rounds. The maximum and minimum blast-hole diameters of 2.95 and 5.9 inches, respectively, were used in various procedures. The effective parameters of boulder blasting and corresponding ranges are reported in Table 2. In addition, the distribution plot of effective parameters listed in Table 2 is depicted in Figure 7.

Table 2. The range of effective parameters on flyrock distance.

Input Parameters	Hole Depth	Burden	Hole Angle	Charge Weight	Stemming	Powder Factor	Output Flyrock Distance
Sign	HD	B	HA	CW	St	PF	Flyrock
Unit	(cm)	(cm)	(°)	(kg)	(cm)	(kg/m^3)	(m)
Min	71	57	22	2.7	31	0.6	157
Average	86.91	77.18	27.46	3.41	39.80	0.79	227.66
Max	101	96	33	4.3	49	1.01	300
Standard Deviation	7.11	10.63	2.95	0.40	5.41	0.10	37.54

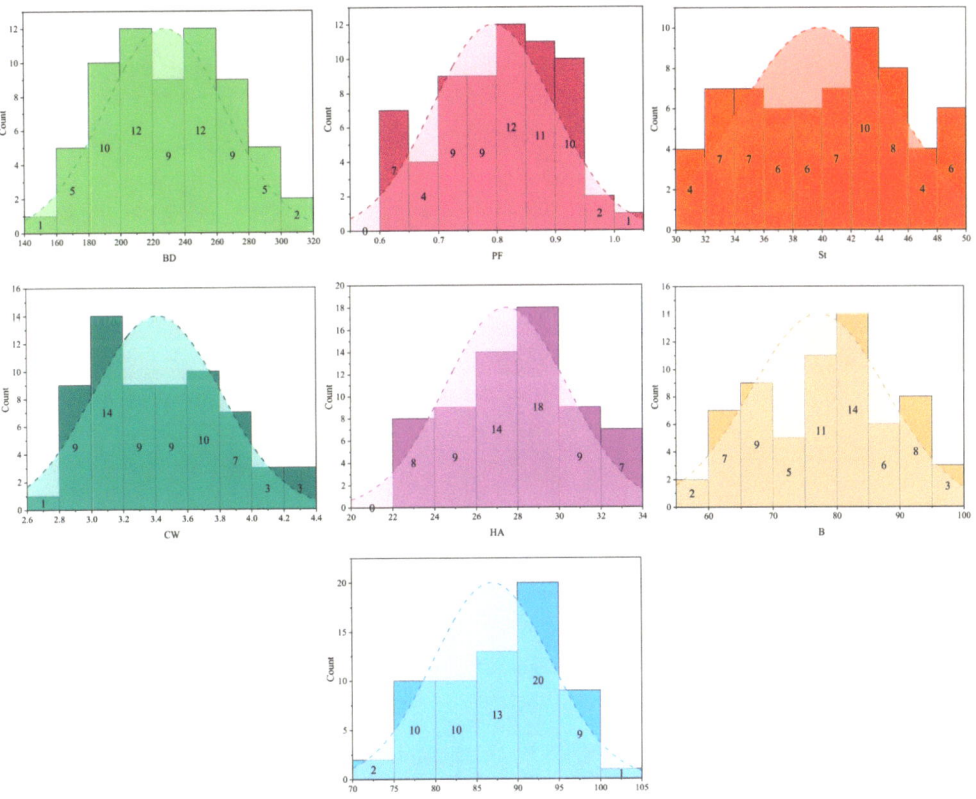

Figure 7. The histogram plot of effective parameters on flyrock distance.

Two video cameras were installed to capture the maximum distance of fragmented boulder pieces. The prepared benched for performing blasting rounds were colored to indicate the spaces between blasted boulders. Utilizing the aforementioned cameras, the pieces of boulders could be distinguished after the explosion. The maximum distance of fragmented boulder pieces was then determined to be the horizontal separation of pieces at their greatest. It is noteworthy that the data collected in this research have not been used in the research literature before, and for the first time in this research, the prediction of the maximum distance of fragmented boulder pieces is addressed. Figure 8 shows the production of a large number of boulders that require secondary blasting to be fragmented into portable sizes. Furthermore, the drilling of holes with a diameter of 8.9 cm in boulders is shown in Figure 9.

Figure 8. Oversize boulders in the case study.

Figure 9. The drilled hole in the oversize boulder for charging and blasting operation.

4. Model Development

In this paper, the modeling and estimation of flyrock distance due to oversize boulder blasting were performed by the ANN model and hybrid systems of PSO–ANN and JSA–ANN. To do this, the four main steps were considered; (1) the available 65 datasets that were collected in a quarry mine in Malaysia were randomly classified into two phases training data (80% of whole data, 52 datasets) and testing data (20% of whole data, 13 datasets). (2 All of the data, including six influential parameters and flyrock data, were converted to normalized values in the range of $[-1,1]$ utilizing the following equation [5]:

$$x_n = \frac{x_i - x_{min}}{x_{max} - x_{min}} \tag{9}$$

in which x_n, x_i, x_{min}, and x_{max} are the normalized values, measured data, and minimum and maximum of datasets, respectively. (3) The capabilities of the developed models were assessed using three evaluation metrics, including R^2, RMSE, and VAF, which can be calculated as follows [48]:

$$R^2 = 1 - \left(\frac{\sum_{i=1}^{n} (O_i - P_i)^2}{\sum_{i=1}^{n} (P_i - \overline{P_i})^2} \right) \tag{10}$$

$$RMSE = \sqrt{\frac{1}{n} \sum_{i=1}^{n} (O_i - P_i)^2} \tag{11}$$

$$VAF = 100 \cdot \left(1 - \frac{var(O_i - P_i)}{var(O_i)} \right) \tag{12}$$

where Oi and Pi indicate actual and anticipated values, respectively; is the average of the anticipated amounts, and n stands the number of data. (4) The determined statistical metrics were rated by a rating system proposed by Zorlu et al. [49], and a color intensity system was used to validate the results of the rating system.

1.1. ANN

In this study, the examination of flyrock distance was the main emphasis. In order to obtain the structure that has the highest efficiency and is capable of forecasting flyrock distance accurately and to the best degree of accuracy, a variety of network models were developed using a variety of hidden neuron sizes and transfer functions. To pass the data from the structured layer to the next layer in an architecture, transfer functions including "LOGSIGMOID", "TANSIGMOID", and "PURELIN" were used, along with a variety of training techniques, including, among others, "trainlm", "trainoss", and "traingdx". This evaluation was the assignment that was provided to the rating approach that was developed by Zorlu et al., and the R^2 and RMSE metrics were the metrics utilized in order to evaluate and choose the optimal architecture among the models that were run with high efficiency and precision. Using this method, the R^2 and RMSE values for the training and testing parts are calculated, and the scores for those quantities are determined. According to this ranking method, the ranking of the architecture is considered to be better when both the values of R^2 and VAF are larger and when the value of RMSE is smaller. Table 3 provides a rundown of the results of these computations in summary form.

It is important to highlight that the outcomes were evaluated using a technique known as color intensity rating (CIR), and the outcomes of both were examined. The CIR technique is a creative and quantitative tool for the problem of selecting the best ANN architecture. Within this approach, the architectures are each allocated a particular coloring (for example, blue), and the model that has a greater rating shows a higher color temperature.

Table 3. Different topology of ANN models in anticipating flyrock distance.

Model No.	Training			Testing			Training Rates			Testing Rates			Total Rate	Rank
	R^2	RMSE	VAF	R^2	RMSE	VAF	R^2	RMSE	VAF	R^2	RMSE	VAF		
1	0.880	13.106	65.783	0.848	11.256	83.126	1	1	1	1	1	1	6	10
2	0.938	8.194	98.110	0.931	7.509	92.166	7	9	9	9	9	9	52	2
3	0.916	10.542	97.858	0.894	10.303	89.412	3	2	8	6	2	8	29	6
4	0.940	8.235	93.983	0.879	9.821	86.232	9	8	4	3	5	4	33	5
5	**0.957**	**7.392**	**99.472**	**0.945**	**7.473**	**93.961**	**10**	**10**	**10**	**10**	**10**	**10**	**60**	**1**
6	0.917	9.934	91.989	0.864	10.027	85.595	4	4	3	2	4	3	20	9
7	0.905	10.215	93.983	0.882	9.055	88.025	2	3	4	4	7	6	26	8
8	0.919	9.559	96.439	0.909	8.771	88.772	5	6	7	7	8	7	40	3
9	0.939	8.544	91.989	0.885	10.130	85.588	8	7	2	5	3	2	27	7
10	0.928	9.611	93.983	0.928	9.699	87.771	6	5	4	8	6	5	34	4

The yellow color indicates the intensity of statistical metrics and their rates. Bold row indicates the best model.

On the other hand, the lower the rate of models, the lower their color temperature becomes, resulting in it becoming almost completely white. All of the numbers in Table 3 have been given the appropriate shading in light of these explanations and the procedure that has been presented. Table 3 presents ten distinct topologies, of which only one was deemed suitable for inclusion in the study as a candidate for the best ANN topology. Among the ten different topologies of ANN, only ANN5, which had received the highest rate possible, i.e., 60, was chosen to serve as the ideal architecture since it performed better than the other models. Furthermore, according to the mentioned scoring tool, the color that was designated to the ANN5 was used to have the maximum intensity. This indicates that all approaches are equivalent and provide very accurate results when selecting the best topology. Because of this, the ANN5 was chosen as the best available ANN model to predict flyrock distance. It has a structure of 6-4-10-1 (with two hidden layers), and the activation function of the input, hidden, and output layers are respectively "tansig", "tansig", and "purelin" type. Figure 10 shows the identified topology that was selected as well as the architecture that was produced by the toolbox of the MATLAB program.

As can be seen in Figure 10, the activation function of all layers was a sigmoid type. Figure 10 also demonstrates that a variable known as "bias" was used in all levels of the network, with the exception of the input layer. As a result, the prediction of the flyrock distance was carried out using the data collected from 65 boulder blasting, which were classified into train and test. The effectiveness of the ANN architectures that were constructed is compared in Table 3. The results indicated that the ANN model presents the R^2 values of 0.957 and 0.945 for the training and testing parts, respectively.

4.2. Hybrid Models

There are instances whenever the algorithms/models/techniques outperform other models when it involves estimating. Therefore, in this case, it could be advantageous for the modeling that was conducted better to be more heavily involved in the optimized hybrid models. The hybrid models are based on the concept that optimized models with more competence ought to have a greater influence on the results. This is accomplished by optimizing the weight and biases in the ANN structures. There are several ways to find these weights and biases. One of these suggestions is the use of metaheuristic optimization algorithms. This section addresses the development of hybrid models, i.e., PSO–ANN and JSA–ANN, for predicting flyrock-induced boulder blasting in open-pit mines. The controllable parameters applied in adjusting PSO and JSA are fixed in the optimization framework to yield the highest performance degree and accuracy level for flyrock estimation.

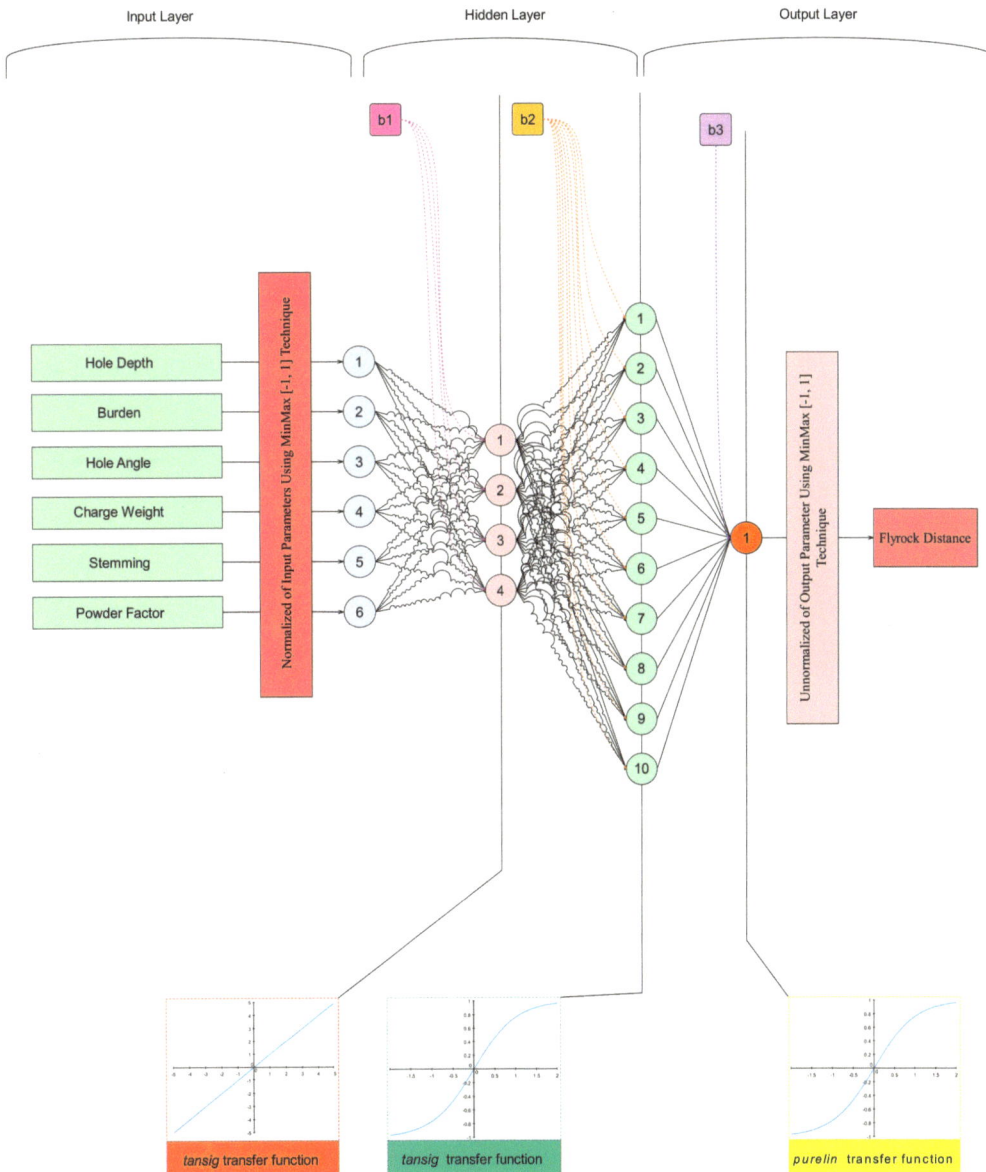

Figure 10. The designed ANN topology for predicting flyrock distance.

4.3. PSO–ANN

As aforementioned in PSO methodology, this metaheuristic algorithm is controlled by various parameters involving a number of particles, inertia weight, and velocity equation's coefficient that the iteration number managed error reduction. These parameters apply a considerable effect on the PSO. In this study, the inertia weight and velocity equation's coefficients are set at 2 and 0.25, respectively, due to the suggestion of previously conducted research [42] that obtained accurate prediction results. Hence, the inertia weight of 2 and the velocity equation's coefficient of 2.5 was employed in PSO–ANN modeling process. Furthermore, the iteration number is considered as 1000 repetitions. Nevertheless, the parameter of the number of particles should be determined by the trial-and-error approach. Therefore, the swarm is defined as various populations, including 50 particles to 500 particles, and the RMSE function is used for evaluating the performance of PSO.

The obtained results of PSO in optimizing weights of neurons and biased values are depicted in Figure 11 and Table 4. Figure 11 illustrates the RMSE value obtained for each PSO swarm size. It can be found that the RMSE values of the PSO–ANN model converge for all swarm sizes in iteration 475. The different PSO–ANN systems were structured for anticipating flyrock distance based on various swarm sizes, as presented in Table 4, and then the best PSO–ANN system was chosen among the ten presented models. For better choosing, Zorlu's rating system was used, as shown in Table 4. The PSO–ANN with swarm sizes of 200 and a total rate of 41 was the superior model compared to other presented PSO–ANN models. The statistical metrics related to this model were the R^2 of (0.972 and 0.954), RMSE of (5.533 and 7.751), and VAF of (99.680 and 93.608), for the training and test phases, respectively.

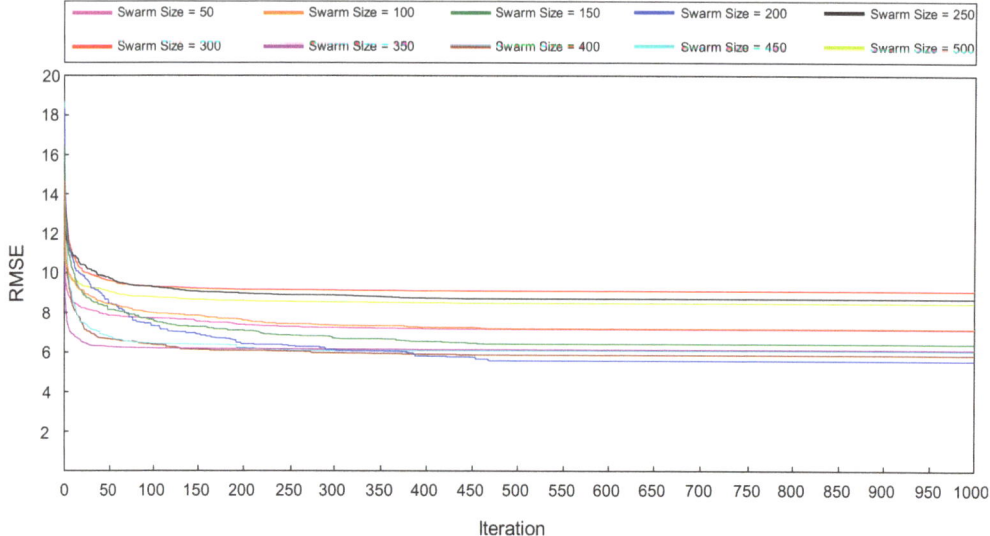

Figure 11. PSO–ANN models with different swarm sizes.

Table 4. Various swarm sizes of PSO in anticipating flyrock distance.

Model No.	Swarm Size	Training			Testing			Training Rates			Testing Rates			Total Rate	Rank
		R^2	RMSE	VAF	R^2	RMSE	VAF	R^2	RMSE	VAF	R^2	RMSE	VAF		
1	50	0.956	7.389	97.116	0.952	6.164	94.832	1	3	2	9	9	10	34	6
2	100	0.961	7.184	95.692	0.946	6.457	93.871	6	6	1	3	5	4	25	9
3	150	0.964	6.963	99.430	0.942	6.906	93.155	7	8	5	1	3	2	26	8
4	**200**	**0.972**	**5.533**	**99.680**	**0.954**	**7.751**	**93.608**	**10**	**10**	**7**	**10**	**1**	**3**	**41**	**1**
5	250	0.957	7.204	99.430	0.944	7.066	92.908	3	4	5	2	2	1	17	10
6	300	0.960	7.192	99.858	0.950	6.385	94.059	5	5	8	8	7	5	38	3
7	350	0.957	7.178	98.255	0.949	6.325	94.287	2	7	3	7	8	7	34	6
8	400	0.957	7.672	100.000	0.948	6.076	94.656	4	1	10	5	10	9	39	2
9	450	0.965	6.587	98.255	0.949	6.427	94.175	8	9	3	6	6	6	38	3
10	500	0.966	7.442	99.964	0.947	6.469	94.628	9	2	9	4	4	8	36	5

The green color indicates the intensity of statistical metrics and their rates. Bold row indicates the best model.

4.4. JSA–ANN

To obtain the optimum value of neuron weights and biases in the ANN architecture (6-4-10-1) that was designed in the previous section, the JAS algorithm was used. Nevertheless, the controllable parameters of JSA should first be adjusted and implemented to achieve the most accurate results. In this regard, the selected topology was employed in developing all hybrid systems. As described in the JSA methodology, the number of populations is considered a controllable parameter of JSA. To specify the best number of jellyfish, several JSA-ANN–ANN models with different populations, i.e., 25, 50, 75, 100, 125, 150, 175, 200, 225, and 250, were trained. The revealed results in Figure 12, the parametric investigation indicated that the number of jellyfish of 200 could achieve the best accuracy and higher system capacity.

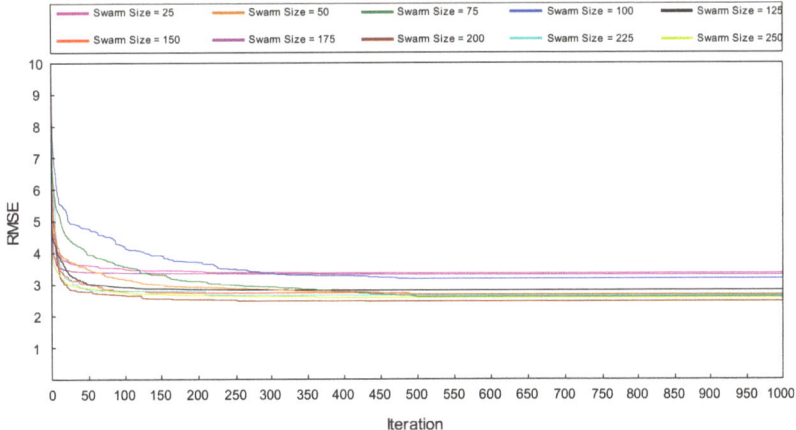

Figure 12. JAS–ANN models with different swarm sizes.

In the present research, the JSA optimization was implemented to identify the ANN model's optimum weights and biases. The JSA algorithm initializes by the originally created initial solution, similar to the existing evolutionary computing algorithms.

The JS algorithm searches the optimum values following the four main stages.

Stage 1. The initial population of the artificial jellyfish, X_i (i = 1, 2, ..., n), is generated using the chaotic map operation:

In the search space, the jellyfish serve as a model. The study's maximum iterations and the population size of the jellyfish are set at 1000 and 250, respectively.

Based on the trial-and-error procedure, beta and gamma have respective values of 4.5 and 0.09.

Stage 2. Finding the X^*:

In this study, the RMSE values are calculated to find the fitness function as shown in the following equation:

$$F_f = \sqrt{\left(\frac{\sum_{i=1}^{n}\left(X_i^O - X_i^E\right)^2}{n_s}\right)} \tag{13}$$

in which X_i^O, X_i^E and n are the measured flyrock, obtained flyrock by the model, and a number of datasets, respectively. An artificial jellyfish with the lowest fitness function is given to the X^* by the algorithm.

Stage 3. Continue as follows until the maximum number of iterations has been reached:

Utilizing Equation (6), ascertain the time control function, $c(t)$.

Perform a local or global search for artificial jellyfish.

Examine the produced values and, when they do not fall inside the given ranges, replace them with new ones.

Considering the new values, and if the fitness function's value is the lowest, add it to X^*.

Here, the JSA method is used to find the weights that will be used to construct the basic models for the JSA–ANN model. Hence, a value between [0, 1] should be selected at random to preserve the $\sum_{i=1}^{n} W_i = 1$. The RMSE works as the cost function in this minimization process.

For selecting the best value for the number of jellyfish, the different JSA–ANN models with different populations were designed, and the results were evaluated based on the RMSE function, as illustrated in Figure 12. Based on Figure 12, RMSE changes are fixed after 500 iterations. Therefore, the JSA–ANN model with the number of jellyfish of 200, beta of 4.5 and gamma of 0.09 was constructed. The various generated results were compared and evaluated using the statistical metrics, i.e., R^2, RMSE, and VAF, as shown in Table 5. Similar to the evaluation of PSO–ANN, the developed JSA–ANN models were evaluated based on the rating system to choose the best JSA–ANN system with a high level of accuracy and acceptable performance prediction level.

Table 5. Different swarm sizes of JSA in anticipating flyrock distance.

Model No.	Swarm Size	Training			Testing			Training Rates			Testing Rates			Total Rate	Rank
		R^2	RMSE	VAF	R^2	RMSE	VAF	R^2	RMSE	VAF	R^2	RMSE	VAF		
1	25	0.988	3.788	99.964	0.990	4.368	98.706	1	1	8	9	2	9	30	6
2	50	0.988	3.629	98.718	0.971	4.197	96.525	2	2	4	2	4	3	17	9
3	75	0.991	3.425	97.721	0.978	4.261	96.460	6	4	3	5	3	2	23	8
4	100	0.990	3.299	99.110	0.979	3.573	97.597	4	5	5	6	6	5	31	5
5	125	0.990	3.214	99.430	0.976	3.453	97.649	5	6	7	4	7	6	35	4
6	150	0.989	3.587	97.116	0.964	4.796	96.313	3	3	2	1	1	1	11	10
7	175	0.995	2.791	99.964	0.992	3.282	98.664	9	9	8	10	8	8	52	2
8	200	0.995	2.449	100.000	0.990	2.602	98.832	10	10	10	8	10	10	58	1
9	225	0.992	3.095	99.110	0.983	3.101	98.300	8	8	5	7	9	7	44	3
10	250	0.992	3.150	96.439	0.975	3.700	97.298	7	7	1	3	5	4	27	7

The blue color indicates the intensity of statistical metrics and their rates. Bold row indicates the best model.

5. Results and Discussion

The purpose of the current research is to propose a precise model for modeling and predicting flyrock distance due to oversize boulder blasting in a quarry mine located in Malaysia. The most effective parameters were six numbers identified and imported into the modeling process. Based on the available data, the ANN model, as well as the two hybrid PSO–ANN and JSA–ANN systems, were developed to determine the superior predictive flyrock model between other proposed models. The obtained results relevant to the considered best models of ANN, PSO–ANN, and JSA–ANN based on R^2, RMSE, and VAF metrics in anticipating flyrock are shown in Table 6—these predictive models train well as a result of their high achievements in terms of the training data. The generated model achieves a high precision level among testing dataset indicates because it is well-developed.

Table 6. Results of the ANN and hybrid models in estimating flyrock distance.

Developed Model	Train			Test			Train Rating			Test Rating			Total Rate	Rank
	R^2	RMSE	VAF	R^2	RMSE	VAF	R^2	RMSE	VAF	R^2	RMSE	VAF		
ANN	0.957	7.392	91.989	0.945	7.473	93.961	1	1	1	1	2	2	8	3
PSO–ANN	0.972	5.533	99.680	0.954	7.751	93.608	2	2	2	2	1	1	10	2
JSA–ANN	0.995	2.791	99.964	0.989	2.896	98.872	3	3	3	3	3	3	18	1

Although all of the predictive models have the ability to predict flyrock, the JSA–ANN predictive model has the potential to deliver greater performance capabilities in terms of R^2 values throughout the training phase as well as the testing phase. According to these findings, the JSA–ANN model has the potential to achieve the lowest overall system error of all the models that have been applied. Figure 13 depicts the anticipated values for flyrock together with the measured values obtained from the application of the ANN, PSO–ANN, and JSA–ANN prediction models. The anticipated findings for both the training dataset and test phases are provided here in this figure. Based on this figure, despite the fact that all models have adequately performed the estimation of flyrock distance, the JSA–ANN model has the potential to establish itself as a novel hybrid system in this field. Table 7 illustrates the results that we have acquired about the effectiveness indicators of the developed model. The information presented in Table 7 shows a comparison between the prediction precision and capability level of our suggested method and that of a number of the most recent studies. According to the findings, the JSA–ANN model provides a higher performance ability in the modeling and prediction of flyrock than the other techniques.

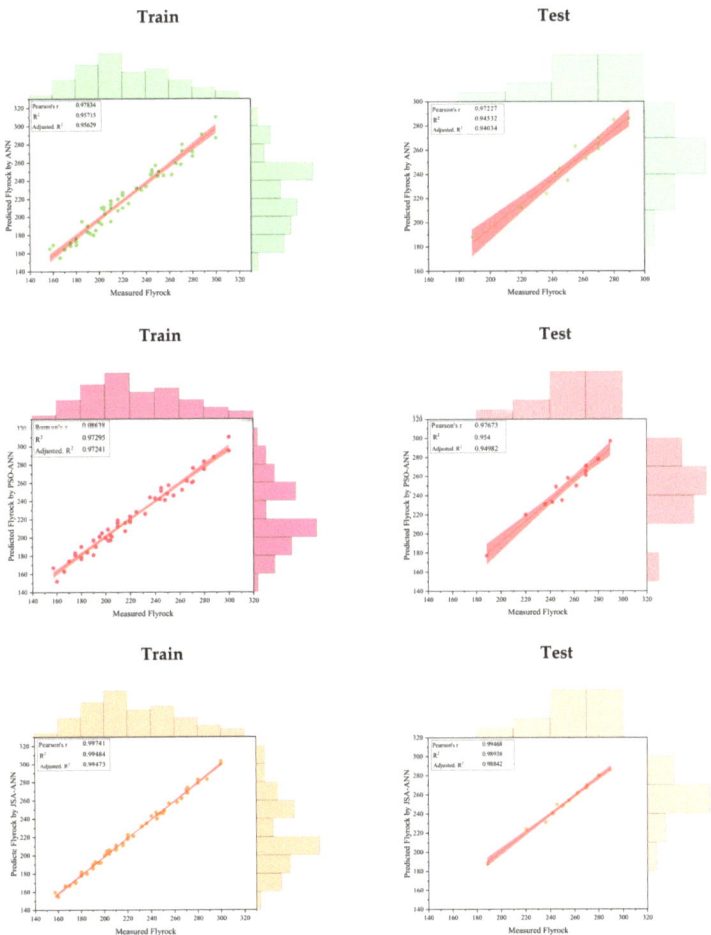

Figure 13. The results of developed models in predicting flyrock distance.

Table 7. Comparative analysis of the precision of our suggested method with that of other research.

Author	Year	Method	R^2
[38]	2020	Extreme Learning Machine	0.955
[39]	2020	FRES	0.981
[6]	2022	Z-FCM–ANN	0.991
[3]	2022	ANN	0.982
[41]	2022	HGSO-ANFIS	0.924
[50]	2022	Ensemble model	0.974
[42]	2023	AdaBoost	0.99
		ANN	0.945
Proposed technique		PSO–ANN	0.954
		JSA–ANN	0.989

6. Sensitivity Analysis

For assessing the impact of all of the influential factors on flyrock, an analysis of sensitivity was conducted employing the cosine amplitude (CA) method (Equation (14)) introduced by Yang and Zhang [51]:

$$r_{ij} = \frac{\sum\limits_{k=1}^{l} g_{ik} \cdot g_{jk}}{\sqrt{\left(\sum\limits_{k=1}^{l} g_{ik}^2\right) \cdot \left(\sum\limits_{k=1}^{m} g_{jk}^2\right)}} \tag{14}$$

in which g_{ik} and g_{jk} indicate the inputs and output(s), respectively. k reveals the number of datasets. Noteworthy, a higher value of r_{ij} signifies inputs that matter most. Figure 14 shows the effect of each parameter on flyrock. The values of 0.993, 0.992, and 0.991 for the effectiveness of charge weight, powder factor, and hole angle demonstrated that this parameter had the highest effect on flyrock intensity; moreover, the burden with the r_{ij} value of 0.973 had the least effect on flyrock intensity. Furthermore, insignificant charge weight changes cause considerable flyrock changes.

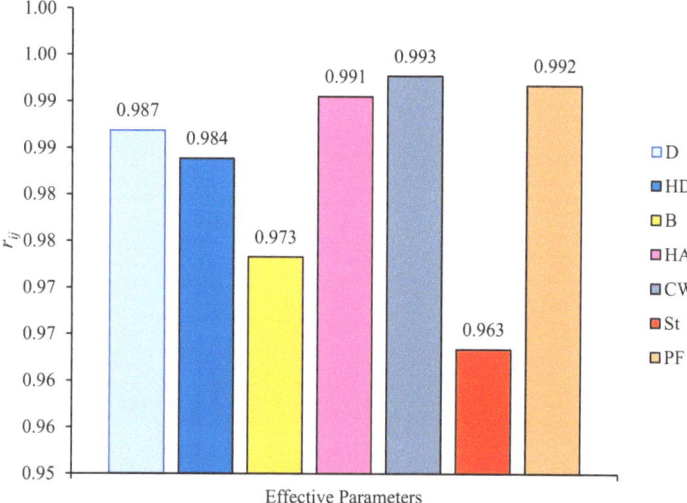

Figure 14. The effectiveness of considered variables on flyrock intensity.

7. Conclusions

This research focuses on the development of an innovative hybrid system for flyrock prediction in a quarry mines. To do this, the most influential variables on the flyrock distance-induced boulder blasting were identified from available literature and imported to the ANN model. The neurons' weights and biases were optimized by two optimization algorithms of PSO and JSA. The JSA–ANN model was first presented for estimating flyrock. For each ANN, PSO–ANN, and JSA–ANN model, the different models with various structures and swarm sizes were designed, and the evaluation indices of R^2, RMSE, and VAF were calculated for them.

To choose the best predictive model, a rating system was employed, and the model with the highest rate was introduced as the superior model. The evaluation of the achieved predictions indicated that both the PSO–ANN and JSA–ANN hybrid models are able to present precise results in estimating flyrock distance. However, the JSA–ANN model yields a higher accuracy prediction level and lower error. The R^2 values of (0.957, 0.972, and 0.995) and (0.945, 0.954, and 0.989) were determined to train and test the ANN, PSO–ANN and JSA–ANN predictive models, respectively. Moreover, the RMSE values of (7.392, 5.533, and 2.791) and (7.473, 7.751, and 2.896) were used to train and test the ANN, PSO–ANN and JSA–ANN models, respectively. These findings reveal the highest capability of the JSA–ANN hybrid model compared to the others.

It can be concluded that a hybrid JSA–ANN system is identified as the best predictive model to estimate flyrock distance if a predictive model with the highest accuracy and lowest error is required. It is worth noting that the results of sensitivity analysis indicated that the largest and smallest impact parameters on flyrock distance were charge weight and burden, respectively.

The current study has some limitations; thus, the following further examinations are suggested as possible next steps. Firstly, the data that was utilized may be extended to incorporate more full data with further blasting that was captured. Second, there is a desire to strengthen both the predictive and optimizing capabilities of the system. Third, since the number of data samples is relatively low, artificial data augmentation techniques can be used to increase the size and diversity of the dataset.

In light of the fact that the estimation and optimization models used in this investigation have room for development, it has been concluded that the utilization of novel approaches that enable the utilize hybrid combinations is the most effective method for improving both the estimation and optimization settings. Based on practical applications, the provided framework can be modified to apply to various sectors of engineering, particularly mining and building engineering. Nevertheless, the ensemble soft computing method can be used to boost the performance capacity of estimation objectives and enhance the accuracy level of soft computing approaches. These suggested techniques can be employed to conduct an analysis of safety data and locate possible dangers, blasting safety regions, and risks associated with blasting activities. The flyrock distance can be anticipated when the blasting activities begin in order to monitor for any possible problems or damages that could happen to the personnel, equipment, and residential area that is close to a safe area. If the anticipated outcomes are higher than those specified in the literature or standards, the blasting pattern or structure can be revised once again such that the anticipated flyrock values remain inside the safe limits that have been advised. In general, soft computing techniques can be applied to evaluate the data related to the environment and analyze the influence of mining activities on the surrounding ecosystem.

Author Contributions: Conceptualization, S.H., D.J.A. and E.T.M.; methodology, X.W., S.H. and D.J.A., software, X.W. and S.H., validation, X.W. and S.H., formal analysis, X.W. and S.H., data curation, D.J.A. writing—original draft preparation, X.W., S.H., D.J.A. and E.T.M., writing—review and editing, X.W., S.H., D.J.A. and E.T.M., supervision, D.J.A. and E.T.M. All authors have read and agreed to the published version of the manuscript.

Funding: This research received no external funding.

Data Availability Statement: The data are available upon reasonable request.

Conflicts of Interest: The authors declare no conflict of interest.

References

1. Lundborg, N.; Persson, A.; Ladegaard-Pedersen, A.; Holmberg, R. Keeping the lid on flyrock in open-pit blasting. *Eng. Min. J.* **1975**, *176*, 95–100.
2. Gupta, R.N.; Bagchi, A.; Singh, B. Optimising drilling and blasting parameters to improve blasting efficiency. In *Status Report*; CBIP Rock Mech: New Delhi, India, 1988; pp. 185–206.
3. Hosseini, S.; Mousavi, A.; Monjezi, M.; Khandelwal, M. Mine-to-crusher policy: Planning of mine blasting patterns for environmentally friendly and optimum fragmentation using Monte Carlo simulation-based multi-objective grey wolf optimization approach. *Resour. Policy* **2022**, *79*, 103087. [CrossRef]
4. Hosseini, S.; Pourmirzaee, R.; Armaghani, D.J.; Sabri Sabri, M.M. Prediction of ground vibration due to mine blasting in a surface lead–zinc mine using machine learning ensemble techniques. *Sci. Rep.* **2023**, *13*, 6591. [CrossRef] [PubMed]
5. Hosseini, S.; Poormirzaee, R.; Hajihassani, M. An uncertainty hybrid model for risk assessment and prediction of blast-induced rock mass fragmentation. *Int. J. Rock Mech. Min. Sci.* **2022**, *160*, 105250. [CrossRef]
6. Hosseini, S.; Poormirzaee, R.; Hajihassani, M.; Kalatehjari, R. An ANN-Fuzzy Cognitive Map-Based Z-Number Theory to Predict Flyrock Induced by Blasting in Open-Pit Mines. *Rock Mech. Rock Eng.* **2022**, *55*, 4373–4390. [CrossRef]
7. Rezaei, M.; Monjezi, M.; Yazdian Varjani, A. Development of a fuzzy model to predict flyrock in surface mining. *Saf. Sci.* **2011**, *49*, 298–305. [CrossRef]
8. Bahrami, A.; Monjezi, M.; Goshtasbi, K.; Ghazvinian, A. Prediction of rock fragmentation due to blasting using artificial neural network. *Eng. Comput.* **2011**, *27*, 177–181. [CrossRef]
9. Monjezi, M.; Bahrami, A.; Varjani, A.Y.; Sayadi, A.R. Prediction and controlling of flyrock in blasting operation using artificial neural network. *Arab. J. Geosci.* **2011**, *4*, 421–425. [CrossRef]
10. Amini, H.; Gholami, R.; Monjezi, M.; Torabi, S.R.; Zadhesh, J. Evaluation of flyrock phenomenon due to blasting operation by support vector machine. *Neural Comput. Appl.* **2012**, *21*, 2077–2085. [CrossRef]
11. Zangoei, A.; Monjezi, M.; Armaghani, D.J.; Mehrdanesh, A.; Ahmadian, S. Prediction and optimization of flyrock and oversize boulder induced by mine blasting using artificial intelligence techniques. *Environ. Earth Sci.* **2022**, *81*, 359. [CrossRef]
12. Mohamad, E.T.; Armaghani, D.J.; Hajihassani, M.; Faizi, K.; Marto, A. A simulation approach to predict blasting-induced flyrock and size of thrown rocks. *Electron. J. Geotech. Eng.* **2013**, *18*, 365–374.
13. Trivedi, R.; Singh, T.N.; Raina, A.K. Prediction of blast-induced flyrock in Indian limestone mines using neural networks. *J. Rock Mech. Geotech. Eng.* **2014**, *6*, 447–454. [CrossRef]
14. Ghasemi, E.; Amini, H.; Ataei, M.; Khalokakaei, R. Application of artificial intelligence techniques for predicting the flyrock distance caused by blasting operation. *Arab. J. Geosci.* **2014**, *7*, 193–202. [CrossRef]
15. McKenzie, C.K. Flyrock range and fragment size prediction. In Proceedings of the 35th Annual Conference on Explosives and Blasting Technique, Denver, CO, USA, 8–11 February 2009; International Society of Explosives Engineers: Cleveland, OH, USA, 2009; Volume 2.
16. Ikram, R.M.A.; Ewees, A.A.; Parmar, K.S.; Yaseen, Z.M.; Shahid, S.; Kisi, O. The viability of extended marine predators algorithm-based artificial neural networks for streamflow prediction. *Appl. Soft. Comput.* **2022**, *131*, 109739. [CrossRef]
17. Ikram, R.M.A.; Dai, H.-L.; Al-Bahrani, M.; Mamlooki, M. Prediction of the FRP Reinforced Concrete Beam shear capacity by using ELM-CRFOA. *Measurement* **2022**, *205*, 112230. [CrossRef]
18. Ikram, R.M.A.; Jaafari, A.; Milan, S.G.; Kisi, O.; Heddam, S.; Zounemat-Kermani, M. Hybridized Adaptive Neuro-Fuzzy Inference System with Metaheuristic Algorithms for Modeling Monthly Pan Evaporation. *Water* **2022**, *14*, 3549. [CrossRef]
19. Ikram, R.M.A.; Goliatt, L.; Kisi, O.; Trajkovic, S.; Shahid, S. Covariance matrix adaptation evolution strategy for improving machine learning approaches in streamflow prediction. *Mathematics* **2022**, *10*, 2971. [CrossRef]
20. Ikram, R.M.A.; Dai, H.-L.; Ewees, A.A.; Shiri, J.; Kisi, O.; Zounemat-Kermani, M. Application of improved version of multi verse optimizer algorithm for modeling solar radiation. *Energy Rep.* **2022**, *8*, 12063–12080. [CrossRef]
21. Adnan, R.M.; Dai, H.-L.; Mostafa, R.R.; Islam, A.R.M.T.; Kisi, O.; Heddam, S.; Zounemat-Kermani, M. Modelling groundwater level fluctuations by ELM merged advanced metaheuristic algorithms using hydroclimatic data. *Geocarto Int.* **2023**, *38*, 2158951. [CrossRef]
22. He, B.; Armaghani, D.J.; Lai, S.H. Assessment of tunnel blasting-induced overbreak: A novel metaheuristic-based random forest approach. *Tunn. Undergr. Sp. Technol.* **2023**, *133*, 104979. [CrossRef]
23. Ghanizadeh, A.R.; Ghanizadeh, A.; Asteris, P.G.; Fakharian, P.; Armaghani, D.J. Developing bearing capacity model for geogrid-reinforced stone columns improved soft clay utilizing MARS-EBS hybrid method. *Transp. Geotech.* **2023**, *38*, 100906. [CrossRef]
24. Yang, H.; Wang, Z.; Song, K. A new hybrid grey wolf optimizer-feature weighted-multiple kernel-support vector regression technique to predict TBM performance. *Eng. Comput.* **2022**, *38*, 2469–2485. [CrossRef]
25. Yang, H.; Song, K.; Zhou, J. Automated Recognition Model of Geomechanical Information Based on Operational Data of Tunneling Boring Machines. *Rock Mech. Rock Eng.* **2022**, *55*, 1499–1516. [CrossRef]
26. Lundborg, N. *The Probability of Flyrock*; Swedish Detonic Research Foundation: Stockholm, Sweden, 1981.

27. Richard, A.B.; Moore, A.J. *Golden Pike Cut Back Fly Rock Control and Calibration of a Predictive Model*; Terrock Consulting Engineers Report; Kalgoorlie Consolidated Gold Mines: Subiaco, Australia, 2005; p. 37.
28. Monjezi, M.; Bahrami, A.; Yazdian Varjani, A. Simultaneous prediction of fragmentation and flyrock in blasting operation using artificial neural networks. *Int. J. Rock Mech. Min. Sci.* **2010**, *47*, 476–480. [CrossRef]
29. Monjezi, M.; Khoshalan, H.A.; Varjani, A.Y. Prediction of flyrock and backbreak in open pit blasting operation: A neuro-genetic approach. *Arab. J. Geosci.* **2012**, *5*, 441–448. [CrossRef]
30. Ghasemi, E.; Sari, M.; Ataei, M. Development of an empirical model for predicting the effects of controllable blasting parameters on flyrock distance in surface mines. *Int. J. Rock Mech. Min. Sci.* **2012**, *52*, 163–170. [CrossRef]
31. Monjezi, M.; Mehrdanesh, A.; Malek, A.; Khandelwal, M. Evaluation of effect of blast design parameters on flyrock using artificial neural networks. *Neural Comput. Appl.* **2013**, *23*, 349–356. [CrossRef]
32. Khandelwal, M.; Monjezi, M. Prediction of backbreak in open-pit blasting operations using the machine learning method. *Rock Mech. Rock Eng.* **2013**, *46*, 389–396. [CrossRef]
33. Trivedi, R.; Singh, T.N.; Gupta, N. Prediction of blast-induced flyrock in opencast mines using ANN and ANFIS. *Geotech. Geol. Eng.* **2015**, *33*, 875–891. [CrossRef]
34. Raina, A.K.; Murthy, V.M.S.R. Prediction of Flyrock Distance in Open Pit Blasting Using Surface Response Analysis. *Geotech. Geol. Eng.* **2016**, *34*, 15–28. [CrossRef]
35. Trivedi, R.; Singh, T.N.; Raina, A.K. Simultaneous prediction of blast-induced flyrock and fragmentation in opencast limestone mines using back propagation neural network. *Int. J. Min. Miner. Eng.* **2016**, *7*, 237–252. [CrossRef]
36. Rad, H.N.; Hasanipanah, M.; Rezaei, M.; Eghlim, A.L. Developing a least squares support vector machine for estimating the blast-induced flyrock. *Eng. Comput.* **2018**, *34*, 709–717. [CrossRef]
37. Hudaverdi, T.; Akyildiz, O. A new classification approach for prediction of flyrock throw in surface mines. *Bull. Eng. Geol. Environ.* **2019**, *78*, 177–187. [CrossRef]
38. Lu, X.; Hasanipanah, M.; Brindhadevi, K.; Bakhshandeh Amnieh, H.; Khalafi, S. ORELM: A Novel Machine Learning Approach for Prediction of Flyrock in Mine Blasting. *Nat. Resour. Res.* **2020**, *29*, 641–654. [CrossRef]
39. Hasanipanah, M.; Bakhshandeh Amnieh, H.; Amnieh, H.B. A fuzzy rule-based approach to address uncertainty in risk assessment and prediction of blast-induced Flyrock in a quarry. *Nat. Resour. Res.* **2020**, *29*, 669–689. [CrossRef]
40. Lawal, A.I.; Ojo, O.J.; Kim, M.; Kwon, S. Determination of blast-induced flyrock using a drone technology: A bibliometric overview with practical soft computing implementation. *Arab. J. Geosci.* **2022**, *15*, 1581. [CrossRef]
41. Ye, J.; He, X. A novel hybrid of ANFIS-based models using optimisation approaches to predict mine blast-induced flyrock. *Int. J. Environ. Sci. Technol.* **2023**, *20*, 3673–3686. [CrossRef]
42. Yari, M.; Armaghani, D.J.; Maraveas, C.; Ejlali, A.N.; Mohamad, E.T.; Asteris, P.G. Several Tree-Based Solutions for Predicting Flyrock Distance Due to Mine Blasting. *Appl. Sci.* **2023**, *13*, 1345. [CrossRef]
43. Chou, J.-S.; Truong, D.-N. A novel metaheuristic optimizer inspired by behavior of jellyfish in ocean. *Appl. Math. Comput.* **2021**, *389*, 125535. [CroooRcf]
44. Chou, J.S.; Tjandrakusuma, S.; Liu, C.Y. Jellyfish Search-Optimized Deep Learning for Compressive Strength Prediction in Images of Ready-Mixed Concrete. *Comput. Intell. Neurosci.* **2022**, *2022*, 9541115. [CrossRef]
45. Kennedy, J.; Eberhart, R.C. Discrete binary version of the particle swarm algorithm. In Proceedings of the 1997 IEEE International Conference on Systems, Man, and Cybernetics. Computational Cybernetics and Simulation, Orlando, FL, USA, 12–15 October 1997; IEEE: New York, NY, USA, 1997. [CrossRef]
46. Bakhtavar, E.; Hosseini, S.; Hewage, K.; Sadiq, R. Green blasting policy: Simultaneous forecast of vertical and horizontal distribution of dust emissions using artificial causality-weighted neural network. *J. Clean. Prod.* **2021**, *283*, 124562. [CrossRef]
47. Hosseini, S.; Monjezi, M.; Bakhtavar, E.; Mousavi, A. Prediction of Dust Emission Due to Open Pit Mine Blasting Using a Hybrid Artificial Neural Network. *Nat. Resour. Res.* **2021**, *30*, 4773–4788. [CrossRef]
48. Hosseini, S.; Monjezi, M.; Bakhtavar, E. Minimization of blast-induced dust emission using gene-expression programming and grasshopper optimization algorithm: A smart mining solution based on blasting plan optimization. *Clean Technol. Environ. Policy* **2022**, *24*, 2313–2328. [CrossRef]
49. Zorlu, K.; Gokceoglu, C.; Ocakoglu, F.; Nefeslioglu, H.A.; Acikalin, S. Prediction of uniaxial compressive strength of sandstones using petrography-based models. *Eng. Geol.* **2008**, *96*, 141–158. [CrossRef]
50. Barkhordari, M.S.; Armaghani, D.J.; Fakharian, P. Ensemble machine learning models for prediction of flyrock due to quarry blasting. *Int. J. Environ. Sci. Technol.* **2022**, *19*, 8661–8676. [CrossRef]
51. Yang, Y.; Zhang, Q. A hierarchical analysis for rock engineering using artificial neural networks. *Rock Mech. Rock Eng.* **1997**, *30*, 207–222. [CrossRef]

Disclaimer/Publisher's Note: The statements, opinions and data contained in all publications are solely those of the individual author(s) and contributor(s) and not of MDPI and/or the editor(s). MDPI and/or the editor(s) disclaim responsibility for any injury to people or property resulting from any ideas, methods, instructions or products referred to in the content.

Article

Modelling Soil Compaction Parameters Using an Enhanced Hybrid Intelligence Paradigm of ANFIS and Improved Grey Wolf Optimiser

Abidhan Bardhan [1], Raushan Kumar Singh [2], Sufyan Ghani [3], Gerasimos Konstantakatos [4] and Panagiotis G. Asteris [4],*

1 Department of Civil Engineering, National Institute of Technology, Patna 800005, India; abidhan@nitp.ac.in
2 Department of Computer Engineering and Applications, GLA University, Mathura 281406, India; raushan.singh@gla.ac.in
3 Department of Civil Engineering, Sharda University, Greater Noida 201310, India; sufyan.ghani@sharda.ac.in
4 Computational Mechanics Laboratory, School of Pedagogical and Technological Education, 14121 Athens, Greece; gkonstantakatos@aspete.gr
* Correspondence: asteris@aspete.gr

Abstract: The criteria for measuring soil compaction parameters, such as optimum moisture content and maximum dry density, play an important role in construction projects. On construction sites, base/sub-base soils are compacted at the optimal moisture content to achieve the desirable level of compaction, generally between 95% and 98% of the maximum dry density. The present technique of determining compaction parameters in the laboratory is a time-consuming task. This study proposes an improved hybrid intelligence paradigm as an alternative tool to the laboratory method for estimating the optimum moisture content and maximum dry density of soils. For this purpose, an advanced version of the grey wolf optimiser (GWO) called improved GWO (IGWO) was integrated with an adaptive neuro-fuzzy inference system (ANFIS), which resulted in a high-performance hybrid model named ANFIS-IGWO. Overall, the results indicate that the proposed ANFIS-IGWO model achieved the most precise prediction of the optimum moisture content (degree of correlation = 0.9203 and root mean square error = 0.0635) and maximum dry density (degree of correlation = 0.9050 and root mean square error = 0.0709) of soils. The outcomes of the suggested model are noticeably superior to those attained by other hybrid ANFIS models, which are built with standard GWO, Moth-flame optimisation, slime mould algorithm, and marine predators algorithm. The results indicate that geotechnical engineers can benefit from the newly developed ANFIS-IGWO model during the design stage of civil engineering projects. The developed MATLAB models are also included for determining soil compaction parameters.

Keywords: soil compaction; adaptive neuro-fuzzy inference system; grey wolf optimiser; swarm intelligence

MSC: 68Txx

Citation: Bardhan, A.; Singh, R.K.; Ghani, S.; Konstantakatos, G.; Asteris, P.G. Modelling Soil Compaction Parameters Using an Enhanced Hybrid Intelligence Paradigm of ANFIS and Improved Grey Wolf Optimiser. *Mathematics* **2023**, *11*, 3064. https://doi.org/10.3390/math11143064

Academic Editor: Gaige Wang

Received: 23 June 2023
Revised: 6 July 2023
Accepted: 7 July 2023
Published: 11 July 2023

Copyright: © 2023 by the authors. Licensee MDPI, Basel, Switzerland. This article is an open access article distributed under the terms and conditions of the Creative Commons Attribution (CC BY) license (https://creativecommons.org/licenses/by/4.0/).

1. Introduction

In the parlance of geotechnical engineering, soil compaction is a method of compressing soil particles by reducing air voids while maintaining steady water content [1,2]. Compaction can be used to enhance the mechanical qualities of soils in a number of different ways. Proctor [3] recommended compacting soil with different water contents at an appropriate compaction energy. As a result, the compaction curve can be used to determine the optimum moisture content (OMC) and maximum dry density (MDD) of soils. To sustain the long-term performance of various engineering structures, such as embankments of railways, highways, and airport runways, these two compaction parameters are commonly

27. Richard, A.B.; Moore, A.J. *Golden Pike Cut Back Fly Rock Control and Calibration of a Predictive Model*; Terrock Consulting Engineers Report; Kalgoorlie Consolidated Gold Mines: Subiaco, Australia, 2005; p. 37.
28. Monjezi, M.; Bahrami, A.; Yazdian Varjani, A. Simultaneous prediction of fragmentation and flyrock in blasting operation using artificial neural networks. *Int. J. Rock Mech. Min. Sci.* **2010**, *47*, 476–480. [CrossRef]
29. Monjezi, M.; Khoshalan, H.A.; Varjani, A.Y. Prediction of flyrock and backbreak in open pit blasting operation: A neuro-genetic approach. *Arab. J. Geosci.* **2012**, *5*, 441–448. [CrossRef]
30. Ghasemi, E.; Sari, M.; Ataei, M. Development of an empirical model for predicting the effects of controllable blasting parameters on flyrock distance in surface mines. *Int. J. Rock Mech. Min. Sci.* **2012**, *52*, 163–170. [CrossRef]
31. Monjezi, M.; Mehrdanesh, A.; Malek, A.; Khandelwal, M. Evaluation of effect of blast design parameters on flyrock using artificial neural networks. *Neural Comput. Appl.* **2013**, *23*, 349–356. [CrossRef]
32. Khandelwal, M.; Monjezi, M. Prediction of backbreak in open-pit blasting operations using the machine learning method. *Rock Mech. Rock Eng.* **2013**, *46*, 389–396. [CrossRef]
33. Trivedi, R.; Singh, T.N.; Gupta, N. Prediction of blast-induced flyrock in opencast mines using ANN and ANFIS. *Geotech. Geol. Eng.* **2015**, *33*, 875–891. [CrossRef]
34. Raina, A.K.; Murthy, V.M.S.R. Prediction of Flyrock Distance in Open Pit Blasting Using Surface Response Analysis. *Geotech. Geol. Eng.* **2016**, *34*, 15–28. [CrossRef]
35. Trivedi, R.; Singh, T.N.; Raina, A.K. Simultaneous prediction of blast-induced flyrock and fragmentation in opencast limestone mines using back propagation neural network. *Int. J. Min. Miner. Eng.* **2016**, *7*, 237–252. [CrossRef]
36. Rad, H.N.; Hasanipanah, M.; Rezaei, M.; Eghlim, A.L. Developing a least squares support vector machine for estimating the blast-induced flyrock. *Eng. Comput.* **2018**, *34*, 709–717. [CrossRef]
37. Hudaverdi, T.; Akyildiz, O. A new classification approach for prediction of flyrock throw in surface mines. *Bull. Eng. Geol. Environ.* **2019**, *78*, 177–187. [CrossRef]
38. Lu, X.; Hasanipanah, M.; Brindhadevi, K.; Bakhshandeh Amnieh, H.; Khalafi, S. ORELM: A Novel Machine Learning Approach for Prediction of Flyrock in Mine Blasting. *Nat. Resour. Res.* **2020**, *29*, 641–654. [CrossRef]
39. Hasanipanah, M.; Bakhshandeh Amnieh, H.; Amnieh, H.B. A fuzzy rule-based approach to address uncertainty in risk assessment and prediction of blast-induced Flyrock in a quarry. *Nat. Resour. Res.* **2020**, *29*, 669–689. [CrossRef]
40. Lawal, A.I.; Ojo, O.J.; Kim, M.; Kwon, S. Determination of blast-induced flyrock using a drone technology: A bibliometric overview with practical soft computing implementation. *Arab. J. Geosci.* **2022**, *15*, 1581. [CrossRef]
41. Ye, J.; He, X. A novel hybrid of ANFIS-based models using optimisation approaches to predict mine blast-induced flyrock. *Int. J. Environ. Sci. Technol.* **2023**, *20*, 3673–3686. [CrossRef]
42. Yari, M.; Armaghani, D.J.; Maraveas, C.; Ejlali, A.N.; Mohamad, E.T.; Asteris, P.G. Several Tree-Based Solutions for Predicting Flyrock Distance Due to Mine Blasting. *Appl. Sci.* **2023**, *13*, 1345. [CrossRef]
43. Chou, J.-S.; Truong, D.-N. A novel metaheuristic optimizer inspired by behavior of jellyfish in ocean. *Appl. Math. Comput.* **2021**, *389*, 125535. [CrossRef]
44. Chou, J.S.; Tjandrakusuma, S.; Liu, C.Y. Jellyfish Search-Optimized Deep Learning for Compressive Strength Prediction in Images of Ready-Mixed Concrete. *Comput. Intell. Neurosci.* **2022**, *2022*, 9541115. [CrossRef]
45. Kennedy, J.; Eberhart, R.C. Discrete binary version of the particle swarm algorithm. In Proceedings of the 1997 IEEE International Conference on Systems, Man, and Cybernetics. Computational Cybernetics and Simulation, Orlando, FL, USA, 12–15 October 1997; IEEE: New York, NY, USA, 1997. [CrossRef]
46. Bakhtavar, E.; Hosseini, S.; Hewage, K.; Sadiq, R. Green blasting policy: Simultaneous forecast of vertical and horizontal distribution of dust emissions using artificial causality-weighted neural network. *J. Clean. Prod.* **2021**, *283*, 124562. [CrossRef]
47. Hosseini, S.; Monjezi, M.; Bakhtavar, E.; Mousavi, A. Prediction of Dust Emission Due to Open Pit Mine Blasting Using a Hybrid Artificial Neural Network. *Nat. Resour. Res.* **2021**, *30*, 4773–4788. [CrossRef]
48. Hosseini, S.; Monjezi, M.; Bakhtavar, E. Minimization of blast-induced dust emission using gene-expression programming and grasshopper optimization algorithm: A smart mining solution based on blasting plan optimization. *Clean Technol. Environ. Policy* **2022**, *24*, 2313–2328. [CrossRef]
49. Zorlu, K.; Gokceoglu, C.; Ocakoglu, F.; Nefeslioglu, H.A.; Acikalin, S. Prediction of uniaxial compressive strength of sandstones using petrography-based models. *Eng. Geol.* **2008**, *96*, 141–158. [CrossRef]
50. Barkhordari, M.S.; Armaghani, D.J.; Fakharian, P. Ensemble machine learning models for prediction of flyrock due to quarry blasting. *Int. J. Environ. Sci. Technol.* **2022**, *19*, 8661–8676. [CrossRef]
51. Yang, Y.; Zhang, Q. A hierarchical analysis for rock engineering using artificial neural networks. *Rock Mech. Rock Eng.* **1997**, *30*, 207–222. [CrossRef]

Disclaimer/Publisher's Note: The statements, opinions and data contained in all publications are solely those of the individual author(s) and contributor(s) and not of MDPI and/or the editor(s). MDPI and/or the editor(s) disclaim responsibility for any injury to people or property resulting from any ideas, methods, instructions or products referred to in the content.

Article

Modelling Soil Compaction Parameters Using an Enhanced Hybrid Intelligence Paradigm of ANFIS and Improved Grey Wolf Optimiser

Abidhan Bardhan [1], Raushan Kumar Singh [2], Sufyan Ghani [3], Gerasimos Konstantakatos [4] and Panagiotis G. Asteris [4,*]

[1] Department of Civil Engineering, National Institute of Technology, Patna 800005, India; abidhan@nitp.ac.in
[2] Department of Computer Engineering and Applications, GLA University, Mathura 281406, India; raushan.singh@gla.ac.in
[3] Department of Civil Engineering, Sharda University, Greater Noida 201310, India; sufyan.ghani@sharda.ac.in
[4] Computational Mechanics Laboratory, School of Pedagogical and Technological Education, 14121 Athens, Greece; gkonstantakatos@aspete.gr
* Correspondence: asteris@aspete.gr

Citation: Bardhan, A.; Singh, R.K.; Ghani, S.; Konstantakatos, G.; Asteris, P.G. Modelling Soil Compaction Parameters Using an Enhanced Hybrid Intelligence Paradigm of ANFIS and Improved Grey Wolf Optimiser. *Mathematics* **2023**, *11*, 3064. https://doi.org/10.3390/math11143064

Academic Editor: Gaige Wang

Received: 23 June 2023
Revised: 6 July 2023
Accepted: 7 July 2023
Published: 11 July 2023

Copyright: © 2023 by the authors. Licensee MDPI, Basel, Switzerland. This article is an open access article distributed under the terms and conditions of the Creative Commons Attribution (CC BY) license (https:// creativecommons.org/licenses/by/ 4.0/).

Abstract: The criteria for measuring soil compaction parameters, such as optimum moisture content and maximum dry density, play an important role in construction projects. On construction sites, base/sub-base soils are compacted at the optimal moisture content to achieve the desirable level of compaction, generally between 95% and 98% of the maximum dry density. The present technique of determining compaction parameters in the laboratory is a time-consuming task. This study proposes an improved hybrid intelligence paradigm as an alternative tool to the laboratory method for estimating the optimum moisture content and maximum dry density of soils. For this purpose, an advanced version of the grey wolf optimiser (GWO) called improved GWO (IGWO) was integrated with an adaptive neuro-fuzzy inference system (ANFIS), which resulted in a high-performance hybrid model named ANFIS-IGWO. Overall, the results indicate that the proposed ANFIS-IGWO model achieved the most precise prediction of the optimum moisture content (degree of correlation = 0.9203 and root mean square error = 0.0635) and maximum dry density (degree of correlation = 0.9050 and root mean square error = 0.0709) of soils. The outcomes of the suggested model are noticeably superior to those attained by other hybrid ANFIS models, which are built with standard GWO, Moth-flame optimisation, slime mould algorithm, and marine predators algorithm. The results indicate that geotechnical engineers can benefit from the newly developed ANFIS-IGWO model during the design stage of civil engineering projects. The developed MATLAB models are also included for determining soil compaction parameters.

Keywords: soil compaction; adaptive neuro-fuzzy inference system; grey wolf optimiser; swarm intelligence

MSC: 68Txx

1. Introduction

In the parlance of geotechnical engineering, soil compaction is a method of compressing soil particles by reducing air voids while maintaining steady water content [1,2]. Compaction can be used to enhance the mechanical qualities of soils in a number of different ways. Proctor [3] recommended compacting soil with different water contents at an appropriate compaction energy. As a result, the compaction curve can be used to determine the optimum moisture content (OMC) and maximum dry density (MDD) of soils. To sustain the long-term performance of various engineering structures, such as embankments of railways, highways, and airport runways, these two compaction parameters are commonly used [4–8]. Understanding and predicting the compaction characteristics of different soils is thus a crucial aspect of every construction project [9–13].

Analytical techniques and laboratory experiments can be used to calculate the OMC and MDD [1,14,15]. However, to precisely characterise the compaction curve, at least 4 to 5 tests must be carried out in the laboratory, which takes a long time [9,14]. In order to conduct tests and obtain accurate results, highly qualified technical staff and expert personnel are needed. The laboratory values of OMC and MDD are utilised to compact soils of sub-base/base layers to achieve 95–98% MDD in the field. Thus, it is important to create smart, data-driven algorithms for calculating the OMC and MDD based on existing experimental records [1,15,16]. To determine the OMC and MDD of soils, a number of prediction models have previously been put forth. Regression analysis and different data from particular soils were used to create the majority of these models. However, according to the literature, the prediction accuracy of these models tends to decrease as the size of the database increased [1,14,17].

In order to address the issue with a larger database and improved accuracy, machine learning techniques (MLTs) have recently been employed to estimate the OMC and MDD of soils. Using evolutionary polynomial regression (EPR) and artificial neural networks (ANNs), the compaction characteristics of 55 soil samples were predicted [18]. The group method of data handling (GMDH) was used by Ardakani and Kordnaeij [19] to estimate the compaction parameters of 212 samples. Based on the results of 451 experiments using the index properties and conventional proctor tests, Kurnaz and Kaya [16] employed GMDH, support vector machine (SVM), extreme learning machine (ELM), and Bayesian regularisation neural network to estimate the OMC and MDD of soils. Recently, Tiwari et al. [17] used hybrid least square support vector machine (LSSVM) approaches to estimate the OMC and MDD of soils, and found satisfactory results.

These prediction models, in comparison to regression analysis models, displayed better determination coefficient (R^2) values, ranging from 0.90 to 0.98 [1,14]. Nevertheless, these studies used only a few different types of soils. Past studies have shown that within a given soil range, forecast accuracy can be ensured; nevertheless, the issue of the limited soil type and the inadequate consideration of soil factors may result in inaccurate predictions. Prediction models constructed and validated with the fewest number of influential parameters, which are typically determined when samples are brought to the laboratory, are also regarded as the most effective. In contrast, the nonlinear stress-strain relationships, the stress-strain time-conditioning response, and the elasto-plastic behaviour under loading and unloading conditions make soil materials highly complex [20–24]. Therefore, a high-performance soft computing model is considered necessary to estimate the OMC and MDD of soils, taking into account a wide range of soil types and the most influential variables (such as grain size analysis, plasticity characteristics, etc.) that can be readily measured in the laboratory.

According to the most recent literature, ensemble-based and hybrid MLTs are the best suited approaches for estimating the anticipated outputs, such as load-carrying capacity assessment of semi-rigid steel structures [25], patch load resistance of stiffened plate girders [26], soil compaction parameters [27], compression index [24], etc. Additionally, due to the complexity of the task at hand, it is required to look at a variety of advanced MLTs in order to find more precise estimating models. A detailed review of the literature reveals that the main advantage of the neuro-fuzzy system is that it combines neural network properties with fuzzy logic; hence, eliminating the limitations of these two MLTs can be found in the literature [28,29]. After ANN, Adaptive neuro-fuzzy inference system (ANFIS) is one of the widely used MLTs and can be implemented easily to estimate the desired output(s). ANFIS has the advantage of knowing both numbers and languages. ANFIS also makes use of ANN's capacity to classify data and recognise patterns. Specifically, ANFIS is more transparent to the user than the ANN model and generates fewer memorisation errors. The fundamental advantage of the neuro-fuzzy system is that it blends neural network properties with fuzzy logic, removing the limitations of both. While fuzzy logic deals with knowledge that can be obtained and comprehended, neural networks deal with knowledge that can be obtained only via optimised learning [28,30]. However, like many other MLTs, ANFIS has some limitations, such as overfitting issues. Additionally, because it is hard to define the exact global optimum, it may produce undesirable outcomes during the validation phase [14,31].

To solve these issues, researchers have employed a number of meta-heuristic algorithms (MHAs), such as GA, PSO, GWO, etc. [28,29,32], and a number of hybrid models of traditional MLTs and MHAs were built for the estimation of desired output(s). It is important to note that construction of an effective ANFIS model requires optimum selection of its consequent and antecedent (C&A) and fuzzy inference system (FIS) parameters. These two parameters significantly affect how the learning phase turns out, which in turn affects how well a hybrid ANFIS model can predict the desired variables. Due to the robust global search capabilities of MHAs, the C&A parameters of ANFIS are iteratively adjusted, resulting in improved performance. Over the past decade, several hybrid ANFIS models have seen widespread use in addressing a wide range of engineering problems, including compressive strength estimation [28,33], flood assessment [34], prophecy of groundwater level [35], and so on.

Nevertheless, a detailed review of the literature reveals that no previous study has employed hybrid ANFIS models constructed with a specific group of MHAs to predict soil compaction parameters. On the other hand, it is important to highlight that no algorithm provides perfect solutions for all optimisation problems due to improper exploration and exploitation (E&E) processes [31,36]. Therefore, implementing a standard version of MHA in hybrid modelling does not ensure optimum hybrid model generation. It may also be noted that researchers reported modified versions of MHAs and demonstrated that the performance of standard MHA could be improved by implementing different strategies [37–39]. Considering these points as a reference, and to fill the gap in the literature, an enhanced hybrid technique of ANFIS and an improved grey wolf optimiser (IGWO), i.e., ANFIS-IGWO, has been constructed and presented in this study for the estimation of OMC and MDD of soils. The performance of the ANFIS-IGWO model was compared to that of three hybrid ANFIS models built using moth-flame optimisation (MFO), slime mould algorithm (SMA), and marine predator algorithm (MPA). The performance of the ANFIS-IGWO model was also compared with the standard hybrid model of ANFIS and GWO, i.e., ANGIS-GWO. Thus, as a part of ongoing research and to extend the work of Bardhan and Asteris [14], a suitable database of various soils was compiled from the studies of Günaydın [15], Wang and Yin [1], and Bardhan and Asteris [14] and a modified database was prepared. Specifically, a total of 251 datasets from 15 different soils were acquired and utilised in the current study for the estimation of the OMC and MDD of soils.

The remainder of this work is organised as follows. The significance of the present study is presented in Section 2. Section 3 details the methodological development of ANFIS-based hybrid models. Section 4 discusses data collection, descriptive details, and the computer modelling procedure. Section 5 provides and discusses the realisations of the developed models, followed by Section 6 with the limitations and future scope of the study. At the end, summary and conclusions are presented.

2. Research Significance

In the last two decades, a multitude of modern computational methods, techniques, and algorithms have been proposed and published with the aim of predicting the response of complex phenomena whose strongly non-linear nature and behaviour make impossible the widely accepted use of deterministic techniques [25,26]. In these methods, artificial intelligence, machine learning, and MHAs have a dominant position. In fact, despite the fact that these techniques started with the first applications in medicine [40], they were particularly applied in the fields of sciences [30,41–43] and engineering [44–48]. The use of contemporary intelligence techniques in geotechnical and geological engineering domains, such as landslide susceptibility mapping [49], reliability analysis [50], and estimation of various geotechnical parameters [24,27] can also be found in the literature. However, the existing literature in the geotechnical engineering area does not demonstrate sufficient implementation of enhanced/improved versions of MHAs in estimating various geotechnical parameters. Taking the above discussion as a reference, this study proposes a high-performance intelligence paradigm built using an upgraded version of MHA for estimating the OMC and MDD of soils.

3. Methodology

This section presented the theoretical details of GWO and IGWO, followed by a short discussion on MFO, SMA, and MPA. Subsequently, the methodological development of hybrid ANFIS models is presented and discussed. However, before presenting the above details, the working principles of the ANFIS are briefly presented.

3.1. Adaptive Neuro-Fuzzy Inference System

ANFIS, proposed by Jang [51], is an ANN-FIS integration, which was intended to eliminate the drawbacks of the individual ANN and FIS approaches. ANFIS is grounded in fuzzy logic and rules produced in the particular training procedure of the model. These inference systems contain five layers (see Figure 1). The nodes of layer 0 are the inputs, while the nodes of layer 5 represent the output in the connection-based structure. The fixed adaptable nodes of the hidden layers stand for the membership functions (MFs).

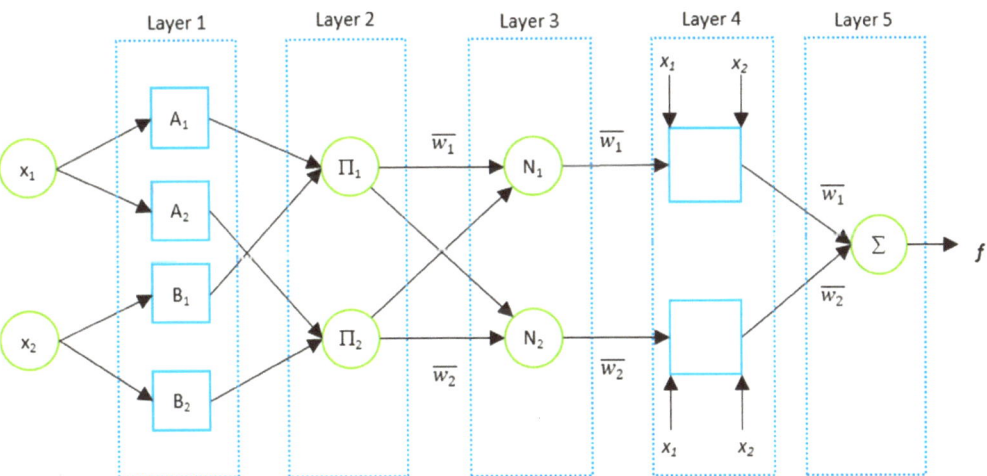

Figure 1. A basic architecture of ANFIS.

For a summarised description of the ANFIS approach, let x_1 and x_2 be the inputs. Additionally, let f be the output. The ANFIS represents the relationship between the inputs and output by fuzzy *if–then* rules. The Takagi–Sugeno fuzzy rules in the model are shown as:

Rule-1: *if* x_1 *is* A_1 *and* x_2 *is* B_1, *then* $f_1 = p_1 x_1 + q_1 x_2 + r_1$
Rule-2: *if* x_1 *is* A_2 *and* x_2 *is* B_2, *then* $f_2 = p_2 x_1 + q_2 x_2 + r_2$

where A_1, A_2, B_1, and B_2 are linguistic symbols, while p_1, q_1, r_1, p_2, q_2, and r_2 are the consequent variables. The layers include:

Layer 1: Fuzzification layer—it is assumed that node i has an adaptive function as: $O_{1,i} = \mu_{A_i}(x)$, where $O_{1,i}$ is the output of node i, while μ_{A_i} denotes the MF.
Layer 2: Ruler layer—Node i within this layer is assumed to be fixed (Π). In addition, the node output is generated by incoming signals, such as $O_{2,i} = w_i = \mu_{A_i}(x) \times \mu_{B_i}(x)$ *for* $i = 1, 2$,

where $O_{2,i}$ denotes the output of the second layer, and w_i represents the firing strength of rule i.

Layer 3: Normalisation layer—Node i undergoes normalisation in the third layer (firing strengths). The ratio of the firing force of rule i to the total firing force can be obtained as: $O_{3,i} = \overline{w}_i = w_i/(w_1 + w_2)$, where $O_{3,i}$ is the output of the third layer, and $\overline{w}_i$ stands for the normalised firing strength.

Layer 4: Defuzzification layer—In this layer, each of the nodes is adaptive and has a function representing the contribution of rule i to the total output.

Layer 5: Output layer—Eventually, this layer yields the final output.

ANFIS can be equipped for MF parameter identification through hybrid learning approaches. Such approaches define the parameters of the defuzzification layer using the forward least squares technique. Errors undergo backpropagation to modify a_i, b_i, and c_i as the premise parameters through gradient descent. For more details, the works of Paryani et al. [49], Piro et al. [30], Golafshani et al. [28], can be referred to.

3.2. Grey Wolf Optimiser

GWO [52] is comes under the category of evolutionary algorithm developed for optimisation based on the imitation of the grey wolves' social behaviour. Specifically, this algorithm mimics the process that grey wolves utilise to capture their prey, along with the structure of their leadership. For the recreation of the hierarchical structure in GWO, grey wolves of four different types are assumed for every wolf pack. The leader and the most significant wolf in the pack are called α, β and δ wolves. ω wolves with minimum responsibility are placed at the bottom of the food. In GWO, the entire hunting process can be classified as searching, encircling, hunting, and attacking. The mathematical expression for encircling prey is given by:

$$D = \left|C.X_{p(t)} - X_{(t)}\right| \quad (1)$$

$$X_{(t+1)} = X_{p(t)} - A.D \quad (2)$$

where X and X_p are the position vectors of the grey wolf and the prey, respectively; t and $t+1$ represent current and subsequent epochs, respectively. A and C are two vectors given by:

$$A = 2a.r_1 - a \quad (3)$$

$$C = 2.r_2 \quad (4)$$

where r_1 and r_2 are the two random vectors that are uniformly distributed [0 1], and the components of a are linearly decreased from 2 to 0. When $|A| > 1$, the exploration of prey location is possible by diverting the search agents. Conversely, with $|A| < 1$, convergence of search agents can be used to achieve exploitation. The hunting process in GWO can be mathematically modelled as follows:

$$D_\alpha = |C_1.X_\alpha - X|;\ D_\beta = |C_2.X_\beta - X|;\ D_\delta = |C_3.X_\delta - X| \quad (5)$$

$$X_{i1} = X_\alpha - A_1.(D_\alpha)\ ;\ X_{i2} = X_\beta - A_2.\left(D_\beta\right);\ X_{i3} = X_\delta - A_3.(D_\delta) \quad (6)$$

$$X_{(t+1)} = (X_{i1} + X_{i2} + X_{i3})/3 \quad (7)$$

In GWO, E&E is handled using parameters a and C, in which the parameter a is decreased from 2 to 0. Additionally, it is seen that the final position would be in a random place within a circle, which is defined by the positions of α, β, and δ in the search space. More mathematical details can be found in the original work of Mirjalili et al. [52].

3.3. Improved Grey Wolf Optimiser

In GWO, α, β, and δ guide ω wolves toward regions of the search space where the optimal solution is likely to be located. This approach may result in entanglement in a locally optimal solution. Another drawback is the decline in population diversity, which causes GWO to approach the local optimum. Nadimi-Shahraki et al. [53] proposed IGWO to address these problems. According to the study of Nadimi-Shahraki et al. [53], the enhancements involve a new search strategy involving a step of selecting and upgrading. Therefore, IGWO consists of three phases, as discussed below.

Initialising phase: During the initialisation phase, N wolves are randomly distributed in $[l_j, u_j]$, as:

$$X_{ij} = l_j + rand_j[0,1] \times (u_j - l_j), \ i \in [1, N], j \in [1, D] \tag{8}$$

The position of the i-th wolf in the t-th iteration, represented by $X_i(t) = \{x_{i1}, x_{i2}, \ldots, x_{iD}\}$, where D is the dimension number. The fitness value of $X_i(t)$ is calculated using f $(X_i(t))$.

Movement phase: The IGWO, proposed by Nadimi-Shahraki et al. [53], includes a different mobility tactic known as the dimension learning-based hunting (DLH) method, in which each wolf is learned by its neighbours to be a different contender for the new position, $X_i(t)$.

Selecting and updating phase: During this stage, the best candidate is first chosen by contrasting the fitness ratings between two candidates $X_{i-GWO}(t+1)$ and $X_{i-DLH}(t+1)$, given by:

$$X_i(t+1) = \begin{cases} X_{i-GWO}(t+1), & \text{if } f(X_{i-GWO}) < f(X_{i-DLH}) \\ X_{i-DLH}(t+1) & \text{otherwise} \end{cases} \tag{9}$$

Then, to update the position of $X_i(t+1)$, if the fitness of the selected candidate is less than $X_i(t)$, $X_i(t)$ is updated by the selected candidate. Otherwise, $X_i(t)$ remains unchanged. After this procedure, the iteration count is increased by 1, and the search operation is repeated until the predetermined number of epochs has been reached.

3.4. Brief Overview of MFO, SMA, and MPA

The other employed MHAs, viz., MFO, SMA, and MPA, are briefly discussed in this sub-section. All of these MHAs are swarm-based and they have been widely used in different engineering disciplines [54–57].

MFO, proposed by Mirjalili [58], is an innovative MHA that draws inspiration from the intriguing behaviour of moths attracted to flames. MFO incorporates the unique phenomenon of moths spiralling around a flame into its search strategy. This behaviour, while seemingly irrational and perilous for the moths, serves as a metaphor for E&E in optimisation problems. MFO leverages a chaotic search mechanism that emulates the unpredictable flight patterns of moths around a flame. This mechanism enables the MFO to efficiently explore diverse solution spaces, avoiding stagnation in the local optima. By introducing chaos, the MFO promotes global exploration while maintaining its ability to exploit promising regions of the search space. The core idea behind MFO is to strike a balance between E&E, mimicking the trade-off faced by moths as they navigate the dangerous allure of flames. By dynamically adjusting the balance between E&E strategies, the MFO adaptively evolves its search behaviour, allowing it to effectively handle complex optimisation problems with varying landscapes. The effectiveness of MFO has been demonstrated across a wide range of applications, including engineering design, data mining, and image processing. Its ability to handle both continuous and discrete optimisation problems make it a versatile tool in the field of MHAs.

SMA [59] simulates the nutritive phase of a slime mould as a unique approach that is grounded in nature (a single-celled eukaryote). The foraging behaviour of slime moulds is simulated by this programme. By smelling potential food sources, slime moulds locate them, wrap them, and then digest them by secreting enzymes. In SMA, the phase of iterations to produce the highest smell concentration is the theoretical description of how to approach the optimal solution. The slime mould's flexible weight ensures rapid convergence and prevents it from becoming stranded in regional extremes. This approach enables the slime mould to advance along any viable path in the direction of the ideal outcome, which mimics the slime mould's eating-related architecture. The next stage is wrapping the meal using contractions of the intravenous framework inside the upper and lower limitations. The vein with the maximum contraction of food generates more bio-oscillator waves, which cause the cytoplasm to flow more quickly through the vein, increasing its thickness. The search patterns in SMA are altered in response to the opposing signals from veins regarding the concentration of food.

MPA [60], a MHA inspired by the natural principles governing optimal foraging strategies and encounter rates between predator and prey in marine ecosystems. Marine predators adopt a Lévy strategy when navigating environments with scarce prey, while employing Brownian movement in areas abundant with prey. Throughout their lifetimes, these predators exhibit a consistent balance of Lévy and Brownian movement as they traverse diverse habitats. Environmental factors, such as eddy formation, influence their behaviour, prompting adaptive changes to explore regions with varying prey distributions. Leveraging their remarkable memory capabilities, they capitalise on the recollection of successful foraging locations and associations with other individuals. MPA harnesses these concepts to guide its search process, mimicking the adaptive foraging behaviour of marine predators. By integrating these nature-inspired mechanisms, MPA demonstrates a powerful optimisation approach capable of addressing complex problems in diverse domains.

Note that the detailed working principles of these OAs are not presented in this study because they are well established, and the original studies of MFO [58], SMA [59], and MPA [60] can be referred to for more details.

3.5. Hybrid Modelling of ANFIS and MHAs

In this work, the C&A parameters of ANFIS were optimised using MHAs. It is important to note that proper setting of the FIS and C&A parameters is necessary for creating an optimum ANFIS model because learning parameters have a significant impact on the model's performance. Notably, the selection of all of the ANFIS hyperparameters at once is a challenging operation because they must be searched in continuous domains, leading to an infinite number of parameters sets. As a result, it is possible to define the problem of ANFIS parameter tweaking as an optimisation problem. Thus, the values of the FIS and C&A parameters were optimised using IGWO, GWO, MFO, SMA, and MPA, and five hybrid ANFIS models, i.e., ANFIS-IGWO, ANFIS-GWO, ANFIS-MFO, ANFIS-SMA, and ANFIS-MPA, were created. A flow chart of the construction procedure of the hybrid ANFIS models is presented in Figure 2.

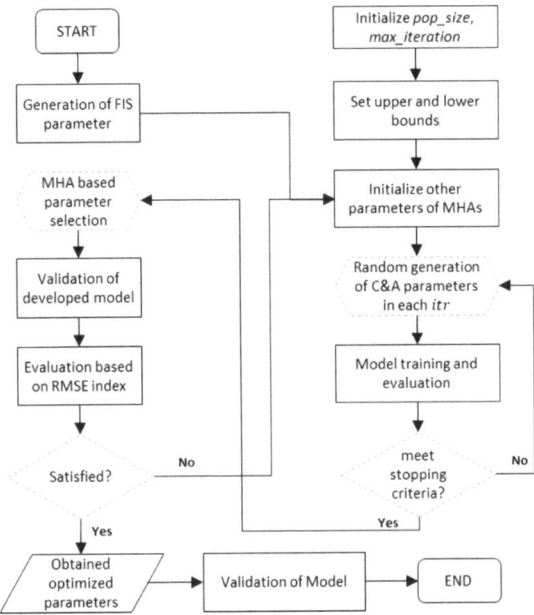

Figure 2. Flow chart of hybrid ANFIS model construction.

4. Data Description and Modelling

A broad variety of experimental results of soil compaction parameters were acquired from the studies of Günaydın [15], Wang and Yin [1], and Bardhan and Asteris [14]. Specifically, a total of 372 results were obtained, the details of which are presented in Table 1. The work of Günaydın [15] consists of 126 compaction results of nine distinct soil types (CH, CI, CL, GC, GM, MH, MI, ML, and SC) with six influencing parameters, viz., fines content (F), sand content (S), gravel content (G), specific gravity, liquid limit (LL), and plastic limit (PL). Wang and Yin [1] gathered a total of 226 records from the literature. The database includes G, S, F, LL, PL, and compaction energy of various soil types, such as CL, CL-ML, CH, MH, ML, SC, SP-SC, SW-SC, SM, GC, GP-GC, GW-GC, and GM. Bardhan and Asteris [14] presented 20 experimental records of soil compaction parameters, including four distinct soil types (CH, CI, CL, and SC) and six influencing parameters, identical to Günaydın [15]. According to the study of Wang and Yin [1], the majority of 226 soil compaction experiments were conducted using either the conventional Proctor or the reduced compaction energy. Additionally, thirty modified Proctor compaction tests were incorporated into the database.

Table 1. Details of data pre-processing for OMC and MDD estimation.

Particulars	No. of Actual Data	Actual Data Dimension	No. of Data Selected	Final Data Dimension
Günaydın [15]	126	126 × 8	126	126 × 7
Wang and Yin [1]	226	226 × 8	105	105 × 7
Bardhan and Asteris [14]	20	20 × 8	20	20 × 7
Final dataset (for this study)	-	-	251	251 × 7

Note: The data dimension also includes OMC and MDD parameters.

In this study, the database presented by Wang and Yin [1] has been revised, and a total of 105 records were chosen. Additionally, all datasets of Günaydın [15] and Bardhan and Asteris [14] were used. Therefore, 126, 105, and 20 experimental records were acquired from the studies of Günaydın [15], Wang and Yin [1], and Bardhan and Asteris [14], respectively.

The details of data dimension are also presented in Table 2. Therefore, the final database includes 251 records and five influential parameters viz., F in %, S in %, G in %, LL in %, and PL in %, of 15 different soil types. These five influential parameters were used to estimate the OMC and MDD of soils. Descriptive details of the final dataset are given in Table 2. In addition, the minimum and maximum values of influential (soil-type wise) and compaction parameters are presented in Table 3. Note that the abbreviations of soil types are presented as per the Indian Standard Soil Classification System (ISSCS) and ASTM [61].

Table 2. Descriptive statistics of the employed dataset.

Particulars	F (%)	S (%)	G (%)	LL (%)	PL (%)	OMC (%)	MDD (kN/m^3)
Min.	8.60	0.00	0.00	16.00	6.10	7.00	13.73
Avg.	63.76	27.95	8.29	40.14	20.63	17.16	17.25
Max.	100.00	83.60	67.10	70.00	32.50	31.00	21.48
Stnd. Error	1.49	1.09	0.74	0.63	0.28	0.24	0.08
Stnd. Dev.	23.62	17.19	11.78	9.93	4.50	3.87	1.29
Variance	557.68	295.50	138.65	98.62	20.21	15.00	1.67
Kurtosis	−0.90	−0.31	3.55	0.20	0.15	0.87	0.54
Skewness	−0.20	0.33	1.85	0.67	−0.06	0.38	0.02

Table 3. Soil type-wise details of the employed dataset.

Soil Types	F		S		G		LL		PL		OMC		MDD	
	Min.	Max.	Min.	Max.	Min.	Max.	Min.	Max.	Min.	Max.	Min.	Max.	Min.	Max.
CH	53.80	100.00	0.00	41.16	0.00	20.00	50.00	70.00	18.00	31.00	17.50	30.80	13.93	17.42
CI	49.00	75.00	21.00	44.95	0.05	23.07	35.15	49.40	14.40	26.72	13.95	23.75	15.19	19.41
CL	33.00	99.00	1.00	65.00	0.00	22.00	23.00	49.30	6.10	27.00	11.00	22.00	15.89	19.28
CL-ML	81.00	81.00	19.00	19.00	0.00	0.00	27.00	27.00	21.00	21.00	17.00	17.00	17.46	17.46
GC	13.00	41.50	19.90	45.61	30.39	67.10	27.60	63.20	13.40	26.11	7.60	18.80	16.43	20.51
GM	40.00	50.00	17.25	28.69	24.69	37.75	40.20	50.90	26.00	26.61	13.85	20.40	16.36	17.55
GP-GC	9.40	9.40	41.90	41.90	48.70	48.70	37.80	37.80	14.70	14.70	8.40	8.40	20.60	20.60
GW-GC	8.60	8.60	44.30	44.30	47.10	47.10	29.50	29.50	14.10	14.10	7.00	7.00	21.48	21.48
MH	60.00	100.00	0.00	36.48	0.00	3.52	36.00	64.00	26.00	32.50	19.40	31.00	13.73	16.09
MI	59.00	74.00	24.24	34.61	1.76	6.39	47.90	49.35	28.41	28.85	18.00	21.95	16.36	16.39
ML	53.00	90.00	10.00	37.00	0.00	10.00	25.00	47.00	14.55	28.00	10.40	22.00	15.89	19.24
SC	15.00	48.00	30.90	71.26	0.00	39.00	16.00	61.10	9.00	26.24	9.00	18.50	16.28	20.50
SM	44.00	44.00	56.00	56.00	0.00	0.00	16.00	16.00	9.00	9.00	9.00	9.00	20.01	20.01
SP-SC	8.80	8.80	83.60	83.60	7.60	7.60	31.20	31.20	19.30	19.30	10.80	10.80	19.13	19.13
SW-SC	9.60	9.60	77.30	77.30	13.10	13.10	30.40	30.40	18.80	18.80	9.80	9.80	19.72	19.72

Figure 3 shows the comparative histograms for each influential variable. To better illustrate, the correlation matrices between influential variables and compaction parameters are presented in Figure 4. From the information given in Table 2, Figures 3 and 4, it can be seen that the OMC has a negative correlation with the contents of S and G, whereas F, LL, and PL show a positive correlation. In contrast, F, LL, and PL exhibit negative correlations, while S and G contents have positive correlations with MDD. Notably, these figures are particularly useful, as they indicate the range of values of the parameters for which the reliability is limited, and further experimental investigation is required for values of the parameters included in these regions and not with the aim of updating the database in the future.

After finalising the database, it was divided into two subsets: a training (TR) subset that contained 80% of the overall dataset and a testing (TS) subset that contained the remaining 20% of the data. The following steps can be used to describe the computational modelling process for estimating soil compaction parameters: (a) choosing the main dataset; (b) data normalisation; (c) data partitioning and selection of TR and TS subsets; (d) model construction using a training subset; (e) check model performance; (f) check terminating criteria; (g) model validation if terminating criteria are satisfied; and (h) performance assessment. The steps of computational modelling are illustrated in Figure 5.

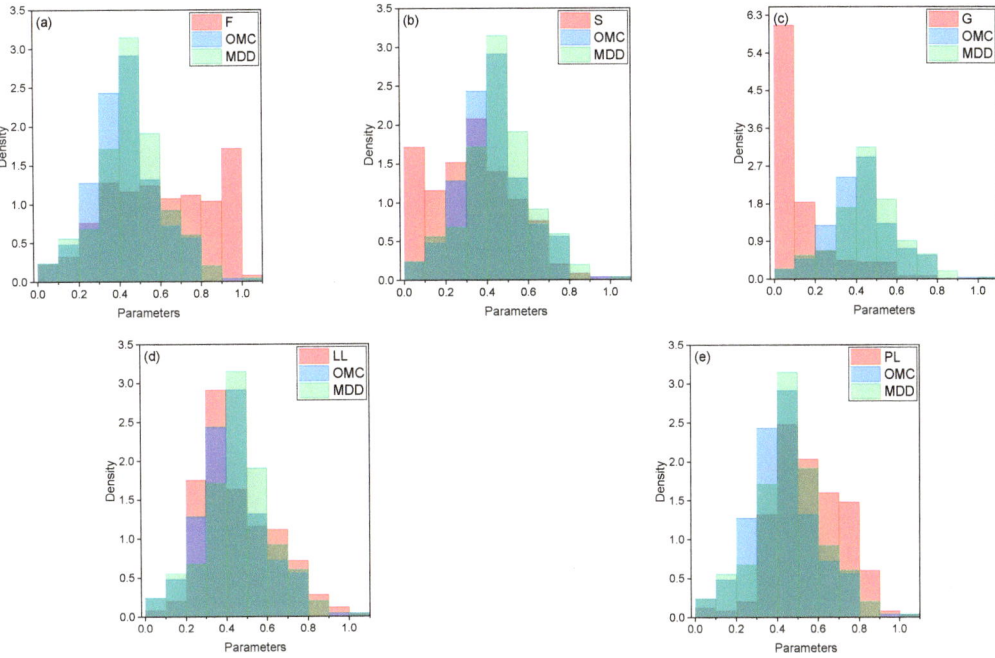

Figure 3. (a–e) Comparative histogram (values are in normalised form).

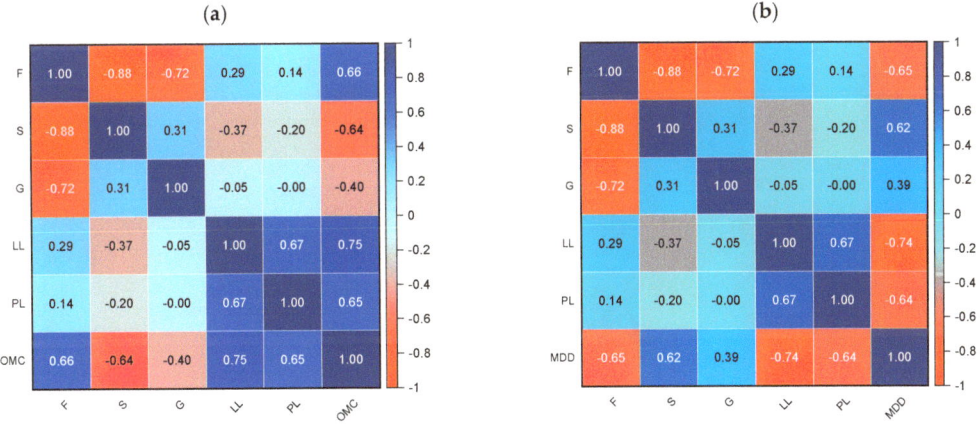

Figure 4. Correlation matrix between soil parameters and OMC (a) and MDD (b).

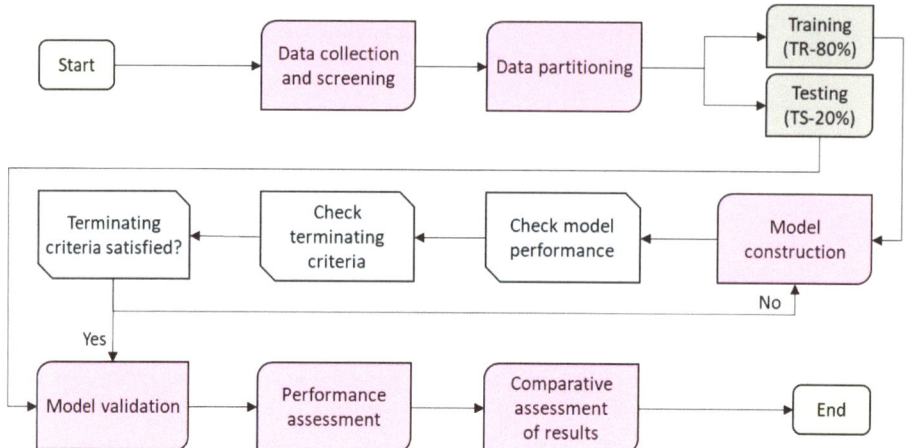

Figure 5. Steps of computational modelling.

5. Results and Discussion

The outcomes of the hybrid ANFIS models used to estimate soil compaction parameters are described in this section. As previously mentioned, the primary dataset was divided into training (201 samples) and testing (50 samples) subsets before the models were built. Note that all models were constructed and validated using identical training and testing subsets. The output of the developed models was then assessed using a number of indices, namely performance index (PFI), correlation coefficient (R), variance account factor (VAF), Willmott's Index of agreement (WI), mean absolute error (MAE), root mean square error (RMSE), RMSE to observation's standard deviation ratio (RSR), and weighted mean absolute percentage error (WMAPE). Notably, these indices are frequently used to evaluate the generalisability of any prediction model from a variety of perspectives, including correlation accuracy, related error, amount of variation, and so on.

In contrast, the deterministic parameters of MHAs, such as swarm size, maximum iteration number, and upper and lower bounds, play a vital part in hybrid modelling; thus, they were calibrated throughout the optimisation process. The details of the deterministic and hyper-parameters of hybrid ANFIS models in estimating soil compaction parameters are described in the following sub-section, followed by a comparative assessment of the results.

$$PFI = adj.R^2 + 0.01 VAF - RMSE \tag{10}$$

$$R = \sqrt{\frac{\sum_{i=1}^{n}(y_i - y_{mean})^2 - \sum_{i=1}^{n}(y_i - \hat{y}_i)^2}{\sum_{i=1}^{n}(y_i - y_{mean})^2}} \tag{11}$$

$$VAF\,(\%) = \left(1 - \frac{var(y_i - \hat{y}_i)}{var(y_i)}\right) \times 100 \tag{12}$$

$$WI = 1 - \left[\frac{\sum_{i=1}^{n}(y_i - \hat{y}_i)^2}{\sum_{i=1}^{n}\{|\hat{y}_i - y_{mean}| + |y_i - y_{mean}|\}^2}\right] \tag{13}$$

$$MAE = \frac{1}{n}\sum_{i=1}^{n}|(\hat{y}_i - y_i)| \tag{14}$$

$$RMSE = \sqrt{\frac{1}{n}\sum_{i=1}^{n}(y_i - \hat{y}_i)^2} \tag{15}$$

$$RSR = \frac{RMSE}{\sqrt{\frac{1}{n}\sum_{i=1}^{n}(y_i - y_{mean})^2}} \tag{16}$$

$$WMAPE = \frac{\sum_{i=1}^{n}\left|\frac{y_i - \hat{y}_i}{y_i}\right| \times y_i}{\sum_{i=1}^{n} y_i} \tag{17}$$

where y_i = actual ith value; $\hat{y}_i$ = estimated ith value; n = is the number of samples; and y_{mean} = mean of the actual value. Note that for a perfect predictive model, the values of the aforementioned indices should be identical to their identical values, the details of which can be obtained from the literature [14,17].

5.1. Model Performance

The results of the hybrid ANFIS models that were built to estimate soil OMC and MDD are presented in this sub-section. As stated above, the optimum selection of hyper-parameters is a challenging operation, and hence, proper tuning of FIS and C&A parameters was performed during the course of hybrid modelling. The number of FIS parameters (N_{FIS}) were investigated between 2 and 15. Using Gaussian MF and RMSE as fitness functions, the most appropriate value of N_{FIS} was determined to be 5. Notably, Gaussian and linear MFs were used in the input and output layers, respectively. A total of 60 C&A membership functions of ANFIS were optimised for the nine-dimensional input space. Note that the optimised values of N_{FIS} and C&A were chosen following a trial-and-error approach and according to the performance during the testing phase. The convergence behaviour and computational time of the developed hybrid ANFIS models are presented in Figures 6 and 7, respectively. It should be noted that the computational time of the developed ANFIS-IGWO model was found to be longer due to the use of an upgraded version of GWO that required changed mathematical calculations to handle E&E operations. Moreover, it is seen that all the developed hybrid models converge within 500 epochs; hence, they are considered to be sufficient as the maximum iteration count.

The performance of the developed ANFIS models is presented in Tables 4 and 5, respectively, for the OMC and MDD estimations. The abilities of the constructed models for training, testing, and total outputs are shown here. It should be underlined that the training subset performance was used to define the goodness of fit of the developed models, while the testing dataset was used to evaluate their generalisation potential. According to Table 4, it is seen that the developed ANFIS-MPA achieved the highest R and lowest RMSE values of 0.9335 and 0.0590, respectively, during the training phase of OMC prediction. However, during the testing phase, the constructed ANFIS-IGWO achieved the most precise precision, with R = 0.8645 and RMSE = 0.0754. According to the overall results of the OMC estimation, the ANFIS-IGWO was determined to be the best-fitted model with R = 0.9203 and RMSE = 0.0635, followed by ANFIS-MFO (R = 0.9191 and RMSE = 0.0636), ANFIS-GWO (R = 0.9167 and RMSE = 0.0647), and ANFIS-MPA (R = 0.9153 and RMSE = 0.0652). The developed ANFIS-SMA model was the least performing model, with R = 0.9139 (lowest among other developed models) and RMSE = 0.0658 (highest among other developed models).

On the contrary, the results of Table 5 exhibit that the developed ANFIS-MPA (R = 0.9142 and RMSE = 0.0692) and ANFIS-MFO (R = 0.9131 and RMSE = 0.0697) models were found to be the top-two models during the training phase of MDD estimation, while the constructed ANFIS-IGWO (R = 0.8619 and RMSE = 0.0738) and ANFIS-GWO (R = 0.8562 and RMSE = 0.0749) models were found to be the best-two models in the testing phase. According to the overall results of the MDD estimation, the ANFIS-IGWO was determined to be the best-fitted model with R = 0.9050 and RMSE = 0.0709, followed by ANFIS-GWO (R = 0.8973 and RMSE = 0.0735), ANFIS-SMA (R = 0.8964 and RMSE = 0.0739), and ANFIS-MFO (R = 0.8935 and RMSE = 0.0752). The developed ANFIS-MPA model was the least performing model, with R = 0.8866 (lowest among other developed models) and

RMSE = 0.0774 (highest among other developed models). These findings demonstrate the good predictive performance of the suggested ANFIS-IGWO model during both the OMC and MDD predictions.

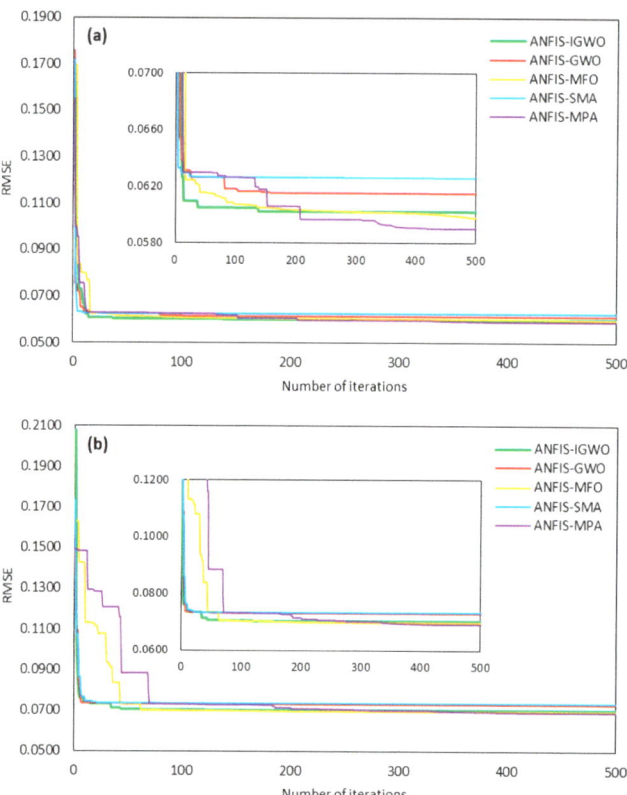

Figure 6. Convergence curve of the developed hybrid ANFIS models for (**a**) OMC and (**b**) MDD estimations.

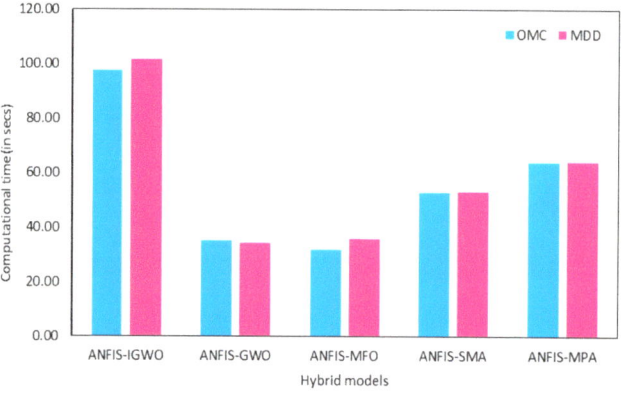

Figure 7. Illustration of the computational time of the developed hybrid ANFIS models.

Table 4. Performance indices for OMC prediction.

Phases	Models	PFI	R	VAF	WI	MAE	RMSE	RSR	WMAPE
Training	ANFIS-IGWO	1.6686	0.9307	86.5973	0.9636	0.0479	0.0602	0.3662	0.1088
	ANFIS-GWO	1.6550	0.9274	86.0065	0.9610	0.0473	0.0615	0.3741	0.1081
	ANFIS-MFO	1.6757	0.9328	86.8809	0.9622	0.0453	0.0598	0.3636	0.1036
	ANFIS-SMA	1.6439	0.9247	85.5093	0.9594	0.0487	0.0626	0.3808	0.1106
	ANFIS-MPA	**1.6801**	**0.9335**	**87.1078**	**0.9638**	**0.0449**	**0.0590**	**0.3591**	**0.1025**
Testing	ANFIS-IGWO	**1.3766**	**0.8645**	73.3267	**0.9167**	0.0604	**0.0754**	**0.5607**	0.1627
	ANFIS-GWO	1.3726	0.8625	**73.3937**	0.9132	0.0602	0.0762	0.5666	0.1623
	ANFIS-MFO	1.3494	0.8560	72.4010	0.9107	**0.0584**	0.0770	0.5729	**0.1573**
	ANFIS-SMA	1.3526	0.8604	71.9109	0.9143	0.0625	0.0772	0.5742	0.1683
	ANFIS-MPA	1.2137	0.8395	62.7992	0.9041	0.0641	0.0854	0.6353	0.1726
Total	ANFIS-IGWO	**1.6265**	**0.9203**	**84.6266**	**0.9577**	0.0504	**0.0635**	**0.3932**	0.1182
	ANFIS-GWO	1.6125	0.9167	84.0233	0.9549	0.0499	0.0647	0.4004	0.1176
	ANFIS-MFO	1.6222	0.9191	84.4224	0.9555	**0.0479**	0.0636	0.3936	**0.1130**
	ANFIS-SMA	1.6012	0.9139	83.5102	0.9536	0.0515	0.0658	0.4071	0.1207
	ANFIS-MPA	1.6066	0.9153	83.7206	0.9551	0.0488	0.0652	0.4032	0.1147

Note: Bold values indicate best-obtained performance.

Table 5. Performance indices for MDD prediction.

Phases	Models	PFI	R	VAF	WI	MAE	RMSE	RSR	WMAPE
Training	ANFIS-IGWO	1.5872	0.9116	83.0798	0.9526	0.0540	0.0702	0.4114	0.1202
	ANFIS-GWO	1.5551	0.9036	81.6465	0.9471	0.0559	0.0731	0.4284	0.1243
	ANFIS-MFO	1.5933	0.9131	83.3592	0.9532	0.0529	0.0697	0.4085	0.1178
	ANFIS-SMA	1.5528	0.9030	81.5383	0.9464	0.0564	0.0734	0.4300	0.1256
	ANFIS-MPA	**1.5981**	**0.9142**	**83.5737**	**0.9535**	**0.0522**	**0.0692**	**0.4053**	**0.1160**
Testing	ANFIS-IGWO	**1.3740**	**0.8619**	**73.4131**	**0.9244**	**0.0620**	**0.0738**	**0.5229**	**0.1257**
	ANFIS-GWO	1.3524	0.8562	72.4607	0.9213	0.0636	0.0749	0.5308	0.1291
	ANFIS-MFO	1.0522	0.7831	57.7198	0.8794	0.0709	0.0943	0.6679	0.1438
	ANFIS-SMA	1.3428	0.8538	72.0656	0.9189	0.0646	0.0759	0.5381	0.1311
	ANFIS-MPA	0.8772	0.7560	45.8550	0.8642	0.0771	0.1042	0.7382	0.1564
Total	ANFIS-IGWO	**1.5630**	**0.9050**	**81.8582**	**0.9493**	**0.0556**	**0.0709**	**0.4256**	**0.1214**
	ANFIS-GWO	1.5328	0.8973	80.5090	0.9442	0.0574	0.0735	0.4407	0.1254
	ANFIS-MFO	1.5161	0.8935	79.7219	0.9429	0.0565	0.0752	0.4514	0.1234
	ANFIS-SMA	1.5292	0.8964	80.3568	0.9431	0.0580	0.0739	0.4433	0.1268
	ANFIS-MPA	1.4878	0.8866	78.3472	0.9401	0.0571	0.0774	0.4644	0.1247

Note: Bold values indicate best-obtained performance.

To better demonstrate the performance of the developed ANFIS models, scatterplots are presented in Figures 8 and 9 for the OMC and MDD estimations, respectively. Herein, the illustrations of actual and estimated values for the best three models (based on RMSE value) are shown. The amount of variance in these diagrams can be visualised by viewing red-coloured dotted lines put at 10% levels. The performance of the generated hybrid models is compared in the following sub-section, and a comparative assessment is presented using a variety of graphical illustrations.

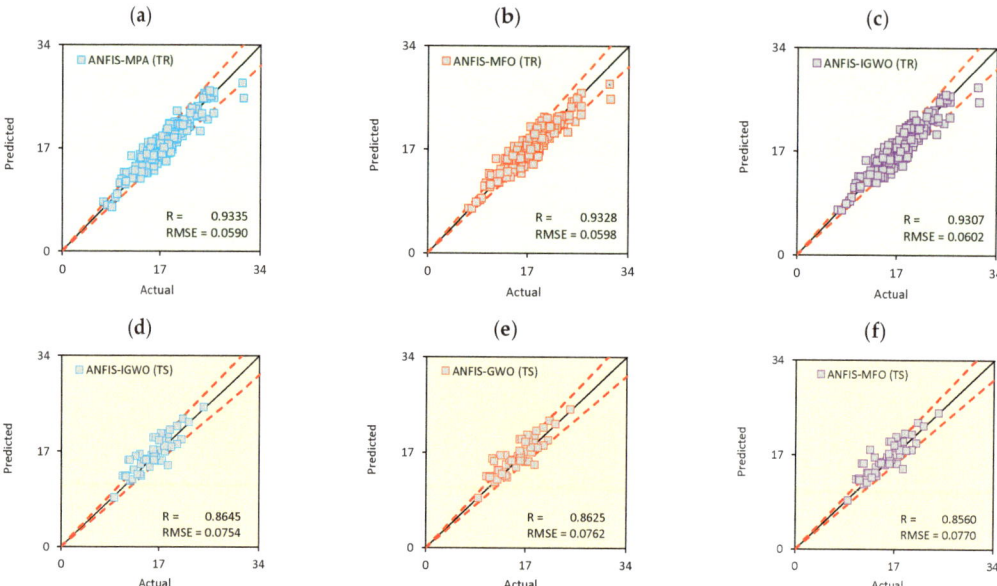

Figure 8. Scatter plot of OMC prediction for the best three models (based on RMSE index) in (**a**–**c**) training and (**d**–**f**) testing phases.

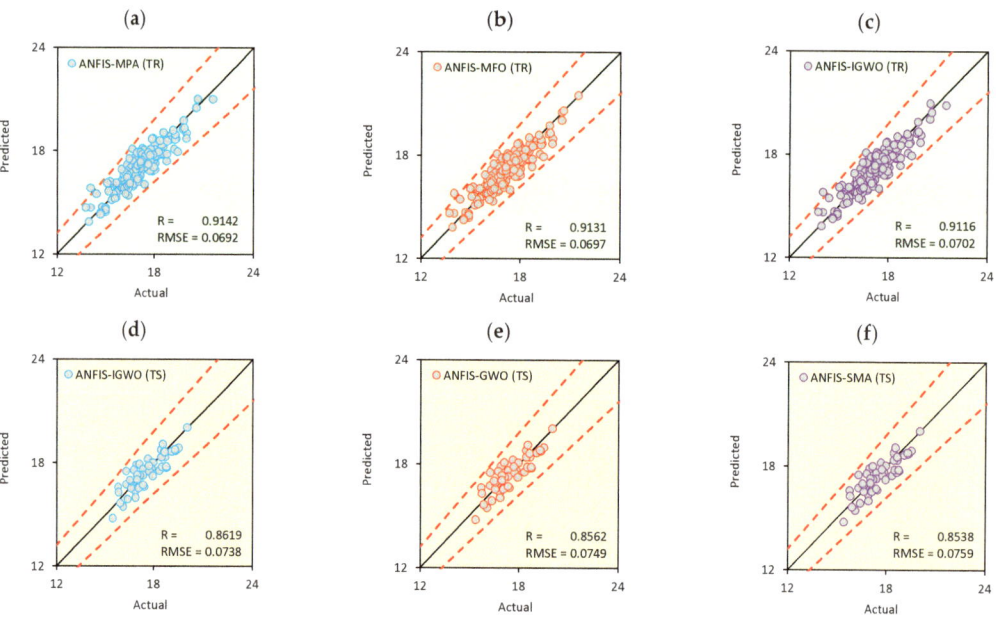

Figure 9. Scatter plot of MDD prediction for the best three models (based on RMSE index) in (**a**–**c**) training and (**d**–**f**) testing phases.

5.2. Discussion of Results

It is critical to highlight that a data-driven model is incomplete without a visual representation of the results. Visualisations enable the identification of the degree of accuracy and associated errors in a model that is easier to comprehend. Therefore, the results are displayed in the form of an accuracy matrix, Taylor diagrams, and radar plots. Notably, the Taylor diagrams are shown for the testing dataset only, since the performance of a data-driven model during the testing dataset should be accepted with more certainty. For thoroughly assessing a model's overall correctness, these diagrams are quite beneficial. An accuracy matrix is a heat map matrix that is used to measure the level of accuracy that a model achieves in terms of certain performance criteria. This matrix makes it simple to evaluate a model's correctness without having to look up each index's value. As previously stated, a number of indices must be created to assess a model's accuracy from multiple angles; however, interpreting results by looking at each index's values takes time and necessitates in-depth observation. Figure 10 shows the accuracy matrix for the models created for the OMC and MDD predictions. The accuracy matrix demonstrates that the constructed ANFIS-IGWO attained higher predictive precision against each index during the testing phase.

On the other hand, the Taylor diagram [62] is used to provide a quick assessment of a model's accuracy in terms of the coefficient of correlation, ratio of standard deviations, and RMSE index. Generally, a point inside a Taylor diagram indicates a model. The position of the point should line up with the reference point for an ideal model. The Taylor diagrams for the hybrid ANFIS models developed for OMC and MDD predictions are shown in Figure 11. In addition to the accuracy matrix and Taylor diagrams, radar plots representing the R value are also presented in Figure 12 for the training, testing, and total cases of OMC and MDD estimations. A ridgeline chart and distribution with Kernel smooth of error between actual and estimated values are presented in Figure 13. From these diagrams, the predictive capability of hybrid ANFIS models can be assessed from different perspectives.

However, according to the aforementioned results, the ANFIS-IGWO model was found to be the best-obtained model in both instances of prediction. As indicated previously, eight indices were used to evaluate the performance of the developed ANFIS models. Based on the overall results against OMC prediction, the developed ANFIS-IGWO achieved the highest level of accuracy, with $R = 0.9203$ and $RMSE = 0.0635$, whereas against MDD prediction, $R = 0.9050$ and $RMSE = 0.0709$ achieved the highest level of accuracy. Therefore, the suggested ANFIS-IGWO model can be used to approximate the OMC and MDD ranges for various soil types. This will aid engineers and practitioners in reducing the operational time required for laboratory compaction experiments. The developed MATLAB models, as well as the employed dataset, are included as Supplementary Materials for future use. The details of MATLAB implementations of the developed models are also presented in Appendix A. For better demonstration, the steps of OMC and MDD estimations using basic soil parameters and the developed MATLAB models are illustrated in Figure 14.

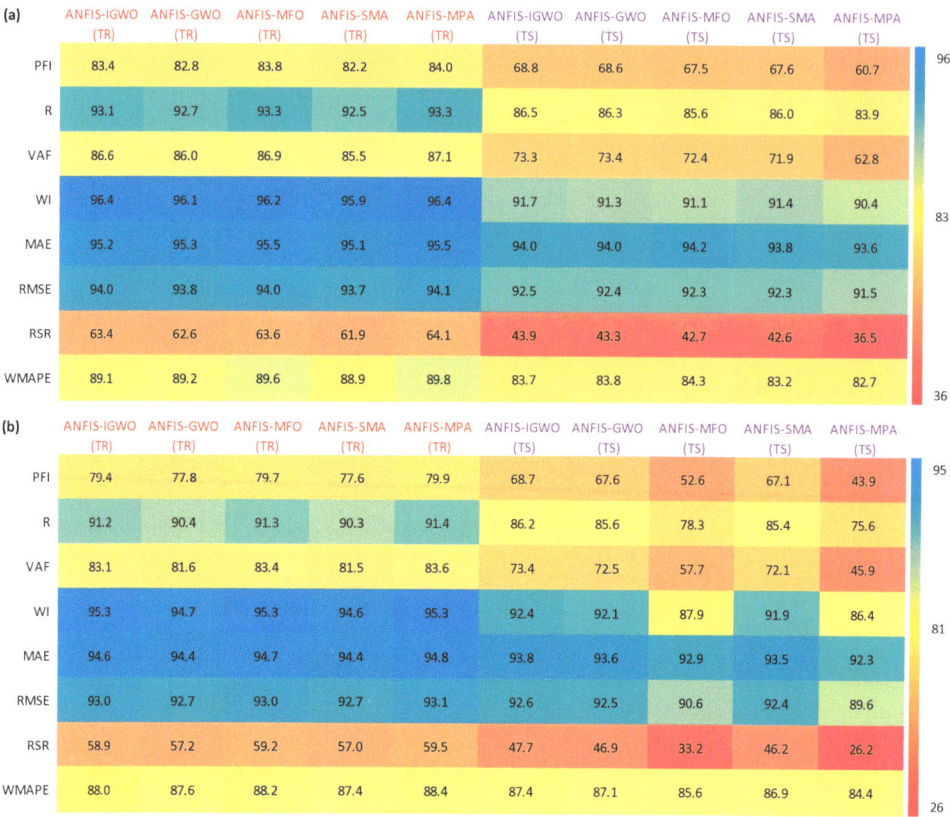

Figure 10. Accuracy matrix (testing phase) for (**a**) OMC and (**b**) MDD predictions.

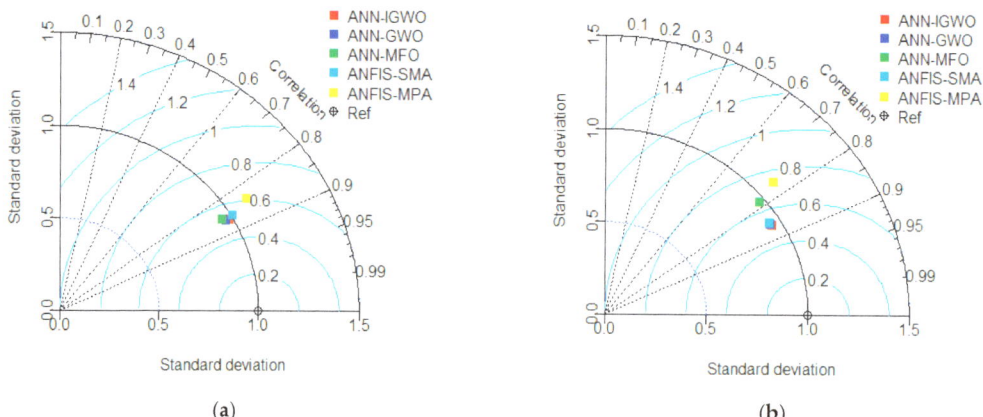

Figure 11. Taylor diagram (testing phase) for (**a**) OMC and (**b**) MDD predictions.

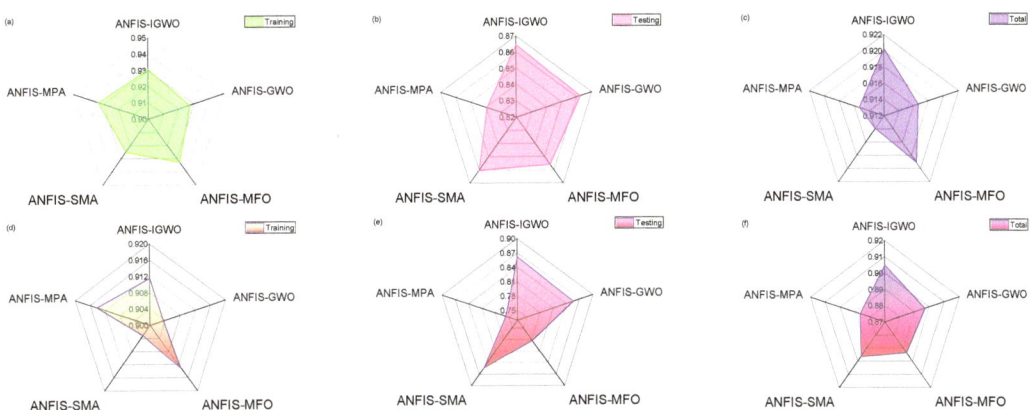

Figure 12. Radar plot representing the R value for (**a**–**c**) OMC and (**d**–**f**) MDD predictions.

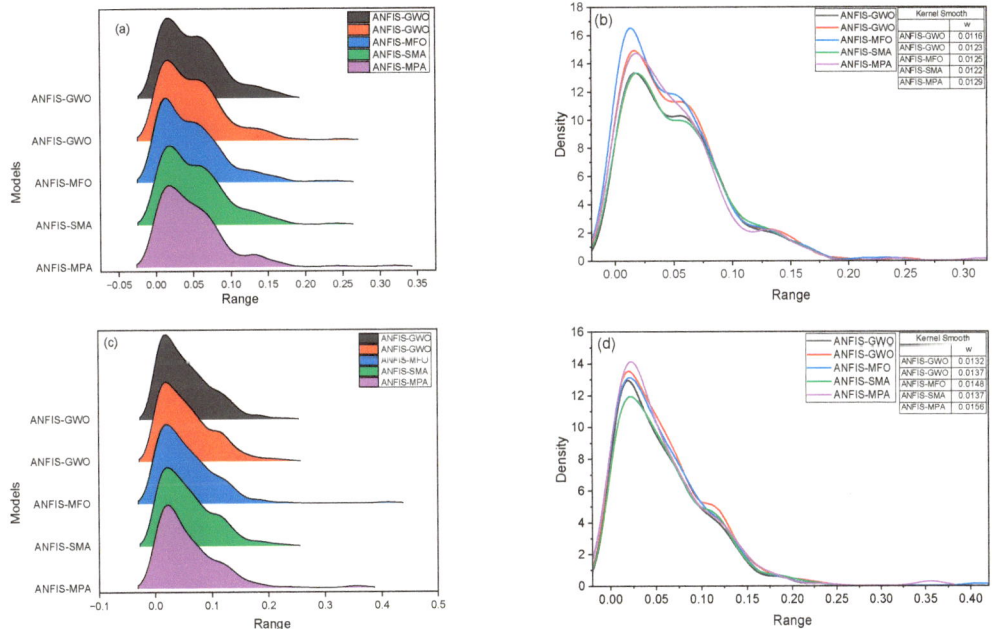

Figure 13. Ridgeline chart (left) and distribution with Kernel smooth (right) plots for (**a**,**b**) OMC and (**c**,**d**) MDD predictions.

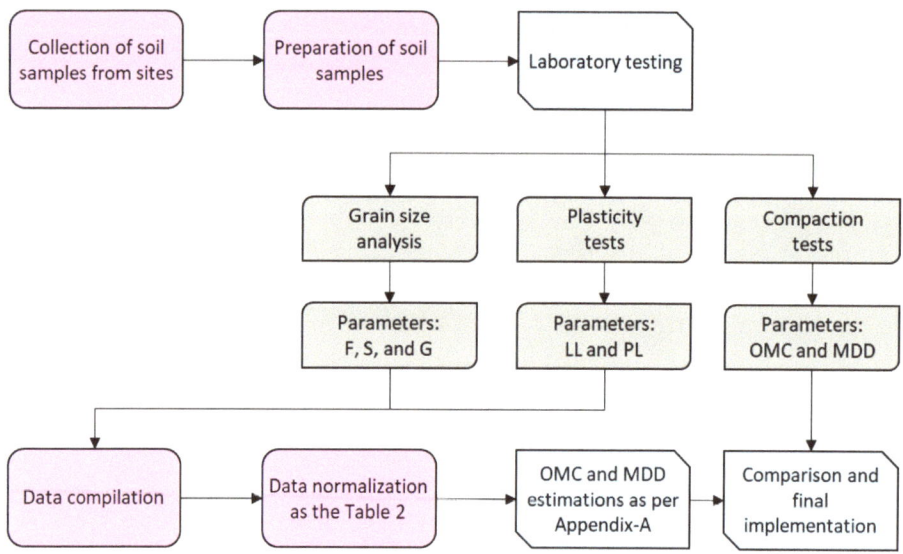

Figure 14. Illustration of the steps of OMC and MDD estimations using basic soil parameters and the developed MATLAB models.

6. Limitations and Future Research

In this section, the limitations of the proposed ANFIS-IGWO model are presented, as well as the main points that need to be further investigated. Regarding the estimation of the OMC and MDD of soils, it is worth noting that despite the excellent prediction it achieves, and which are presented in the previous section, it only applies to values of the input parameters between the minimum and the maximum values (refer to Table 2) that have the corresponding parameters of the database used to train and develop the model. Additionally, the reliability of the proposed model is limited for parameter value ranges, where the number of experimental data and soil types are not sufficient. That is, in cases in which the number of data is very small, and thus unable to satisfactorily describe the soil compaction. For example, based on the histograms of Figure 3, it was found that there is not enough data in some regions. Such value ranges, where there is a shortage of each of the input parameters, should be studied experimentally in the near future and updated the database with the aim of future development of more efficient forecasting soft computing models.

7. Summary and Conclusions

Soil compaction parameters play a vital role in construction projects. They are crucial for comparing the level of compaction achieved in the field. However, the traditional laboratory method for determining OMC and MDD is time consuming. Therefore, the main objective of this study is to sidestep the need for multiple laboratory tests by leveraging the predictive capabilities of high-performance hybrid intelligence paradigms. Taking these points into consideration, the current study proposes a high-performance hybrid model to sidestep the operation of typical laboratory testing of soil compaction parameters. To achieve this goal, an ANFIS-IGWO model was constructed, and the performance of this model was compared with four hybrid ANFIS models, namely ANFIS-GWO, ANFIS-MFO, ANFIS-SMA, and ANFIS-MPA. The experimental results clearly demonstrate that the proposed ANFIS-IGWO model effectively predicts soil compaction parameters. With an accuracy range of 92.5% to 94%, according to the RMSE index, the developed ANFIS-IGWO model exhibits superior generalisation abilities for estimating soil compaction parameters.

According to the overall outcomes, the proposed ANFIS-IGWO model offers a significant advantage by transforming the C&A parameters of the model into the coordinates of individual wolves within the community. Each wolf's position represents a result of the ANFIS-IGWO model, with N_{FIS} = 5 and 500 epochs utilised. However, a drawback of the ANFIS-IGWO model is its high computational cost due to the implementation of a modified approach. Multiple runs were performed to identify the most suitable search space for accurate output estimation, further increasing the time required. Other limitations encompass no external validation performed and the exclusion of factors such as compaction energy and the parental significance of soils during modelling. Therefore, additional research is needed to expand the application of the suggested ANFIS-IGWO model in estimating soil compaction parameters. Future directions should involve (a) a comprehensive assessment of the model's superiority using real-life data from diverse construction sites; (b) external validation using a real-life database of different soil types; (c) consideration of compaction energy as an influencing variable; (d) the implementation of newly introduced MHAs and their improved/enhanced, and (e) a comprehensive analysis of hybrid and traditional ANFIS paradigms in estimating soil compaction parameters. Nevertheless, the employed dataset and the MATLAB models developed in this study are provided as Supplementary Materials to encourage further research.

Supplementary Materials: The following supporting information can be downloaded at: https://www.mdpi.com/article/10.3390/math11143064/s1.

Author Contributions: Conceptualisation, A.B.; methodology, A.B.; software, A.B. and P.G.A.; formal analysis, A.B.; validation, G.K.; writing—original draft preparation, A.B., R.K.S., S.G. and G.K.; writing—review and editing, A.B. and P.G.A. All authors have read and agreed to the published version of the manuscript.

Funding: This research received no external funding.

Data Availability Statement: Attached as a Supplementary Materials.

Conflicts of Interest: The authors declare no conflict of interest.

Nomenclature

ANFIS	Adaptive neuro-fuzzy inference system	MF	Membership function
ANFIS-GWO	Hybrid model of ANFIS and GWO	MFO	Moth-flame optimisation
ANFIS-IGWO	Hybrid model of ANFIS and IGWO	MHA	Meta-heuristic algorithm
ANFIS-MFO	Hybrid model of ANFIS and MFO	MLT	Machine learning technique
ANFIS-MPA	Hybrid model of ANFIS and MPA	MPA	Marine predators algorithm
ANFIS-SMA	Hybrid model of ANFIS and SMA	N_{FIS}	Number of FIS parameters
ANN	Artificial neural network	OMC	Optimum moisture content
C&A	Consequent and antecedent	PFI	Performance index
E&E	Exploration and exploitation	PL	Plastic limit
ELM	Extreme learning machine	R	Correlation coefficient
EPR	Evolutionary polynomial regression	R^2	Determination coefficient
F	Fines content	RMSE	Root mean square error
FIS	Fuzzy inference system	RSR	RMSE to observation's standard deviation ratio
G	Gravel content	S	Sand content
GMDH	Group method of data handling	SMA	Slime mould algorithm
GWO	Grey wolf optimiser	SVM	Support vector machine
IGWO	Improved grey wolf optimiser	TR	Training subset
LL	Liquid limit	TS	Testing subset

LSSVM	Least square support vector machine	VAF	Variance account factor
MAE	Mean absolute error	WI	Willmott's Index of agreement
MDD	Maximum dry density	WMAPE	Weighted mean absolute percentage error

Appendix A

- MATLAB implementation for the developed ANFIS-IGWO model.

%% Dataset uploading: For dataset uploading via an Excel sheet named 'PROJECT.' The training dataset should be kept in the TR sheet, and the testing dataset should be kept in the TS sheet. The output value should be placed in the right-most column. All the values are given in normalised form.

train=xlsread('PROJECT', 'TR');
test=xlsread('PROJECT', 'TS');
xtrain = train(:,1:end-1); ytrain = train(:,end);
xtest = test(:,1:end-1); ytest = test(:,end);

%% Loading of the ANFIS-IGWO model for OMC estimation
%% Loading of anfis_igwo_mdd is necessary for MDD estimation

load anfis_igwo_omc
load anfis_igwo_mdd

%% Prediction of training and testing outputs (normalised values)

Pr_train_norm=evalfis(xtrain,fis);
Pr_test_norm=evalfis(xtest,fis);

%% Generation of de-normalisation values of OMC

Pr_train_act=(Pr_train_norm*24) + 7;
Pr_test_act=(Pr_test_norm*24) + 7;

%% Generation of de-normalisation values of MDD

Pr_train_act=(Pr_train_norm*7.7499) + 13.7340;
Pr_test_act=(Pr_test_norm*7.7499) + 13.7340;

References

1. Wang, H.-L.; Yin, Z.-Y. High performance prediction of soil compaction parameters using multi expression programming. *Eng. Geol.* **2020**, *276*, 105758. [CrossRef]
2. Tatsuoka, F.; Correia, A.G. Importance of controlling the degree of saturation in soil compaction linked to soil structure design. *Transp. Geotech.* **2018**, *17*, 3–23. [CrossRef]
3. Proctor, R. Fundamental principles of soil compaction. *Eng. News Record.* **1933**, *111*.
4. Xu, C.; Chen, Z.; Li, J.; Xiao, Y. Compaction of subgrade by high-energy impact rollers on an airport runway. *J. Perform. Constr. Facil.* **2014**, *28*, 4014021. [CrossRef]
5. Chen, R.-P.; Qi, S.; Wang, H.-L.; Cui, Y.-J. Microstructure and hydraulic properties of coarse-grained subgrade soil used in high-speed railway at various compaction degrees. *J. Mater. Civ. Eng.* **2019**, *31*, 4019301. [CrossRef]
6. Xu, Z.; Li, X.; Li, J.; Xue, Y.; Jiang, S.; Liu, L.; Luo, Q.; Wu, K.; Zhang, N.; Feng, Y. Characteristics of source rocks and genetic origins of natural gas in deep formations, Gudian Depression, Songliao Basin, NE China. *ACS Earth Space Chem.* **2022**, *6*, 1750–1771. [CrossRef]
7. Wu, Z.; Xu, J.; Li, Y.; Wang, S. Disturbed state concept–based model for the uniaxial strain-softening behavior of fiber-reinforced soil. *Int. J. Geomech.* **2022**, *22*, 4022092. [CrossRef]

8. Ren, C.; Yu, J.; Liu, S.; Yao, W.; Zhu, Y.; Liu, X. A plastic strain-induced damage model of porous rock suitable for different stress paths. *Rock Mech. Rock Eng.* **2022**, *55*, 1887–1906. [CrossRef]
9. Najjar, Y.M.; Basheer, I.A.; Naouss, W.A. On the identification of compaction characteristics by neuronets. *Comput. Geotech.* **1996**, *18*, 167–187. [CrossRef]
10. Nagaraj, H.B.; Reesha, B.; Sravan, M.V.; Suresh, M.R. Correlation of compaction characteristics of natural soils with modified plastic limit. *Transp. Geotech.* **2015**, *2*, 65–77. [CrossRef]
11. Peng, J.; Xu, C.; Dai, B.; Sun, L.; Feng, J.; Huang, Q. Numerical investigation of brittleness effect on strength and microcracking behavior of crystalline rock. *Int. J. Geomech.* **2022**, *22*, 4022178. [CrossRef]
12. Fu, Q.; Gu, M.; Yuan, J.; Lin, Y. Experimental study on vibration velocity of piled raft supported embankment and foundation for ballastless high speed railway. *Buildings* **2022**, *12*, 1982. [CrossRef]
13. Cheng, F.; Li, J.; Zhou, L.; Lin, G. Fragility analysis of nuclear power plant structure under real and spectrum-compatible seismic waves considering soil-structure interaction effect. *Eng. Struct.* **2023**, *280*, 115684. [CrossRef]
14. Bardhan, A.; Asteris, P.G. Application of hybrid ANN paradigms built with nature inspired meta-heuristics for modelling soil compaction parameters. *Transp. Geotech.* **2023**, *41*, 100995. [CrossRef]
15. Günaydın, O. Estimation of soil compaction parameters by using statistical analyses and artificial neural networks. *Environ. Geol.* **2009**, *57*, 203–215. [CrossRef]
16. Kurnaz, T.F.; Kaya, Y. The performance comparison of the soft computing methods on the prediction of soil compaction parameters. *Arab. J. Geosci.* **2020**, *13*, 159. [CrossRef]
17. Tiwari, L.B.; Burman, A.; Samui, P. Modelling soil compaction parameters using a hybrid soft computing technique of LSSVM and symbiotic organisms search. *Innov. Infrastruct. Solut.* **2023**, *8*, 2. [CrossRef]
18. Sinha, S.K.; Wang, M.C. Artificial neural network prediction models for soil compaction and permeability. *Geotech. Geol. Eng.* **2008**, *26*, 47–64. [CrossRef]
19. Ardakani, A.; Kordnaeij, A. Soil compaction parameters prediction using GMDH-type neural network and genetic algorithm. *Eur. J. Environ. Civ. Eng.* **2019**, *23*, 449–462. [CrossRef]
20. Yu, J.; Zhu, Y.; Yao, W.; Liu, X.; Ren, C.; Cai, Y.; Tang, X. Stress relaxation behaviour of marble under cyclic weak disturbance and confining pressures. *Measurement* **2021**, *182*, 109777. [CrossRef]
21. Wang, W.; Li, D.-Q.; Tang, X.-S.; Du, W. Seismic fragility and demand hazard analyses for earth slopes incorporating soil property variability. *Soil Dyn. Earthq. Eng.* **2023**, *173*, 108088. [CrossRef]
22. Ran, C.; Bai, X.; Tan, Q.; Luo, G.; Cao, Y.; Wu, L.; Chen, F.; Li, C.; Luo, X.; Liu, M. Threat of soil formation rate to health of karst ecosystem. *Sci. Total Environ.* **2023**, *887*, 163911. [CrossRef] [PubMed]
23. Liu, Y.; Li, J.; Lin, G. Seismic performance of advanced three-dimensional base-isolated nuclear structures in complex-layered sites. *Eng. Struct.* **2023**, *289*, 116247. [CrossRef]
24. Bui, D.T.; Nhu, V.-H.; Hoang, N.-D. Prediction of soil compression coefficient for urban housing project using novel integration machine learning approach of swarm intelligence and multi-layer perceptron neural network. *Adv. Eng. Inform.* **2018**, *38*, 593 604.
25. Truong, V.-H.; Pham, H.-A.; Van, T.H.; Tangaramvong, S. Evaluation of machine learning models for load-carrying capacity assessment of semi-rigid steel structures. *Eng. Struct.* **2022**, *273*, 115001. [CrossRef]
26. Truong, V.-H.; Papazafeiropoulos, G.; Vu, Q.-V.; Pham, V.-T.; Kong, Z. Predicting the patch load resistance of stiffened plate girders using machine learning algorithms. *Ocean Eng.* **2021**, *240*, 109886. [CrossRef]
27. Benbouras, M.A.; Lefilef, L. Progressive machine learning approaches for predicting the soil compaction parameters. *Transp. Infrastruct. Geotechnol.* **2023**, *10*, 211–238. [CrossRef]
28. Golafshani, E.M.; Behnood, A.; Arashpour, M. Predicting the compressive strength of normal and High-Performance Concretes using ANN and ANFIS hybridized with Grey Wolf Optimizer. *Constr. Build. Mater.* **2020**, *232*, 117266. [CrossRef]
29. Le, L.T.; Nguyen, H.; Dou, J.; Zhou, J. A comparative study of PSO-ANN, GA-ANN, ICA-ANN, and ABC-ANN in estimating the heating load of buildings' energy efficiency for smart city planning. *Appl. Sci.* **2019**, *9*, 2630. [CrossRef]
30. Piro, N.S.; Mohammed, A.; Hamad, S.M.; Kurda, R. Artificial neural networks (ANN), MARS, and adaptive network-based fuzzy inference system (ANFIS) to predict the stress at the failure of concrete with waste steel slag coarse aggregate replacement. *Neural Comput. Appl.* **2023**, *35*, 13293–13319. [CrossRef]
31. Ojha, V.K.; Abraham, A.; Snášel, V. Metaheuristic design of feedforward neural networks: A review of two decades of research. *Eng. Appl. Artif. Intell.* **2017**, *60*, 97–116. [CrossRef]
32. Behnood, A.; Golafshani, E.M. Predicting the compressive strength of silica fume concrete using hybrid artificial neural network with multi-objective grey wolves. *J. Clean. Prod.* **2018**, *202*, 54–64. [CrossRef]
33. Ly, H.-B.; Pham, B.T.; Le, L.M.; Le, T.-T.; Le, V.M.; Asteris, P.G. Estimation of axial load-carrying capacity of concrete-filled steel tubes using surrogate models. *Neural Comput. Appl.* **2021**, *33*, 3437–3458. [CrossRef]
34. Smys, S.; Balas, V.E.; Kamel, K.A.; Lafata, P. *Inventive Computation and Information Technologies*; Springer: Berlin/Heidelberg, Germany, 2021.
35. Samantaray, S.; Sumaan, P.; Surin, P.; Mohanta, N.R.; Sahoo, A. Prophecy of groundwater level using hybrid ANFIS-BBO approach. In *Proceedings of International Conference on Data Science and Applications: ICDSA 2021*; Springer: Berlin/Heidelberg, Germany, 2022; Volume 1, pp. 273–283.

36. Joshi, H.; Arora, S. Enhanced grey wolf optimization algorithm for global optimization. *Fundam. Informaticae* **2017**, *153*, 235–264. [CrossRef]
37. Qais, M.H.; Hasanien, H.M.; Alghuwainem, S. Augmented grey wolf optimizer for grid-connected PMSG-based wind energy conversion systems. *Appl. Soft Comput.* **2018**, *69*, 504–515. [CrossRef]
38. Gupta, S.; Deep, K.; Mirjalili, S. An efficient equilibrium optimizer with mutation strategy for numerical optimization. *Appl. Soft Comput.* **2020**, *96*, 106542. [CrossRef]
39. Ding, Q.; Xu, X. Improved GWO Algorithm for UAV Path Planning on Crop Pest Monitoring. Issue Special Issue on Multimedia Streaming and Processing in Internet of Things with Edge Intelligence. *Int. J. Interact. Multimed. Artif. Intell.* **2022**, *7*, 30–39. [CrossRef]
40. Rosenblatt, F. The perceptron: A probabilistic model for information storage and organization in the brain. *Psychol. Rev.* **1958**, *65*, 386. [CrossRef]
41. Chen, H.; Asteris, P.G.; Armaghani, D.J.; Gordan, B.; Pham, B.T. Assessing dynamic conditions of the retaining wall: Developing two hybrid intelligent models. *Appl. Sci.* **2019**, *9*, 1042. [CrossRef]
42. Armaghani, D.J.; Ming, Y.Y.; Mohammed, A.S.; Momeni, E.; Maizir, H. Effect of Different Kernels of the Support Vector Machine to Forecast the Bearing Capacity of Deep Foundation. *J. Soft Comput. Civ. Eng.* **2023**, *7*, 111–128.
43. Ahmed, H.U.; Mohammed, A.S.; Faraj, R.H.; Abdalla, A.A.; Qaidi, S.M.A.; Sor, N.H.; Mohammed, A.A. Innovative modeling techniques including MEP, ANN and FQ to forecast the compressive strength of geopolymer concrete modified with nanoparticles. *Neural Comput. Appl.* **2023**, *35*, 12453–12479. [CrossRef]
44. Asteris, P.G.; Tsaris, A.K.; Cavaleri, L.; Repapis, C.C.; Papalou, A.; Di Trapani, F.; Karypidis, D.F. Prediction of the fundamental period of infilled RC frame structures using artificial neural networks. *Comput. Intell. Neurosci.* **2016**, *2016*, 20. [CrossRef] [PubMed]
45. He, B.; Armaghani, D.J.; Lai, S.H. Assessment of tunnel blasting-induced overbreak: A novel metaheuristic-based random forest approach. *Tunn. Undergr. Space Technol.* **2023**, *133*, 104979. [CrossRef]
46. Indraratna, B.; Armaghani, D.J.; Correia, A.G.; Hunt, H.; Ngo, T. Prediction of resilient modulus of ballast under cyclic loading using machine learning techniques. *Transp. Geotech.* **2023**, *38*, 100895. [CrossRef]
47. Shan, F.; He, X.; Armaghani, D.J.; Zhang, P.; Sheng, D. Success and challenges in predicting TBM penetration rate using recurrent neural networks. *Tunn. Undergr. Space Technol.* **2022**, *130*, 104728. [CrossRef]
48. Li, D.; Liu, Z.; Xiao, P.; Zhou, J.; Armaghani, D.J. Intelligent rockburst prediction model with sample category balance using feedforward neural network and Bayesian optimization. *Undergr. Space* **2022**, *7*, 833–846. [CrossRef]
49. Paryani, S.; Neshat, A.; Javadi, S.; Pradhan, B. Comparative performance of new hybrid ANFIS models in landslide susceptibility mapping. *Nat. Hazards.* **2020**, *103*, 1961–1988. [CrossRef]
50. Mustafa, R.; Samui, P.; Kumari, S. Reliability Analysis of Gravity Retaining Wall Using Hybrid ANFIS. *Infrastructures* **2022**, *7*, 121. [CrossRef]
51. Jang, J.-S. ANFIS: Adaptive-network-based fuzzy inference system. *IEEE Trans. Syst. Man. Cybern.* **1993**, *23*, 665–685. [CrossRef]
52. Mirjalili, S.; Mirjalili, S.M.; Lewis, A. Grey Wolf Optimizer. *Adv. Eng. Softw.* **2014**, *69*, 46–61. [CrossRef]
53. Nadimi-Shahraki, M.H.; Taghian, S.; Mirjalili, S. An improved grey wolf optimizer for solving engineering problems. *Expert Syst. Appl.* **2021**, *166*, 113917. [CrossRef]
54. Tumar, I.; Hassouneh, Y.; Turabieh, H.; Thaher, T. Enhanced binary moth flame optimization as a feature selection algorithm to predict software fault prediction. *IEEE Access* **2020**, *8*, 8041–8055. [CrossRef]
55. Tiachacht, S.; Khatir, S.; Le Thanh, C.; Rao, R.V.; Mirjalili, S.; Wahab, M.A. Inverse problem for dynamic structural health monitoring based on slime mould algorithm. *Eng. Comput.* **2021**, *38*, 2205–2228. [CrossRef]
56. AlRassas, A.M.; Al-Qaness, M.A.A.; Ewees, A.A.; Ren, S.; Sun, R.; Pan, L.; Elaziz, M.A. Advance artificial time series forecasting model for oil production using neuro fuzzy-based slime mould algorithm. *J. Pet. Explor. Prod. Technol.* **2022**, *12*, 383–395. [CrossRef]
57. Al-Qaness, M.A.A.; Ewees, A.A.; Fan, H.; Abualigah, L.; Elaziz, M.A. Marine predators algorithm for forecasting confirmed cases of COVID-19 in Italy, USA, Iran and Korea. *Int. J. Environ. Res. Public Health* **2020**, *17*, 3520. [CrossRef]
58. Mirjalili, S. Moth-flame optimization algorithm: A novel nature-inspired heuristic paradigm. *Knowl. Based Syst.* **2015**, *89*, 228–249. [CrossRef]
59. Li, S.; Chen, H.; Wang, M.; Heidari, A.A.; Mirjalili, S. Slime mould algorithm: A new method for stochastic optimization. *Futur. Gener. Comput. Syst.* **2020**, *111*, 300–323. [CrossRef]
60. Faramarzi, A.; Heidarinejad, M.; Mirjalili, S.; Gandomi, A.H. Marine Predators Algorithm: A nature-inspired metaheuristic. *Expert Syst. Appl.* **2020**, *152*, 113377. [CrossRef]
61. ASTM Committee D-18 on Soil and Rock. *Standard Practice for Classification of Soils for Engineering Purposes (Unified Soil Classification System)*; ASTM International: West Conshohocken, PA, USA, 2017.
62. Taylor, K.E. Summarizing multiple aspects of model performance in a single diagram. *J. Geophys. Res. Atmos.* **2001**, *106*, 7183–7192. [CrossRef]

Disclaimer/Publisher's Note: The statements, opinions and data contained in all publications are solely those of the individual author(s) and contributor(s) and not of MDPI and/or the editor(s). MDPI and/or the editor(s) disclaim responsibility for any injury to people or property resulting from any ideas, methods, instructions or products referred to in the content.

Article

Slope Stability Prediction Using k-NN-Based Optimum-Path Forest Approach

Leilei Liu, Guoyan Zhao and Weizhang Liang *

School of Resources and Safety Engineering, Central South University, Changsha 410083, China; leilei_liu@csu.edu.cn (L.L.)
* Correspondence: wzlian@csu.edu.cn

Abstract: Slope instability can lead to catastrophic consequences. However, predicting slope stability effectively is still challenging because of the complex mechanisms and multiple influencing factors. In recent years, machine learning (ML) has received great attention in slope stability prediction due to its strong nonlinear prediction ability. In this study, an optimum-path forest algorithm based on k-nearest neighbor (OPF_{k-NN}) was used to predict the stability of slopes. First, 404 historical slopes with failure risk were collected. Subsequently, the dataset was used to train and test the algorithm based on randomly divided training and test sets, respectively. The hyperparameter values were tuned by combining ten-fold cross-validation and grid search methods. Finally, the performance of the proposed approach was evaluated based on accuracy, F_1-score, area under the curve (AUC), and computational burden. In addition, the prediction results were compared with the other six ML algorithms. The results showed that the OPF_{k-NN} algorithm had a better performance, and the values of accuracy, F_1-score, AUC, and computational burden were 0.901, 0.902, 0.901, and 0.957 s, respectively. Moreover, the failed slope cases can be accurately identified, which is highly critical in slope stability prediction. The slope angle had the most important influence on prediction results. Furthermore, the engineering application results showed that the overall predictive performance of the OPF_{k-NN} model was consistent with the factor of safety value of engineering slopes. This study can provide valuable guidance for slope stability analysis and risk management.

Keywords: slope stability prediction; machine learning (ML); optimum path forest (OPF); k-nearest neighbor (k-NN); hyperparameter tuning

MSC: 86-10

1. Introduction

Slope instability is a global geological problem, which is one of the three major geological problems in nature besides earthquakes and volcanoes. Many geotechnical projects, such as open-pit mining, mountain roads, tailings dams, and landfills, are seriously threatened by slope instability. A serious slope instability disaster can cause casualties, building damages, and huge economic losses. For example, on 20 December 2015, a catastrophic landslide occurred at the Hong'ao landfill in Shenzhen, China, resulting in 77 deaths, 33 buildings buried, and direct economic losses of more than 880 million RMB [1]. On the evening of 11 March 2017, a landslide at the Koshe landfill in Ethiopia's capital, Yah, caused 113 deaths and more than 80 people missing [2]. Due to heavy rainfall on 18 October 2020, a landslide occurred in Vietnam's Quang Tri province, claiming the lives of 22 soldiers [3]. Because of its serious consequences, predicting the risk of slope instability is crucial and plays a significant role in disaster prevention.

The prediction methods of slope stability can be classified into four categories. The first one is instrumental monitoring technology. Currently, many on-site monitoring techniques of slope deformation have been applied to monitor the early warning signs of slope instability. For example, Zhang et al. [4] used distributed fiber optic strain sensors to monitor the shear displacement in the Three Gorges Reservoir region in China, and two potential circular sliding surfaces were successfully identified. Dixon et al. [5], Shiotani [6], and Codeglia et al. [7] adopted the acoustic emissions (AE) technology to monitor the signals generated by the fracture of soil and rock materials in the slope. By analyzing the relationship between AE characteristics and slope deformation, AE-based criteria were used to evaluate the long-term stability of slopes. In addition, some other techniques, such as remote sensing [8], terrestrial laser scanning [9], synthetic aperture radar [10], and time domain reflectometry [11], were applied to slope stability monitoring. These technologies have relatively high prediction accuracy because the precursor information of slope instability can be obtained directly, but the installation process is complicated, and the cost is high.

The second one is the theoretical analysis method. It is proposed from the view of mechanical mechanisms. Many theoretical and analytical approaches have been used to analyze slope stability, such as the limit equilibrium method (LEM) [12], the strength reduction method (SRM) [13], and the limit analysis method [14]. The factor of safety (FOS), calculated by the ratio of resisting force to driving force, is used to evaluate the stability of the slope. When the value of FOS is larger than 1, the slope is stable; otherwise, it is unstable [15]. Faramarzi et al. [16] employed LEM to calculate the FOS and analyzed the rock slope stability of the Chamshir dam pit. Liu [17] adopted the SRM to obtain the FOS of the established slope model. Mbarka et al. [18] combined the Monte Carlo approach, LEM, and SRM for the reliability analysis of homogeneous slopes with circular-type failure. Although the theoretical and analytical methods are simple, they are unsuitable for slopes with complex conditions due to the simplified formulas and assumptions.

The third one is the numerical simulation technique. With the rapid development of numerical simulation methods, finite element method (FEM) [19], boundary element method [20], discrete element method [21], numerical manifold method [22], and other methods have been widely used in slope stability analysis. Sun et al. [23] simulate the progressive failure process of jointed rock slopes based on the combined finite-discrete element method. Ma et al. [24] analyzed the slope stability under a complex stress state with saturated and unsaturated seepage using the fast Lagrangian analysis of continua. Wei et al. [25] investigated the kinetic features of slope instability based on particle flow code. Haghnejad et al. [26] analyzed the effect of blast-induced vibration on slope stability using dynamic pressure in three dimensions distinct element codes. Song et al. [27] adopted an improved smoothed-particle hydrodynamics method to calculate the slope safety factor. Zhang et al. [28] adopted a realistic failure process analysis to evaluate the stability and investigated the failure mode of the high rock slope during excavations. In addition, some researchers have integrated numerical simulation and mathematical methods to analyze the slope stability. For example, Dyson and Tolooiyan [29] adopted FEM and Monte Carlo to determine the FOS and damage probability of slopes. Although the numerical simulation methods are convenient to operate, the accuracy strongly depends on constitutive models and mechanical parameters [30].

The fourth one is the machine learning (ML) algorithm. With the accumulation of slope cases, some researchers attempted to develop slope stability prediction models using ML algorithms. There are two types of predicted outputs: FOS and stability status. Lu and Rosenbaum [31] adopted an artificial neural network to estimate the FOS and SS on 46 slope cases collected by Sah et al. [32]. Based on the same database, Samui [33] and Yang et al. [34] used a support vector machine (SVM) and genetic programming to determine FOS, respectively. Amirkiyaei and Ghasemi [35] constructed two tree-based models to assess circular-type failure slopes based on 87 cases. Zhou et al. [36] collected 221 slope cases and employed the gradient-boosting machine to predict the SS. Wang et al. [37] hybridized a genetic algorithm with a multi-layer perceptron to predict FOS using 630 cases. In addition, several researchers performed a comparative analysis of multiple ML algorithms. Hoang and Tien Bui [38] carried out a comparative study of SS prediction using a radial basis function neural network, an extreme learning machine, and least squares SVM. Mahmoodzadeh et al. [39] adopted Gaussian process regression, support vector regression, decision trees (DT), long-short-term memory, deep neural networks, and k-nearest neighbors (k-NN) to determine FOS. All the above ML algorithms performed well on slope stability prediction. However, a large number of slope stability cases are required to improve its credibility.

Compared with other approaches, ML algorithms can obtain reliable prediction results by establishing the nonlinear relationship between input and output. It is a promising method for predicting slope stability. But to date, there is no one ML algorithm that can be applied to all slope engineering conditions under the consensus of the geotechnical industry. Accordingly, it is meaningful to investigate more robust ML algorithms to achieve better prediction results. Recently, the optimum-path forest (OPF) algorithm has been successfully applied in many fields, such as face recognition [40], Parkinson's disease identification [41], laryngeal cancer pathology detection [42], land use classification [43], and network intrusion detection [44]. However, the OPF algorithm is susceptible to outliers. In response to this deficiency, Papa et al. [45] proposed the OPF algorithm based on k-NN (OPF$_{k\text{-NN}}$), and the discriminative performance of the OPF model was improved. In combination with the k-NN algorithm, the OPF$_{k\text{-NN}}$ algorithm can provide better performance for classification tasks by leveraging the topological properties of the data [46]. Compared to other classification algorithms, the OPF$_{k\text{-NN}}$ algorithm has several advantages, including (1) it is free of hyperparameters, (2) it does not assume separability of the feature space, (3) it has a unique feature selection and classification mechanism that can effectively handle the high-dimensional and nonlinear data with outliers, (4) and its training step is usually much faster than traditional ML approaches.

Considering that the OPF$_{k\text{-NN}}$ has great predictive performance and has not yet been employed to predict the stability of slopes, this study aims to investigate the feasibility of OPF$_{k\text{-NN}}$ for predicting slope stability. In addition, a comparison against OPF, radial basis function support vector machine (RBF-SVM), random forest (RF), DT, k-NN, and logistic regression (LR) classifiers is performed.

2. Methodology
2.1. k-NN Based OPF Classifier

The OPF is a graph-based classifier [47,48]. Its classification principle is to denote the training samples as nodes and connect them by path. Then, the optimal path tree (OPT) is constructed by executing the shortest path algorithm on the graph. Finally, the test sample is mapped onto the OPT, and its class is determined. Figure 1 shows the schematic diagram of the OPF-based classifiers. The nodes with different colors in the set S represent different classes, and the nodes outside the set S are the samples to be classified. A series of adjacent nodes are defined as path π. Among all paths, the one with the maximum path-cost function $f(\pi_t)$ is called OPT, and all OPTs constitute OPF. There are three different classes in Figure 1; the blue sample s is the root node of the OPT where sample t is located, so sample t is classified as blue.

The OPF$_{k\text{-NN}}$ is a variant of the OPF algorithm, and the main difference between them is the adjacency of the samples in the training set. The latter is to construct a complete graph, while the former is to construct a k-NN graph [45]. The OPF$_{k\text{-NN}}$ algorithm is divided into training and classification phases.

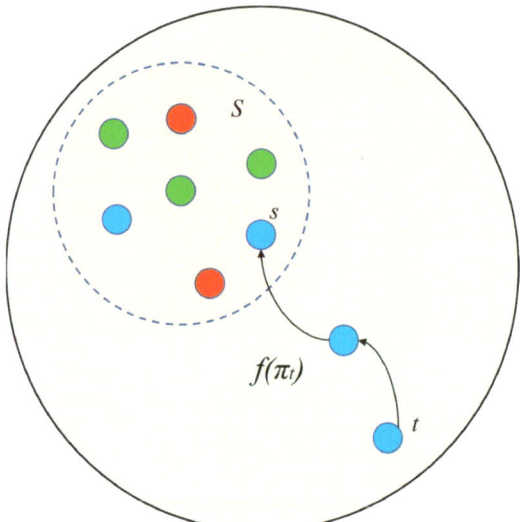

Figure 1. Schematic diagram of OPF-based classifiers [49].

2.1.1. Training Phase

The first step is to construct a k-NN graph G_k based on the training set Z_1. The sample s is weighed by a probability density function $\rho(s)$:

$$\rho(s) = \frac{1}{\sqrt{2\pi\sigma^2}|G_k^*(s)|} \sum_{\forall t \in G_k^*(s)} \exp\left(\frac{-d^2(s,t)}{2\sigma^2}\right), \qquad (1)$$

where $\sigma = \frac{d_f}{3}$, d_f is the maximum arc weight in G_k, and $d(s, t)$ is the distance between sample s and sample t.

The second step is to calculate the path cost function $f_{\min}$, which is defined as:

$$\begin{aligned} f_{\min}(\langle t \rangle) &= \begin{cases} \rho(t) & \text{if } t \in S \\ \rho(t) - 1 & \text{otherwise} \end{cases}, \\ f_{\min}(\pi_s \cdot \langle s, t \rangle) &= \min\{f_{\min}(\pi_s), \rho(t)\} \end{aligned} \qquad (2)$$

According to the method proposed by Papa et al. [50], the k value of k-NN is determined by maximizing the accuracy of the training set in the range $[1, k_{\max}]$. The value of $k_{\max}$ defaults to 5. After determining the value of k, the algorithm is applied to retrain the classifier. The function $f_{\min}$ is replaced by $f'_{\min}$, which is defined as:

$$\begin{aligned} f'_{\min}(\langle t \rangle) &= \begin{cases} \rho(t) & \text{if } t \in S \\ \rho(t) - 1 & \text{otherwise} \end{cases} \\ f'_{\min}(\pi_s \cdot \langle s, t \rangle) &= \begin{cases} -\infty & \text{if } \lambda(t) \neq \lambda(s) \\ \min\{f'_{\min}(\pi_s), \rho(t)\} & \text{otherwise} \end{cases} \end{aligned} \qquad (3)$$

Figure 2 is the schematic diagram of the training phase, where Figure 2a indicates the k-NN graph generated from the training set, Figure 2b represents the minimum spanning tree calculated by the k-NN graph, Figure 2c denotes the two samples of different colors labeled as prototype samples (marked by black dashed circles), and Figure 2d signifies the OPF$_{k\text{-NN}}$ classifier composed by all the OPTs. The red squares and green circles represent different classes, respectively.

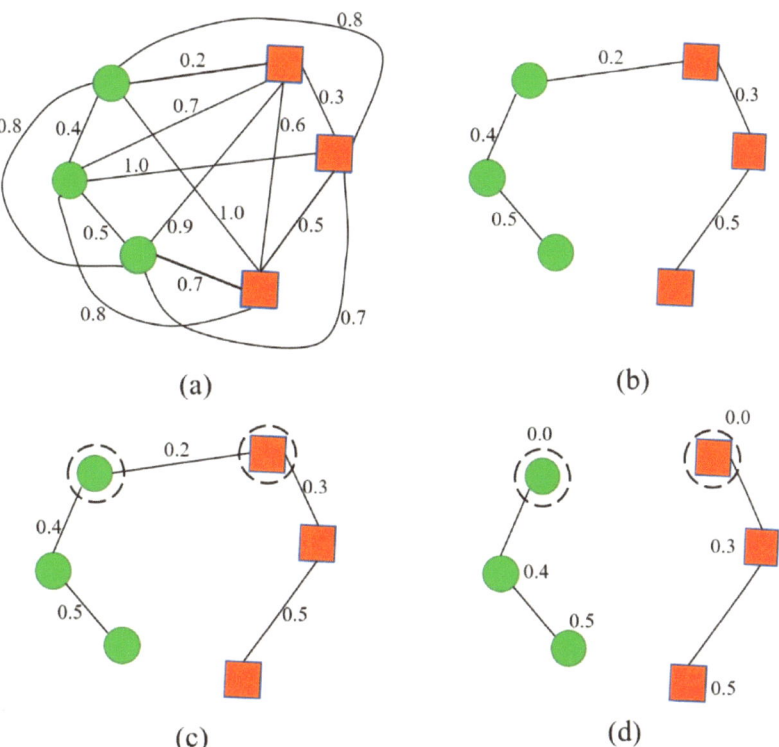

Figure 2. Schematic diagram of the training phase [50], (**a**) a two-class ("green circles" and "red squares") complete graph, (**b**) minimum spanning tree (MST), (**c**) labeled prototypes (marked by black dashed circles), (**d**) optimal path forest.

2.1.2. Classification Phase

After training the OPF$_{k\text{-NN}}$ classifier, the sample t in the test set Z_2 is classified. The k-NN is first calculated from Z_1 to a testing sample t. Then, it is verified which sample $s \in Z_1$ satisfies the equation below:

$$V(t) = \max\{\min[V(s), \rho(t)]\} \forall s \in Z_1 \qquad (4)$$

Figure 3 indicates the classification process of OPF$_{k\text{-NN}}$. The blue triangle is the sample to be classified. Figure 3a shows that the blue triangle is connected to the k-nearest training samples in the generated OPF, and Figure 3b illustrates that the triangle is conquered by the samples of the red squares class and labeled as red.

2.2. Proposed Approach

Figure 4 depicts the flowchart of the proposed approach. First, due to the different units of indicators and the diversity of data distribution, the raw data is pre-processed. The dataset is standardized using a Gaussian distribution with zero mean and unit standard deviation. Subsequently, 80% of samples are used for training, and the remaining 20% are adopted for testing [51,52]. For the k-NN, RBF-SVM, RF, DT, and LR algorithms, the grid search and ten-fold cross-validation (CV) methods are used to select the optimal hyperparameters. Finally, the test set is predicted, and the optimal classifier is determined according to the evaluation metrics.

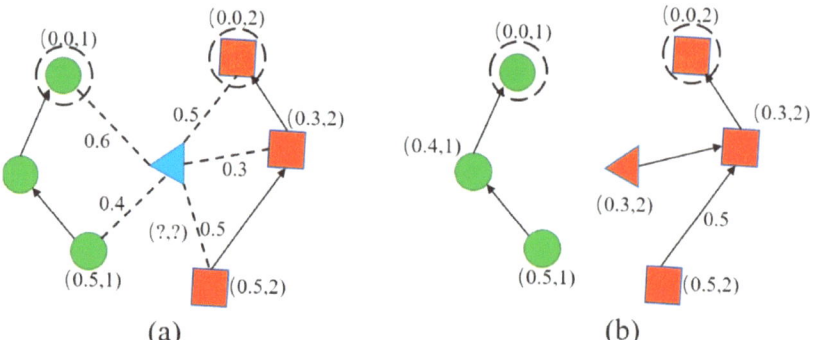

Figure 3. Schematic diagram of classification phase [50], (**a**) the sample to be classified (blue triangle) is connected to all training nodes in the generated optimal path forest, and the connection strength $f$max is calculated for each path, (**b**) the triangle is conquered by "red squares" class samples and classified as "red".

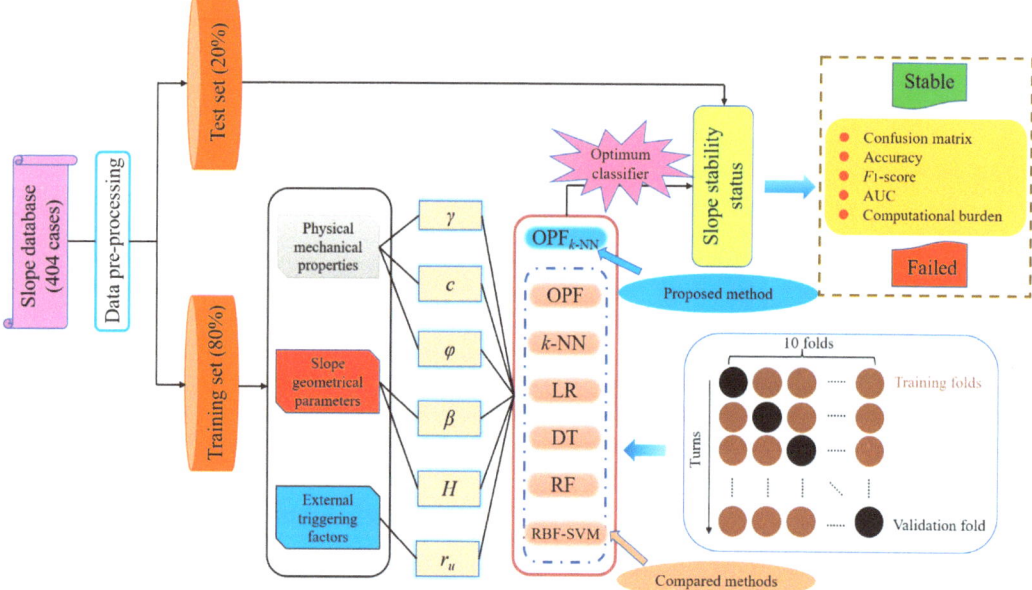

Figure 4. Flowchart of the proposed approach.

The $OPF_{k\text{-NN}}$ and OPF are implemented based on the Python library "opfython" [53], and the k-NN, RBF-SVM, RF, DT, and LR are conducted on the Python library "scikit-learn" [54]. All experiments are conducted using a Windows10 64 bits computer with 8Gb of RAM running an Intel® Core™ i7-9700F CPU @ 3.00 GHz × 2.

If the predictive performance of our proposed approach is acceptable, it can be used for engineering applications in several ways. For example, it can be integrated into slope monitoring systems to provide real-time alerts for potential instability. The model can also be used to evaluate slope stability during the design phase of construction projects to ensure the safety and stability of the slope. Additionally, the model can be applied to slope stability analysis and risk management, which can be used by geotechnical engineers in various projects related to slope instability.

2.3. Performance Evaluation Metrics

In this study, several metrics are used to evaluate the performance of classifiers and figure out the optimal classifier for slope stability prediction [30,55].

A confusion matrix, which can also be called a likelihood table or error matrix, is used to visually represent whether the performance is ideal or not. Table 1 shows the confusion matrix for the slope-stability prediction, where true positive (*TP*) means the number of stable cases predicted correctly, false positive (*FP*) means the number of stable cases predicted incorrectly, true negative (*TN*) means the number of failed cases predicted correctly, and false negative (*FN*) means the number of failed cases predicted incorrectly. According to Table 1, true negative rate (*TN*/(*TN* + *FP*)) and false positive rate (*FP*/(*FP* + *TN*)) can be defined.

Table 1. Confusion matrix for slope stability prediction.

Actual Condition	Predicted Condition	
	Stable	Failed
Stable	True positive	False negative
Failed	False positive	True negative

Accuracy indicates the ratio of the cases correctly predicted to the total cases, which can be calculated by: $accuracy = (TP + TN)/(TP + TN + FP + FN)$.

F_1-score indicates the harmonic mean of precision and recall, which can be calculated by: $F_1\text{-}score = 2 precision \cdot recall/(precision + recall)$, where $precision = TP/(TP + FP)$, $recall = TP/(TP + FN)$.

The area under the curve (AUC) is defined as the area under the receiver operating characteristic (ROC) curve, which is commonly used to evaluate the performance of classifiers. Bradley [56] proposed classification criteria of AUC as follows: not discriminating (0.5–0.6), poor (0.6–0.7), fair (0.7–0.8), good (0.8–0.9), and excellent (0.9–1).

Computational burden is used to evaluate the computational efficiency of algorithms. The mean and standard deviation of computation time are used as the evaluation metrics in this study.

2.4. Hyperparameter Tuning

In general, the performance of most ML algorithms is highly dependent on the hyperparameters. There are several hyperparameter tuning methods, such as manual search, grid search, random search, Bayesian optimization, gradient-based optimization, and evolutionary optimization [57]. In this study, the grid search algorithm is combined with the *k*-fold CV method to select the optimal hyperparameters.

The grid search algorithm is to grid the hyperparameters in a fixed range in equal steps, compare all hyperparameter combinations exhaustively, and then select the optimal hyperparameters. To avoid the risk of overfitting or selection bias in the model, the *k*-fold CV method is used in the hyperparameter tuning process, illustrated in Figure 5. The original training set is randomly split into *k* folds, of which $k - 1$ folds are used as the training sub-set, and the remaining fold is used as the validation set in turn. Then, the average accuracy of *k* rounds is calculated to evaluate the performance and determine the optimal hyperparameters [58]. In this study, *k* was selected as 10 after considering the calculation time and variance [59].

Figure 5. Flowchart of *k*-fold CV.

3. Data Collection

3.1. Dataset Description

The failure surfaces of the slopes are prone to occur near the potential slip surface. Because of the excavation at the foot of the slope or water seepage at the top of the slope, the shear stress on the potential slip surface exceeds the shear strength, causing the local slope instability, as shown in Figure 6. A large number of engineering cases and theoretical analyses indicate that there are three main aspects that affect slope stability: the physical–mechanical properties of the potential slip surface, the basic geometrical parameters, and the external triggering factors. [12,18,60–62]. Considering the independent correlation between indicators and the easy availability of indicator values, six indicators were selected in this study, including the unit weight (γ), the cohesion (c), the internal friction angle (φ), the slope angle (β), the slope height (H), and the pore pressure ratio (r_u). The detailed descriptions of these indicators are displayed in Table 2.

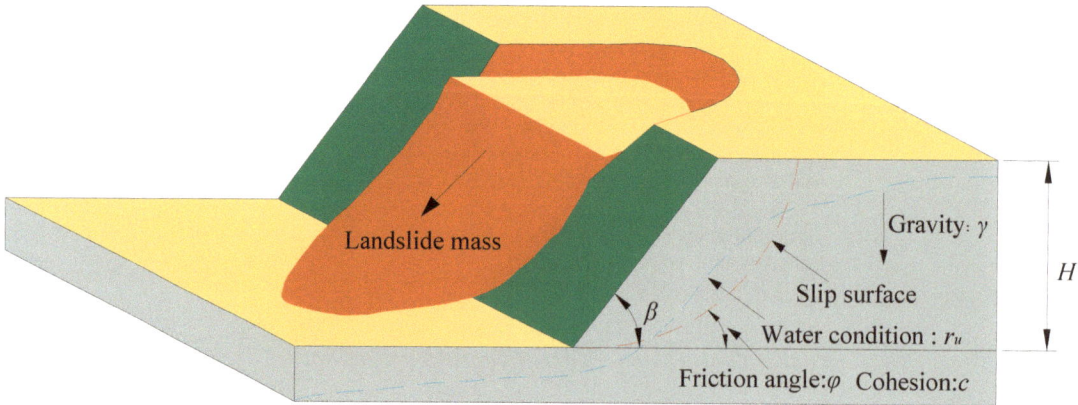

Figure 6. The 3D schematic diagram of slope failure.

Table 2. Descriptions of input indicators.

Indicator	Description	Measurement Method
γ (kN/m^3)	It indicates the weight of soil/rock per unit volume.	It can be measured by performing the standard mass volume method, mercury displacement method, or gravimeter method in the laboratory.
c (kPa)	It indicates the attraction between molecules on the surface of adjacent material particles within the soil/rock.	It can be determined by performing direct shear tests and triaxial compression tests in the laboratory.
φ (°)	It indicates a measure of the ability of a unit of soil/rock to withstand shear stress.	It can be determined by performing direct shear tests and triaxial compression tests in the laboratory.
β (°)	It indicates the angle between the slope plane and the slope bottom.	It can be measured in the field by an inclinometer.
H (m)	It indicates the vertical distance from the slope bottom to the slope top.	It can be measured in the field using a surveying instrument such as a total station.
r_u	It is defined as the ratio of the pore pressure and normal stress at a certain point within a slope.	It can be measured by installing pore water piezometers on-site or by performing immersion tests or infiltration tests in the laboratory.

In this study, a database of 404 slopes with failure risk from various countries was collected (available in "Appendix A") [32,36,57,63–72]. There are two statuses of slope stability: stable (207 cases) and failed (197 cases). Among them, most of the failed slopes were circular-type failures. The distribution of slope SS on the overall dataset is given in Figure 7, and the statistical values of data samples are illustrated in Table 3.

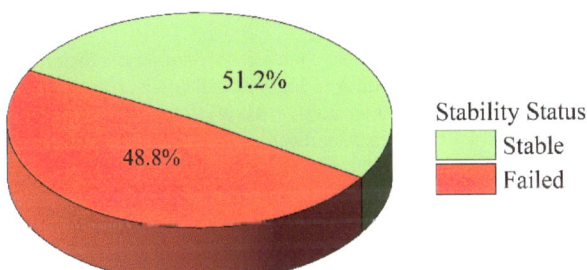

Figure 7. Distribution of slope stability status.

Table 3. Statistical values of slope stability dataset.

Value Type	γ (kN/m^3)	c (kPa)	φ (°)	β (°)	H (m)	r_u
Minimum	10.06	0	0	4.24	3.45	0
Median	21.38	29.7	28.27	34.03	51	0.2
Maximum	31.3	300	57.36	59.35	565	0.75
Mean	21.69	39.38	27.74	34.19	84.26	0.18
Standard	3.84	40.54	9.63	10.86	94.97	0.17

3.2. Dataset Analysis

The violin plots of six indicators are shown in Figure 8. They were a combination of box plots and density plots and indicated the overall distribution of the dataset. For each violin plot, the white dot in the center was the median of the samples, the top and bottom of the thick black line represented the third and first quartile of the samples, and the top and bottom of the thin black line indicated the upper and lower adjacent value. From Figure 8, it can be seen that the distribution of γ, φ, β was relatively balanced, and the medians were basically in the middle of the violin plots. While for c, H, r_u, there were some individual outliers.

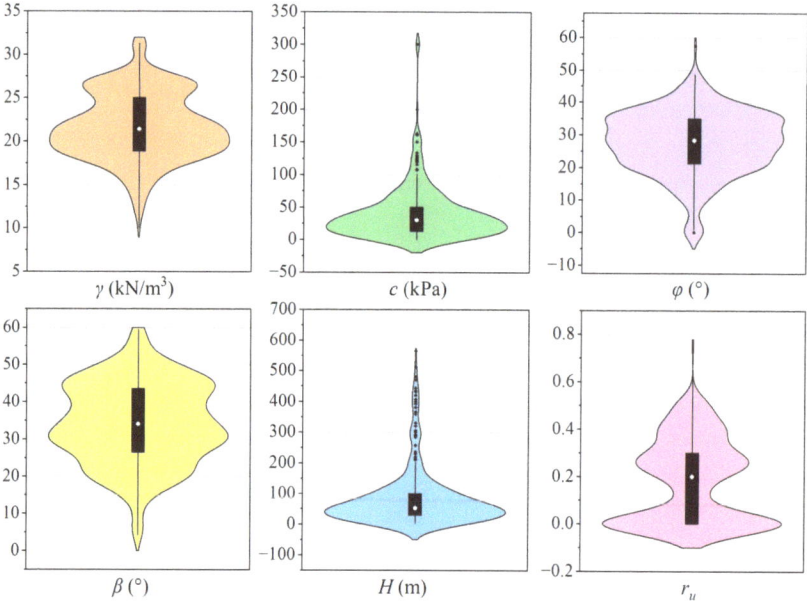

Figure 8. Violin plots of the dataset.

The heatmap of the Pearson correlation coefficient between each indicator is shown in Figure 9. According to Figure 9, all correlation coefficients were less than 0.5, and the highest correlation was only 0.41, which indicated that the correlation between indicators was poor. Therefore, all indicators were relatively independent and important for predicting slope stability.

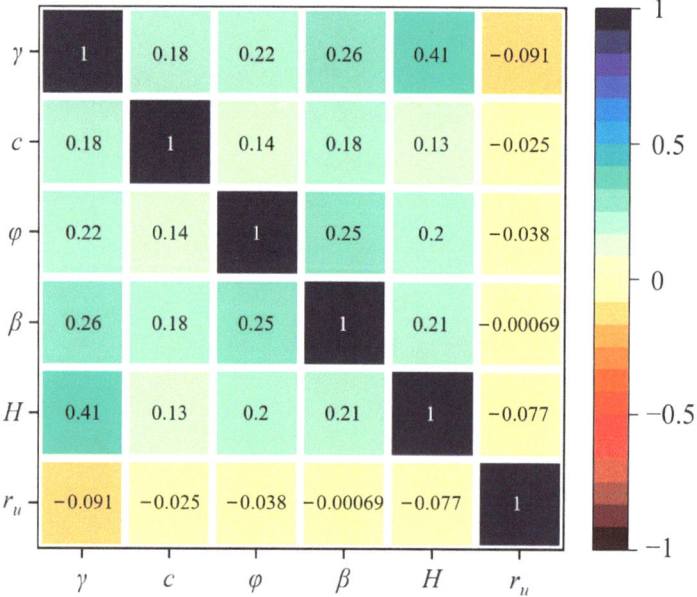

Figure 9. Correlation matrix of six indicators.

To visualize the distribution of the dataset, the correlation pair plots of the two slope SS were displayed in Figure 10. The distribution plots of these six indicators were shown on the diagonal line, and the correlation scatter plots between indicators were shown on the non-diagonal line. It can be seen that the differences in the distribution of indicators for both slope statuses were slight, and there was no apparent correlation among the indicators. Therefore, it was difficult to classify the slope SS only using one indicator, and the effect of all indicators should be incorporated for better accuracy.

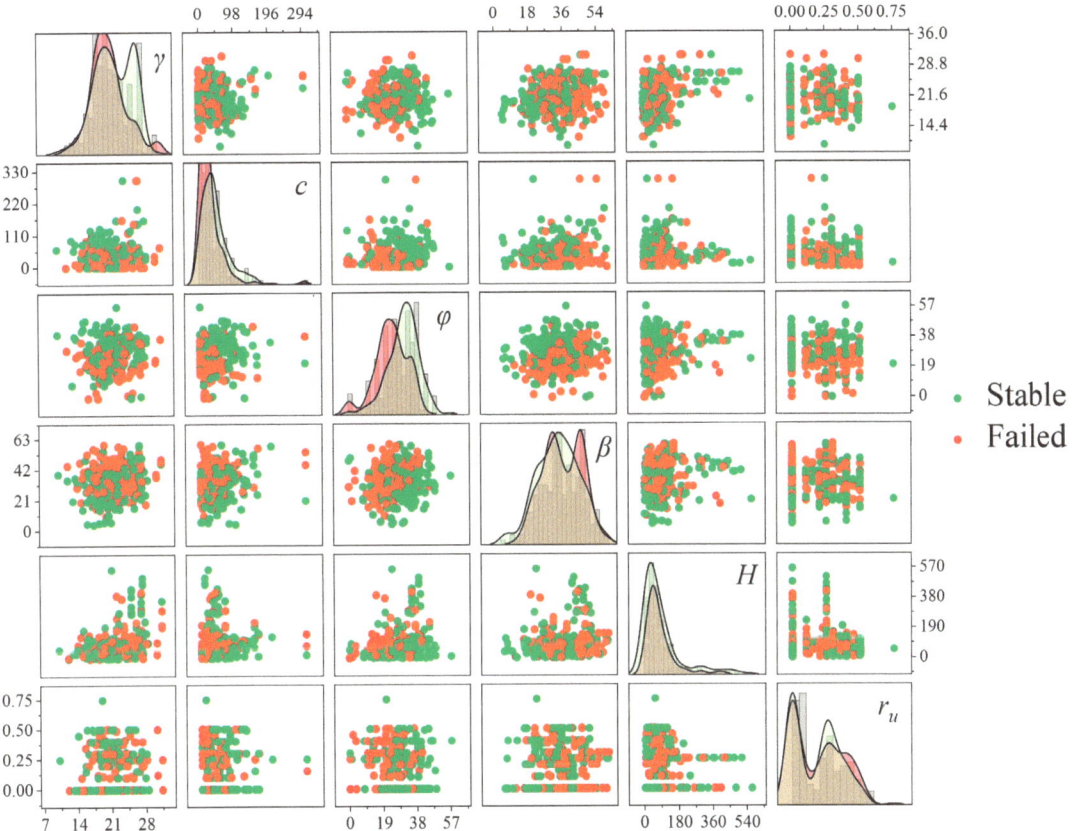

Figure 10. Correlation pair plots of six indicators.

4. Results and Analysis

4.1. Results of Hyperparameters Tuning

The average accuracy of ten-fold CV corresponding to different hyperparameters for k-NN, LR, DT, RF, and RBF-SVM algorithms is shown in Figure 11. According to Figure 11, the overall performance can be observed. With the increase of hyperparameter values, the average accuracy of LR decreased, but the other models had several peaks. Compared with other models, the results of RF were more stable. Based on the best average accuracy of ten-fold CV, the optimal hyperparameter values were determined. The scope, interval, and final optimization results of hyperparameter values are indicated in Table 4.

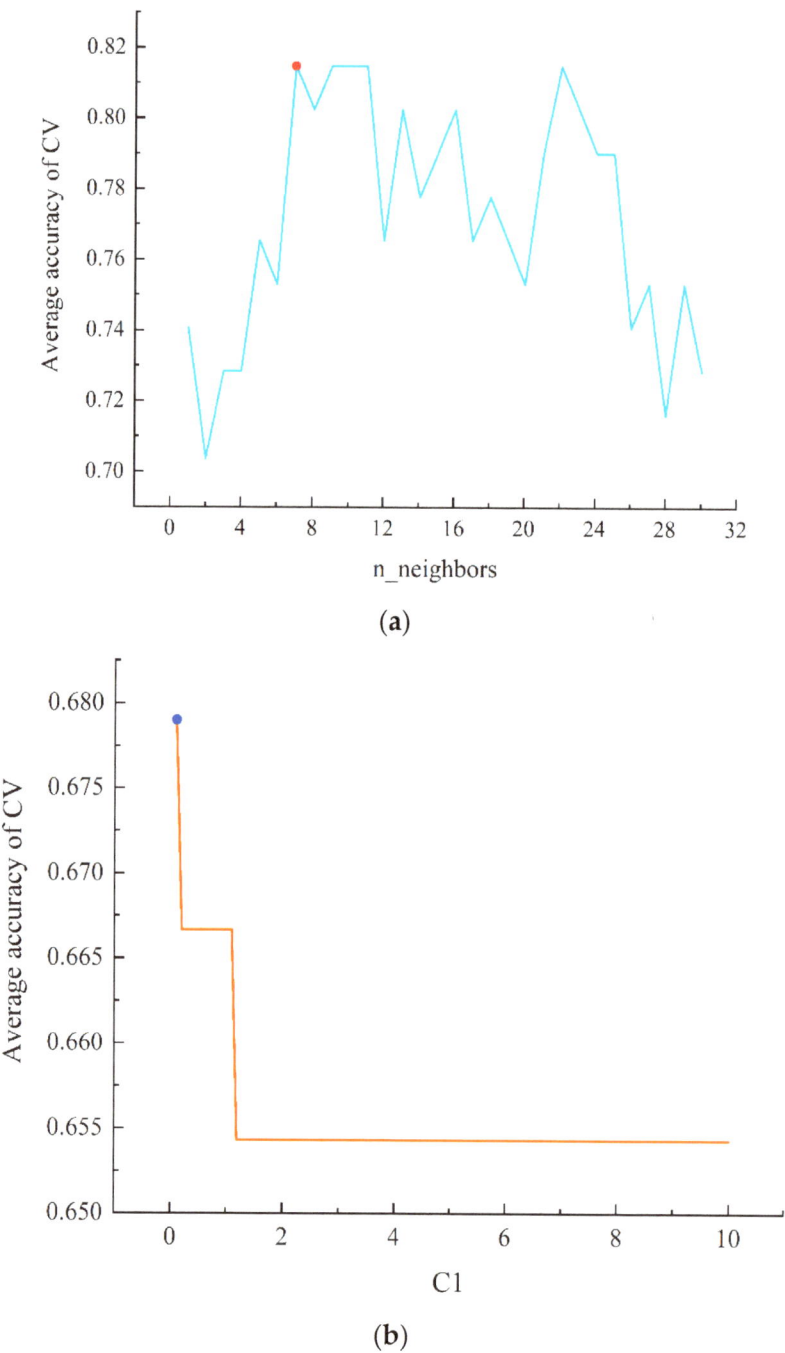

Figure 11. *Cont.*

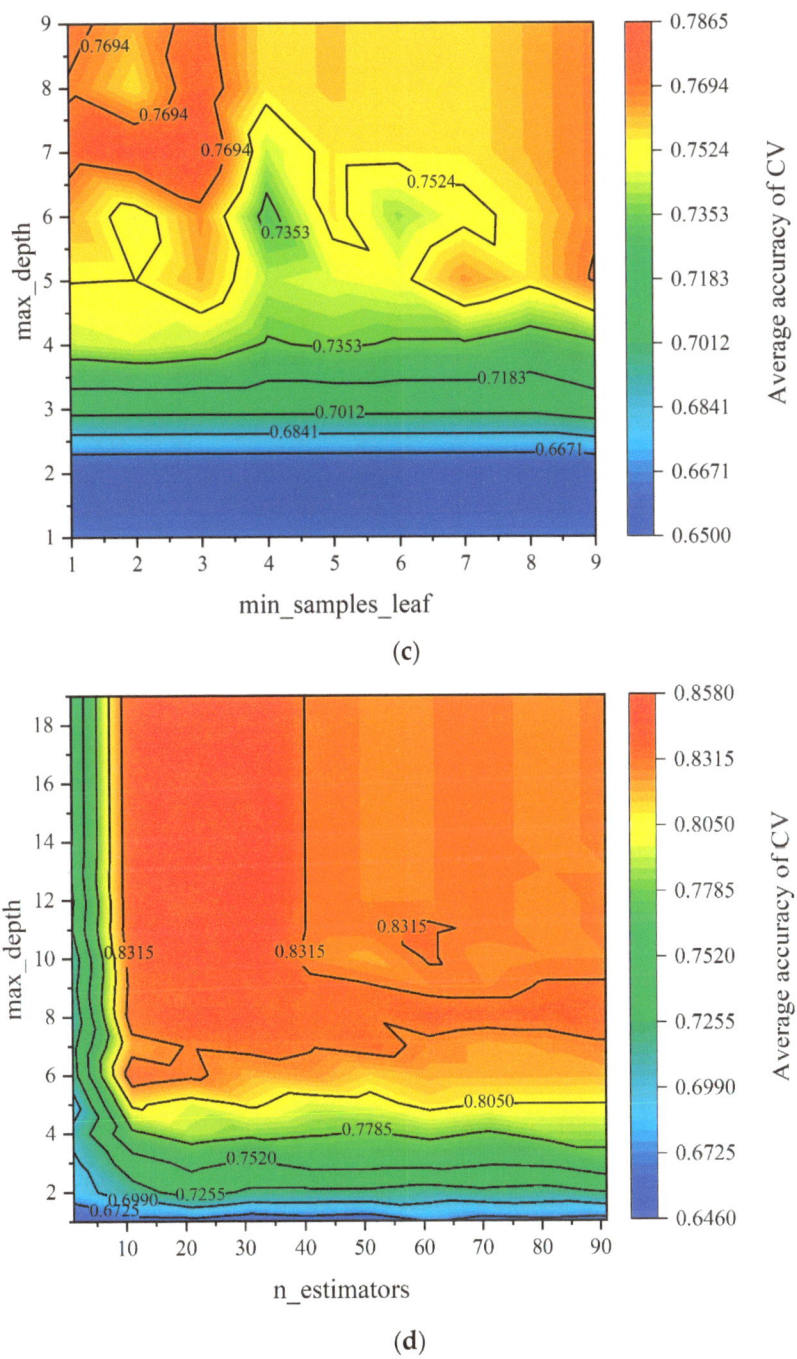

Figure 11. Cont.

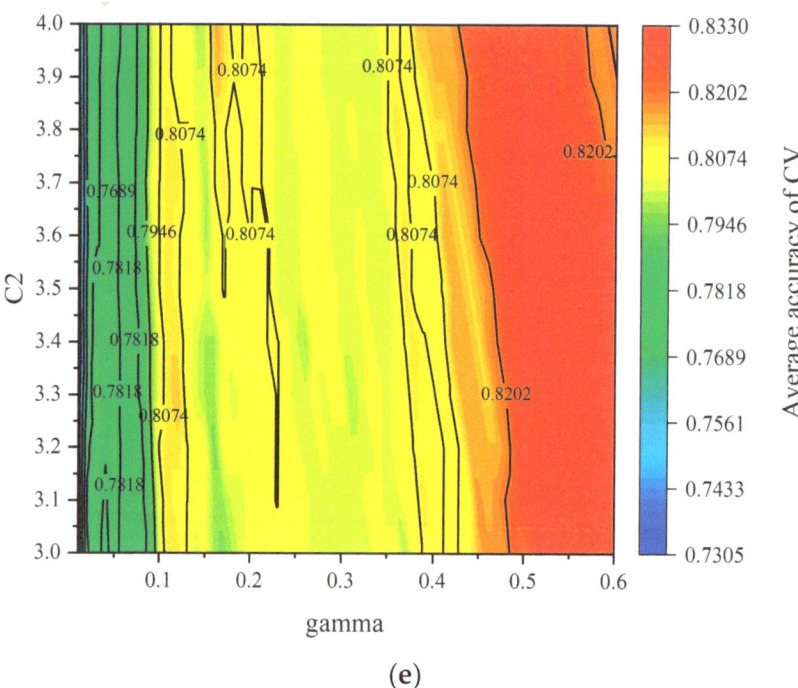

(e)

Figure 11. Grid search of hyperparameters tuning: (**a**) *k*-NN, (**b**) LR, (**c**) DT, (**d**) RF, and (**e**) RBF-SVM.

Table 4. Results of hyperparameters tuning.

ML Algorithms	Hyperparameters	Scope of Values	Interval of Values	Optimal Values
k-NN	n_neighbors	(1, 31)	1	7
LR	Inverse of regularization strength C1	(0.1, 10)	0.1	0.1
DT	max_depth	(1, 10)	1	7
	min_samples_leaf	(1, 10)	1	3
RF	n_estimators	(1, 101)	10	31
	max_depth	(1, 20)	1	11
RBF-SVM	gamma	(0.01, 0.6)	0.01	0.55
	Penalty coefficient C2	(3, 4)	0.1	3.3

4.2. Models Comparison and Evaluation

After the hyperparameters were tuned, these seven ML algorithms were used to predict slope stability based on the test set. The confusion matrix, accuracy, and F_1-score were calculated to compare the performance of each algorithm, which were illustrated in Table 5. It can be observed that $OPF_{k\text{-NN}}$ performed best with the highest accuracy of 0.901, followed by OPF, RF, *k*-NN, RBF-SVM, and DT with an accuracy of 0.876, 0.827, 0.815, 0.802, and 0.765, respectively. LR performed worst with an accuracy of 0.679. Furthermore, the rank was the same when using the F_1-score. Therefore, based on the overall prediction performance, the rank was $OPF_{k\text{-NN}}$ > OPF > RF > *k*-NN > RBF-SVM > DT > LR.

The ROC curves and AUC values of these seven classifiers are presented in Figure 12. It can be seen that the ROC curve of the $OPF_{k\text{-NN}}$ classifier was closer to the left and upper axes than others, indicating better performance. The AUC values of $OPF_{k\text{-NN}}$, RBF-SVM, RF, OPF, *k*-NN, DT, and LR were 0.895, 0.885, 0.876, 0.870, 0.783, and 0.720, respectively. According to the AUC classification criterion mentioned in Section 2.3, only $OPF_{k\text{-NN}}$

performed excellently, RBF-SVM, RF, OPF, and *k*-NN performed well, while DT and LR performed fair.

Table 5. Confusion matrix, accuracy, and F_1-score of the classifiers.

Classifiers	Actual Condition	Predicted Condition		Accuracy	F_1-Score
		Stable	Failed		
OPF$_{k\text{-NN}}$	Stable	37	4	0.901	0.902
	Failed	4	36		
OPF	Stable	38	3	0.876	0.884
	Failed	7	33		
RF	Stable	37	7	0.827	0.841
	Failed	7	30		
k-NN	Stable	36	8	0.815	0.828
	Failed	7	30		
RBF-SVM	Stable	35	9	0.802	0.814
	Failed	7	30		
DT	Stable	33	11	0.765	0.776
	Failed	8	29		
LR	Stable	28	16	0.679	0.683
	Failed	10	27		

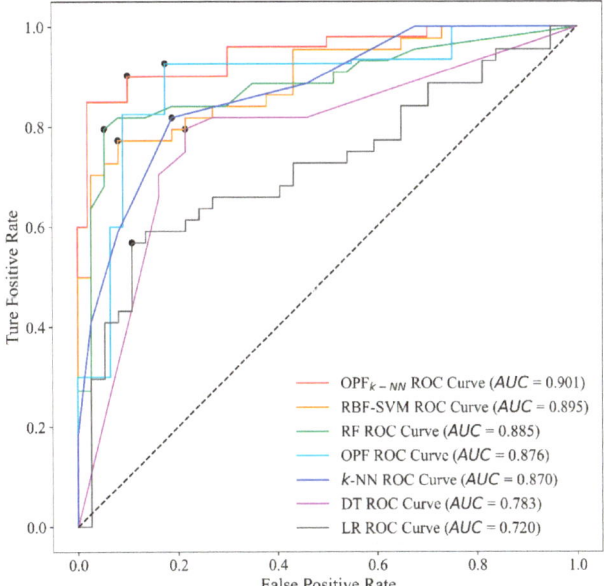

Figure 12. ROC curves and AUC of seven classifiers.

The average computation time for each classifier during the training and testing phases over 20 runs was calculated, as listed in Table 6. The results were presented in the following format: $x \pm y$, where x and y indicated the average time and standard deviation, respectively—noted that the values in bold indicated the minimum time consumed. It can be observed that the *k*-NN took the least time in the training phase, followed by LR, OPF, OPF$_{k\text{-NN}}$, RBF-SVM, and RF. In the testing phase, the time consumed by each classifier was not significantly different, and the difference between the maximum and minimum values was less than 0.2 s. For the total time, the rank was *k*-NN > LR > OPF > OPF$_{k\text{-NN}}$ > DT > RBF-SVM > RF. The total computation time of the OPF$_{k\text{-NN}}$ classifier was less than 1 s.

Table 6. Average computation time of classifiers over 20 runs.

Time	OPF$_{k\text{-NN}}$	OPF	RF	RBF-SVM	DT	LR	k-NN
Train	0.915 ± 0.027	0.322 ± 0.034	117.751 ± 1.163	82.326 ± 1.149	2.162 ± 0.067	0.402 ± 0.035	**0.187 ± 0.011**
Test	0.042 ± 0.002	0.097 ± 0.004	0.055 ± 0.003	0.171 ± 0.005	**0.008 ± 0.001**	**0.008 ± 0.001**	0.011 ± 0.002
Total	0.957 ± 0.026	0.419 ± 0.033	117.806 ± 1.164	82.497 ± 1.149	2.170 ± 0.067	0.410 ± 0.036	**0.198 ± 0.011**

4.3. Relative Importance of Indicators

The relative importance of indicators was significant for the design of support structures in slope engineering. In this study, the relative importance of each indicator was calculated by combining the OPF$_{k\text{-NN}}$ model with the permutation feature importance technique [73]. The permutation feature importance is a model inspection technique available in the Python library "scikit-learn" [54]. Values of indicators were shuffled in turn within the test set, the slope stability prediction results were generated by the OPF$_{k\text{-NN}}$ model, and the accuracy changes were recorded. Then, the prediction accuracy changes of indicators were ranked, and the relative importance was derived. As shown in Figure 13, the slope angle was the most important indicator with an importance value of 30.5%, followed by internal friction angle (22%), cohesion (19.7%), unit weight (12.3%), slope height (7.93%), and pore pressure ratio (7.63%).

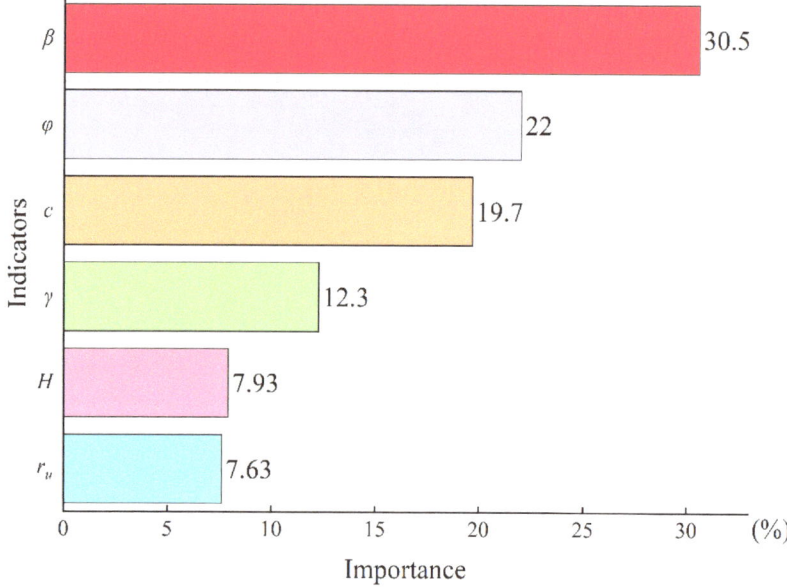

Figure 13. Relative importance of indicators.

5. Discussions

The prediction of failed cases is particularly important, which may lead to the development of slope instability if predicted incorrectly [74]. Therefore, the false positive rate and true negative rate were presented together in Figure 14. It can be seen that the false positive rate and true negative rate of RBF-SVM, k-NN, and RF were the same, and the OPF$_{k\text{-NN}}$ had the largest true negative rate and the lowest false positive rate. From this view, the OPF$_{k\text{-NN}}$ classifier performed better. The reason is that the OPF$_{k\text{-NN}}$ algorithm can effectively process high-dimensional and nonlinear slope data with outliers, improve the data quality of the model in the training phase, and predict the failed slope cases more accurately.

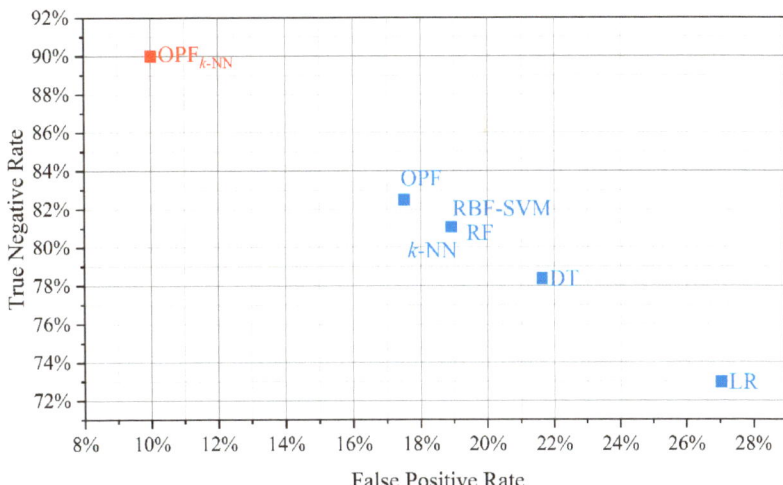

Figure 14. False positive rate and true negative rate of each classifier.

When the trade-off between AUC and the computational burden was considered, the OPF$_{k\text{-NN}}$ classifier was the most prominent because it demonstrated the optimal performance (AUC = 0.901) in less computation time (total time < 1 s) among the seven classifiers. It is worth noting that the OPF$_{k\text{-NN}}$ classifier was pretty much faster than RBF-SVM (86.2 times faster) and RF (123.1 times faster), although the difference in their performance was not significant. Therefore, the OPF$_{k\text{-NN}}$ classifier achieved the best trade-off between performance and efficiency.

According to the importance scores, all indicators were non-negligible for slope stability prediction. The physical–mechanical properties had the greatest influence on the slope stability (φ = 22%, c = 19.7%, γ = 12.3%), followed by the geometrical parameters (β = 30.5%, H = 7.93%). Some measures can be adopted to improve the slope stability from two directions. One is to optimize the slope geometry parameters, especially the slope angle. Another is to improve the physical–mechanical properties by using grouting-reinforcement techniques.

Although the OPF$_{k\text{-NN}}$ approach obtained excellent results in the slope stability prediction, there are also some limitations:

(1) More indicators should be considered. Although the six indicators in this study affect the slope stability significantly, other factors such as excavation, the properties of clay minerals, vegetation coverage, earthquake, and rainfall also have an effect on the slope stability. It is significant to analyze the influences of these indicators on the prediction results;

(2) The dataset is relatively small. The performance of ML algorithms greatly depends on the quantity and quality of data. Although the OPF$_{k\text{-NN}}$ algorithm performs well on this dataset, a better dataset might further improve the predictive performance. Therefore, it is necessary to build a larger slope database;

(3) Slopes are typically composed of multiple layers of various geotechnical materials whose properties and spatial distribution can significantly affect slope stability. As the number of slope failure cases increases, a comprehensive and diverse slope dataset should be expanded in future work. Such efforts are crucial for advancing the field of geotechnical engineering and ensuring the safety of human lives and infrastructure;

(4) The safety factor of slope stability can reflect the percentage of slope instability, and the slope stability analysis can be better considered a regression problem. Therefore, it is necessary to compile relevant data and develop relevant ML models for slope FOS value estimation in future work.

6. Engineering Application

In order to further verify the reliability of the proposed $OPF_{k\text{-NN}}$ model, it was necessary to apply it to evaluate the stability of engineering slopes. For this, eight typical slopes were collected from the Jing-xin expressway in Hebei Province, China, where landslides frequently occurred [75].

The FOS values of these eight slopes and the estimation results of the $OPF_{k\text{-NN}}$ model were recorded in Table 7. It can be seen that the overall prediction performance of the $OPF_{k\text{-NN}}$ model was consistent with the FOS values of the slopes.

Table 7. Predictive results of $OPF_{k\text{-NN}}$ model on engineering slopes.

Slopes	γ (kN/m^3)	c (kPa)	φ (°)	β (°)	H (m)	r_u	FOS	Status
1	22.4	20.0	27.0	30.0	54.0	0.12	1.208	Stable
2	21.4	31.5	42.0	34.0	18.0	0.23	2.448	Stable
3	19.0	50.0	32.0	42.0	26.0	0.17	1.786	Stable
4	19.6	17.8	29.2	41.2	50.0	0.31	0.979	Failed
5	20.2	16.7	22.3	42.4	26.6	0.47	0.869	Failed
6	20.4	25.0	20.4	35.0	65.9	0.42	0.833	Failed
7	20.0	20.0	36.0	45.0	50.0	0.14	1.102	Stable
8	23.0	18.3	25.2	39.6	61.2	0.30	0.824	Failed

7. Conclusions

Slope stability prediction is a crucial task in geotechnical engineering. This study investigated the performance of the $OPF_{k\text{-NN}}$ algorithm for the stability prediction of slopes. A total of 404 historical slope cases with failure risk from various countries were collected after considering the slope damage mechanism and geological conditions simultaneously. The $OPF_{k\text{-NN}}$, OPF, RBF-SVM, RF, k-NN, DT, and LR were used to evaluate and compare the predictive performance. To avoid the risk of overfitting or selection bias, ten-fold CV and grid search methods were selected to tune the hyperparameters. Overall, the prediction results of the $OPF_{k\text{-NN}}$ algorithm were better and more reliable, and its prediction accuracy and F_1-score were 0.901 and 0.902, respectively. According to the ROC curves and AUC values, the performance rank of the seven classifiers was $OPF_{k\text{-NN}}$ > RBF-SVM > RF > OPF > k-NN > DT > LR. In addition, the $OPF_{k\text{-NN}}$ achieved the highest TNR and the lowest FPR, which indicated that it could predict failed slope cases better. After considering the total calculation time, the $OPF_{k\text{-NN}}$ classifier achieved the optimal trade-off between performance and efficiency. Based on the importance scores of indicators, the slope angle was the most influential indicator on prediction results. Furthermore, the engineering application results showed that the overall predictive performance of the $OPF_{k\text{-NN}}$ model was consistent with the FOS value of engineering slopes.

In the future, more parameters such as excavation, the properties of clay minerals, geological formation, vegetation coverage, earthquake, and rainfall can be considered so that the feasibility of the $OPF_{k\text{-NN}}$ classifier can be further validated using more comprehensive and diverse slope datasets. In addition, the proposed methodology can be recommended for the application of other mining and geotechnical engineering projects, such as rockburst risk prediction and pillar stability prediction.

Author Contributions: Conceptualization, L.L.; methodology, L.L.; software, L.L.; validation, W.L. and G.Z.; formal analysis, L.L.; investigation, L.L.; resources, L.L.; data curation, L.L.; writing—original draft preparation, L.L.; writing—review and editing, W.L.; visualization, W.L.; supervision, G.Z.; project administration, G.Z.; funding acquisition, G.Z. and W.L. All authors have read and agreed to the published version of the manuscript.

Funding: This research was funded by the National Key Research and Development Program of China (2018YFC0604606) and the National Natural Science Foundation of China (52204117).

Data Availability Statement: The data presented in this study are available upon request from the corresponding author.

Conflicts of Interest: The authors declare no conflict of interest.

Nomenclature

Abbreviation	Full Name
AE	Acoustic emissions
LEM	Limit equilibrium method
SRM	Strength reduction method
FOS	Factor of safety
FEM	Finite element method
ML	Machine learning
RBF-SVM	Radial basis function support vector machine
DT	Decision trees
OPF	Optimum-path forest
k-NN	k-nearest neighbors
RF	Random forest
LR	Logistic regression
OPT	Optimal path tree
CV	Cross-validation
TP	True positive
FP	False positive
TN	True negative
FN	False negative
TNR	True negative rate
FPR	False positive rate
AUC	Area under the curve
ROC	Receiver operating characteristic

Appendix A. Database of Slope Cases

No.	Location	γ (kN/m^3)	c (kPa)	φ (°)	β (°)	H (m)	r_u	Status	Instability Type
1	Congress street, open cut slope, Chicago, USA	18.68	26.34	15	35	8.23	0	Failed	Circular
2	Brightlingsea slide, UK	16.5	11.49	0	30	3.66	0	Failed	Circular
3	Unknown	18.84	14.36	25	20	30.5	0	Stable	-
4	Unknown	18.84	57.46	20	20	30.5	0	Stable	-
5	Case 1: open pit iron ore mine, India	28.44	29.42	35	35	100	0	Stable	-
6	Case 2: open pit iron ore mine, India	28.44	39.23	38	35	100	0	Stable	-
7	Open pit chromite mine, Orissa, India	20.6	16.28	26.5	30	40	0	Failed	Circular
8	Sarukuygi landslide, Japan	14.8	0	17	20	50	0	Failed	Circular
9	Open pit iron ore mine, Goa, India	14	11.97	26	30	88	0	Failed	Circular
10	Mercoirol open pit coal mine, France	25	120	45	53	120	0	Stable	-
11	Marquesade open pit iron ore mine, Spain	26	150.05	45	50	200	0	Stable	-
12	Unknown	18.5	25	0	30	6	0	Failed	Circular
13	Unknown	18.5	12	0	30	6	0	Failed	Circular
14	Case 1: Highvale coal mine, Alberta, Canada	22.4	10	35	30	10	0	Stable	-
15	Case 2: Highvale coal mine, Alberta, Canada	21.4	10	30.34	30	20	0	Stable	-
16	Case 1: open pit coal mine, Newcastle coalfield, Australia	22	20	36	45	50	0	Failed	Circular
17	Case 2: open pit coal mine, Newcastle coalfield, Australia	22	0	36	45	50	0	Failed	Circular
18	Unknown	12	0	30	35	4	0	Stable	-

No.	Location	γ (kN/m^3)	c (kPa)	φ (°)	β (°)	H (m)	r_u	Status	Instability Type
19	Unknown	12	0	30	45	8	0	Failed	Circular
20	Pima open pit mine, Arizona, USA	23.47	0	32	37	214	0	Failed	Circular
21	Case 1: Wyoming, USA	16	70	20	40	115	0	Failed	Circular
22	Seven Sisters Landslide, UK	20.41	24.9	13	22	10.67	0.35	Stable	-
23	Case 1: The Northolt slide, UK	19.63	11.97	20	22	12.19	0.405	Failed	Circular
24	Selset Landslide, Yorkshire, UK	21.82	8.62	32	28	12.8	0.49	Failed	Circular
25	Saskatchewan dam, Canada	20.41	33.52	11	16	45.72	0.2	Failed	Circular
26	Case 2: The Northolt slide, UK	18.84	15.32	30	25	10.67	0.38	Stable	-
27	Sudbury slide, UK	18.84	0	20	20	7.62	0.45	Failed	Circular
28	Folkstone Warren slide, Kent, UK	21.43	0	20	20	61	0.5	Failed	Circular
29	River bank side, Alberta, Canada	19.06	11.71	28	35	21	0.11	Failed	Circular
30	Unknown	18.84	14.36	25	20	30.5	0.45	Failed	Circular
31	Unknown	21.51	6.94	30	31	76.81	0.38	Failed	Circular
32	Case 2: open pit iron ore mine, Goa, India	14	11.97	26	30	88	0.45	Failed	Circular
33	Athens slope, Greece	18	24	30.15	45	20	0.12	Failed	Circular
34	Open pit coal mine Allori coalfield, Italy	23	0	20	20	100	0.3	Failed	Circular
35	Case 1: open pit coal mine, Alberta, Canada	22.4	100	45	45	15	0.25	Stable	-
36	Case 2: open pit coal mine, Alberta, Canada	22.4	10	35	45	10	0.4	Failed	Circular
37	Case 3: open pit coal mine, Newcastle coalfield, Australia	20	20	36	45	50	0.25	Failed	Circular
38	Case 4: open pit coal mine, Newcastle coalfield, Australia	20	20	36	45	50	0.5	Failed	Circular
39	Case 5: open pit coal mine, Newcastle coalfield, Australia	20	0	36	45	50	0.25	Failed	Circular
40	Case 6: open pit coal mine, Newcastle coalfield, Australia	20	0	36	45	50	0.5	Failed	Circular
41	Case 1: Harbour slope, Newcastle, Australia	22	0	40	33	8	0.35	Stable	-
42	Case 2: Harbour slope, Newcastle, Australia	24	0	40	33	8	0.3	Stable	-
43	Case 3: Harbour slope, Newcastle, Australia	20	0	24.5	20	8	0.35	Stable	-
44	Case 4: Harbour slope, Newcastle, Australia	18	5	30	20	8	0.3	Stable	-
45	Unknown	27	40	35	47.1	292	0	Failed	Circular
46	Unknown	25	46	35	50	284	0	Stable	-
47	Unknown	31.3	68	37	46	366	0	Failed	Circular
48	Unknown	25	46	36	44.5	299	0	Stable	-
49	Unknown	27.3	10	39	40	480	0	Stable	-
50	Unknown	25	46	35	46	393	0	Stable	-
51	Unknown	25	48	40	49	330	0	Stable	-
52	Unknown	31.3	68.6	37	47	305	0.25	Failed	Circular
53	Unknown	25	55	36	45.5	299	0.25	Stable	-
54	Unknown	31.3	68	37	47	213	0.25	Failed	Circular
55	Three Gorges hydropower project, China	26.49	150	33	45	73	0.15	Stable	-
56	Three Gorges hydropower project, China	26.7	150	33	50	130	0.25	Stable	-
57	Three Gorges hydropower project, China	26.89	150	33	52	120	0.25	Stable	-
58	Three Gorges hydropower project, China	26.57	300	38.7	45.3	80	0.15	Failed	Unknown

No.	Location	γ (kN/m³)	c (kPa)	φ (°)	β (°)	H (m)	r_u	Status	Instability Type
59	Three Gorges hydropower project, China	26.78	300	38.7	54	155	0.25	Failed	Unknown
60	Three Gorges hydropower project, China	26.81	200	35	58	138	0.25	Stable	Unknown
61	Three Gorges hydropower project, China	26.43	50	26.6	40	92.2	0.15	Stable	Unknown
62	Three Gorges hydropower project, China	26.69	50	26.6	50	170	0.25	Stable	Unknown
63	Three Gorges hydropower project, China	26.81	60	28.8	59	108	0.25	Stable	Unknown
64	Dingjiahe phosphorus mine, China	27.8	27.8	27	41	236	0.1	Stable	-
65	Guilin-Liuzhou highway, China	27.1	22	18.6	25.6	100	0.19	Failed	Unknown
66	Xiaolangdi reservoir, China	22.3	0	40	26.5	78	0.25	Stable	-
67	Jingzhumiao reservoir, China	18.6	0	32	26.5	46	0.25	Stable	-
68	Jingzhumiao reservoir, China	18.6	0	32	21.8	46	0.25	Stable	-
69	Yuecheng reservoir, China	18.8	9.8	21	19.29	39	0.25	Failed	Unknown
70	Yuecheng reservoir, China	21.2	0	35	18.43	73	0.25	Stable	-
71	Gushan reservoir, China	17.2	10	24.25	17.07	38	0.4	Stable	-
72	Laobu reservoir, China	19	11.9	20.4	21.04	54	0.75	Stable	-
73	Wenyuhe reservoir, China	18	5	26.5	15.52	53	0.4	Failed	Unknown
74	Wenyuhe reservoir, China	18	5	22	15.52	53	0.4	Failed	Unknown
75	Hongwuyi reservoir, China	17.4	20	24	18.43	51	0.4	Failed	Unknown
76	Hongwuyi reservoir, China	17.8	21.2	13.92	18.43	51	0.4	Stable	-
77	Lingli reservoir, China	18.8	8	26	21.8	40	0.4	Failed	Unknown
78	Lingli reservoir, China	18	21	21.33	21.8	40	0.4	Failed	Unknown
79	Zhejiang sea wall, China	17.6	10	16	21.8	9	0.4	Stable	-
80	Zhejiang sea wall, China	17.6	10	8	21.8	9	0.4	Stable	-
81	Hunan anxiang reservoir, China	17.4	14.95	21.2	45	15	0.4	Failed	Unknown
82	A reservoir dam in Jiangxi, China	18.82	25	14.6	20.32	50	0.4	Failed	Unknown
83	Qing River area landslide, China	22	29	15	18	400	0	Failed	Circular
84	Qing River area landslide, China	23	24	19.8	23	380	0	Failed	Circular
85	Qing River area landslide, China	22	40	30	30	196	0	Stable	-
86	Qing River area landslide, China	22.54	29.4	20	24	210	0	Stable	-
87	Qing River area landslide, China	22	21	23	30	257	0	Failed	Circular
88	Qing River area landslide, China	23.5	10	27	26	190	0	Failed	Circular
89	Qing River area landslide, China	22.5	18	20	20	290	0	Stable	-
90	Qing River area landslide, China	22.5	20	16	25	220	0	Stable	-
91	Qing River area landslide, China	21	20	24	21	565	0	Stable	-
92	Guzhang gaofeng slope, China	27	27.3	29.1	35	150	0.26	Failed	Circular
93	Guzhang gaofeng slope, China	27	27.3	29.1	37	184	0.22	Failed	Circular
94	Guzhang gaofeng slope, China	27	27.3	29.1	34	126.5	0.3	Failed	Circular
95	Chengmenshan open pit copper mine, China	25	46	35	50	285	0.25	Stable	-
96	Baijiagou earth slope, China	20.45	16	15	30	36	0.25	Stable	-
97	Jingping first stage hydropower station, China	27	70	22.8	45	60	0.32	Stable	-
98	Left bank accumulation body of Xiaodongjiang hydropower station, China	22	10	35	45	10	0.403	Failed	Unknown
99	Longxi landslide of Longyangxia hydropower Station, China	20	20	36	45	30	0.503	Failed	Unknown
100	Chana landslide of Longyangxia hydropower Station, China	20	0.1	36	45	50	0.25	Failed	Unknown
101	Canal slope of Baoji gorge with Wei River diversion project, China	20	0.1	36	45	50	0.503	Failed	Unknown

No.	Location	γ (kN/m³)	c (kPa)	φ (°)	β (°)	H (m)	r_u	Status	Instability Type
102	Yellowstone landslide in the Three Gorges of the Yangtze River, China	22	0	40	33	8	0.393	Stable	-
103	Baiyian landslide in the Three Gorges reservoir area, China	24	0	40	33	8	0.303	Stable	-
104	Baihuanping landslide in the Three Gorges reservoir area, China	20	0	24.5	20	8	0.35	Stable	-
105	Gaojiazui landslide in the Three Gorges reservoir area, China	18	0	30	33	8	0.303	Stable	-
106	Songshan ancient landslide at Lechangxia hydropower station, China	27	43	35	43	420	0.25	Failed	Unknown
107	Back channel landslide in the Three Gorges reservoir area, China	27	50	40	42	407	0.25	Stable	-
108	Jipazi landslide in the Three Gorges reservoir area, China	27	35	35	42	359	0.25	Stable	-
109	Jiuxianping Landslide in the Three Gorges reservoir area, China	27	37.5	35	37.8	320	0.25	Stable	-
110	Heishe landslide, China	27	32	33	42.6	301	0.25	Failed	Unknown
111	Liujiawuchang landslide in the Three Gorges reservoir area, China	27	32	33	42.2	289	0.25	Stable	-
112	Majiaba landslide in the Three Gorges Reservoir Area, China	27.3	14	31	41	110	0.25	Stable	-
113	Sandengzi landslide in the Three Gorges Reservoir Area, China	27.3	31.5	29.703	41	135	0.25	Stable	-
114	Yaqianwan landslide in the Three Gorges Reservoir Area, China	27.3	16.8	28	50	90.5	0.25	Stable	-
115	No. 3 landslide of Sanbanxi hydropower station, China	27.3	36	1	50	92	0.25	Stable	-
116	Shijiapo landslide, China	27.3	10	39	41	511	0.25	Stable	-
117	Tanggudong landslide, China	27.3	10	39	40	470	0.25	Stable	-
118	Tianbao landslide, China	25	46	35	47	443	0.25	Stable	-
119	Shipingtai landslide of Xiaoxi hydropower station, China	25	46	35	44	435	0.25	Stable	-
120	Dongyemiao landslide, China	25	46	35	46	432	0.25	Stable	-
121	Hongtupo landslide, China	26	150	45	30	230	0.25	Failed	Unknown
122	Lianziya landslide in the Three Gorges reservoir area, China	18.5	25	0	30	6.003	0.25	Failed	Unknown
123	No. 6 landslide of Jishixia hydropower station, China	18.5	12	0	30	6.003	0.25	Failed	Unknown
124	Unknown	21.4	10	30.343	30	20	0.25	Stable	-
125	No. 1 landslide of Jishixia hydropower station, China	22	20	36	45	50	0	Failed	Unknown
126	Daxi landslide, China	22	0	36	45	50	0	Failed	Unknown
127	Right Bank landslide of Zihong reservoir, China	12	0	30	35	4	0	Stable	-
128	Zhongyangcun landslide, China	12	0	30	45	8	0	Failed	Unknown
129	Yangdagou landslide of Xunyang hydropower station, China	31.3	68	37	49	200.5	0.25	Failed	Unknown
130	Unknown	20	20	36	45	50	0.29	Failed	Unknown
131	Maidipo Landslide, China	19.6	21.8	29.5	37.8	40.3	0.25	Stable	-
132	Maidipo Landslide, China	23.1	25.2	29.2	36.5	61.9	0.4	Stable	-
133	Shaling Landslide, China	23.8	31	38.7	47.5	23.5	0.31	Stable	-
134	Niugunhan Landslide, China	22.3	20.1	31	40.2	88	0.19	Stable	-
135	Xieliupo Landslide, China	23.5	25	20	49.1	115	0.41	Stable	-
136	Zhaojiatang Landslide, China	23	20	20.3	46.2	40.3	0.25	Stable	-
137	Touzhaigou Landslide, China	21.5	15	29	41.5	123.6	0.36	Stable	-

No.	Location	γ (kN/m^3)	c (kPa)	φ (°)	β (°)	H (m)	r_u	Status	Instability Type
138	Shenzhen reservoir diversion tunnel landslide, China	23.4	15	38.5	30.3	45.2	0.28	Failed	Unknown
139	Taipingyi hydropower station diversion tunnel landslide, China	19.6	17.8	29.2	46.8	201.2	0.37	Stable	-
140	Bawangshan Landslide, China	22.1	24.2	39.7	45.8	49.5	0.21	Stable	-
141	Unknown	18.9	17.5	31	33.5	90.5	0.26	Stable	Circular
142	Unknown	20.2	16.7	22.3	42.4	26.6	0.25	Stable	Circular
143	Unknown	21.5	14	19.3	35	65.9	0.32	Stable	Circular
144	KSH Slope in Tailie elementary school, China	20	8	20	10	10	0	Failed	Unknown
145	KSH Slope on the right of Circle E of Tailie Overpass, China	27.3	37.3	31	30	30	0	Stable	-
146	KSH Landslide on the left of K71 + 625~K71 + 700, China	20.6	26.31	22	25	35	0	Failed	Unknown
147	KSH Slope of Pingxite Bridge, China	21.6	6.5	19	40	50	0	Failed	Unknown
148	KSH Slope on the right of K76 + 085~K76 + 200, China	22.4	28.9	24	28	35	0	Failed	Unknown
149	KSH Slope on the left of K77 + 920~K78 + 100, China	23.2	31.2	23	30	33	0	Failed	Unknown
150	KSH Slope on the left of K79 + 165~K79 + 300, China	26.8	37.5	32	30	26	0	Stable	-
151	KSH Slope on the right of K79 + 920~K80 + 035, China	27.4	38.1	31	25	42	0	Stable	-
152	KSH Landslide on the right of ZAK0 + 315~ZAK0 + 407, China	21.8	32.7	27	50	50	0	Failed	Unknown
153	KSH Slope on the left of K83 + 260~K83 + 360, China	21.8	27.6	25	35	60	0	Failed	Unknown
154	KSH Slope on the right of K88 + 300~K88 + 420, China	26.5	35.4	32	30	21	0	Stable	-
155	KSH Slope on the right of K88 + 700~K88 + 876, China	26.5	36.1	31	35	39	0	Stable	-
156	KSH Slope on the right of K89 + 730~K89 + 841, China	27	35.8	32	30	69	0	Stable	-
157	KSH Slope on the right of K90 + 225~K90 + 345, China	27	38.4	33	25	22	0	Stable	-
158	KSH Slope on the right of K90 + 225~K90 + 345, China	21.4	28.8	20	50	52	0	Failed	Unknown
159	KSH Slope on the left of K99 + 120~K99 + 260, China	26	42.4	37	38	55	0	Stable	-
160	KSH Slope on the left of K100 + 280~K100 + 410, China	26	39.4	36	25	30	0	Stable	-
161	KSH Slope on the left of K100 + 615~K100 + 915, China	25.6	38.8	36	25	26	0	Stable	-
162	KSH Landslide on the left of K103 + 330~K103 + 450, China	20	30.3	25	45	53	0	Failed	Unknown
163	KSH Landslide on the left of K103 + 330~K103 + 450, China	25.8	34.7	33	30	50	0	Stable	-
164	KSH Landslide on the left of K104 + 892~K105 + 052, China	21.8	28.8	26	35	99	0	Failed	Unknown
165	KSH Landslide on the left of K105 + 260~K105 + 330, China	21.8	31.2	25	30	60	0	Failed	Unknown
166	KSH Slope on the left of K106 + 268~K106 + 577, China	24	41.5	36	30	51	0	Stable	-
167	KSH Slope on the left of K106 + 992~K107 + 085, China	24	40.8	35	35	50	0	Stable	-

No.	Location	γ (kN/m^3)	c (kPa)	φ (°)	β (°)	H (m)	r_u	Status	Instability Type
168	KSH Landslide on the left of K107 + 856~K107 + 968, China	20.6	27.8	27	35	70	0	Failed	Unknown
169	KSH Landslide on the left of K108 + 960~K109 + 010, China	20.6	32.4	26	35	55	0	Failed	-
170	KSH Landslide on the left of K108 + 960~K109 + 010, China	25.8	38.2	33	27	40	0	Stable	Unknown
171	KSH Landslide on the left of K108 + 960~K109 + 010, China	25.8	39.4	33	25	45	0	Stable	Unknown
172	KSH Landslide on the left of K110 + 421~K110 + 500, China	21.1	33.5	28	40	31	0	Failed	-
173	KSH Landslide on the left of K110 + 980~K110 + 240, China	21.1	34.2	26	30	75	0	Failed	-
174	KSH Slope on the right of K112 + 720~K112 + 815, China	26.6	42.4	37	25	52	0	Stable	Unknown
175	KSH Slope on the left of K113 + 500~K113 + 580, China	26.6	44.1	38	35	42	0	Stable	Unknown
176	KSH Slope on the left of K113 + 500~K113 + 580, China	26.6	40.7	35	35	60	0	Stable	Unknown
177	KSH Slope on the left of K114 + 224~K114 + 258, China	25.8	41.2	35	30	40	0	Stable	Unknown
178	KSH Slope on the left of K117 + 200~K117 + 412, China	25.8	43.3	37	30	33	0	Stable	Unknown
179	KSH Front slope of tunnel in Songjieya K122 + 310, China	21.7	32	27	45	60	0	Failed	-
180	KSH Landslide on the right of K122 + 350~K122 + 455, China	20.6	28.5	27	40	65	0	Failed	-
181	KSH Landslide on the left of K127 + 440~K127 + 590, China	21.5	29.8	26	40	70	0	Failed	-
182	KSH Landslide on the left of K127 + 440~K127 + 590, China	26.5	42.9	38	34	36	0	Stable	Unknown
183	KSH Landslide on the left of K137 + 650~K137 + 730, China	20.8	15.6	20	30	45	0	Failed	-
184	KSH Landslide on the left of K138 + 624~K138 + 797, China	20.8	14.8	21	30	40	0	Failed	-
185	KSH Landslide on the right of K75 + 760~K76 + 000, China	19.6	29.6	23	40	58	0	Failed	-
186	KSH Slope on the right of ZBK0 + 000~ZBK0 + 185, China	25.4	33	33	20	35	0	Failed	-
187	KSH Landslide on the left of K84 + 602~K85 + 185, China	22.4	29.3	26	50	50	0	Failed	Unknown
188	KSH Slope on the right of K91 + 614~K91 + 660, China	26.2	41.5	36	35	30	0	Stable	-
189	KSH Slope on the right of K91 + 720~K91 + 771, China	26.2	42.3	36	23	36	0	Stable	-
190	KSH Slope on the left of K100 + 950~K101 + 300, China	25.6	39.8	36	30	32	0	Stable	-
191	KSH Slope on the left of K102 + 691~K102 + 880, China	25.6	36.8	34	35	60	0	Stable	-
192	KSH Slope on the right of K118 + 360~K118 + 549, China	26.2	42.8	37	30	37	0	Stable	-
193	KSH Slope on the right of K119 + 823~K119 + 951, China	26.2	43.8	38	35	68	0	Stable	-
194	KSH Landslide on the right of K124 + 340~K124 + 562, China	20.6	32.4	26	30	42	0	Failed	Unknown
195	KSH Slope on the right of K131 + 280~K131 + 380, China	26.5	41.8	36	42	54	0	Stable	-

No.	Location	γ (kN/m³)	c (kPa)	φ (°)	β (°)	H (m)	r_u	Status	Instability Type
196	KSH Landslide on the left of K138 + 840~K138 + 930, China	20.8	15.4	21	30	53	0	Failed	Unknown
197	Unknown	17.98	4.95	30.02	19.98	8	0.3	Stable	-
198	Unknown	21.47	6.9	30.02	31.01	76.8	0.38	Failed	Circular
199	Unknown	21.78	8.55	32	27.98	12.8	0.49	Failed	Circular
200	Unknown	21.4	10	30.34	30	20	0	Stable	-
201	Unknown	21.36	10.05	30.33	30	20	0	Stable	-
202	Unknown	19.97	10.05	28.98	34.03	6	0.3	Stable	-
203	Unknown	22.38	10.05	35.01	30	10	0	Stable	-
204	Unknown	22.38	10.05	35.01	45	10	0.4	Failed	Circular
205	Unknown	19.08	10.05	9.99	25.02	50	0.4	Failed	Circular
206	Unknown	19.08	10.05	19.98	30	50	0.4	Failed	Circular
207	Unknown	18.83	10.35	21.29	34.03	37	0.3	Failed	Circular
208	Unknown	16.47	11.55	0	30	3.6	0	Failed	Circular
209	Unknown	19.03	11.7	27.99	34.98	21	0.11	Failed	Circular
210	Unknown	19.06	11.71	28	35	21	0.11	Failed	Circular
211	Unknown	19.6	12	19.98	22	12.2	0.41	Failed	Circular
212	Unknown	13.97	12	26.01	30	88	0	Failed	Circular
213	Unknown	18.46	12	0	30	6	0	Failed	Circular
214	Unknown	13.97	12	26.01	30	88	0.45	Failed	Circular
215	Unknown	18.84	14.36	25	20.3	50	0.45	Failed	Circular
216	Unknown	18.8	14.4	25.02	19.98	30.6	0	Stable	-
217	Unknown	18.8	14.4	25.02	19.98	30.6	0.45	Failed	Circular
218	Unknown	18.8	15.31	30.02	25.02	10.6	0.38	Stable	-
219	Unknown	20.56	16.21	26.51	30	40	0	Failed	Circular
220	Unknown	27.3	16.8	28	50	90.5	0.25	Stable	-
221	Unknown	27	16.8	28	50	90.5	0.25	Stable	-
222	Unknown	20.96	19.96	40.01	40.02	12	0	Stable	-
223	Unknown	21.98	19.96	36	45	50	0	Failed	Circular
224	Unknown	19.97	19.96	36	45	50	0.25	Failed	Circular
225	Unknown	19.97	19.96	36	45	50	0.5	Failed	Circular
226	Unknown	18.77	19.96	9.99	25.02	50	0.3	Failed	Circular
227	Unknown	18.77	19.96	19.98	30	50	0.3	Failed	Circular
228	Unknown	21.98	19.96	22.01	19.98	180	0.1	Failed	Circular
229	Unknown	22	20	36	45	50	0	Failed	Circular
230	Unknown	18	24	30.15	45	20	0.12	Failed	Circular
231	Unknown	18.83	24.76	21.29	29.2	37	0.5	Failed	Circular
232	Unknown	18.77	25.06	19.98	30	50	0.2	Failed	Circular
233	Unknown	18.77	25.06	9.99	25.02	50	0.2	Failed	Circular
234	Unknown	27.3	26	31	50	92	0.25	Stable	-
235	Unknown	20.96	30.01	35.01	40.02	12	0.4	Stable	-
236	Unknown	18.97	30.01	35.01	34.98	11	0.2	Stable	-
237	Unknown	27	32	33	42.4	289	0.25	Stable	-
238	Unknown	20.39	33.46	10.98	16.01	45.8	0.2	Failed	Circular
239	Unknown	20.96	34.96	27.99	40.02	12	0.5	Stable	-
240	Unknown	27	40	35	43	420	0.25	Failed	Circular
241	Unknown	19.97	40.06	30.02	30	15	0.3	Stable	-
242	Unknown	19.97	40.06	40.01	40.02	10	0.2	Stable	-
243	Unknown	20.96	45.02	25.02	49.03	12	0.3	Stable	-
244	Unknown	17.98	45.02	25.02	25.02	14	0.3	Stable	-
245	Unknown	26.7	50	26.6	50	170	0.25	Stable	-
246	Unknown	18.8	57.47	19.98	19.98	30.6	0	Stable	-
247	Unknown	26.8	60	28.8	59	108	0.25	Stable	-
248	Unknown	31.3	68	37	47	213	0.25	Failed	Circular
249	Unknown	31.3	68	37	46	366	0.25	Stable	-
250	Unknown	31.3	68.6	37	47	305	0.25	Failed	Circular

No.	Location	γ (kN/m³)	c (kPa)	φ (°)	β (°)	H (m)	r_u	Status	Instability Type
251	Unknown	15.99	70.07	19.98	40.02	115	0	Failed	Circular
252	Unknown	22.38	99.93	45	45	15	0.25	Stable	-
253	Unknown	19.8	10	8	30	10	0.25	Stable	-
254	Unknown	19.63	11.97	20	22	21.19	0.4	Failed	Circular
255	Simulated by finite element analysis	17.93	78.2	18.49	33.42	120.79	0	Failed	Circular
256	Simulated by finite element analysis	18.02	40.92	21.18	21.86	34.65	0.1	Stable	-
257	Simulated by finite element analysis	25.76	64.11	21.4	15.76	30.38	0.5	Stable	-
258	Simulated by finite element analysis	25.55	14.8	3.44	41.06	33.31	0.4	Failed	Circular
259	Simulated by finite element analysis	23.85	78.48	33.9	22.88	118.09	0.1	Stable	-
260	Simulated by finite element analysis	18.34	92.2	40.51	40.89	139.48	0	Stable	-
261	Simulated by finite element analysis	25.15	33.36	39.25	45.48	148.37	0.3	Failed	Circular
262	Simulated by finite element analysis	19.24	65.34	34.2	21.8	64.56	0	Stable	-
263	Simulated by finite element analysis	19.91	46.83	32.8	18.15	77.25	0.2	Stable	-
264	Simulated by finite element analysis	24.36	0.41	27.04	28.44	99.28	0.3	Failed	Circular
265	Simulated by finite element analysis	20.04	67.59	42.91	25.86	4.06	0	Stable	-
266	Simulated by finite element analysis	20.31	71.43	31.46	28.18	110.81	0.2	Stable	-
267	Simulated by finite element analysis	19.26	43.88	34.26	44.16	122.49	0	Failed	Circular
268	Simulated by finite element analysis	17.99	7.2	19.23	55.56	82.75	0	Failed	Circular
269	Simulated by finite element analysis	17.85	73.21	22.22	46.32	77.08	0	Failed	Circular
270	Simulated by finite element analysis	19.14	94.52	14.6	33.78	105.01	0.5	Failed	Circular
271	Simulated by finite element analysis	21.01	44.08	26.49	28.94	97.57	0	Failed	Circular
272	Simulated by finite element analysis	19.33	99.3	33.1	34.82	55.54	0	Stable	-
273	Simulated by finite element analysis	16.1	65.25	20.21	20.17	17.27	0.3	Stable	-
274	Simulated by finite element analysis	19.9	73.05	45.46	32.99	9.53	0.4	Stable	-
275	Simulated by finite element analysis	19.62	3.67	31.06	5.87	92.13	0.4	Stable	-
276	Simulated by finite element analysis	20.71	28.37	14.49	26.49	63.78	0	Failed	Circular
277	Simulated by finite element analysis	22.12	37.55	38.11	33.33	29.93	0.1	Stable	-
278	Simulated by finite element analysis	21.54	32.07	18.89	27.06	58.89	0.3	Failed	Circular
279	Simulated by finite element analysis	17.4	108.19	30.04	47.3	111.28	0.3	Failed	Circular
280	Simulated by finite element analysis	17.39	20.26	26.6	56.38	34.45	0.3	Failed	Circular
281	Simulated by finite element analysis	18.63	106.66	14.27	38.62	68.73	0.5	Failed	Circular
282	Simulated by finite element analysis	17.68	94.92	25.4	45.11	65.97	0.4	Failed	Circular
283	Simulated by finite element analysis	14.59	10.92	27.55	47.11	141.66	0.1	Failed	Circular
284	Simulated by finite element analysis	18.72	87.53	23.28	33.15	61.82	0	Stable	-
285	Simulated by finite element analysis	15.17	35.57	42.06	14.6	183.27	0	Stable	-
286	Simulated by finite element analysis	15.79	31.63	28.09	48.97	12.09	0.5	Stable	-
287	Simulated by finite element analysis	15.87	69.53	48.47	27.1	17.83	0	Stable	-
288	Simulated by finite element analysis	16.56	74.15	18.33	37.2	31.92	0	Stable	-
289	Simulated by finite element analysis	16.27	44.32	21.6	27.07	151.39	0.4	Failed	Circular
290	Simulated by finite element analysis	17.09	52.7	26	42.55	17.87	0.4	Stable	-
291	Simulated by finite element analysis	19.49	100.82	31.34	54.81	21.06	0.3	Stable	-
292	Simulated by finite element analysis	23.46	56.15	31.06	43.67	53.54	0	Failed	Circular
293	Simulated by finite element analysis	15.48	46.54	43.56	39.42	14.92	0.2	Stable	-
294	Simulated by finite element analysis	24.36	64.7	39.14	46.87	141.85	0.3	Failed	Circular
295	Simulated by finite element analysis	22.39	59.91	11.89	22.7	94.67	0.2	Failed	Circular
296	Simulated by finite element analysis	22.42	161.55	20.7	39.03	15.89	0	Stable	-
297	Simulated by finite element analysis	19.51	63.27	37.01	18.77	90.45	0.4	Stable	-
298	Simulated by finite element analysis	21.16	124	21.92	30.41	116.84	0.5	Stable	-
299	Simulated by finite element analysis	22.53	34.61	26.81	58	102.93	0	Failed	Circular
300	Simulated by finite element analysis	22.77	27.51	25.23	14.95	67.59	0.2	Stable	-
301	Simulated by finite element analysis	19.2	55.28	24.02	29.8	91.59	0.3	Failed	Circular
302	Simulated by finite element analysis	23.17	17.75	23.6	53.51	24.8	0.3	Failed	Circular
303	Simulated by finite element analysis	24.89	121.63	30.2	35.32	16.18	0.5	Stable	-
304	Simulated by finite element analysis	24.03	72.37	28.77	37.74	59.21	0.1	Stable	-
305	Simulated by finite element analysis	23.05	12.16	14	23.3	89.05	0	Failed	Circular
306	Simulated by finite element analysis	18.22	77.64	46.58	43.19	24.52	0.4	Stable	-

No.	Location	γ (kN/m^3)	c (kPa)	φ (°)	β (°)	H (m)	r_u	Status	Instability Type
307	Simulated by finite element analysis	20.47	16.87	35.48	27.58	17.86	0	Stable	-
308	Simulated by finite element analysis	20.99	63.58	48.54	30.91	68.82	0	Stable	-
309	Simulated by finite element analysis	18.74	49.05	17.54	14.34	118.98	0	Failed	Circular
310	Simulated by finite element analysis	21.26	9.78	43.23	17.42	90.73	0	Stable	-
311	Simulated by finite element analysis	21.07	29.89	14.46	21.98	22.31	0	Failed	Circular
312	Simulated by finite element analysis	20.27	25.33	23.75	8.37	42.76	0	Stable	-
313	Simulated by finite element analysis	19.9	25.05	25.46	44.15	37.03	0	Failed	Circular
314	Simulated by finite element analysis	20.32	14.9	14.35	42.66	80.26	0	Failed	Circular
315	Simulated by finite element analysis	20.57	34.55	44.41	38.36	122.28	0	Stable	-
316	Simulated by finite element analysis	19.1	133.38	41.5	31.38	109.11	0	Stable	-
317	Simulated by finite element analysis	18.88	9.77	21.01	51.49	33.34	0	Failed	Circular
318	Simulated by finite element analysis	20.26	122.61	23.44	24.92	114.17	0	Stable	-
319	Simulated by finite element analysis	16.3	91.72	27.7	41.82	87.53	0	Failed	Circular
320	Simulated by finite element analysis	13.6	58.07	38.63	36.61	32.97	0	Stable	-
321	Simulated by finite element analysis	19.65	28.79	17.38	35.79	68.78	0	Failed	Circular
322	Simulated by finite element analysis	16.1	81.18	30.16	4.84	125.44	0	Stable	-
323	Simulated by finite element analysis	26.52	68.74	20.76	24.86	123.99	0	Failed	Circular
324	Simulated by finite element analysis	23.12	57.21	29.96	26.39	94.95	0	Stable	-
325	Simulated by finite element analysis	25.06	14.97	14.86	47.79	142.71	0	Failed	Circular
326	Simulated by finite element analysis	23.15	46.41	23.56	48.54	22.44	0	Failed	Circular
327	Simulated by finite element analysis	19.27	129.46	27.54	34.61	87.63	0	Stable	-
328	Simulated by finite element analysis	22.3	40.64	21.93	24.05	103.19	0	Failed	Circular
329	Simulated by finite element analysis	22.37	43.37	19.15	45.03	119.95	0	Failed	Circular
330	Simulated by finite element analysis	15.37	53.03	28.06	40.94	79	0.35	Failed	Circular
331	Simulated by finite element analysis	23.35	29.97	16.38	39.73	33.92	0.405	Failed	Circular
332	Simulated by finite element analysis	17.14	127.05	41.92	31.87	114.99	0.49	Stable	-
333	Simulated by finite element analysis	16.1	71.69	20.81	52.77	70.06	0.2	Failed	Circular
334	Simulated by finite element analysis	23.18	17.74	13.86	26.71	60.39	0.38	Failed	Circular
335	Simulated by finite element analysis	18.34	36.34	30.19	29.44	143.1	0.45	Failed	Circular
336	Simulated by finite element analysis	16.9	31.8	33.65	29.21	81.74	0.5	Stable	-
337	Simulated by finite element analysis	24.83	119.28	13.24	26.86	113.91	0.11	Failed	Circular
338	Simulated by finite element analysis	13.93	80.9	37.13	34.16	58.25	0.45	Stable	-
339	Simulated by finite element analysis	17.61	59.31	19.1	43.28	31.25	0.38	Failed	Circular
340	Simulated by finite element analysis	24.6	11.36	1.7	20.19	11.06	0.45	Failed	Circular
341	Simulated by finite element analysis	30.31	22	23.94	36.99	104.02	0.12	Failed	Circular
342	Simulated by finite element analysis	20.69	69.68	40.34	49.39	111.42	0.3	Failed	Circular
343	Simulated by finite element analysis	23.82	300	21.77	20.57	23.9	0.25	Stable	-
344	Simulated by finite element analysis	16.77	24.09	34	22.53	26.72	0.4	Stable	-
345	Simulated by finite element analysis	28.11	0.69	21	18.22	99.46	0.25	Failed	Circular
346	Simulated by finite element analysis	18.27	6.45	20.69	26.3	17.04	0.5	Failed	Circular
347	Simulated by finite element analysis	10.06	62.41	39.99	39.04	58.31	0.25	Stable	-
348	Simulated by finite element analysis	20.85	74.42	11.34	39.57	13.17	0.5	Stable	-
349	Simulated by finite element analysis	20.98	52.5	23.55	33.67	49.7	0.35	Failed	Circular
350	Simulated by finite element analysis	17.56	27.82	17.23	37.23	67.61	0.3	Failed	Circular
351	Simulated by finite element analysis	21.4	67.99	38.11	32.72	132.33	0.35	Stable	-
352	Simulated by finite element analysis	25.29	125.82	0	48.07	56	0.3	Stable	-
353	Simulated by finite element analysis	15.47	79.39	47.88	32.46	81.14	0.15	Stable	-
354	Simulated by finite element analysis	22.3	38.64	31.01	43.92	47	0.25	Failed	Circular
355	Simulated by finite element analysis	16.82	0.05	23.92	29.45	36.22	0.25	Failed	Circular
356	Simulated by finite element analysis	25.93	13.72	22.36	35.79	53.37	0.15	Stable	-
357	Simulated by finite element analysis	22.56	63.51	31.13	38.36	49.54	0.25	Stable	-
358	Simulated by finite element analysis	18.56	21.04	24.82	5.3	45.92	0.25	Stable	-
359	Simulated by finite element analysis	21.47	41.59	18.76	45.73	48.47	0.15	Failed	Circular
360	Simulated by finite element analysis	19.01	29.34	12.19	30.35	12.07	0.25	Stable	-
361	Simulated by finite element analysis	22.84	68.46	10.91	35.94	63.73	0.25	Failed	Circular
362	Simulated by finite element analysis	20.36	11.89	36.6	16.58	108.92	0	Stable	-

No.	Location	γ (kN/m³)	c (kPa)	φ (°)	β (°)	H (m)	r_u	Status	Instability Type
363	Simulated by finite element analysis	25.28	83.67	18.4	36.46	106.8	0.1	Failed	Circular
364	Simulated by finite element analysis	30.27	38.55	22.46	39	29.53	0.5	Failed	Circular
365	Simulated by finite element analysis	21.71	16.57	19.68	29	60.8	0.4	Failed	Circular
366	Simulated by finite element analysis	23.67	55.72	38.36	38.68	100.02	0.1	Stable	-
367	Simulated by finite element analysis	21.84	53.21	35.12	15.3	108.67	0	Stable	-
368	Simulated by finite element analysis	18.58	82.65	21.89	31.64	20.11	0.3	Stable	-
369	Simulated by finite element analysis	22.23	30.81	21.8	31.44	3.45	0	Stable	-
370	Simulated by finite element analysis	24.05	30.89	28.57	36.87	71.36	0.2	Failed	Circular
371	Simulated by finite element analysis	23.57	162.62	12.59	56.79	155.28	0.3	Failed	Circular
372	Simulated by finite element analysis	21.03	8.32	28.22	31.63	49.25	0	Failed	Circular
373	Simulated by finite element analysis	19.88	30.86	21.47	50.14	38.23	0.2	Failed	Circular
374	Simulated by finite element analysis	27.2	53.62	28.3	21.82	56.78	0	Stable	-
375	Simulated by finite element analysis	23.88	43.5	26.48	43.07	13.52	0	Stable	-
376	Simulated by finite element analysis	25.55	64.91	16.97	33.45	97.58	0	Failed	Circular
377	Simulated by finite element analysis	18.04	38.49	43.96	32.44	27.54	0.5	Stable	-
378	Simulated by finite element analysis	25.7	84.49	18.66	42.65	7.75	0	Stable	-
379	Simulated by finite element analysis	15.07	3.58	35.12	36.52	22.1	0	Failed	Circular
380	Simulated by finite element analysis	22.21	86.74	27.43	25.2	13.37	0.3	Stable	-
381	Simulated by finite element analysis	20.56	46.9	13.47	10.75	3.88	0.4	Stable	-
382	Simulated by finite element analysis	21.05	95.94	36.24	37.34	132.92	0.4	Stable	-
383	Simulated by finite element analysis	18.93	9.28	31.46	43.31	33.06	0	Failed	Circular
384	Simulated by finite element analysis	23.88	10.07	22.75	28.3	23.92	0.1	Failed	Circular
385	Simulated by finite element analysis	22.44	10.48	31.88	26.22	101.93	0.3	Stable	-
386	Simulated by finite element analysis	21.17	12.58	40.51	49.4	111.54	0.3	Failed	Circular
387	Simulated by finite element analysis	28.07	160.77	26.2	24.64	162.76	0.3	Stable	-
388	Simulated by finite element analysis	24.3	45.96	44.35	38.12	56.21	0.5	Stable	-
389	Simulated by finite element analysis	21.13	76.34	37.55	19.9	5.05	0.4	Stable	-
390	Simulated by finite element analysis	20.41	44.66	28.23	33.89	86.39	0.1	Failed	Circular
391	Simulated by finite element analysis	13.12	94.38	8.11	20.66	34.42	0	Stable	-
392	Simulated by finite element analysis	18.09	11.87	3.46	34.43	78.52	0	Failed	Circular
393	Simulated by finite element analysis	18.67	115.4	27.1	14.56	91.16	0.5	Stable	-
394	Simulated by finite element analysis	17.46	99.03	24.1	4.24	42.94	0	Stable	-
395	Simulated by finite element analysis	20.05	91.29	32.17	39.26	70.97	0	Stable	-
396	Simulated by finite element analysis	27.17	14.55	15.02	44.82	19.18	0.4	Failed	Circular
397	Simulated by finite element analysis	22.35	0	57.36	37.5	15.1	0.4	Stable	-
398	Simulated by finite element analysis	19.58	0	14.6	27.18	77.83	0.3	Failed	Circular
399	Simulated by finite element analysis	16.44	0	29.22	40.24	21.74	0	Stable	-
400	Simulated by finite element analysis	23.96	0	28.04	32.4	74.58	0.2	Failed	Circular
401	Simulated by finite element analysis	19.6	0	22.79	59.35	155.73	0.3	Failed	Circular
402	Simulated by finite element analysis	27.35	0	33.92	34.03	5.7	0.2	Failed	Circular
403	Simulated by finite element analysis	21.03	0	17.72	5.79	57.31	0	Stable	-
404	Simulated by finite element analysis	25.74	0	17.23	30.03	80.53	0.4	Failed	Circular

Case 1–44 reported by [32]. Case 45–54 reported by [63]. Case 55–63 reported by [64]. Case 64 reported by [65]. Case 65–82 reported by [70]. Case 83–91 reported by [66]. Case 92–94 reported by [67]. Case 95–97 reported by [36]. Case 98–140 reported by [68]. Case 141–143 reported by [36]. Case 144–196 reported by [72]. Case 197–254 reported by [69]. Case 255–404 reported by [57]. KSH denotes Kaili-Sansui highway.

References

1. Zhan, L.-T.; Guo, X.-G.; Sun, Q.-Q.; Chen, Y.-M.; Chen, Z.-Y. The 2015 Shenzhen catastrophic landslide in a construction waste dump: Analyses of undrained strength and slope stability. *Acta Geotech.* **2021**, *16*, 1247–1263. [CrossRef]
2. Asnakew, S.; Shumet, S.; Ginbare, W.; Legas, G.; Haile, K. Prevalence of post-traumatic stress disorder and associated factors among Koshe landslide survivors, Addis Ababa, Ethiopia: A community-based, cross-sectional study. *BMJ Open* **2019**, *9*, e028550. [CrossRef] [PubMed]
3. Van Tien, P.; Luong, L.H.; Duc, D.M.; Trinh, P.T.; Quynh, D.T.; Lan, N.C.; Thuy, D.T.; Phi, N.Q.; Cuong, T.Q.; Dang, K.; et al. Rainfall-induced catastrophic landslide in Quang Tri Province: The deadliest single landslide event in Vietnam in 2020. *Landslides* **2021**, *18*, 2323–2327. [CrossRef]

4. Zhang, C.-C.; Zhu, H.-H.; Liu, S.-P.; Shi, B.; Zhang, D. A kinematic method for calculating shear displacements of landslides using distributed fiber optic strain measurements. *Eng. Geol.* **2018**, *234*, 83–96. [CrossRef]
5. Dixon, N.; Smith, A.; Flint, J.A.; Khanna, R.; Clark, B.; Andjelkovic, M. An acoustic emission landslide early warning system for communities in low-income and middle-income countries. *Landslides* **2018**, *15*, 1631–1644. [CrossRef]
6. Shiotani, T. Evaluation of long-term stability for rock slope by means of acoustic emission technique. *NDT E Int.* **2006**, *39*, 217–228. [CrossRef]
7. Codeglia, D.; Dixon, N.; Fowmes, G.J.; Marcato, G. Analysis of acoustic emission patterns for monitoring of rock slope deformation mechanisms. *Eng. Geol.* **2017**, *219*, 21–31. [CrossRef]
8. Akbar, T.A.; Ha, S.R. Landslide hazard zoning along Himalayan Kaghan Valley of Pakistan—By integration of GPS, GIS, and remote sensing technology. *Landslides* **2011**, *8*, 527–540. [CrossRef]
9. Marsella, M.; D'Aranno, P.J.V.; Scifoni, S.; Sonnessa, A.; Corsetti, M. Terrestrial laser scanning survey in support of unstable slopes analysis: The case of Vulcano Island (Italy). *Nat. Hazard.* **2015**, *78*, 443–459. [CrossRef]
10. Atzeni, C.; Barla, M.; Pieraccini, M.; Antolini, F. Early Warning Monitoring of Natural and Engineered Slopes with Ground-Based Synthetic-Aperture Radar. *Rock Mech Rock Eng.* **2015**, *48*, 235–246. [CrossRef]
11. Ho, S.-C.; Chen, I.H.; Lin, Y.-S.; Chen, J.-Y.; Su, M.-B. Slope deformation monitoring in the Jiufenershan landslide using time domain reflectometry technology. *Landslides* **2019**, *16*, 1141–1151. [CrossRef]
12. Chen, Z.Y.; Mi, H.L.; Zhang, F.M.; Wang, X.G. A simplified method for 3D slope stability analysis. *Can. Geotech. J.* **2003**, *40*, 675–683. [CrossRef]
13. Nie, Z.; Zhang, Z.; Zheng, H. Slope stability analysis using convergent strength reduction method. *Eng. Anal. Boundary Elem.* **2019**, *108*, 402–410. [CrossRef]
14. Wang, L.; Sun, D.; Li, L. Three-dimensional stability of compound slope using limit analysis method. *Can. Geotech. J.* **2019**, *56*, 116–125. [CrossRef]
15. Liu, H.; Xu, D.; Min, Y. Discussion on the Multi-Solution of Three-Dimensional Slope Safety Factor. *Geotech. Geol. Eng.* **2021**, *39*, 3361–3370. [CrossRef]
16. Faramarzi, L.; Zare, M.; Azhari, A.; Tabaei, M. Assessment of rock slope stability at Cham-Shir Dam Power Plant pit using the limit equilibrium method and numerical modeling. *Bull. Eng. Geol. Environ.* **2017**, *76*, 783–794. [CrossRef]
17. Liu, F. Stability Analysis of Geotechnical Slope Based on Strength Reduction Method. *Geotech. Geol. Eng.* **2020**, *38*, 3653–3665. [CrossRef]
18. Mbarka, S.; Baroth, J.; Ltifi, M.; Hassis, H.; Darve, F. Reliability analyses of slope stability. *Eur. J. Environ. Civ. Eng.* **2010**, *14*, 1227–1257. [CrossRef]
19. Ma, Z.; Liao, H.; Dang, F.; Cheng, Y. Seismic slope stability and failure process analysis using explicit finite element method. *Bull. Eng. Geol. Environ.* **2021**, *80*, 1287–1301. [CrossRef]
20. Nie, Z.; Zhang, Z.; Zheng, H.; Lin, S. Stability analysis of landslides using BEM and variational inequality based contact model. *Comput. Geotech.* **2020**, *123*, 103575. [CrossRef]
21. Zhao, Y.; Zhao, G.; Zhou, J.; Ma, J.; Cai, X. Failure mechanism analysis of rock in particle discrete element method simulation based on moment tensors. *Comput. Geotech.* **2021**, *136*, 104215. [CrossRef]
22. Yang, Y.; Xu, D.; Liu, F.; Zheng, H. Modeling the entire progressive failure process of rock slopes using a strength-based criterion. *Comput. Geotech.* **2020**, *126*, 103726. [CrossRef]
23. Sun, L.; Grasselli, G.; Liu, Q.; Tang, X.; Abdelaziz, A. The role of discontinuities in rock slope stability: Insights from a combined finite-discrete element simulation. *Comput. Geotech.* **2022**, *147*, 104788. [CrossRef]
24. Ma, Z.; Zhu, C.; Yao, X.; Dang, F. Slope Stability Analysis under Complex Stress State with Saturated and Unsaturated Seepage Flow. *Geofluids* **2021**, *2021*, 6637098. [CrossRef]
25. Wei, J.; Zhao, Z.; Xu, C.; Wen, Q. Numerical investigation of landslide kinetics for the recent Mabian landslide (Sichuan, China). *Landslides* **2019**, *16*, 2287–2298. [CrossRef]
26. Haghnejad, A.; Ahangari, K.; Moarefvand, P.; Goshtasbi, K. Numerical investigation of the impact of geological discontinuities on the propagation of ground vibrations. *Geomech. Eng.* **2018**, *14*, 545–552. [CrossRef]
27. Song, X.; Zhang, X.; Wu, S. Study on slope stability analysis and large deformation characteristics of failure based on SPH method. *Comput. Part. Mech.* **2023**. [CrossRef]
28. Zhang, Y.W.; Tang, L.X.; Bai, D.C.; Zhou, P. Numerical Simulation of Failure Process on Soil Slope with Different Support Measures. *Appl. Mech. Mater.* **2014**, *580–583*, 665–668. [CrossRef]
29. Dyson, A.P.; Tolooiyan, A. Comparative Approaches to Probabilistic Finite Element Methods for Slope Stability Analysis. *Simul. Modell Pract. Theory* **2020**, *100*, 102061. [CrossRef]
30. Liang, W.; Luo, S.; Zhao, G.; Wu, H. Predicting Hard Rock Pillar Stability Using GBDT, XGBoost, and LightGBM Algorithms. *Mathematics* **2020**, *8*, 765. [CrossRef]
31. Lu, P.; Rosenbaum, M.S. Artificial neural networks and Grey Systems for the prediction of slope stability. *Nat. Hazard.* **2003**, *30*, 383–398. [CrossRef]
32. Sah, N.K.; Sheorey, P.R.; Upadhyaya, L.N. Maximum likelihood estimation of slope stability. *Int. J. Rock Mech. Mining Sci. Geomech. Abstracts* **1994**, *31*, 47–53. [CrossRef]
33. Samui, P. Slope stability analysis: A support vector machine approach. *Environ. Geol.* **2008**, *56*, 255–267. [CrossRef]

34. Yang, C.X.; Tham, L.G.; Feng, X.T.; Wang, Y.J.; Lee, P.K.K. Two-stepped evolutionary algorithm and its application to stability analysis of slopes. *J. Comput. Civ. Eng.* **2004**, *18*, 145–153. [CrossRef]
35. Amirkiyaei, V.; Ghasemi, E. Stability assessment of slopes subjected to circular-type failure using tree-based models. *Int. J. Geotech. Eng.* **2020**, *16*, 301–311. [CrossRef]
36. Zhou, J.; Li, E.; Yang, S.; Wang, M.; Shi, X.; Yao, S.; Mitri, H.S. Slope stability prediction for circular mode failure using gradient boosting machine approach based on an updated database of case histories. *Saf. Sci.* **2019**, *118*, 505–518. [CrossRef]
37. Wang, H.; Moayedi, H.; Kok Foong, L. Genetic algorithm hybridized with multilayer perceptron to have an economical slope stability design. *Eng. Comput.* **2021**, *37*, 3067–3078. [CrossRef]
38. Hoang, N.-D.; Tien Bui, D. Chapter 18—Slope Stability Evaluation Using Radial Basis Function Neural Network, Least Squares Support Vector Machines, and Extreme Learning Machine. In *Handbook of Neural Computation*; Samui, P., Sekhar, S., Balas, V.E., Eds.; Academic Press: Cambridge, MA, USA, 2017; pp. 333–344.
39. Mahmoodzadeh, A.; Mohammadi, M.; Ali, H.F.H.; Ibrahim, H.H.; Abdulhamid, S.N.; Nejati, H.R. Prediction of safety factors for slope stability: Comparison of machine learning techniques. *Nat. Hazard.* **2021**, *111*, 1771–1799. [CrossRef]
40. Papa, J.P.; Falcao, A.X.; Levada, A.L.; Corrêa, D.C.; Salvadeo, D.H.; Mascarenhas, N.D. Fast and accurate holistic face recognition using optimum-path forest. In Proceedings of the 2009 16th International Conference on Digital Signal Processing, Santorini, Greece, 5–7 July 2009; pp. 1–6.
41. Bernardo, L.S.; Quezada, A.; Munoz, R.; Maia, F.M.; Pereira, C.R.; Wu, W.; de Albuquerque, V.H.C. Handwritten pattern recognition for early Parkinson's disease diagnosis. *Pattern Recognit Lett.* **2019**, *125*, 78–84. [CrossRef]
42. Papa, J.P.; Spadotto, A.A.; Falcao, A.X.; Pereira, J.C. Optimum path forest classifier applied to laryngeal pathology detection. In Proceedings of the 2008 15th International Conference on Systems, Signals and Image Processing, Bratislava, Slovakia, 25–28 June 2008; pp. 249–252.
43. Pisani, R.J.; Mizobe Nakamura, R.Y.; Riedel, P.S.; Lopes Zimback, C.R.; Falcao, A.X.; Papa, J.P. Toward Satellite-Based Land Cover Classification Through Optimum-Path Forest. *IEEE Trans Geosci. Remote Sens.* **2014**, *52*, 6075–6085. [CrossRef]
44. Bertoni, M.A.; de Rosa, G.H.; Brega, J.R.F. Optimum-path forest stacking-based ensemble for intrusion detection. *Evol. Intell.* **2021**, *15*, 2037–2054. [CrossRef]
45. Papa, J.P.; Nachif Fernandes, S.E.; Falcao, A.X. Optimum-Path Forest based on k-connectivity: Theory and applications. *Pattern Recognit Lett.* **2017**, *87*, 117–126. [CrossRef]
46. Hensel, F.; Moor, M.; Rieck, B. A Survey of Topological Machine Learning Methods. *Front. Artif. Intell.* **2021**, *4*, 681108. [CrossRef]
47. Papa, J.P.; Falcao, A.X.; Suzuki, C.T.N. Supervised Pattern Classification Based on Optimum-Path Forest. *Int. J. Imaging Syst. Technol.* **2009**, *19*, 120–131. [CrossRef]
48. Papa, J.P.; Falcao, A.X.; de Albuquerque, V.H.C.; Tavares, J.M.R.S. Efficient supervised optimum-path forest classification for large datasets. *Pattern Recognit.* **2012**, *45*, 512–520. [CrossRef]
49. Chen, S.; Sun, T.; Yang, F.; Sun, H.; Guan, Y. An improved optimum-path forest clustering algorithm for remote sensing image segmentation. *Comput. Geosci.* **2018**, *112*, 38–46. [CrossRef]
50. Papa, J.P.; Falcao, A.X. A New Variant of the Optimum-Path Forest Classifier. In Proceedings of the 4th International Symposium on Visual Computing, Las Vegas, NV, USA, 16–18 October 2008; pp. 935–944.
51. Zhao, G.; Wang, M.; Liang, W. A Comparative Study of SSA-BPNN, SSA-ENN, and SSA-SVR Models for Predicting the Thickness of an Excavation Damaged Zone around the Roadway in Rock. *Mathematics* **2022**, *10*, 1351. [CrossRef]
52. Liang, W.; Sari, A.; Zhao, G.; McKinnon, S.D.; Wu, H. Short-term rockburst risk prediction using ensemble learning methods. *Nat. Hazard.* **2020**, *104*, 1923–1946. [CrossRef]
53. de Rosa, G.H.; Papa, J.P. OPFython: A Python implementation for Optimum-Path Forest. *Software Impacts* **2021**, *9*, 100113. [CrossRef]
54. Pedregosa, F.; Varoquaux, G.; Gramfort, A.; Michel, V.; Thirion, B.; Grisel, O.; Blondel, M.; Prettenhofer, P.; Weiss, R.; Dubourg, V.; et al. Scikit-learn: Machine Learning in Python. *J. Mach. Learn Res.* **2011**, *12*, 2825–2830.
55. Yuan, C.; Moayedi, H. The performance of six neural-evolutionary classification techniques combined with multi-layer perception in two-layered cohesive slope stability analysis and failure recognition. *Eng. Comput.* **2020**, *36*, 1705–1714. [CrossRef]
56. Bradley, A.P. The use of the area under the ROC curve in the evaluation of machine learning algorithms. *Pattern Recognit.* **1997**, *30*, 1145–1159. [CrossRef]
57. Kardani, N.; Zhou, A.; Nazem, M.; Shen, S.-L. Improved prediction of slope stability using a hybrid stacking ensemble method based on finite element analysis and field data. *J. Rock Mech. Geotech. Eng.* **2021**, *13*, 188–201. [CrossRef]
58. Moayedi, H.; Osouli, A.; Nguyen, H.; Rashid, A.S.A. A novel Harris hawks' optimization and k-fold cross-validation predicting slope stability. *Eng. Comput.* **2021**, *37*, 369–379. [CrossRef]
59. Liang, W.; Sari, Y.A.; Zhao, G.; McKinnon, S.D.; Wu, H. Probability Estimates of Short-Term Rockburst Risk with Ensemble Classifiers. *Rock Mech Rock Eng.* **2021**, *54*, 1799–1814. [CrossRef]
60. Bishop, A.W.; Morgenstern, N. Stability Coefficients for Earth Slopes. *Geotechnique* **1960**, *10*, 129–153. [CrossRef]
61. Fellenius, W. Calculation of stability of Earth dam. In *Transactions of the Second Congress Large Dams*; International Commission on Large Dams: Washington, DC, USA, 1936; pp. 445–462.
62. Morgenstern, N.R.; Price, V.E. The Analysis of the Stability of General Slip Surfaces. *Geotechnique* **1965**, *15*, 79–93. [CrossRef]

63. Feng, X.-T.; Hudson, J.A. The ways ahead for rock engineering design methodologies. *Int. J. Rock Mech. Min. Sci.* **2004**, *41*, 255–273. [CrossRef]
64. Xu, W.; Shao, J.F. Artificial Neural Network Analysis for the Evaluation of Slope Stability. In *Application of Numerical Methods to Geotechnical Problems*; Cividini, A., Ed.; Springer: Vienna, Austria, 1998; pp. 665–672.
65. Li, W.-X.; Yang, S.-C.; Chen, E.-Z.; Qiao, J.-L.; Dai, L.-F. Neural network method of analysis of natural slope failure due to underground mining in mountainous areas. *Yantu Lixue Rock Soil Mech.* **2006**, *27*, 1563–1566.
66. Wang, H.B.; Xu, W.Y.; Xu, R.C. Slope stability evaluation using back propagation neural networks. *Eng. Geol.* **2005**, *80*, 302–315. [CrossRef]
67. Jin, L.; Feng, W.; Zhang, J. Maximum likelihood estimation on safety coefficients of rocky slope near DAM of Fengtan project. *Yanshilixue Yu Gongcheng Xuebao/Chinese J. Rock Mech. Eng.* **2004**, *23*, 1891–1894.
68. Wang, C. Study on Prediction Methods for High Engineering Slope. Master's Thesis, Beijing Jiaotong University, Beijing, China, 2009.
69. Qi, C.; Tang, X. Slope stability prediction using integrated metaheuristic and machine learning approaches: A comparative study. *Comput. Ind. Eng.* **2018**, *118*, 112–122. [CrossRef]
70. Chen, L.-Q.; Peng, Z.-B.; Chen, W.; Peng, W.-X.; Wu, Q.-H. Artificial neural network simulation on prediction of clay slope stability based on fuzzy controller. *Zhongnan Daxue Xuebao Ziran Kexue Ban J. Central South Univ. Sci. Technol.* **2009**, *40*, 1381–1387.
71. Lin, S.; Zheng, H.; Han, B.; Li, Y.; Han, C.; Li, W. Comparative performance of eight ensemble learning approaches for the development of models of slope stability prediction. *Acta Geotech.* **2022**, *17*, 1477–1502. [CrossRef]
72. Chen, C.; Xiao, Z.; Zhang, G. Stability assessment model for epimetamorphic rock slopes based on adaptive neuro-fuzzy inference system. *Electron. J. Geotech. Eng.* **2011**, *16 A*, 93–107.
73. Altmann, A.; Tolosi, L.; Sander, O.; Lengauer, T.J.B. Permutation importance: A corrected feature importance measure. *Bioinformatics* **2010**, *26*, 1340–1347. [CrossRef] [PubMed]
74. Viet-Ha, N.; Nhat-Duc, H.; Hieu, N.; Phuong Thao Thi, N.; Tinh Thanh, B.; Pham Viet, H.; Samui, P.; Dieu Tien, B. Effectiveness assessment of Keras based deep learning with different robust optimization algorithms for shallow landslide susceptibility mapping at tropical area. *Catena* **2020**, *188*, 104458. [CrossRef]
75. Sun Jishu, X.J.; Wang, J.; Li, W. Application of Relevance Vector Machine Model in Slope Stability Prediction. *Sci. Tech. Eng.* **2021**, *21*, 12234–12242.

Disclaimer/Publisher's Note: The statements, opinions and data contained in all publications are solely those of the individual author(s) and contributor(s) and not of MDPI and/or the editor(s). MDPI and/or the editor(s) disclaim responsibility for any injury to people or property resulting from any ideas, methods, instructions or products referred to in the content.

MDPI AG
Grosspeteranlage 5
4052 Basel
Switzerland
Tel.: +41 61 683 77 34

Mathematics Editorial Office
E-mail: mathematics@mdpi.com
www.mdpi.com/journal/mathematics

Disclaimer/Publisher's Note: The statements, opinions and data contained in all publications are solely those of the individual author(s) and contributor(s) and not of MDPI and/or the editor(s). MDPI and/or the editor(s) disclaim responsibility for any injury to people or property resulting from any ideas, methods, instructions or products referred to in the content.